The
Crimean War

ALSO BY ORLANDO FIGES

Peasant Russia, Civil War:
The Volga Countryside in Revolution, 1917–1921

A People's Tragedy:
The Russian Revolution, 1891–1924

Interpreting the Russian Revolution:
The Language and Symbols of 1917
(with Boris Kolonitskii)

Natasha's Dance:
A Cultural History of Russia

The Whisperers:
Private Life in Stalin's Russia

The Crimean War

A History

Orlando Figes

Metropolitan Books
Henry Holt and Company
New York

m

Metropolitan Books
Henry Holt and Company, LLC
Publishers since 1866
175 Fifth Avenue
New York, New York 10010
www.henryholt.com

Library of Congress Cataloging-in-Publication Data

Figes, Orlando.
  The Crimean War : a history / Orlando Figes. — 1st ed.
      p.   cm.
  "Published simultaneously in the United Kingdom by Penguin Books,
London"—T.p. verso.
  Includes bibliographical references and index.
  ISBN 978-0-8050-7460-4
  1. Crimean War, 1853–1856.   I. Title.
  DK214.F53 2010
  947'.0738—dc22

                                                    2010023152

ISBN: 978-0-8050-7460-4

First Edition 2010

Printed in the United States of America

10 9 8 7 6 5 4 3 2 1

For Seren

Contents

CONTENTS

List of Plates

1. Easter at the Holy Sepulchre, Jerusalem, *c.* 1900. G. Eric and Edith Matson Photograph Collection, Library of Congress Prints and Photographs Division, Washington, DC.

2. Russian barracks for pilgrims, Jerusalem, by B. W. Kilburn, *c.* 1899. Library of Congress Prints and Photographs Division, Washington, DC.

3. An artillery park on the shores of the Bosporus with the Nusretiye Mosque in the background, 1855, by James Robertson. National Army Museum, London. Photo: The Bridgeman Art Library.

4. Nicholas I, 1852, by Franz Kruger. Hermitage, St Petersburg. Photo: The Bridgeman Art Library.

5. *Russians Firing at a Statue*, 1854, by Gustave Doré, from *The Rare and Extraordinary History of Holy Russia* (*Histoire pittoresque, dramatique et caricaturale de la Sainte Russie*).

6. 'Now For It! A Set to between Pam, the Downing Street Pet, and the Russian Spider', from *Punch*, February 1855.

7. 'Saint Nicholas of Russia' by John Tenniel, from *Punch*, 18 March 1854.

8. Turkish troops on the Danube Front, 1854, by Carol Szathmari. The Royal Collection © 2010, Her Majesty Queen Elizabeth II.

List of Illustrations

Note on Dates and Proper Names

DATES

From 1700 until 1918 Russia adhered to the Julian calendar, which ran thirteen days behind the Gregorian calendar in use in Western Europe. To avoid confusion, all dates in this book are given according to the Gregorian calendar.

PROPER NAMES

Russian names are spelled in this book according to the standard (Library of Congress) system of transliteration, but common English spellings of well-known Russian names (Tsar Alexander, for example) are retained.

Acknowledgements

The research for this book took place over many years and thanks are due to a large number of people.

In the early stages of research Helen Rappaport helped me to compile a working bibliography from the potentially endless list of books, published memoirs, diaries and letters by participants in the Crimean War. She also gave invaluable advice on the social history of the war, sharing information from her own research for *No Place for Ladies: The Untold Story of Women in the Crimean War.*

At the National Army Museum in London I am grateful to Alastair Massie, whose own works, *The National Army Museum Book of the Crimean War: The Untold Stories* and *A Most Desperate Undertaking: The British Army in the Crimea, 1854–56*, were an inspiration to my own. I gratefully acknowledge the permission of Her Majesty Queen Elizabeth II to make use of the materials from the Royal Archives, and am thankful to Sophie Gordon for her advice on the photographs of the Royal Collection at Windsor. In the Basbanlik Osmanlik Archive in Istanbul, I was helped by Murat Siviloglu and Melek Maksudoglu, and in the Russian State Military History Archive in Moscow by Luisa Khabibulina.

Various people commented on all or sections of the draft – Norman Stone, Sean Brady, Douglas Austin, Tony Margrave, Mike Hinton, Miles Taylor, Dominic Lieven and Mark Mazower – and I am grateful to them all. Douglas Austin and Tony Margrave, in particular, were a mine of information on various military aspects. Thanks are also due to Mara Kozelsky for allowing me to read the typescript of her then unfinished book on the Crimea, to Metin Kunt and Onur Önul for help on Turkish matters, to Edmund Herzig on Armenian affairs, to

ACKNOWLEDGEMENTS

Lucy Riall for advice on Italy, to Joanna Bourke for her thoughts on
military psychology, to Antony Beevor for his help on the hussars,
to Ross Belson for background information on the resignation of
Sidney Herbert, to Keith Smith for his generous donation of the extraordinary photograph 'Old Scutari and Modern Üsküdar' by James
Robertson, and to Hugh Small, whose book *The Crimean War: Queen
Victoria's War with the Russian Tsars* made me change my mind on
many things.

As always, I am indebted to my family, to my wife, Stephanie, and
our daughters, Lydia and Alice, who could never quite believe that I
was writing a war book but indulged my interests nonetheless; to my
wonderfully supportive agent, Deborah Rogers, and her superb team
at Rogers, Coleridge and White, especially Ruth McIntosh, who talks
me through my VAT returns, and to Melanie Jackson in New York; to
Cecilia Mackay for her thoughtful work on the illustrations; to Elizabeth Stratford for the copy-editing; to Alan Gilliland for the excellent
maps; and above all to my two great editors, Simon Winder at Penguin and Sara Bershtel at Metropolitan.

Introduction

In the parish church of Witchampton in Dorset there is a memorial to commemorate five soldiers from this peaceful little village who fought and died in the Crimean War. The inscription reads:

DIED IN THE SERVICE OF THEIR COUNTRY.
THEIR BODIES ARE IN THE CRIMEA.
MAY THEIR SOULS REST IN PEACE. MDCCCLIV

In the communal cemetery of Héricourt in south-eastern France, there is a gravestone with the names of the nine men from the area who died in the Crimea:

ILS SONT MORTS POUR LA PATRIE.
AMIS, NOUS NOUS REVERRONS UN JOUR

At the base of the memorial somebody has placed two cannonballs, one with the name of the 'Malakoff' (Malakhov) Bastion, captured by the French during the siege of Sevastopol, the Russian naval base in the Crimea, the other with the name 'Sebastopol'. Thousands of French and British soldiers lie in unmarked and long-neglected graves in the Crimea.

In Sevastopol itself there are hundreds of memorials, many of them in the military cemetery (*bratskoe kladbishche*), one of three huge burial grounds established by the Russians during the siege, where a staggering 127,583 men killed in the defence of the town lie buried. The officers have individual graves with their names and regiments but the ordinary soldiers are buried in mass graves of fifty or a hundred men. Among the Russians there are soldiers who had come from Serbia, Bulgaria or Greece, their co-religionists in the

The Héricourt Memorial

Eastern Church, in response to the Tsar's call for the Orthodox to defend their faith. One small plaque, barely visible in the long grass where fifteen sailors lie underground, commemorates their 'heroic sacrifice during the defence of Sevastopol in 1854–5':

> THEY DIED FOR THEIR FATHERLAND,
> FOR TSAR AND FOR GOD

Elsewhere in Sevastopol there are 'eternal flames' and monuments to the unknown and uncounted soldiers who died fighting for the town. It is estimated that a quarter of a million Russian soldiers, sailors and civilians are buried in mass graves in Sevastopol's three military cemeteries.[1]

Two world wars have obscured the huge scale and enormous human cost of the Crimean War. Today it seems to us a relatively minor war; it is almost forgotten, like the plaques and gravestones in those churchyards. Even in the countries that took part in it (Russia, Britain, France, Piedmont-Sardinia in Italy and the Ottoman Empire, including those territories that would later make up Romania and Bulgaria) there are not many people today who could say what the Crimean War was all about. But for our ancestors before the First World War the Crimea was the major conflict of the nineteenth century, the most important war of their lifetimes, just as the world wars of the twentieth century are the dominant historical landmarks of our lives.

The losses were immense – at least three-quarters of a million soldiers killed in battle or lost through illness and disease, two-thirds of them Russian. The French lost around 100,000 men, the British a small fraction of that number, about 20,000, because they sent far fewer troops (98,000 British soldiers and sailors were involved in the Crimea compared to 310,000 French). But even so, for a small agricultural community such as Witchampton the loss of five able-bodied men was felt as a heavy blow. In the parishes of Whitegate, Aghada and Farsid in County Cork in Ireland, where the British army recruited heavily, almost one-third of the male population died in the Crimean War.[2]

Nobody has counted the civilian casualties: victims of the shelling; people starved to death in besieged towns; populations devastated by disease spread by the armies; entire communities wiped out in the massacres and organized campaigns of ethnic cleansing that accompanied the fighting in the Caucasus, the Balkans and the Crimea. This was the first 'total war', a nineteenth-century version of the wars of our own age, involving civilians and humanitarian crises.

It was also the earliest example of a truly modern war – fought with new industrial technologies, modern rifles, steamships and railways, novel forms of logistics and communication like the telegraph, important innovations in military medicine, and war reporters and photographers directly on the scene. Yet at the same time it was the last war to be conducted by the old codes of chivalry, with 'parliamentaries' and truces in the fighting to clear the dead and wounded from the killing fields. The early battles in the Crimea, on the River Alma and at Balaklava, where the famous Charge of the Light Brigade took place, were not so very different from the sort of fighting that went on during the Napoleonic Wars. Yet the siege of Sevastopol, the longest and most crucial phase of the Crimean War, was a precursor of the industrialized trench warfare of 1914–18. During the eleven and a half months of the siege, 120 kilometres of trenches were dug by the Russians, the British and the French; 150 million gunshots and 5 million bombs and shells of various calibre were exchanged between the two sides.[3]

The name of the Crimean War does not reflect its global scale and huge significance for Europe, Russia and that area of the world – stretching from the Balkans to Jerusalem, from Constantinople to the Caucasus – that came to be defined by the Eastern Question, the great international problem posed by the disintegration of the Ottoman Empire. Perhaps it would be better to adopt the Russian name for the Crimean War, the 'Eastern War' (*Vostochnaia voina*), which at least has the merit of connecting it to the Eastern Question, or even the 'Turco-Russian War', the name for it in many Turkish sources, which places it in the longer-term historical context of centuries of warfare between the Russians and the Ottomans, although this omits the crucial factor of Western intervention in the war.

The war began in 1853 between Ottoman and Russian forces in the Danubian principalities of Moldavia and Wallachia, the territory of today's Romania, and spread to the Caucasus, where the Turks and the British encouraged and supported the struggle of the Muslim tribes against Russia, and from there to other areas of the Black Sea. By 1854, with the intervention of the British and the French on Turkey's side and the Austrians threatening to join this anti-Russian alliance, the Tsar withdrew his forces from the principalities, and the fighting shifted to the Crimea. But there were several other theatres of the war in 1854–5: in the Baltic Sea, where the Royal Navy planned to attack St Petersburg, the Russian capital; on the White Sea, where it bombarded the Solovetsky Monastery in July 1854; and even on the Pacific coastline of Siberia.

The global scale of the fighting was matched by the diversity of people it involved. Readers will find here a broad canvas populated less than they might have hoped (or feared) by military types and more by kings and queens, princes, courtiers, diplomats, religious leaders, Polish and Hungarian revolutionaries, doctors, nurses, journalists, artists and photographers, pamphleteers and writers, none more central to the story from the Russian perspective than Leo Tolstoy, who served as an officer on three different fronts of the Crimean War (the Caucasus, the Danube and the Crimea). Above all, through their own words in letters and memoirs, the reader will find here the viewpoint of the serving officers and ordinary troops, from the British 'Tommy' to the French-Algerian Zouaves and the Russian serf soldiers.

There are many books in English on the Crimean War. But this is the first in any language to draw extensively from Russian, French and Ottoman as well as British sources to illuminate the geo-political, cultural and religious factors that shaped the involvement of each major power in the conflict. Because of this concentration on the historical context of the war, readers eages for the fighting to begin will need to be patient in the early chapters (or even skip over them). What I hope emerges from these pages is a new appreciation of the war's importance as a major turning point in the history of Europe, Russia and the Middle East, the consequences of which are still felt today. There is no room here for the widespread British view that it was a 'senseless' and 'unnecessary' war – an idea going back to the public's disappointment with the poorly managed military campaign and its limited achievements at the time – which has since had such a detrimental impact on the historical literature. Long neglected and often ridiculed as a serious subject by scholars, the Crimean War has been left mainly in the hands of British military historians, many of them amateur enthusiasts, who have constantly retold the same stories (the Charge of the Light Brigade, the bungling of the English commanders, Florence Nightingale) with little real discussion of the war's religious origins, the complex politics of the Eastern Question, Christian–Muslim relations in the Black Sea region, or the influence of European Russophobia, without which it is difficult to grasp the conflict's true significance.

The Crimean War was a crucial watershed. It broke the old conservative alliance between Russia and the Austrians that had upheld the existing order on the European continent, allowing the emergence of new nation states in Italy, Romania and Germany. It left the Russians with a deep sense of resentment of the West, a feeling of betrayal that the other Christian states had sided with the Turks, and with frustrated ambitions in the Balkans that would continue to destabilize relations between the powers in the 1870s and the crises leading to the outbreak of the First World War. It was the first major European conflict to involve the Turks, if we discount their brief participation in the French Revolutionary and Napoleonic Wars. It opened up the Muslim world of the Ottoman Empire to Western armies and technologies, accelerated its integration into the global capitalist economy, and sparked an Islamic reaction against the West which continues to this day.

Each power entered the Crimean War with its own motives. Nationalism and imperial rivalries combined with religious interests. For the Turks, it was a question of fighting for their crumbling empire in Europe, of defending their imperial sovereignty against Russia's claims to represent the Orthodox Christians of the Ottoman Empire, and of averting the threat of an Islamic and nationalist revolution in the Turkish capital. The British claimed they went to war to defend the Turks against Russia's bullying, but in fact they were more concerned to strike a blow against the Russian Empire, which they feared as a rival in Asia, and to use the war to advance their own free-trade and religious interests in the Ottoman Empire. For the Emperor of the French, Napoleon III, the war was an opportunity to restore France to a position of respect and influence abroad, if not to the glory of his uncle's reign, and perhaps to redraw the map of Europe as a family of liberal nation states along the lines envisaged by Napoleon I – though the influence of the Catholics on his weak regime also pushed him towards war against the Russians on religious grounds. For the British and the French, this was a crusade for the defence of liberty and European civilization against the barbaric and despotic menace of Russia, whose aggressive expansionism represented a real threat, not just to the West but to the whole of Christendom. As for the Tsar, Nicholas I, the man more than anyone responsible for the Crimean War, he was partly driven by inflated pride and arrogance, a result of having been tsar for twenty-seven years, partly by his sense of how a great power such as Russia should behave towards its weaker neighbours, and partly by a gross miscalculation about how the other powers would respond to his actions; but above all he believed that he was fighting a religious war, a crusade, to fulfil Russia's mission to defend the Christians of the Ottoman Empire. The Tsar vowed to take on the whole world in accordance with what he believed was his holy mission to extend his empire of the Orthodox as far as Constantinople and Jerusalem.

Historians have tended to dismiss the religious motives of the war. Few devote more than a paragraph or two to the dispute in the Holy Land – the rivalry between the Catholics or Latins (backed by France) and the Greeks (supported by Russia) over who should have control of the Church of the Holy Sepulchre in Jerusalem and the Church of the Nativity in Bethlehem – even though it was the starting point (and for the Tsar a sufficient cause) of the Crimean War. Until the religious wars of our own age, it seemed implausible that a petty quarrel over some churchwarden's keys should entangle the great powers in a major war. In some histories the Holy Lands dispute is used to illustrate the absurd nature of this 'silly' and 'unnecessary war'. In others, it appears as no more than a trigger for the real cause of the war: the struggle of the European powers for influence in the Ottoman Empire. Wars are caused by imperial rivalries, it is argued in these histories, by competition over markets, or by the influence of nationalist opinions at home. While all this is true, it underestimates the importance of religion in the nineteenth century (if the Balkan wars of the 1990s and the rise of militant Islam have taught us anything, it is surely that religion plays a vital role in fuelling wars). All the powers used religion as a means of leverage in the Eastern Question, politics and faith were closely intertwined in this imperial rivalry, and every nation, none more so than Russia, went to war in the belief that God was on its side.

The Eastern Question's conflict zone

The Danube conflict zone

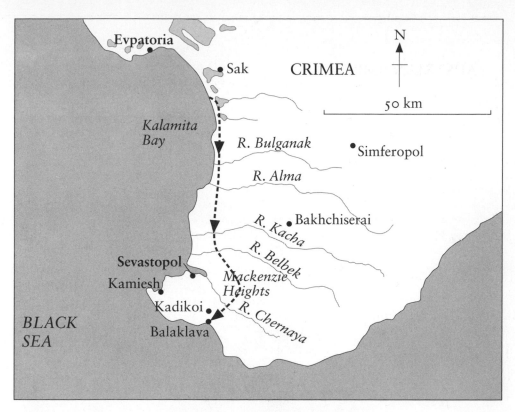

The Allied advance towards Sevastopol

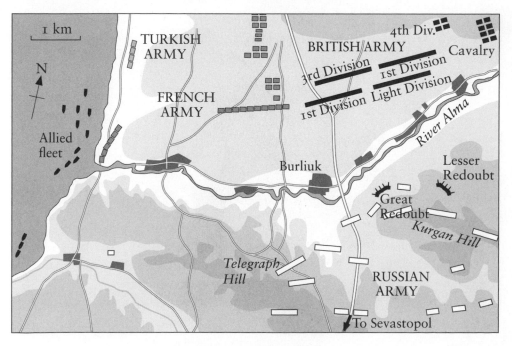

The battle of the Alma

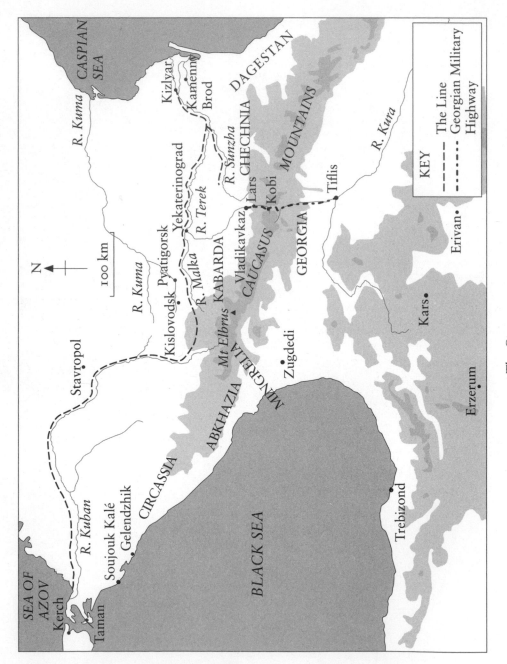

The Caucasus

KEY

— — — The Line
········ Georgian Military Highway

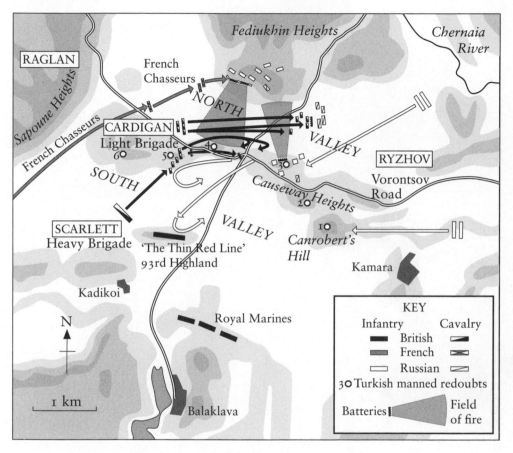

The battle of Balaklava

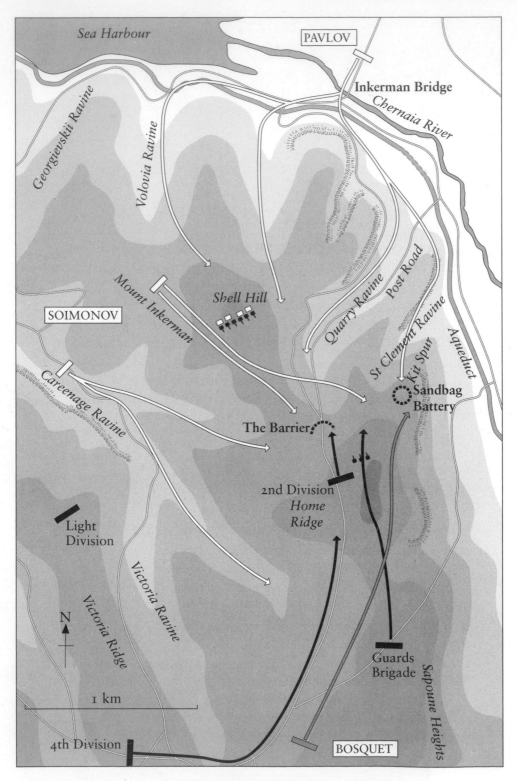

The battle of Inkerman

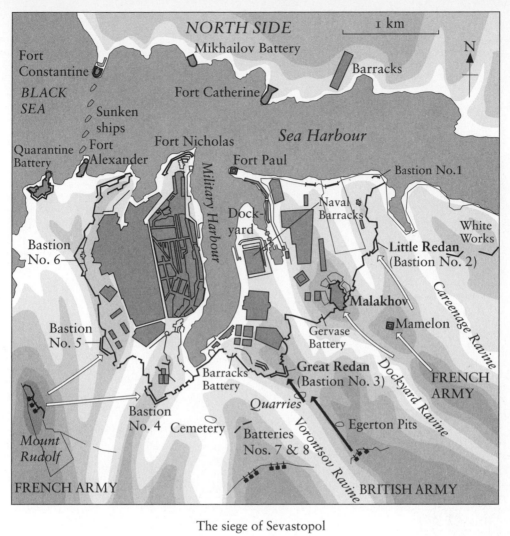

The siege of Sevastopol

I

Religious Wars

For weeks the pilgrims had been coming to Jerusalem for the Easter festival. They came from every corner of Eastern Europe and the Middle East, from Egypt, Syria, Armenia, Anatolia, the Greek peninsula, but most of all from Russia, travelling by sea to the port of Jaffa where they hired camels or donkeys. By Good Friday, on 10 April 1846, there were 20,000 pilgrims in Jerusalem. They rented any dwelling they could find or slept in family groups beneath the stars. To pay for their long journey nearly all of them had brought some merchandise, a handmade crucifix or ornament, strings of beads or pieces of embroidery, which they sold to European tourists at the holy shrines. The square before the Church of the Holy Sepulchre, the focus of their pilgrimage, was a busy marketplace, with colourful displays of fruit and vegetables competing for space with pilgrims' wares and the smelly hides of goats and oxen left out in the sun by the tanneries behind the church. Beggars, too, collected here. They frightened strangers into giving alms by threatening to touch them with their leprous hands. Wealthy tourists had to be protected by their Turkish guides, who hit the beggars with heavy sticks to clear a path to the church doors.

In 1846 Easter fell on the same date in the Latin and Greek Orthodox calendars, so the holy shrines were much more crowded than usual, and the mood was very tense. The two religious communities had long been arguing about who should have first right to carry out their Good Friday rituals on the altar of Calvary inside the Church of the Holy Sepulchre, the spot where the cross of Jesus was supposed to have been inserted in the rock. During recent years the rivalry between the Latins and the Greeks had reached such fever pitch that Mehmet Pasha, the Ottoman governor of Jerusalem, had been forced to position soldiers inside and outside the church to preserve order. But even this had not prevented fights from breaking out.

On this Good Friday the Latin priests arrived with their white linen altar-cloth to find that the Greeks had got there first with their silk embroidered cloth. The Catholics demanded to see the Greeks' firman, their decree from the Sultan in Constantinople, empowering them to place their silk cloth on the altar first. The Greeks demanded to see the Latins' firman allowing them to remove it. A fight broke out between the priests, who were quickly joined by monks and pilgrims on either side. Soon the whole church was a battlefield. The rival groups of worshippers fought not only with their fists, but with crucifixes, candlesticks, chalices, lamps and incense-burners, and even bits of wood which they tore from the sacred shrines. The fighting continued with knives and pistols smuggled into the Holy Sepulchre by worshippers of either side. By the time the church was cleared by Mehmet Pasha's guards, more than forty people lay dead on the floor.[1]

'See here what is done in the name of religion!' wrote the English social commentator Harriet Martineau, who travelled to the Holy Lands of Palestine and Syria in 1846.

> This Jerusalem is the most sacred place in the world, except Mekkeh, to the Mohammedan: and to the Christian and the Jew, it is the most sacred place in the world. What are they doing in this sanctuary of their common Father, as they all declare it to be? Here are the Mohammedans eager to kill any Jew or Christian who may enter the Mosque of Omar. There are the Greeks and Latin Christians hating each other, and ready to kill any Jew or Mohammedan who may enter the Church of the Holy Sepulchre. And here are the Jews, pleading against their enemies, in the vengeful language of their ancient prophets.[2]

The rivalry between the Christian Churches was intensified by the rapid growth in the number of pilgrims to Palestine in the nineteenth century. Railways and steamships made mass travel possible, opening up the region to tour-groups of Catholics from France and Italy and to the devout middle classes of Europe and America. The various Churches vied with one another for influence. They set up missions to support their pilgrims, competed over purchases of land, endowed bishoprics and monasteries, and established schools to convert the Orthodox Arabs (mainly Syrian and Lebanese), the largest but least educated Christian community in the Holy Lands.

'Within the last two years considerable presents have been sent to Jerusalem to decorate the Church of the Holy Sepulchre by the Russian, French, Neapolitan and Sardinian governments,' reported William Young, the British consul in Palestine and Syria, to Lord Palmerston at the Foreign Office in 1839.

> There are many symptoms of increasing jealousy and inimical feeling among the churches. The petty quarrels that have always existed between the Latin, Greek and Armenian convents were of little moment so long as their differences were settled from time to time by the one giving a larger bribe to the Turkish authorities than the other. But that day passes by, for these countries are now no longer closed against European intrigue in church matters.[3]

Between 1842 and 1847 there was a flurry of activity in Jerusalem: the Anglicans founded a bishopric; the Austrians set up a Franciscan printing press; the French established a consulate in Jerusalem and pumped money into schools and churches for the Catholics; Pope Pius IX re-established a resident Latin patriarch, the first since the Crusades of the twelfth century; the Greek patriarch returned from Constantinople to tighten his hold on the Orthodox; and the Russians sent an ecclesiastical mission, which led to the foundation of a Russian compound with a hostel, hospital, chapel, school and marketplace to support the large and growing number of Russian pilgrims.

In the early decades of the nineteenth century, the Russian Orthodox Church sent more pilgrims to Jerusalem than any other branch of the Christian faith. Every year up to 15,000 Russian pilgrims would arrive in Jerusalem for the Easter festival, some even making the long trek on foot across Russia and the Caucasus, through Anatolia and Syria. For the Russians, the holy shrines of Palestine were objects of intense and passionate devotion: to make a pilgrimage to them was the highest possible expression of their faith.

In some ways the Russians saw the Holy Lands as an extension of their spiritual motherland. The idea of 'Holy Russia' was not contained by any territorial boundaries; it was an empire of the Orthodox with sacred shrines throughout the lands of Eastern Christianity and with the Holy Sepulchre as its mother church. 'Palestine', wrote one Russian theologian in the 1840s, 'is our native land, in which we do not recognize ourselves as foreigners.'[4] Centuries of pilgrimage had laid the basis of this claim, establishing a link between the Russian Church and the Holy Places (connected with the life of Christ in Bethlehem, Jerusalem and Nazareth) which many Russians counted more important – the basis of a higher spiritual authority – than the temporal and political sovereignty of the Ottomans in Palestine.

Nothing like this ardour could be found among the Catholics or Protestants, for whom the Holy Places were objects of historical interest and romantic sentiment rather than religious devotion. The travel writer and historian Alexander Kinglake thought that 'the closest likeness of a pilgrim which the Latin Church could supply was often a mere French tourist with a journal and a theory and a plan of writing a book'. European tourists were repelled by the intense passion of the Orthodox pilgrims, whose strange rituals struck them as 'barbaric' and as 'degrading superstitions'. Martineau refused to go to the Holy Sepulchre to see the washing of the pilgrims' feet on Good Friday. 'I could not go to witness mummeries done in the name of Christianity,' she wrote, 'compared with which the lowest fetishism on the banks of an African river would have been inoffensive.' For the same reason, she would not go to the ceremony of the Holy Fire on Easter Saturday, when thousands of Orthodox worshippers squeezed into the Holy Sepulchre to light their torches from the miraculous flames that appeared from the tomb of Christ. Rival groups of Orthodox – Greeks, Bulgarians, Moldavians, Serbians and Russians – would jostle with each other to light their candles first; fights would start; and sometimes worshippers were crushed to death or suffocated in the smoke. Baron Curzon, who witnessed one such scene in 1834, described the ceremony as a 'scene of disorder and profanation' in which the pilgrims, 'almost in a state of nudity, danced about with frantic gestures, yelling and screaming as if they were possessed'.[5]

It is hardly surprising that a Unitarian such as Martineau or an Anglican like Curzon should have been so hostile to such rituals: demonstrations of religious emotion had long been effaced from the Protestant Church. Like many tourists in the Holy Land, they sensed that they had less in common with the Orthodox pilgrims, whose wild

4

behaviour seemed barely Christian at all, than with the relatively secular Muslims, whose strict reserve and dignity were more in sympathy
with their own private forms of quiet prayer. Attitudes like theirs were
to influence the formation of Western policies towards Russia in the —
diplomatic disputes about the Holy Land which would eventually
lead to the Crimean War.

Unaware of and indifferent to the importance of the Holy Lands
to Russia's spiritual identity, European commentators saw only a
growing Russian menace to the interests of the Western Churches
there. In the early 1840s, Young, now the British consul, sent regular
reports to the Foreign Office about the steady build-up of 'Russian
agents' in Jerusalem – their aim being, in his view, to prepare a 'Russian conquest of the Holy Lands' through sponsored pilgrimage
and purchases of land for Orthodox churches and monasteries. This
was certainly a time when the Russian ecclesiastical mission was
exerting its influence on the Greek, Armenian and Arab Orthodox
communities by financing churches, schools and hostels in Palestine
and Syria (an activism resisted by the Foreign Ministry in St Petersburg, which rightly feared that such activities might antagonize the
Western powers). Young's reports about Russia's conquest plans were
increasingly hysterical. 'The pilgrims of Russia have been heard to
speak openly of the period being at hand when this country will be
under the Russian government,' he wrote to Palmerston in 1840. 'The
Russians could in one night during Easter arm 10,000 pilgrims
within the walls of Jerusalem. The convents in the city are spacious
and, at a trifling expense, might be converted into fortresses.' British
fears of this 'Russian plan' accelerated Anglican initiatives, eventually leading to the foundation of the first Anglican church in Jerusalem
in 1845.[6]

But it was the French who were most alarmed by the growing
Russian presence in the Holy Lands. According to French Catholics,
France had a long historical connection to Palestine going back to the
Crusades. In French Catholic opinion, this conferred on France,
Europe's 'first Catholic nation', a special mission to protect the faith
in the Holy Lands, despite the marked decline of Latin pilgrimage in
recent years. 'We have a heritage to conserve there, an interest to defend,'
declared the Catholic provincial press. 'Centuries will pass before

the Russians shed a fraction of the blood that the French spilled in the Crusades for the Holy Places. The Russians took no part in the Crusades. . . . The primacy of France among the Christian nations is so well established in the Orient that the Turks call Christian Europe Frankistan, the country of the French.'[7]

To counteract the growing Russian presence and cement their role as the main protector of the Catholics in Palestine, the French set up a consulate in Jerusalem in 1843 (an outraged Muslim crowd, hostile to the influence of the Western powers, soon tore the godless tricolour from its mast). At Latin services in the Holy Sepulchre and the Church of the Nativity in Bethlehem the French consul began to appear in full dress uniform with a large train of officials. For the midnight Christmas Mass in Bethlehem he was accompanied by a large force of infantry furnished by Mehmet Pasha but paid for by France.[8]

Fights between the Latins and the Orthodox were as common at the Church of the Nativity as they were at the Holy Sepulchre. For years they had squabbled about whether Latin monks should have a key to the main church (of which the Greeks were the guardians) so that they could pass through it to the Chapel of the Manger, which belonged to the Catholics; whether they should have a key to the Grotto of the Nativity, an ancient cave beneath the church thought to be the place where Christ was born; and whether they should be allowed to put into the marble floor of the Grotto, on the supposed location of the Nativity, a silver star adorned with the arms of France and inscribed in Latin: 'Here Jesus Christ was born of the Virgin Mary'. The star had been placed there by the French in the eighteenth century, but had always been resented as a 'badge of conquest' by the Greeks. In 1847 the silver star was stolen; the tools used to wrench it from the marble floor were abandoned at the site. The Latins immediately accused the Greeks of carrying out the crime. Only recently the Greeks had built a wall to prevent the Latin priests from accessing the Grotto, and this had ended in a brawl between the Latin and Greek priests. After the removal of the silver star, the French launched a diplomatic protest to the Porte, the Ottoman government in Constantinople, citing a long-neglected treaty of 1740 which they claimed secured the rights of the Catholics to the Grotto for the upkeep of the silver star. But the Greeks had rival claims based on custom and concessions by the Porte.[9] This small conflict over a church key was in fact the start of a diplomatic crisis over the control of the Holy Places that would have profound consequences.

Along with the keys to the church at Bethlehem, the French claimed for the Catholics a right to repair the roof of the Holy Sepulchre, also based on the treaty of 1740. The roof was in urgent need of attention. Most of the lead on one side had been stripped off (the Greeks and the Latins each accusing the other side of having done this). Rain came through the roof and birds flew freely in the church. Under Turkish law, whoever owned the roof of a house was the owner of that house. So the right to carry out the repairs was fiercely disputed by the Latins and the Greeks on the grounds that it would establish them in the eyes of the Turks as the legitimate protectors of the Holy Sepulchre. Against the French, Russia backed the counterclaims of the Orthodox, appealing to the 1774 Treaty of Kuchuk Kainarji, signed by the Turks after their defeat by Russia in the war of 1768–74. According to the Russians, the Treaty of Kuchuk Kainarji had given them a right to represent the interests of the Orthodox in the Ottoman Empire. This was a long way from the truth. The language of the treaty was ambiguous and easily distorted by translations into various languages (the Russians signed the treaty in Russian and Italian, the Turks in Turkish and Italian, and then it was translated by the Russians into French for diplomatic purposes).[10] But Russian pressure on the Porte ensured that the Latins would not get their way. The Turks temporized and fudged the issue with conciliatory noises to both sides.

The conflict deepened in May 1851, when Louis-Napoleon appointed his close friend the Marquis Charles de La Valette as ambassador in the Turkish capital. Two and a half years after his election as President of France, Napoleon was still struggling to assert his power over the National Assembly. To strengthen his position he had made a series of concessions to Catholic opinion: in 1849 French troops had returned the Pope to Rome after he had been forced out of the Vatican by revolutionary crowds; and the Falloux Law of 1850 had opened the way to an increase in the number of Catholic-run schools. The appointment of La Valette was another major concession to clerical opinion. The Marquis was a zealous Catholic, a leading figure in the shadowy 'clerical party' which was widely viewed as pulling the hidden strings of France's foreign policy. The influence of this clerical faction was particularly strong on France's policies towards the Holy Places, where it called for a firm stand against the Orthodox menace. La Valette went well beyond his remit when he took up his position as ambassador. On his way to Constantinople he made an unscheduled stop in Rome to persuade the Pope to support the French claims for the Catholics in the Holy Lands. Installed in Constantinople, he made a point of using aggressive language in his dealings with the Porte – a tactic, he explained, to 'make the Sultan and his ministers recoil and capitulate' to French interests. The Catholic press rallied behind La Valette, especially the influential *Journal des débats*, whose editor was a close friend of his. La Valette, in turn, fed the press with quotations that inflamed the situation and enraged the Tsar, Nicholas I.[11]

In August 1851 the French formed a joint commission with the Turks to discuss the issue of religious rights. The commission dragged on inconclusively as the Turks carefully weighed up the competing Greek and Latin claims. Before its work could be completed, La Valette proclaimed that the Latin right was 'clearly established', meaning that there was no need for the negotiations to go on. He talked of France 'being justified in a recourse to extreme measures' to support the Latin right, and boasted of 'her superior naval forces in the Mediterranean' as a means of enforcing French interests.

It is doubtful whether La Valette had the approval of Napoleon for such an explicit threat of war. Napoleon was not particularly interested in religion. He was ignorant about the details of the Holy Lands dispute, and basically defensive in the Middle East. But it is possible and perhaps even likely that Napoleon was happy for La Valette to provoke a crisis with Russia. He was keen to explore anything that would come between the three powers (Britain, Russia, Austria) that had isolated France from the Concert of Europe and subjected it to the 'galling treaties' of the 1815 settlement following the defeat of his uncle, Napoleon Bonaparte. Louis-Napoleon had reasonable grounds for hoping that a new system of alliances might emerge from the dispute in the Holy Lands: Austria was a Catholic country, and might be persuaded to side with France against Orthodox Russia, while Britain had its own imperial interests to defend against the Russians in the Near East. Whatever lay behind it, La Valette's premeditated act of aggression infuriated the Tsar, who warned the Sultan that any recognition of the Latin claims would violate existing treaties between the Porte and Russia, forcing him to break off diplomatic relations with the Ottomans. This sudden turn of events alerted Britain, which had previously encouraged France to reach a compromise, but now had to prepare for the possibility of war.[12]

The war would not actually begin for another two years, but when it did the conflagration it unleashed was fuelled by the religious passions that had been building over centuries.

*

More than any other power, the Russian Empire had religion at its heart. The tsarist system organized its subjects through their confessional status; it understood its boundaries and international commitments almost entirely in terms of faith.

In the founding ideology of the tsarist state, which gained new force through Russian nationalism in the nineteeth century, Moscow was the last remaining capital of Othodoxy, the 'Third Rome', following the fall of Constantinople, the centre of Byzantium, to the Turks in 1453. According to this ideology, it was part of Russia's divine mission in the world to liberate the Orthodox from the Islamic empire of the Ottomans and restore Constantinople as the seat of Eastern Christianity. The Russian Empire was conceived as an Orthodox crusade. From the defeat of the Mongol khanates of Kazan and Astrakhan in the sixteenth century to the conquest of the Crimea, the Caucasus and Siberia in the eighteenth and nineteenth centuries, Russia's imperial identity was practically defined by the conflict between Christian settlers and Tatar nomads on the Eurasian steppe. This religious boundary was always more important than any ethnic one in the definition of the Russian national consciousness: the Russian was Orthodox and the foreigner was of a different faith.

Religion was at the heart of Russia's wars against the Turks, who by the middle of the nineteenth century had 10 million Orthodox subjects (Greeks, Bulgarians, Albanians, Moldavians, Wallachians and Serbs) in their European territories and something in the region of another 3 to 4 million Christians (Armenians, Georgians and a small number of Abkhazians) in the Caucasus and Anatolia.[13]

On the northern borders of the Ottoman Empire a defensive line of fortresses stretched from Belgrade in the Balkans to Kars in the Caucasus. This was the line along which all of Turkey's wars with Russia had been fought since the latter half of the seventeenth century (in 1686–99, 1710–11, 1735–9, 1768–74, 1787–92, 1806–12 and 1828–9). The Crimean War and the later Russo-Turkish war of 1877–8 were no exceptions to the rule. The borderlands defended by these fortresses were religious battlegrounds, the fault-line between Orthodoxy and Islam.

Two regions, in particular, were vital in these Russo-Turkish wars: the Danube delta (encompassing the principalities of Moldavia and Wallachia) and the Black Sea northern coast (including the Crimean peninsula). They were to become the two main theatres of the Crimean War.

With its wide rivers and pestilent marshes, the Danube delta was a crucial buffer zone protecting Constantinople from a land attack by the Russians. Danubian food supplies were essential for the Turkish fortresses, as they were for any Russian army attacking the Ottoman capital, so the allegiance of the peasant population was a vital factor in these wars. The Russians appealed to the Orthodox religion of the peasantry in an attempt to get them on their side for a war of liberation against Muslim rule, while the Turks themselves adopted scorched-earth policies. Hunger and disease repeatedly defeated the advancing Russians, as they marched into the Danubian lands whose crops had been destroyed by the retreating Turks. Any attack on the Turkish capital would thus depend on the Russians setting up a sea route – through the Black Sea – to bring supplies to the attacking troops.

But the Black Sea northern coast and the Crimea were also used by the Ottomans as a buffer zone against Russia. Rather than colonize the area, the Ottomans relied on their vassals there, the Turkic-speaking Tatar tribes of the Crimean khanate, to protect the borders of Islam against Christian invaders. Ruled by the Giray dynasty, the direct descendants of Genghiz Khan himself, the Crimean khanate was the last surviving outpost of the Golden Horde. From the fifteenth to the eighteenth century its army of horsemen had the run of the southern steppes between Russia and the Black Sea coast. Raiding into Muscovy, the Tatars provided a regular supply of Slavic slaves for sale in the sex-markets and rowing-galleys of Constantinople. The tsars of Russia and the kings of Poland paid tribute to the khan to keep his men away.[14]

From the end of the seventeenth century, when it gained possession of Ukraine, Russia began a century-long struggle to wrench these buffer zones from Ottoman control. The warm-water ports of the Black Sea, so essential for the development of Russian trade and naval power, were the strategic objects in this war, but religious interests were never far behind. Thus, after the defeat of the Ottomans by Russia and its allies in 1699, Peter the Great demanded from the Turks a guarantee of the Greek rights at the Holy Sepulchre and free access for all Russians to the Holy Lands. The struggle for the Danubian principalities (Moldavia and Wallachia) was also in part a religious war. In the Russo-Turkish conflict of 1710–11 Peter ordered Russian troops to cross the River Pruth and invade the principalities in the hope of provoking an uprising by their Christian population against the Turks. The uprising did not materialize. But the idea that Russia could appeal to its co-religionists in the Ottoman Empire to undermine the Turks remained at the centre of tsarist policy for the next two hundred years.

The policy took formal shape in the reign of Catherine the Great (1762–96). After their decisive defeat of the Ottomans in the war of 1768–74, during which they had reoccupied the principalities, the Russians demanded relatively little from the Turks in terms of territory, before withdrawing from the principalities. The resulting Treaty of Kuchuk Kainarji granted them only a small stretch of the Black Sea coastline between the Dnieper and Bug rivers (including the port of Kherson), the Kabarda region of the Causasus, and the Crimean ports of Kerch and Enikale, where the Sea of Azov joins the Black Sea, although the treaty forced the Ottomans to surrender their sovereignty over the Crimean khanate and give independence to the Tatars. The treaty also gave Russian shipping free passage through the Dardanelles, the narrow Turkish Straits connecting the Black Sea to the Mediterranean. But if the Russians did not gain a lot of territory, they gained substantial rights to interfere in Ottoman affairs for the protection of the Orthodox. Kuchuk Kainarji restored the principalities to their former status under Ottoman sovereignty, but the Russians assumed the right of protection over the Orthodox population. The treaty also granted Russia permission to build an Orthodox church in Constantinople – a treaty right the Russians took to mean a broader right to represent the sultan's Orthodox subjects. It allowed the Christian merchants of the Ottoman Empire (Greeks, Armenians, Moldavians and Wallachians) to sail their ships in Turkish waters with a Russian flag, an important concession that allowed the Russians to advance their commercial and religious interests at the same time. These religious claims had some interesting pragmatic ramifications. Since the Russians could not annex the Danubian principalities without incurring the opposition of the great powers, they looked instead to win concessions from the Porte that would turn the principalities into semi-autonomous regions under Russian influence. Shared religious loyalties would, in time, they hoped, lead to alliances with the Moldavians and Wallachians which would weaken Ottoman authority and ensure Russian domination over south-east Europe should the Ottoman Empire collapse.

Encouraged by victory against Turkey, Catherine also pursued a policy of collaboration with the Greeks, whose religious interests she claimed Russia had a treaty right and obligation to protect. Catherine sent military agents into Greece, trained Greek officers in her military schools, invited Greek traders and seamen to settle in her new towns on the Black Sea coast, and encouraged Greeks in their belief that Russia would support their movement for national liberation from the Turks. More than any other Russian ruler, Catherine identified with the Greek cause. Under the growing influence of her most senior military commander, statesman and court favourite Prince Grigory Potemkin, Catherine even dreamed of re-creating the old Byzantine Empire on the ruins of the Ottoman. The French philosopher Voltaire, with whom the Empress corresponded, addressed her as 'votre majesté impériale de l'église grecque', while Baron Friedrich Grimm, her favourite German correspondent, referred to her as 'l'Impératrice des Grecs'. Catherine conceived this Hellenic empire as a vast Orthodox imperium protected by Russia, whose Slavonic tongue had once been the lingua franca of the Byzantine Empire, according (erroneously) to the first great historian of Russia, Vasily Tatishchev. The Empress gave the name of Constantine – after both the first and the final emperor of Byzantium – to her second grandson. To commemorate his birth in 1779, she had minted special silver coins with the image of the great St Sophia church (Hagia Sophia) in Constantinople, cruelly converted into a mosque since the Ottoman conquest. Instead of a minaret, the coin showed an Orthodox cross on the cupola of the former Byzantine basilica. To educate her grandson to become the ruler of this resurrected Eastern Empire, the Russian Empress brought nurses from Naxos to teach him Greek, a language which he spoke with great facility as an adult.[15]

It was always unclear how serious she was about this 'Greek Project'. In the form that it was drawn up by Count Bezborodko, her private secretary and virtual Foreign Minister, in 1780, the project involved nothing less than the expulsion of the Turks from Europe, the division of their Balkan territories between Russia and Austria, and the 're-establishment of the ancient Greek empire' with Constantinople as its capital. Catherine discussed the project with the Austrian Emperor Joseph II in 1781. They agreed on its desirability in an exchange of letters over the next year. But whether they intended to carry out the plan remains uncertain. Some historians have concluded that the Greek project was no more than a piece of neoclassical iconography, or political theatre, like the 'Potemkin villages', which played no real part in Russia's foreign policy. But even if there was no concrete plan for immediate action, it does at least seem fairly clear that the project formed a part of Catherine's general aims for the Russian Empire as a Black Sea power linked through trade and religion to the Orthodox world of the eastern Mediterranean, including Jerusalem. In the words of Catherine's favourite poet, Gavril Derzhavin, who was also one of Russia's most important statesmen in her reign, the aim of the Greek project was

> To advance through a Crusade,
> To purify the Jordan River,
> To liberate the Holy Sepulchre,
> To return Athens to the Athenians,

Constantinople – to Constantine
And re-establish Japheth's Holy Land.*
'Ode on the Capture of Izmail'

It was certainly more than political theatre when Catherine and Joseph, accompanied by a large international entourage, toured the Black Sea ports. The Empress visited the building sites of new Russian towns and military bases, passing under archways erected by Potemkin in her honour and inscribed with the words 'The Road to Byzantium'.[16] Her journey was a statement of intent.

Catherine believed that Russia had to turn towards the south if it was to be a great power. It was not enough for it to export furs and timber through the Baltic ports, as in the days of medieval Muscovy. To compete with the European powers it had to develop trading outlets for the agricultural produce of its fertile southern lands and build up a naval presence in the warm-water ports of the Black Sea from which its ships could gain entry to the Mediterranean. Because of the odd geography of Russia, the Black Sea was crucial, not just to the military defence of the Russian Empire on its southern frontier with the Muslim world, but also to its viability as a power on the European continent. Without the Black Sea, Russia had no access to Europe by the sea, except via the Baltic, which could easily be blocked by the other northern powers in the event of a European conflict (as indeed it would be by the British during the Crimean War).

The plan to develop Russia as a southern power had begun in earnest in 1776, when Catherine placed Potemkin in charge of New Russia (*Novorossiia*), the sparsely populated territories newly conquered from the Ottomans on the Black Sea's northern coastline, and ordered him to colonize the area. She granted enormous tracts of land to her nobility and invited European colonists (Germans, Poles, Italians, Greeks, Bulgarians and Serbs) to settle on the steppelands as agriculturalists. New cities were established there – Ekaterinoslav, Kherson, Nikolaev and Odessa – many of them built in the French and Italian rococo style. Potemkin personally oversaw the construction of Ekaterinoslav (meaning 'Catherine's Glory') as a Graeco-Roman

---

* According to medieval Russian chronicles, the lands of Japheth were settled by the Rus' and other tribes after the Flood in the Book of Genesis.

fantasy to symbolize the classical inheritance that he and the supporters of the Greek project had envisaged for Russia. He dreamed up
grandiose neoclassical structures, most of which were never built,
such as shops 'built in a semicircle like the Propylaeum or threshold
of Athens', a governor's house in the 'Greek and Roman style', law
courts in the shape of 'ancient basilicas', and a cathedral, 'a kind of
imitation of St Paul's outside the walls of Rome', as he explained in a
letter to Catherine. It was, he said, 'a sign of the transformation of this
land by your care, from a barren steppe to an ample garden, and from
the wilderness of animals to a home welcoming people from all
lands'.[17]

Odessa was the jewel in Russia's southern crown. Its architectural
beauty owed a great deal to the Duc de Richelieu, a refugee from the
French Revolution, who for many years served as the city's governor.
But its importance as a port was the work of the Greeks, who were
first encouraged to settle in the town by Catherine. Thanks to the freedom of movement afforded Russian shipping by the Treaty of Kuchuk
Kainarji, Odessa soon became a major player in the Black Sea and
Mediterranean trade, to a large degree supplanting the domination of
the French.

Russia's incorporation of the Crimea followed a different course.
As part of the Treaty of Kuchuk Kainarji, the Crimean khanate had
been made independent of the Ottomans, although the Sultan had
retained a nominal religious authority in his role as caliph. Despite
their signature on the treaty, the Ottomans had been reluctant to
accept the independence of the Crimea, fearing it would soon be swallowed up by the Russians, like the rest of the Black Sea coast. They
held on to the powerful fortress of Ochakov at the mouth of the
Dnieper river from which to attack the Russians if they intervened in
the peninsula. But they had little defence against Russia's policy of
political and religious infiltration.

Three years after the signing of the treaty, Şagin Giray was elected
khan. Educated in Venice and semi-Westernized, he was Russia's preferred candidate (as the head of a Crimean delegation to St Petersburg,
he had impressed Catherine with his 'sweet character' and handsome
looks). Şagin was supported by the Crimea's sizeable Christian population (Greek, Georgian and Armenian traders) and by many of the

Nogai nomads on the mainland steppe, who had always been fiercely independent of the Ottoman khanate and owed their allegiance to Şagin as Commander of the Nogai Horde. Şagin, however, was unacceptable to the Ottomans, who sent a fleet with their own khan to replace him and encouraged the Crimean Tatars to rise up against Şagin as an 'infidel'. Şagin fled, but soon returned to carry out a slaughter of the rebellious Tatars that appalled even the Russians. In response, and encouraged by the Ottomans, the Tatars began a religious war of retribution against the Christians of the Crimea, prompting Russia to organize the latter's hurried exodus (30,000 Christians were moved to Taganrog, Mariupol and other towns on the Black Sea coast, where most of them became homeless).

The departure of the Christians seriously weakened the Crimean economy. Şagin became even more dependent on the Russians, who began to pressure him to accept annexation. Anxious to secure the Crimea before the rest of Europe could react, Potemkin prepared for a quick war against the Turks, while procuring Şagin's abdication in return for a magnificent pension. With the Khan removed to St Petersburg, the Tatars were persuaded to submit to Catherine. Throughout the Crimea there were stage-managed ceremonies where the Tatars gathered with their mullahs to swear an oath on the Koran to the Orthodox Empress a thousand kilometres away. Potemkin was determined that the annexation should at least appear to be the will of the people.

The Russian annexation of the Crimea, in 1783, was a bitter humiliation for the Turks. It was the first Muslim territory to be lost to Christians by the Ottoman Empire. The Grand Vizier of the Porte reluctantly accepted it. But other politicians at the Sultan's court saw the loss of the Crimea as a mortal danger to the Ottoman Empire, arguing that the Russians would use it as a military base against Constantinople and Ottoman control of the Balkans, and they pressed for war against Russia. But it was unrealistic for the Turks to fight the Russians on their own, and Turkish hopes of Western intervention were not great: Austria had aligned itself with Russia in anticipation of a future Russian–Austrian partition of the Ottoman Empire; France was too exhausted by its involvement in the American War of Independence to send a fleet to the Black Sea; while the British, deeply wounded by their losses in America, were essentially indifferent (if

'France means to be quiet about the Turks', noted Lord Grantham, the Foreign Secretary, 'why should we meddle? Not time to begin a fresh broil').[18]

Ottoman forbearance broke four years later, in 1787, shortly after Catherine's provocative procession through her newly conquered Black Sea coastal towns, which came just as the Turks were facing further losses to the Russians in the Caucasus.* Hopeful of a Prussian alliance, the pro-war party at the Porte prevailed, and the Ottomans declared war on Russia, which was then supported by its ally Austria with its own declaration of war against Turkey. At first the Ottomans had some success. On the Danube front, they pushed back the Austrian forces into the Banat. But military help from Prussia never came, and after a long siege the Turks lost their strategic fortress at Ochakov to the Russians, followed by Belgrade and the Danubian principalities to an Austrian counter-offensive, before the Russians took the important Turkish forts in the Danube estuary. The Turks were forced to sue for peace. By the Treaty of Iaşi, in 1792, they regained a nominal control of the Danubian principalities, but ceded the area of Ochakov to Russia, thereby making the Dniester river the new Russo-Turkish boundary. They also declared their formal recognition of the Russian annexation of the Crimea. But in reality they never fully accepted its loss and waited for revenge.

*

In Russia's religious war against its Muslim neighbours, the Islamic cultures of the Black Sea area were regarded as a particular danger. Russia's rulers were afraid of an Islamic axis, a broad coalition of Muslim peoples under Turkish leadership, threatening Russia's southern borderlands, where the Muslim population was increasing fast, partly as a result of high birth rates, and partly from conversions to Islam by nomadic tribes. It was to consolidate imperial control in these unsettled borderlands that the Russians launched a new part of

---

* The Russians were steadily extending their system of fortresses along the Terek river (the 'Caucasus Line') and using their newly won protectorate over the Orthodox Georgian kingdom of Kartli-Kacheti to build up a base of operations against the Ottomans, occupying Tbilisi and laying the foundations for the Georgian Military Highway to link Russia to the southern Caucasus.

their southern strategy in the early decades of the nineteenth century: clearing Muslim populations and encouraging Christian settlers to colonize the newly conquered lands.

Bessarabia was conquered by the Russians during the war against Turkey in 1806–12. It was formally ceded by the Turks to Russia through the Treaty of Bucharest in 1812, which also placed the Danubian principalities under the joint sovereignty of Russia and the Ottoman Empire. The new tsarist rulers of Bessarabia expelled the Muslim population, sending thousands of Tatar farmers as prisoners of war to Russia. They resettled the fertile plains of Bessarabia with Moldavians, Wallachians, Bulgarians, Ruthenians and Greeks attracted to the area by tax breaks, exemptions from military service, and by loans to skilled craftsmen from the Russian government. Under pressure to populate the area, which brought Russia to within a few kilometres of the Danube, the local tsarist authorities even turned a blind eye to the runaway Ukrainian and Russian serfs, who arrived in growing numbers in Bessarabia after 1812. There was an active programme of church-building, while the establishment of an eparchy in Kishinev locked the local Church leaders into the Russian (as opposed to the Greek) Orthodox Church.[19]

The Russian conquest of the Caucasus, too, was part of this crusade. To a large extent, it was conceived as a religious war against the Muslim mountain tribes, the Chechens, Ingush, Circassians and Daghestanis, and for the Christianization of the Caucasus. The Muslim tribes were mainly Sunni, fiercely independent of political control by any secular power but aligned by religion to the Ottoman sultan in his capacity as 'supreme caliph of Islamic law'. Under the command of General Alexander Ermolov, appointed as governor of Georgia in 1816, the Russians fought a savage war of terror, raiding villages, burning houses, destroying crops and clearing the forests, in a vain attempt to subjugate the mountain tribes. The murderous campaign gave rise to an organized resistance movement by the tribes, which soon assumed a religious character of its own.

The main religious influence, known as Muridism, came from the Naqshbandiya (Sufi) sect, which began to flourish in Daghestan in the 1810s and spread from there to Chechnya, where preachers organized the resistance as a jihad (holy war) led by the Imam Ghazi

Muhammad, in defence of shariah law and the purity of Islamic faith. Muridism was a powerful mixture of holy and social war against the infidel Russians and the princes who supported them. It brought a new unity to the mountain tribes, previously divided by blood-feuds and vendettas, enabling the imam to introduce taxes and universal military service. The imam's rule was enforced through the murids (religious disciples), who provided local officials and judges in the rebel villages.

The more religious the resistance grew, the more the Russian invasion's religious character intensified. The Christianization of the Caucasus became one of the primary goals, as the Russians rejected any compromise with the rebel movement's Muslim leadership. 'A complete rapprochement between them and us can be expected only when the Cross is set up on the mountains and in the valleys, and when churches of Christ the Saviour have replaced the mosques,' declared an official Russian document. 'Until then, force of arms is the true bastion of our rule in the Caucasus.' The Russians destroyed mosques and imposed restrictions on Muslim practices – the greatest outcry being caused by the prohibition of the pilgrimage to Mecca and Medina. In many areas, the destruction of Muslim settlements was connected to a Russian policy of what today would be known as 'ethnic cleansing', the forced resettlement of mountain tribes and the reallocation of their land to Christian settlers. In the Kuban and the northern Caucasus, Muslim tribes were replaced by Slavic settlers, mainly Russian or Ukrainian peasants and Cossacks. In parts of the southern Caucasus, the Christian Georgians and Armenians sided with the Russian invasion and took a share of the spoils. During the conquest of the Ganja khanate (Elizavetopol), for example, Georgians joined the invading Russian army as auxiliaries; they were then encouraged by the Russians to move into the occupied territory and take over lands abandoned by the Muslims after a campaign of religious persecution had encouraged them to move away. The province of Erivan, which roughly corresponds to modern Armenia, had a largely Turkish-Muslim population until the Russo-Turkish war of 1828–9, during which the Russians expelled around 26,000 Muslims from the area. Over the next decade they moved in almost twice that number of Armenians.[20]

But it was in the Crimea that the religious character of Russia's southern conquests was most clear. The Crimea has a long and complex religious history. For the Russians, it was a sacred place. According to their chronicles, it was in Khersonesos, the ancient Greek colonial city on the south-western coast of the Crimea, just outside modern Sevastopol, that Vladimir, the Grand Prince of Kiev, was baptized in 988, thereby bringing Christianity to Kievan Rus'. But it was also home to Scythians, Romans, Greeks, Goths, Genoese, Jews, Armenians, Mongols and Tatars. Located on a deep historical fault-line separating Christendom from the Muslim world of the Ottomans and the Turkic-speaking tribes, the Crimea was continuously in contention, the site of many wars. Religious shrines and buildings in the Crimea themselves became battlefields of faith, as each new wave of settlement claimed them as their own. In the coastal town of Sudak, for example, there is a St Matthew church. It was originally built as a mosque, but subsequently destroyed and rebuilt by the Greeks as an Orthodox church. It was later converted into a Catholic church by the Genoese, who came to the Crimea in the thirteenth century, and then turned back into a mosque by the Ottomans. It remained a mosque until the Russian annexation, when it was reconverted into an Orthodox church.[21]

The Russian annexation of the Crimea had created 300,000 new imperial subjects, nearly all of them Muslim Tatars and Nogais. The Russians attempted to co-opt the local notables (beys and mirzas) into their administration by offering to convert them to Christianity and elevate them to noble status. But their invitation was ignored. The power of these notables had never been derived from civil service but from their ownership of land and from clan-based politics: as long as they were allowed to keep their land, most of them preferred to keep their standing in the local community rather than serve their new imperial masters. The majority had ties through kin or trade or religion to the Ottoman Empire. Many of them emigrated there following the Russian takeover.

Russian policy towards the Tatar peasants was more brutal. Serfdom was unknown in the Crimea, unlike most of Russia. The freedom of the Tatar peasants was recognized by the new imperial government, which made them into state peasants (a separate legal category from the serfs). But the continued allegiance of the Tatars to the Ottoman caliph, to whom they appealed in their Friday prayers, was a constant provocation to the Russians. It gave them cause to doubt the sincerity of their new subjects' oath of allegiance to the tsar. Throughout their many wars with the Ottomans in the nineteenth century, the Russians remained terrified of Tatar revolts in the Crimea. They accused Muslim leaders of praying for a Turkish victory and Tatar peasants of hoping for their liberation by the Turks, despite the fact that, for the most part, until the Crimean War, the Muslim population remained loyal to the tsar.

Convinced of Tatar perfidy, the Russians did what they could to get their new subjects to leave. The first mass exodus of Crimean Tatars to Turkey occurred during the Russo-Turkish war of 1787–92. Most of it was the panic flight of peasants frightened of reprisals by the Russians. But the Tatars were also encouraged to depart by a variety of other Russian measures, including the seizure of their land, punitive taxation, forced labour and physical intimidation by Cossack squads. By 1800 nearly one-third of the Crimean Tatar population, about 100,000 people, had emigrated to the Ottoman Empire with another 10,000 leaving in the wake of the Russo-Turkish war of 1806–12. They were replaced by Russian settlers and other Eastern Christians: Greeks, Armenians, Bulgarians, many of them refugees from the Ottoman Empire who wanted the protection of a Christian state. The exodus of the Crimean Tatars was the start of a gradual retreat of the Muslims from Europe. It was part of a long history of demographic exchange and ethnic conflict between the Ottoman and Orthodox spheres which would last until the Balkan crises of the late twentieth century.[22]

The Christianization of the Crimea was also realized in grand designs for churches, palaces and neoclassical cities that would eradicate all Muslim traces from the physical environment. Catherine envisaged the Crimea as Russia's southern paradise, a pleasure-garden where the fruits of her enlightened Christian rule could be enjoyed and exhibited to the world beyond the Black Sea. She liked to call the peninsula by its Greek name, Taurida, in preference to Crimea (*Krym*), its Tatar name: she thought that it linked Russia to the Hellenic civilization of Byzantium. She gave enormous tracts of land to Russia's

nobles to establish magnificent estates along the mountainous southern coast, a coastline to rival the Amalfi in beauty; their classical
buildings, Mediterranean gardens and vineyards were supposed to be
the carriers of a new Christian civilization in this previously heathen
land.

Urban planning reinforced this Russian domination of the Crimea:
ancient Tatar towns like Bakhchiserai, the capital of the former
khanate, were downgraded or abandoned completely; ethnically
mixed cities such as Theodosia or Simferopol, the Russian administrative capital, were gradually reordered by the imperial state, with
the centre of the city shifted from the old Tatar quarter to new areas
where Russian churches and official buildings were erected; and new
towns like Sevastopol, the Russian naval base, were built entirely in
the neoclassical style.[23]

Church-building in the newly conquered colony was relatively
slow, and mosques continued to dominate the skyline in many towns
and villages. But in the early nineteenth century there was an intense
focus on the discovery of ancient Christian archaeological remains,
Byzantine ruins, ascetic cave-churches and monasteries. It was all part
of a deliberate effort to reclaim the Crimea as a sacred Christian site,
a Russian Mount Athos, a place of pilgrimage for those who wanted
to make a connection to the cradle of Slavic Christianity.[24]

The most important holy site was, of course, the ruin of Khersonesos, excavated by the imperial administration in 1827, where a
church of St Vladimir was later built to mark the notional spot where
the Grand Prince had converted Kievan Rus' to Christianity. It was
one of those symbolic ironies of history that this sacred shrine was
only a few metres from the place where the French forces landed and
set up their camp during the Crimean War.

2

Eastern Questions

The Sultan rode on a white horse at the head of the procession, followed by his retinue of ministers and officials on foot. To the sound of an artillery salute, they emerged from the main Imperial Gate of the Topkapi Palace into the midday heat of a July day in Constantinople, the Turkish capital. It was Friday, 13 July 1849, the first day of the Muslim holy month of Ramadan. The Sultan Abdülmecid was on his way to reinaugurate the great mosque of Hagia Sophia. For the past two years it had been shut down for urgent restorations, the building having fallen into chronic disrepair after many decades of neglect. Riding through the crowd assembled in the square on the northern side of the former Orthodox basilica, where his mother, children and harem awaited him in gilded carriages, the Sultan arrived at the entrance of the mosque, where he was met by his religious officials and, in a break from Islamic tradition which specifically excluded non-Muslims from such holy ceremonies, by two Swiss architects, Gaspare and Giuseppe Fossati, who had overseen the restoration work.

The Fossatis led Abdülmecid through a series of private chambers to the sultan's loge in the main prayer hall which they had rebuilt and redecorated in a neo-Byzantine style on the orders of the Sultan, whose insignia was fixed above the entry door. When the dignitaries had gathered in the hall, the rites of consecration were carried out by the Sheikh ül-Islam, the supreme religious official in the Ottoman Empire, who was (wrongly) equated with the Pope by European visitors.[1]

It was an extraordinary occasion – the sultan-caliph and religious leaders of the world's largest Muslim empire consecrating one of its most holy mosques in chambers rebuilt by Western architects in the style of the original Byzantine cathedral from which it was converted

Hagia Sophia, early 1850s

following the conquest of Constantinople by the Turks. After 1453 the Ottomans had taken down the bells, replaced the cross with four minarets, removed the altar and iconostasis, and over the course of the next two centuries plastered over the Byzantine mosaics of the Orthodox basilica. The mosaics had remained concealed until the Fossati brothers had discovered them by accident while restoring the revetments and plasterwork in 1848. Having cleared a part of the mosaics on the north aisle vault, they showed them to the Sultan, who was so impressed by their brilliant colours that he ordered all of them to be liberated from their plaster covering. The hidden Christian origins of the mosque had been revealed.

Realizing the significance of their discovery, the Fossati brothers made drawings and watercolours of the Byzantine mosaics, which they presented to the Tsar in the hope of receiving a subvention for the publication of their work. The architects had previously worked in

St Petersburg, and the elder brother, Gaspare, had originally come to Constantinople to build the Russian embassy, a neoclassical palace completed in 1845, where he was joined by Giuseppe. This was a time when many European architects were constructing buildings in the Turkish capital, many of them foreign embassies, a time when the young Sultan was giving his support to a whole series of Westernizing liberal reforms and opening up his empire to the influence of Europe in the pursuit of economic modernization. Between 1845 and 1847 the Fossatis were employed by the Sultan to erect a massive three-storey complex for Constantinople University. Built entirely in the Western neoclassical style and placed awkwardly between the Hagia Sophia and Sultan Ahmet mosques, the complex was burned down in 1936.[2]

The Tsar of Russia, Nicholas I, was bound to be excited by the discovery of these Byzantine mosaics. The church of Hagia Sophia was a focal point in the religious life of tsarist Russia – a civilization built upon the myth of Orthodox succession to the Byzantine Empire. Hagia Sophia was the Mother of the Russian Church, the historic link between Russia and the Orthodox world of the eastern Mediterranean and the Holy Lands. According to the *Primary Chronicle*, the first recorded history of Kievan Rus ', compiled by monks in the eleventh century, the Russians were originally inspired to convert to Christianity by the visual beauty of the church. Sent to various countries to search for the True Faith, the emissaries of the Grand Prince Vladimir reported of Hagia Sophia: 'We knew not whether we were in heaven or on earth. For on earth there is not such splendour or such beauty, and we are at a loss how to describe it. We only know that God dwells there among them, and their service is fairer than the ceremonies of other nations. For we cannot forget that beauty.'[3] The reclamation of the church remained a persistent and fundamental aim of Russian nationalists and religious leaders throughout the nineteenth century. They dreamed of the conquest of Constantinople and its resurrection as the Russian capital ('Tsargrad') of an Orthodox empire stretching from Siberia to the Holy Lands. In the words of the Tsar's leading missionary, Archimandrite Uspensky, who had led the ecclesiastical mission to Jerusalem in 1847, 'Russia from eternity has been ordained to illuminate Asia and to unite the Slavs. There will be a union of all Slav races with Armenia, Syria, Arabia and Ethiopia, and they will praise God in Saint Sophia.'[4]

The Tsar rejected the Fossatis' application for a grant to publish plans and drawings of the great Byzantine church and its mosaics. Although Nicholas expressed great interest in their work, this was not the time for a Russian ruler to get involved in the restoration of a mosque that was so central to the religious and political claims of the Ottoman Empire on the former territories of Byzantium. But at the heart of the conflict that eventually led to the Crimean War was Russia's own religious claim to lead and protect the Christians of the Ottoman Empire, a demand that centred on its aspiration to reclaim Hagia Sophia as the Mother Church and Constantinople as the capital of a vast Orthodox imperium connecting Moscow to Jerusalem.

Mosaic panel above the royal doors of the Hagia Sophia. The Fossatis painted the eight-point star over a whitewashed mosaic panel depicting the Byzantine emperor kneeling before Christ enthroned.

The Fossatis' studies would not be published until more than a century later, although some drawings of the Byzantine mosaics by the German archaeologist Wilhelm Salzenberg were commissioned by the Prussian King Friedrich Wilhelm IV, the brother-in-law of Nicholas I, and published in Berlin in 1854.[5] It was only through these drawings that the nineteenth-century world would learn about the hidden Christian treasures of the Hagia Sophia mosque. On the Sultan's orders, the figural mosaic panels were re-covered with plaster and painted in accordance with Muslim religious customs prohibiting the representation of humans. But the Fossatis were allowed to leave the purely ornamental Byzantine mosaics exposed, and they even painted decorations matching the surviving mosaic patterns onto whitewashed panels covering the human images.

The fortunes of the Byzantine mosaics offered a graphic illustration of the complex intermingling and competing claims of Muslim and Christian cultures in the Ottoman Empire. At the beginning of the nineteenth century Constantinople was the capital of a sprawling multinational empire stretching from the Balkans to the Persian Gulf, from Aden to Algeria, and comprising around 35 million people. Muslims were an absolute majority, accounting for about 60 per cent of the population, virtually all of them in Asiatic Turkey, North Africa and the Arabian peninsula; but the Turks themselves were a minority, perhaps 10 million, mostly concentrated in Anatolia. In the Sultan's European territories, which had been largely conquered from Byzantium, the majority of his subjects were Orthodox Christians.[6]

From its origins in the fourteenth century, the empire's ruling Osman dynasty had drawn its legitimacy from the ideal of a continuous holy war to extend the frontiers of Islam. But the Ottomans were pragmatists, not religious fundamentalists, and in their Christian lands, the richest and most populous in the empire, they tempered their ideological animosity towards the infidels with a practical approach to their exploitation for imperial interests. They levied extra taxes on the non-Muslims, looked down on them as inferior 'beasts' (*rayah*), and treated them unequally in various humiliating ways (in Damascus, for example, Christians were forbidden to ride animals of any kind).[7] But they let them keep their religion, did not generally persecute or try to convert them, and, through the *millet* system of religious segregation, which gave Church leaders powers within their separate, faith-based 'nations' or *millets*, they even allowed non-Muslims a certain measure of autonomy.

The *millet* system had developed as a means for the Osman dynasty to use religious élites as the intermediaries in newly conquered territories. As long as they submitted to Ottoman authority, ecclesiastical leaders were allowed to exercise a limited control over education, public order and justice, tax collection, charity and Church affairs, subject to the approval of the Sultan's Muslim officials (even for such matters, for example, as the repair of a church roof). In this sense, the *millet* system not only served to reinforce the ethnic and religious hierarchy of the Ottoman Empire – with the Muslims at the top and all the other *millets* (Orthodox, Gregorian Armenian, Catholic and Jewish) below them – which encouraged Muslim prejudice against the Christians and the Jews; it also encouraged these minorities to express their grievances and organize their struggle against Muslim rule through their national Churches, which was a major source of instability in the empire.

Nowhere was this more apparent than among the Orthodox, the largest Christian *millet* with 10 million of the Sultan's subjects. The patriarch in Constantinople was the highest Orthodox authority in the Ottoman Empire. He spoke for the other Orthodox patriarchs of Antioch, Jerusalem and Alexandria. In a wide range of secular affairs he was the real ruler of the 'Greeks' (meaning all those who observed the Orthodox rite, including Slavs, Albanians, Moldavians and Wallachians) and represented their interests against both the Muslims and the Catholics. The patriarchate was controlled by the Phanariots, a powerful caste of Greek (and Hellenized Romanian and Albanian) merchant families originally from the Phanar district of Constantinople (from which they derived their name). Since the beginning of the eighteenth century the Phanariots had provided the Ottoman government with the majority of its dragomans (foreign secretaries and interpreters), purchased many other senior posts, assumed control of the Orthodox Church in Moldavia and Wallachia, where they were the main provincial governors (hospodars), and used their domination of the patriarchate to promote their Greek imperial ideals. The Phanariots saw themselves as the heirs of the Byzantine Empire and dreamed of restoring it with Russian help. But they were hostile to the influence of the Russian Church, which had promoted the Bulgarian clergy as a Slavic rival to Greek control of the patriarchate, and they were afraid of Russia's own ambitions in Ottoman Europe.

During the first quarter of the nineteenth century the other national Churches (Bulgarian and Serb) gradually assumed an equal importance to the Greek-dominated patriarchy in Constantinople. Greek domination of Orthodox affairs, including education and the courts, was unacceptable to many Slavs, who looked increasingly to their own Churches for their national identity and leadership against the Turks. Nationalism was a potent force among the different groups of Balkan Christians – Serbs, Montenegrins, Bulgarians, Moldavians, Wallachians and Greeks – who united on the basis of their language, culture and religion to break free from Ottoman control. The Serbs were the first to win their liberation, by means of Russian-sponsored uprisings between 1804 and 1817, leading to the Turkish recognition of Serb autonomy and eventually to the establishment of a principality of Serbia with its own constitution and a parliament headed by the Obrenović dynasty. But such was the weakness of the Ottoman Empire that its collapse in the rest of the Balkans appeared to be only a question of time.

*

Long before the Tsar described the Ottoman Empire as the 'sick man of Europe', on the eve of the Crimean War, the idea that it was about to crumble had become a commonplace. 'Turkey cannot stand, she is falling of herself,' the Prince of Serbia told the British consul in Belgrade in 1838; 'the revolt of her misgoverned provinces will destroy her.'[8]

That misgovernment was rooted in the empire's failure to adapt to the modern world. The domination of the Muslim clergy (the mufti and the ulema) acted as a powerful brake on reform. 'Meddle not with things established, borrow nothing from the infidels, for the law forbids it' was the motto of the Muslim Institution, which made sure that the sultan's laws conformed to the Koran. Western ideas and technologies were slow to penetrate the Islamic parts of the empire: trades and commerce were dominated by the non-Muslims (the Christians and Jews); there was no Turkish printing press until the 1720s; and as late as 1853 there were five times as many boys studying traditional Islamic law and theology in Constantinople as there were in the city's modern schools with a secular curriculum.[9]

The stagnation of the economy was matched by the proliferation of corrupt bureaucracy. The purchasing of offices for the lucrative business of tax-farming was almost universal in the provinces. Powerful pashas and military governors ruled whole regions as their personal fiefdoms, squeezing from them as many taxes as they could. As long as they passed on a share of their revenues to the Porte, and paid off their own financial backers, no one questioned or cared much about the arbitrary violence they employed. The lion's share of the empire's taxes was extracted from the non-Muslims, who had no legal protection or means of redress in the Muslim courts, where the testimony of a Christian counted for nothing. It is estimated that by the early nineteenth century the average Christian farmer and trader in the Ottoman Empire was paying half his earnings in taxes.[10]

But the key to the decline of the Ottoman Empire was its military backwardness. Turkey had a large army in the early nineteenth century, and it accounted for as much as 70 per cent of treasury expenditure, but it was technically inferior to the modern conscript armies of Europe. It lacked their centralized administration, command structures and military schools, was poorly trained and was still dependent on the recruitment of mercenaries, irregulars and tribal forces from the periphery of the empire. Military reform was essential, and recognized as such by reformist sultans and their ministers, particularly after the repeated defeats by Russia, followed by the loss of Egypt to Napoleon. But to build a modern conscript army was impossible without a fundamental transformation of the empire to centralize control of the provinces and overcome the vested interests of the 40,000 janizaries, the sultan's salaried household infantry, who represented the outmoded traditions of the military establishment and resisted all reforms.[11]

Selim III (1789–1807) was the first sultan to recognize the need to Westernize the Ottoman army and navy. His military reforms were guided by the French, the major foreign influence on the Ottomans in the final decades of the eighteenth century, mainly because their enemies (Austria and Russia) were also the enemies of the Ottoman Empire. Selim's concept of Westernization was similar to the Westernization of Russia's institutions carried out by Peter the Great in the early eighteenth century, and the Turks were conscious of this parallel.

It involved little more than the borrowing of new technologies and practices from foreigners, and certainly not the adoption of Western cultural principles that might challenge the dominant position of Islam in the empire. The Turks had invited the French to advise them, partly because they assumed they were the least religious of the European nations and therefore the least likely to threaten Islam – an impression gained from the anti-clerical policies of the Jacobins.

Selim's reforms were defeated by the janizaries and the Muslim clergy, who were opposed to any change. But they were continued by Mahmud II (1808–39), who built up the military schools established by Selim to undermine the janizaries' domination of the army by promoting officers on a meritocratic basis. He pushed through reforms of military dress, introduced Western equipment, and abolished the janizaries' fiefdoms in an effort to create a centralized European-style army into which the Sultan's household guards would eventually be merged. When the janizaries rebelled against the reforms, in 1826, they were put down, with several thousand killed by the Sultan's new army, and then liquidated by imperial decree.

As the Sultan's empire weakened to the point where it seemed in danger of imminent collapse, the great powers intervened increasingly in its affairs – ostensibly to protect the Christian minorities but in reality to advance their own ambitions in the area. European embassies were no longer content to limit their contacts to the Ottoman administration, as they had done previously, but took a hand directly in the empire's politics, supporting nationalities, religious groups, political parties and factions, and even interfering in the Sultan's appointment of individual ministers to promote their own imperial interests. To advance their country's trade they developed direct links with merchants and financiers and established consuls in the major trading towns. They also began to issue passports to Ottoman subjects. By the middle of the nineteenth century as many as one million inhabitants of the Sultan's empire were using the protective powers of the European legations to escape the jurisdiction and taxes of the Turkish authorities. Russia was the most active in this respect, developing its Black Sea commerce by granting passports to large numbers of the Sultan's Greeks and allowing them to sail under the Russian flag.[12]

For the Orthodox communities of the Ottoman Empire, Russia
was their protector against the Turks. Russian troops had helped the
Serbs to gain autonomy. They had brought Moldavia and Wallachia
under Russian protection, and liberated the Moldavians from Turkish
rule in Bessarabia. But the Russians' part in the Greek independence
movement showed how far they were prepared to go in their support
of their co-religionists to exert their hold over Turkey's European
territories.

The Greek revolution really began in Russia. In its early stages it
was led by Greek-born Russian politicians who had never even been
to mainland Greece (a 'geographical expression' if ever there was one)
but who dreamed of uniting all the Greeks through a series of uprisings against the Turks, which they planned to begin in the Danubian
principalities. In 1814 a Society of Friends (*Philiki Etaireia*) was set
up by Greek nationalists and students in Odessa, with affiliated
branches established soon thereafter in all the major areas where the
Greeks lived – Moldavia, Wallachia, the Ionian islands, Constantinople, the Peloponnese – as well as in other Russian cities where the
Greeks were strong. It was the Society that organized the Greek uprising in Moldavia in 1821 – an uprising led by Alexander Ypsilantis, a
senior officer in the Russian cavalry and the son of a prominent
Phanariot family in Moldavia that had fled to St Petersburg on the
outbreak of the Russo-Turkish war in 1806. Ypsilantis had close connections to the Russian court, where he had received the patronage of
the Empress Maria Fedorovna (the widow of Paul I) from the age of
15. Tsar Alexander I had appointed him his aide-de-camp in 1816.

There was a powerful Greek lobby in the ruling circles of St Petersburg. The Foreign Ministry contained a number of Greek-born
diplomats and activists of the Greek cause. None was more important
than Alexandru Sturdza from Moldavia, a Phanariot on his mother's
side, who became the first Russian governor of Bessarabia, or Ioannis
Kapodistrias, a Corfu nobleman who was appointed Russia's Foreign
Minister jointly with Karl Nesselrode in 1815. The Greek Gymnas-
ium in St Petersburg had been training Greek-born youths for military
and diplomatic service since the 1770s, and many of its graduates had
fought in the Russian army against the Turks in the war of 1806–12
(as did thousands of Greek volunteers from the Ottoman Empire,

who fled to Russia at the war's end). By the time Ypsilantis planned his uprising in Moldavia, there was a large cohort of Russian-trained, experienced Greek fighters on which he could count.

The plan was to start the uprising in Moldavia and then move to Wallachia. The insurgents would combine their attacks with the pandur (guerrilla) militia led by the Wallachian revolutionary Tudor Vladimirescu, another veteran of the Tsar's army in the Russo-Turkish war of 1806–12, whose peasant followers were in practice more opposed to their Phanariot rulers and landlords than they were to the distant Ottomans. The Treaty of Bucharest had placed the principalities under the joint sovereignty of Russia and the Ottoman Empire. They did not have any Turkish garrisons but the local hospodars were allowed to maintain small armies, which Ypsilantis expected to join the uprising as soon as his army of Greek volunteers from Russia crossed the River Pruth. Ypsilantis hoped that the revolt would spark a Russian intervention to defend the Greeks once the Turks took repressive measures against them. In the Moldavian capital of Iaşi he appeared in a Russian uniform and announced to the local boyars that he had 'the support of a great power'. There was certainly a great deal of support in the élite circles of St Petersburg, where philhellenic sentiment ran high, as well as among military and Church leaders. The Russian consulates in the principalities even became recruiting centres for the revolt. But neither Kapodistrias nor the Tsar knew anything about the preparations for the uprising, and both men denounced it as soon as it began. However much they might have sympathized with the Greek cause, Russia was the founder of the Holy Alliance, the conservative union formed with the Austrians and Prussians in 1815, whose *raison d'être* was to combat revolutionary and nationalist movements on the European continent.

Without Russian support, the Greek uprising in the principalities was soon crushed by 30,000 Turkish troops. The Wallachian peasant army retreated to the mountains, and Ypsilantis fled to Transylvania, where he was arrested by the Austrian authorities. The Turks occupied Moldavia and Wallachia, and carried out reprisals against the Christian population there. Turkish soldiers looted churches, murdered priests, men, women and children and mutilated their bodies, cutting off their noses, ears and heads, while their officers looked on.

Thousands of terrified civilians fled into neighbouring Bessarabia, presenting the Russian authorities with a massive refugee problem. The violence even spread to Constantinople, where the patriarch and several bishops were publicly hanged by a group of janizaries on Easter Sunday 1821.

As news spread of the atrocities, causing ever-stronger Russian sympathy for the Greek cause, the Tsar felt increasingly obliged to intervene, despite his commitment to the principles of the Holy Alliance. As Alexander saw it, the actions of the Turks had gone well beyond the legitimate defence of Ottoman sovereignty; they were in a religious war against the Greeks, whose religious rights the Russians had a duty to protect, according to their interpretation of the Treaty of Kuchuk Kainarji. The Tsar issued an ultimatum calling on the Turks to evacuate the principalities, restore the damaged churches, and acknowledge Russia's treaty rights to protect the Sultan's Orthodox subjects. This was the first time any of the powers had spoken out on behalf of the Greeks. The Turks responded by seizing Russian ships, confiscating their grain, and imprisoning their sailors in Constantinople.

Russia broke off diplomatic relations. Many of the Tsar's advisers favoured war. The Greek revolt had spread to central Greece, the Peloponnese, Macedonia and Crete. Unless the Russians intervened, they feared that in these regions it would be repressed with similar atrocities to those in the principalities. In 1822 Ottoman troops brutally crushed a Greek uprising on the island of Chios, hanging 20,000 islanders and deporting into slavery almost all the surviving population of 70,000 Greeks. Europe was outraged by the massacre, whose horrors were depicted by the French painter Eugène Delacroix in his great masterpiece *The Massacre of Chios* (1824). In the Russian Foreign Ministry, Kapodistrias and Sturdza argued for military intervention on religious grounds. In a rehearsal of the arguments employed in 1853 for Russia's invasion of the principalities, they reasoned that the defence of Christians against Muslim violence should outweigh any considerations about the sovereignty of the Ottoman Empire. To support revolts in, say, Spain or Austria, they maintained, would be a betrayal of the principles of the Holy Alliance, because these two nations were both ruled by lawful Christian sovereigns; but no Muslim power could be recognized as lawful or legitimate, so the same principles did not apply to the Greek uprising against the Ottomans. The rhetoric of Holy Russia's duty to its co-religionists was also employed by Pozzo di Borgo, the Tsar's ambassador to France, though he was more interested in promoting Russia's strategic ambitions, calling for a war to expel the Turks from Europe and establish a new Byzantine Empire under Russian protection.

Such ideas were widely shared by high officials, army officers and intellectuals, who were increasingly united in the early 1820s by their Russian nationalism and at times by an almost messianic commitment to the Orthodox cause. There was talk of 'crossing the Danube and delivering the Greeks from the cruelties of Muslim rule'. One leader in the southern army called for a war against the Turks to unite the Balkan Christians in a 'Greek Kingdom'. The pro-war lobby also had supporters at the court, where the legitimist principles of the Holy Alliance were more strictly recognized. The most enthusiastic was Baroness von Krüdener, a religious mystic who encouraged Tsar Alexander to believe in his messianic role and campaigned for an Orthodox crusade to drive the Muslims out of Europe and raise the cross in Constantinople and Jerusalem. She was dismissed from the court and ordered by the Tsar to leave St Petersburg.[13]

Alexander was far too committed to the Concert of Europe to give serious consideration to the idea of unilateral Russian intervention to liberate the Greeks. He stood firmly by the Congress System established at Vienna by which the great powers had agreed to resolve major crises through international negotiation, and realized that any action in the Greek crisis was bound to be opposed. By October 1821 a European policy of international mediation over Greece had already been coordinated by Prince Metternich, the Austrian Foreign Minister and chief conductor of the Concert of Europe, together with the British Foreign Secretary, Lord Castlereagh. So when the Tsar appealed to them for support against Turkey, in February 1822, it was agreed to convene an international congress to resolve the crisis.

Alexander called for the creation of a large autonomous Greek state under Russian protection, much like Moldavia and Wallachia. However, Britain feared that this would be a means for Russia to advance its own interests and intervene in Ottoman affairs on the pretext of protecting its co-religionists. Austria was equally afraid that a successful Greek revolt would set off uprisings in parts of central Europe under its control. Since Alexander prized the Austrian alliance above all, he held back assistance to the Greeks, while continuing to urge collective European action to help them. None of the powers would support the Greeks. But two things happened in 1825 to change their minds: first, the Sultan called in Mehmet Ali, his powerful vassal in Egypt, to put down the Greeks, which the Egyptians did with new atrocities, giving rise to an ever-growing wave of pro-Greek sympathy and ever-louder calls for intervention in liberal Europe; and then Alexander died.

*

The new tsar – the man responsible, more than anyone, for the Crimean War – was 29 when he succeeded his brother to the Russian throne. Tall and imposing, with a large, balding head, long sideburns and an officer's moustache, Nicholas I was every inch a 'military man'. From an early age he had developed an obsessive interest in military affairs, learning all the names of his brother's generals, designing uniforms, and attending with excitement military parades and manoeuvres. Having missed out on his boyhood dream of fighting in the war against Napoleon, he prepared himself for a soldier's life. In 1817 he received his first appointment, Inspector-General of Engineers, from which he derived a lifelong interest in army engineering and artillery (the strongest elements of the Russian military during the Crimean War). He loved the routines and discipline of army life: they appealed to his strict and pedantic character as well as to his spartan tastes (throughout his life he insisted on sleeping on a military campbed). Courteous and charming to those in his intimate circle, to others Nicholas was cold and stern. In later life he grew increasingly irritable and impatient, inclined to rash behaviour and angry rages, as he succumbed to the hereditary mental illness that troubled Alexander and Nicholas's other older brother, the Grand Duke Constantine, who renounced the throne in 1825.[14]

More than Alexander, Nicholas placed the defence of Orthodoxy at the centre of his foreign policy. Throughout his reign he was governed by an absolute conviction in his divine mission to save

Orthodox Europe from the Western heresies of liberalism, rational-
ism and revolution. During his last years he was led by this calling
to fantastic dreams of a religious war against the Turks to liberate
the Balkan Christians and unite them with Russia in an Orthodox empire with its spiritual centres in Constantinople and Jerusalem. Anna Tiutcheva, who was at his court from 1853, described
Nicholas as 'the Don Quixote of autocrats – terrible in his chivalry
and power to subordinate everything to his futile struggle against
History'.[15]

Nicholas had a personal connection to the Holy Land through
the New Jerusalem Monastery near Moscow. Founded by Patriarch
Nikon in the 1650s, the monastery was situated on a site chosen for
its symbolic resemblance to the Holy Land (with the River Istra sym-
bolizing the Jordan). The ensemble of the monastery's churches was
laid out in a sacred topographical arrangement to represent the Holy
Places of Jerusalem. Nikon also took in foreign monks so that the
monastery would represent the multinational Orthodoxy linking
Moscow to Jerusalem. Nicholas had visited the monastery in 1818 –
the year his first son, the heir to the throne, was born (a coincidence
he took to be a sign of divine providence). After the monastery was
partially destroyed by fire Nicholas directed plans to reconstruct its
centrepiece, the Church of the Resurrection, as a replica of the Church
of the Holy Sepulchre in Jerusalem, even sending his own artist on a
pilgrimage to make drawings of the original, so that it could be rebuilt
on Russian soil.[16]

None of Nicholas's religious ambitions were immediately obvious
in 1825. There was a gradual evolution in his views from the first years
of his reign, when he upheld the legitimist principles of the Holy Alliance, to the final period before the Crimean War, when he made the
championing of Orthodoxy the primary goal of his aggressive foreign
policy in the Balkans and the Holy Lands. But from the start there
were clear signs that he was determined to defend his co-religionists
and take a tough position against Turkey, beginning with the struggle
over Greece.

Nicholas restored relations with Kapodistrias, whose active support for the Greek cause had forced him to resign from the Foreign
Ministry and leave Russia for exile in 1822. He threatened war against

the Turks unless they evacuated the Danubian principalities, and accepted plans from his military advisers to occupy Moldavia and Wallachia in support of the Greek cause. The Tsar was closely guided by his Foreign Minister, Karl Nesselrode, who had lost patience with the Concert of Europe and joined the war party, not out of love for the Greek rebels, but because he realized that a war against the Turks would promote Russian goals in the Near East. At the very least, reasoned Nesselrode, the threat of Russian intervention would force the British into joining Russia in efforts to resolve the Greek Question, if only to prevent the Tsar from exercising overwhelming influence in the region.[17]

In 1826 the Duke of Wellington, the commander of the allied forces against Napoleon, who was now a senior statesman in the British government, travelled to St Petersburg to negotiate an Anglo-Russian accord (later joined by France in the Treaty of London in 1827) that would mediate between the Greeks and Turks. Britain, Russia and France agreed to call for the establishment of an autonomous Greek province under Ottoman sovereignty. When the Sultan rejected their proposals, the three powers sent a combined naval force under the command of the fiery British philhellene Admiral Edward Codrington, with instructions to impose a resolution by peaceful means if possible, and 'by cannon' as a last resort. Codrington was not known for diplomacy, and in October 1827 he destroyed the entire Turkish and Egyptian fleets in the battle of Navarino. Enraged by this action, the Sultan refused any further mediation, declared a jihad, and rejected the Russian ultimatum to withdraw his troops from the Danubian principalities. His defiance played into Russia's hands.

Nicholas had long suspected that the British were unwilling to go to war for the Greek cause. He had been considering an occupation of the principalities to force the Turks into submission, but feared that would encourage the British to renounce the Treaty of London. Now the Sultan's rejection of his ultimatum had given him a legitimate excuse to declare war against Turkey without the British or the French. Russia would fight on its own to secure a 'national government in Greece', Nesselrode wrote to Kapodistrias in January 1828. The Tsar sent money and weapons to Kapodistrias's revolutionary government, and received from him an assurance that Russia would enjoy an 'exclusive influence' in Greece.[18]

In April 1828 a Russian attack-force of 65,000 fighting men and Cossacks crossed the Danube and struck in three directions, against Vidin, Silistria and Varna, on the road to Constantinople. Nicholas insisted on joining the campaign: it was his first experience of war. The Russians advanced quickly (the land was full of forage for their horses) but then got bogged down in fighting around Varna, where they succumbed to the pestilent conditions of the Danube delta and suffered severe losses. Half the Russian soldiers died from illness and diseases during 1828–9. Reinforcements soon got sick as well. Between May 1828 and February 1829 a staggering 210,000 soldiers received treatment in military hospitals – twice the troop strength of the whole campaign.[19] Such huge losses were not unusual in the tsarist army, where there was little care for the welfare of the serf soldiers.

Renewing the offensive in the spring of 1829, the Russians captured the Turkish fortress of Silistria, followed by the city of Edirne (Adrianople), a short march from Constantinople, where the cannons of the nearby Russian fleet could be heard. At this point the Russians could easily have seized the Turkish capital and overthrown the Sultan. Their fleet controlled the Black Sea and the Aegean, they had reinforcements on which they could draw from Greek or Bulgarian volunteers, and the Turkish forces were in complete disarray. In the Caucasus, where the Russians had advanced simultaneously, they had captured the Turkish fortresses of Kars and Erzurum, opening the way for an attack on Turkish territories in Anatolia. The collapse of the Ottoman Empire appeared so imminent that the French King Charles X proposed partitioning its territories between the great powers.[20]

Nicholas, too, was convinced that the collapse of the Ottoman Empire was at hand. He was prepared to hasten its demise and liberate the Balkan Christians, provided he could get the other powers, or at least Austria (his closest ally with interests in the Balkans), on his side. As his troops advanced towards the Turkish capital, Nicholas informed the Austrian ambassador in St Petersburg that the Ottoman Empire was 'about to fall', and suggested that it would be in Austria's interests to join Russia in the partition of its territories in order to 'forestall the people who would fill the vacuum'. The Austrians, however, mistrusted Russia and chose instead to preserve the Concert of Europe. Without their support, Nicholas held back from dealing the fatal blow to the Ottoman Empire in 1829. He was afraid of a European war against Russia should his attack on Turkey move the other powers to unite in its defence, and even more afraid that the collapse of the Ottoman Empire would result in a frantic rush by the European powers to seize Turkish territories. Either way, Russia would lose out. For this reason, Nicholas abided by the viewpoint of his cool and calculating Foreign Minister: that it would best serve Russia's interests to keep the Ottoman Empire in existence, but in a weakened state, where its dependence on Russia for survival would enable the promotion of Russian interests in the Balkans and the Black Sea area. A sick Turkey was more useful to Russia than a dead one.[21]

Consequently, the Treaty of Adrianople was surprisingly kind to the defeated Turks. Imposed by the Russians in September 1829, the treaty established the virtual autonomy of Moldavia and Wallachia under Russian protection. It gave the Russians some islands in the mouth of the Danube, a couple of forts in Georgia and the Sultan's recognition of their possession of the rest of Georgia as well as the south Caucasian khanates of Erivan and Nakhichevan, which they had wrested from the Persians in 1828, but compared to what the Russians might have forced out of the defeated Turks, these were relatively minor gains. The two most important clauses of the treaty secured concessions from the Porte that had been wanted by all the signatories of the Treaty of London: Turkish recognition of Greek autonomy; and the opening of the Straits to all commercial ships.

The Western powers did not trust these appearances of Russian moderation, however. The treaty's silence on warship movements through the Straits led them to conclude that Russia must have gained some secret clause or verbal promise from the Turks, allowing them exclusive control of this crucial waterway between the Black Sea and the Mediterranean. Western fears of Russia had been growing since the outbreak of the Greek revolt, and the treaty fuelled their Russophobia. The British were especially alarmed. Wellington, by now the Prime Minister, thought the treaty had transformed the Ottoman Empire into a Russian protectorate – an outcome worse than its partition (which at least would have been done by a concert of powers). Lord Heytesbury, the British ambassador in St Petersburg, declared (without any intended irony) that the Sultan would soon become as 'submissive to the orders of the Tsar as any of the Princes of India to those of the [East India] Company'.[22] The British may have totally supplanted the Mughal Empire in India, but they were determined to stop the Russians doing the same to the Ottomans, presenting themselves as the honest defenders of the status quo in the Near East.

Fearful of the perceived Russian threat, the British began to shape a policy towards the Eastern Question. To prevent Russia from gaining the initiative in Greece, they gave their backing to the independence of the new Greek state, as opposed to mere autonomy under Turkish sovereignty (which they feared would make it a dependant of Russia). British fears were not unwarranted. Encouraged by the Russian intervention, Kapodistrias had been calling on the Tsar to expel the Turks from Europe and create a larger Greece, a confederation of Balkan states under Russian protection, on the model once proposed by Catherine the Great. However, the Tsar's position was seriously weakened by the assassination of Kapodistrias in 1831, followed by the decline of his pro-Russian party and the rise of new Greek liberal parties aligned with the West. These changes moderated Russian expectations and cleared the way for an international settlement at the Convention of London in 1832: the modern Greek state was established under the guarantee of the great powers and with Britain's choice of sovereign, the young Otto of Bavaria, as its first king.

*

The 'weak neighbour' policy dominated Russia's attitude to the Eastern Question between 1829 and the Crimean War. It was not shared by everyone: there were those in the Tsar's army and Foreign Ministry who favoured a more aggressive and expansionist policy in the Balkans and the Caucasus. But it was flexible enough to satisfy both the ambitions of Russian nationalists as well as the concerns of those who wanted to avoid a European war. The key to the 'weak neighbour' policy was the use of religion – backed up by a constant military threat – to increase Russian influence within the Sultan's Christian territories.

To enforce the Treaty of Adrianople, the Russians occupied Molda-via and Wallachia. During the five years of the occupation, from 1829 to 1834, they introduced a constitution (*Règlement organique*) and reformed the administration of the principalities on relatively liberal principles (far more so than anything allowed in Russia at that time) to undermine the remaining vestiges of Ottoman control. The Russians tried to ease the burden of the peasantry and win their sympathy through economic concessions; they brought the Churches under Russian influence; recruited local militias; and improved the infra-structure of the region as a military base for future operations against Turkey. For a while, the Russians even thought of turning occupation into permanent annexation, though they finally withdrew in 1834, leaving behind a significant Russian force to control the military roads, which also served to remind the native princes who took over government that they ruled the principalities at the mercy of St Peters-burg. The princes placed in power (Michael Sturdza in Moldavia and Alexander Ghica in Wallachia) had been chosen by the Russians for their affiliations with the tsarist court. They were closely watched by the Russian consulates, which often intervened in the boyar assem-blies and princely politics to advance Russia's interests. According to Lord Ponsonby, the British ambassador to Constantinople, Sturdza and Ghica were 'Russian subjects disguised as hospodars'. They were 'merely nominal governors . . . serving only as executors of such meas-ures as may be dictated to them by the Russian government'.[23]

The desire to keep the Ottoman Empire weak and dependent some-times required intercession *on behalf* of the Turks, as happened in 1833, when Mehmet Ali challenged the Sultan's power. Having helped the Sultan fight the Greek rebels, Mehmet Ali demanded hereditary title to Egypt and Syria. When the Sultan refused, Mehmet Ali's son Ibrahim Pasha marched his troops into Palestine, Lebanon and Syria. His powerful army, which had been trained by the French and organ-ized on European principles, easily swept aside the Ottoman forces. Constantinople lay at the mercy of the Egyptians. Mehmet Ali had modernized the Egyptian economy, integrating it into the world mar-ket as a supplier of raw cotton to the textile mills of Britain, and even building factories, mainly to supply his large army. In many ways, the invasion of Syria was prompted by a need to expand his base of cash crops, as Egyptian exports came under pressure from competitors in the globalized economy. Yet Mehmet also came to represent a powerful religious revival among Muslim traditionalists and an alternative to the more accommodating religious leadership of the Sultan. He called his army the *Cihadiye* – the Jihadists. According to contemporary observers, had he seized the Turkish capital, Mehmet Ali would have established a 'new Muslim empire' hostile to the growing intervention of the Christian powers in the Middle East.[24]

The Sultan appealed to the British and the French, but neither showed much interest in helping him, so he turned in desperation to the Tsar, who promptly sent a fleet of seven ships with 40,000 men to defend the Turkish capital against the Egyptians. The Russians considered Mehmet Ali a French lackey who posed a significant danger to Russian interests in the Near East. Since 1830 the French had been engaged in the conquest of Ottoman Algeria. They had the only army in the region capable of checking Russian ambitions. The Russians, moreover, had been disturbed by reports from their agents that Mehmet Ali had promised to 'resurrect the former greatness of the Muslim people' and take revenge on Russia for the humiliation suffered by the Turks in 1828–9. They were afraid that the Egyptian leader would stop at nothing less than 'the conquest of the whole of Asia Minor' and the establishment of a new Islamic empire supplanting the Ottomans. Instead of a weak neighbour, the Russians would be faced by a powerful Islamic threat on their southern border with strong religious connections to the Muslim tribes of the Caucasus.[25]

Alarmed by the Russian intervention, the British and French moved their fleets to Besika Bay, just beyond the Dardanelles, and in May 1833 brokered an agreement known as the Convention of Kütahya between Mehmet Ali and the Turks by which the Egyptian leader agreed to withdraw his forces from Anatolia in exchange for the territories of Crete and the Hijaz (in western Arabia). Ibrahim was appointed lifetime governor of Syria but Mehmet Ali was denied his main demand of a hereditary kingdom for himself in Egypt, leaving him frustrated and eager to renew his war against the Turks should another chance present itself. The British strengthened their Levant fleet and put it on alert to serve the Sultan if Mehmet Ali threatened him again. Their arrival on the scene was enough to force the Russians to withdraw, but only after they had, in recognition of Russia's role in rescuing the Ottoman Empire, managed to extract from the Sultan major new concessions through the Treaty of Unkiar-Skelessi, signed in July 1833. The treaty basically reaffirmed the Russian gains of 1829, but it contained a secret article guaranteeing Russia's military protection of Turkey in exchange for a Turkish promise to close the Straits to foreign warships when demanded by Russia. The effect of the secret clause was to keep out the British navy and put the Russians in control of the Black Sea; but more importantly, as far as the Russians were concerned, it gave them an exclusive legal right to intervene in Ottoman affairs.[26]

The British and the French soon found out about the secret clause after it was leaked by Turkish officials. There was outrage in the Western press, which immediately suspected that the Russians had obtained not just the right to close the Straits to other powers but also the right to keep them open to their own warships – in which case they would be able to land a major force in the Bosporus and seize Constantinople in a lightning strike before any Western fleet would have time to intervene (the Black Sea Fleet at Sevastopol was only four days' sailing from the Turkish capital). In fact, the secret clause had left this point unclear. The Russians claimed that all they had wanted from the controversial clause was a means of self-defence against the possibility of an attack by France or Britain, the major naval powers in the Mediterranean, whose fleets could otherwise sail through the Straits and destroy the Russian bases at Sevastopol and Odessa before their entry into the Black Sea was discovered in St Petersburg. The Straits were 'the keys to Russia's house'. If they were unable to close them, the Russians would be vulnerable to an attack on their weakest frontier – the Black Sea littoral and the Caucasus – as indeed they were when Turkey and the Western powers attacked during the Crimean War.

*

Such arguments were discounted in the West, where Russia's good intentions were increasingly mistrusted by informed opinion. Now, almost every Russian action on the Continent was interpreted as constituting part of a reactionary and aggressive plan of imperial expansion. 'No reasonable doubt can be entertained that the Russian Government is intently engaged in the prosecution of those schemes of aggrandizement towards the South which, ever since the reign of Catherine, have formed a prominent feature of Russian policy,' Palmerston wrote to Lord John Ponsonby in December 1833.

> The cabinet of St Petersburg, whenever its foreign policy is adverted to, deals largely in the most unqualified declarations of disinterestedness; and protests that, satisfied with the extensive limits of the empire, it desires no increase of territory, and has renounced all those plans of aggrandizement which were imputed to Russia . . .
>
> But notwithstanding these declarations, it has been observed that the encroachments of Russia have continued to advance on all sides with a steady march and a well-directed aim, and that almost every transaction of much importance, in which of late years Russia has been engaged, has in some way or other been made conducive to an alteration either of her influence or of her territory.
>
> The recent events in the Levant have, indeed, by an unfortunate combination of circumstances, enabled her to make an enormous stride towards the accomplishment of her designs upon Turkey, and it becomes an object of great importance for the interests of Great Britain, to consider how Russia can be prevented from pushing her advantage further, and to see whether it be possible to deprive her of the advantage she has already gained.

The French statesman François Guizot maintained that the 1833 treaty had converted the Black Sea into a 'Russian lake' guarded by Turkey, the Tsar's 'vassal state', 'without anything hindering Russia herself from passing through the Straits and hurling her ships and soldiers into the Mediterranean'. The chargé d'affaires in St Petersburg lodged a protest with the Russian government warning that if the treaty led to Russia intervening in 'the internal affairs of the Ottoman Empire, the French government would hold itself wholly at liberty to adopt such a line of conduct as circumstances might suggest'. Palmerston empowered Ponsonby to summon the British fleet from the Mediterranean for the defence of Constantinople, if he felt that it was threatened by Russia.[27]

The events of 1833 were a turning point in British policy towards

Russia and Turkey. Until then, Britain's main concern in the Ottoman Empire had been to preserve the status quo, mainly from fears that its breakup would affect the balance of power in Europe and possibly lead to a European war, rather than from any firm commitment to the sovereignty of the Sultan (their support for Greece had not demonstrated much of that). But once the British woke up to the danger that the Ottoman Empire might be taken over by the Egyptians at the head of a powerful Muslim revival, or, even worse, that it might become a Russian protectorate, they took an active interest in Turkey. They increasingly intervened in Ottoman affairs, encouraging economic and political reforms by which the British hoped to restore the health of the Ottoman Empire and expand their influence.

Britain's interests were mainly commercial. The Ottoman Empire was a growing market for the export of British manufactures and a valuable source of raw materials. As the dominant industrial power in the world, Britain generally threw its weight behind the opening up of global markets to free trade; as the dominant naval power, it was prepared to use its fleet to force foreign governments to open up their markets. This was a type of 'informal empire', an 'imperialism of free trade', in which Britain's military power and political influence advanced its commercial hegemony and curtailed the independence of foreign governments without the direct controls of imperial rule.

Nowhere was this more in evidence than in the Ottoman Empire. Ponsonby was at pains to stress the economic dividends of increased British influence in Constantinople. 'Protection given to our political interests', the ambassador wrote to Palmerston in 1834, 'will throw open sources of commercial prosperity perhaps hardly to be hoped for from our intercourse with any other country upon earth.' By this time there was a large and powerful body of British traders with extensive interests in Turkey who put growing pressure on the government to intervene. Their viewpoint was expressed in influential periodicals, such as *Blackwood's* and the *Edinburgh Review*, both of which depended on their patronage; and it found an echo in the arguments of Turcophiles, such as David Urquhart, the leader of a secret trade mission to Turkey in 1833, who saw a huge potential for British commerce in the development of the Ottoman economy. 'The progress of Turkey,' Urquhart wrote in 1835, 'if undisturbed by political events, bids fair to render it, in a few years, the largest market in the world for English manufacturers.'[28]

In 1838, through a series of military threats and promises, Britain imposed on the Porte a Tariff Convention which in effect transformed the Ottoman Empire into a virtual free-trade zone. Deprived of tariff revenues, the Porte's ability to protect its nascent industries was seriously handicapped. From this moment the export of British manufactured goods to Turkey rose steeply. There was an elevenfold increase by 1850, making it one of Britain's most valuable export markets (surpassed only by the Hanseatic towns and the Netherlands). After the repeal of the protectionist Corn Laws in 1846, British imports of cereals from Turkey, chiefly from Moldavia and Wallachia, increased as well. The advent of ocean steamships, steam river-boats and railroads opened up the Danube for the first time as a busy commercial highway. The river's trade was dominated by British merchant ships exporting grain to western Europe and importing manufactures from Britain. The British were in direct competition with the merchants of Odessa, Taganrog and other Black Sea ports, from which the grain of Russia's breadbasket in the Ukraine and south Russia was exported to the West. The cereal export market was increasingly important to Russia as the value of its timber trade declined during the steam age. By the middle of the nineteenth century the Black Sea ports were handling one-third of all Russian exports. The Russians tried to give their traders an advantage over their British rivals through their control of the Danube delta after 1829 by subjecting foreign ships to time-consuming quarantine controls and even allowing the Danube to silt up and become once more unnavigable.

On the eastern side of the Black Sea the commercial interests of Britain were increasingly bound up with the port of Trebizond, in north-eastern Turkey, from which Greek and Armenian merchants imported large quantities of British manufactured goods for sale in the interior of Asia. The growing value of this trade to Britain, observed Karl Marx in the *New York Tribune*, 'may be seen at the Manchester Exchange, where dark-complexioned Greek buyers are increasing in numbers and importance, and where Greek and South Slav dialects are heard along with German and English'. Until the 1840s, the Russians had a near-monopoly of trade in manufactured goods in this part of Asia. Russian textiles, rope and linen products dominated the bazaars of Bayburt, Baghdad and Basra. But steamships and railways made it possible to open up a shorter route to India – either through the Mediterranean to Cairo and then from Suez to the Red Sea, or via the Black Sea to Trebizond and the Euphrates river to the Persian Gulf (sailing ships could not readily cope with the high winds and monsoons of the Gulf of Suez or with the narrow waters of the Euphrates). The British favoured the Euphrates route, mainly because it ran through territories ruled by the Sultan (as opposed to Mehmet Ali); developing the route was seen as a way to increase British influence and check the growing power of Russia in this part of the Ottoman Empire. In 1834 Britain received permission from the Porte for General Francis Chesney to survey the Euphrates route. The survey was a failure, and British interest in the route declined. But plans for a Euphrates Valley Railway from the Mediterranean to the Persian Gulf via Aleppo and Baghdad were revived in the 1850s, when the British government was looking for a way to increase its presence in an area where they perceived a growing Russian threat to India (the railway was never developed by the British, for lack of financial guarantees, but the Baghdad Railway built by Germany from 1903 followed much of the same route).

The danger Russia posed to India was the *bête noire* of British Russophobes. For some, this would become the underlying aim of the Crimean War: to stop a power bent not just on the conquest of Turkey but on the domination of the whole of Asia Minor right up to Afghanistan and India. In their alarmed imagination there were no bounds on the designs of Russia, the fastest growing empire in the world.

In truth, there was never any serious danger of the Russians reaching India in the years before the Crimean War. It was much too far and difficult to march an army all that way – though the Russian Emperor Paul I had once entertained a madcap scheme to send a combined French and Russian force there. The idea had been taken up again by Napoleon in his talks with Tsar Alexander in 1807. 'The more unrealistic the expedition is,' Napoleon explained, 'the more it can be used to terrorize the Englishmen.' The British government always knew that such an expedition was not feasible. One British intelligence officer thought that any Russian invasion of India 'would amount to little more than the sending of a caravan'. But while few in official British circles thought that Russia was a serious threat to India, this did not prevent the Russophobic British press from whipping up that fear, emphasizing the potential danger posed by Russia's conquest of the Caucasus and its 'underhand activities' in Persia and Afghanistan.[29]

The theory made its first appearance in 1828, in a pamphlet, *On the Designs of Russia,* written by Colonel George de Lacy Evans (a general by the time he took up the command of the British army's 2nd Infantry Division during the Crimean War). Speculating on the outcome of the Russo-Turkish war, de Lacy Evans conjured up a nightmare fantasy of Russian aggression and expansion, leading to the conquest of the whole of Asia Minor and the collapse of British trade with India. De Lacy's working principle – that the rapid growth of the Russian Empire since the beginning of the eighteenth century proved the iron law that Russian expansion must continue until checked – reappeared in a second pamphlet he published, in 1829, *On the Practicality of an Invasion of British India,* in which he claimed, without any evidence of Russia's actual intentions, that a Russian force could be built up on India's north-west frontier. The pamphlet was widely read in official circles. Wellington took it as a warning and told Lord Ellenborough, the president of the Board of Control for India, that he was 'ready to take up the question in Europe, if the Russians [should] move towards India with views of evident hostility'. After 1833, with Russia's domination of the Ottoman Empire seemingly secured, these fears took on the force of a self-fulfilling prophecy. In 1834 Lieutenant Arthur Connolly (who coined the term 'the Great Game' to describe Anglo-Russian rivalry in Asia Minor) published a best-selling travelogue, *Journey to the North of India,* in which he argued that the Russians could attack the north-west frontier if they were supported by the Persians and Afghans.[30]

The Russians had in fact been steadily increasing their presence in Asia Minor in line with their policy of keeping neighbours weak. Russian agents advised Persia on foreign policy and organized support for the Shah's army. In 1837, when the Persians took the Afghan city of Herat, many British politicians had no doubt that it was part of Russia's preparation for an invasion of India. 'Herat, in the hands of Persia,' wrote a former British ambassador to Tehran, 'can never be considered in any other light than as an advanced *point d'appui* for the Russians toward India.' The Russophobic press criticized the inactivity of British governments that had failed to see the 'underhand' and 'nefarious' activities of the Russians in Persia. 'For several years,' warned the *Herald*, 'we have endeavoured to make them understand that the ambitious designs of Russia extended beyond Turkey and Circassia and Persia, even to our East Indian dependencies, which Russia has not lost sight of since Catherine threatened to march her armies in that direction, and rally the native Indian princes round the standard of the Great Mogul.' The *Standard* called for more than watchful vigilance against Russia: 'It is of little use to *watch* Russia, if our care and exertion are to end with that exercise of vigilance. We have been *watching* Russia during eight years, and within that time she has pushed her acquisitions and military posts nearly 2000 miles on the road to India.'[31]

The view that Russia, by its very nature, was a threat to India became widespread among the British broadsheet-reading classes. It was expressed by the anonymous author of a widely read pamphlet of 1838 called *India, Great Britain, and Russia*, in a passage that is reminiscent of the domino theory of the Cold War:

> The unparalleled aggressions of Russia in every direction must destroy all confidence in her pacific protestations, and ought to satisfy every reasonable inquirer that the only limit on her conquests will be found in the limitation of her power. On the West, Poland has been reduced to the state of a vassal province. In the South, the Ottoman sovereign has been plundered of part of his possessions, and holds the rest subject to the convenience of his conqueror. The Black Sea cannot be navigated but by permission of the Muscovite. The flag of England, which was wont to wave proudly over all the waters of the world, is insulted, and the commercial enterprise of her merchants crippled and defeated. In the East, Russia is systematically pursuing the same course: Circassia is to be crushed; Persia to be made first a partisan, then a dependent province, finally an integral part of the Russian Empire. Beyond Persia lies Afghanistan, a country prepared by many circumstances to furnish a ready path for the invader. The Indus crossed, what is to resist the flight of the Russian eagle into the heart of British India? It is thither that the eyes of Russia are directed. Let England look to it.[32]

To counteract the perceived Russian threat, the British attempted to create buffer states in Asia Minor and the Caucasus. In 1838 they occupied Afghanistan. Officially, their aim was to reinstall the recently deposed Emir Shah Shuja on the Afghan throne, but after that had been achieved, in 1839, they maintained their occupation to support his puppet government – ultimately as a means of moving towards British rule – until they were forced to withdraw by tribal rebellions and disastrous military reverses in 1842. The British also stepped up their diplomatic presence in Tehran, attempting to wean the Persians *Iran* off the Russians through a defensive alliance and promises of aid for their army. Under British pressure the Persians left Herat and signed a new commercial treaty with Britain in 1841. The British even considered the occupation of Baghdad, believing that it would be welcomed by the Arabs as a liberation from the Turks, or at least that any resistance would be undermined by the division between Sunni and Shia, – who in the words of Henry Rawlinson, the British consul-general in Baghdad, 'could always be played off against each other'. An army officer of the East India Company and a distinguished orientalist who first deciphered the ancient Persian cuneiform inscriptions of Behistun, Rawlinson was one of the most important figures arguing for an active British policy to check the expansion of Russia into Central Asia, Persia and Afghanistan. He thought that Britain should set up a Mesopotamian empire under European protection to act as a buffer against Russia's growing presence in the Caucasus and prevent a Russian conquest of the Tigris and Euphrates valleys on the route to India. He even advocated sending the Indian army to attack the Russians in Georgia, Erivan and Nakhichevan, territories the British had never recognized as Russian, as the Turks had done through the Treaty of Adrianople.[33]

Rawlinson was also instrumental in getting British aid to the Muslim tribes of the Caucasus, whose war against the Russians gained new force from the charismatic leadership of the Imam Shamil after 1834. To his followers Shamil seemed invincible: a warlord sent by God. There were stories of his legendary bravery, his famous victories against the Russians, and of his miraculous escapes from certain capture and defeat. Having such a leader gave new confidence to the Muslim tribes, uniting them around the imam's call for a jihad against the Russian occupation of their lands. The strength of Shamil's army derived from its close ties with the mountain villages: this enabled them to carry out the guerrilla-type operations which so confounded the Russians. With the support of the local population, Shamil's army was ubiquitous and practically invisible. Villagers could become soldiers and soldiers villagers at a moment's notice. The mountain people were the army's ears and eyes – they served as scouts and spies – and everywhere the Russians were vulnerable to ambush. Shamil's fighters literally ran circles around the tsarist army – launching sudden raids on exposed Russian troops, forts and supply lines before vanishing into the mountains or merging with the tribesmen in the villages. They seldom engaged with the Russians in the open, where they knew they ran the risk of being defeated by superior numbers and artillery. It was difficult to cope with such tactics, especially since none of the Russian commanders had ever come across anything like them before, and for a long time they simply threw in ever-growing numbers of their troops in a fruitless effort to defeat Shamil in his main base in Chechnya. By the end of the 1830s Shamil's way of fighting had become so effective that he began to appear as invincible to the Russians as he did to the Muslim tribes. As one tsarist general lamented, Shamil's rule had acquired a 'religious-military character, the same by which at the beginning of Islam Muhammed's sword shook three-quarters of the Universe'.[34]

*

But it was in Turkey that the British sought to create their main buffer state against Russia. It did not take them long to realize that by ignoring the Sultan's call for help against the Egyptian invasion they had missed a golden opportunity to secure their position as the dominant foreign power in the Ottoman Empire. Palmerston said it was 'the greatest miscalculation in the field of foreign affairs ever made by a British cabinet'. Having missed that chance, they redoubled their efforts to influence the Porte and impose on it a series of reforms to resolve the problems of its Christian population which had given Russia cause to intervene on their behalf.

The British were believers in political reform and thought that with their gunboats in support they could export their liberal principles across the globe. In their view, the reform of the Ottoman Empire was the only real solution to the Eastern Question, which was rooted in the decay of the Sultan's realm: cure the 'sick man' and the problem of the East would go away. But the motives of the British in promoting liberal reforms were not just to secure the independence of the Ottoman Empire against Russia. They were also to promote the influence of Britain in Turkey: to make the Turks dependent on the British for political advice and financial loans, and to bring them under the protection of the British military; to 'civilize' the Turks under British tutelage, teaching them the virtues of British liberal principles, religious toleration and administrative practices (though stopping short of parliaments and constitutions, for which the Turks were deemed to lack the necessary 'European' qualities); to promote British free-trade interests (which may have sounded splendid but was arguably damaging to the Ottoman Empire); and to secure the route to India (where Britain's free-trade policies were not of course pursued).

The British were encouraged in their reformist mission by the outward signs of Westernization they had noted in the culture of the Turks during the last years of Mahmud's reign. Although the Sultan's military reforms had yielded limited success, changes had been made in the dress and customs of the Ottoman élites in the Turkish capital: the tunic and the fez had replaced robes and turbans; beards had been removed; and women had been brought into society. These cosmetic changes were reflected in the rise of a new type of Turkish official or gentleman, the European Turk, who had picked up foreign languages, Western habits, manners and vices, while in other ways remaining rooted in the traditional culture of Islam.

Travellers to Turkey were impressed by the manifestations of progress they observed in Turkish manners, and their writings transformed British attitudes. The best-selling and most influential of these publications was undoubtedly Julia Pardoe's *The City of the Sultan; and Domestic Manners of the Turks in 1836*, which sold over 30,000 copies in four editions between 1837 and the start of the Crimean War. Pardoe set out to correct what she saw as the prejudices of earlier accounts by travellers to the Ottoman Empire. On the surface Turkey seemed to conform to all the European stereotypes – exotic, indolent, sensual, superstitious, obscurantist and religiously fanatical – but on closer inspection it was seen to possess 'noble qualities' that made it fertile soil for liberal reform. 'Who that regards with unprejudiced eyes the moral state of Turkey can fail to be struck by the absence of capital crime, the contented and even proud feelings of the lower ranks, and the absence of all assumption and haughtiness among the higher?' The only obstacle to the 'civilization of Turkey', Pardoe argued, was 'the policy of Russia to check every advance towards enlightenment among a people she has already trammelled, and whom she would fain subjugate'.[35]

By the 1840s such ideas were the common currency of numerous travelogues and political pamphlets by Turcophiles. In *Three Years in Constantinople; or, Domestic Manners of the Turks in 1844*, Charles White encouraged the idea of Britain setting out to 'civilize the Turks' by citing examples of improvements in their habits and behaviour, such as the adoption of Western dress, the decline of religious fanaticism, and a growing appetite for education among the 'middling and inferior classes'. Among these two classes

> the ascendancy of good over evil is unquestionable. In no city are social or moral ties more tenaciously observed than by them. In no city can more numerous examples be found of probity, mild single-heartedness, and domestic worth. In no city is the amount of crime against property or persons more limited: a result that must be attributed to inherent honesty, and not to preventive measures.[36]

Closely connected to such ideas was a romantic sympathy for Islam as a basically benign and progressive force (and preferable to the deeply superstitious and only 'semi-Christian' Orthodoxy of the Russians) that took hold of many British Turcophiles. Urquhart, for example, saw the role of Islam, much as the Turks would have it seen themselves, as a tolerant and moderating force which kept the peace between the warring Christian sects in the Ottoman Empire:

> What traveller has not observed the fanaticism, the antipathy, of all these sects – their hostility to each other? Who has traced their actual repose to the *toleration* of Islamism? Islamism, calm, absorbed, without spirit of dogma, or views of proselytism, imposes at present on the other creeds the reserve and silence which characterise itself. But let this

moderator be removed, and the humble professions now confined to the sanctuary would be proclaimed in the court and the military camp; political power and political emnity would combine with religious domination and religious animosity; the empire would be deluged in blood, until a nervous arm – the arm of Russia – appears to restore harmony, by despotism.[37]

Some of these ideas were shared by Lord Stratford de Redcliffe (1786–1880), known as Stratford Canning until his elevation in 1852, who served no less than five times as Britain's ambassador to Constantinople, directly guiding the reform programme of the young Sultan Abdülmecid and his main reformist minister Mustafa Reshid Pasha after 1839. The first cousin of George Canning, who had been Foreign Secretary and briefly Prime Minister before his death in 1827, Stratford Canning was a domineering and impatient character – a consequence perhaps of never having had to wait for advancement (he was only 24, fresh out of Eton and Cambridge, when he took up his first office as Minister-Plenipotentiary in Constantinople). It is an irony that at the time of his first appointment as ambassador to the Porte, in 1824, Stratford had a profound dislike of Turkey – the country he said it would be his mission to save 'from itself'. In his letters to his cousin George, he wrote of a 'secret wish' to expel the Turks 'bags and baggage' from Europe, and confessed that he 'had a mind to curse the balance of Europe for protecting those horrid Turks'. But Stratford's Russophobia far outweighed his dislike of the Turks (in 1832, the Tsar, knowing this, took the extraordinary step of refusing to receive him as ambassador in St Petersburg). Russia's growing domination of Turkey persuaded Stratford that only liberal reform could save the Ottoman Empire.

Unlike Urquhart and the Turcophiles, Stratford Canning had limited knowledge of Turkey. He did not speak Turkish. He did not travel widely in the country, spending nearly all his time in the seclusion of the British embassy at Pera or its summer residence in Therapia. Stratford had no faith in modernizing the old Turkish institutions, and no sympathy for or even understanding of Islam. In his view the only hope for Turkey was to be given a complete injection of European civilization – and Christian civilization at that – to rescue it from religious obscurantism and steer it on the path towards rational

enlightenment. He, too, was encouraged by the signs of Westernization in Turkish dress and manners that he observed on his second
posting as ambassador, in 1832. They convinced him that, if the Turks
were not perfectible, at least they could be improved. 'The Turks have
undergone a complete metamorphosis since I was last here, at least as
to costume,' he wrote to Palmerston.

> They are now in a middle state from turbans to hats, from petticoats to
> breeches. How far these changes may extend below the surface I will
> not take upon myself to say. I know no conceivable substitute but
> civilization in the sense of Christendom. Can the sultan attain it? I have
> my doubts. At all events it must be an arduous and slow process, if not
> an impracticable one.[38]

On and off for the next quarter of a century, Stratford lectured the
Sultan and tutored his reformist ministers about how to liberalize
Turkey along English lines.

Mustafa Reshid (1800–58) was a perfect illustration of the European Turk that Stratford Canning hoped to see emerge in the forefront
of Ottoman reform. 'By birth and education a gentleman, by nature of
a kind and liberal disposition, Reshid had more to engage my sympathies than any other of his race and class,' Stratford Canning wrote
in his memoirs. A short and stocky man with lively features framed by
a black beard, Reshid had been the Porte's ambassador in London
and Paris, where he cut a striking figure in French theatres and salons,
before becoming Foreign Minister in 1837. He spoke both French and
English well. Like many Turkish reformers of the nineteenth century,
Reshid had connections to the European Freemasons. He was admitted to a London lodge during the 1830s. Flirting with Freemasonry
was a way for Western-oriented Turks like Reshid to embrace secular
ideas without giving up their Muslim faith and identity or laying
themselves open to the charge of apostasy from Islam (a crime that
carried the death sentence until 1844). Inspired by the West, Reshid
wanted to transform the Ottoman Empire into a modern monarchy,
in which the sultan would reign but not rule, the power of the clergy
would be limited, and a new caste of enlightened bureaucrats would
run the affairs of the imperial state.[39]

In 1839, the 16-year-old new Sultan Abdülmecid issued a decree, the Hatt-i Sharif of Gülhane (Noble Decree of the Rose Chamber), announcing a number of reforms, the first in a series, the Tanzimat reforms, which would span the entire period of his reign (1839–61) and lead eventually to the establishment of the first Ottoman parliament in 1876. The decree was the work of Reshid Pasha, who had drafted it in his London residence in Bryanston Square and shown it first to Stratford Canning for his personal approval on his brief second posting as ambassador to Britain in 1838. The English values of the Magna Carta were clearly evident in its wording. The Hatt-i Sharif promised everyone in the Sultan's empire security of life, honour, property, regardless of their faith; it stressed the rule of law, religious toleration, the modernization of the empire's institutions, and a just and rational system of centralized taxation and military conscription. In essence, the decree assumed that the commonwealth would be promoted by giving guarantees of personal liberty to the empire's most dynamic elements, the non-Muslim *millets*, whose unfair treatment by the Muslim majority had created instability.[40]

How far the decree was motivated by a desire to enlist British support for the Ottoman Empire at a time of crisis is a matter of controversy. There was certainly an element of English window dressing in the liberal language of the Hatt-i Sharif, whose final wording also owed much to Ponsonby, the British ambassador. But this does not mean that the Hatt-i Sharif was insincere, reluctantly conceded as a tactical device to secure British support. At the heart of the decree was a genuine belief in the need to modernize the Ottoman Empire. Reshid and his followers were convinced that to rescue the empire they ultimately needed to create a new secular concept of imperial unity (Ottomanism) based on the equality of all the Sultan's subjects, regardless of their faith. It was a mark of the seriousness with which the reformers took their task, as well as a sign of their concern to pacify the potential opposition of conservatives, that the concessions of the Hatt-i Sharif were couched in terms of the defence of Islamic traditions and the precepts of the 'glorious Koran'. Indeed, the Sultan and many of his most prominent reformist ministers, including Mustafa Reshid and Mehmet Hüsrev, the Grand Vizier in 1839–41, had close connections to the Naqshbandi lodges (*tekkes*), where a strict emphasis on the teachings of Islamic law was preached. In many ways the Tanzimat reforms were an attempt to create a more centralized but more tolerant Islamic state.[41]

The Ottoman government did very little to implement its lofty declarations, however. Its promise to improve the conditions of the Christian population was the main sticking point, inciting as it did the opposition of the traditional Muslim clergy and conservatives. There were only minor improvements. The death penalty for apostasy was renounced by the Sultan in 1844, although a small number of Muslims who had converted to Christianity (and Christians who had reversed conversion to Islam) were still executed on the authority of local governors. Blasphemy continued to be punished by the death sentence. Christians were admitted to some of the military schools and were liable to conscription, but since they were not likely to be promoted to the senior ranks, most chose to pay a special tax for exemption from service. From the late 1840s Christians were allowed to become members of the provincial councils that checked the work of governors. They also began to sit on juries alongside Muslims in the commercial courts where Western legal principles were liberally applied. But otherwise there was not much change. The slave trade continued, most of it involving the capture of Christian boys and girls from the Caucasus for sale in Constantinople. The Turks continued to regard the Christians as inferior, and thought that Muslim privileges should not be given up. The informal rules and practices of the administration, if not all the written laws, continued to ensure that the Christians were treated as second-class citizens, although they were rapidly emerging as the dominant economic group in the Ottoman Empire, which became a growing source of tension and envy – especially when they evaded taxes by acquiring foreign passports and protection.

Returning to Constantinople for his third term as ambassador in 1842, Stratford Canning became increasingly despondent about the prospects of reform. The Sultan was too young, and Reshid too weak, to stand up to the conservatives, who gradually gained the upper hand against the reformers in the Council (Divan) of the Porte. The reform agenda was increasingly entangled in personal rivalries, in particular between Reshid and Mehmet Ali Pasha,* one of Reshid's reformist

* Not to be confused with Mehmet Ali, the Egyptian ruler.

protégés, who served as ambassador in London from 1841 to 1844, and then as Foreign Minister from 1846 to 1852, when he replaced Reshid as Grand Vizier. Such was Reshid's jealousy of Mehmet Ali that, by the early 1850s, he had even joined the Muslim opposition to granting equal rights to the Sultan's Christian subjects in the hope of stopping his rival. The reforms were also hampered by practical difficulties. The Ottoman government in Constantinople was far too distant and too weak to force through laws in a society without railways, post offices, telegraphs or newspapers.

But the main obstacle was the opposition of traditional élites – the religious leaders of the *millets* – who felt beleaguered by the Tanzimat reforms. All the *millets* protested, especially the Greeks, and there was a sort of secularist coup in the Armenian one; but the reforms were most opposed by Islamic leaders and élites. This was a society where the interests of the local pashas and the Muslim clergy were heavily invested in the preservation of the traditional *millet* system with all its legal and civil disabilities against the Christians. The more the Porte attempted to become an agency of centralization and reform, the more these leaders stirred up local grievances and reactionary Muslim feeling against a state which they denounced as 'infidel' because of its increasing dependence on foreigners. Incited by their clergy, Muslims demonstrated against the reforms in many towns: there were acts of violence against Christians; churches were destroyed; and there were even threats to burn the Latin Quarter in Constantinople.

For Stratford Canning, who was no friend of Islam, this reaction raised a moral dilemma: could Britain continue to support a Muslim government that failed to stop the persecution of its Christian citizens? In February 1850 he was thrown into despair after hearing of 'atrocious massacres' of the Christian population in Rumelia (in a region later part of Bulgaria). He wrote in gloomy terms to Palmerston, the Foreign Secretary, explaining that 'the great game of improvement is altogether up for the present'.

The master mischief in this country is dominant religion ... Though altogether effete as a principle of national strength and reviving power, the spirit of Islamism, thus perverted, lives in the supremacy of the conquering race and in the prejudices engendered by a long tyrannical domination. It may not be too much to say that the progress of the empire towards a firm re-establishment of its prosperity and independence is to be measured by the degree of its emancipation from that source of injustice and weakness.

Palmerston agreed that the persecution of the Christians not only invited but even justified the policy pursued by the Russians. In his view, it gave Britain little choice but to withdraw support for the Ottoman government. Writing to Reshid the following November, he foresaw that the Ottoman Empire was 'doomed to fall by the timidity and weakness and irresolution of its sovereign and his ministers, and it is evident we shall ere long have to consider what other arrangement can be set up in its place'.[42]

British intervention in Turkish politics had meanwhile brought about a Muslim reaction against Western interference in Ottoman affairs. By the early 1850s Stratford Canning had become far more than an ambassador or adviser to the Porte. The 'Great Elchi', or Great Ambassador, as he was known in Constantinople, had a direct influence on the policies of the Turkish government. Indeed, at a time when there was no telegraph between London and the Turkish capital and several months could pass before instructions arrived from Whitehall, he had considerable leeway over British policy in the Ottoman Empire. His presence was a source of deep resentment among the Sultan's ministers, who lived in terror of a personal visit from the dictatorial ambassador. Local notables and the Muslim clergy were equally resentful of his efforts on behalf of the Christians, and saw his influence on the government as a loss of Turkish sovereignty. This hostility to foreign intervention in Ottoman affairs – by Britain, France or Russia – would come to play an important role in Turkish politics on the eve of the Crimean War.

3

The Russian Menace

The Dutch steamer pulled into the docks at Woolwich late on a Saturday evening, 1 June 1844. Its only passengers were 'Count Orlov' – the pseudonym of Tsar Nicholas – and his entourage of courtiers who had travelled incognito from St Petersburg. Ever since Russia's brutal suppression of the Polish insurrection in 1831, Nicholas had lived in fear of assassination by Polish nationalists opposed to Russian rule in their homeland, so it was his custom to travel in disguise. London had a large community of Polish exiles, and there were concerns for the Tsar's safety from the moment the trip had been discussed with the British government in January. To increase his personal security, Nicholas had told no one of his travel plans. Stopping only briefly in Berlin, the Tsar's coaches sped across the Continent, without anyone in Britain even knowing of his imminent arrival until he had boarded the steamer in Hamburg on 30 May, less than two days before his landing at Woolwich.

Even Baron Brunov, the Russian ambassador in London, was not told the precise details of the Tsar's itinerary. Not knowing when his steamer would arrive, Brunov had spent the whole of Saturday at the Woolwich docks. Finally, at ten o'clock in the evening, the steamer pulled in. The Tsar disembarked – barely recognizable in a grey cloak he had worn during the Turkish campaign of 1828 – and hurried off with Brunov to the Russian embassy at Ashburnham House in Westminster. Despite the late hour, he sent a note to the Prince Consort requesting a meeting with the Queen at her earliest convenience. Accustomed as he was to summoning his ministers at all hours of the day and night, it had not occurred to him that it might be rude to wake Prince Albert in the early hours of the morning.[1]

This was not the Tsar's first trip to London. He had fond memories of his previous visit, in 1816, when as a 20-year-old and still a Grand Duke, he had been a great success with the female half of the English aristocracy. Lady Charlotte Campbell, a famous beauty and lady-in-waiting to the Princess of Wales, had declared of him: 'What an amiable creature! He is devilish handsome! He will be the handsomest man in Europe.' From that trip, Nicholas had gained the impression that he had an ally in the English monarchy and aristocracy. As the despotic ruler of the world's greatest state, Nicholas had little sense of the limitations on a constitutional monarchy. He presumed that he could come to Britain and decide matters of foreign policy directly with the Queen and her most senior ministers. It was 'an excellent thing', he told Victoria at their first meeting, 'to see now and then with one's own eyes, as it did not do always to trust to diplomatists only'. Such meetings created 'a feeling of friendship and interest' between reigning sovereigns, and more could be achieved 'in a single conversation to explain one's feelings, views and motives than in a host of messages and letters'. The Tsar thought that he could strike a 'gentlemen's agreement' with Britain about how to deal with the Ottoman Empire in the event of its collapse.[2]

Nor was this the first attempt that Nicholas had made to enlist the support of another power in his partition plans for the Ottoman Empire. In 1829 he had suggested to the Austrians a bilateral division of its European territories to forestall the chaos which he feared would follow its collapse, but they had turned him down to preserve the Concert of Europe. Then, in the autumn of 1843 he again approached the Austrians, resurrecting the idea of a Greek empire backed by Russia, Austria and Prussia (the Triple Alliance of 1815) to prevent the British and the French from dividing the spoils of the crumbling Ottoman Empire between themselves. Insisting that Russia did not want to expand into the Balkans, Nicholas proposed that the Austrians should be given all the Turkish lands between the Danube and the Adriatic, and that Constantinople should become a free city under Austrian guardianship. But nothing he said had been able to dispel Vienna's deep mistrust of Russia's ambitions. The Austrian ambassador in St Petersburg believed that the Tsar was trying to engineer a situation where Russia could use the excuse of defending Turkey to intervene in its affairs and impose its own partition plans by military force. What the Tsar really wanted, the ambassador maintained, was not a Greek empire backed by the three powers but a 'state tied to Russia by interests, principles and religion, and governed by a Russian prince.... Russia can never lose sight of this aim. It is a necessary condition for the fulfilment of her destiny ... Present-day Greece would be swallowed up in the new state.'[3] Deeply suspicious, the Austrians would have nothing to do with the Tsar's partition plans without the agreement of the British and the French. So Nicholas now came to London in the hope of winning over Britain to his point of view.

On the face of it, there was not much to suggest that Nicholas could forge a new alliance with Britain. The British were committed to their liberal reform plans to save the Ottoman Empire, and saw the ambitions of the Russians as a major threat. But the Tsar was encouraged by the diplomatic rapprochement between Russia and Britain during recent years, prompted by their shared alarm at France's growing involvement in the Middle East.

In 1839 the French had given their support to a second insurrection by the Egyptian ruler Mehmet Ali against the Sultan's rule in Syria. With French backing, the Egyptians defeated the Ottoman army, raising renewed fears that they would march against the Turkish capital, as they had done six years before. The young Sultan Abdülmecid appeared too weak to resist Mehmet Ali's renewed demands for a hereditary dynasty in Egypt and Syria, especially after the Ottoman navy defected to the Egyptians at Alexandria, and once again the Porte was forced to ask for foreign help. In 1833 the Russians had intervened on their own to rescue the Ottoman Empire, but in this second crisis they looked to work with Britain for the restoration of the Sultan's rule – their aim being to come between the British and the French.

Like the Russians, the British were alarmed by the growing French involvement in Egypt. This was where Napoleon had threatened to bring down the British Empire in 1798. France had invested heavily in the booming cotton cash crop and industrial economy of Egypt during the 1830s. It had sent advisers to help train the Egyptian army and navy. With French support, the Egyptians were not only a major threat to Turkish rule. As head of a powerful Islamic revival movement against the intervention of the Christian nations in the Ottoman Empire, Mehmet Ali was also an inspiration to the Muslim rebels against tsarist rule in the Caucasus.

Consequently, Russia and Britain with Austria and Prussia urged Mehmet Ali to withdraw from Syria and accept their terms for a settlement with the Sultan. These terms, set down in the London Convention of 1840 and ratified by the four powers with the Ottoman Empire, allowed Mehmet Ali to establish a hereditary dynasty in Egypt. To ensure his withdrawal, a British fleet sailed to Alexandria, and an Anglo-Austrian force was sent to Palestine. For a while the Egyptian leader held out, in the expectation of French support; there were scares of a war in Europe when the French government rejected the peace terms proposed by the four powers and pledged to help Ali. But at the final moment the French, unwilling to be drawn into war, backed down and Mehmet Ali withdrew from Syria. By the terms of a subsequent London Convention of 1841, which the French signed reluctantly, Mehmet Ali was recognized as the hereditary ruler of Egypt in exchange for his recognition of the Sultan's sovereignty in the rest of the Ottoman Empire.

The importance of the 1841 Convention extended beyond securing Mehmet Ali's surrender. Agreement had also been reached to close the Turkish Straits to all warships except those of the Sultan's allies during wartime – a very big concession by the Russians because potentially it allowed the British navy into the Black Sea, where it could attack their vulnerable southern frontiers. By signing the convention, the Russians had given up their privileged position in the Ottoman Empire and their control of the Straits, all in the hope of improving relations with Britain and isolating France.

From the Tsar's point of view, propping up the Sultan's power could only be a temporary measure. With the French weakened by their support for this insurrection, and Russia having reached what Nicholas believed was a new understanding with the British in the Middle East, he concluded that the London Convention opened the possibility of a more formal alliance between Russia and Britain. The election of a Conservative government headed by Sir Robert Peel in 1841 gave the Tsar some added grounds to be hopeful on this score, for the Tories were less hostile to the Russians than the previous Whig administration of Lord Melbourne (1835–41). The Tsar was convinced that the Tory government would listen favourably to his suggestion that Russia and Britain should take the lead in Europe and decide the future of the Ottoman Empire. In 1844, confident that he could bring the British round to his partition plans, the Tsar departed for London.

The suddenness of his June arrival took everybody by surprise. There had been vague talk of his visit since the spring. Peel had welcomed the idea at a banquet for the Russian Trading Company in the London Tavern on 2 March, and three days later Lord Aberdeen, the Foreign Secretary, had sent a formal invitation via Baron Brunov, reassuring the Tsar that his presence would 'dispel any Polish prejudices' against Russia in Britain. 'For such a reserved and nervous man as Aberdeen to speak so confidently on this matter is significant,' Brunov wrote to Nesselrode. As for the Queen, at first she was reluctant to receive the Tsar, on the grounds of his long-standing conflict with her uncle Leopold, king of the newly independent Belgium, who had attracted many Polish exiles to his army during the 1830s. Determined to uphold the legitimist principles of the Holy Alliance, Nicholas had wanted to restore the monarchies deposed by the French and Belgian revolutions of 1830, and had been prevented only by the outbreak of the Polish uprising in Warsaw in November of that year. His threats of intervention had earned him the mistrust of West European liberals, who labelled him the 'gendarme of Europe', while the Polish rebels who fled abroad after the suppression of their uprising had found a welcome refuge in Paris, Brussels and London. These were the developments that worried Queen Victoria, but eventually she was persuaded by her husband, Prince Albert (who was also a nephew of King Leopold), that a visit by the Tsar would help to mend relations between the ruling houses on the Continent. In her invitation to the Tsar, Victoria had said that she would welcome him in late May or early June, but no date had been set. In mid-May it was still not clear if Nicholas would come. In the end, the Queen learned of his arrival a few hours before his steamer landed at Woolwich. Her staff were thrown into a panic, not least because they were expecting a visit from the King of Saxony on the same day, and hasty preparations to receive the Tsar needed to be improvised.[4]

The Tsar's impromptu visit was one of many signs of a growing rashness in his behaviour. After eighteen years on the throne he had begun to lose those qualities that had characterized his early rule: caution, conservatism and reserve. Increasingly affected by the hereditary mental illness that had troubled Alexander in his final years, Nicholas became impatient and impetuous, and inclined to impulsive behaviour, like rushing off to London to impose his will on the British. His erratic nature was noted by Prince Albert and the Queen, who wrote to her uncle Leopold: 'Albert thinks he is a man inclined to give way too much to impulse and feeling which makes him act wrongly often.'[5]

The day after his arrival, the Queen received the Tsar at Buckingham Palace. There was a meeting with the dukes of Cambridge, Wellington and Gloucester, followed by a tour of London's fashionable West End streets. The Tsar inspected the building work at the Houses of Parliament, which at that time were being reconstructed after the fire of 1834, and visited the newly finished Regent's Park. In the evening the royal party travelled by train to Windsor, where they remained for the next five days. The Tsar astonished the servants with his spartan habits. The first thing his valets did on being shown his bedroom at Windsor Castle was to send to the stable for some straw to stuff the leather sack which served as the mattress of the military campbed on which the Tsar always slept.[6]

Because the Queen was heavily pregnant and the Saxe-Coburgs were in mourning for Prince Albert's father, there was no royal ball in the Tsar's honour. But there were plenty of other amusements: hunting parties; military reviews; outings to the races at Ascot (where the Gold Cup was renamed the Emperor's Plate in honour of the Tsar*); an evening with the Queen at the opera; and a glittering banquet where more than sixty guests ate their way through fifty-three different dishes served from the Grand Service, possibly the finest collection of silver-gilt dining plate in the world. On his last two evenings, there were large dinners where the male guests dressed in military uniform, in line with the wishes of the Tsar, who felt uncomfortable *en frac* and admitted to the Queen that he was embarrassed when not dressed in a uniform.[7]

---

* The name reverted to the Gold Cup after the outbreak of the Crimean War.

As an exercise in public relations, the Tsar's visit was a great success. Society women were charmed and delighted by his good looks and manners. 'He is still a great devotee to female beauty,' noted Baron Stockmar, 'and to his old English flames he showed the greatest attention.' The Queen also warmed to him. She liked his 'dignified and graceful' demeanour, his kindness to children, and his sincerity, though she thought him rather sad. 'He gives Albert and myself the impression of a man who is not happy, and on whom the burden of his immense power and position weighs heavily and painfully,' she wrote to Leopold on 4 June. 'He seldom smiles, and when he does, the expression is not a happy one.' A week later, at the end of the trip, she wrote again to her uncle with a penetrating assessment of the Tsar's character:

> There is much about him which I cannot help liking, and I think his character is one which should be understood, and looked upon for once as it is. He is stern and severe – with fixed principles of *duty* which *nothing* on earth will make him change; very *clever* I do *not* think him, and his mind is an uncivilized one; his education has been neglected; politics and military concerns are the only things he takes great interest in; the arts and all softer occupations he is insensible to, but he is sincere, I am certain, *sincere* even in his most despotic acts, from a sense that that *is* the *only* way to govern.

Lord Melbourne, one of the most anti-Russian of the Whigs, got on very well with Nicholas at a breakfast at Chiswick House, the centre of the Whig establishment. Even Palmerston, the former Whig spokesman on foreign policy, who was well known for his hard line against Russia, thought it was important for a 'favourable impression of England' to be given to the Tsar: 'He is very powerful and may act in our favour, or bring us harm, depending on whether he is well disposed or hostile towards us.'[8]

During his stay in England the Tsar had a number of political discussions with the Queen and Prince Albert, with Peel and Aberdeen. The British were surprised by the frankness of his views. The Queen even thought he was 'too frank, for he talks so openly before people, which he should not do, and with difficulty restrains himself', as she wrote to Leopold. The Tsar had come to the conclusion that openness was the only way to overcome British mistrust and prejudice against Russia. 'I know that I am taken for an actor,' he told Peel and Aberdeen, 'but indeed I am not; I am thoroughly straightforward; I say what I mean, and what I promise I fulfil.'[9]

On the question of Belgium, the Tsar declared that he would like to mend his relations with Leopold, but 'while there are Polish officers in the service of the king, that is completely impossible'. Exchanging views with Aberdeen, 'not as an emperor with a minister, but as two gentlemen', he explained his thinking, voicing his resentment of Western double standards against Russia:

> The Poles were and still remain in rebellion against my rule. Would it be acceptable for a gentleman to take into service people who are guilty of rebellion against his friend? Leopold took these rebels under his protection. What would you say if I became the patron of [the Irish independence leader Daniel] O'Connell and thought of making him my minister?

When it came to France, Nicholas wanted Britain to join Russia in a policy of containment. Appealing to their mistrust of the French after the Napoleonic Wars, he told Peel and Aberdeen that France 'should never be allowed again to create disorder and march its armies beyond its borders'. He hoped that with their common interests against France, Britain and Russia might become allies. 'Through our friendly intercourse,' he said with feeling, 'I hope to annihilate the prejudices between our countries. For I value highly the opinion of Englishmen. As to what the French say of me, I care not. I spit on it.'[10]

Nicholas particularly played on Britain's fear of France in the Middle East – the main subject of his talks with Peel and Aberdeen. 'Turkey is a dying man,' he told them.

> We may endeavour to keep him alive, but we shall not succeed. He will, he must, die. That will be a critical moment. I foresee that I shall have to put my armies into motion and Austria must do the same. In this crisis I fear only France. What does she want? I expect her to make a move in many places: in Egypt, in the Mediterranean, and in the East. Remember the French expedition to Ancona [in 1832]? Why could they not undertake the same in Crete or Smyrna? And if they did

wouldn't the English mobilize their fleet? And so in these territories there would be the Russian and the Austrian armies, and all the ships of the English fleet. A major conflagration would become unavoidable.

The Tsar argued that the time had come for the European powers, led by Russia and Britain, to step in and manage a partition of the Turkish territories to avoid a chaotic scramble over their division, possibly involving national revolutions and a Continental war, when the Sultan's empire finally collapsed. He impressed on Peel and Aberdeen his firm conviction that the Ottoman Empire would soon cave in and that Russia and Britain should act together to plan for that eventuality, if only to prevent the French from taking over Egypt and the eastern Mediterannean, a concern uppermost in British thinking at that time. As Nicholas told Peel,

> I do not claim one inch of Turkish soil, but neither will I allow that any other, especially the French, shall have an inch of it. . . . We cannot now stipulate as to what shall be done with Turkey when she is dead. Such stipulations would only hasten her death. I shall therefore do all in my power to maintain the status quo. But we should keep the possible and eventual case of her collapse honestly and reasonably before our eyes. We ought to deliberate reasonably, and endeavour to come to a straightforward and honest understanding on the subject.[11]

Peel and Aberdeen were ready to agree on the need to plan ahead for the possible partition of the Ottoman Empire, but only when that need arose, and they did not see that yet. A secret memorandum containing the conclusions of the conversations was drafted by Brunov and agreed (though not signed) by Nicholas and Aberdeen.

The Tsar left England with the firm conviction that the conversations he had held with Peel and Aberdeen were statements of policy, and that he could now look forward to a partnership with Britain the aim of which was to devise a coordinated plan for the partition of the Ottoman Empire whenever that should become necessary to safeguard the interests of the two powers. It was not an unreasonable assumption to make, given that he had a secret memorandum to show for his efforts in London. But in fact it was a fatal error for Nicholas to think that he had a 'gentlemen's agreement' with the British government on the Eastern Question. The British saw the conversations as no more than an exchange of opinions on matters of concern to both powers and not as something binding in any formal sense. Convinced that all that mattered was the viewpoint of the Queen and her senior ministers, Nicholas failed to appreciate the influence of Parliament, opposition parties, public opinion and the press on the foreign policy of the British government. This misunderstanding was to play a crucial role in the diplomatic blunders made by Nicholas on the eve of the Crimean War.

*

The Tsar's visit to London did nothing to dispel the British mistrust of Russia that had been building for decades. Despite the fact that the threat of Russia to British interests was minimal, and trade and diplomatic relations between the two countries were not bad at all in the years leading up to the Crimean War, Russophobia (even more than Francophobia) was arguably the most important element in Britain's outlook on the world abroad. Throughout Europe, attitudes to Russia were mostly formed by fears and fantasies, and Britain in this sense was no exception to the rule. The rapid territorial expansion of the Russian Empire in the eighteenth century and the demonstration of its military might against Napoleon had left a deep impression on the European mind. In the early nineteenth century there was a frenzy of European publications – pamphlets, travelogues and political treatises – on 'the Russian menace' to the Continent. They had as much to do with the imagination of an Asiatic 'other' threatening the liberties and civilization of Europe as with any real or perceived threat. The stereotype of Russia that emerged from these fanciful writings was that of a savage power, aggressive and expansionist by nature, yet also sufficiently cunning and deceptive to plot with 'unseen forces' against the West and infiltrate societies.*

The documentary basis of this 'Russian menace' was the so-called 'Testament of Peter the Great', which was widely cited by Russophobic writers, politicians, diplomats and military men as prima facie

---

* There is an obvious comparison with the Western view of Russia during the Cold War. The Russophobia of the Cold War era was partly shaped by nineteenth-century attitudes.

evidence of Russia's ambitions to dominate the world. Peter's aims for Russia in this document were megalomaniac: to expand on the Baltic and Black seas, to ally with the Austrians to expel the Turks from Europe, to 'conquer the Levant' and control the trade of the Indies, to sow dissent and confusion in Europe and become the master of the European continent.

The 'Testament' was a forgery. It was created sometime in the early eighteenth century by various Polish, Hungarian and Ukrainian figures connected to France and the Ottomans, and it went through several drafts before the finished version ended up in the French Foreign Ministry archives during the 1760s. For reasons of foreign policy, the French were disposed to believe in the authenticity of the 'Testament': their main allies in Eastern Europe (Sweden, Poland and Turkey) had all been weakened by Russia. The belief that the 'Testament' reflected Russia's aims formed the basis of France's foreign policy throughout the eighteenth and early nineteenth centuries.[12]

Napoleon I was particularly influenced by the 'Testament'. His senior foreign policy advisers freely cited its ideas and phraseology, claiming, in the words of Charles Maurice de Talleyrand, the Foreign Minister of the Directory and the Consulate (1795–1804), that 'the entire system [of the Russian Empire] constantly followed since Peter I . . . tends to crush Europe anew under a flood of barbarians'. Such ideas were expressed even more explicitly by Alexandre d'Hauterive, an influential figure in the Foreign Ministry who had the confidence of Bonaparte:

> Russia in time of war seeks to conquer her neighbours; in time of peace she seeks to keep not only her neighbours but all the countries of the world in a confusion of mistrust, agitation and discord . . . All that this power has usurped in Europe and Asia is well known. She tries to destroy the Ottoman Empire; she tries to destroy the German Empire. Russia will not proceed directly to her goal . . . but she will in an underhanded manner undermine the bases [of the Ottoman Empire]; she will foment intrigues; she will promote rebellion in the provinces . . . In so doing, she will not cease to profess the most benevolent sentiments for the Sublime Porte; she will constantly call herself the friend, the

protectress of the Ottoman Empire. Russia will similarly attack ... the
house of Austria ... Then there will be no more the court of Vienna
[*sic*]; then we, the Western nations, we will have lost one of the barriers
most capable of defending us against the incursions of Russia.[13]

The 'Testament' was published by the French in 1812, the year of
their invasion of Russia, and from that point on was widely reproduced and cited throughout Europe as conclusive evidence of Russia's
expansionist foreign policy. It was republished on the eve of every war
involving Russia on the European continent – in 1854, 1878, 1914
and 1941 – and was cited during the Cold War to explain the aggressive intentions of the Soviet Union. On the Soviet invasion of
Afghanistan in 1979 it was cited in the *Christian Science Monitor*,
Time magazine and the British House of Commons as an explanation
of the origins of Moscow's aims.[14]

Nowhere was its influence more evident than in Britain, where
fantastic fears of the Russian threat – and not just to India – were a
journalistic staple. 'A very general persuasion has long been entertained by the Russians that they are destined to be the rulers of the
world, and this idea has been more than once stated in publications in
the Russian language,' declared the *Morning Chronicle* in 1817. Even
serious periodicals succumbed to the view that Russia's defeat of
Napoleon had set it on a course to dominate the world. Looking back
on the events of recent years, the *Edinburgh Review* thought in 1817
that it 'would have seemed far less extravagant to predict the entry
of a Russian army into Delhi, or even Calcutta, than its entry into
Paris'.[15] British fears were supported by the amateur opinions and
impressions of travel writers on Russia and the East, a literary genre
that enjoyed something of a boom in the early nineteenth century.
These travel books not only dominated public perceptions of Russia
but also provided a good deal of the working knowledge on which
Whitehall shaped its policies towards that country.

One of the earliest and most controversial of such travelogues was
*A Sketch of the Military and Political Power of Russia in the Year
1817* by Sir Robert Wilson, a veteran of the Napoleonic Wars who
had served briefly as a commissioner in the Russian army. Wilson
made a number of extravagant claims – incapable of demonstration or

disproof – which he presented as the fruit of his inside knowledge of the tsarist government: that Russia was determined to drive the Turks from Europe, conquer Persia, advance on India, and dominate the world. Wilson's speculations were so wild that in some quarters they were ridiculed (*The Times* suggested that Russia might advance to the Cape of Good Hope, the South Pole and the Moon) but the extremity of his argument guaranteed attention for his pamphlet, and it was widely debated and reviewed. The *Edinburgh Review* and the *Quarterly Review* – the most read and respected journals in government circles – agreed that Wilson had overestimated the immediate threat of Russia but nonetheless praised him for raising the issue and thought that the conduct of that country henceforth merited the 'careful scrutiny of distrust'.[16] In other words, the general premise of Wilson's extreme views – that Russian expansionism was a danger to the world – was now to be accepted.

From this point on the phantom threat of Russia entered into the political discourse of Britain as a reality. The idea that Russia had a plan for the domination of the Near East and potentially the conquest of the British Empire began to appear with regularity in pamphlets, which in turn were later cited as objective evidence by Russophobic propagandists in the 1830s and 1840s.

The most influential of these pamphlets was *On the Designs of Russia*, previously discussed, by the future Crimean War commander George de Lacy Evans, which first laid out the danger posed by Russia's activities in Asia Minor. But this pamphlet was notable for another reason as well: it was here that de Lacy Evans advanced the earliest detailed plan for the dismemberment of the Russian Empire, a programme that would be taken up again by the cabinet during the Crimean War. He advocated a preventive war against Russia to block its aggressive intentions. He proposed attacking Russia in Poland, Finland, the Black Sea and the Caucasus, where it was most vulnerable. His eight-point plan reads almost like a blueprint of the larger British aims against Russia during the Crimean War:

1. Cut off trade to Russia so that the nobles would lose their profits and turn against the tsarist government.
2. Destroy the naval depots at Kronstadt, Sevastopol, etc.

3. Launch a series of 'predatory and properly supported incursions along her maritime frontiers, especially in the Black Sea, within the shores of which, and even in the rear of her line of military posts, she has a host of unsubdued, armed, indomitable mountaineer enemies ...'.
4. Help the Persians to reclaim the Caucasus.
5. Send a large corps of troops and a fleet to the Gulf of Finland 'to menace the flanks and reserve of the Russian armies of Poland and Finland'.
6. Finance revolutionaries to 'create insurrections and a serf war'.
7. Bombard St Petersburg, 'if that be practicable'.
8. Send arms to Poland and Finland 'for their liberation from Russia'.[17]

David Urquhart, the famous Turcophile, also advocated a preventive war against Russia. No writer did more to prepare the British public for the Crimean War. A Scotsman educated at Oxford in Classics, Urquhart first encountered the Eastern Question in 1827, when, at the age of 22, he enrolled in a group of volunteers to fight for the Greek cause. He travelled widely in European Turkey, became enamoured of the virtues of the Turks, learned Turkish and modern Greek, adopted Turkish dress, and quickly gained a reputation as something of an expert on Turkey through his reports on that country which were published in the *Morning Courier* during 1831. Making use of a family friendship with Sir Herbert Taylor, private secretary to King William IV, Urquhart got himself attached to Stratford Canning's mission to Constantinople to negotiate a final settlement of the Greek boundary in November 1831. During his time there he became convinced of the threat posed by Russian intervention in Turkey. Encouraged by his patrons at the court, he wrote *Turkey and Its Resources* (1833), in which he denied that the Ottoman Empire was about to collapse and highlighted the commercial opportunities awaiting Britain if it gave aid to Turkey and protected it from Russian aggression. The success of the book earned Urquhart the favour of Lord Palmerston, the Foreign Secretary in Lord Grey's government (1830–34), and a new appointment to the Turkish capital as part of a secret mission to examine the possibilities for British trade in the Balkans, Turkey, Persia, southern Russia and Afghanistan.

In Constantinople, Urquhart became a close political ally of the British ambassador, Lord John Ponsonby, an ardent Russophobe who was unshakeable in his conviction that Russia's aim was the subjugation of Turkey. Ponsonby urged the British government to send warships into the Black Sea and to aid the Muslim tribes of the Caucasus in their fight against Russia (in 1834 he even won from Palmerston a 'discretionary order' granting him authority to summon British warships into the Black Sea if he deemed it necessary but this was soon cancelled by the Duke of Wellington, who thought better of giving so much power to make war to such a notorious Russophobe). Under the influence of Ponsonby, Urquhart became increasingly political in his activities. He did not stop at writing but actually did things to make war against the Russians more likely. In 1834 he visited the Circassian tribes, pledging British support for their war against the Russian occupation, an act of provocation against Russia that obliged Palmerston to recall him to London.

There, Urquhart stepped up his campaign for British military intervention against Russia in Turkey. A pamphlet he had written with Ponsonby, *England, France, Russia and Turkey*, was published in December 1834. It went through five editions within a year and received very positive reviews. Encouraged by this success, in November 1835 Urquhart launched a periodical, *The Portfolio*, in which he aired his Russophobic views, of which the following is typical: 'The ignorance of the Russian people separates them from all community with the feelings of other nations, and prepares them to regard every denunciation of the injustice of their rulers as an attack upon themselves, and the Government has already announced by its Acts a determination to submit to no moral influences which may reach it from without.'[18]

In another act of provocation Urquhart published in *The Portfolio* what purported to be copies of Russian diplomatic documents captured from the palace of Grand Duke Constantine, the governor of Poland, during the Warsaw insurrection in November 1830 and passed on by Polish émigrés to Palmerston. Most, if not all, of these documents were fabricated by Urquhart, including a 'suppressed passage of a speech' in which Tsar Nicholas was said to have declared that Russia would not stop its repressive measures until it had achieved the complete subjugation of Poland, and a 'Declaration of Independence' supposedly proclaimed by the Circassian tribes. But such was the climate of Russophobia that they were widely accepted as authentic documents by the British press.[19]

In 1836 Urquhart returned to Constantinople as secretary of the embassy. His growing fame and influence in British diplomatic and political circles had forced Palmerston to bring him back into office, although his role in the Turkish capital was rather limited. Once again, Urquhart took up the Circassian cause and attempted to stir up a conflict between Russia and Britain. In his most brazen act yet, Urquhart conspired to send a British schooner, the *Vixen*, to Circassia in deliberate contravention of the Russian embargo against foreign shipping on the eastern Black Sea coast imposed as part of the Treaty of Adrianople. The *Vixen* belonged to a shipping company, George and James Bell of Glasgow and London, that had already clashed with the Russians over their obstructive quarantine regulations on the Danube. Officially, the *Vixen* was transporting salt, but in fact it was loaded with a large supply of weapons for the Circassians. Ponsonby in Constantinople had been informed of the ship's intended journey and did nothing to discourage it; nor did he reply to the Bells' enquiries about whether the Foreign Office recognized the embargo and whether Britain would defend their shipping rights, as Urquhart had assured them that it would. The Russians were aware of Urquhart's plans: in the summer of 1836 the Tsar had already complained to the British ambassador in St Petersburg after one of Urquhart's followers had travelled to Circassia and promised British support for their war against Russia. The *Vixen* sailed in October. As Urquhart had anticipated, a Russian warship seized the *Vixen* on the Caucasian coast, at Soujouk Kalé, prompting loud denunciations of the Russian action and calls for war in *The Times* and other newspapers. Ponsonby urged Palmerston to send a fleet into the Black Sea. Although he was reluctant to recognize Russia's embargo or its claims to Circassia, Palmerston was nevertheless not ready to be pushed into a war by Urquhart, Ponsonby and the British press. He acknowledged that the *Vixen* had contravened Russian regulations, which Britain recognized, but only in so far as these related to Soujouk Kalé, not to the whole Caucasian coastline.

Recalled once again from Constantinople, Urquhart was dismissed from the foreign service and charged with a breach of official secrecy by Palmerston in 1837. Urquhart always claimed that Palmerston had known about the *Vixen* plan. For years he harboured a deep grudge against the Foreign Secretary for supposedly betraying him. As Britain moved towards *entente* with Russia, Urquhart became increasingly frustrated and extreme in his Russophobia, calling for an even stronger anti-Russian line – not discounting war – to defend Britain's trade and its interests in India. He even accused Palmerston of being in the pay of the Russian government, a charge taken up by his supporters in the press, including in *The Times*, a major influence on middle-class opinion, which joined the Urquhart camp in opposition to the 'pro-Russian' foreign policy of Palmerston. In 1839 a long series of letters to *The Times* by 'Anglicus' – a pseudonym of Henry Parish, one of Urquhart's acolytes – almost took on the status of editorials, warning of the dangers of any compromise with an empire bent on the domination of Europe and Asia.

Urquhart continued his attacks on Russia in the House of Commons, to which he was elected in 1847 as an independent candidate (taking as his colours the green and yellow of Circassia). By this time Palmerston was the Foreign Secretary in Lord John Russell's Whig administration, which took office in 1846, following the split of the Conservatives over the repeal of import tariffs on cereal products (the Corn Laws). Urquhart renewed his charges against him. In 1848 he even led a campaign to impeach Palmerston for his failure to pursue a more aggressive policy against Russia. In a five-hour speech in the House of Commons, Urquhart's main ally, the MP Thomas Anstey, accused him of a shameful foreign policy that had endangered Britain's national security by failing to defend the liberty of Europe against Russian aggression – in particular, the constitutional liberties of Poland, whose maintenance had been made a condition for the transfer of the Polish kingdom to the Tsar's protection by the other powers at the Congress of Vienna in 1815. Russia's brutal crushing of the Warsaw uprising in 1831 had obliged Britain to intervene in Poland in support of the rebels, even at the risk of a European war against Russia, Anstey maintained. In self-defence, Palmerston explained why it had been unrealistic to take up arms in favour of the Poles, while laying out the general principles of liberal interventionism which he would call on again when Britain entered the Crimean War:

> I hold that the real policy of England – apart from questions which involve her own particular interests, political or commercial – is to be the champion of justice and right; pursuing that course with moderation and prudence, not becoming the Quixote of the world, but giving the weight of her moral sanction and support wherever she thinks that justice is, and wherever she thinks that wrong has been done.[20]

Urquhart's Russophobia may have been at odds with Britain's foreign policy in the 1840s but it had considerable support in Parliament, where there was a powerful lobby of politicians who backed his calls for a tougher line against Russia, including Lord Stanley and Stratford Canning, who replaced Ponsonby as ambassador to Constantinople in 1842. Outside Parliament, Urquhart's backing for free trade (the major reform issue of the 1840s) won him a broad following among Midlands and northern businessmen, who were persuaded by his frequent public speeches that Russian tariffs were a major cause of Britain's economic depression. He also had the support of influential diplomats and men of letters, including Henry Bulwer, Sir James Hudson and Thomas Wentworth Beaumont, co-founder of the *British and Foreign Review*, which became increasingly hostile to Russia under Urquhart's influence.

As the decade wore on, a mood of growing Russophobia was to be found in even the most moderate intellectual circles. Highbrow periodicals like the *Foreign Quarterly Review*, which had previously discounted the 'alarmist' warnings of a Russian threat to the liberty of Europe and British interests in the East, succumbed to the anti-Russian atmosphere. Meanwhile, among the broader public – in churches, taverns, lecture halls and Chartist conventions – hostility to Russia was rapidly becoming a central reference point in a political discourse about liberty, civilization and progress that helped shape the national identity.

*

Sympathies for Turkey, fears for India – nothing fuelled Russophobia in Britain as intensely as the Polish cause. Championed by liberals throughout Europe as a just and noble fight for freedom against Russian tyranny, the Polish uprising – and its brutal suppression – did more than any other issue to involve the British in the affairs of the Continent and exacerbate the tensions that led to the Crimean War.

Poland's history could hardly have been more tormented. During the previous half-century the large old Polish Commonwealth (the Kingdom of Poland united with the Grand Duchy of Lithuania) had been partitioned no less than three times: twice (in 1772 and 1795) by all three neighbouring powers (Russia, Austria and Prussia) and once (in 1792) by the Russians and the Prussians on the grounds that Poland had become a stronghold of revolutionary sentiment. As a result of these partitions the Polish kingdom had lost more than two-thirds of its territory. Despairing of ever regaining their independence, the Poles turned to Napoleon in 1806, only to see their territory further carved up on his defeat. In 1815, in the Treaty of Vienna, the European powers established Congress Poland (an area roughly corresponding to the Napoleonic Duchy of Warsaw) and placed it under the protection of the Tsar on condition that he maintain Poland's constitutional liberties. But Alexander never fully recognized the new state's political autonomy – it was a tall order to combine autocracy in Russia and constitutionalism in Poland – while the repressive rule of Nicholas I further alienated many Poles. Throughout the 1820s the Russians violated the terms of the treaty – rolling back the freedoms of the press, imposing taxes without the consent of the Polish parliament, and using special powers to persecute the liberals opposed to tsarist rule. The final straw came in November 1830 when the viceroy of Poland, the Tsar's brother, Grand Duke Constantine, issued an order to conscript Polish troops for the suppression of revolutions in France and Belgium.

The uprising began when a group of Polish officers from the Russian Military Academy in Warsaw rebelled against the Grand Duke's order. Taking arms from their garrison, the officers attacked the Belvedere Palace, the main seat of the Grand Duke, who managed to escape (disguised in women's clothes). The rebels took the Warsaw arsenal and, supported by armed civilians, forced the Russian troops to withdraw from the Polish capital. The Polish army joined the uprising. A provisional government was established, headed by Prince Adam Czartoryski, and a national parliament was called. The radicals who took control declared a war of liberation against Russia and in a ceremony to dethrone the Tsar proclaimed Polish independence in January 1831. Within days of the proclamation, the Russian army crossed the Polish border and advanced towards the capital. The troops were led by General Ivan Paskevich, a veteran of the wars against the Turks and the Caucasian mountain tribes, whose brutal measures of repression made his name a byword for Russian cruelty in Poland's national memory. On 25 February a Polish force of 40,000 men fought off 60,000 Russians on the Vistula to save Warsaw. But Russian reinforcements soon arrived and gradually wore down the Polish resistance. They surrounded the city, where hungry citizens began to loot and riot against the provisional government. Warsaw fell on 7 September after heavy fighting in the streets. Rather than submit to the Russians, the remainder of the Polish army, some 20,000 men, fled to Prussia, where they were captured by the Prussian government, another ruler of annexed Polish territory and an ally of Russia; Prince Czartoryski made his way to Britain, while many other rebels escaped to France and Belgium, where they were welcomed as heroes.

The reaction of the British public was just as sympathetic. After the suppression of the uprising, there were mass rallies, public meetings and petitions to protest against the Russian action and demand intervention by Britain. The call for war against Russia was joined by many sections of the press, including *The Times*, which asked in July 1831: 'How long will Russia be permitted, with impunity, to make war upon the ancient and noble nation of the Poles, the allies of France, the friends of England, the natural, and, centuries ago, the tried and victorious protectors of civilized Europe against the Turkish and Muscovite barbarians?' Associations of Friends of Poland were set up in London, Nottingham, Birmingham, Hull, Leeds, Glasgow and Edinburgh to organize support for the Polish cause. Radical MPs (many of them Irish) called for British action to defend the 'downtrodden Poles'. Chartist groups of working men and women (engaged in the struggle for democratic rights) declared their solidarity with the Polish fight for freedom, sometimes even stating their readiness to go to war for the defence of liberty at home and abroad. 'Unless the English nation rouses itself,' declared the Chartist *Northern Liberator*, 'we shall see the damnable spectacle of a Russian fleet armed to the teeth and crammed with soldiers, daring to sail through the English Channel, and probably to anchor at Spithead or Plymouth Sound!'[21]

The fight for freedom in Poland captured the imagination of the British public, who readily assimilated it to the ideals they liked to think of as 'British' – in particular, a love of liberty and the commitment to defend the 'little man' against 'bullies' (the principle upon which the British told themselves they went to war in 1854, 1914 and 1939). At a time of liberal reforms and new freedoms for the British middle class, powerful emotions were stirred by this association with the Polish cause. Shortly after the passing of the parliamentary Reform Act in 1832, the editor of the *Manchester Times* told a meeting of the Association of Friends of Poland that the British and the Poles were fighting the same battle for freedom:

> It was our own fight (*Hear, hear*). We were fighting abroad upon the same principle as we were fighting against the boroughmongers at home. Poland was only one of our outposts. All the distresses of England and the continent might be traced to the first division of Poland. If that people could have remained free and unshackled, we should never have seen the barbarian hordes of Russia ravaging all Europe; and the Kalmyks and Cossacks of the despot bivouacking in the streets and gardens of Paris ... Was there a single sailor in our navy, or a single marine, who would not rejoice to be sent forth to lift up his hand in the cause of freedom and in aid of the unfortunate Poles? (*Cheers*) The expense would not be great to blow the castle of Kronstadt around the Russian despot's ears. (*Cheers*) In a month ... our navy should have swept every Russian merchant vessel from every sea upon the face of the globe. (*Cheers*) Let a fleet be sent to the Baltic to close up the Russian ports, and what would the Emperor of Russia be then? A Kalmyk surrounded by a few barbarian tribes (*Cheers*), a savage, with no more power upon the sea, when opposed by England and France, than the Emperor of China had (*Cheers*).[22]

The presence of Prince Czartoryski, 'Poland's uncrowned king', in London increased British sympathy for the Polish cause. The fact that the exiled Pole was a former Russian foreign minister gave his warnings about Russia's menace to Europe even greater credibility.

Czartoryski had entered the foreign service of Tsar Alexander I at the age of 33 in 1803. He thought that Poland could regain her independence and a good deal of her land by fostering friendly relations with the Tsar. As a member of the Tsar's Secret Committee he had once submitted an extensive memorandum aiming at the complete transformation of the European map: Russia would be protected from the Austrian and Prussian threat by a restored and reunited Kingdom of Poland under the protection of the Tsar; European Turkey would become a Balkan kingdom dominated by the Greeks with Russia in control of Constantinople and the Dardanelles; the Slavs would gain their freedom from the Austrians under the protection of Russia; Germany and Italy would become independent nation states organized on federal lines like the United States; while Britain and Russia together were to maintain the equilibrium of the Continent. The plan was unrealistic (no tsar would consent to the restoration of the old Polish-Lithuanian kingdom).

After Poland's national aspirations were dashed with Napoleon's defeat, Czartoryski found himself in exile in Europe, but returned to Poland in time for the November uprising. He joined the revolutionary executive committee, was elected president of the provisional government, and convened the national parliament. After the suppression of the insurrection, he fled to London, where he and other Polish émigrés carried on the fight against Russia. Czartoryski tried to persuade the British government to intervene in Poland and, if necessary, to fight a European war against Russia. What was now at hand, he told Palmerston, was an unavoidable struggle between the liberal West and the despotic East. He was vocally supported by several influential liberals and Russophobes, including George de Lacy Evans, Thomas Attwood, Stratford Canning and Robert Cutlar Fergusson, who all made speeches in the House of Commons calling for a war against Russia. Palmerston was sympathetic to the Polish cause and joined in condemnations of the Tsar's actions, but, given the position of the Austrians and Prussians, who were unlikely to oppose Russia as they also owned chunks of Poland, he did not think it 'prudent to support by force of arms the view taken by England' and risk 'involving Europe in a general war'. The appointment of the anti-Russian Stratford Canning as ambassador to St Petersburg (an appointment refused by the Tsar) was about as far as the British government would go in demonstrating its opposition to the Russian actions in Poland. Disillusioned by Britain's inaction, Czartoryski left for Paris in the autumn of 1832. 'They do not care about us now,' he wrote. 'They look to their own interests and will do nothing for us.'[23]

Czartoryski next took up residence at the Hôtel Lambert, the centre of the Polish emigration in Paris and in many ways the seat of the unofficial government of Poland in exile. The Hôtel Lambert group kept alive the constitutional beliefs and culture of the émigrés who gathered there, among them the poet Adam Mickiewicz and the composer Frédéric Chopin. Czartoryski maintained close relations with British diplomats and politicians calling for a war against Russia. He developed a strong friendship with Stratford Canning, in particular, and no doubt influenced his increasingly Russophobic views during the 1830s and 1840s. Czartoryski's chief agent in London, Władisław Zamoyski, a former aide-de-camp to the Grand Duke Constantine who had played a leading part in the Polish uprising, kept good ties to Ponsonby and the Urquhart camp – he even helped to finance the *Vixen* adventure. Through Stratford Canning and Zamoyski, there is no doubt that Czartoryski exercised a major influence on the evolution of Palmerston's thinking during the 1830s and 1840s, when the future British Crimean War leader gradually came round to the idea of a European alliance against Russia. Czartoryski also cultivated close relations with the liberal leaders of the July Monarchy in France, in particular with Adolphe Thiers, the Prime Minister of 1836–9, and François Guizot, the Foreign Minister of the 1840s and last Prime Minister of the July Monarchy, from 1847 to 1848. Both French statesmen realized the value of the Polish émigré as a friendly link to the British government and public opinion, which at that time were cool in their relations towards France. In this sense, through his exertions in London and Paris, Czartoryski was to play a signficant part in bringing about the Anglo-French alliance that would go to war with Russia in 1854.

Czartoryski and the Polish exiles of the Hôtel Lambert group also played a significant role in the rise of French Russophobia, which gained strength in the two decades before the Crimean War. Until 1830, French views of Russia were relatively moderate. Enough

Frenchmen had been to Russia with Napoleon and returned with favourable impressions of its people's character to counteract the writings of Russophobes, such as the Catholic publicist and statesman François-Marie de Froment, who warned against the dangers of Russian expansionism in *Observations sur la Russie* (1817), or the priest and politician Dominique-Georges-Frédéric de Pradt, who represented Russia as the 'Asiatic enemy of liberty in Europe' in his best-selling polemic *Parallèle de la puissance anglaise et russe relativement à l'Europe* (1823).[24] But the Tsar's opposition to the July 1830 Revolution had made him hated by the liberals and the Left, while Russia's traditional allies, the legitimist supporters of the Bourbon dynasty, had strong Catholic opinions, which alienated them from the Russians on the question of Poland.

The image of Poland as a martyred nation was firmly established in the French Catholic imagination by a series of works on Polish history and culture in the 1830s, none more influential than Mickiewicz's *Livre des pèlerins polonais* (Book of Polish Pilgrims), translated from the Polish with a preface by the extreme Catholic publicist Charles Montalembert, and published with the addition of a 'Hymn to Poland' by the priest and writer Félicité de Lamennais.[25] French support for Poland's national liberation was strongly reinforced by religious solidarity, which extended to the Ruthenian (Uniate) Catholics of Belarus and western Ukraine, territories once dominated by Poland, where Catholics were forcibly converted to the Russian Church after 1831. The religious persecution of the Ruthenians attracted little attention in France during the 1830s, but when that persecution spread to Congress Poland in the early 1840s Catholic opinion was outraged. Pamphlets called for a holy war to defend the 'five million' Polish Catholics forced by Russia to renounce their faith. Encouraged by a papal manifesto – 'On the Persecution of the Catholic Religion in the Russian Empire and Poland' – in 1842, the French press joined in condemnations of Russia. 'Since today all that remains of Poland is its Catholicism, the Tsar Nicholas has picked on it,' declared the influential *Journal des débats* in an editorial in October 1842. 'He wants to destroy the Catholic religion as the last and strongest principle of Polish nationality, as the last freedom and sign of independence that this unhappy people has, and as the last obstacle to the establishment in his vast empire of a unity of laws and morals, of ideas and faith.'[26]

French anger at the Tsar's persecution of the Catholics reached fever pitch in 1846, when reports arrived of the brutal treatment of the nuns of Minsk. In 1839, the Synod of Polotsk, in Belarus, had proclaimed the dissolution of the Greek Catholic Church, whose pro-Latin clergy had actively supported the Polish insurrection of 1831, and ordered all its property to be transferred to the Russian Orthodox Church. The leader of the Polotsk Synod was a pro-Russian bishop called Semashko, who had previously been chaplain to a convent of 245 nuns in Minsk. One of his first acts on taking over the episcopate was to order the nuns to submit to the Russian Church. According to the reports that arrived in France, when the nuns refused, Semashko had them arrested. With their hands and feet bound in irons, the nuns were taken to Vitebsk, where fifty of them were imprisoned and forced to perform heavy manual labour in their iron chains, and suffered dreadful torture and beatings by the guards. Then, in the spring of 1845, four of the sisters managed to escape. One of them, the abbess of the convent, Mother Makrena Mieczysławska, then aged 61, made her way to Poland, where she was helped by the Archbishop of Poznan, and then taken by his Church officials to Paris. She recounted her appalling tale to the Polish émigrés of the Hôtel Lambert group. Makrena next brought her account to Rome, and met with Pope Gregory XVI just before the Tsar's visit to the Vatican in December 1845. It is said that Nicholas emerged from his audience with the Pope covered with shame and confusion, having had his denials of the persecution of the Catholic Ruthenians refuted by documents in which he himself had praised the 'holy deeds' of Semashko.

The story of the 'martyred nuns' of Minsk was first published in the French newspaper *Le Correspondant* in May 1846 and retold many times in popular pamphlets. It quickly spread throughout the Catholic world. Russian diplomats and government agents in Paris tried to discredit Makrena's version of events, but a medical examination by papal authorities confirmed that she had indeed been beaten over many years. The story had a powerful and lasting impact on French Catholics as an illustration of how the Tsar was 'spreading Orthodoxy to the West' and converting Catholics 'by force of arms'.[27] This idea was a major influence on French opinion in the Holy Lands dispute against Russia.*

The fear of religious persecution was matched by the fear of a gargantuan Russia sweeping away European civilization. One of Czartoryski's fellow-exiles, Count Valerian Krasinki, was the author of a series of pamphlets warning of the dangers to the West of a Russian Empire stretching from the Baltic and Adriatic seas to the Pacific Ocean. 'Russia is an aggressive power,' Krasinki wrote in one of his most widely circulated books, 'and a single glance at the acquisitions she has made in the course of one century is sufficient to establish this fact beyond every controversy.' Since the time of Peter the Great, he argued, Russia had swallowed up more than half of Sweden, territories from Poland equal to the size of the Austrian Empire, Turkish lands greater in size than the Kingdom of Prussia, and lands from Persia equal to the size of Great Britain. Since the first partition of Poland in 1772, Russia had advanced her frontier 1,370 kilometres towards Vienna, Berlin, Dresden, Munich and Paris; 520 kilometres towards Constantinople; to within a few kilometres of the Swedish capital; and it had taken the Polish capital. The only way to safeguard the West from this Russian menace, he concluded, was through the restoration of a strong and independent Polish state.[28]

The perception of Russian aggression and threat was amplified in France by the Marquis de Custine, whose entertaining travelogue *La Russie en 1839* did more than any other publication to shape European attitudes towards Russia in the nineteenth century. An account of the nobleman's impressions and reflections from a journey to Russia, it first appeared in Paris in 1843, was reprinted many times, and quickly went on to become an international best-seller. Custine had

---

* It also influenced British public opinion on the eve of the Crimean War. In May 1854, 'The True Story of the Nuns of Minsk' was published in Charles Dickens's journal *Household Words*. The author of the article, Florence Nightingale, had met Makrena in Rome in 1848 and had written an account of her ordeal which she then put in a drawer. After the battle of Sinope, when the Russians destroyed the Turkish fleet in the Black Sea, Nightingale brought out the article, which she thought might help to drum up popular support against Russia, and sent it to Dickens, who shortened it into the version that appeared in *Household Words*.

travelled to Russia with the specific purpose of writing a popular travel book to make his name as a writer. He had previously tried his hand at novels, plays and dramas without much success, so travel literature was his last chance to make a reputation for himself.

The Marquis was a devout Catholic with many friends among the Hôtel Lambert group. Through one of his Polish contacts, who had a half-sister at the Russian court, he gained entrée to the highest circles of St Petersburg society and even had an audience with the Tsar – a guarantee of Western interest in his book. Custine's Polish sympathies turned him against Russia from the start. In St Petersburg and Moscow he spent a lot of time in the company of liberal noblemen and intellectuals (several of them converts to the Roman Church) who were deeply disenchanted with the reactionary policies of Nicholas I. The suppression of the Polish uprising, which came just six years after the crushing of the Decembrist revolt in Russia, had made these men despair of their country ever following the Western constitutional path. Their pessimism no doubt left its mark on Custine's dark impressions of contemporary Russia. Everything about it filled the Frenchman with contempt and dread: the despotism of the Tsar; the servility of the aristocracy, who were themselves no more than slaves; their pretentious European manners, a thin veneer of civilization to hide their Asiatic barbarism from the West; the lack of individual liberty and dignity; the pretence and contempt for truth that seemed to pervade society. Like many travellers to Russia before him, the Marquis was struck by the huge scale of everything the government had built. St Petersburg itself was a 'monument created to announce the arrival of Russia in the world'. He saw this grandiosity as a sign of Russia's ambition to overtake and dominate the West. Russia envied and resented Europe, 'as the slave resented his master', Custine argued, and therein lay the threat of its aggression:

> An ambition inordinate and immense, one of those ambitions which could only possibly spring in the bosoms of the oppressed, and could find nourishment only in the miseries of an entire nation, ferments in the heart of the Russian people. That nation, essentially aggressive, greedy under the influence of privation, expiates beforehand, by a debasing submission, the design of exercising a tyranny over other

nations: the glory, the riches, which are the objects of its hopes, console it for the disgrace to which it submits. To purify himself from the foul and impious sacrifice of all public and personal liberty, the slave, sunk to his knees, dreams of world domination.

Russia had been put on earth by Providence to 'chastise the corrupt civilization of Europe by the agency of a new invasion', Custine argued. It served as a warning and a lesson to the West, and Europe would succumb to its barbarism 'if our extravagances and iniquities render us worthy of the punishment'. As Custine concluded in the famous last passage of his book:

To have a feeling for the liberty enjoyed in the other European countries one must have sojourned in that solitude without repose, in that prison without leisure, that is called Russia. If ever your sons should be discontented with France, try my recipe: tell them to go to Russia. It is a journey useful to every foreigner; whoever has well examined that country will be content to live anywhere else.[29]

Within a few years of its publication, *La Russie en 1839* went through at least six editions in France; it was pirated and republished in several other editions in Brussels; translated into German, Danish and English; and abridged in pamphlet form in various other European languages. Overall it must have sold several hundred thousand copies, making it by far the most popular and influential work by a foreigner on Russia on the eve of the Crimean War. The key to its success was its articulation of the fears and prejudices about Russia widely held in Europe at that time.

Throughout the Continent there were deep anxieties about the rapid growth and military power of Russia. The Russian invasion of Poland and the Danubian principalities, combined with Russia's growing influence in the Balkans, gave rise to fears of a Slavic threat to Western civilization that *La Russie* had expressed. In the German lands, in particular, where Custine's book was very well received, it was widely argued in the pamphlet press that Nicholas was plotting to become the emperor of the Slavs throughout Europe, and that German unity could not be gained without a war to push back Russian influence. Such ideas were further fuelled by the appearance of *Russ-*

land und die Zivilisation, a pamphlet published anonymously in various German editions in the early 1830s and translated into French as the work of Count Adam Gurowski in 1840. As one of the earliest published expressions of a pan-Slav ideology, the pamphlet excited much discussion on the Continent. Gurowski maintained that European history until the present time had known just two civilizations, the Latin and German, but that Providence had assigned to Russia the divine mission of giving to the world a third, Slavic, civilization. Under German domination, the Slav nations (Czechs, Slovaks, Serbs, Slovenes and so on) were all in decline. But they would be united and reinvigorated under Russian leadership, and would dominate the Continent.[30]

In the 1840s Western fears of pan-Slavism focused specifically on the Balkans, where Russian influence seemed to be on the rise. The Austrians were increasingly wary of Russia's intentions in Serbia and the Danubian principalities, as were the British, who set up consulates in Belgrade, Braila and Iaşi to promote British trade and keep a check on Russia. Of particular concern was Russia's interference in Serbian politics. In 1830 Serbia had become self-governing under Ottoman sovereignty, with Prince Milos of the Obrenović family as its hereditary prince. The 'Russian Party' in Belgrade – Slavophiles who wanted Russia to adopt a more aggressive foreign policy in support of Balkan Slavs – quickly built up its support among Serbian notables, the clergy, the army and even among members of the Prince's court, who were disgruntled with his dictatorial policies. The British responded by buttressing the Milos regime, on the grounds that a pro-British despot was preferable to a Russian-controlled oligarchy of Serbian notables, and exerted pressure on the Prince to strengthen his position through constitutional reforms. But Russia used its influence to threaten Milos with rebellion, and to extract from the Ottoman authorities in 1838 an Organic Statute as an alternative to the British constitutional model. The Statute granted civil liberties but established life-appointed noble councillors rather than elected assemblies to counteract the power of the Prince. Since most of the councillors were pro-Russian, the tsarist government was able to exert considerable pressure on the Serbian government during the 1840s.[31]

What the Tsar's motives in the Balkans were is difficult to say. He insisted that he was opposed to any pan-Slav or nationalist movement that challenged the legitimate sovereigns of the Continent, the Ottomans and Milos included. The aim of his intervention in the Balkans was merely to stamp out the possibility of national revolutions arising there which might spread to the Slav nations under his own rule (the Poles in particular). At home, he openly condemned the pan-Slavs as dangerous liberals and revolutionaries. 'Under the guise of sympathy for the oppression of the Slavs in other states,' he wrote, 'they conceal the rebellious idea of union with these tribes, despite their legitimate citizenship in neighbouring and allied states; and they expect this to be brought about not through God's will but from violent attempts that will make for the ruin of Russia herself.'[32] The 'Russian Party' were deemed a major threat by Nicholas and kept under a close watch by the Third Section, the political police, during the 1830s and 1840s. In 1847 the Brotherhood of Sts Cyril and Methodius, the centre of the pan-Slav movement in Kiev, was closed down by the police.[33]

Yet the Tsar was pragmatic in his adherence to legitimist principles. He applied them to Christian states but not necessarily to Muslim ones, if this involved siding against Orthodox Christians, as demonstrated by his support for the Greek uprising against the Ottoman Empire. As the years passed, Nicholas placed more importance on the defence of the Orthodox religion and Russia's interests – which in his view were practically synonymous – than on the Concert of Europe or the international principles of the Holy Alliance. Thus, while he shared the reactionary ideology of the Habsburgs and supported their empire, this did not prevent him from encouraging the nationalist sympathies of the Serbs, Romanians and Ukrainians within the Austrian Empire, because they were Orthodox. His attitude towards the Catholic Slavs under Habsburg rule (Czechs, Slovenes, Slovaks, Croats and Poles) was less encouraging.

As for the Slavs within the Ottoman Empire, Nicholas's initial reluctance to support their liberation gradually weakened, as he became convinced that the collapse of European Turkey was unavoidable and imminent and that the promotion of Russia's interests involved building up alliances with the Slav nations in readiness for its eventual partition. The shift in the Tsar's thinking was a change of strategy rather than a fundamental alteration of his ideology: if Russia did not intervene in the Balkans, the Western powers would do so, as they had in Greece, to turn the Christian nations against Russia and into Western-oriented states. But there is also evidence that in the course of the 1840s Nicholas began to feel a certain sympathy for the religious and nationalist sentiments of the Slavophiles and the pan-Slavs, whose mystical ideas of Holy Russia as an empire of the Orthodox increasingly appealed to his own understanding of his international mission as a Tsar:

> Moscow, and the city of Peter, and the city of Constantine –
> These are the sacred capitals of Russian tsardom . . .
> But where is its end? and where are its borders
> To the North, to the East, to the South and toward sunset?
> They will be revealed by the fates of future times . . .
> Seven internal seas and seven great rivers!
> From the Nile to the Neva, from Elbe to China –
> From the Volga to the Euphrates, from the Ganges to the Danube . . .
> This is Russian tsardom . . . and it will not disappear with the ages.
> The Holy Spirit foresaw and Daniel foretold this.
>
> (Fedor Tiutchev, 'Russian Geography', 1849)[34]

The leading pan-Slav ideologist was Mikhail Pogodin, a professor of Moscow University and founding editor of the influential journal *Moskvitianin* (Muscovite). Pogodin had an entry to the court and high official circles through the Minister of Education, Sergei Uvarov, who protected him from the police and brought many of his minister-ial colleagues round to Pogodin's idea that Russia should support the liberation of the Slavs on religious grounds. At the court Pogodin had an active supporter in Countess Antonina Bludova, the daughter of a highly placed imperial statesman. He also had a sympathetic ear in the Grand Duke Alexander, the heir to the throne. In 1838 Pogodin laid out his ideas in a memorandum to the Tsar. Arguing that history advanced by means of a succession of chosen people, he maintained that the future belonged to the Slavs, if Russia took upon itself its providential mission to create a Slavic empire and lead it to its destiny. In 1842 he wrote to him again:

> Here is our purpose – Russian, Slavic, European, Christian! As Rus-sians, we must capture Constantinople for our own security. As Slavs

we must liberate millions of our older kinsmen, brothers in faith, educators and benefactors. As Europeans we must drive out the Turks. As Orthodox Christians, we must protect the Eastern Church and return to St Sophia its ecumenical cross.[35]

Nicholas remained opposed to these ideas officially. His Foreign Minister, Karl Nesselrode, was adamant that giving any signs of encouragement to the Balkan Slavs would alienate the Austrians, Russia's oldest ally, and ruin the *entente* with the Western powers, leaving Russia isolated in the world. But judging from the notes that the Tsar made in the margins of Pogodin's writings, it appears that privately, at least, he sympathized with his ideas.

*

Western fears of Russia were intensified by its violent reaction to the revolutions of 1848. In France, where the revolutionary wave began in February with the downfall of the July Monarchy and the establishment of the Second Republic, the Left was united by the fear of Russian forces coming to the aid of the counter-revolutionary Right and restoring 'order' in Paris. Everybody waited for the Russian invasion. 'I am learning Russian,' wrote the playwright Prosper Mérimée to a friend in Italy. 'Perhaps it will help me to converse with the Cossacks in the Tuileries.' As democratic revolutions spread through the German and Habsburg lands that spring, it seemed to many (as Napoleon had once said) that either Europe would become republican, or it would be overrun by the Cossacks. The Continental revolutions appeared destined for a life-or-death struggle against Russia and Tsar Nicholas, the 'gendarme of Europe'. In Germany, the newly elected deputies of the Frankfurt National Assembly, the first German parliament, appealed for a union with France and for the creation of a European army to defend the Continent against a Russian invasion.[36]

For the Germans and the French, Poland was the first line of defence against Russia. Throughout the spring of 1848, there were declarations of support and calls for a war for the restoration of an independent Poland in the National Assembly in Paris. On 15 May the Assembly was invaded by a crowd of demonstrators angry at the rumours (which were true) that Alphonse de Lamartine, the Foreign Minister, had reached an understanding with the Russians over Poland. To cries of 'Vive la Pologne!' from the crowd, radical deputies took turns to declare their passionate support for a war of liberation to restore Poland to her pre-partition frontiers and expel the Russians from all Polish soil.[37]

Then, in July, the Russians moved against the Romanian revolution in Moldavia and Wallachia, which further inflamed the West. The revolution in the principalities had been anti-Russian from the start. Romanian liberals and nationalists were opposed to the Russian-dominated administration that had been left in place by the departing tsarist troops following their occupation of Moldavia and Wallachia in 1829–34. The liberal opposition was first centred in the boyar assemblies whose political rights had been severely limited by the *Règlement organique* imposed by the Russians before handing back the principalities to the sovereignty of the Ottomans. The rulers of the principalities, for instance, were no longer elected by the assemblies, but appointed by the Tsar. During the 1840s, when moderate leaders like Ion Campineanu were in exile, the national movement passed into the hands of a younger generation of activists – many of them boyar sons educated in Paris – who organized themselves in secret revolutionary societies along the lines of the Carbonari and the Jacobins.

It was the largest of these secret societies, the *Fratja* or 'Brotherhood', that burst onto the scene in the spring of 1848. In Bucharest and Iaşi there were public meetings calling for the restoration of old rights annulled by the *Règlement organique*. Revolutionary committees were formed. In Bucharest, huge demonstrations organized by the *Fratja* forced Prince Gheorghe Bibescu to abdicate in favour of a provisional government. A republic was declared and a liberal constitution promulgated to replace the *Règlement organique*. The Russian consul fled to Austrian Transylvania. The Romanian tricolour was paraded through the streets of Bucharest by cheering crowds, whose leaders called for the union of the principalities as an independent national state.

Alarmed by these developments, and fearing that the spirit of rebellion might spread to their own territories, in July the Russians occupied Moldavia with 14,000 troops to prevent the establishment of a revolutionary government like the one in Bucharest. They also brought up 30,000 soldiers from Bessarabia to the Wallachian border in preparation for a strike against the provisional government.

The revolutionaries in Bucharest appealed to Britain for support. The British consul, Robert Colquhoun, had been actively encouraging the national opposition against Russia, not because the Foreign Office wanted to promote Romanian independence but because it wanted to roll back the domination of Russia and restore Turkish sovereignty on a more liberal basis so that British interests could be better promoted in the principalities. The consulate in Bucharest had been one of the main meeting places for the revolutionaries. Britain had even smuggled in Polish exiles to organize an anti-Russian movement uniting Poles, Hungarians, Moldavians and Wallachians under British tutelage.[38]

Recognizing that the only hope for Wallachian independence was to prevent a Russian intervention, Colquhoun acted as a mediator between the revolutionary leaders and the Ottoman authorities in the hope of securing Turkish recognition of the provisional government. He assured the Ottoman commissioner Suleiman Pasha that the government in Bucharest would remain loyal to the Sultan – a calculated deception – and that its hatred of the Russians would serve Turkey well in any future war against Russia. Suleiman accepted Colquhoun's reasoning and made a speech to cheering crowds in Bucharest in which he toasted the 'Romanian nation' and spoke about the possibility of the 'union between Moldavia and Wallachia as a stake in the entrails of Russia'.[39]

This was a red rag to the Russian bull. Vladimir Titov, the Russian ambassador in Constantinople, demanded that the Sultan cease negotiations with the revolutionaries and restore order in Wallachia, or Russia would intervene. This was enough to bring about a Turkish volte-face at the start of September. A new commissioner, Fuad Efendi, was sent to put an end to the revolt with the help of the Russian General Alexander Duhamel. Fuad crossed into Wallachia and camped outside Bucharest with 12,000 Turkish soldiers, while Duhamel brought up the 30,000 Russian troops who had been mobilized in Bessarabia. On 25 September they moved together into Bucharest and easily defeated the small groups of rebels who fought them in the streets. The revolution was over.

The Russians took control of the city and carried out a series of mass arrests, forcing thousands of Romanians to flee abroad. British citizens too were arrested. No public meetings were allowed by the pro-Russian government installed in power by the occupying troops. To write on political matters became a punishable offence; even personal letters were perused by the police. 'A system of espionage has been established here,' Colquhoun reported. 'No person is allowed to converse on politics, German and French newspapers are prohibited ... The Turkish commissioner feels compelled to enjoin all to cease speaking on political subjects in public places.'[40]

Having restored order in the principalities, the Tsar demanded for his services a new convention with the Ottomans to increase Russian control of the territories. This time his conditions were extortionate: the Russian military occupation was to last for seven years; the two powers would appoint the rulers of the principalities; and Russian troops would be allowed to pass through Wallachia to crush the ongoing Hungarian revolution in Transylvania. Suspecting that the Russians aimed at nothing less than the annexation of the principalities, Stratford Canning urged the Turks to stand firm against the Tsar. But he could not promise British intervention if it came to a war between Turkey and Russia. He called on Palmerston to deter Russia and demonstrate support for the Ottoman Empire by sending in a fleet – a measure he regarded as essential to prevent the outbreak of hostilities. If Palmerston had followed his advice, Britain might have gone to war with Russia six years before the Crimean War. But once again the Foreign Secretary was not prepared to act. Despite his hard line against Russia, Palmerston (for the moment) was prepared to trust the Tsar's motives in the principalities, did not think that he would try to annexe them, and perhaps even welcomed the Russian restoration of order in the increasingly tumultuous and chaotic Ottoman and Habsburg lands.

Without support from Britain, the Turkish government had little option but to negotiate with the Russians. By the Act of Balta Liman, signed in April 1849, the Tsar got most of his demands: the rulers of the principalities would be chosen by the Russians and the Turks; the boyar assemblies would be replaced altogether by advisory councils nominated and overseen by the two powers; and the Russian occupation would last until 1851. The provisions of the Act amounted in effect to the restoration of Russian control and to a substantial reduction of the autonomy previously enjoyed by the principalities, even under the restrictions of the *Règlement organique*.[41] The Tsar concluded that the principalities were henceforth areas of Russian influence, that the Turks retained them only at his discretion, and that even after 1851 he would still be able to enter them at will to force more concessions from the Porte.

The success of the Russian intervention in the Danubian principalities influenced the Tsar's decision to intervene in Hungary in June 1849. The Hungarian revolution had begun in March 1848, when, inspired by the events in France and Germany, the Hungarian Diet, led by the brilliant orator Lajos Kossuth, proclaimed Hungary's autonomy from the Habsburg Empire and passed a series of reforms, abolishing serfdom and establishing Hungarian control of the national budget and Hungarian regiments in the imperial army. Faced with a popular revolution in Vienna, the Austrian government at first accepted Hungarian autonomy, but once the revolution in the capital had been suppressed the imperial authorities ordered the dissolution of the Hungarian Diet and declared war on Hungary. Supported by the Slovak, German and Ruthenian minorities of Hungary, and by a large number of Polish and Italian volunteers who were equally opposed to Habsburg rule, the Hungarians were more than a match for the Austrian forces, and in April 1849, after a series of military stalemates, they in turn declared a war of independence against Austria. The newly installed 18-year-old Emperor Franz Joseph appealed to the Tsar to intervene.

Nicholas agreed to act against the revolution without conditions. It was basically a question of solidarity with the Holy Alliance – the collapse of the Austrian Empire would have dramatic implications for the European balance of power – but there was also a connected issue of Russia's self-interest. The Tsar could not afford to stand aside and watch the spread of revolutionary movements in central Europe that might lead to a new uprising in Poland. The Hungarian army had many Polish exiles in its ranks. Some of its best generals were Poles, including General Jozef Bem, one of the main military leaders of the 1830 Polish uprising and in 1848–9 the commander of the victorious Hungarian forces in Transylvania. Unless the Hungarian revolution was defeated, there was every danger of its spreading to Galicia (a largely Polish territory controlled by Austria), which would reopen the Polish Question in the Russian Empire.

On 17 June 1849, 190,000 Russian troops crossed the Hungarian frontier into Slovakia and Transylvania. They were under the command of General Paskevich, the leader of the punitive campaign against the Poles in 1831. The Russians carried out a series of ferocious repressions against the population, but themselves succumbed in enormous numbers to disease, especially cholera, in a campaign lasting just eight weeks. Vastly outnumbered by the Russians, most of the Hungarian army surrendered at Vilagos on 13 August. But about 5,000 soldiers (including 800 Poles) fled to the Ottoman Empire – mostly to Wallachia, where some Turkish forces were fighting against the Russian occupation in defiance of the Balta Liman convention.

The Tsar favoured clemency for the Hungarian leaders. He was opposed to the brutal reprisals carried out by the Austrians. But he was determined to pursue the Polish refugees, in particular the Polish generals in the Hungarian army who might become the leaders of another insurrection for the liberation of Poland from Russia. On 28 August the Russians demanded from the Turkish government the extradition of those Poles who were subjects of the Tsar. The Austrians demanded the extradition of the Hungarians, including Kossuth, who had been welcomed by the Turks. International law provided for the extradition of criminals, but the Turks did not regard these exiles in those terms. They were pleased to have these anti-Russian soldiers on their soil and granted them political asylum, as liberal Western states had done on certain conditions for the Polish refugees in 1831. Encouraged by the British and the French, the Turks refused to bow to the threats of the Russians and the Austrians, who broke off relations with the Porte. Responding to Turkish calls for military aid, in October the British sent their Malta squadron to Besika Bay, just outside the Dardanelles, where they were later joined by a French fleet. The Western powers were on the verge of war against Russia.

By this stage the British public was up in arms about the Hungarian refugees. Their heroic struggle against the mighty tsarist tyranny had captured the British imagination and once again fired up its passions against Russia. In the press, the Hungarian revolution was idealized as a mirror image of the Glorious Revolution of 1688, when the British

Parliament had overthrown King James II and established a constitutional monarchy. Kossuth was seen as a very 'British type' of revolutionary – a liberal gentleman and supporter of enlightened aristocracy, a fighter for the principles of parliamentary rule and constitutional government (two years later he was welcomed as a hero by enormous crowds in Britain when he went there for a speaking tour). The Hungarian and Polish refugees were seen as romantic freedom-fighters. Karl Marx, who had come to London as a political exile in 1849, began a campaign against Russia as the enemy of liberty. Reports of repression and atrocities by Russian troops in Hungary and the Danubian principalities were received with disgust, and the British public was delighted when Palmerston announced that he was sending warships to the Dardanelles to help the Turks stand up against the Tsar. This was the sort of robust foreign policy – a readiness to intervene in any place around the world in defence of British liberal values – that the middle class expected from its government, as the Don Pacifico affair would show.*

The mobilization of the British and French fleets persuaded Nicholas to reach a compromise with the Ottoman authorities on the refugee issue. The Turks undertook to keep the Polish refugees a long way from the Russian border – a concession broadly in line with the principles of political asylum recognized by Western states – and the Tsar dropped his demand for extradition.

But just as a settlement was being reached, news arrived from Constantinople that Stratford Canning had improvised a reading of the 1841 Convention so as to allow the British fleet to move into the shelter of the Dardanelles if heavy winds in Besika Bay demanded this – exactly what transpired in fact when its ships arrived at the end of October. Nicholas was furious. Titov was ordered to inform the Porte that Russia had the same rights in the Bosporus as Britain had just claimed in the Dardanelles – a brilliant rejoinder because from the Bosporus

---

* In 1850 the British public applauded the decision by Palmerston to send the Royal Navy to block the port of Athens in support of Don Pacifico, a British subject who had appealed to the Greek government for compensation after his home was burned down in an anti-Semitic riot in Athens. Don Pacifico was serving as the Portuguese consul in Athens at the time of the attack (he was a Portuguese Jew by descent) but he had been born in Gibraltar and was thus a British subject. On this basis ('Civis Britannicus Sum'), Palmerston defended his decision to dispatch the fleet.

Russian ships would be able to attack Constantinople long before the British fleet could reach them from the remote Dardanelles. Palmerston backed down, apologized to Russia, and reaffirmed his government's commitment to the convention. The allied fleets were sent away, and the threat of war was averted – once again.

Before Palmerston's apology arrived, however, the Tsar gave a lecture to the British envoy in St Petersburg. What he said reveals a lot about the Tsar's state of mind just four years before he went to war against the Western powers:

> I do not understand the conduct of Lord Palmerston. If he chooses to wage war against me, let him declare it freely and loyally. It will be a great misfortune for the two countries, but I am resigned to it and ready to accept it. But he should stop playing tricks on me right and left. Such a policy is unworthy of a great power. If the Ottoman Empire still exists, this is due to me. If I pull back the hand that protects and sustains it, it will collapse in an instant.

On 17 December, the Tsar instructed Admiral Putiatin to prepare a plan for a surprise attack on the Dardanelles in the event of another crisis over Russia's presence in the principalities. He wanted to be sure that the Black Sea Fleet could prevent the British entering the Dardanelles again. As a sign of his determination, he gave approval to the construction of four expensive new war steamers required by the plan.[42]

Palmerston's decision to back down from conflict was a severe blow to Stratford Canning, who had wanted decisive military action to deter the Tsar from undermining Turkish sovereignty in the principalities. After 1849, Canning became even more determined to strengthen Ottoman authority in Moldavia and Wallachia by speeding up the process of liberal reform in these regions – despite his growing doubts about the Tanzimat in general – and bolstering the Turkish armed forces to counteract the growing menace of Russia. The importance he attached to the principalities was shared increasingly by Palmerston, who was moved by the crisis of 1848–9 to support a more aggressive defence of Turkey's interests against Russia.

The next time the Tsar invaded the principalities, to force Turkey to submit to his will in the Holy Lands dispute, it would lead to war.

4

The End of Peace in Europe

The Great Exhibition opened in Hyde Park on 1 May 1851. Six million people, a third of the entire population of Britain at that time, would pass through the mammoth exhibition halls in the specially contructed Crystal Palace, the largest glasshouse yet built, and marvel at the 13,000 exhibits – manufactures, handicrafts and various other objects from around the world. Coming as it did after two decades of social and political upheaval, the Great Exhibition seemed to hold the promise of a more prosperous and peaceful age based upon the British principles of industrialism and free trade. The architectural wonder of the Crystal Palace was itself proof of British manufacturing ingenuity, a fitting place to house an exhibition whose aim was to show that Britain held the lead in almost every field of industry. It symbolized the Pax Britannica which the British expected to dispense to Europe and the world.

The only possible threat to peace appeared to come from France. Through a *coup d'état* on 2 December 1851, the anniversary of Napoleon's coronation as Emperor in 1804, Louis-Napoleon, the President of the Second Republic, overthrew the constitution and established himself as dictator. By a national referendum the following November, the Second Republic became the Second Empire, and on 2 December 1852 Louis-Napoleon became the Emperor of the French, Napoleon III.

The appearance of a new French emperor put the great powers on alert. In Britain, there were fears of a Napoleonic revival. MPs demanded the recall of the Lisbon Squadron to guard the English Channel against the French. Lord Raglan, the future leader of the British forces in the Crimean War, spent the summer of 1852 planning the defences of London against a potential attack by the French navy, and that remained the top priority of British naval planning throughout 1853. Count Buol, the Austrian Foreign Minister, demanded confirmation of Napoleon's peaceful intentions. The Tsar wanted him to make a humiliating disclaimer of any aggressive plans, and promised Austria 60,000 troops if it was attacked by France. In an attempt to reassure them all, Napoleon made a declaration in Bordeaux in October 1852: 'Mistrustful people say, the empire means war, but I say, the empire means peace.'[1]

Louis-Napoleon, 1854

In truth, there were reasons to be mistrustful. It was hardly likely that Napoleon III would remain content with the existing settlement of Europe, which had been set up to contain France after the Napoleonic Wars. His genuine and extensive popularity among the French rested on his stirring of their Bonapartist memories, even though in almost every way he was inferior to his uncle. Indeed, with his large and awkward body, short legs, moustache and goatee beard, he looked more like a banker than a Bonaparte ('extremely short, but with a head and bust which ought to belong to a much taller man', is how Queen Victoria described him in her diary after she had met him for the first time in 1855[2]).

Napoleon's foreign policy was largely driven by his need to play to this Bonapartist tradition. He aimed to restore France to a position of respect and influence abroad, if not to the glory of his uncle's reign, by revising the 1815 settlement and reshaping Europe as a family of liberal nation states along the lines supposedly envisaged by Napoleon I. This was an aim he thought he could achieve by forging an alliance with Britain, the traditional enemy of France. His close political ally and Minister of the Interior, the Duc de Persigny, who had spent some time in London in 1852, persuaded him that Britain was no longer dominated by the aristocracy but a new 'bourgeois power' that was set to dominate the Continent. By allying with Britain, France would be able to 'develop a great and glorious foreign policy and avenge our past defeats more effectively than through any gain that we might make by refighting the battle of Waterloo'.[3]

Russia was the one country the French could fight to restore their national pride. The memory of Napoleon's retreat from Moscow, which had done so much to hasten the collapse of the First Empire, the subsequent military defeats and the Russian occupation of Paris were constant sources of pain and humiliation to the French. Russia was the major force behind the 1815 settlement and the restoration of the Bourbon dynasty in France. The Tsar was the enemy of liberty and a major obstacle to the development of free nation states on the European continent. He was also the only sovereign not to recognize the new Napoleon as emperor. Britain, Austria and Prussia were all prepared to grant him that status, albeit reluctantly in the case of the last two, but Nicholas refused, on the grounds that emperors were made by God, not elected by referendums. The Tsar showed his contempt for Napoleon by addressing him as 'mon ami' rather than 'mon frère', the customary greeting to another member of the European family of ruling sovereigns.* Some of Napoleon's advisers, Persigny in particular, wanted him to seize on the insult and force a break with Russia. But the French Emperor would not begin his reign with a personal quarrel, and he passed it off with the remark: 'God gives us brothers, but we choose our friends.'[4]

For Napoleon, the conflict with Russia in the Holy Lands served as a means of reuniting France after the divisions of 1848–9. The revolutionary Left could be reconciled to the *coup d'état* and the Second Empire if it was engaged in a patriotic fight for liberty against the 'gendarme of Europe'. As for the Catholic Right, it had long been pushing for a crusade against the Orthodox heresy that was threatening Christendom and French civilization.

It was in this context that Napoleon appointed the extreme Catholic La Valette as French ambassador to Constantinople. La Valette was part of a powerful clerical lobby at the Quai d'Orsay, the French Foreign Ministry, which used its influence to raise the stakes in the Holy Lands dispute, according to Persigny.

> Our foreign policy was often troubled by a clerical lobby (*coterie cléricale*) which wormed its way into the secret recesses of the Foreign Ministry. The 2 December had not succeeded in dislodging it. On the contrary, it became even more audacious, profiting from our preoccupation with domestic matters to entangle our diplomacy in the complications of the Holy Places, where it hailed its infantile successes as national triumphs.

La Valette's aggressive proclamation that the Latin right to the Holy Places had been 'clearly established', backed up by his threat of using the French navy to support these claims against Russia, was greeted with approval by the ultra-Catholic press in France. Napoleon himself was more moderate and conciliatory in his approach to the Holy Lands dispute. He confessed to the chief of the political directorate, Édouard-Antoine de Thouvenel, that he was ignorant about the details of the contested claims and regretted that the religious conflict had been

---

* The Austrians and Prussians had agreed to follow Russia's example, but then backed down, fearing it would cause a break with France. They found a compromise, addressing Napoleon as 'Monsieur mon frère.'

'blown out of all proportion', as indeed it had. But his need to curry favour with Catholic opinion at home, combined with his plans for an
alliance with Britain against Russia, also meant that it was not in his
interests to restrain La Valette's provocative behaviour. It was not until
the spring of 1852 that he finally recalled the ambassador from the Turkish capital, and then only following complaints about La Valette by Lord
Malmesbury, the British Foreign Secretary. But even after his recall, the
French continued with their gunboat policy to pressure the Sultan into
concessions, confident that it would enrage the Tsar and hopeful that it
would force the British to ally with France against Russian aggression.[5]

The policy paid dividends. In November 1852 the Porte issued a
new ruling granting to the Catholics the right to hold a key to the
Church of the Nativity in Bethlehem, allowing them free access to the
Chapel of the Manger and the Grotto of the Nativity. With Stratford
Canning away in England, the British chargé d'affaires in Constantinople, Colonel Hugh Rose, explained the ruling by the fact that the
latest gunship in the French steam fleet, the *Charlemagne*, could sail at
eight and a half knots from the Mediterranean, while its sister ship, the
Napoleon, could sail at twelve – meaning that the French could defeat
the technologically backward Russian and Turkish fleets combined.[6]

The Tsar was furious with the Turks for caving in to French pressure, and threatened violence of his own. On 27 December he ordered
the mobilization of 37,000 troops from the 4th and 5th Army Corps
in Bessarabia in preparation for a lightning strike on the Turkish capital, and a further 91,000 soldiers for a simultaneous campaign in the
Danubian principalities and the rest of the Balkans. It was a sign of
his petulance that he made the order on his own, without consulting
either Nesselrode, the Foreign Minister, Prince Dolgorukov, the Minister of War, or even Count Orlov, the chief of the Third Section, with
whom he conferred nearly every day. At the court there was talk of
dismembering the Ottoman Empire, starting with the Russian occupation of the Danubian principalities. In a memorandum written in
the final weeks of 1852, Nicholas set out his plans for the partition of
the Ottoman Empire: Russia was to gain the Danubian principalities
and Dobrudja, the river's delta lands; Serbia and Bulgaria would
become independent states; the Adriatic coast would go to Austria;
Cyprus, Rhodes and Egypt to Britain; France would gain Crete; an

enlarged Greece would be created from the archipelago; Constantinople would become a free city under international protection; and the Turks were to be ejected from Europe.[7]

At this point Nicholas began a new round of negotiations with the British, whose overwhelming naval power would make them the decisive factor in any showdown between France and Russia in the Near East. Still convinced that he had forged an understanding with the British during his 1844 visit, he now believed that he could call on them to restrain the French and enforce Russia's treaty rights in the Ottoman Empire. But he also hoped to convince them that the time had come for the partition of Turkey. The Tsar held a series of conversations with Lord Seymour, the British ambassador in St Petersburg, during January and February 1853. 'We have a sick man on our hands,' he began on the subject of Turkey, 'a man gravely ill; it will be a great misfortune if he slips through our hands, especially before the necessary arrangements are made.' With the Ottoman Empire 'falling to pieces', it was 'very important' for Britain and Russia to reach an agreement on its organized partition, if only to prevent the French from sending an expedition to the East, an eventuality that would force him to order his troops into Ottoman territory. 'When England and Russia are agreed,' the Tsar told Seymour, 'it is immaterial what the other powers think or do.' Speaking 'as a gentleman', Nicholas assured the ambassador that Russia had renounced the territorial ambitions of Catherine the Great. He had no desire to conquer Constantinople, which he wanted to become an international city, but for that reason he could not allow the British or the French to seize control of it. In the chaos of an Ottoman collapse he would be forced to take the capital on a temporary basis (*en dépositaire*) to prevent 'the breaking up of Turkey into little republics, asylums for the Kossuths and Mazzinis and other revolutionists of Europe', and to protect the Eastern Christians from the Turks. 'I cannot recede from the discharge of a sacred duty,' the Tsar emphasized. 'Our religion as established in this country came to us from the East, and these are feelings, as well as obligations, which never must be lost sight of.'[8]

Seymour was not shocked by the Tsar's partition plans, and in his first report to Lord John Russell, the Foreign Secretary, he even seemed to welcome the idea. If Russia and Britain, the two Christian powers 'most interested in the destinies of Turkey', could take the place of Muslim rule in Europe, 'a noble triumph would be obtained by the civilization of the nineteenth century', he argued. There were many in the coalition government of Lord Aberdeen, including Russell and William Gladstone, the Chancellor of the Exchequer, who wondered whether it was right to go on propping up the Ottoman Empire while Christians were being persecuted by the Turks. But others were committed to the Tanzimat reforms and wanted time for them to work. Procrastination certainly suited the British, since they were caught between the Russians and the French, whom they distrusted equally. 'The Russians accuse us of being too French,' the astute Queen Victoria remarked, 'and the French accuse us of being too Russian.' The cabinet rejected the Tsar's notion that an Ottoman collapse was imminent and agreed not to plan ahead for hypothetical contingencies – a course of action likely in itself to hasten the demise of the Ottoman Empire by provoking Christian uprisings and inspiring repressions by the Turks. Indeed, the Tsar's insistence on an imminent collapse raised suspicions in Westminster that he was plotting and precipitating it by his actions. As Seymour noted of his conversation with the Tsar on 21 February, 'it can hardly be otherwise but that the Sovereign who insists with such pertinacity upon the impending fate of a neighbouring state must have settled in his own mind that the hour of its dissolution is at hand'.[9]

In his later conversations with Seymour, Nicholas became more confident and even more revealing about his partition plans. He talked of reducing Turkey to a vassal state, as he had done with Poland, and of giving independence to the Danubian principalities, Serbia and Bulgaria, under Russian protection; and he claimed that he had the support of Austria. 'You must understand,' he told Seymour, 'that when I speak of Russia, I speak of Austria as well. What suits the one, suits the other, our interests as regards Turkey are perfectly identical.' Seymour for his part was increasingly put off by the Tsar's 'rash and reckless' plans – he seemed prepared to gamble everything on a war against Turkey – and put them down to the arrogance of autocratic power accumulated over nearly thirty years.[10]

The Tsar's confidence was surely also based on his misapprehension that he enjoyed the support of the British government; he felt that he had formed a bond with Lord Aberdeen in 1844, when Aberdeen, now

Prime Minister and the most pro-Russian of all the British leaders, was Foreign Secretary. Nicholas assumed that Aberdeen's backing for Russia's position in the Holy Lands dispute implied British agreement with his partition plans. In a dispatch from London in early February, the Russian ambassador Baron Brunov informed the Tsar that Aberdeen had remarked off the cuff that the Ottoman government was the worst in the world and that the British had little inclination to support it any longer. The report encouraged Nicholas to speak more freely to Seymour and (in the belief that an Anglo-French alliance was no longer to be feared) to take a more aggressive line against the French and the Turks in the spring of 1853.[11] He had no idea of the growing isolation of Aberdeen within his own cabinet on the Eastern Question; no appreciation of the general drift in British policy against Russia.

To force the Sultan to restore Russia's rights in the Holy Places, the Tsar dispatched his own envoy to Constantinople in February 1853. The choice of envoy was deliberate and itself a sign of his militant intentions for the mission. Instead of choosing a seasoned diplomat who might have furthered peace, Nicholas decided on a military man with a fearful reputation. Prince Alexander Menshikov was 65 years old, a veteran of the wars against the French in 1812, and an admiral in the war against the Turks in 1828–9, when he was castrated by a cannonball. He had experience as a naval minister involved in plans to seize the Turkish Straits, as governor-general of occupied Finland in 1831 and as a negotiator with Persia. Menshikov was a 'remarkably well informed man', in Seymour's estimation, 'with more independence of character than perhaps belongs to any of the Emperor's associates, his peculiar turn of thought constantly showing itself by sarcastic observations which make him a little dreaded in St Petersburg'. But he lacked the necessary tact and patience to act as an appeaser with the Turks, which, as Seymour wrote, was noteworthy.

> If it were necessary to send a military man to Constantinople the Emperor could hardly have made a better selection . . . than he has done; it is however impossible not to reflect that the choice of a soldier has in itself a certain significance, and that should a negotiation . . . prove ineffectual, the negotiator may readily become the commander who has authority to call in 100,000 soldiers and to place himself at their head.[12]

Menshikov's mission was to demand from the Sultan the nullification of the November ruling in favour of the Catholics, the restoration of Greek privileges in the Holy Sepulchre, and reparation in the form of a formal convention or *sened* that would guarantee the treaty rights of Russia (supposedly dating back to the 1774 Treaty of Kuchuk Kainarji) to represent the Orthodox not just in the Holy Lands but throughout the Ottoman Empire. If the French resisted Greek control of the Holy Sepulchre, Menshikov was to propose a secret defensive alliance in which Russia would put a fleet and 400,000 Russian troops at the Sultan's disposal, should he ever need them against a Western power, on condition that he exercised his sovereignty in favour of the Orthodox. According to his diary, Menshikov was given the command of the army and the fleet 'and the post of envoy-plenipotentiary of peace or war'. His instructions were to combine persuasion with military threats. The Tsar had already approved plans to occupy the Danubian principalities and grant them independence if the Turks rejected Menshikov's demands. He had ordered the advance of 140,000 soldiers to the frontiers of the principalities, and was prepared to use these troops with the Black Sea Fleet to seize Constantinople if that should be needed to force the Sultan into submission. There was a flamboyant review of the fleet at Sevastopol to coincide with Menshikov's departure for the Turkish capital, where he arrived on the aptly named steam frigate *Thunderer* on 28 February. Cheered by a huge crowd of Greeks who had gathered at the port to welcome him, Menshikov was accompanied by a large suite of military and naval officers, including General Nepokoichitsky, chief of staff of the 4th Army Corps, and Vice-Admiral Vladimir Kornilov, chief of staff of the Black Sea Fleet, whose mission was to spy on the defences of the Bosporus and Constantinople in preparation for a lightning attack.[13]

Menshikov's demands stood little chance of being met in their original form. The fact that the Tsar had even thought they might succeed suggests how far removed he was from political reality. The draft of the *sened* prepared by Nesselrode went well beyond the dispute in the Holy Lands. In effect, Russia was demanding a new treaty that would reassert its rights of protection of the Greek Church throughout the Ottoman Empire and (in so far as the Orthodox patriarchs were to be appointed for life) without any control by the Porte. European Turkey would become a Russian protectorate, and the Ottoman Empire would in practical terms become a dependency of Russia, always threatened by her military might.

But whatever chances of diplomatic success the admiral might have had, they were ruined by the way Menshikov behaved in the Turkish capital. Two days after he arrived he broke with diplomatic precedent and insulted the Turks by appearing in civilian clothes and an overcoat instead of full uniform for his ceremonial welcome by the Porte. Meeting the Grand Vizier Mehmet Ali, Menshikov immediately demanded the dismissal of Fuad Efendi, the Foreign Minister, who had caved in to the French in November, and refused to begin negotiations until a new Foreign Minister, more amenable to Russia's interests, had been appointed. In a calculated affront to Fuad, Menshikov refused to speak with him, in full view of a large crowd; it was an act to demonstrate that a minister hostile to Russia 'would be humiliated and punished even in the midst of the sultan's court'.[14]

The Turks were appalled by Menshikov's behaviour, but the build-up of Russian troops in Bessarabia was worrying enough to make them acquiesce to his demands. Swallowing their pride, they even allowed the Russian dragoman to interview Fuad's successor, Rifaat Pasha, on behalf of Menshikov before appointing him as Foreign Minister. But Menshikov's continued bullying, his threats to break off relations with the Porte unless it satisfied his demands at once, also alienated the Turkish ministers and made them more inclined to resist his pressure by turning to the British and the French for help. It was a question of defending Turkey's sovereignty.

By the end of the first week of Menshikov's mission, the gist of his instructions had been leaked or sold by Turkish officials to all the Western embassies, and a nervous Mehmet Ali had consulted with the French and British chargés d'affaires, secretly requesting them to call up their fleets to the Aegean in case they were needed to defend the Turkish capital against an attack by the Russians. Colonel Rose was particularly alarmed at Menshikov's actions. He feared that the Russians were about to impose on the Turks a new Treaty of Unkiar-Skelessi, 'or something worse', by the occupation of the Dardanelles (a clear abrogation of the 1841 Straits Convention). He believed he had to act, without waiting until the return of Stratford Canning, who had resigned the ambassadorship in January but had been reappointed by the Aberdeen government in February. On 8 March Rose sent a message by fast steamer to Vice-Admiral Sir James Dundas in Malta calling on him to bring up his squadron to Urla near İzmir. Dundas refused to obey the order without confirmation from the government in London, where a group of ministers, who were later to become the 'inner cabinet' of the Crimean War,* met to discuss Rose's appeal on 20 March. The ministers were concerned by the Russian military build-up in Bessarabia, by the 'vast naval preparations at Sevastopol', and the 'hostile language' used by Menshikov towards the Porte. Convinced that the Russians were preparing to destroy Turkey, Russell was inclined to let their fleets advance into the Bosporus and seize the Turkish capital so that Britain and France could use the defence of the Straits Convention as a reason to launch a full-out naval war against Russia in the Black Sea and the Baltic. Supported by Palmerston, Russell would have had the majority of the British public on his side. But the other ministers were more cautious. They were wary of the French, whom they still regarded as a military threat, and disagreed with Russell that an Anglo-French alliance would counteract the challenge of the French steam fleet to British maritime power. They took the view that the French had provoked the Russians, who deserved a concession in the Holy Lands, and trusted the assurances of Baron Brunov ('as a gentleman') that the Tsar's intentions remained peaceful. On this basis they rejected Rose's request for a squadron. It was not up to chargés d'affaires, it seemed to them, to call up fleets or decide matters of war and peace; and Rose had allowed himself to be swayed by 'the alarm of the Turkish government . . . and the rumours that obtained general credit at Constantinople of the advancing army and fleet of Russia'. The ministers decided that they would wait for Stratford Canning to return to the Turkish capital and sort out a peaceful settlement.[15]

News of Rose's summons to Dundas arrived in Paris on 16 March.

---

* The Prime Minister, Lord Aberdeen; Lord John Russell, leader of the House of Commons; Foreign Secretary Lord George Clarendon; Sir James Graham, First Lord of the Admiralty; and Palmerston, at that time Home Secretary.

In a cabinet meeting to discuss the situation three days later, Drouyn de Lhuys, the Foreign Minister, painted a picture of imminent catastrophe: 'The last hour of Turkey has been tolled, and we must expect to see the double-headed eagle [of the Romanovs] planted on the towers of St Sophia.' Drouyn rejected the idea of sending in a fleet, at least not until the British did, in case they should be isolated in Europe, which feared the reassertion of Napoleonic France. This was also the position of the other ministers, except Persigny, who claimed that Britain 'would rejoice and join our side' if France took a stand 'to stop the march of Russia towards Constantinople'. For Persigny it was a question of national honour. The army that had carried out the *coup d'état* of 2 December was an 'army of praetorians' with a heritage of glory to defend. He warned Napoleon that if he temporized, as his ministers advised, 'the first time you pass before your troops, you will see their faces saddened, the ranks silenced, and you will feel the ground shake beneath your feet. So, as you well know, to win back the army you must take some risks; and you, Messieurs, who would have peace at any price, you will be thrown into a terrible conflagration.' At this point the Emperor, who had been wavering over what to do, succumbed to the argument of Persigny and ordered the advance of the French fleet, not as far as the Dardanelles, but to Salamis, in Greek waters, as a warning to the Russians that 'France was not disinterested in what took place in Constantinople'.[16]

There were three main reasons behind his decision to mobilize the fleet. First, as Persigny had intimated, there were rumours of a plot against Napoleon in the army, and a show of force was a good way to nip this in the bud. 'I must tell you', Napoleon wrote to Empress Eugénie in the winter of 1852, 'that serious plots are afoot in the army. I am keeping my eye on all this, and I reckon that by one means or another, I can prevent any outbreak: perhaps by means of a war.' Secondly, Napoleon was anxious to restore France as a naval power in the Mediterranean – for everybody knew, in the words of Horace de Viel-Castel, the director of the Louvre, that 'the day when the Mediterranean is partitioned between Russia and England, France will no longer be counted among the great powers'. In a conversation with Stratford Canning, who passed through Paris on his way from London to Constantinople, Napoleon was concerned to highlight France's

interests in the Mediterranean. Stratford wrote this memorandum of
their conversation on 10 March:

> He said that he had no wish to make the Mediterranean a *French* lake –
> to use a well-known expression – but that he should like to see it made a
> *European* one. He did not explain the meaning of this phrase. If he meant
> that the shores of the Mediterranean should be exclusively in the hands
> of Christendom, the dream is rather colossal.... The impression left
> upon my mind ... is that Louis Napoleon, meaning to be well with us, at
> least for the present, is ready to act politically in concert with England at
> Constantinople; but it remains to be seen whether he looks to the restor-
> ation of Turkish power, or merely to the consequences of its decay,
> preparing to avail himself of them hereafter in the interests of France.

But above all, it was Napoleon's desire to 'act ... in concert with England' and establish an Anglo-French alliance that led him to mobilize
the fleet. 'Persigny is right,' he told his ministers on 19 March. 'If we
send our fleet to Salamis, England will be forced to do as much, and
the union of the two fleets will lead to the union of the two nations
against Russia.' According to Persigny, the Emperor reasoned that the
dispatch of the fleet would appeal to British Russophobia, win support from the bourgeois press and force the hand of the more cautious
Aberdeen government to join France.[17]

In fact, the British fleet remained at Malta while the French sailed
from Toulon on 22 March. The British were furious with the French
for escalating the crisis, and urged them not to advance beyond
Naples, giving Stratford time to get to Constantinople and arrange a
settlement, before moving their gunboats into the Aegean Sea. Stratford arrived in the Turkish capital on 5 April. He found the Turks
already in a mood to stand up to Menshikov – nationalist and religious emotions had become highly charged – although there were
divisions about how far they should go and how long they should
wait for the military backing of the West. These arguments became
entangled in the long-standing personal rivalry between the Grand
Vizier Mehmet Ali and Reshid, Stratford's old ally, who was then out
of power. Hearing that Mehmet Ali was about to make a compromise
with Menshikov, Stratford urged him to stand firm against the Russians, assuring him (on his own authority) that the British fleet would

back him if need be. The key thing, he advised, was to separate the conflict in the Holy Lands (where Russia had a legitimate claim for the restoration of its treaty rights) and the broader demands of the draft *sened* that had to be rejected to maintain Turkish sovereignty. It was vital for the Sultan to grant religious rights by direct sovereign authority rather than by any mechanism dictated by Russia. In Stratford's view, the Tsar's real intention was to use his protection of the Greek Church as a Trojan horse for the penetration and dismemberment of the Ottoman Empire.[18]

The Grand Council heeded his advice when it met to discuss Menshikov's demands on 23 April. It agreed to negotiate on the Holy Places but not on the broader question concerning Russia's protection of the Sultan's Orthodox subjects. On 5 May Menshikov came back with a revised version of the *sened* (without the life appointment of the patriarchs) but with an ultimatum that if it was not signed within five days he would leave Constantinople and break off diplomatic relations. Stratford urged the Sultan to hold firm, and the Ottoman cabinet rejected the ultimatum on 10 May. In a desperate bid to satisfy the Tsar's demands without recourse to war, Menshikov gave the Turks four more days to sign the revised *sened*. During this reprieve, Stratford and Reshid engineered the dismissal of Mehmet Ali, allowing Reshid to take over at the Foreign Ministry. Following the advice of the British ambassador, Reshid was in favour of a firmer line against the Russians on the understanding that this was the surest way to reach a settlement on the religious question without compromising the sovereignty of the Sultan. Reshid asked for five more days from Menshikov. News had come from the Ottoman ambassador in London, Kostaki Musurus, that Britain would defend the sovereign rights of the Ottoman Empire, and this emboldened the new Turkish Foreign Minister, who needed time to win support for a firm stand against the Russians among his fellow-ministers.

On 15 May the Grand Council met again. The ministers and Muslim leaders were fired up with anti-Russian sentiment, much of it encouraged by Stratford, who had called on many of them personally to urge them to stand firm. The Council refused Menshikov's demands. Receiving the news that evening, Menshikov replied that Russia would now break off relations with the Porte but that he would wait a few more days in the Turkish capital, citing storms in the Black Sea as a reason to delay his departure, though really he was hoping for a last-minute deal. Finally, on 21 May, the Russian coat of arms was taken down from the embassy and Menshikov departed for Odessa on the *Thunderer*.[19]

*

The failure of the Menshikov mission convinced the Tsar that he needed to resort to military means. On 29 May he wrote to Field Marshal Paskevich that if he had been more aggressive from the start he might have been successful in extracting concessions from the Turks. He did not want a war – he feared the intervention of the Western powers – but he was now prepared to use the threat of war, to shake the Turkish Empire to its foundations, to get his way and enforce what he saw as Russia's treaty rights to protect the Orthodox. He revealed his thinking (and state of mind) to Paskevich:

> The consequence [of Menshikov's failure] is war. However, before I get to that, I have decided to send my troops into the [Danubian] principalities – to show the world how far I would go to avoid war – and send a final ultimatum to the Turks to satisfy my demands within eight days, and if they don't, I shall declare war on them. My aim is to occupy the principalities without a war, if the Turks do not meet us on the left bank of the Danube ... If the Turks resist, I shall blockade the Bosporus and seize Turkish ships on the Black Sea; and I shall propose to Austria to occupy Herzegovina and Serbia. If that does not take effect, I shall declare the independence of the principalities, Serbia and Herzegovina – and then the Turkish Empire will begin to crumble, for everywhere there will be Christian uprisings and the last hour of the Ottoman Empire will sound. I do not intend to cross the Danube, the [Turkish] Empire will collapse without that, but I shall keep my fleet prepared, and the 13th and 14th Divisions will remain on a war footing in Sevastopol and Odessa. Canning's actions ... do not put me off: I must go by my own path and fulfil my duty according to my faith as befits the honour of Russia. You cannot imagine how much all this saddens me. I have grown old, but I would like to end my life in peace![20]

The Tsar's plan was the result of a compromise between his own initial inclination to seize Constantinople in a surprise attack (before the Western powers could react) and the more cautious thinking of Paskevich. Paskevich had commanded the punitive campaign against the Hungarians and the Poles and was the Tsar's most trusted military adviser. He was sceptical about such an offensive and fearful that it would entangle Russia in a European-wide war. The key difference between the two centred on their views of Austria. Nicholas put excessive faith in his personal link to Franz Joseph. He was convinced that the Austrians – whom he had saved from the Hungarians in 1849 – would join him in his threats against the Turks and, if necessary, in the partition of the Ottoman Empire. That is what had made him so aggressive in his foreign policy: the belief that with Austria on his side there could be no European war and the Turks would be forced to capitulate. Paskevich, by contrast, was doubtful about Austrian support. As he correctly understood, the Austrians could hardly be expected to welcome Russian troops in the principalities and the Balkans, where they already feared uprisings against them by the Serbs and other Slavs; they might even join the Western powers against Russia if these revolts materialized, if and when the Tsar's troops crossed the Danube.

Determined to limit the Tsar's offensive plans, Paskevich played to his pan-Slav fantasies. He persuaded Nicholas that it would be enough for Russian troops to occupy the principalities in a defensive war for the Balkan Slavs to rise up and force the Turks to give in to the Tsar's demands. He spoke of occupying the principalities for several years, if necessary, and claimed that Russian propaganda would raise as many as 50,000 Christian soldiers for the Tsar's army in the Balkans – enough to deter the intervention of the Western powers and at least neutralize the Austrians. In a memorandum to the Tsar in early April, Paskevich outlined his vision of the religious war that would unfold in the Balkans as the Russian troops advanced:

> The Christians of Turkey are from warring tribes and, if the Serbs and Bulgarians have remained peaceful, it is only because they have not yet felt Turkish rule in their villages ... But their warrior spirit will be roused by the first conflicts between Christians and Muslims, they will not stand for the atrocities that the Turks will carry out against their villages ... when our armies begin the war. There is not a village, perhaps not a family, where there won't be oppressed Christians ... willing

to join us in our fight against the Turks. . . . We will have a weapon that can bring the Turkish Empire down.[21]

Towards the end of June the Tsar ordered his two armies in Bessarabia to cross the River Pruth and occupy Moldavia and Wallachia. Paskevich still hoped that the invasion of the principalities would not lead to a European war, but feared that the Tsar would not pull back from it if that should be the case, as he explained to General Gorchakov, the commander of the Russian forces, on 24 June. The Tsar's troops advanced to Bucharest, where their command established headquarters. In every town, they posted copies of a manifesto from the Tsar in which it was stated that Russia did not want to make territorial gains and was only occupying the principalities as a 'guarantee' for the satisfaction of its religious grievances by the Ottoman government. 'We are ready to stop our troops if the Porte guarantees the inviolable rights of the Orthodox Church. But if it continues to resist, then, with God on our side, we shall advance and fight for our true faith.'[22]

The occupying troops had little understanding of the dispute in the Holy Lands. 'We did not think of anything, we knew nothing. We let our commanders think for us and did what they told us,' recalled Teofil Klemm, a veteran of the Danubian campaign. Klemm was just 18, a literate serf who had been chosen for training as an officer in Kremenchug in the Ukraine, when he was called up by the infantry in 1853. Klemm was unimpressed by the pan-Slav pamphlets that circulated widely among the troops and officers of the 5th Army Corps. 'None of us were interested in such ideas,' he wrote. But like every soldier in the Russian army, Klemm went off to battle with a cross around his neck and with an understanding of his calling as a fight for God.[23]

The Russian army was a peasant army – serfs and state peasants were the main groups subject to the military draft – and that was its main problem. It was by far the biggest army in the world, with over a million infantry, a quarter of a million irregulars (mainly Cossack cavalry) and three-quarters of a million reservists in special military settlements. But even this was not enough to defend the enormous borders of Russia, where there were so many vulnerable points, such as the Baltic coast, or Poland, or the Caucasus, and the army could not recruit more without running down the serf economy and sparking peasant uprisings. The weakness of the population base in European Russia – a territory the size of the rest of Europe but with less than a fifth of its population – was compounded by the concentration of the serf population in the central agricultural zone of Russia, a long way from the Empire's borders where the army would be needed at short notice in the event of war. Without railways it took months for serfs to be recruited and sent by foot or cart to their regiments. Even before the Crimean War, the Russian army was already overstretched. Virtually all the serfs eligible for conscription had been mobilized, and the quality of the recruits had declined significantly, as landowners and villages, desperate to hold on to their last able farmers, sent inferior men to the army. A report of 1848 showed that during recent levies one-third of the conscripts had been rejected because they had failed to meet the necessary height requirement (a mere 160 centimetres); and another half had been rejected because of chronic illness or other physical deficiencies. The only way to solve the army's shortages of manpower would have been to widen its social base of conscription and move towards a European system of universal military service, but this would have spelled the end of serfdom, the foundation of the social system, to which the aristocracy was firmly committed.[24]

Despite two decades of reform, the Russian military remained far behind the armies of the other European states. The officer corps was poorly educated and almost all the troops illiterate: official figures of the 1850s showed that in a group of six divisions, numbering approximately 120,000 men, only 264 (0.2 per cent) were able to read or write. The ethos of the army was dominated by the eighteenth-century parade-ground culture of the tsarist court, in which promotion, to quote Karl Marx, was limited to 'martinets, whose principal merit consists of stolid obedience and ready servility added to accuracy of eyesight in detecting a fault in the buttons and buttonholes of the uniform'. There was more emphasis on the drilling and appearance of the troops than on their battleworthiness. Even during fighting there were elaborate rules for the posture, length of stride, line and movement of the troops, all set out in army manuals, which were quite irrelevant to the actual conditions of the battlefield:

> When a battle formation is advancing or retiring it is necessary to observe a general alignment of the battalions in each line and to maintain

correctly the intervals between battalions. In this case it is not enough for each battalion separately to keep alignment, it is necessary that the pace be alike in all battalions, so that the guidon sergeants marching before the battalions shall keep alignment among themselves and march parallel to one another along lines perpendicular to the common formation.

The domination of this parade culture was connected to the backwardness of the army's weaponry. The importance attached to keeping troops in tight columns was partly to maintain their discipline and prevent chaos when there were large formations on the move, as in other armies of the time. But it was also necessitated by the inefficiency of the Russian musket and the consequent reliance on the bayonet (justified by patriotic myths about the 'bravery of the Russian soldier', who was at his best with the bayonet). Such was the neglect of small-arms fire in the infantry that 'very few men even knew how to use their muskets', according to one officer. 'With us, success in battle was entirely staked on the art of marching and the correct stretching of the toe.'[25]

These outdated means of fighting had brought Russia victory in all the major wars of the early nineteenth century – against the Persians and the Turks, and of course in Russia's most important war, against Napoleon (a triumph that convinced the Russians that their army was invincible). So there had been little pressure to update them for the needs of warfare in the new age of steam and the telegraph. Russia's economic backwardness and financial weakness compared to the new industrial powers of the West also placed a severe brake on the modernization of its vast and expensive peacetime army. It was only during the Crimean War – when the musket was shown to be useless against the Minié rifle of the British and the French – that the Russians ordered rifles for their own army.

Of the 80,000 Russian troops who crossed the River Pruth, the border between Russia and Moldavia, less than half would survive for a year. The tsarist army lost men at a far higher rate than any of the other European armies. Soldiers were sacrificed in huge numbers for relatively minor gains by aristocratic senior officers, who cared little for the welfare of their peasant conscripts but a great deal for their own promotion if they could report a victory to their superiors. The vast majority of Russian soldiers were not killed in battle but died from wounds and diseases that might not have been fatal had there been a proper medical service. Every Russian offensive told the same sad tale: in 1828–9, half the army died from cholera and illnesses in the Danubian principalities; during the Polish campaign of 1830–31, 7,000 Russian soldiers were killed in combat but 85,000 were carried off by wounds and sickness; during the Hungarian campaign of 1849, only 708 men died in the fighting but 57,000 Russian soldiers were admitted to Austrian hospitals. Even in peacetime the average rate of sickness in the Russian army was 65 per cent.[26]

The appalling treatment of the serf soldier lay behind this high rate of illness. Floggings were a daily aspect of the disciplinary system; beatings so common that entire regiments could be made up of men who carried wounds inflicted by their own officers. The supply system was riddled with corruption because officers were very badly paid – the whole army was chronically underfunded by the cash-strapped tsarist government – and by the time they had taken their profit from the sums they were allowed to buy provisions with, there was little money left for the rations of the troops. Without an effective system of supply, soldiers were expected to fend largely for themselves. Each regiment was responsible for the manufacturing of its uniforms and boots with materials provided by the state. Regiments not only had their own tailors and cobblers, but their own barbers, bakers, blacksmiths, carpenters and metal workers, joiners, painters, singers and bandsmen, all of them bringing their own village trades into the army. Without these peasant skills, a Russian army, let alone an army on the offensive, would not have been feasible. The Russian soldier on the march drew on all his peasant know-how and resourcefulness. He carried bandages in his knapsack so that he could treat himself for wounds. He was very good at improvising ways to sleep in the open – using leaves and branches, haystacks, crops, and even digging himself into a hole in the ground – a crucial skill that helped the army to go on long marches without the need to carry tents.[27]

As the Russians crossed the Pruth, the Turkish government ordered Omer Pasha, the commander of the Rumelian army, to strengthen the

Turkish forts along the Danube and prepare for their defence. The Porte also called for reinforcements from the Ottoman dominions of Egypt and Tunis. By mid-August there were 20,000 Egyptian troops and 8,000 Tunisians encamped around Constantinople and ready to depart for the Danubian forts. A British embassy official described them in a letter to Lady Stratford de Redcliffe:

> 'Tis a pity you can't see the Bosphorus about Therapia, swarming with ships of war, and the opposite heights crowned with the green tents of the Egyptian camp. Constantinople has itself gone back fifty years, and the strangest figures swarm in from the distant provinces to have a cut at the Muscov[ite]. Turbans, lances, maces, and battle-axes jostle each other in the narrow streets, and are bundled off immediately to the camp at Shumla for the sake of a quiet life.[28]

The Turkish army was made up of many nationalities. It included Arabs, Kurds, Tatars, Egyptians, Tunisians, Albanians, Greeks, Armenians and other peoples, many of them hostile to the Turkish government or unable to understand the commands of their Turkish or European officers (Omer Pasha's staff contained many Poles and Italians). The most colourful of the Turkish forces were the Bashi Bazouks, irregulars from North Africa, Central Asia and Anatolia, who left their tribes in bands of twenty or thirty at a time, a motley bunch of cavalrymen of all ages and appearances, and made their way to the Turkish capital to join the jihad against the Russian infidels. In his memoirs of the Crimean War, the British naval officer Adolphus Slade, who helped to train the Turkish navy, described a parade of the Bashi Bazouks in Constantinople before they were sent off to the Danubian front. They were mostly dressed in old tribal gear, 'sashed and turbaned, and picturesquely armed with pistols, yataghan [Turkish sword] and sabre. Some carried pennoned lances. Each squadron had its colours and its kettle-drums of the fashion of those, if not the same, carried by their ancestors who had marched to the siege of Vienna.' They spoke so many different languages that, even within small units, translators and criers had to be employed to shout out the orders of the officers.[29]

Language was not the only problem of command. Many Muslim soldiers were unwilling to obey Christian officers, even Omer Pasha, a Croatian Serb and Orthodox by birth (his real name was Mihailo Latas) who had been educated in an Austrian military school before fleeing from corruption charges to the Ottoman province of Bosnia and converting to Islam. Jocular and talkative, Omer Pasha enjoyed the luxurious lifestyle that his command of the Rumelian army had afforded him. He dressed in a uniform decorated with gold braid and precious stones, kept a private harem, and employed an orchestra of Germans to accompany his troops (in the Crimea he had them play 'Ah! Che la morte' from Verdi's recent opera *Il Trovatore*). Omer Pasha was not an outstanding commander. It was said that he had been promoted on the basis of his beautiful handwriting (he had been the writing-master of the young Abdülmecid and had been made a colonel when his pupil became Sultan in 1839). In this sense, despite his Christian birth, Omer Pasha was typical of the Ottoman officer class, which still depended on personal patronage for promotion rather than on military expertise. The military reforms of Mahmud's reign and the Tanzimat had yet to create the foundations of a modern professional army, and the majority of Turkish officers were tactically weak on the battlefield. Many still adhered to the outmoded strategy of dispersing their troops to cover every bit of ground rather than deploying them in larger and more compact groups. The Ottoman army was good at 'small-war' ambushes and skirmishing, and excellent at siege warfare, but it had long lacked the discipline and training to master close-order formations using smooth-bore muskets, unlike the Russians.[30]

In terms of pay and conditions there was a huge gulf between the officers and the soldiers, a divide even wider than in the Russian army, with many senior commanders living like pashas and their troops left unpaid for several months, sometimes even years, during a war. The Russian diplomat and geographer Pyotr Chikhachev reported on the problem when he worked at the Russian embassy in Constantinople in 1849. In his calculation, the annual cost of the Turkish infantry soldier (salary, rations and clothing) was 18 silver roubles; the equivalent costs for the Russian soldier were 32 roubles; for the Austrian, 53 roubles; for the Prussian, 60 roubles; for the French, 85 roubles; and for the British foot soldier, 134 roubles. European soldiers were shocked by the conditions of the Turkish troops on the Danubian front. 'Poorly fed and dressed in rags, they were the most wretched specimens of humanity,' according to one British officer. The Egyptian reinforcements were described by a Russian officer as 'old men and country boys without any training for battle'.[31]

*

The British were divided in their reaction to the Russian occupation of the principalities. The most pacific member of the cabinet was the Prime Minister Lord Aberdeen. He refused to see the occupation as an act of war – he even thought it had been partly justified to press the Porte to recognize the Russians' legitimate demands in the Holy Lands – and looked for diplomatic ways to help the Tsar retreat without losing face. He certainly was not inclined to encourage Turkish resistance. His greatest fear was being drawn into a war against Russia by the Turks, whom he generally mistrusted. In February he had written to Lord Russell to warn against the sending of a British fleet to help the Turks:

> These Barbarians hate us all, and would be delighted to take their chance of some advantage, by embroiling us with the other Powers of Christendom. It may be necessary to give them our moral support, and to endeavour to prolong their existence; but we ought to regard as the greatest misfortune any engagement which compelled us to take up arms for the Turks.

At the more belligerent end of the cabinet, Palmerston thought the occupation was a 'hostile act' that demanded immediate action by Britain 'for the protection of Turkey'. He wanted British warships in the Bosporus to put pressure on the Russians to withdraw from the principalities. Palmerston was supported by the Russophobic British press, and by anti-Russian diplomats, such as Ponsonby and Stratford Canning, who saw the occupation of the principalities as an opportunity for Britain to make good on its failure to oppose the Russians on the Danube in 1848–9.[32]

London had a large community of Romanian exiles from the previous Russian occupation of the principalities who formed an influential pressure-group for British intervention that enjoyed the support of several members of the cabinet, including Palmerston and Gladstone, and many more MPs who lobbied Parliament with questions about the Danube. The Romanian leaders had close connections to the Italian exiles in London and were part of the Democratic Committee established by Mazzini which by this time had also been joined by Greek and Polish exiles in the British capital. The Romanians were careful to distance themselves from the revolutionary politics of these nationalists, and were well aware of the need to tailor their arguments to the liberal interests of the British middle classes. With the support of several national newspapers and periodicals, they succeeded in getting across to the British public the idea that the defence of the principalities against Russian aggression was vitally important for the broader interests of liberty and free trade on the Continent. In a series of almost daily articles in the *Morning Advertiser*, Urquhart joined their calls for intervention in the principalities, although he was more concerned about the defence of Turkish sovereignty and Britain's free-trade interests than about the Romanian national cause. As the Russian invasion of the principalities progressed, Romanian propagandists grew bolder and made direct appeals to the public on speaking tours. In all their speeches the main theme was the European crusade for freedom against Russian tyranny – a rallying cry that was at times extremely fanciful in its vision of a Christian uprising for liberty in the Ottoman Empire. Constantine Rosetti, for example, told a crowd in Plymouth that 'an army of 100,000 Romanians stood ready on the Danube to join the soldiers of democracy'.[33]

While the nature of the Russian occupation of the principalities remained unclear, the British government hestitated over where to send the Royal Navy. Palmerston and Russell wanted British warships in the Bosporus to prevent the Russian fleet attacking Constantinople; but Aberdeen preferred to hold the navy back in order not to threaten a negotiated peace. In the end a compromise was reached and the fleet was kept on a war footing at Besika Bay, just outside the Dardanelles, close enough, so the thinking went, to deter a Russian attack on the Turkish capital but not close enough to provoke a conflict between Britain and Russia. Then in July the Russian occupation of the principalities began to assume a more serious character. Reports reached the European capitals that the hospodars of Moldavia and Wallachia had been ordered by the Russians to break off relations with the Porte and to pay tribute to the Tsar instead. The news caused alarm because it suggested that Russia's real intention was to take possession of the principalities on a permanent basis, despite the assurances of the Tsar's manifesto to the contrary.[34]

The reaction of the European powers was immediate. The Austrians mobilized 25,000 troops on their southern frontiers, mainly as a warning to the Serbs and other Habsburg Slavs not to rise up in support of the Russian invasion. The French put their fleet on a war footing, and the British followed them. Stratford Canning, who had first heard the news of the order to the hospodars, and who was eager to make amends for the failure of the British to make a stand against the last Russian invasion in 1848–9, called for decisive military action to defend the principalities. He warned the Foreign Office that 'the whole of European Turkey, from the frontier of Austria to that of Greece', was about to fall to the Russians; that if they crossed the Danube there would be uprisings by Christians everywhere in the Balkans; that the Sultan and his Muslim subjects were prepared for war against Russia, provided they could rely on the support of Britain and France; and that while it would be a misfortune for Britain to be dragged into a war whose consequences were so unpredictable, it would be better to deal with the danger of Russia now than later on, when it would be too late.[35]

The threatening nature of the Russian occupation raised a bundle of security concerns for the European powers, none of which could afford to stand by while Russia dismantled the Ottoman Empire. Britain, France, Austria and Prussia (which basically followed Austria's lead) now agreed to act together in a peace initiative. The diplomatic lead was taken by Austria, the key guarantor of the Vienna Settlement, of which it was the major beneficiary. The Austrians were heavily dependent on the Danube for their foreign trade and could not tolerate the Russian annexation of the principalities, yet could least afford a European war against Russia in which they were likely to bear the heaviest burden. What the Austrians proposed was probably impossible: a diplomatic solution that would allow the Tsar to drop his demands and withdraw from the principalities without losing face.

The peace process involved an elaborate exchange of diplomatic notes between the European capitals with endless variations on the precise wording of a formula to satisfy the interests of Russia and underline the independence of Turkey. The culmination of this activity was the Vienna Note drafted by the foreign ministers of the four powers at a conference in Vienna on behalf of the Turkish government on 28 July. Like all diplomatic documents designed to end hostilities, the wording of the Note was deliberately vague: the Porte agreed to uphold the treaty rights of Russia to protect the Orthodox subjects of the Sultan. The Tsar saw the Note as a diplomatic victory and agreed to sign it at once 'without modifications' on 5 August. The trouble started when the Turks (who had not even been consulted on the drafting of the Note) asked for details to be clarified. They were concerned that the Note had not set proper limits on the Russian right to intervene in Ottoman affairs – a concern that was soon proved to be justified when a private diplomatic document was leaked to a Berlin newspaper showing that the Russians had interpreted the Note to mean that they could intervene to protect the Orthodox anywhere throughout the Ottoman Empire and not just in areas where a specific conflict had occurred, as in the Holy Lands. The Sultan suggested a couple of minor verbal alterations to the Note – forms of words but important to a government that was being asked to sign the Note as a concession to Russia or face the loss of two of its richest provinces. He also wanted the Russians to evacuate the principalities before the re-establishment of diplomatic relations, and a guarantee from the four powers that Russia would not invade them again. These were reasonable demands for a sovereign power to insist upon, but the Tsar refused to accept the Turkish modifications, on the grounds that he had agreed to sign the Note unchanged, although his suspicion that Stratford Canning had encouraged the Turks to dig in their heels was also not irrelevant. In early September the Vienna Note was reluctantly abandoned by the four powers and, with Turkey on the brink of declaring war on Russia, negotiations had to start again.[36]

In fact, contrary to the Tsar's suspicions, Stratford Canning had played a minor role in the Turkish decision to reject the Note. The British ambassador was well known for his fierce defence of Turkish sovereignty and his hatred of Russia, so it was not surprising that he was held responsible for the unexpected refusal of the Turks to go along with the diplomatic solution imposed on them by the Western powers to appease the Tsar. The idea that Stratford had pushed the Turks towards a war against Russia was later taken up by the Foreign Office, which took the view that the ambassador might have persuaded the Turks to accept the Note, if he had gone about it in the right manner, but that he had chosen not to because 'he is himself no better than a Turk, and has lived there so long, and is animated with such personal hatred of the [Russian] Emperor, that he is full of the Turkish spirit; and this and his temper together have made him take a part directly contrary to the wishes and instructions of his government'.[37] Looking back on the failure of peace on 1 October, Foreign Secretary Lord George Clarendon concluded that it would have been better to have had a more moderate man than Stratford as ambassador in the Turkish capital. The game of deceit the Russians played 'called forth all his Russian antipathies and made him from the first look to war as the best thing for Turkey. In fact no settlement would have been satisfactory to him that did not humiliate Russia.'[38] But this was unfair to Stratford, who took the blame for the failure of the government. The truth is that Stratford did his best to get the Porte to accept the Note, but his influence on the Turks was steadily declining in the summer months, as Constantinople was swept by demonstrations calling for a 'holy war' against Russia.

The invasion of the principalities stirred a powerful combination of Muslim feeling and Turkish nationalism in the Ottoman capital. The Porte had roused the Muslim population against the invasion, and now could not contain the ensuing religious emotions. The language of the metropolitan ulema was increasingly belligerent, raising fears among the devout that the invaders would destroy their mosques and build churches in their place. Meanwhile the Porte kept the public ignorant about the Vienna initiative, claiming that any peace would come 'solely from the Tsar's awe of the Sultan' – an idea that encouraged nationalist feelings of Muslim superiority. Rumours circulated that the Sultan was paying the British and French navies to fight for Turkey; that Europe had been chosen by Allah to defend the Muslims; that the Tsar had sent his wife to Constantinople to beg for peace and had offered to repay Turkey for the invasion of the principalities by giving up the Crimea. Many of these rumours were engineered or promoted by the recently dimissed Grand Vizier Mehmet Ali to undermine Reshid. By the end of August, Mehmet Ali had emerged as the head of a 'war party', which had gained the ascendancy within the Grand Council. Backed by Muslim leaders, he enjoyed the support of a large group of younger Turkish officials, who were nationalist and religious, and opposed to Western intervention in Ottoman affairs, but calculated, nonetheless, that if they could involve the British and the French on their side in a war against Russia, this would be hugely to their advantage and might even reverse a hundred years of military defeats by the Russians. To secure the support of the Western fleets, they were prepared to promise sound administration to interfering Europeans like Stratford, but they rejected the Tanzimat reforms, because they saw the granting of more civil rights to Christians as a potential threat to Muslim rule.[39]

The war mood in the Turkish capital reached fever pitch during the second week of September, when there was a series of pro-war demonstrations and a mass petition with 60,000 signatures calling on the government to launch a 'holy war' against Russia. The theological schools (*medrese*) and mosques were the organizing centres of the protests, and their influence was clearly marked in the religious language of the posters that appeared throughout the capital:

> O Glorious Padishah! All your subjects are ready to sacrifice their lives, property and children for the sake of your majesty. You too have now incurred the duty of unsheathing the sword of Muhammad that you girded in the mosque of Eyyub-i Ansari like your grandfathers and predecessors. The hesitations of your ministers on this question stem from their addiction to the disease of vanity and this situation has the possibility (God forbid) of leading us all into a great danger. Therefore your victorious soldiers and your praying servants want war for the defence of their clear rights, O My Padishah!

There were 45,000 religious students in the *medrese* of the Turkish capital. They were discontented as a group – the Tanzimat reforms had reduced their status and career prospects by promoting graduates of the new secular schools – and this social grievance gave a cutting edge to their protests. The Turkish government was terrified of the possibility of an Islamic revolution if it failed to declare war against Russia.[40]

On 10 September, thirty-five religious leaders submitted a petition to the Grand Council, which discussed it the next day. According to the London *Times*:

> The petition was principally composed of numerous quotations from the Koran, enjoining war on the enemies of Islam, and contained covert threats of disturbance were it not listened to and complied with. The tone of the petition is exceedingly bold, and bordering on the insolent. Some of the principal Ministers endeavoured to reason with those who presented it, but the answers they obtained were short and to the point. 'Here are the words of the Koran: if you are Mussulmans you are bound to obey. You are now listening to foreign and infidel ambassadors who are the enemies of the Faith; we are the children of the Prophet; we have an army and that army cries out with us for war, to avenge the insults which the Giaours have heaped upon us.' It is said that on each attempt to reason with these fanatics, the Ministers were met by the answer 'These are the words of the Koran.' The present Ministers are undoubtedly in a state of alarm, since they look upon the present circumstance (a very unusual event in Turkey) as but the commencement of a revolution, and fear to be forced at the present inopportune juncture into a war.

On 12 September the religious leaders gained an audience with the Sultan. They gave him an ultimatum: either declare war or abdicate. Abdülmecid turned for help to Stratford and the French ambassador, Edmond de Lacour, who both agreed to bring up their fleets if they were needed to put down a revolution in the Turkish capital.[41]

That evening, the Sultan called a meeting of his ministers. They agreed to declare war against Russia, although not until the Porte had time to firm up the support of the Western fleets and put down the religious protests in Constantinople. The policy was formally agreed at an enlarged session of the Grand Council on 26–7 September attended by the Sultan's ministers, leading Muslim clerics and the military establishment. It was the religious leaders who insisted on the need to fight, despite the hesitations of the military commanders, who had their doubts about the capacity of the Turkish forces to win a war against Russia. Omer Pasha thought that 40,000 more troops would be needed on the Danube, where it would require several months to prepare the forts and bridges for a war against Russia. Mehmet Ali, who had recently been appointed commander-in-chief of the army, would not say whether it was possible to win against Russia, despite his association with the 'war party'. Nor would Mahmud Pasha, the grand admiral of the navy, who said the Turks could match the Russian fleet but would not take responsibility for these words if later called to account for a defeat. In the end, it was Reshid who came round to the viewpoint of the Muslim leaders, perhaps sensing that to oppose war at this late stage would spark a religious revolution and destroy the Tanzimat reforms, upon which the support of the Western powers in any war with Russia would depend. 'Better to die fighting than not to fight at all,' declared Reshid. 'God willing, we will be victorious.'[42]

5

Phoney War

The Turkish declaration of war appeared in the official newspaper *Takvim-i Vekayi* on 4 October. It was quickly followed by a 'Manifesto of the Sublime Porte' stating that the government had been forced to declare war because of Russia's refusal to evacuate the principalities but adding that, as a sign of its peaceful intentions, the commander of the Rumelian army, Omer Pasha, would give the Russian forces an extra fifteen days to carry out the evacuation before the commencement of hostilities.[1]

Even at this stage there were hopes for a diplomatic settlement. The Turkish declaration was a means of buying time for one to work by calming the war fever of the religious crowds in Constantinople and placing pressure on the Western governments to intervene. Unprepared for a real war against Russia, the Ottomans began a phoney one to avert the threat of an Islamic revolution in the Turkish capital and to force the West to send their fleets to make the Russians back down.

On 19 October the Turkish ultimatum expired. Against the advice of the British and the French, who tried to hold them back, the Turks went on the attack in the principalities, calculating that the Western press would drum up public support for their cause against Russia. The Turkish government was very conscious of the power of the British press in particular, perhaps even thinking that it was the same as the government, and tried very hard to win it over to its side. Throughout the autumn of 1853 the Porte directed considerable funds to its London embassy so that it could 'pay for and organize in secret a series of public demonstrations and newspaper articles' calling on the British government to intervene against Russia.[2]

Ordered by the Porte to commence hostilities, on 23 October Omer

Pasha's forces crossed the Danube at Kalafat and took the town from the Cossacks in the first skirmish of the war. The villagers of the Kalafat region – an anti-Russian stronghold of the 1848 Wallachian revolution – armed themselves with hunting guns and joined the fight against the Cossack troops. The Turks also crossed the river at Olten-itsa, where they engaged in heavier but indecisive fighting with the Russians, both sides claiming victory.[3]

These initial skirmishes made up the Tsar's mind to launch a major offensive against the Turks, as he had outlined in his letter to Paskevich on 29 May. But his chief commander had become even more opposed to the idea than he had been in the spring. Paskevich thought the Turks too strong and the Western fleets too close for the Russians to attack the Turkish capital. On 24 September he had sent a memo to the Tsar, urging him to adopt a more defensive position on the northern side of the Dan-ube, while organizing Christian militias to rise up against the Turks south of the river. His aim was to pressure the Turks into making concessions to Russia without the need to fight a war. 'We have the most deadly weapon to use against the Ottoman Empire,' Paskevich wrote. 'Its success cannot even be prevented by the Western powers. Our most terrifying weapon is our influence among our Christian tribes in Turkey.'

Paskevich was mainly worried that the Austrians would oppose a Russian offensive in the Balkans, where they were vulnerable to Slav uprisings in their own neighbouring territories. He did not want to commit Russian troops to battle with the Turks if they might be needed against an attack by the Austrians, most likely in Poland, whose loss might lead to the collapse of the Russian Empire in Europe. Paskevich lacked the courage to confront the Tsar. So instead he dragged his heels, ignoring orders to advance south as soon as possible and con-centrating instead on the consolidation of the Russian positions along the Danube. His aim was twofold: to turn the river into a supply line from the Black Sea into the Balkans, and to organize the Christians into militias in preparation for a future offensive against the Turks, perhaps in the spring of 1854. 'The idea is new and beautiful,' Paske-vich wrote. 'It will bring us into close relations with the most belligerent tribes of Turkey: the Serbs, Herzegovians, Montenegrins and Bulgar-ians, who, if not for us, are at least against the Turks, and who with some help from our side may indeed destroy the Turkish empire ...

without loss of Russian blood.'[4] Aware that it went against the legitimist principles of the Tsar to stir revolts in foreign lands, Paskevich
defended his idea on religious grounds – the protection of the Orthodox from Muslim persecution – and cited precedents from previous
wars with Turkey (in 1773–4, 1788–91 and 1806–12) when the Russian army had raised Christian troops in Ottoman territories.[5]

The Tsar did not need much convincing. In a revealing memorandum written at the start of November 1853, Nicholas outlined his
strategy for the war against Turkey. Circulated to his ministers and
senior commanders, the memorandum was clearly influenced by
Paskevich, his most trusted general. The Tsar was counting on the
Serbs to rebel against the Turks, followed sometime later by the Bulgarians. The Russian army would consolidate a defensive position on
the Danube and then move further south to liberate the Christians
when they rose against the Turks. The strategy depended on the long-
term occupation of the principalities to give the Russians time to
organize the Christians into militias. The Tsar looked ahead at least a
year:

> The beginning of 1855 will show us how much hope we can place on
> the Christians of Turkey and whether England and France will remain
> opposed to us. There is no other way for us to move ahead, except
> through a popular uprising (*narodnoe vosstanie*) for independence on
> the widest and most general scale; without this popular collaboration
> we cannot even think of an offensive; the fight should be between the
> Christians and the Turks – with us, so to speak, remaining in reserve.[6]

Nesselrode, the Tsar's cautious Foreign Minister, tried to pour cold
water on this revolutionary strategy, and his caution was shared by
most Russian diplomats. In a memo to the Tsar on 8 November, he
argued that the Balkan Slavs would not rise up in large numbers;*

---

* Nesselrode was supported by Baron Meyendorff, the Russian ambassador in Vienna,
who reported to the Tsar on 29 November that the 'little Christian peoples' would not
fight on Russia's side. They had never received any help from Russia in the past and
had been left in 'a state of military destitution', unable to resist the Turks (*Peter von
Meyendorff: Ein russischer Diplomat an den Höfen von Berlin und Wien. Politischer
und privater Briefwechsel 1826–1863*, ed. O. Hoetzsch, 3 vols. (Berlin and Leipzig,
1923), vol. 3, pp. 100–104).

that inciting revolts would make Europe suspicious of Russia's ambitions in the Balkans; and that it was a dangerous game to play in any case, for Turkey too could stir revolts by the Tsar's Muslims in the Caucasus and the Crimea.[7]

But Nicholas would not be diverted from his goal of a religious war. He saw himself as the defender of the Orthodox faith and refused to be dissuaded from his mission by a Foreign Minister whose Protestant background diminished his standing on religious matters in the Tsar's opinion. Nicholas saw it as his sacred duty to free the Slavs from Muslim rule. In all his manifestos to the Balkan Slavs he made it clear that Russia was fighting a religious war for their liberation from the Turks. On his instructions, his army commanders donated bells to churches in the Christian towns and villages they occupied as a means of winning popular support. Mosques were converted into churches by the Russian troops.[8]

The Tsar's religious fervour became entangled in the broader military calculation – foremost in the more tactical thinking of Paskevich – that the Balkan Christians might provide a cheap army and plentiful resources to fight the Russian cause. By 1853, Nicholas had moved much closer to the Slavophiles and the pan-Slavs, who had a number of patrons at the court as well as the support of Barbette Nelidov, the long-term mistress of the Tsar. According to Anna Tiutcheva, the daughter of the poet Fedor Tiutchev and a lady-in-waiting at the court, the ideas of the pan-Slavs were now openly expressed by the Grand Duke Alexander, the heir to the throne, and his wife, the Grand Duchess Maria Alexandrovna. On several occasions she heard them say in conversation that Russia's natural allies were the Balkan Slavs, who should be supported in their fight for independence by the Russian troops once they had crossed the Danube. Countess Bludova, another pan-Slav at court, urged the Tsar to declare war on Austria as well as Turkey for the liberation of the Slavs. She passed on many of Pogodin's letters to the Tsar in which the pan-Slav leader called on Nicholas to unite the Slavs under Russian leadership and found a Slavic Christian empire based in Constantinople.[9]

The Tsar's notes in the margins of a memorandum by Pogodin reveal much about his thinking in December 1853, when he came closest to embracing the pan-Slav cause. Pogodin had been asked by

Nicholas to give his thoughts on Russia's policy towards the Slavs in the war against Turkey. His answer was a detailed survey of Russia's relations with the European powers which was filled with grievances against the West. The memorandum clearly struck a chord with Nicholas, who shared Pogodin's sense that Russia's role as the protector of the Orthodox had not been recognized or understood and that Russia was unfairly treated by the West. Nicholas especially approved of the following passage, in which Pogodin railed against the double standards of the Western powers, which allowed them to conquer foreign lands but forbade Russia to do the same:

> France takes Algeria from Turkey, and almost every year England annexes another Indian principality: none of this disturbs the balance of power; but when Russia occupies Moldavia and Wallachia, albeit only temporarily, that disturbs the balance of power. France occupies Rome and stays there several years in peacetime:* that is nothing; but Russia only thinks of occupying Constantinople, and the peace of Europe is threatened. The English declare war on the Chinese,† who have, it seems, offended them: no one has a right to intervene; but Russia is obliged to ask Europe for permission if it quarrels with its neighbour. England threatens Greece to support the false claims of a miserable Jew and burns its fleet:‡ that is a lawful action; but Russia demands a treaty to protect millions of Christians, and that is deemed to strengthen its position in the East at the expense of the balance of power. We can expect nothing from the West but blind hatred and malice, which does not understand and does not want to understand (*comment in the margin by Nicholas I*: 'This is the whole point').

Having stirred the Tsar's own grievances against the West, Pogodin encouraged him to act alone, according to his conscience before God, to defend the Orthodox and promote Russia's interests in the Balkans. Nicholas expressed his approval:

---

* A reference to the expeditionary force of General Oudinot in 1849–50 which attacked the anti-papal Roman Republic and brought back Pius IX to Rome. The French troops remained in Rome to protect the Pope until 1870.
† In the Opium Wars of 1839–42.
‡ A reference to the Don Pacifico affair.

Who are our allies in Europe (*comment by Nicholas*: 'No one, and we don't need them, if we put our trust in God, unconditionally and willingly'). Our only true allies in Europe are the Slavs, our brothers in blood, language, history and faith, and there are ten million of them in Turkey and millions in Austria ... The Turkish Slavs could provide us with over 200,000 troops – and what troops! And that is not counting the Croatians, Dalmatians and Slovenians, etc. (*comment by Nicholas*: 'An exaggeration: reduce to one-tenth and it is true') ...

By declaring war on us, the Turks have destroyed all the old treaties defining our relations, so we can now demand the liberation of the Slavs, and bring this about by war, as they themselves have chosen war (*comment by Nicholas*: 'That is right').

If we do not liberate the Slavs and bring them under our protection, then our enemies, the English and the French ... will do so instead. In Serbia, Bulgaria and Bosnia, they are active everywhere among the Slavs, with their Western parties, and if they succeed, where will we be then? (*comment by Nicholas*: 'Absolutely right').

Yes! If we fail to use this favourable opportunity, if we sacrifice the Slavs and betray their hopes, or leave their fate to be decided by other powers, then we will have ranged against us not one lunatic Poland but ten of them (which our enemies desire and are working to arrange) ... (*comment by Nicholas*: 'That is right').

With the Slavs as enemies, Russia would become a 'second-rate power', argued Pogodin, whose final sentences were three times underlined by Nicholas:

The greatest moment in Russia's history has arrived – greater perhaps even than the days of Poltava* and Borodino. If Russia does not advance it will fall back – that is the law of history. But can Russia really fall? Would God allow that? No! He is guiding the great Russian soul, and we see that in the glorious pages we have dedicated to Him in the History of our Fatherland. Surely He would not allow it to be said: Peter founded the dominion of Russia in the East, Catherine consolidated it, Alexander expanded it, and Nicholas betrayed it to the Latins.

---

* In the battle of Poltava (1709) Peter the Great defeated Sweden and established Russia as a Baltic power.

No, that cannot be, and will not be. With God on our side, we cannot go back.[10]

To get him to embrace his pan-Slav ideology Pogodin had cleverly appealed to the Tsar's belief in his divine mission to defend the Orthodox as well as to his growing alienation from the West. In his November memorandum to his ministers, Nicholas had declared that Russia had no option but to turn towards the Slavs, because the Western powers, and Britain in particular, had sided with the Turks against Russia's 'holy cause'.

> We call on all the Christians to join us in the struggle for their liberation from centuries of Ottoman oppression. We declare our support for the independence of the Moldavian-Wallachians, Serbs, Bulgarians, Bosnians and Greeks.... I see no other way to bring an end to the hostility of the British, because it is unlikely that after such a declaration they would continue to ally with the Turks and fight with them against Christians.[11]

Nicholas continued to have doubts about the pan-Slav cause: he did not share Pogodin's illusions about the number of Slav troops it was possible to mobilize in the Balkans; and ideologically he remained opposed to the idea of stirring revolutionary uprisings, preferring instead to proclaim his support for the liberation of the Slavs on religious principles. But the more the West expressed its opposition to Russia's occupation of the principalities, the more he was inclined to gamble everything on a grand alliance of the Orthodox, even threatening to support Slav revolts against the Austrians, if they should join the West against Russia. Religious conviction made the old Tsar rash and reckless, risking all the gains Russia had made in the Near East over many decades of diplomacy and fighting on a gamble with the Slavs.[12]

Hopeful of a Serb uprising, the Tsar favoured marching south-west from Bucharest towards Rusçuk, so that his troops would be close enough to aid the Serbs if they rose up, instead of concentrating on the Turkish fortress of Silistria, further to the east on the Danube, as preferred by Paskevich. As Nicholas explained in a letter to Paskevich, he wanted to subordinate his military strategy to the larger cause of the liberation of the Slavs, which a Serb uprising would begin:

Of course Silistria is an important point ... but it seems to me that if we are to advance our cause through the Christians, and keep ourselves in reserve, it would make more sense to take Rusçuk, from which we can strike into the centre of Wallachia while remaining among the Bulgarians and close to the Serbs, on whom surely we need to depend. To advance further than Rusçuk will depend on a general uprising of the Christians, which should break out shortly after we have occupied Rusçuk; capturing Silistria, I suggest, would not have such an effect [on the Serbs], for it is far away from them.[13]

But Paskevich was more cautious. He was nervous that a Serb uprising would force the Austrians to intervene in order to prevent it from spreading to Habsburg lands. In December he advised the Tsar to keep reserves in Poland in case of an Austrian attack, and to march south-east from Bucharest towards Silistria, where the Russians could rely on the support of the Bulgarians without fear of Austria. Paskevich thought Silistria could be taken in three weeks, allowing the Tsar to launch a spring attack on Adrianople and bring Turkey to its knees before the Western powers had time to intervene, and on this basis Nicholas deferred to the plan of his commander.[14]

However, as the Russian troops advanced towards Silistria there was no mass uprising by the Bulgarians, nor by any other Slavs, although the Bulgarians were generally pro-Russian and had taken part in large-scale revolts against Muslim rule in Vidin, Nish and other towns during recent years. The Bulgarians welcomed the Russian troops as liberators from the Turks, they joined them in attacks on Turkish positions, but few signed up as volunteers, and there were only small, sporadic uprisings, nearly all of them put down with brutal violence by Omer Pasha's men. In Stara Zagora, where the largest Bulgarian revolt took place, dozens of women and young girls were raped by Turkish troops.[15]

In January 1854 the British consul in Wallachia noted that the occupying force was 'actively engaged in enrolling a corps of volunteers comprised principally of Greeks, Albanians, Serbs and Bulgarians'. They were incorporated into the Russian army as a 'Greek-Slavonic Legion'. So far only a thousand volunteers had been recruited, the consul reported. Called up to fight a 'holy war' against the Turks, 'they are to form a body of crusaders, to be equipped and armed at the expense of the Russian military authorities', he noted. The volunteers were known as the 'cross-carriers', because they wore on their shakos a 'red Orthodox cross on a white background'. According to a Russian officer, nearly all these volunteers had to be employed as police auxiliaries to maintain order in the rear, although they had received training for military purposes. The repressive nature of the Russian occupation, with public meetings closed, local councils taken over by the military, censorship tightened and food and transport requisitioned by the troops, bred widespread resentment. The Russians were despised by the Moldavians and Wallachians, the British consul reported, 'and everybody laughs at them when it can be done with safety'. There were dozens of uprisings in the countryside against the requisitioning, some of them repressed by the Cossacks with ruthless violence, killing peasants and burning villages. Omer Pasha's Turkish forces also carried out a war of terror against dozens of Bulgarian settlements – destroying churches, beheading priests, mutilating murder victims and raping girls – to deter others from rising up against them or sending volunteers to the Russians.[16]

Omer Pasha was even more concerned to prevent the Russians breaking through to Serbia, on the Turkish flank, where there was strong support for an uprising in favour of the Russians among the Serbian Orthodox clergy and some sections of the peasantry (suggesting that the Tsar's assessment and preference for an attack towards Serbia had been right). The commander of the Turkish forces concentrated his defences in the strategic area around Vidin, the eastern gateway to Serb lands on the Danube, and in late December used 18,000 troops to drive 4,000 Russians from Cetatea on the other side of the river (in a foretaste of the sort of fighting yet to come in the Crimean War the Turks killed more than a thousand wounded Russians left behind on the battlefield).[17]

The urgency with which the Turks defended Serbia was dictated by the country's instability. Prince Alexander, who ruled under licence from the Porte, had lost all authority, and pro-Russian elements in the Serbian Church and court were actively preparing for an uprising against his government timed to coincide with the anticipated arrival of Russian troops in Serbia. The leaders of the Serb army were resigned to and even colluding in a Russian takeover, according to the British consul in Belgrade. In January 1854 the commander-in-chief of the Serbian army told him that it was 'pointless to resist a power as invincible as Russia, which would conquer the Balkans and turn Constantinople into the capital of Orthodox Slavdom'.[18]

If Serbia was lost, there was a real danger that the entire Balkans would rebel against the Ottomans. From Serbia it was not far to Thessaly and Epirus, where 40,000 Greeks were already organized in armed rebellion against the Turks and were supported by the government in Athens, which took the opportunity provided by the Russian occupation of the principalities to start a war with Turkey for the rebellious territories. Warned by the British not to intervene in Thessaly and Epirus, King Otto chose to ignore them. Gambling on a Russian victory, or at least a prolonged war on the Danube, Otto hoped to win support for his monarchical dictatorship by establishing a greater Greece. Nationalist feelings were running high in Greece in 1853, the 400th anniversary of the fall of Constantinople to the Turks, and many Greeks were looking towards Russia to restore a new Greek empire on the ruins of Byzantium.[19]

*

Afraid of losing all their Balkan territories, the Turks decided to hold a defensive line on the Danube and attack the Russians in the Caucasus, where they could draw on the support of the Muslim tribes, to force them to withdraw some of their troops from the Danubian front. They could count on the support of the Muslim rebels against Russian rule in the Caucasus. In March 1853, Shamil, the imam of the rebel tribesmen, had appealed to the Ottomans for help in his war against the Tsar. 'We your subjects', he had written to the Sultan, 'have lost our strength, having fought the enemies of our Faith for a long time. . . . We have lost all our means and now stand in a disastrous position.' Shamil's army had been squeezed out of its guerrilla bases in Chechnya and Daghestan by the Russian forces, which had steadily increased their numbers since 1845, when Mikhail Vorontsov, the governor-general of New Russia and the Crimea, was appointed commander-in-chief and viceroy of the Caucasus.* Instead of attacking the rebel strongholds directly, Vorontsov had encircled them and starved them out of existence by burning crops and villages; his troops had cut down forests to flush the rebels out and built roads into the insurgent areas. By 1853, the strategy was showing signs of real success: hundreds of Chechen villages had gone over to the Russian side in the hope of being left alone to farm their land; and the rebels had become demoralized. Thinking they had contained the insurgency, the Russians started to reduce their forces in the Caucasus, transferring most of them to the Danubian front. They closed down many of their smaller forts along the Circassian coast.[20]

This was the opportunity the Turks now decided to exploit. A successful war against the Russians in the Caucasus would encourage the Persians and Muslims throughout the Black Sea area, perhaps even leading to the downfall of the Russian Empire in the region. It was also bound to attract the support of the British, who for several years had secretly been running guns and money to the rebels in Circassia and Georgia, and had long been planning to link up with Shamil.[21]

Before 1853, the Turks had not dared support Shamil. By the Treaty of Adrianople (1829), the Porte had agreed to give up all its claims on Russian territories in the Caucasus; and since then the Russians had protected it from Mehmet Ali of Egypt (who had good relations with Shamil). But everything was changed by the Turkish declaration of war. On 9 October the Sultan answered Shamil's appeal, calling on him to launch a 'holy war' for the defence of Islam and to attack the Russians in the Caucasus in collaboration with the Anatolian army under the command of Abdi Pasha. Anticipating this, Shamil had al-

---

* It is one of the ironies of the Crimean War that Sidney Herbert, the British Secretary at War in 1852–5, was the nephew of this senior Russian general and Anglophile. Mikhail was the son of Count Semyon Vorontsov, who lived for forty-seven years in London, most of them after his retirement as Russia's ambassador. Semyon's daughter Catherine married George Herbert, the Earl of Pembroke. A general in the war against Napoleon, Mikhail was appointed governor-general of New Russia in 1823. He did a great deal to establish Odessa, where he built a magnificent palace, promoted the development of steamships on the Black Sea and fought in the war against the Turks in 1828–9. Following the Anglophile traditions of his family, Vorontsov built a fabulous Anglo-Moorish palace at Alupka on the Crimea's southern coast, where the British delegation to the Yalta Conference stayed in 1945.

ready marched with 10,000 men towards Tbilisi, and further volunteers were moved up from Circassia and Abkhazia for an assault on the Russian military capital. On 17 October the British consul in Erzurum told the Foreign Office in London that Shamil had placed 20,000 troops at the disposal of Abdi Pasha to fight against Russia. Eight days later the Turkish campaign in the Caucasus began when the Bashi Bazouks of Abdi Pasha's army in Ardahan captured the important Russian fortress of St Nicholas (Shekvetili in Georgian), to the north of Batumi, killing up to a thousand Cossacks and, according to a report by Prince Menshikov, the commander-in-chief, torturing hundreds of civilians, raping women and taking shiploads of Georgian boys and girls to sell as slaves in Constantinople.[22]

To support their land offensive in the Caucasus the Turks depended on their Black Sea fleet to bring in supplies. The Turkish fleet had never fully recovered from its crushing defeat at Navarino in 1827. According to the British naval adviser to the Porte, Adolphus Slade, the Turkish navy in 1851 had 15,000 sailors and 68 vessels in more or less seaworthy condition, but it lacked good officers and most of its sailors were untrained. Although no match for the Russian fleet, the Turkish navy grew in confidence in late October, when the French and British fleets dropped anchor in Beykoz, a suburb of Constantinople in the Bosporus: with five line-of-battle ships (two- or three-decked vessels with at least seventy guns each), eleven twin-deckers, four frigates and thirteen steamers, their combined power was more than enough to keep the Russian fleet at bay. The Russian Black Sea Fleet was divided into two squadrons: one under Admiral Vladimir Kornilov patrolled the western half of the Black Sea; the other under Vice-Admiral Pavel Nakhimov patrolled the eastern half. Both had orders from Menshikov to destroy any Turkish ships carrying supplies to the Caucasus. The Turkish ministers and senior commanders were aware of the enemy's patrols but resolved nonetheless to send a small fleet into the Black Sea. The Russians had every reason to believe that the Turkish ships were carrying arms and men to the Caucasus, as indeed they were. But the Turks were confident that if their ships were attacked by the Russians, the British and the French would come to their rescue. Perhaps that was indeed their aim – to provoke an attack by the Russians and thereby force the Western powers to become involved in a naval war in the Black Sea. They certainly seemed indifferent to the precarious situation of their fleet, which lay anchored in Sinope on the Anatolian coast, within easy range of Nakhimov's larger and more powerful squadron (six modern battleships, two frigates and three steamers).[23]

On 30 November Nakhimov gave the order of attack. The heavy guns and explosive shells of his squadron obliterated the Turkish fleet. It was the first time explosive shells were used in a sea battle. The Russians had designed an advanced type of shell that penetrated into the wooden planking of the Turkish ships before releasing its explosive charge, ripping them apart from the inside. Slade was on the single Turkish ship that got away, a paddle steamer called *Taif*. He left this account:

> In one hour or one hour and a half, the action had virtually ceased, save dropping shot here and there from the want of means on one side to continue it, half the crews of the Turkish Ships were slain, their guns were mostly dismounted and their sides literally beaten in by the number and weight of the enemy's shot. Some of the ships were on fire. . . . The Russians cheered, they had obtained the object for which they had come into the bay, the destruction of the Turkish Squadron, and on every consideration they should then have ceased firing, and had they done so, they would have avoided merited censure, but they reopened their fire on the stranded hulks, and in addition to the ships already engaged, their frigates came into the Bay to range close to them and complete their demolition. Many men thus lost their lives either by the shot or by drowning in their attempts to reach the shore . . . Together with the ships the Russians destroyed the Turkish quarter of Sinope with shells and carcasses, the ruin is complete, not a house is standing, the inhabitants having followed the Governor in their flights from the town at the first shot.

According to Slade, the Russian attack killed 2,700 Turkish sailors, out of a total of 4,200 at Sinope. In the town there was chaos and destruction everywhere. Cafés became makeshift hospitals. There were hundreds of wounded civilians but just three doctors in the town. Six days passed before the Russians ceased their bombardment and the wounded could be taken off in ships to Constantinople.[24]

A few days later Slade related the details of the battle to the Porte. He found the ministers strangely unaffected by the news – reinforcing the suspicion that the Turks had provoked the attack by the Russians to bring the Western powers into the war:

> Their cheerful cushioned apartment and sleek fur-robed persons deepened in imagination, by the force of contrast, the gloom of the dingy cafés of Sinope with their writhing occupants. They listened, apparently unconcerned, to the woeful tale; they regarded composedly a panoramic view of the Bay of Sinope, taken a few days after the action by Lieutenant O'Reilly of the *Retribution*. A stranger, ignorant of the *nil admirari* of Ottomans, would have fancied them listening to an account and looking at a picture of a disaster in Chinese waters.[25]

In fact, the defeat gave new life to diplomatic efforts from the Porte. It was a sign of Reshid's influence and his determination to prevent an escalation of the war. In his view, one last effort to involve the Western powers in a settlement was needed if they were to be won over to the Turkish side in the event of a general war.

On 5 December, Count Buol, the Austrian Foreign Minister, presented to the Russians a set of peace terms from the Porte which had been agreed by the four powers (Austria, Prussia, Britain and France) at the Vienna Conference. If the Tsar agreed to the immediate evacuation of the Danubian principalities, the Turks would send representatives to negotiate a peace directly with the Russians under international supervision. They promised to renew their treaties with Russia and accept her proposals regarding the Holy Lands. On 18 December the Grand Council resolved to accept peace on these conditions.

In Constantinople, there were angry demonstrations by religious students against the decision of the Grand Council. 'For the last three days the Turkish capital has been in a state of insurrection,' reported Stratford Canning on the 23rd. The students gathered in illegal assemblies and threatened Reshid Pasha and the other ministers. There were rumours of a massacre of Christians in the European quarters of the city. Stratford invited diplomats and their families to take shelter in the British embassy. He wrote to Reshid Pasha urging him to stand firm against the students, but Reshid, who was not known for his personal courage, had resigned and was hiding from the mob in his son's house at Besiktas. Stratford was unable to reach him. Fearing a religious revolution, he brought up several steamers from the British fleet at Beykoz to the centre of the capital, and went to the Sultan to demand firm measures against the potential insurrectionaries. The next day, 160 religious students were arrested by the police and brought before the Grand Council. Asked to account for their insurrection, their leaders replied 'that the conditions prescribed by the Koran for peace after war had been disregarded' by the Grand Council. After it was explained that the Porte had not made peace, only set the conditions for negotiations, the students were asked whether they would like to go to the battlefront, if they wanted war so much, but they replied that their duty was to preach and not to fight. They were sent into exile in Crete instead.[26]

News of Sinope reached London on 11 December. The destruction of the Turkish fleet was a justified action by the Russians, who were after all at war with Turkey, but the British press immediately declared it a 'violent outrage' and a 'massacre', and made wildly exaggerated claims of 4,000 civilians killed by the Russians. 'Sinope', declared *The Times*, 'dispels the hopes we have been led to entertain of pacification . . . We have thought it our duty to uphold and defend the cause of peace as long as peace was compatible with the honour and dignity of our country . . . but the Emperor of Russia has thrown down the gauntlet to the maritime Powers . . . and now war has begun in earnest.' The *Chronicle* declared: 'We shall draw the sword, if draw it we must, not only to preserve the independence of an ally, but to humble the ambitions and thwart the machinations of a despot whose intolerable pretensions have made him the enemy of all civilized nations.' The provincial press followed the bellicose and Russophobic line of Fleet Street. 'Mere talking to the Tsar will do nothing,' argued an editorial in the *Sheffield and Rotherham Independent*. 'The time appears to be at hand when we must act so as to dissipate the evil designs and efforts of Russia.' In London, Manchester, Rochdale, Sheffield, Newcastle and many other towns, there were public meetings in defence of Turkey. In Paisley, the anti-Russian propagandist David Urquhart addressed a crowd for two hours, ending with a plea to 'the people of England . . . to call on their Sovereign to require that either war shall be proclaimed against Russia, or the British squadron withdrawn from the Turkish waters'. Newspapers published petitions to the Queen demanding a more active stand against Russia.[27]

The position of the British government – a fragile coalition of Liberals and free-trade Conservatives weakly held together by Lord Aberdeen – was dramatically altered by the public reaction to Sinope. At first the government reacted calmly to the news. Most of the cabinet took the view of the Prime Minister that more time should be given to the peace initiatives promoted by the Austrians. It was agreed that the British and French fleets would have to make their presence felt in the Black Sea, but that this show of naval strength should be used to force the Russians to accept peace talks rather than provoke a war. There was a general feeling that Britain should not be dragged into a war by the Turks, who had brought the disaster on themselves. As Queen Victoria herself had warned:

> we have taken on ourselves in conjunction with France all the risks of a European war without having bound Turkey to any conditions with respect to provoking it. The hundred and twenty fanatical Turks constituting the Divan at Constantinople are left sole judges of the line of policy to be pursued, and made cognisant at the same time of the fact that England and France have bound themselves to defend the Turkish territory! This is entrusting them with a power which Parliament has been jealous to confide even to the hands of the British Crown.[28]

At this stage the Queen agreed with Aberdeen that the invasion of the principalities should not be taken as a cause of war against Russia. Like him, she was still inclined to trust the Tsar, whom she had met and come to like ten years before, and thought that his aggressive actions might be curbed. Her private views were anti-Turk, which also had a bearing on her attitude to the Russian invasion. Before Sinope, Victoria had written in her journal that it 'would be in the interest of peace, and a great advantage generally, were the Turks to be well beaten'. Afterwards she took a different view of the invasion, hoping that a Russian beating of the Turks would make both sides more amenable to European peace initiatives. 'A decided victory of the Russians by *land*, may, and I *trust will* have a pacifying effect by rendering the Emperor magnanimous and the Turks amenable to reason,' she noted in her journal on 15 December.[29]

Standing up to the Turkish war mood was one thing; it was quite another to resist the war cries of the British press, especially when Palmerston, who had resigned from the cabinet on 14 December, ostensibly over parliamentary reform, was adding his own voice to the chorus of demands for military action – his aim being to challenge the peace-loving Aberdeen from outside the government by rallying public opinion behind his own campaign for a more aggressive foreign policy. Palmerston maintained that the action at Sinope was an indirect attack upon the Western powers, which had sent their warships into the Bosporus as a warning to Russia. 'The sultan's squadron was destroyed in a Turkish harbour where the English and French fleets, if they had been present, would have protected it,' he explained to Seymour. Sinope was proof of Russian aggression – it was the moral pretext Britain needed (and Palmerston had been looking for) to destroy the Russian menace in the East – and continuing with the peace talks in Vienna would only make it harder for the Western powers to fight this 'just and necessary war'. In the cabinet, Palmerston was supported by Russell, the Leader of the Commons, and crucially by Clarendon, the Foreign Secretary, who swung round to Palmerston's position when he sensed the public reaction to the destruction of the Turkish fleet (the Queen noted in her journal on 15 December that he had become 'more warlike than he was, from fear of the newspapers'). 'You think I care too much for public opinion,' he wrote to Aberdeen on 18 December, 'but really when the frightful carnage at Sinope comes to be known we shall be utterly disgraced if upon the mere score of humanity we don't take active measures to prevent any more such outrages.'[30]

With Palmerston out of the cabinet, it fell to Clarendon to make the running for the war party. Sinope had demonstrated that the Russians had 'no real intention of making peace even if the Turks propose reasonable terms', Clarendon told Aberdeen, so there was no point in talking to them any more. He urged the Prime Minister to use Sinope as a 'moral argument' to reject the Austrian peace initiative and take strong measures against Russia. Determined to undermine the peace negotiations, he told Stratford to instruct the Turks to toughen their position, and warned Buol that Austria was too soft on Russia. It was too late for talks, he told Lord Cowley, the British ambassador in

Paris; the time had come for the Western powers to 'finish up Russia as a naval power in the East'.[31]

French support was crucial to Palmerston and the war party in the British cabinet. Napoleon was determined to use Sinope as a pretext to take strong action against Russia, partly from the calculation that it was an opportunity to cement an alliance with Britain, and partly from the belief that an emperor of France should not tolerate the humiliation of his fleet, should the Russian action go unpunished. On 19 December Napoleon proposed that the French and British fleets should enter the Black Sea and force all Russian warships to return to Sevastopol. He even threatened that the French would act alone, if Britain refused. This was enough to make Aberdeen reluctantly capitulate: fear of a resurgent France, if not fear of Russia, had forced his hand. On 22 December it was agreed that a combined fleet would protect Turkish shipping in the Black Sea. Palmerston returned to the cabinet, the undisputed leader of the war party, on Christmas Eve.[32]

*

But the origins of the Crimean War cannot be understood by studying only the motives of statesmen and diplomats. This was a war – the first war in history – to be brought about by the pressure of the press and by public opinion. With the development of the railways enabling the emergence of a national press in the 1840s and 1850s, public opinion became a potent force in British politics, arguably overshadowing the influence of Parliament and the cabinet itself. *The Times*, the country's leading newspaper, had long been closely associated with the Conservative Party; but increasingly it acted and perceived itself as nothing less than a national institution, a 'Fourth Estate', in the words of Henry Reeve, its chief for foreign affairs, who wrote of his profession in 1855: 'Journalism is not the instrument by which the various divisions of the ruling class express themselves: it is rather the instrument by means of which the aggregate intelligence of the nation criticizes and controls them all. It is indeed the "Fourth Estate" of the Realm: not merely the written counterpart and voice of the speaking Third.' The government had little choice but to recognize this new reality. 'An English Minister must please the newspapers,' lamented

Aberdeen, a Conservative of the old school who moved between the palace and his Pall Mall club. 'The newspapers are always bawling for interference. They are bullies, and they make the Government a bully.'[33]

Palmerston

Palmerston was the first really modern politician in this sense. He understood the need to cultivate the press and appeal in simple terms to the public in order to create a mass-based political constituency. The issue that allowed him to achieve this was the war against Russia. His foreign policy captured the imagination of the British public as the embodiment of their own national character and popular ideals: it was

Protestant and freedom-loving, energetic and adventurous, confident and bold, belligerent in its defence of the little man, proudly British, and contemptuous of foreigners, particularly those of the Roman Catholic and Orthodox religion, whom Palmerston associated with the worst vices and excesses of the Continent. The public loved his verbal commitment to liberal interventionism abroad: it reinforced their John Bull view that Britain was the greatest country in the world and that the task of government should be to export its way of life to those less fortunate who lived beyond its shores.

Palmerston became so popular, and his foreign policy became so closely linked to the defence of 'British values' in the public mind, that anyone who tried to halt the drift to war was likely to be vilified by the patriotic press. That was the fate of the pacifists, the radical free-traders Richard Cobden and John Bright, whose refusal to see Russia as a threat to British interests (which in their view were better served by trading with Russia) led to the press denouncing them as 'pro-Russian' and therefore 'un-English'. Even Prince Albert, whose Continental habits were disliked, found himself attacked as a German or Russian (many people seemed incapable of distinguishing between the two). He was accused of treason by the press, notably by the *Morning Advertiser* (the 'red top' of its day), after it was rumoured that a court intrigue had been responsible for the resignation of Palmerston in December. When Palmerston returned to office it was widely reported by the more scurrilous end of the press that Albert had been sent as a traitor to the Tower of London, and crowds assembled there to catch a glimpse of the imprisoned Prince. The *Morning Advertiser* even called for his execution, adding for good measure: 'Better that a few drops of guilty blood should be shed on a scaffold on Tower Hill than that a country should be baulked of its desire for war!' Queen Victoria was so outraged that she threatened to abdicate. Aberdeen and Russell talked to the editors of all the major papers on the Queen's behalf, but the answer they received held out little hope of an end to the campaign: the editors themselves had approved the stories, and in some cases had even written them, because they sold newspapers.[34]

In the popular imagination the struggle against Russia involved 'British principles' – the defence of liberty, civilization and free trade. The protection of Turkey against Russia was associated with the gallant

British virtue of championing the helpless and the weak against tyrants and bullies. Hatred of the Russians turned the Turks into paragons of virtue in the public estimation – a romantic view that had its origins in 1849 when the Turks had given refuge to the Hungarian and Polish freedom-fighters against tsarist oppression. When an Association for the Protection of Turkey and Other Countries from Partition was established by the Turcophile Urquhart at the start of 1854 it was quickly joined by several thousand radicals.

The issue of defending the Muslim Turks against the Christian Russians represented a major obstacle for Anglican Conservatives like Aberdeen and Gladstone and indeed the Queen, whose religious sympathies made her hostile to the Turks (privately, she wanted the establishment of a 'Greek empire' to replace the Ottomans in Europe and hoped the Turks in time 'would *all* become Christians').[35] The obstacle was brushed aside by Evangelical radicals who pointed to the Tanzimat reforms as evidence of Turkish liberalism and religious tolerance. Some Church leaders even argued that the Turks had contributed to the spread of Protestantism in the Near East – an idea largely based on the missionary work of the Protestants in the Ottoman Empire. Forbidden by the Porte to convert Muslims, Anglican missionaries had concentrated instead on the Orthodox and Catholics, and every convert came with tales of the evil conduct of their priests. The issue was addressed by Lord Shaftesbury in a debate in the House of Lords on the Ottoman suppression of the Greek revolts in Thessaly and Epirus. In a speech inspired by Evangelical missionary zeal, Shaftesbury argued that the Balkan Christians were as much the victims of the Greek Orthodox priesthood and their Russian backers as they were of the Turkish authorities. From the viewpoint of converting Christians to the Protestant religion, Shaftesbury concluded, Turkish rule was preferable to the increased influence of the Tsar, who did not even allow the circulation of the Bible in Russian in his own lands.* Should the Russians conquer the Balkans, the same darkness would descend and all hopes for the Protestant religion would be lost in the region. The Porte, by contrast, Shaftesbury maintained, was not hostile to the missionary work of the Anglicans: it had

---

* There was no Russian Bible – only a Psalter and a Book of Hours – until the 1870s.

intervened to protect Protestant converts from persecution by other Christians, and had even granted *millet* status to the Protestant religion in 1850 (he failed to mention that converts from Islam were put to death under Ottoman law). Like many Anglicans, Shaftesbury drew a sympathetic picture of Islam, whose quiet rituals seemed more in keeping with their own forms of contemplative prayer than the loud and semi-pagan rituals of the Orthodox. Such ideas were commonplace in the Evangelical community. At a public meeting to discuss the Russo-Turkish conflict in December, for example, one speaker insisted that 'The Turk was not infidel. He was Unitarian.' 'As to the Russian Greeks or Greek Christians,' it was reported by the *Newcastle Guardian*, 'he said nothing against their creed, but they were a besotted, dancing, fiddling race. He spoke from personal observation.'[36]

The mere mention of the Sultan's name was enough to evoke tumultuous applause. At one meeting in a theatre in Chester, for example, two thousand people passed by acclamation a resolution calling on the government to assist the Sultan 'by the strongest warlike measures', on the grounds that

> there is no sovereign in Europe who has higher claims than the Sultan to the support of this country: no sovereign who has done more for religious toleration; for he has established religious equality in his dominions. It would be no dishonour to Englishmen if they were to rank him with the Alfreds and Edwards; and if properly supported at the present crisis by the nations of West Europe, he will make his dominions happy and prosperous and establish commercial relations of mutual advantage between them and Great Britain.

When *The Times* suggested that the Balkan Christians might prefer the protection of the Tsar to the continued rule of the Sultan, it was rounded on with vehement nationalistic overtones by the *Morning Herald* and the *Morning Advertiser*, which accused it of being un-English: 'It is printed in the English language, but that is the only thing English about it. It is, where Russia is concerned, Russian all over.'[37]

In France, too, the press was an active influence on Napoleon's foreign policy. The greatest pressure came from the Catholic provincial press, which had been calling for war against Russia since the beginning of the Holy Lands dispute. Their calls became ever louder after the news of Sinope. 'A war with Russia is regrettable but necessary and unavoidable,' argued an editorial in the *Union franc-comtoise* on 1 January 1854, because 'if France and Britain fail to stop the Russian menace in Turkey, they too will be enslaved to the Russians like the Turks'.

The leitmotif of this anti-Russian propaganda was 'the crusade of civilization against barbarism' – a theme that also dominates the Russophobic best-seller of 1854, Gustave Doré's *Histoire pittoresque, dramatique et caricaturale de la Sainte Russie*. The main idea of Doré's prototype cartoon – that Russia's barbarism was the source of her aggression – was a commonplace of the pro-war lobby on both sides of the Channel. In Britain, it was used to counteract the argument of Cobden and Bright that Russia was too backward to invade England: a campaign of publicity was launched to document the case that *because* Russia was so backward it needed to increase its resources through territorial expansion. In France the argument had stronger cultural overtones, inviting comparison between the Russians and the Huns. 'The Emperor Nicholas is rather like Attila,' claimed an editorial in the newspaper the *Impartial* in late January 1854.

> To pretend otherwise is to overturn all notions of order and justice. Falsity in politics and falsity in religion – that is what Russia represents. Its barbarity, which tries to ape our civilization, inspires our mistrust; its despotism fills us with horror ... Its despotism is suitable perhaps for a population that crawls on the boundary of animality like a herd of fanatical beasts; but it is not suitable for a civilized people. ... The policies of Nicholas have raised a storm of indignation in all the civilized states of Europe; these are the policies of rape and pillage; they are brigandage on a vast scale.[38]

For the Ultramontane press, the greatest threat to Western civilization was Russia's religion. If the westward march of the Tsar's armies was not stopped, it was argued, Christendom would be taken over by the Orthodox and a new age of religious persecution would enslave the Catholics. 'If we allow the Russians to take over Turkey,' wrote the editor of the *Union franc-comtoise*, 'we will soon see the Greek heresy imposed by Cossack arms on all of us; Europe will lose not just its liberty but its religion ... We will be forced to watch our children become educated in the Greek schism and the Catholic religion will perish in the frozen deserts of Siberia where those who raise their voices to defend it will be sent.' Echoing the words of the Cardinal of Paris, the *Spectateur de Dijon* called on the Catholics of France to fight a 'holy war' against the Russians and the Greeks in defence of their religious heritage:

> Russia represents a special menace to all Catholics and none of us should misunderstand it. The Emperor Nicholas talks of privileges for the Greeks at the Holy Sepulchre, privileges bought with Russian blood. Centuries will pass before the Russians shed a fraction of the blood that the French spilled in the crusades for the Holy Places ... We have a heritage to conserve there, an interest to defend. But that is not all. We are directly threatened by the proselytism of the Greek-Russian Church. We know that in St Petersburg they harbour dreams of imposing a religious autocracy on the West. They hope to convert us to their heresy by the limitless expansion of their military power. If Russia is installed in the Bosporus, it will conquer Rome as quickly as Marseilles. A swift attack would be enough to remove the Pope and cardinals before anyone could intervene.

For the Catholic provincial press, this holy war would also be a chance to reinforce religious discipline at home – to counteract the Revolution's secularizing influence and restore the Church to the centre of national life. Frenchmen who had been divided by the barricades in 1848 would now be reunited through the defence of their faith.[39]

Napoleon seized on this idea. No doubt he imagined that a glorious war would reconcile the nation to the repressive army of his *coup d'état*. But his enthusiasm was never really shared by the French people, who remained on the whole indifferent to the Holy Lands dispute and the Eastern Question, even after news had reached them of the battle of Sinope. It was Napoleon who talked of following the 'path of honour' and fighting against Russian aggression; it was the press that voiced the 'outrage of the French public'; but according to the reports of the local prefects and procurators, the ordinary people were unmoved. Although the French would fight – and die – in the Crimea in far greater numbers than the British, they were never as excited by the causes of the war as their allies were. If anything, the French were hostile to the idea of a war in which they would be allied with the English, their traditional enemy. It was widely felt that France was being dragged into a war that would be fought for British imperial interests – a theme constantly invoked by the opposition to Napoleon – and that France would pay the price for it. The business world was especially opposed to the idea of war, fearing higher taxes and a drain on the economy. There were predictions that before a year was out any war would become so unpopular that France would be forced to sue for peace.

By the end of January, anti-war feelings had spread to the Emperor's entourage. At a council of senior officials assembled by Napoleon to discuss Russia's protest against the arrival of the French and British fleets in the Black Sea on 4 January, two of the Emperor's closest political allies, Jean Bineau, the Minister of Finance, and Achille Fould, a councillor of state, argued for an accommodation with Russia to avoid sliding into war. They were concerned by the lack of military preparations: the army was not mobilized or ready for a war in the early months of 1854, having been reduced to calm British fears of a French invasion after the *coup d'état* of December 1851. Bineau even threatened to resign if war broke out, on the grounds that it would become impossible to raise the necessary taxes without major social upheavals (a threat he did not carry out). Napoleon was sufficiently sobered by these dissenting voices to think again about his plans for war and renew the search for a diplomatic resolution of the crisis. On 29 January he wrote directly to the Tsar, offering to negotiate a settlement with the mediation of the Austrians and suggesting as the basis of negotiations that the French and British might withdraw their fleets from the Black Sea if the Tsar withdrew his troops from the Danubian principalities. Napoleon's letter was publicized at once – a move designed to prove to the anxious French public that he was doing everything he could for peace, as he himself confided to Baron Hübner, the Austrian ambassador in Paris.[40]

Palmerston and his war party kept a close eye on the French. They were worried that Napoleon would try to back out of a military showdown with Russia at the last minute, and used every means at their disposal to stiffen his resolve and undermine his efforts at a diplomatic settlement. It was the British, not the French, who wanted war and pushed hardest for it in the early months of 1854.

*

Their task was made easier by the Tsar's intransigence. On 16 February Russia broke off relations with Britain and France, withdrawing its ambassadors from London and Paris. Five days later the Tsar rejected Napoleon's proposal for a quid pro quo on the Black Sea and the principalities. He proposed instead that the Western fleets should stop the Turks from carrying weapons to Russia's Black Sea coasts – a clear allusion to the causes of Sinope. On this condition, and on it alone, he offered to negotiate with the Porte's envoy in St Petersburg. Realizing that his defiant stand invited war, he warned Napoleon that Russia would be the same in 1854 as it had been in 1812.

It was an astonishingly blunt rebuff for the Tsar to make towards the French, who had offered him his best way to escape a showdown with the British and the Turks. The French approach was his last chance to avoid total isolation on the Continent. He had tried to build ties with the Austrians and Prussians at the end of January, sending Count Orlov to Vienna with a proposal that Russia would defend Austria against the Western powers (an obvious reference to Franz Joseph's fears that Napoleon would stir up trouble for the Habsburgs in Italy) if they signed a declaration of neutrality together with Prussia and the other German states. But the Austrians were alarmed by the Russian offensive in the Balkans – they would not listen to the Tsar's suggestion that they join in the partition of the Ottoman Empire – and made it clear that they would not cooperate with the Russians unless the Turkish borders remained unchanged. They were so concerned by the threat of a Serb rising in support of the Russian offensive that they placed 25,000 additional troops on their frontier with Serbia.[41]

By 9 February the Tsar knew that Orlov had failed in his mission. He had also learned that the Austrians were preparing to send their troops actually into Serbia to prevent its occupation by his troops. So it seems extraordinary that he should reject the one chance he had left – Napoleon's overture – to avoid a war against the Western powers, a war he must have feared that he would lose, if Austria opposed

Russia. It is tempting to believe, as some historians do, that Nicholas had finally lost all sense of proportion, that the tendency to mental disturbance with which he had been born – his impulsiveness and rash behaviour and melancholic irritability – had become mixed with the arrogance acquired by an autocratic ruler after almost thirty years of listening to sycophants.[42] In the crisis of 1853–4 he behaved at times like a reckless gambler who overplays his hand: after years of patient play to build up Russia's position in the Near East, he was risking everything on a war against the Turks, desperately staking his entire winnings on a single turn of the wheel.

But was this really gambling from his point of view? We know from Nicholas's private writings that he took confidence from comparisons with 1812. He constantly referred to his older brother's war against Napoleon as a reason why it was possible for Russia to fight alone against the world. 'If Europe forces me to go to war,' he wrote in February, 'I will follow the example of my brother Alexander in 1812, I will venture into uncompromising war against it, I will retreat if necessary to behind the Urals, and will not put down arms as long as the feet of foreign forces trample anywhere on Russian land.'[43]

This was not a reasoned argument. It was not based on any calculation of the armed forces at his disposal or any careful thought about the practical difficulties the Russians would face in fighting against the superior forces of the European powers, difficulties often pointed out by Menshikov and his other senior commanders, who had warned him several times not to provoke war with Turkey and the Western powers by invading the Danubian principalities. It was a purely emotional reaction, based on the Tsar's pride and arrogance, on his inflated sense of Russian power and prestige, and perhaps above all on his deeply held belief that he was engaged in a religious war to complete Russia's providential mission in the world. In all sincerity Nicholas believed that he had been called by God to wage a holy war for the liberation of the Orthodox from Muslim rule, and nothing would divert him from this 'divine cause'. As he explained to Frederick William, the Prussian king, in March 1854, he was prepared to fight this war alone, against the Western powers, if they sided with the Turks:

Waging war neither for worldly advantages nor for conquests, but for a solely Christian purpose, must I be left alone to fight under the banner of the Holy Cross and to see the others, who call themselves Christians, all unite around the Crescent to combat Christendom? . . . Nothing is left to me but to fight, to win, or to perish with honour, as a martyr of our holy faith, and when I say this I declare it in the name of all Russia.[44]

These were not the words of a reckless gambler; they were the calculations of a believer.

Rebuffed by the Tsar, Napoleon had no option but to add his signature to the British ultimatum to the Russians to withdraw from the principalities: for him it was an issue of national honour and prestige. Sent to the Tsar on 27 February, the ultimatum stated that, if he did not reply within six days, a state of war would automatically come into existence between the Western powers and Russia. There was no reference to peace talks any more – no opportunity was given to the Tsar to come back with terms – so the purpose of the ultimatum was clearly to precipitate a war. It was a foregone conclusion that the Tsar would reject the ultimatum – he considered it beneath his dignity even to make a reply – so as soon as they had sent their ultimatum the Western powers were in effect acting as if war had already been declared. By the end of February, troops were being mobilized.

Antoine Cetty, the quartermaster of the French army, wrote to Marshal de Castellane on 24 February:

The Tsar has replied negatively [to Napoleon's letter]; it only now remains to prepare for war. The Emperor's thinking was to do everything in his power not to send an expeditionary force to the East, but England carried us away in its headlong rush to war. It was impossible to permit an English flag to hang without our own on the walls of Constantinople. Wherever England treads alone, she rapidly becomes the sole mistress and does not let go of her prey.

This was about the sum of it. At the moment of decision, Napoleon had hesitated over war. But in the end he needed the alliance with the British, and feared losing out in the share-out of the spoils if he did not join them in a war for the defence of Western interests in the Near East. The French Emperor confessed as much in a speech to the Senate and Legislative Assembly on 2 March:

> France has as great an interest as England – perhaps a greater interest – to ensure that the influence of Russia does not permanently extend to Constantinople; because to reign at Constantinople means to reign over the Mediterranean; and I think that none of you, gentlemen, will say that only England has vital interests in this sea, which washes three hundred leagues of our shores. ... Why are we going to Constantinople? We are going there with England to defend the Sultan's cause, and no less to protect the right of the Christians; we are going there to defend the freedom of the seas and our rightful influence in the Mediterranean.[45]

In fact, it was far from clear what the allies would be fighting for. Like so many wars, the allied expedition to the East began with no one really knowing what it was about. The reasons for the war would take months for the Western powers to work out through long-drawn-out negotiations between themselves and the Austrians during 1854. Even after they had landed in the Crimea, in September, the allies were a long way from agreement about the objectives of the war.

The French and the British had different ideas from the start. During March there was a series of conferences in Paris to discuss their aims and strategy. The French argued for a Danubian campaign as well as a Crimean one. If Austria and Prussia could be persuaded to join the war on the allies' side, the French favoured a large-scale land offensive in the principalities and southern Russia, combined with an Austrian-Prussian campaign in Poland. But the British mistrusted the Austrians – they thought they were too soft on Russia – and did not want to be committed to an alliance with them which might inhibit their own more ambitious plans against Russia.

The British cabinet was divided over its war aims and strategy. Aberdeen insisted on a limited campaign to restore the sovereignty of Turkey, while Palmerston and his war party argued for a more aggressive offensive to roll back Russian influence in the Near East and bring Russia to its knees. The two sides reached a sort of compromise through the naval strategy drawn up by Sir James Graham, the First

Lord of the Admiralty, which had taken shape in reaction to Sinope in December 1853. Graham's plan was to launch a swift attack on Sevastopol to destroy the Russian Black Sea Fleet and seize the Crimea before the opening of the more important spring campaign in the Baltic which would bring British forces to St Petersburg – a strategy developed from plans already made in the event of a war against France (for Sevastopol read Cherbourg).[46]

As Britain moved onto a military footing in the early months of 1854, the idea of a limited campaign for the defence of Turkey became lost in the war fever that swept the country. Britain's war aims escalated, not just from the bellicose chauvinism of the press but from the belief that the war's immense potential costs demanded larger objectives, 'worthy of Britain's honour and greatness'. Palmerston was always returning to this theme. His war aims changed in detail but never in their anti-Russian character. In a memorandum to the cabinet on 19 March, he outlined an ambitious plan for the dismemberment of the Russian Empire and the redrawing of the European map: Finland and the Aaland Islands would be transferred from Russia to Sweden; the Tsar's Baltic provinces would be given to Prussia; Poland would be enlarged as an independent kingdom and buffer state for Europe against Russia; Austria would gain the Danubian principalities and Bessarabia from the Russians (and be forced to give up northern Italy); the Crimea and Georgia would be given to Turkey; while Circassia would become independent under Turkish protection. The plan called for a major European war against Russia, one involving Austria and Prussia, and ideally Sweden, on the anti-Russian side. It was greeted with a good deal of scepticism in the cabinet. Aberdeen, who was hoping for a short campaign so that his government could 'return zealously to the task of domestic reform', objected that it would require another Thirty Years War. But Palmerston continued to promote his plans. Indeed, the longer the war went on, the more determined he became to advance it, on the grounds that anything less than 'great territorial changes' would not be enough to justify the war's enormous loss of life.[47]

By the end of March, the idea of expanding the defence of Turkey into a broader European war against Russia had gained much support in the British political establishment. Prince Albert was doubtful whether Turkey could be saved, but confident that Russia's influence in Europe could be curbed by a war to deprive her of her western territories. He thought that Prussia could be drawn into this war by promises of 'territory to guard against Russia's pouncing upon her', and advocated measures to get the German states on side as well as to tame the Russian bear, 'whose teeth must be drawn and claws pared'. He wrote to Leopold, the Belgian king: 'All Europe, Belgium and Germany included, have the greatest interest in the integrity and independence of the Porte being secured for the future, but a still greater interest in Russia being defeated and chastised.' Sir Henry Layard, the famous Assyriologist and MP, who served as Under-Secretary of State for Foreign Affairs, called for war until Russia had been 'crippled'. Stratford Canning proposed a war to break up the Tsar's empire 'for the benefit of Poland and other spoliated neighbours to the lasting delivery of Europe from Russian dictation'. In a later letter to Clarendon, Stratford emphasized the need to curb the will of Russia, not just by checking its 'present outbreak' but 'by bringing home to its inner sense a feeling of permanent restraint'. The aim of any war by the European powers should be to destroy the threat of Russia once and for all, argued Stratford, and they should go on fighting until Russia was surrounded by a buffer zone of independent states (the Danubian principalities, the Crimea, Circassia and Poland) to ensure that feeling of restraint. As the government prepared to declare war on Russia, Russell called on Clarendon not to include anything in the Queen's message to Parliament that would commit the Western powers to the existing territorial boundaries of Europe.[48]

Even at this stage Aberdeen was reluctant to declare war. On 26 March, the eve of the British declaration, he told the Queen and Prince Albert that he had been '*dragged* into a *war*' by Palmerston, who had the support of the press and public opinion. Three months earlier, the Queen had shared Aberdeen's reluctance to commit British troops to the defence of the Turks. But now she saw the necessity of war, as she and Albert both explained to the Prime Minister:

> We both repeated our conviction that it was necessary *now*, which he could not deny, and I observed that I thought we could not have avoided it, even if there had been mistakes and misfortunes, that the power and

encroachments of Russia must be resisted. He could not see this, and thought it was a 'bugbear' – that the only Power to be feared was France! – that the 3 Northern Powers ought to keep together, though he could not say on what basis. Of course we were unable to agree with him, and spoke of the state Germany had been placed in by the Empr Nicholas & the impossibility of looking upon the present times as the former ones. Everything has changed. Ld Aberdeen did not like to agree in this, saying that no doubt in a short time this country would have changed its feelings regarding the war, and would be all for Peace.[49]

What she meant by 'everything has changed' is not entirely clear. Perhaps she was thinking of the fact that France had joined in Britain's ultimatum to the Russians and that the first British and French troops had already set sail for Turkey. Or perhaps, like Albert, she thought the time had come to involve the German states in a European war against Russia, whose invasion of the principalities represented a new and present danger to the Continent. But it is also possible that she had in mind the xenophobic press campaign against the Prince Consort – a constant worry in her journal in these months – and had come to realize that a short victorious war would secure public support for the monarchy.

That evening the Queen gave a small family ball to celebrate the birthday of her cousin, the Duke of Cambridge, who was shortly to depart for Constantinople to take up the command of the British 1st Division. Count Vitzthum von Eckstadt, Saxon Minister to London, was invited to the ball:

> The Queen took an active part in the dances, including a Scotch reel with the Duke of Hamilton and Lord Elgin, both of whom wore the national dress. As I had given up waltzing, the Queen danced a quadrille with me, and spoke to me with the most amiable unconstraint of the events of the day, telling me she would be compelled the next morning, to her great regret, to declare war against Russia.

The following morning – a day before the French made their own declaration of war on Russia – the Queen's declaration was read out by Clarendon in Parliament. As the great historian of the Crimean

War Alexander Kinglake wrote (and his words could be applied to any war):

> The labour of putting into writing the grounds for a momentous course of action is a wholesome discipline for statesmen; and it would be well for mankind if, at a time when the question were really in suspense, the friends of a policy leading towards war were obliged to come out of the mist of oral intercourse and private notes, and to put their view into a firm piece of writing.

If such a document had been recorded by those responsible for the Crimean War, it would have disclosed that their real aim was to reduce the size and power of Russia for the benefit of 'Europe' and the Western powers in particular, but this could not be said in the Queen's message, which spoke instead in the vaguest terms of defending Turkey, without any selfish interests, 'for the cause of right against injustice'.[50]

*

As soon as the declaration became public, Church leaders seized upon the war as a righteous struggle and crusade. On Sunday, 2 April pro-war sermons were preached from pulpits up and down the land. Many of them were published in pamphlet form, some even selling tens of thousands of copies, for this was an age when preachers had the status of celebrities in both the Anglican and Nonconformist Church.[51] In Trinity Chapel in Conduit Street, Mayfair, in London, the Reverend Henry Beamish told his congregation that it was a 'Christian duty' for England

> to interpose her power to maintain the independence of a weak ally against the unjustifiable aggression of an ambitious and perfidious despot, and to punish with the arm of her power an act of selfish and barbarous oppression – an oppression the more hateful and destructive, because it is attempted to be justified on the plea of promoting the cause of religious liberty and the highest interests of Christ's kingdom.

On Wednesday, 26 April, a fast-day set aside for 'national humiliation and prayer on the declaration of war', the Reverend T. D. Harford

Battersby preached a sermon in St John's Church, Keswick, in which he declared that

> the conduct of our ambassadors and statesmen has been so honourable and straightforward, so forbearing and moderate in the transactions which have led to this war that there is no cause for humiliation at this time, but rather of strengthening ourselves in our righteousness, and that we should rather present ourselves before God with words of self congratulation and say, 'We thank thee, O God, that we are not as other nations are: unjust, covetous, oppressive, cruel; we are a religious people, we are a Bible-reading, church-going people, we send missionaries into all the earth.'

In Brunswick Chapel, Leeds, on the same day, the Reverend John James said that Russia's offensive against Turkey was an attack 'on the most sacred rights of our common humanity; an outrage standing in the same category as the slave trade, and scarcely inferior to it in crime'. The Balkan Christians, James maintained, had more religious freedom under the Sultan than they would ever have under the Tsar:

> Leave Turkey to the Sultan and, aided by the good offices of France and England, these humble Christians will, by God's blessing, enjoy perfect liberty of conscience.... Hand it over to Russia and their establishments will be broken up; the school-houses closed; and their places of prayer either demolished, or converted into temples of a faith as impure, demoralizing, and intolerant, as Popery itself. What British Christian can hesitate as to the course proper for such a country as ours, in such a case as this? ... It is a Godly war to drive back at any hazard the hordes of the modern Attila, who threatens the liberty and Christianity, not of Turkey only, but of the civilized world.[52]

To mark the embarkation of Britain's 'Christian soldiers' for the East, the Reverend George Croly preached a sermon in St Stephen's Church, Walbrook, in London, in which he maintained that England was engaging in a war for 'the defence of mankind' against the Russians, a 'hopeless and degenerate people' bent upon the conquest of the world. This was a 'religious war' for the defence of the true Western religion against the Greek faith; the 'first Eastern war since the Crusades'. 'If England in the last war [against Napoleon] was the refuge of the principles of freedom, in the next she may be appointed for the refuge of the principles of Religion. May it not be the Divine will that England, after having triumphed as the champion, shall be called to the still loftier distinction of the teacher of mankind?' England's destiny in the East, the Reverend Croly argued, might be advanced by the coming war: it was nothing less than to convert the Turks to Christianity: 'The great work may be slow, difficult, and interrupted by the casualties of kingdoms, or the passions of men – but it will prosper. Why should not the Church of England aid this work? Why not offer up solemn and public prayer at once for the success of our righteous warfare, the return of peace, and the conversion of the infidel?'[53]

To varying degrees, the major parties to the Crimean War – Russia, Turkey, France and Britain – all called religion to the battlefield. Yet by the time the war began, its origins in the Holy Lands had been forgotten and subsumed by the European war against Russia. The Easter celebrations in the Holy Sepulchre 'passed off very quietly' in 1854, according to James Finn, the British consul in Jerusalem. There were few Russian pilgrims because of the outbreak of the war and the Greek services were tightly managed by the Ottoman authorities to prevent a recurrence of the religious fighting that had become common in recent years. Within a few months, the world's attention would be turned to the battlefields of the Crimea, and Jerusalem would disappear from Europe's view, but from the Holy Lands these distant events appeared in a different light. As the British consul in Palestine put it:

> In Jerusalem it was otherwise. These important transactions seemed but superstructures upon the original foundation; for although in diplomacy the matter (the Eastern question) had nominally shifted into a question of religious protection . . . still it had become a settled creed among us that the kernel of it all lay with us in the Holy Places; that the pretensions of St Petersburg to an ecclesiastical protection by virtue of treaty aimed still, as at the very first, at an actual possession of the sanctuaries at the local well-spring of Christianity – that these sanctuaries were in very truth the meed contended for by gigantic athletes at a distance.[54]

6

First Blood to the Turks

In March 1854 a young artillery officer by the name of Leo Tolstoy arrived at the headquarters of General Mikhail Gorchakov. He had joined the army in 1852, the year he had first come to the attention of the literary world with the publication of his memoir *Childhood* in the literary journal the *Contemporary*, the most important monthly periodical in Russia at that time. Dissatisfied with his frivolous way of life as an aristocrat in St Petersburg and Moscow, he had decided to make a fresh start by following his brother Nikolai to the Caucasus when he returned from leave to his army unit there. Tolstoy was attached to an artillery brigade in the Cossack village of Starogladskaya in the northern Caucasus. He took part in raids against Shamil's Muslim army, narrowly escaping capture by the rebels on more than one occasion, but after the outbreak of the war against Turkey, he requested a transfer to the Danubian front. As he explained in a letter to his brother Sergei in November 1853, he wanted to take part in a real war: 'For almost a year now I've been thinking only of how I might sheathe my sword, and I can't do it. But since I'm compelled to fight somewhere or other, I would find it more agreeable to fight in Turkey than here.'[1]

In January Tolstoy passed the officer's examination for the rank of ensign, the lowest-ranking commissioned officer in the tsarist army, and departed for Wallachia, where he was attached to the 12th Artillery Brigade. He travelled sixteen days by sledge through the snows of southern Russia to his estate at Yasnaya Polyana, arriving there on 2 February, and set off again on 3 March, travelling again by sledge, and then, when the snows turned to mud, by horse and cart through the Ukraine to Kishinev, reaching Bucharest on 12 March. Two days later, Tolstoy was received by Prince Gorchakov himself, who treated the young Count as one of the family. 'He embraced me, made me promise to dine with him every day, and wants to put me on his staff,' Tolstoy wrote to his aunt Toinette on 17 March.

Leo Tolstoy in 1854

Aristocratic connections went a long way in the Russian army staff. Tolstoy was quickly caught up in the social whirl of Bucharest, attending dinners at the Prince's house, games of cards and musical soirées in drawing rooms, evenings at the Italian opera and French theatre – a world apart from the bloody battlefields of the Danubian front just a few miles away. 'While you are imagining me exposed to all the dangers of war, I have not yet smelt Turkish powder, but am very quietly at Bucharest, strolling about, making music, and eating ice-creams,' he wrote to his aunt at the start of May.[2]

Tolstoy arrived in Bucharest in time for the start of the spring offensive on the Danube. The Tsar was determined to push south to Varna and the Black Sea coast as soon as possible, before the Western powers had time to land their troops and stop the Russian advance towards Constantinople. The key to this offensive was the capture of the Turkish fortress at Silistria. It would give the Russians a dominant stronghold in the Danube area, allowing them to convert the river into a supply line from the Black Sea into the interior of the Balkans, and giving them a base from which to recruit the Bulgarians to fight against the Turks. This was the plan that Paskevich had persuaded the Tsar to adopt in order not to alienate the Austrians, who might intervene against a Russian offensive through the Serb-dominated areas of the Danube further to the west, where Serbian uprisings in favour of the Russians might spread into Habsburg lands. 'The English and the French cannot land their troops for at least another fortnight,' Nicholas wrote to Gorchakov on 26 March, 'and I suppose that they will land at Varna to rush towards Silistria. . . . We must take the fortress before they arrive . . . With Silistria in our hands, there will be time for volunteers to raise more troops from the Bulgarians, but we must not touch the Serbs, in case we alarm the Austrians.'[3]

The Tsar was hopeful of mobilizing troops from the Bulgarians and other Slavs. Although he was wary of inflaming Serb passions against the Austrians, he hoped that his offensive would trigger Christian uprisings, leading to the collapse of the Ottoman Empire, when a victorious Russia would impose a new religious settlement on the Balkans. 'All the Christian parts of Turkey', he wrote in the spring of 1854, 'must necessarily become independent, they must become again what they previously were, principalities, Christian states, and as such rejoin the family of the Christian states of Europe.' Such was his commitment to this religious cause that he was prepared to exploit revolutions against even Austria, should this be necessitated by the opposition of the Austrians to a Russian settlement of the Eastern Question. 'It is highly likely that our victories will lead to Slav revolts in Hungary,' he wrote to the Russian ambassador in Vienna. 'We shall use them to threaten the heart of the Austrian Empire and force her government to accept our conditions.' Indeed the Tsar was ready by now to abandon virtually all his legitimist principles in the interests of his holy war. Angered by the anti-Russian stance of the European powers, he talked of stirring up the revolutionary disturbances in Spain to divert French troops from the east, and even thought of forming an alliance with Mazzini's liberation movement in Lombardy and Venice to undermine the Austrians. But in both cases the Tsar was dissuaded from supporting revolutionary democrats.[4]

The start of the spring offensive was hailed by Slavophiles as the dawning of a new religious era in the history of the world, the first step towards the resurrection of the Eastern Christian empire with its capital in Tsargrad, the name they gave to Constantinople. In 'To Russia' (1854), the poet Khomiakov greeted the beginning of the offensive with 'A call to holy war':

> Arise my motherland!
> For our Brothers! God calls you
> To cross the waves of the fiery Danube . . .

In an earlier poem by the same title, written in 1839, Khomiakov had referred to Russia's mission to bring the true Orthodox religion to the peoples of the world, but had warned Russia against pride. Now, in his poem of 1854, he called on Russia to engage in 'bloody battles' and 'Smite with the sword – the sword of God'.[5]

The Russians advanced slowly, fighting against stubborn Turkish resistance at several points on the northern side of the Danube, before coming to a virtual halt. At Ibrail, 20,000 Russian grenadiers, supported by river gunboats and steamers, were unable to defeat the well-defended Turkish fortresses. At Maçin there were 60,000 Russian troops encamped in bivouacs outside the fortress town but unable to take it. Held up by the Turks, the Russians spent their time constructing rafts and pontoon bridges from pine masts in preparation for a surprise crossing of the Danube at Galaţi, which they completed unopposed at the end of March.[6]

Advancing south towards Silistria, the Russians got bogged down in the marshlands of the Danube delta, the place where so many of them had been struck down by cholera and typhus in 1828–9. These were sparsely populated lands without food supplies for the invading troops, who soon succumbed to the effects of hunger and disease. Of 210,000 Russian troops in the principalities, 90,000 were too sick for action by April. Soldiers were fed on rations of dry bread that were so devoid of nutrition that not even rats and dogs would eat them, according to a French officer, who saw these husks abandoned in the fortress town of Giurgevo after the retreat of the Russian forces in the summer of 1854. A German doctor in the tsarist army thought that 'the bad quality of food habitually served to the Russian troops' was one of the main reasons why they 'dropped like flies' once they were wounded or exposed to illnesses. 'The Russian soldier has such a small nervous system that he sinks under the loss of a few ounces of blood and frequently dies of wounds such as would be sure to heal if inflicted on persons better constituted.'[7]

Soldiers wrote home to their families about the terrible conditions in the ranks, many begging them to send money. Some of these letters were intercepted and sent to Gorchakov by the police, who considered them politically dangerous, and they ended up in the archives. These simple letters give a unique insight into the world of the ordinary Russian troops. Grigory Zubianka, a foot soldier in the 8th Hussars Squadron, wrote to his wife Maria on 24 March:

> We are in Wallachia on the banks of the Danube and face our enemy on the other side. . . . Every day there is shooting across the river, and every hour and every minute we expect to die, but we pray to God that we may be saved, and every day that passes and we are still alive and healthy, we thank the Lord the Maker of all things for that blessing. But we are made to spend all day and night in hunger and the cold, because they give us nothing to eat and we have to live as best we can by fending for ourselves, so help us God.

Nikifor Burak, a soldier in the 2nd Battalion of the Tobol'sk Infantry Regiment, wrote to his parents, wife and children in the village of Sidorovka in Kiev Province:

> We are now a very long way from Russia, the land is not like Russia at all, we are almost in Turkey itself, and every hour we expect to die. To tell the truth, nearly all our regiment was destroyed by the Turks, but by the

grace of the highest creator I am still alive and well . . . I hope to return
home and see you all again, I will show myself to you and talk with you,
but now we are in the gravest danger, and I am afraid to die.[8]

As the Russian losses mounted, Paskevich became increasingly
opposed to the offensive. Though he had previously advocated the
march on Silistria, he was worried by the build-up of Austrian troops
on the Serbian frontier. With the British and the French expected to
land on the coast at any moment, with the Turks holding their line in
the south, and the Austrians mobilizing in the west, the Russians were
in serious danger of being surrounded by hostile armies in the principalities. Paskevich urged the Tsar to order a retreat. He delayed the
offensive against Silistria, in defiance of the Tsar's command to push
ahead as fast as possible, for fear that an attack by the Austrians
should find him without sufficient reserves.

Paskevich was right to be anxious about the Austrians, who were
alarmed by the growing Russian threat to Serbia. They had mobilized
their troops on the Serb frontier in readiness to put down any Serb
uprisings in favour of the Russians and oppose Russian forces
approaching Habsburg-controlled Serb lands from the east. Throughout the spring, the Austrians demanded a Russian withdrawal from
the principalities, threatening to join the Western powers if the Tsar
did not comply. The British were equally concerned by Russia's influence on Serbia. According to their consul in Belgrade, the Serbs were
being 'taught to expect Russian troops in Serbia as soon as Silistria
had fallen – and to join an expedition against the south-Slavonic
provinces of Austria'. On Palmerston's instructions, the consul warned
the Serbs that Britain and France would oppose with military force
any armament by Serbia in support of the Russians.[9]

Meanwhile, on 22 April, Easter Saturday in the Orthodox calendar,
the Western fleets began their first direct attack on Russian soil by bombarding Odessa, the important Black Sea port. The British had received
reports from captured merchant seamen that the Russians had collected
60,000 troops and large stockpiles of munitions at Odessa for trans-
portation to the Danubian front (in fact the port had little military
significance and only half a dozen batteries to defend itself against the
allied fleets). They sent an ultimatum to the governor of the town,

General Osten-Sacken, demanding the surrender of all his ships, and when there was no reply, began their bombardment with a fleet of nine steamers, six rocket boats and a frigate. The shelling continued for eleven hours, causing massive damage to the port, destroying several ships and killing dozens of civilians. It also hit Vorontsov's neoclassical palace on the cliff top above the port, with one ball hitting the statue of the Duc de Richelieu, the first governor of Odessa, though ironically the building damaged most was the London Hotel on the Primorsky Boulevard.

During a second bombardment, on 12 May, one of the British ships, a steamer called the *Tiger*, ran hard aground in dense fog and was heavily shelled from the shore. Her crew was captured by a small platoon of Cossacks commanded by a young ensign called Shchegolov. The British attempted to burn their ship, while Odessa ladies with their parasols watched the action from the embankment, where bits of shipwreck, including boxes of English rum, were later washed ashore. The Cossacks marched off the British crew (24 officers and 201 men) and imprisoned them in the town, where they were subjected to humiliating taunts from Russian sailors and civilians, whose sense of outrage at the timing of the attack over the Easter period had been encouraged by their priests, though the captain of the ship, Henry Wells Giffard, who had been injured by shellfire and died of gangrene on 1 June, was given a full military burial in Odessa and, in an act of chivalry from a bygone age, a lock of his hair was sent to his widow in England. The cannon of the *Tiger* were displayed in Odessa as war trophies.*

Priests declared the capture of the British steamer a symbol of divine revenge for the attack on Holy Saturday, which they pronounced had begun a religious war. The washed-up liquor was soon consumed by the Russian sailors and workers at the docks. There were drunken brawls, and several men were killed. Parts of the ship were later sold as souvenirs. The Cossack ensign Shchegolov became a popular hero overnight. He was commemorated almost as a saint. Bracelets and medallions were made with his image and sold as far away as Moscow and St Petersburg. There was even a new brand of cigarettes manufactured in Shchegolov's name with his picture on the box.[10]

---

* One of them now stands in front of the City Duma building on the Primorsky Boulevard.

The bombardment of Odessa announced the arrival of the Western powers near the Danubian front. Now the question was how soon the British and the French would come to the aid of the Turks against the Russians at Silistria. Fearful that a continuation of the offensive towards Constantinople would end badly for Russia, Paskevich wanted to retreat. On 23 April he wrote to Menshikov, the newly appointed commander-in-chief of Russian forces in the Crimea:

> Unfortunately we now find marshalled against us not only the maritime powers but also Austria, supported, so it appears, by Prussia. England will spare no money to bring Austria in on her side, for without the Germans they can do nothing against us. . . . If we are going to find all Europe ranged against us then we will not fight on the Danube.

Throughout the spring, Paskevich dragged his heels over the Tsar's orders to lay siege to Silistria. By mid-April, 50,000 troops had occupied the Danubian islands opposite the town, but Paskevich delayed the commencement of the siege. Nicholas was furious with the lack of vigour his commander showed. Although he himself admitted that Austria might join Russia's foes, Nicholas sent an angry note to Paskevich, urging him to begin the assault. 'If the Austrians treacherously atttack us,' he wrote on 29 April, 'you have to engage them with 4 Corps and the dragoons; that will be quite enough for them! Not one word more, I have nothing more to add!'

It was only on 16 May, after three weeks of skirmishing had given them control of the high ground to the south-west of Silistria, that the Russians at last began their bombardment of the town, and even then Paskevich focused his attack on its outer defences, a semicircle of stone forts and earthworks several kilometres from the fortress of Silistria itself. Paskevich hoped to wear down the opposition of the Turks and allow his troops to assault the town without major losses. But the officers in charge of the siege operations knew this was to hope in vain. The Turks had used the months since the Porte's declaration of war against Russia to build up their defences. The Turkish forts had been greatly strengthened by the Prussian Colonel Grach, an expert on entrenchments and mining, and they were relatively little damaged by the Russian guns, although the key redoubt, the earthworks known as the Arab Tabia, was so battered by the Russian shells and mines that it had to be rebuilt by the Turks several times during the siege. There were 18,000 troops in the Turkish forts, most of them Egyptians and Albanians, and they fought with a spirit of defiance that took the Russians by surprise. In the Arab Tabia the Ottoman forces were led by two experienced British artillery officers, Captain James Butler of the Ceylon Rifles and Lieutenant Charles Nasmyth of the Bombay Artillery. 'It was impossible not to admire the cool indifference of the Turks to danger,' Butler thought.

> Three men were shot in the space of five minutes while throwing up earth for the new parapet, at which only two men could work at a time so as to be at all protected; and they were succeeded by the nearest bystander, who took the spade from the dying man's hands and set to work as calmly as if he were going to cut a ditch by the road-side.

Realizing that the Russians needed to get closer to cause any damage to the forts, Paskevich ordered General Shil'der to begin elaborate engineering work, digging trenches to allow artillery to be brought up to the walls. The siege soon settled into a monotonous routine of dawn-to-dusk bombardment by the Russian batteries, supported by the guns of a river fleet. There had never been a time in the history of warfare when soldiers were subjected to so much constant danger for so long. But there was no sign of a breakthrough.[11]

Butler kept a diary of the siege. He thought the power of the heavy Russian guns had 'been much exaggerated' and that the lighter Turkish artillery were more than a match for them, although everything was conducted by the Turks 'in a slovenly manner'. Religion played an important role on the Turkish side, according to Butler. Every day, at morning prayers by the Stamboul Gate, the garrison commander Musa Pasha would call upon his soldiers to defend Silistria 'as becomes the descendants of the Prophet', to which 'the men would reply with cries of "Praise Allah!"'* There were no safe buildings in the town but the inhabitants had built caves where they took shelter during the day's bombardment. The town 'appeared deserted with only dogs and soldiers to be seen'. At sunset Butler watched the closing round of Russian

---

* Their determination was given more religious force when Musa Pasha was later killed by a shell that landed directly on him while he was conducting evening prayers for divine intervention to save Silistria.

shots come in from the fortress walls: 'I saw several little urchins, about 9 or 10 years old, actually chasing the round shot as they ricocheted, as coolly as if they had been cricket balls; they were racing to see who would get them first, a reward of 20 peras being given by the Pasha for every cannon ball brought in.' After dark, he could hear the Russians singing in their trenches, and 'when they made a night of it, they even had a band playing polkas and waltzes'.

Under growing pressure from the Tsar to seize Silistria, Paskevich ordered more than twenty infantry assaults between 20 May and 5 June, but still the breakthrough did not come. 'The Turks fight like devils,' reported one artillery captain on 30 May. Small groups of men would scale the ramparts of the forts, only to be repulsed by the defenders in hand-to-hand fighting. On 9 June there was a major battle outside the main fortress walls, after a large-scale Russian assault had been beaten back and the Turkish forces followed up with a sortie against the Russian positions. By the end of the fighting there were 2,000 Russians lying dead on the battlefield. The next day, Butler noted,

> numbers of the townspeople went out and cut off the heads of the slain and brought them in as trophies for which they hoped to get a reward, but the savages were not allowed to bring them within the gates. A heap of them however were left for a long time unburied just outside the gate. While we were sitting with Musa Pasha, a ruffian came out and threw at his feet a pair of ears, which he had cut from a Russian soldier; another boasted to us that a Russian officer had begged him for mercy in the name of the Prophet, but that he had drawn his knife and in cold blood had cut his throat.

The unburied Russians lay on the ground for several days, until the townspeople had stripped them of everything. Albanian irregulars also took part in the mutilation and looting of the dead. Butler saw them a few days later. It was 'a disgusting sight', he wrote. 'The smell was already becoming very offensive. Those who were in the ditch had all been stripped and were lying in various attitudes, some headless trunks, others with throats half out, arms extended in the air or pointing upwards as they fell.'[12]

Tolstoy arrived at Silistria on the day of this battle. He had been transferred there as an ordnance officer with the staff of General

Serzhputovsky, which set up its headquarters in the gardens of Musa Pasha's hilltop residence. Tolstoy enjoyed the spectacle of battle from this safe vantage point. He described it in a letter to his aunt:

> Not to mention the Danube, its islands and its banks, some occupied by us, others by the Turks, you could see the town, the fortress and the little forts of Silistria as though on the palm of your hand. You could hear the cannon-fire and rifle shots which continued day and night, and with a field-glass you could make out the Turkish soldiers. It's true it's a funny sort of pleasure to see people killing each other, and yet every morning and evening I would get up on to my cart and spend hours at a time watching, and I wasn't the only one. The spectacle was truly beautiful, especially at night . . . At night our soldiers usually set about trench work and the Turks threw themselves upon them to stop them; then you should have seen and heard the rifle-fire. The first night . . . . I amused myself, watch in hand, counting the cannon shots that I heard, and I counted 100 explosions in the space of a minute. And yet, from near by, all this wasn't at all as frightening as might be supposed. At night, when you could see nothing, it was a question of who would burn the most powder, and at the very most 30 men were killed on both sides by these thousands of cannon shots.[13]

Paskevich claimed that he had been hit by a shell fragment during the fighting on 10 June (in fact he was unwounded) and gave up the command to General Gorchakov. Relieved no longer to be burdened with responsibility for an offensive he had come to oppose, he rode off in his carriage back across the Danube to Iaşi.

On 14 June the Tsar received news that Austria was mobilizing its army and might join the war against Russia by July. He also had to contend with the possibility that at any moment the British and the French might arrive to relieve Silistria. He knew that time was running out but ordered one last assault on the fortress town, which Gorchakov prepared for the early hours of 22 June.[14]

*

By this time the British and the French were assembling their armies in the Varna area. They had begun to land their forces at Gallipoli at the beginning of April, their intention being to protect Constantinople from possible attack by the Russians. But it soon became apparent that the area was unable to support such a large army, so after a few weeks of foraging for scarce supplies, the allied troops moved on to set up other camps in the vicinity of the Turkish capital, before relocating well to the north at the port of Varna, where they could be supplied by the French and British fleets.

The two armies set up adjacent camps on the plains above the old fortified port – and eyed each other warily. They were uneasy allies. There was so much in their recent history to make them suspicious. Famously, Lord Raglan, the near-geriatric commander-in-chief of the British army, who had served as the Duke of Wellington's military secretary during the Peninsular War of 1808–14 and had lost an arm at Waterloo,* would on occasion refer to the French rather than the Russians as the enemy.

Lord Raglan

* After it was amputated (without anaesthetic) Raglan had asked to have the arm so that he could retrieve a ring given to him by his wife. The incident had sealed his reputation for personal bravery.

From the start there had been disputes over strategy – the British favouring the landing at Gallipoli followed by a cautious advance into the interior, whereas the French had wanted a landing at Varna to forestall the Russian advance towards Constantinople. The French had also sensibly suggested that the British should control the sea campaign, where they were superior, while they should take command of the land campaign, where they could apply the lessons of their war of conquest in Algeria. But the British had shuddered at the thought of taking orders from the French. They mistrusted Marshal Saint-Arnaud, the Bonapartist commander of the French forces, whose notorious speculations on the Bourse had led many in Britain's ruling circles to suppose that he would put his own selfish interests before the allied cause (Prince Albert thought that he was even capable of accepting bribes from the Russians). Such ideas filtered down to the officers and men. 'I hate the French,' wrote Captain Nigel Kingscote, who like most of Raglan's aides-de-camp was also one of his nephews. 'All Saint-Arnaud's staff, with one or two exceptions, are just like monkeys, girthed up as tight as they can be and sticking out above and below like balloons.'[15]

The French took a dim view of their British allies. 'Visiting the English camp makes me proud to be a Frenchman,' wrote Captain Jean-Jules Herbé to his parents from Varna.

> The British soldiers are enthusiastic, strong and well-built men. I admire their elegant uniforms, which are all new, their fine comportment, the precision and regularity of their manoeuvres, and the beauty of their horses, but their great weakness is that they are used to comfort far too much; it will be difficult to satisfy their numerous demands when we get on the march.[16]

Louis Noir, a soldier in the first battalion of Zouaves, the élite infantry established during the Algerian War,* recalled his miserable impression of the British troops at Varna. He was particularly shocked by the floggings that were often given by their officers for indiscipline and

---

* The first Zouave battalions were recruited from a Berber mountain tribe called the Zouaoua. Later Zouave battalions of Frenchmen adopted their Moorish costumes and green turbans.

drunkenness – both common problems among the British troops – which reminded him of the old feudal system that had disappeared in France:

> The English recruiters seemed to have brought out the dregs of their society, the lower classes being more susceptible to their offers of money. If the sons of the better-off had been conscripted, the beatings given to the English soldiers by their officers would have been outlawed by the military penal code. The sight of these corporal punishments disgusted us, reminding us that the Revolution of [17]89 abolished flogging in the army when it established universal conscription. . . . The French army is made up of a special class of citizens subject to the military laws, which are severe but applied equally to all the ranks. In England, the soldier is really just a serf – he is no more than the property of the government. It drives him on by two contradictory impulses. The first is the stick. The second is material well-being. The English have a developed instinct for comfort; to live well in a comfortable tent with a nice big side of roast-beef, a flagon of red wine and a plentiful supply of rum – that is the *desideratum* of the English trooper; that is the essential precondition of his bravery. . . . But if these supplies do not arrive on time, if he has to sleep out in the mud, find his firewood, and go without his beef and grog, the English become battle-shy, and demoralization spreads through the ranks.[17]

The French army was superior to the British in many ways. Its schools for officers had produced a whole new class of military professionals, who were technically more advanced, tactically superior and socially far closer to their men than the aristocratic officers of the British army. Armed with the advanced Minié rifle, which could fire rapidly with lethal accuracy up to 1,600 metres, the French infantry was celebrated for its attacking élan. The Zouaves, in particular, were masters of the fast attack and tactical retreat, a type of fighting they had developed in Algeria, and their courage was an inspiration to the rest of the French infantry, who invariably followed them into battle. The Zouaves were seasoned campaigners, experienced in fighting in the most difficult and mountainous terrain, and united by strong bonds of comradeship, formed through years of fighting together in Algeria (and in many cases on the revolutionary barricades of Paris in

1848). Paul de Molènes, an officer in one of the Spahi cavalry regiments recruited by Saint-Arnaud in Algeria, thought the Zouaves exerted a 'special power of seduction' over the young men of Paris, who flocked to join their ranks in 1854. 'The Zouaves' poetic uniforms, their free and daring appearance, their legendary fame – all this gave them an image of popular chivalry unseen since the days of Napoleon.'[18]

The experience of fighting in Algeria was a decisive advantage for the French over the British army, which had not fought in a major battle since Waterloo, and in many ways remained half a century behind the times. At one point a third of the French army's 350,000 men had been deployed in Algeria. From that experience, the French had learned the crucial importance of the small collective unit for maintaining discipline and order on the battlefield – a commonplace of twentieth-century military theorists that was first advanced by Ardant du Picq, a graduate of the École spéciale militaire de Saint-Cyr, the élite army school at Fontainebleau near Paris, who served as a captain in the Varna expedition and developed his ideas from observations of the French soldiers during the Crimean War. The French had also learned how to supply an army on the march efficiently – an area of expertise where their superiority over the British became apparent from the moment the two armies landed at Gallipoli. For two and a half days, the British troops were not allowed to disembark, 'because nothing was ready for them', reported William Russell of *The Times*, the pioneering correspondent who had joined the expedition to the East, whereas the French were admirably prepared with a huge flotilla of supply ships: 'Hospitals for the sick, bread and biscuit bakeries, wagon trains for carrying stores and baggage – every necessary and every comfort, indeed, at hand, the moment their ship came in. On our side not a British pendant was afloat in the harbour! Our great naval state was represented by a single steamer belonging to a private company.'[19]

The outbreak of the Crimean War had caught the British army by surprise. The military budget had been in decline for many years, and it was only in the early weeks of 1852, following Napoleon's *coup d'état* and the eruption of the French war scare in Britain, that the Russell government was able to obtain parliamentary approval for a modest increase in expenditure. Of the 153,000 enlisted men, two-thirds were serving overseas in various distant quarters of the Empire in the spring of 1854, so troops for the Black Sea expedition had to be recruited in a rush. Without the conscription system of the French, the British army relied entirely on the recruitment of volunteers with the inducement of a bounty. During the 1840s the pool of able-bodied men had been severely drained by great industrial building projects and by emigration to the United States and Canada, leaving the army to draw upon the unemployed and poorest sections of society, like the victims of the Irish famine, who took the bounty in a desperate attempt to clear their debts and save their families from the poorhouse. The main recruiting grounds for the British army were pubs and fairs and races, where the poor got drunk and fell into debt.[20]

If the British trooper came from the poorest classes of society, the officer corps was drawn mostly from the aristocracy – a condition almost guaranteed by the purchasing of commissions. The senior command was dominated by old gentlemen with good connections to the court but little military experience or expertise; it was a world apart from the professionalism of the French army. Lord Raglan was 65; Sir John Burgoyne, the army's chief engineer, 72. Five of the senior commanders at Raglan's headquarters were relatives. The youngest, the Duke of Cambridge, was a cousin to the Queen. This was an army, rather like the Russian, whose military thinking and culture remained rooted in the eighteenth century.

Raglan insisted on sending British soldiers into battle in tight-fitting tunics and tall shakos that might have made them look spectacular when marched in strict formation on the parade ground but which in a battle were quite impractical. When Sidney Herbert, the Secretary at War, wrote to him in May suggesting that the dress code ought to be relaxed and that perhaps the men might be excused from shaving every day, Raglan replied:

> I view your proposition for the introduction of beards in somewhat a
> different light, and it cannot be necessary to adopt it at present. I am
> somewhat old-fashioned in my ideas, and I cling to the desire that an
> Englishman should look like an Englishman, notwithstanding that the

French are endeavouring to make themselves appear as Africans, Turks, and Infidels. I have always remarked in the lower orders in England, that their first notion of cleanliness is shaving, and I dare say this feeling prevails in a great deal in our ranks, though some of our officers may envy the hairy men amongst our Allies. However, if when we come to march and are exposed to great heat and dirt, I remark that the sun makes inroads on the faces of the men, I will consider whether it be desirable to relax or not, but let us appear as Englishmen.[21]

The sanction against beards did not last beyond the July heat, but the British soldier was still ridiculously overdressed compared to the light and simple uniforms of the Russians and the French, as Lieutenant Colonel George Bell of the 1st (Royal) Regiment complained:

A suit on his back & a change in his pack is all the men require but still he is loaded like a donkey – Great coat & blanket, tight . . . belts that cling to his lungs like death, his arms and accoutrements, 60 rounds of Minié ammunition, pack & contents. The stiff leather choker we have abolished thanks to 'Punch' and the 'Times'. The reasoning of 40 years experience would not move the military authorities to let the soldier go into the field until he was half strangled & unable to move under his load until public opinion and the Newspapers came in to relieve him. The next thing I want to pitch aside is the abominable Albert,* as it is called, whereon a man may fry his ration beef at mid-day in this climate, the top being patent leather to attract a 10 fold more portion of the sun's rays to madden his brain.[22]

Encamped on the plains around Varna, with nothing much to do but wait for news from the fighting at Silistria, the British and French troops sought out entertainments in the drinking-places and brothels of the town. The hot weather and warnings not to drink the local water resulted in a monstrous drinking binge, especially of the local *raki*, which was very cheap and strong. 'Thousands of Englishmen and Frenchmen thronged together in the improvised taverns,' wrote Paul de Molènes, 'where all the wines and liquors of our countries poured out into noisy drunkenness . . . The Turks stood outside their

* A tall shako, named after Prince Albert, who supposedly designed it.

doors and watched without emotion or surprise these strange defenders that Providence had sent to them.' Drunken fighting between the
men was a daily problem in the town. Hugh Fitzhardinge Drummond,
an adjutant of the Scots Fusilier Guards, wrote to his father from
Varna:

> Our friends, the Highlanders, drink like fishes, and our men . . . drink
> more than they did at Scutari. The Zouaves are the most ill-behaved
> and lawless miscreants you can imagine; they commit every crime.
> They executed another man the day before yesterday. Last week a
> Chasseur de Vincennes was nearly cut in half by one of these ruffians,
> with a short sword, in a fit of mad drunkenness. The French drink a
> great deal – I think as much as our men – and when drunk are more
> insubordinate.

Complaints from the residents of Varna multiplied. The town was
populated mainly by Bulgarians, but there was a sizeable Turkish
minority. They were irritated by soldiers demanding alcohol from
Muslim-owned cafés and becoming violent when they were told that
it was not sold. They might have been excused for wondering whether
their defenders were a greater danger to them than the menace of
Russia, as British naval officer Adolphus Slade observed from his vantage point in Constantinople:

> French soldiers lounged in the mosques during prayers, ogled licen-
> tiously the veiled ladies, poisoned the street dogs . . . shot the gulls in
> the harbour and the pigeons in the streets, mocked the *muezzins* chant-
> ing *ezzan* from the minarets, and jocosely broke up carved tombstones
> for pavement . . . The Turks had heard of civilization: they now saw it,
> as they thought, with amazement. Robbery, drunkenness, gambling,
> and prostitution revelled under the glare of an eastern sun.[23]

The British quickly formed an ill opinion of the Turkish soldiers,
who set up camp beside them on the plains around Varna. 'The little I
have seen of the Turks makes me think they are very poor allies,' Raglan's aide-de-camp Kingscote wrote to his father. 'I am certain they are
the greatest liars on the face of the earth. If they say they have 150,000
men you will find that on enquiry there are only 30,000. Everything
in the same proportion, and from all I hear, I cannot make out why

the Russians have not walked over them.' The French also did not think much of the Turkish troops, although the Zouaves, who contained a large contingent of Algerians, established good relations with the Turks. Louis Noir thought the British soldiers had a racist and imperial attitude towards the Turks that made them widely hated by the Sultan's troops.

> The English soldiers believed they had come to Turkey, not to save it, but to conquer it. At Gallipoli they would often have their fun by accosting a Turkish gentleman along the beach; they would draw a circle around him and tell him that this circle was Turkey; then they would make him leave the circle and cut it into two, naming one half 'England' and the other 'France', before pushing the Turk away into something which they called 'Asia'.[24]

Colonial prejudice limited the use the Western powers were prepared to make of the Turkish troops. Napoleon III thought the Turks were lazy and corrupt while Lord Cowley, the British ambassador in Paris, advised Raglan that 'no Turk was to be trusted' with any military responsibility essential to national security. The Anglo-French commanders thought the Turks were only good at fighting behind fortifications. They were ready to use them for auxiliary tasks such as digging trenches, but assumed they lacked the discipline or courage to fight alongside European troops on the open battlefield.[25] The success of the Turks in holding off the Russians at Silistria (which was largely put down to the British officers) did not change these racist attitudes, which would become even more pronounced when the campaign shifted to the Crimea.

*

As it was, the Turks were doing more than hold their own against the Russians, who launched one last assault against Silistria on 22 June. On the morning of the 21st, Gorchakov went with his staff to inspect the trenches before the Arab Tabia, where the attack would begin. Tolstoy was impressed by Gorchakov (he would later draw on him for his portrait of General Kutuzov in *War and Peace*). 'I saw him under fire for the first time that morning,' he wrote to his brother Nikolai. 'You can see he's so engrossed in the general course of events

that he simply doesn't notice the bullets and cannon-balls.' Throughout that day, to weaken the resistance of the Turks, 500 Russian guns
bombarded their fortifications; the firing continued late into the
night. The assault was set for three in the morning. 'There we all were,'
Tolstoy wrote, and, 'as always on the eve of a battle, we were all
pretending not to think of the following day as anything more than an
ordinary day, while all of us, I'm quite sure, at the bottom of our
hearts felt a slight pang (and not even slight, but pronounced) at the
thought of the assault'.

> As you know, Nikolai, the period that precedes an engagement is the
> most unpleasant – it's the only period when you have the time to be
> afraid, and fear is one of the most unpleasant feelings. Towards morn-
> ing, the nearer the moment came, the more this feeling diminished, and
> towards 3 o'clock, when we were all waiting to see the shower of rockets
> let off as the signal for the attack, I was in such a good humour that I
> would have been very upset if someone had come to tell me that the
> assault wouldn't take place.

What he feared most happened. At two o'clock in the morning, an
aide-de-camp brought Gorchakov a message, ordering him to raise
the siege. 'I can say without fear of error', Tolstoy told his brother,

> that this news was received by all – soldiers, officers and generals – as
> a real misfortune, all the more so since we knew through spies who
> came to us very often from Silistria, and with whom I very often had
> occasion to talk myself, that once this fort was taken – something of
> which nobody had any doubt – Silistria couldn't hold out for more
> than two or three days.[26]

What Tolstoy did not know, or refused to take into account, was
that by this stage there were 30,000 French, 20,000 British and 20,000
Turkish troops ready to reinforce the defence of Silistria, and that
Austria, which had massed 100,000 troops along the Serbian frontier,
had served an ultimatum to the Tsar to withdraw from the Danubian
principalities. Austria had effectively adopted a policy of armed neutrality in favour of the allies, mobilizing Habsburg troops to force the
Russians to withdraw from the Danube. Fearful of uprisings among
their own Slavs, the Austrians were worried by the Russian presence

in the principalities, which looked more like annexation every day. If the Austrians attacked the Russians from the west, there was a real possibility that they would cut them off from their lines of supply on the Danube and block their main path of retreat, leaving them exposed to the allied armies attacking from the south. The Tsar had no choice but to retreat before his army was destroyed.

Nicholas felt a deep sense of betrayal by the Austrians, whose empire he had saved from the Hungarians in 1849. He had developed a paternal affection for the Emperor Franz Joseph, more than thirty years his junior, and felt that he deserved his gratitude. Visibly saddened and shaken by the news of the ultimatum, he turned Franz Joseph's portrait to the wall and wrote on the back of it in his own hand: 'Du Undankbarer!' (You ungrateful man!) He told the Austrian envoy Count Esterhazy in July that Franz Joseph had completely forgotten what he had done for him and that 'because the confidence which had existed until now between the two sovereigns for the happiness of their empires was destroyed, the same intimate relations could not exist between them any more'.[27]

The Tsar wrote to Gorchakov to explain his reasons for calling off the siege. It was an unusually personal letter that revealed a lot about his thinking:

> How sad and painful it is for me, my dear Gorchakov, to be forced into agreement with the persistent arguments of Prince Ivan Fedorovich [Paskevich] ... and to retreat from the Danube after having made so many efforts and having lost so many brave souls without gain – I do not need to tell you what that means to me. Judge that for yourself!!! But how can I disagree with him when I look at the map. Now the danger is not so much, for you are in a position to exact a severe punishment on the impudent Austrians. I am fearful only that the retreat may damage the morale of our troops. You must raise their spirits, make it clear to every one of them that it is better to retreat in time so that we can attack later on, as it was in 1812.[28]

The Russians retreated from the Danube, fighting off the Turks, who pursued them, smelling blood. The Russian troops were tired and demoralized, many of the soldiers had not eaten for days, and there were so many sick and wounded that they could not all be taken back by cart. Thousands were abandoned to the Turks. At the fortress town of Giurgevo, on 7 July, the Russians lost 3,000 men in a battle with the Turkish forces (some of them commanded by British officers) who crossed the river from Rusçuk and attacked the Russians with the support of a British gunboat. Gorchakov arrived with reinforcements from the abandoned siege of Silistria, but was soon forced to order a retreat. The Union Jack was planted on the fortress of Giurgevo, where the Turks then took savage revenge on the Russians, killing more than 1,400 wounded men, cutting off their heads and mutilating their bodies, while Omer Pasha and the British officers looked on.[29]

The Turkish reprisals had a clear religious character. As soon as the town was cleared of Russians troops, the Turkish troops (Bashi Bazouks and Albanians) ransacked the homes and churches of its Christian population, most of them Bulgarians. The entire Christian population left Giurgevo with the Russian infantry, hurriedly packing their belongings onto carts and heading north with their columns. A French officer described the scene he found in Giurgevo a few weeks after its abandonment:

> The Russians, in departing, left only 25 inhabitants out of a population of 12,000 people! Only a handful of houses were intact . . . The looters were not content to pillage only houses. Several churches were ransacked. I saw with my own eyes a Greek church which I found in a dreadful state. An old Bulgarian sacristan was clearing up the broken icons and church windows, the sculptures, lamps and other sacred objects piled up in the sanctuary. I asked him in sign language who had committed these atrocities, the Russians or the Turks. 'Turkos' he replied in a single word, his teeth clenched and in a tone that promised no redemption for the first Bashi Bazouk who fell into his hands.[30]

In every town and village the Russian troops passed through, they were joined by other refugees afraid of Turkish reprisals. There were scenes of chaos and panic on the roads, as thousands of Bulgarian peasants left their villages with their livestock and joined the ever-growing columns of humanity in flight. The roads became so badly blocked with peasant carts that the Russian retreat was slowed down, and Gorchakov considered using troops to hold back the refugees. But he was talked out it by his senior officers, and in the end some

7,000 Bulgarian families were evacuated to Russia. Tolstoy described the scene in one village in a letter to his aunt which he wrote on reaching Bucharest on 19 July:

> There was one village that I went into from the camp to fetch milk and fruit that had been destroyed [by the Turks]. As soon as the Prince [Gorchakov] had let the Bulgarians know that those who wanted to could cross the Danube with the army and become Russian subjects, the whole country rose up, and all of them, with their wives, children, horses and cattle, came down to the bridge, but as it was impossible to take them all, the Prince was obliged to refuse those who came last, and you should have seen how much that grieved him; he received all the deputations coming from these poor people, he chatted with each of them, tried to explain to them the impossibility of the thing, proposed to them that they cross without their carts and cattle, and, taking upon himself their means of subsistence until they should reach Russia, paid out of his own purse for private vessels to transport them.[31]

In Bucharest, there were similar scenes of confusion. Many of the disaffected Russian troops took the opportunity to desert from their units and went into hiding in the city, prompting the military authorities to issue dire threats to the population to give up any deserters or risk punishment. The Wallachian volunteers, who had joined the Russian troops on their occupation of the principality, now melted away, many of them fleeing south to join the allies. Evacuating the city, the Russians issued a dark warning to the 'treacherous Wallachians' in a manifesto from the Tsar:

> His Majesty the Tsar does not believe that those who profess the same religion as the Orthodox Emperor can submit to a government that is not Christian. If the Wallachians cannot understand that, because they are too much influenced by Europe, and given over to false beliefs, the Tsar nonetheless cannot renounce the mission that God has given him as the leader of the Orthodox, to remove for ever from the sovereignty of the Ottomans those who profess the true Christian faith, that is to say the Greek. That thought has preoccupied the Tsar since the beginning of his glorious reign, and the moment has arrived when His Majesty will carry out the project he has planned for many years,

whatever may be the intentions of the powerless European states in the hold of false beliefs. The time will come when the rebellious Wallachians, who have incurred the wrath of His Majesty, will pay dearly for their disloyalty.

On 26 July the proclamation was read out to the assembled boyars in Bucharest by Gorchakov, who added his own parting words: 'Gentlemen, we are leaving Bucharest for the moment, but I hope to return soon – remember 1812.'[32]

News of the withdrawal was a huge shock to the Slavophiles in Moscow and St Petersburg who had seen the Russian advance into the Balkans as a war of liberation for the Slavs. They now became despondent at what they saw as the abandonment of their ideals. Konstantin Aksakov had dreamed of a Slavic federation under Russian leadership. He thought the war would end with the planting of a cross on the Hagia Sophia in Constantinople. But the retreat from the Danube filled him 'with feelings of disgust and shame', as he wrote to his brother Ivan to explain:

> It feels as if we are retreating from our Orthodox belief. If this is because we distrust, or because we are withdrawing from a holy war, then since the foundation of Russia there has never been such a shameful moment in our history – we have defeated enemies but not our own fear. And now what! ... We are retreating from Bulgaria, but what will happen to the poor Bulgarians, to the crosses on the churches of Bulgaria? ... Russia! If you leave God then God will leave you! You have renounced the holy mission with which He entrusted you to defend the holy faith and deliver your suffering brothers, and now God's wrath will come to you, Russia!

Like many Slavophiles, the Aksakovs blamed the decision to retreat on Nesselrode, the 'German' Foreign Minister, who was now denounced in nationalist circles as a traitor to Russia and an 'Austrian agent'. With the pan-Slav leader Pogodin, they mounted a campaign in the salons of St Petersburg and Moscow to persuade the Tsar to reverse the retreat and fight alone against the Austrians and the Western powers. They rejoiced in the fact that Russia would be fighting on its own against Europe, believing that a holy war for the Slavs' liberation from Western influence would be the fulfilment of Russia's messianic role.[33]

As the Russians withdrew from Wallachia, the Austrians moved in to restore order in the principality. An Austrian contingent of 12,000 troops under General Coronini pushed on as far as Bucharest, where they clashed with the Turks, who had already occupied the city following the retreat of the Russians. Omer Pasha, who had pronounced himself the 'Governor of the Reoccupied Principalities', refused to relinquish Bucharest to the Austrian commander. As a former Austrian subject who had joined the Turks, he could hardly be expected to hand over his hard-earned conquests to a courtier such as Coronini, who had been the personal tutor of the Emperor and stood for everything in the Habsburg world that Omer Pasha had rejected when he crossed over to the Ottomans. The Turkish commander was supported by the British and the French. Having spent so long attempting to involve the Austrians in the principalities, the allies now regarded the Austrian intervention as something of a mixed blessing. They were pleased that the Austrians had helped to liberate the principalities from Russian control, but they also suspected them of intending a long-term occupation of the principalities, either in the hope of substituting their own rule for the political vacuum left by the departure of the Russian troops, or in the belief that they might impose their own solution to the Russo-Turkish conflict at the expense of the West. Their suspicions were increased when the Austrians prevented Omer Pasha's forces from pursuing the Russians into Bessarabia (the preferred tactics of Napoleon III); and even further when they reinstalled in power the Russian-nominated hospodars in a move evidently intended to smooth the ruffled feathers of the Tsar. To the British and the French, it seemed obvious that the Austrians had come to the rescue of the Danubian principalities, not as gendarmes of the European Concert, nor as champions of Turkish sovereignty, but with political motives of their own.[34]

It was partly to counteract the Austrian threat, and partly to secure the Black Sea coastline for an attack on southern Russia and the Crimea, that the French sent an expeditionary force into the Dobrudja region of the Danube delta in late July. The force was made up of Bashi Bazouk irregulars (called the Spahis d'Orient by the French) under the command of General Yusuf as well as infantry from the 1st (General

Canrobert's), 2nd (General Bosquet's) and 3rd (Prince Napoleon's) Divisions. Captured as the 6-year-old Giuseppe Vantini in Elba in 1815 by the Barbary corsairs and brought up in the palace of the Bey of Tunis, Yusuf was the founder and commander of the Spahi cavalry employed by the French in their conquest of Algeria. His success there made him the ideal candidate to organize the Bashi Bazouks under French command. By 22 July he had assembled at Varna a cavalry brigade of 4,000 Bashi Bazouks given to the French by the Ottomans, along with various other detachments of irregulars, including a Kurdish band of horsemen commanded by Fatima Khanum. Known as the Virgin of Kurdistan, the 70-year-old Khanum led her tribal followers, armed with swords and knives and pistols, under the green banner of a Muslim war. Yusuf too appealed to the idea of a jihad to motivate his men against the Russians and give them something to fight for other than the prospect of plunder, their traditional incentive, which the French were determined to stamp out. 'We have come to save the Sultan, our caliph,' a group of Bashi Bazouks told Louis Noir, whose Zouave brigade joined Yusuf's force on its march north from Varna; 'if we die fighting for him without payment, we will go directly to heaven; if we were paid to fight, none of us would have a right to paradise, for we would have received our recompense on earth.'[35]

But not even the promise of paradise could ensure the discipline of Yusuf's cavalry. As soon as they were ordered to set off from Varna, the Bashi Bazouks began to desert, claiming they would not fight for foreign officers (Yusuf spoke a Tunisian Arabic which the Syrians, Turks and Kurds under his command could not understand). An advance squadron of cavalry ran away en masse on their first sighting of the Cossacks near Tulcea, leaving the French officers to fight them on their own (they were all killed). On the 28th, Yusuf's troops beat the Cossacks and forced them to retreat, but then they lost all discipline, plundering the villages, killing Christians and bringing their heads back to General Yusuf, in the hope of a reward (the Turkish army customarily paid a bounty for the heads of infidels, including civilians, defeated in a holy war). Some men even murdered Christian women and children, cutting their bodies into pieces also in exchange for a reward.[36]

The next day, the first of Yusuf's troops succumbed to cholera. The marshes and lakes of the Danube delta were infested with disease. The death toll was alarming. Dehydrated by the disease and by days of marching in the scorching heat, men fell down and died beside the road. Yusuf's force disintegrated rapidly, as soldiers fled to escape the cholera or lay down in the shelter of a tree to die. Yusuf ordered a retreat to Varna, and the remnants of his force, some 1,500 men, arrived there on 7 August.

They found cholera at Varna, too. They would have found it anywhere, for the whole of south-east Europe was struck by cholera in the summer of 1854. The French camp was infected first, followed shortly after by the British. A hot wind blew in from the land, covering the campsites with a white limestone powder and a blanket of dead flies. Men began to suffer from nausea and diarrhoea, and then lay down in their tents to die. Ignorant of the causes, soldiers went on drinking water in the summer heat, though some, like the Zouaves, who had come across the disease in Algeria, knew to stick to wine or to boil the water for coffee (of which the French drank enormous quantities). Cholera epidemics were a regular occurrence in London and other British cities in the 1830s and 1840s, but it was not until the 1880s that the link to sanitation was really understood. A London doctor by the name of John Snow had discovered that boiling drinking water could prevent cholera, but his findings were generally ignored. Instead, the disease was put down to miasmas from the lakes around Varna, excessive drinking, or the consumption of soft fruit. The elementary rules of sanitation were disregarded by the military authorities: latrines were allowed to overflow; carcasses were left to putrefy in the sun. The sick were carted off to a rat-infested barrack in Varna, where they were cared for by exhausted orderlies, who were joined in August by a small group of French nuns. The dead were wrapped in blankets and buried in mass graves (which were later dug up by the Turks to steal the blankets). By the second week of August, 500 British troops had died of the disease, and deaths among the French were spiralling to a rate of more than sixty every day.[37]

Then came the fire at Varna. It began in the evening of 10 August in the old trading quarters of the town and spread quickly to the neighbouring port, where the supplies of the allied armies were waiting to be loaded onto ships. The fire had almost certainly been started by Greek and Bulgarian arsonists sympathetic to the Russian cause (several men were apprehended with lucifer matches in the area where the fire had begun). Half the town was engulfed in flames by the time the French and British troops arrived with water pumps. Shops and wharfs loaded up with crates of rum and wine exploded in the flames, and alcoholic rivers ran through the streets, where firefighters gorged themselves from the gutters. By the time the fire was contained, the supply base of the allied armies was severely damaged. 'Varna housed all the munitions, all the supplies and provisions needed by an army on campaign,' Herbé wrote to his parents on 16 August. 'The powder magazines of the French, the English and the Turks were at the centre of the conflagration. Much of the town disappeared, and with it the hopes of the soldiers encamped on the plain.'[38]

*

After the fire, there were only enough supplies in the town to feed the allied armies for eight days. It was clear that the soldiers needed to get out of the Varna area before they were totally destroyed by cholera and starvation.

With the Russians forced to retreat from the Danube, the British and the French could have gone home, claiming victory against Russia. It would have been feasible to end the war at this stage. The Austrians and the Turks could have occupied the principalities as a peacekeeping force (by mid-August they had drawn up separate zones of occupation and agreed to share control of Bucharest), while the Western powers could have used the threat of intervention to make the Russians promise not to invade Turkish soil again. So why did the allies not pursue a peace once the Russians had left the principalities? Why did they decide to invade Russia when the war against the Russians had been won? Why was there a Crimean War at all?

The allied commanders were frustrated by the retreat of the Russians. Having brought their armies all this way, they felt they had been 'robbed of victory', as Saint-Arnaud put it, and wanted to achieve a military goal to justify the efforts they had made. In the six months that had passed since their mobilization the allied troops had barely used their weapons against the enemy. They were mocked by the Turks and ridiculed at home. 'There they are,' wrote Karl Marx in an editorial in the *New York Times* on 17 August, 'eighty or ninety thousand

1. Easter at the Holy Sepulchre.

How the Russians aspire to all that is well-established.

5. One of the Russophobic images in Gustav Doré's
History of Holy Russia, 1854.

NOW FOR IT!
A Set-to between "Pam, the Downing Street Pet," and "The Russian Spider."

6. Palmerston and
Nicholas I prepare
for a fight (*Punch*).

SAINT NICHOLAS OF RUSSIA.

7. *Punch*'s view
of Nicholas I.

8. One of the earliest photographs of war: Turkish troops on the Danube Front, 1854, by Carol Szathmari.

9. Coldstream guards at Scutari, 1854. The skyline of Constantinople is visible on the far side of the Bosporus. Note the army wives, who look as strong as their husbands.

10. Part of the British camp outside Sevastopol, 1855.

11. Balaklava Harbour, 1855.

12. The French base at Kamiesh Bay, 1855.

13. French soldiers standing by a group of Zouaves, 1855.

14. Crimean Tatars at work in Balaklava, 1855.

HOW JACK MAKES THE TURK USEFUL AT BALACLAVA.

15. An illustration of British racist attitudes towards their
Turkish allies from *Punch*, 1855.

English and French soldiers at Varna, commanded by old Wellington's late military secretary and by a Marshal of France (whose greatest exploits, it is true, were performed in London pawnshops) – there they are, the French doing nothing and the British helping them as fast as they can.'[39]

Back in London, the British cabinet also felt that forcing Russia out of the Danube area was not enough to justify the sacrifices made so far. Palmerston and his 'war party' were not prepared to negotiate a peace when the Russian armed forces remained intact. They wanted to inflict serious damage on Russia, to destroy her military capacity in the Black Sea, not just to secure Turkey but to end the Russian threat to British interests in the Near East. As the Duke of Newcastle, the gung-ho Secretary of State for War, had put it back in April, expelling the Russians from the principalities 'without crippling their future means of aggression upon Turkey is not now an object worthy of the great efforts of England and France'.[40]

But what would inflict serious damage? The cabinet had considered various options. They saw little point in pursuing the Russians into Bessarabia, where the allied troops would be exposed to the cholera, while the French proposal of a Continental war for the liberation of Poland was bound to be obstructed by the Austrians, even if (and it was a big 'if') the conservative members of the British cabinet could be persuaded of the virtues of a revolutionary war. Nor were they convinced that the naval campaign in the Baltic would bring Russia to its knees. Soon after the beginning of the campaign in the spring, Sir Charles Napier, the admiral in charge of the allied Baltic fleet, had come to the conclusion that it would be practically impossible to overcome the almost impregnable Russian defences at Kronstadt, the fortress naval base guarding St Petersburg, or even the weaker fortress at Sveaborg, just outside the harbour of Helsingfors (Helsinki), without new gunboats and mortar vessels capable of navigating the shallow reefs around these fortresses.* For a while there was talk of

---

* Events would prove them right. On 8 August Napier launched an allied attack against the Russian fortress at Bomarsund in the Aaland Islands, between Sweden and Finland, mainly with the aim of involving Sweden in the war. The support of Swedish troops was necessary for any move on the Russian capital. After a heavy bombardment that reduced the fortress to rubble, the Russian commander and his 2,000 men

mounting an attack against Russia in the Caucasus. A delegation of Circassian rebels visited the allies in Varna and promised to raise a Muslim war against Russia throughout the Caucasus if the allies sent their armies and their fleets. Omer Pasha supported this idea.[41] But none of these plans were deemed as damaging to Russia as the loss of Sevastopol and its Black Sea Fleet would be. By the time the Russians had retreated from the principalities, the British cabinet had settled on the view that an invasion of the Crimea was the only obvious way to strike a decisive blow against Russia.

The Crimean plan had originally been advanced in December 1853, when, in reaction to Sinope, Graham had devised a naval strategy to knock out Sevastopol in one swift blow. 'On this my heart is set,' the First Lord of the Admiralty wrote; 'the eye tooth of the Bear must be drawn: and 'til his fleet and naval arsenal in the Black Sea are destroyed there is no safety for Constantinople, no security for the peace of Europe.'[42] Graham's plan was never formally placed before the cabinet, but it was accepted as the basis of its strategy. And on 29 June the Duke of Newcastle transmitted to Raglan the cabinet instructions for an invasion of the Crimea. His dispatch was emphatic: the expedition was to start as soon as possible and 'nothing but insuperable impediments' should delay the siege of Sevastopol and the destruction of the Russian Black Sea Fleet, although some secondary attacks against the Russians in the Caucasus might also be necessary. The language of the dispatch left Raglan with the impression that there was no disagreement in the cabinet, and no alternative to an invasion of the Crimea.[43] But in fact there were conflicting views on the practicality of the Crimean plan, and its acceptance was a compromise between those in the cabinet, like

---

surrendered to the allies. But Bomarsund was a minor victory – it was not Kronstadt or St Petersburg – and the Swedes were not impressed, despite strong approaches from the British. Until the allies committed more serious resources to the campaign in the Baltic, there was no real prospect of involving Sweden in the war, let alone threatening St Petersburg. But the allies were divided on the significance of the Baltic. The French were far less keen on it than the British – Palmerston in particular, who dreamed of taking Finland as part of his broader plans to dismantle the Russian Empire – and they were reluctant to commit more troops to a war aim which they saw as serving mainly British interests. For Napoleon, the campaign in the Baltic could be no more than a minor diversion to prevent the Tsar from deploying an even bigger army in the Crimea, the main focus of their war campaign.

Aberdeen, who wanted a more limited campaign to restore Turkish sovereignty and those, like Palmerston, who saw the expedition to the Crimea as an opportunity to launch a broader war against Russia. By this time, the British press was piling pressure on the cabinet to strike a mortal blow against Russia, and the destruction of the Black Sea Fleet at Sevastopol had become the symbolic victory that the warlike public sought. The idea of desisting from the invasion of the Crimea merely on the grounds that, with the retreat of the Russians from the Danube, it had become unnecessary was practically unthinkable.

'The main and real object of the war', Palmerston admitted in 1855, 'was to curb the aggressive ambition of Russia. We went to war not so much to keep the Sultan and the Muslims in Turkey as to keep the Russians out of it.' Palmerston envisaged the attack on the Crimea as the first stage of a long-term crusade against tsarist power in the Black Sea region and the Caucasus, Poland and the Baltic, in line with his memorandum to the cabinet on 19 March, in which he had outlined his ambitious plan for the dismemberment of the Russian Empire. By the end of August he had won considerable support within the cabinet for this enlarged war. He also had an unofficial agreement with Drouyn de Lhuys, the French Foreign Minister, that 'small results' would not be enough to compensate for the inevitable human losses of the war, and that only 'great territorial changes' in the Danube region, the Caucasus, Poland and the Baltic could justify a campaign in the Crimea.[44]

But as long as Aberdeen was Prime Minister it was impossible for Palmerston to get such plans accepted as allied policy. The Four Points agreed by the Western powers with the Austrians after several months of negotiation on 8 August laid out more limited objectives. Peace could not be agreed between Russia and the allied powers unless:

1. Russia renounced any special rights in Serbia and the Danubian principalities, whose protection would be guaranteed by the European powers with the Porte;
2. the navigation of the Danube was free to all commerce;
3. the Straits Convention of 1841 was revised 'in the interests of the Balance of Power in Europe' (ending Russian naval domination of the Black Sea);
4. the Russians abandoned their claim to a protectorate over the

Christian subjects of Turkey, whose security would be guaranteed
by the five great powers (Austria, Britain, France, Prussia and
Russia) in agreement with the Turkish government.

The Four Points were conservative in character (nothing else would
satisfy the Austrians) but vague enough to allow the British (who
wanted to reduce the power of Russia but had no real idea how to
translate this into concrete policies) to add more conditions as the
war went on. Indeed, unknown to the Austrians, there was a secret
fifth point agreed between the British and the French allowing them
to raise further demands depending on the outcome of the war. For
Palmerston, the Four Points were a way of binding Austria and France
to a grand European alliance for the pursuit of an open-ended war
against Russia, a war that could be expanded even after the conquest
of the Crimea had been achieved.[45]

Palmerston even went so far as to articulate a broad long-term plan
for the Crimea. He proposed turning the area over to the Turks, and
linking it to new Turkish territories captured from the Russians
around the Sea of Azov, Circassia, Georgia and the Danube delta. But
few others were prepared to think in such ambitious terms. Napoleon
largely wanted to capture Sevastopol as a symbol of the 'glorious victory' he desired and as a means of punishing the Russians for their
aggression in the principalities. And most of the British cabinet felt
the same way. It was generally assumed that the fall of Sevastopol
would bring Russia to its knees, allowing the Western powers to claim
victory and impose their conditions on the Russians. But this did not
make much sense. Compared to Kronstadt and the other Baltic fortresses defending the Russian capital, Sevastopol was a relatively
distant outpost in the Tsar's Empire, and there was no logical reason
to suppose that its capture by the allies would force him to submit.
The consequence of this unquestioned assumption was that during
1855, when the fall of Sevastopol did not happen quickly, the allies
went on battering the town in what was at that time the longest and
most costly siege in military history to date rather than develop other
strategies to weaken Russia's land armies, which rather than her Black
Sea Fleet were after all the real key to her power over Turkey.[46]

The Crimean campaign was not only wrongly conceived but also badly planned and prepared. The decision to invade the Crimea was taken without any real intelligence. The allied commanders had no maps of the region. They took their information from outdated travelogues, such as Lord de Ros's diary of his Crimean travels and Major-General Alexander Macintosh's *Journal of the Crimea*, both dating back to 1835, which led them to believe that the Crimean winters were extremely mild, even though there were more recent books that pointed out the cold, such as *The Russian Shores of the Black Sea in the Autumn of 1852* by Laurence Oliphant, which was published in 1853. The result was that no winter clothing or accommodation was prepared, partly on the hopeful assumption that it would be a brief campaign and that victory would be achieved before any frost set in. They had no idea how many Russian troops were in the Crimea (estimates ranged between 45,000 and 80,000 men), and no idea where they were located on the peninsula. The allied fleets could transport only 60,000 of the 90,000 troops at Varna to the Crimea – on the most optimistic calculation less than half the three-to-one ratio recommended by military textbooks for a siege – and even that would have to be at the expense of ambulance wagons, draught animals and other essential supplies. The allies suspected that the Russian troops retreating from the Danubian front were going to be brought to the Crimea, and that the best outcome for them would be the seizure of Sevastopol by a lightning *coup de main* and the destruction of its military facilities and the Black Sea Fleet before they arrived. They reasoned that a less successful attack on Sevastopol would very probably require the occupation of Perekop, the isthmus separating the Crimea from the mainland, to block those Russian reinforcements and supplies. In his dispatch of 29 June, Newcastle had ordered Raglan to carry out this task 'without delay'. But Raglan refused to carry out the order, claiming that his troops would suffer in the heat of the Crimean plain.[47]

As the launching of the invasion approached, military leaders got cold feet. The French, in particular, had their doubts. Newcastle's instructions to Raglan were copied by Marshal Vaillant, the Minister of War, to Saint-Arnaud, but the commander of the French forces was sceptical about the plan. His reservations were shared by the majority of his officers, who thought the attack would benefit Britain as a naval power more than France. But such doubts were brushed aside, as pressure was applied by the politicians in London and Paris, eager for an offensive to satisfy the public mood, and increasingly concerned to get the troops away from the cholera-infested Varna zone. By late August Saint-Arnaud had come to the conclusion that fewer men would be lost in an attack on Sevastopol than had died already from cholera.[48]

The embarkation order came as a relief to most of the troops, who 'preferred to fight like men rather than waste away from hunger and disease', according to Herbé. 'The men and officers are getting daily more disgusted with their fate,' wrote Robert Portal, a British cavalry officer, in late August.

> They do nothing but bury their comrades. They say loudly that they have not been brought out to fight, but to waste away and die in this country of cholera and fever. . . . We hear that there is a mutiny in the French encampment, the soldiers swearing that they will go anywhere and do anything, but remain here to die they will not.

Rumours of a mutiny in the French camp were confirmed by Colonel Rose, attached to the French staff, who reported to London on 6 September that the French command did 'not think well of the stability and power of resistance of the French soldiers'.[49]

It was time to pack them off to war before they succumbed to disease or rose up against their officers. On 24 August the embarkation started. The infantry were ferried onto ships, followed by the cavalry and their horses, ammunition carts, wagons with supplies, draught livestock, and finally the heavy guns. Many of the men who marched down to the wharfs were too sick and weak to carry their own knapsacks or their guns, which were taken for them by the stronger men. The French did not have enough troopships for their 30,000 men and crammed them into their ships of war, rendering these useless if they were attacked by the Russian Black Sea Fleet. The defence of the convoy thus fell entirely to the Royal Navy, whose warships flanked the 29 steamers and 56 ships of the line carrying the British troops. On the quaysides there were disturbing scenes when it was announced that not all the soldiers' wives who had travelled out from Britain could be taken to the Crimea.* The grief-stricken women who were to be separated from their men fought to get on board the ships. Some were smuggled on. At the final moment, the commanders took pity on the women, having been informed that no provision had been made for them at Varna, and let many of them board the ships.

By 2 September the embarkation was complete, but bad weather delayed the departure until 7 September. The flotilla of 400 ships – steamers, men-of-war, troop transports, sailing ships, army tugs and other smaller vessels – was led by Rear Admiral Sir Edmund Lyons in HMS *Agamemnon*, the Royal Navy's first screw-propelled steamship, capable of sailing at 11 knots and armed with 91 guns. 'Men remember the beauteous morning of the 7th of September,' wrote Kinglake.

> The moonlight was still floating on the waters, when men, looking from numberless decks towards the east, were able to hail the dawn. There was a summer breeze blowing fair from the land. At a quarter before five a gun from the *Britannia* gave the signal to weigh. The air was obscured by the busy smoke of the engines, and it was hard to see how and whence due order would come; but presently the *Agamemnon* moved through, and with signals at all her masts – for Lyons was on board her, and was governing and ordering the convoy. The French steamers of war went out with their transports in tow, and their great vessels formed the line. The French went out more quickly than the English, and in better order. Many of their transports were vessels of very small size; and of necessity they were a swarm. Our transports went out in five columns of only thirty each. Then – guard over all – the English war-fleet, in single column, moved slowly out of the bay.[50]

---

* The British army had allowed four wives per company to go with their men to Gallipoli. Provided for by the army ('on the strength') the women performed cooking and laundry services.

7

Alma

Soon the allied fleets were strung out across the Black Sea, a moving forest of ships' masts interspersed with huge black clouds of smoke and steam. It was a fantastic sight, 'like a vast industrial city on the waters', noted Jean Cabrol, doctor to the French commander, Marshal Saint-Arnaud, who was now mortally sick on the *Ville de France*. Each French soldier carried rations for eight days in his kitbag – rice, sugar, coffee, lard and biscuit – and on boarding the transports he was given a large blanket which he laid out on the deck to sleep. The British had much less. 'The worst of it all', wrote John Rose, a private in the 50th Regiment, to his parents from Varna, 'is we cannot get a glass of groggy for money. We have living on 1 pound and a half of brown bread and 1 pound of meat per day but it is not for men.'[1]

The soldiers on the ships had no clear idea where they were going. At Varna they had been kept in the dark about the war plans, and all sorts of rumours had circulated among the men. Some thought they were going to Circassia, others to Odessa or the Crimea, but no one knew for sure what to expect. Without maps or any direct knowledge of the Russian southern coast, which they viewed from the ships as they might have looked upon the shores of Africa, the enterprise assumed the character of an adventure from the voyages of discovery. Ignorance gave free rein to the imagination of the men, some of whom believed that they would have to deal with bears and lions when they landed in 'the jungle' of Russia. Few had any idea of what they were fighting for – other than to 'beat the Russians' and 'do God's will', to quote just two French soldiers in their letters home. If the ideas of Private Rose are anything to go by, many of the soldiers did not even know who their allies were. 'We are 48 hours sail from

Seebastepol,' he wrote to his parents, his West Country accent affecting his spelling:

> and the place whear we have going to land is 6 myles from Seebastepol and the first ingagement will be with the Turkes and the russians. Thair is 30,000 Turkes and 40,000 Hasterems [Austrians] besides the Frinch and English and it will not be long before we comance and we hall think that the enemany will ground their harms when they se all the pours [powers] thairs is againest them and I hope it will please god to bring safe ought at the trouble and spare me to return to my materne home again and than I will be able to tell you abought the war.[2]

When the expedition left for the Crimea its leaders were uncertain where it was to land. On 8 September Raglan in the steamer *Caradoc* conferred with Saint-Arnaud in the *Ville de France* (with only one arm, Raglan could not board the French vessel, and Saint-Arnaud, who had stomach cancer, was too ill to leave his bed, so their conversations had to be conducted by intermediaries). Saint-Arnaud finally agreed to Raglan's choice of a landing site, at Kalamita Bay, a long sandy beach 45 kilometres north of Sevastopol, and on 10 September the *Caradoc* set off with a group of senior officers, including Saint-Arnaud's second-in-command, General François Canrobert, to undertake a reconnaissance of the Crimea's western coast. The allied plan had been to capture Sevastopol in a surprise attack, but this was ruled out by deciding to land as far away as Kalamita Bay.

To protect the landing parties from a possible attack by the Russians on their flank, the allied commanders decided first to occupy the town of Evpatoria, the only secure anchorage on that part of the coastline and a useful source of fresh water and supplies. From the sea, the most striking thing about the town was its large number of windmills. Evpatoria was a prosperous trading and grain-processing centre for the farms of the Crimean steppe. Its population of 9,000 people was made up mainly of Crimean Tatars, Russians, Greeks, Armenians and Karaite Jews, who had built a handsome synagogue in the centre of the town.[3]

The occupation of Evpatoria – the first landing by the allied armies on Russian soil – was comically straightforward. At noon on 13 September the allied fleets drew near to the harbour. The people of the town assembled on the quayside or watched from windows and roof-tops, as the small white-haired figure of Nikolai Ivanovich Kaznacheev, the commandant and governor and quarantine and customs officer of Evpatoria, stood at the end of the main pier in full dress uniform and regalia with a group of Russian officers to receive the French and British 'parliamentarians', intermediaries, who came ashore with their interpreter to negotiate the surrender of the town. There were no Russian forces in Evpatoria, except a few convalescent soldiers, so Kaznacheev had nothing to oppose the armed navies of the Western powers except the regulations of his offices; but on these he now relied, calmly, if pointlessly, insisting that the occupying forces land their troops at the Lazaretto so that they could go through quarantine. The next day the town was occupied by a small force of allied troops. They gave the population guarantees of their personal safety, undertook to pay for everything they took from them, and allowed them a day to leave, if they preferred. Many people from the region had already left, especially the Russians, the main administrators and landowners of the area, who in the days since the first sighting of the Western ships had packed their possessions onto carts and fled to Perekop, hoping to return to the mainland before the Crimea was cut off by the enemy. The Russians were as afraid of the Tatars – 80 per cent of the Crimean population – as they were of the invaders. When the allied fleets were seen from the Crimean coast, large groups of Tatar villagers had risen up against their Russian rulers and formed armed bands to help the invasion. On their way towards Perekop, many of the Russians were robbed and killed by these Tatar bands claiming to be confiscating property for the newly installed 'Turkish government' in Evpatoria.[4]

All along the coast, the Russian population fled in panic, followed by the Greeks. The roads were clogged with refugees, the carts and livestock heading north, against the flow of Russian soldiers moving south from Perekop. Simferopol was swamped by refugees from the coastal areas who brought fantastic stories about the size of the Western fleets. 'Many residents lost their heads and did not know what to do,' recalled Nikolai Mikhno, who lived in Simferopol, the administrative capital of the peninsula. 'Others began to pack their things as fast as they could and to leave the Crimea ... They began to talk in frightening terms about how the allies would continue their invasion by marching straight on Simferopol, which could not protect itself.'[5]

It was this feeling of defencelessness that fuelled the panic flight. Menshikov, the commander of the Russian forces in the Crimea, had been taken by surprise. He had not thought the allies would attack so close to the onset of winter, and had failed to mobilize sufficient forces to defend the Crimea. There were 38,000 soldiers and 18,000 sailors along the south-western coast, and 12,000 troops around Kerch and Theodosia – far less than the numbers of attackers imagined by the frightened population of the Crimea. Simferopol had only one battalion.[6]

On 14 September, the same date as the French had entered Moscow in 1812, the allied fleets dropped anchor in Kalamita Bay, south of Evpatoria. From the Alma Heights, further to the south, where Menshikov had positioned his main forces to defend the road to Sevastopol, Robert Chodasiewicz, the captain of a Cossack regiment, described the impressive sight:

> On reaching our position on the heights, one of the most beautiful sights it was ever my lot to behold lay before us. The whole of the allied fleet was lying off the salt lakes to the south of Evpatoria, and at night their forest of masts was illuminated with various-coloured lanterns. Both men and officers were lost in amazement at the sight of such a large number of ships together, especially as many of them had hardly ever seen the sea before. The soldiers said, 'Behold, the infidel has built another holy Moscow on the waves!', comparing the masts of the ships to the church spires of that city.[7]

The French were the first to disembark, their advance parties scrambling ashore and erecting coloured tents at measured distances along the beach to designate the separate landing points for the infantry divisions of Canrobert, General Pierre Bosquet and Prince Napoleon, the Emperor's cousin. By nightfall they had all been disembarked with their artillery. The men put up the French flag and went off to hunt for firewood and food, some of them returning with ducks and chickens, their water cans refilled with wine they had discovered in the nearby farms. Paul de Molènes and his Spahi cavalry had neither meat nor bread for their first meal on Russian soil, 'but we had some biscuit and a bottle of champagne which we had set aside to celebrate our victory'.[8]

The British landing was a shambles compared to the French – a contrast that would become all too familiar during the Crimean War. No plans had been made for a peaceful landing unopposed (it was assumed that they would have to fight their way onto the beach), so the infantry was landed first, when the sea was calm; by the time the British tried to get their cavalry ashore, the wind was up, and the horses struggled in the heavy surf. Saint-Arnaud, set up comfortably in a chair with his newspaper on the beach, watched the scene with mounting frustration, as his plans for a surprise attack on Sevastopol were undermined by the delay. 'The English have the unpleasant habit of always being late,' he wrote to the Emperor.[9]

It took five days for the British troops and cavalry to disembark. Many of the men were sick with cholera and had to be carried off the boats. There were no facilities for moving baggage and equipment overland, so parties had to be sent out to collect carts and wagons from the local Tatar farms. There was no food or water for the men, except the three days' rations they had been given at Varna, and no tents or kitbags were offloaded from the ships, so the soldiers spent their first nights without shelter, unprotected from the heavy rain or the blistering heat of the next days. 'We brought nothing on shore with us excepting our blankets and great coats,' George Lawson, an army surgeon, wrote home to his family. 'We suffer dreadfully from want of water. The first day was very hot; we had nothing to drink but water drained out of puddles from the previous night's rain; and even now the water is so thick that, if put into a glass, you cannot see the bottom of it at all.'[10]

At last, on 19 September, the British were prepared and, at day-break, the advance on Sevastopol began. The French marched on the right, nearest the sea, their blue uniforms contrasting with the scarlet tunics of the British, while the fleet moved south alongside them as they advanced. Six and a half kilometres wide and just under 5 kilometres long, the advancing column was 'all bustle and activity', wrote Frederick Oliver, bandmaster of the 20th Regiment, in his diary. Apart from the compact lines of soldiers, there was an enormous train of 'cavalry, guns, ammunition, horses, bullocks, pack-horses, mules, herds of dromedaries, a drove of oxen, and a tremendous drove of sheep, goats and bullocks, all of which had been taken from the surrounding countryside by the foraging parties'. By midday, with the sun beating down, the column began to break up, as thirsty soldiers fell behind or left to search for water in the nearby Tatar settlements. When they reached the River Bulganak, 12 kilometres from Kalamita Bay, in the middle of the afternoon, discipline broke down altogether, as the British soldiers threw themselves into the 'muddy stream'.[11]

Ahead of them, on the slopes rising south from the river, the British got their first sight of the Russians – 2,000 Cossack cavalry who opened fire on a scouting party from the 13th Light Dragoons. The rest of the Light Brigade, the pride of the British cavalry, prepared to charge the Cossacks, who outnumbered them by two to one, but Raglan saw that behind the Russian horsemen there was a sizeable infantry force that could not be seen by his cavalry commanders, Lord Lucan and Lord Cardigan, who were further down the hill. Raglan ordered a retreat, and the Light Brigade withdrew, while the Cossacks jeered and shot at them, wounding several cavalrymen,* before themselves retreating to the River Alma, further south, where the Russians had prepared their positions on the heights. The incident was a humiliation for the Light Brigade, which had been forced to back down from a fight with the ragged-looking Cossacks in full view of the British infantry, men from poor and labouring families, who took malicious pleasure from the embarrassment of the elegantly tailored and comfortably mounted cavalry. 'Serve them bloody right, silly peacock bastards,' wrote one private in a letter home.[12]

The British bivouacked on the southern slopes of the Bulganak, from which they could make out the Russian troops amassed on the Alma Heights, 5 kilometres away. The next morning they would march down the valley and engage the Russians, whose defences were on the other side of the Alma.

Menshikov had decided to commit the majority of his land forces to the defence of the Alma Heights, the last natural barrier on the

---

* The first British casualty of the fighting was Sergeant Priestley of the 13th Light Dragoons, who lost a leg. Evacuated to England, he was later presented with a cork leg by the Queen (A. Mitchell, *Recollections of One of the Light Brigade* (London, 1885), p. 50).

enemy's approach to Sevastopol, which his troops had occupied since 15 September, but his fears of a second allied landing at Kerch or Theodosia (fears which the Tsar shared) led him to keep back a large reserve. Thus there were 35,000 Russian soldiers on the Alma Heights – less than the 60,000 Western troops but with the crucial advantage of the hills – and more than 100 guns. The heaviest guns were deployed on a series of redoubts above the road to Sevastopol that crossed the river 4 kilometres inland, but there were none on the cliffs facing the sea, which Menshikov assumed were too steep for the enemy to climb. The Russians had made themselves at home, pillaging the nearby village of Burliuk after forcing the Tatars out, and carrying off bedding, doors, planks of wood and tree branches up onto the heights, where they constructed makeshift cabins for themselves and gorged on grapes from the abandoned farms. They stuffed the village houses with hay and straw in preparation for burning them when the enemy advanced. The Russian commanders were confident of holding their positions for at least a week – Menshikov had written to the Tsar promising that he could hold the heights for six times as long – winning precious time for the defences of Sevastopol to be strengthened and shifting the campaign on towards winter, the Russians' greatest weapon against the invading army. Many officers were sure of victory. They joked about the British being only good for fighting 'savages' in their colonies, drank toasts to the memory of 1812 and talked of driving the French back into the sea. Menshikov was so confident that he invited parties of Sevastopol ladies to watch the battle with him from the Alma Heights.[13]

The Russian troops themselves were not so confident. Ferdinand Pflug, a German doctor in the tsarist army, thought that 'each one seemed convinced that the next day's battle would end in defeat'.[14] Few if any of these men had ever engaged in a battle with the army of a major European power. The sight of the mighty allied fleet anchored just off shore and ready to support the enemy's land forces with its heavy guns made it clear to them that they were going to fight an army stronger than their own. While most of their senior commanders could hark back to their memories of battle in the wars against Napoleon, the younger men, who would do the actual fighting, had no such experience on which to draw.

Like all soldiers on the eve of a big battle, they tried to hide their fear from their comrades. As the heat of the day gave way to a cold night, the men of both the armies prepared themselves for the next morning: for many of the men these would be their last hours. They lit fires, cooked their dinners and waited. Most of the soldiers ate little. Some went through the ritual of cleaning their muskets. Others wrote letters to their families. Many of them prayed. The next day was a religious holiday in the Orthodox calendar, the date on which the Russians marked the birth of the Blessed Virgin, and services were held to pray for her protection. Groups of soldiers sat around the fires, talking late into the night, the older ones recounting tales of past battles to the younger men. They drank and smoked, and told jokes, trying to seem calm. Now and then the sound of men singing would drift across the plain. From the Sevastopol Road, where Menshikov had set up his tent, the band and choir of the Tarutinsky Regiment could be heard – their deep bass voices rendering the lines of a song composed by General Gorchakov:

> He alone is worthy of life
> Who is always ready to die;
> The Russian Orthodox warrior
> Strikes his foes without thinking twice.
> The French, the English – what of them?
> So what about the stupid Turkish lines?
> Come out, you infidels,
> We challenge you to fight!
> We challenge you to fight!

Gradually, as the dark sky filled with stars, the fires died down and the hum of talking became quieter. The men lay down and tried to sleep, though few did, and an eerie silence settled over the valley, broken only by the barking of hungry dogs roaming the deserted village.[15]

At three o'clock in the morning, Chodasiewicz could not sleep. It was still dark. In the Russian camp the soldiers 'were collected around the huge fires they had kindled with the plunder of the village of Burliuk'.

After a short time I went up the hill (for our battalion was stationed in a ravine) to take a peep at the bivouac of the allied armies. Little, however, was to be seen but the fires, and now and then a dark shadow as someone moved past them. All was still and had little appearance of the coming strife. These were both armies lying, as it were, side by side. How many, or who, would be sent to their last account, it would be impossible to say. The question involuntarily thrust itself upon me, should I be one of that number?[16]

By four o'clock the French camp was stirring. The men prepared their coffee and joked about the beating they were going to give to the Russians, and then the order came for them to put on their kitbags and fall into line to listen to the orders of their officers. 'By thunder!' the captain of the 22nd Regiment addressed his men. 'Are we Frenchmen or not? The 22nd will earn distinction for itself today, or you are all scoundrels. If any one of you lags behind today, I will run my sabre through his guts. Line up to the Right!' In the Russian camp the men were also up with the first light and listening to speeches from their commanders: 'Now, lads, the good time has come at last, though we have waited some time for it; we will not disgrace our Russian land; we will drive back the enemy, and please our good father, Batiushka the Tsar; then we can return to our homes with the laurels we have earned.' At seven o'clock in the Russian camp prayers were said to the Mother of God calling on her aid against the enemy. Priests carried icons through the ranks as soldiers bowed down to the ground and crossed themselves in prayer.[17]

*

By mid-morning the allied armies were assembling on the plain, the British on the left of the Sevastopol Road, the French and Turks on the right, stretching out towards the coastal cliffs. It was a clear and sunny day, and the air was still. From Telegraph Hill, where Menshikov's well-dressed spectators had arrived in carriages to watch the scene, the details of the French and British uniforms could be clearly seen; the sound of their drums, their bugles and bagpipes, even the clinking of metal and the neighing of the horses could be heard.[18]

The Russians opened fire when the allies came within 1,800 metres – a spot marked with poles to let their gunners know the advancing troops were within range – but the British and the French continued marching forward towards the river. According to the plan that the allies had agreed the day before, the two armies were to advance simultaneously on a broad front and try to turn the enemy's flank on the left – the inland side. But at the final moment Raglan decided to delay the British advance until the French had broken through on the right; he made his troops lie on the ground, within range of the Russian guns, in a position from which they could scramble to the river when the time was right. There they lay for an hour and a half, from 1.15 to 2.45 p.m., losing men as the Russian gunners found their range. It was an astonishing example of Raglan's indecisiveness.[19]

While the British were lying on the ground, Bosquet's division arrived at the river near the sea, where the cliffs rose so steeply to the heights, almost 50 metres above the river, that Menshikov had thought it was unneccessary to defend the position with artillery. At the head of Bosquet's division was a regiment of Zouaves, most of them North Africans, who had experience of mountain fighting in Algeria. Leaving their kitbags on the riverbank, they swam across the river and quickly climbed the cliffs under heavy cover of the trees. The Russians were amazed by the agility of the Zouaves, comparing them to monkeys in the way they used the trees to scale the cliffs. Once they had reached the plateau, the Zouaves hid behind rocks and bushes to pick off the defending forces of the Moscow Regiment one by one until reinforcements could arrive. 'The Zouaves were so well hidden', recalled Noir, who was among the first to reach the top, 'that a well-trained officer arriving on the scene would hardly have been able to pick them out with his own eyes.' Inspired by the Zouaves, more French soldiers climbed the cliffs. They hauled twelve guns up a ravine – the men hit their horses with their swords if they refused to climb the rocky path – arriving just in time to engage the extra soldiers and artillery that Menshikov had transferred from the centre in a desperate attempt to stop his left flank being turned.[20]

The Russian position was more or less hopeless. By the time their artillery arrived, the whole of Bosquet's division and many of the Turks had reached the plateau. The Russians had more guns – 28 to the French 12 – but the French guns were of larger calibre and longer range, and Bosquet's riflemen kept the Russian gunners at a distance where only the heavier French guns could take effect. Sensing their advantage, some of the Zouaves, exalted by the fighting, danced a polka on the battlefield to taunt the enemy, knowing that the Russian guns could not reach them. Meanwhile, the guns of the allied fleet were pounding the Russian positions on the cliffs, undermining the morale of many of their troops and officers. When the first Russian battery of artillery arrived, it found the remnants of the Moscow Regiment already in retreat under heavy fire from the Zouaves, whose Minié rifles had a longer range and greater accuracy than the out-dated muskets of the Russian infantry. The commanding officer on the left flank, Lieutenant General V. I. Kiriakov, was one of the most incompetent in the tsarist army, and was rarely in a sober state. Hold-ing a bottle of champagne in his hand, Kiriakov ordered the Minsk Regiment to shoot at the French but misdirected them towards the Kiev Hussars, who fell back under the fire. Lacking confidence in their drunken commander, and unnerved by the lethal accuracy of the French rifles, the Minsk Regiment also began to retreat.[21]

Meanwhile, in the centre of the battlefield, the two other French divisions, led by Canrobert and Prince Napoleon, were unable to cross the Alma in the face of heavy Russian fire from Telegraph Hill directly opposite. Prince Napoleon sent word to General de Lacy Evans, on his left, calling on the British to advance and take some pressure off the French. Raglan was still waiting for the French attack to succeed before committing British troops, and at first told Evans not to take orders from the French, but under pressure from Evans he finally gave way. At 2.45 p.m., he ordered the infantry of the Light, 1st and 2nd Divisions to advance – though what else they should do he did not say. The order was typical of Raglan's think-ing, which remained rooted in the bygone age of Napoleonic battles, when the infantry was used for primitive direct attacks on prepared positions.

As soon as the men rose from their lying positions on the ground, the Russian Cossack skirmishers, who had been hiding in the vine-yards, set alight the village of Burliuk to obstruct their advance – though in fact all this did was raise a cloud of smoke, which made it more difficult for the Russian gunners to hit them. The British advanced in thin lines to maximize their rifle power, although in this formation it was hard to keep the men together over rough terrain without effective commanders of the line. The Russians were amazed by the sight of the thin red line emerging from the smoke. 'This was the most extraordinary thing to us,' recalled Chodasiewicz; 'we had never before seen troops fight in lines of two deep, nor did we think it possible for men to be found with sufficient firmness of morale to be able to attack in this apparently weak formation our massive columns.'

The advancing lines broke up as they passed through the burning village and vineyards. A greyhound ran around them chasing hares. Moving forward in small groups, the British cleared the village of the Russian skirmishers and drove them out of the vineyards. 'We rushed on driving the enemy's skirmishers before us,' recalled Private Bloomfield of the Derbyshire Regiment. 'Some of these skirmishers even got up trees, so they could get a good shot at us, but we saw them and brought them off their perch. Some of these when falling from the trees . . . would catch their feet or clothes in some parts of the tree and hang there for hours.' As they neared the river, the British came within firing range of the Russian guns. Men fell silently as they were hit but the rest of the line kept moving forward. 'The most striking thing to me', recalled Lieutenant General Brown of the Light Division, 'was the silent way in which death did its work. No sight or sound betrayed the cause; a man dropped, rolled over, or fell out of ranks to the dust. One knew the little bullet had found its destination, but it seemed to happen in mysterious silence – they disappeared, were left, as we went past them.'[22]

Under heavy fire, the men reached the river, collecting in groups at the water's edge to unload their equipment, unsure of the water's depth. Holding their rifles and ammunition pouches above their heads, some men managed to wade across, but others had to swim, and some drowned in the fast current. All the time, the Russians fired at them with grape-shot and shell. There were 14 Russian guns in the earthworks and 24 on either side of the road bridge. By the time Private Bloomfield reached the Alma near the bridge, 'the river was red with blood'. Many men were too frightened to get into the water, which was full of dead bodies. They hugged the ground on the riverbank while mounted officers galloped up and down, shouting at the men to swim across, and sometimes even threatening to cut them with their swords. Once they had crossed the river, all order was lost. Companies and regiments became jumbled together, and where there had been lines two men deep there was now just a crowd. The Russians began to advance down the hill from either side of the Great Redoubt, firing on the British down below, where mounted officers galloped round their men, urging them to reform lines; but it was impossible, the men were exhausted from crossing the river, and happy to be in the shelter of the riverbank where they could not be seen from the heights. Some sat down and took out their water cans; others got out bread and meat and began to eat.

Aware of the danger of the situation, Major-General Codrington, in command of the 1st Brigade of the Light Division, made a desperate effort to regroup his men. Spurring his white Arab charger up the hill, he bellowed at the crowd of infantry: 'Fix bayonets! Get up the bank and advance to the attack!' Soon the whole of Codrington's brigade – the regiments all jumbled up – began scrambling up the Kurgan Hill in a thick crowd. Junior commanders gave up forming lines – there was no time – but urged their men to 'Come on anyhow!' Once they had climbed onto the open slopes, most of the men began to charge with yells and screams towards the Russian guns in the Great Redoubt, 500 metres up the slope. The Russian gunners were astonished by the sight of this British mob – 2,000 men running up the hill – and found easy targets. Some of the Light Division's advance guard reached the entrenchments of the Great Redoubt. Soldiers clambered over the parapets and through the embrasures, only to be shot or cut down by the Russians, who hurriedly withdrew their guns. Within a few minutes, the Great Redoubt was a swarm of men, pockets of them fighting on the parapets, others cheering and waving their colours, as two Russian guns were captured in the confusion.

But suddenly the British were confronted by four battalions (some 3,000 men) of the Vladimirsky Regiment pouring into the Redoubt from the open higher ground, while more Russian guns were pitching shell at them from higher up the Kurgan Hill. With one loud 'Ooorah!' the Russian infantry began charging with their bayonets, driving out the British, and firing at them as they retreated down the hill. The Light Division 'made a front' to fire back, but suddenly and unexpectedly there was a bugle call to cease firing, copied by the buglers of every regiment. For a few fatal moments there was a confused pause in the firing on the British side: an unnamed officer had thought that the Russians were the French and had ordered his men to stop firing. By the time the mistake was corrected, the Vladimirsky soldiers had gained the upper hand; they were steadily advancing down the hill and British troops were lying dead and wounded everywhere. Now buglers truly did give the order to retreat, and the whole rabble of the Light Division, or what was left of it, was soon running down the hill towards the shelter of the riverbank.

The charge had partly failed because there had been no second wave, the Duke of Cambridge having stopped the Guards from advancing in support of the Light Division for lack of further orders from Raglan (another blunder on his part). Evans, on his right, got the Guards marching once again by giving the Duke an order to advance which he pretended had come from Raglan, who in fact was nowhere to be seen.*

The three regiments of the Guards Brigade (Grenadiers, Scots Fusiliers and Coldstream) waded across the river. In their red tunics and bearskins they were an imposing sight. On the other side of the river they took an age to reassemble into lines. Irritated by their dithering, Sir Colin Campbell, the commander of the Highland Brigade, ordered an immediate advance. A firm believer in the charge with bayonets, Campbell told his men not to fire their rifles until they were 'within a yard of the Russians'. The Scots Fusiliers, who had crossed the river before the other Guards, at once began charging up the hill, repeating the mistake of the Light Division, which at that moment was running down the hill pursued by the Russian infantry. The two crowds of men ran straight through each other – the Scots Fusiliers bearing the main brunt of the collision, with men knocked over and bearskins

---

* Having given the order to advance, Raglan had taken the incredible decision to ride up ahead and get a better view of the attack. With his staff, Raglan crossed the Alma and occupied a position on an exposed spur of Telegraph Hill, well ahead of the British troops and practically adjacent to the Russian skirmishers. 'It seems marvellous how one escaped,' wrote Captain Gage, a member of Raglan's staff, from the Alma the next day. 'Shells burst close to me, round shot passed to the right, left & over me. Minié and musket whistled by my ears, horses & riders of Ld R's staff (where I was) fell dead & wounded by my side, & yet I am quite safe & can hardly realize what I have gone thro'' (NAM 1968–07–484–1, 'Alma Heights Battle Field, Sept. 21st 1854').

flying everywhere, so that when they emerged on the other side and continued running towards the Great Redoubt they were only half their number and in a chaotic state. In the centre of this mob was Hugh Annesley, a 23-year-old ensign, who recalled what happened next:

> Suddenly the Russians seemed to line the redoubt again and their fire grew hotter and then the 23rd came down in one mass, right on top of our line. . . . I kept on shouting, 'Forward, Guards', and we had got within 30 or 40 yards of the intrenchment, when a musket ball hit me full in the mouth, and I thought it was all over with me; just then our Adjutant rode up with his revolver in his hand and gave us the order to retire; I turned round and ran as fast as I could down the hill to the river, the balls were coming through us now even hotter than ever, and I felt sure that I should never get away without being struck again; half-way down I stumbled and fell, then I was quite certain I was hit again, but I got up all right, and went on. I lost my sword and bearskin here; at last I reached the riverbank and got under shelter, there were crowds of soldiers here.

Annesley had been badly wounded: the bullet that had entered his left cheek had come out at the right corner of his mouth, taking away twenty-three of his teeth and part of his tongue. Around him was the rest of his shattered regiment, which remained in the shelter of the riverbank for the rest of the battle, ignoring repeated orders to advance.[23]

The other two regiments (the Grenadiers and Coldstream Guards) filled the gap left by the Scots Fusiliers, but refused orders to advance up the hill. Instead, on their own initiative, the 2,000 Guards formed into lines and fired fourteen volleys of Minié rifle shot into the Russian infantry. The volleys delivered an intensity of fire achieved by half a dozen machine guns. They stunned the Russian infantry, who fell in heaps upon the ground, and then withdrew up the hill. By disobeying their commanders, who had ordered them to charge with bayonets, the Guards had demonstrated a crucial innovation – the long-range firepower of the modern rifle – which would prove decisive in all the early battles of the Crimean War. The Minié was a new weapon. Most regiments had been issued with it only on their way to the Crimea, and had received a hurried training in how to use it. They had no idea of its tactical significance – its ability to fire with a lethal accuracy from well beyond the range of the Russian muskets and artillery – until the Guards discovered it for themselves on the Alma. Reflecting on the impact of the Minié rifle, the Russian military engineer Eduard Totleben wrote in his history of the Crimean War:

> Left to themselves to perform the role of sharpshooters, the British troops did not hesitate under fire and did not require orders or supervision. Troops thus armed were full of confidence once they found out the accuracy and immense range of their weapon . . . Our infantry with their muskets could not reach the enemy at greater than 300 paces, while they fired on us at 1,200. The enemy, perfectly convinced of the superiority of his small arms, avoided close combat; every time our battalions charged, he retired for some distance, and began a murderous fusillade. Our columns, in pressing the attack, only succeeded in suffering terrible losses, and finding it impossible to pass through the hail of bullets which overwhelmed them, were obliged to fall back before reaching the enemy.

Without entrenchments to protect their infantry and artillery, the Russians were unable to defend their positions on the heights against the deadly Minié rifles. Soon the fire of the Guards was joined by that of the 2nd Division under Evans, on the British right, whose 30th Regiment could clearly see the gunners of three Russian batteries from the riverbank and take them out with their Minié rifles without the Russians even knowing where the firing was from. As the Russian infantry and artillery withdrew, the British slowly advanced up the hill, stepping over the dead and wounded bodies of the enemy. 'Most of the wounded were crying out for water,' Private Bloomfield wrote. 'A man of my company gave a wounded Russian a drink of water, and as he left him, the Russian rose on his elbow, took his musket in his hand, and fired at the man that gave him the water. The bullet passed close by the man's head. The man turned round immediately and ran his bayonet through the body of the Russian.' By four o'clock in the afternoon, the British were converging on the Russian positions from all directions – the Guards on the left overcoming the last Russian reserves on the Kurgan Hill, Codrington's men and the other Guards closing in on the Great Redoubt, and the 2nd Division pushing up the Sevastopol Road. With the French in command of the cliffs above the Alma, it was clear that the battle had been won.[24]

By this stage, on the Russian side, there were signs of panic, as the enemy closed in and the devastating effect of their long-range rifle fire became apparent. Priests went round the lines to bless the troops, and soldiers prayed with growing fervency, while mounted officers used the knout to whip them forward into line. But otherwise there was a general absence of authority among the Russian commanders. 'Nobody gave any direction what to do,' recalled Chodasiewicz. 'During the five hours that the battle went on we neither saw nor heard of our general of division, or brigadier, or colonel: we did not receive any orders from them either to advance or to retire; and when we retired, nobody knew whether we ought to go to the right or left.' The drunken Kiriakov gave a general order to retreat from the left flank of the heights, but then lost his nerve and went missing for several hours (he was discovered later hiding in a hollow in the ground). It was left to the junior commanders to organize the retreat from the heights, but 'we had the greatest difficulty to keep our men in order', recalled Chodasiewicz, who had to threaten 'to cut down the first man who should break out of the ranks' – a threat he had to carry out more than once.

With no clear idea of where they were to go, the Russians fled in all directions, running down the hill into the valley, away from the enemy. Mounted officers tried in vain to stop the panic flight, riding round the men and whipping them, like cowboys rounding up cattle; but the men had lost all patience with their commanders. Chodasiewicz overheard a conversation between two soldiers:

> 1st soldier: 'Yes, during the fights we saw nothing of these great folks [the officers] but now they are as thick as imps with their shouting "Silence! Keep step!"'
>
> 2nd soldier: 'You are always grumbling, just like a Pole; you are enough to anger Providence, whom we ought to thank for our lives.'
>
> 1st soldier: 'It's all the same to you, provided you are not flogged.'

Chodasiewicz spoke of chaos and confusion, of barely sober officers, 'of the ten minutes of fear and trembling on the second line of heights, when we saw the enemy's cavalry coming forward to cut down the retreating stragglers, for the most part wounded men'.[25]

In the end the Russians were defeated, not just by the superior fire-power of the Minié rifle, but by a loss of nerve among their men. For Ardant du Picq, who would develop his military theories from questionnaires he sent to the Frenchmen who had fought at the Alma, this moral factor was the decisive element in modern war. Large groups of men rarely engaged physically, he maintained, because at the final moment before the point of contact one side nearly always lost its nerve and ran away. The key thing on the battlefield was military discipline – the ability of officers to hold their men together and stop them fleeing out of fear – because it was when they turned their backs to the enemy that soldiers were most likely to be killed. The suppression of fear was thus the main task of the officer, something he could achieve only through his own authority and the unity he instilled in his men.

> What makes the soldier capable of obedience and direction in action is the sense of discipline. This includes: respect for and confidence in his chiefs; confidence in his comrades and fear of their reproaches and retaliation if he abandons them in danger; his desire to go where others do without trembling more than they; in a word, the whole of *esprit de corps*. Organization only can produce these characteristics. Four men equal a lion.

These ideas, which were to become central to the military theories of the twentieth century, first became apparent to du Picq in a letter written to him in 1869 by a veteran of the Alma. The soldier had recalled the crucial intervention of his company commander, who had halted the panic of his men after a senior commander had mistakenly assumed that the Russian cavalry was about to charge and had ordered the bugler to signal a retreat:

> Happily, a level-headed officer, Captain Daguerre, seeing the gross mistake, commanded 'Forward' in a stentorian tone. This halted the retreat and caused us again to take up the attack. The attack made us masters of the telegraph-line, and the battle was won. At this second charge the Russians gave, turned, and hardly any of them were wounded with the

bayonet. So then a Major commanding a battalion, without orders, sounds a bugle call and endangers success. A simple Captain commands 'Forward', and decides the victory.[26]

By half past four the battle was over. Most of the Russians had retreated towards the River Kacha in small groups, without leaders or any clear idea of what to do or where to go. Many men would not be reunited with their regiments for several days. At the top of Telegraph Hill the French captured the abandoned carriage of Prince Menshikov, which was being driven off by some Cossacks. In the carriage they found a field kitchen, letters from the Tsar, 50,000 francs, porno-graphic French novels, the general's boots, and some ladies' underwear. On the hill were abandoned picnics, parasols and field glasses left behind by parties of spectators from Sevastopol.[27]

On the battlefield itself the ground was covered with the wounded and the dead – 2,000 British, 1,600 French and perhaps 5,000 Russians, though the exact numbers are impossible to calcu-late, since so many of them were abandoned there. It took the British two full days to clear the battlefield of the wounded. They had neglected to bring any medical supplies on the ships from Varna – the ambulance corps with its carts and wagons and stretchers was still in Bulgaria – so doctors had to plead with the commissariat for military carts to remove the wounded from the battlefield. Store-keeper John Rowe of the commissariat emptied his cart of its saddles to help with the wounded, and on his way back to collect his cargo came across a group of wounded officers, among them Hugh Annesley:

An officer of the 30th with a damaged arm was partly supporting an officer of the Scots Fusilier Guards. This officer was leaning forward and dripping blood from his mouth. He could not speak but wrote with a pencil in a small book that he was the Hon[oura]ble Annesley and that a ball was lodged in his throat after having knocked away some of his teeth and part of his tongue. He wanted to know what part of the field (if I may so call it) the Fusilier Doctor had his stand and whether I could convey him there. I could not tell him anything of the Doctor . . . I also told him I had no discretion as to the use of the mule cart but to fulfil the duty I was there upon.

Hugh Annesley after his return from the Crimea,
the black patch covering his wound

Annesley was left to find a doctor on his own. What treatment he received remains unknown, but it would not have involved more than
cutting out the ball, probably without the use of proper dressings or
any chloroform to dull the shock and pain. Treatments on the battlefield were rudimentary. The staff surgeon of the Light Division, George
Lawson, carried out his operations on the ground, until an old door
was discovered which he made into an improvised operating table.[28]

Early the next morning, Somerset Calthorpe, a nephew of Lord

Raglan and one of his aides-de-camp, filled his flask with brandy and 'sallied out to walk over the field of battle'.

> The poor wounded were far more quiet than the previous evening; many doubtless had died during the night, and many were too weak and exhausted to do more than moan. I found all glad of something to drink . . . It was a horrible scene – death in every shape and form. I particularly observed that those shot through the heart or forehead appeared all to have died with a smile on their faces, generally speaking lying flat on their backs, with the arms spread out and the legs rather apart . . . Those who appeared to have died in the greatest pain were those shot through the stomach; these had always their legs and arms bent, and with all expression of agony on their faces.[29]

The Russians were unable to collect their wounded from the battle-field.* Those who could walk were left to look for treatment on their own, many of them staggering to the dressing stations set up on the River Kacha, 15 kilometres south of the Alma, or limping back to Sevastopol over the next days. A Russian orderly recalled the scene on the first evening, as he set off with his vehicles for the Kacha:

* A lone Russian woman, Daria Mikhailova, cared for the wounded with a cart and supplies purchased at her own expense. Daria was the 18-year-old daughter of a Sevastopol sailor killed at the battle of Sinope. At the time of the invasion, she was working as a laundress in the Sevastopol naval garrison. According to popular legend, she sold everything she had inherited from her father, bought a horse and cart from a Jewish trader, cut her hair and dressed up as a sailor, and went with the army to the Alma, where she distributed water, food and wine to the wounded soldiers, even tearing her own clothes to make dressings for their wounds, which she cleaned with vinegar. The soldiers saw through Daria's disguise, but she was allowed to carry on with her heroic work in the dressing station at Kacha and then as a nurse in the hospitals of Sevastopol during the siege. Legends spread about the 'heroine of Sevastopol'. She came to symbolize the patriotic spirit of the common people as well as the Russian female 'spirit of sacrifice' that poets such as Alexander Pushkin had romanticized. Not knowing her family name, the soldiers in the hospitals of Sevastopol called her Dasha Sevastopol-skaia, and that is how she has gone down in history. In December 1854 she was awarded the Gold Medal for Zeal by the Tsar, becoming the only Russian woman of non-noble origin ever to receive that honour; the Empress gave her a silver cross with the inscription 'Sevastopol'. In 1855 Daria married a retired wounded soldier and opened a tavern in Sevastopol, where she lived until her death in 1892 (H. Rappaport, *No Place for Ladies: The Untold Story of Women in the Crimean War* (London, 2007), p. 77).

Hundreds of wounded had been deserted by their regiments, and these, with heart-rending cries and moans and pleading gestures, begged to be lifted into the carts and carriages. But what could I do for them? We were already packed to overloading. I tried to console them by telling them that their regimental wagons were coming back for them, although of course they did not. One man could hardly drag himself along – he was without arms and his belly was shot through; another had his leg blown off and his jaw smashed, with his tongue torn out and his body covered with wounds – only the expression on his face pleaded for a mouthful of water. But where to get even that?

Those who could not walk, about 1,600 wounded Russian soldiers, were abandoned on the battlefield, where they lay for several days, until the British and the French, having cleared their own, took care of them, burying the dead and carting off the wounded to their hospitals in Scutari on the outskirts of Constantinople.[30]

Three days after the battle, William Russell described the Russians 'groaning and palpitating as they lay around'.

Some were placed together in heaps, that they might be more readily removed. Others glared upon you from the bushes with the ferocity of wild beasts, as they hugged their wounds. Some implored, in an unknown tongue, but in accents not to be mistaken, water, or succour; holding out their mutilated and shattered limbs, or pointing to the track of the lacerating ball. The sullen, angry scowl of some of these men was fearful. Fanaticism and immortal hate spoke through their angry eyeballs, and he who gazed on them with pity and compassion could at last (unwillingly) understand how these men could in their savage passion kill the wounded, and fire on the conqueror who, in his generous humanity, had aided them as he passed.[31]

There had been incidents of wounded Russians shooting at the British and French soldiers who had given them water. There were also some reported cases of the Russians killing wounded soldiers on the battlefield. Fear and hatred of the enemy were behind these incidents. French interrogations of the Russian soldiers captured at the Alma revealed that the Russians had been 'told the most fantastic stories by their priests – that we were monsters capable of the most ferocious savagery and even

cannibals'. Reports of these 'dishonourable' killings outraged British soldiers and public opinion, reinforcing their belief that the Russians were
'no better than savages'. But such outrage was hypocritical. There were
many incidents of British soldiers killing wounded Russians, and disturbing cases of the British shooting Russian prisoners because they were
'troublesome'. It should also be remembered that the British walked
among the Russian wounded, not only to give them water, but sometimes
to steal from them. They took silver crosses from their necks, rooted
through their kitbags for souvenirs, and helped themselves to what they
fancied from the living and the dead. 'I have got a beautiful trophy for
you from the Alma, just one to suit you,' wrote Hugh Drummond of the
Scots Guards to his mother, 'a large silver Greek cross with engravings on
it – our Saviour and some Russian words; it came off a Russian Colonel's
neck we killed, and, poor fellow, it was next to his skin.'[32]

*

If the allies had pushed on directly from the Alma, they would have
taken Sevastopol by surprise. In all probability, they would have captured it in a few days, at relatively little cost in human lives compared
to the many tens of thousands who were to die during the 349-day
siege that followed from their errors and delays.

The Russian forces were in disarray, and Sevastopol virtually
defenceless, on 21 September. To make matters worse, Menshikov
decided that it was not worth committing any more of his demoralized troops to the defence of the city. Once he had gathered the
remnants of his army at the Kacha, he set off on a march towards
Bakhchiserai to prevent the allies from cutting off the Crimea at Perekop and to wait for reinforcements from the Russian mainland,
leaving Sevastopol in the hands of just 5,000 troops and 10,000 sailors, who were completely untrained for this sort of war. The Russians
had not thought that the allies would invade before the spring, and
had not reinforced the defences of Sevastopol. The city's northern
fortifications had not been greatly improved since they were built in
1818.* The Star Fort's walls were falling down from years of neglect

* The engineering department of the War Ministry had failed to implement a plan of
1834 to reinforce the city's defensive works, claiming lack of finance, though at the

and disrepair and not defended by sufficient guns to withstand a serious attack. On the southern side, Menshikov had ordered the construction of three new batteries in January 1854, but the defences there were in only slightly better shape. Facing the sea were extensive walls, armed with formidable batteries, and at the entrance to the harbour there were two well-armed fortresses, the Quarantine Battery and the Alexander Fort, which taken all together were enough to nullify the gunpower of the allied fleet. But on the land side the defences to the south of Sevastopol were relatively weak. A single stone wall about 4 metres high and 2 metres thick – with earthworks and stone batteries in the most commanding positions – protected only parts of the town. Not all these fortifications were able to withstand bombardment by mortar shells, and the stone wall was only good against musketry. Overall, the city was extremely vulnerable, and the expectation was that it could fall at any time. According to Totleben, who was placed in charge of the defensive works, 'there was practically nothing to stop the enemy from walking into the city'.[33]

Instead of moving swiftly to Sevastopol to take up its defence, the Russian troops retreating from the Alma battlefield allowed themselves to be diverted and delayed by looting the estates abandoned by landowners on hearing news of the defeat. Separated from their regimental units and their officers, the troops lost all discipline. 'The Cossacks were the worst offenders,' recalled one eyewitness; 'there was nothing that they would not steal.'

> Finding a house that had been locked up, they would smash the doors, break the windows, and rampage through the rooms, stealing anything they could carry. Assuming that the owners had hidden money, diamonds and other precious items in the house, the soldiers turned over everything – even pillows and cushions on the divans and armchairs. Books and libraries were destroyed. Large mirrors that could not be

---

same time millions were spent on the fortification of Kiev, several hundred kilometres from the border. Afraid of an Austrian attack through south-west Russia, Nicholas I had kept a large reserve of troops in the Kiev area, but saw no need to do so in Sevastopol since he dismissed the danger of an attack by the Turks or the Western powers in the Black Sea. He had overlooked the huge significance of steamships, which made it possible to carry large armies by sea.

used by the soldiers were broken up so that they could put a piece of it into their pockets.[34]

The allied commanders had no idea of this weakness and disorder on the Russian side. Raglan had wanted to press on as fast as possible to Sevastopol, as the allies had agreed in their war plans, but now the French were not ready, having left their kitbags on the other side of the Alma before they had scaled the heights, and needed time to collect them. Unlike the British, they did not have sufficient cavalry to give chase to the Russians, so were less inclined to rush ahead. Once the initiative was lost, the allied commanders began to hesitate about what they should do next. Tatar spies had misinformed them that the Star Fort was impregnable, that Menshikov intended to defend it with all his might, and that the city was almost undefended on its southern side. This encouraged the allied commanders to abandon their initial plan to attack the city quickly from the north, and instead march right round the city to the southern side, a plan of action strongly urged by Sir John Burgoyne, the chief engineering officer.*

The change of plan was also driven by the Russians' bold decision to blow up their own fleet. Recognizing that they could not match the allied ships in speed or gunpower, the commanders of the Black Sea Fleet sank five sailing ships and two frigates in the mouth of the harbour to block the entrance and so prevent allied ships from supporting an attack from the north. The designated vessels were towed into place, their flags were taken down, and there were religious services to commit them to the sea. Then, at midnight on 22 September, the ships were destroyed. One frigate, *The Three Saints*, would not go down. The next morning it was shelled at close range by a gunboat for two hours until it sank. The noise was heard by the allied armies, which at that time were on the Kacha, prompting Saint-Arnaud to pronounce in amazement, once it was discovered what the noise was from, 'What a parody of Moscow 1812.'[35]

With the harbour blocked and no possibility of back-up from their ships, the allied commanders decided that it was too dangerous to

---

* According to a Russian source, the Tatar spies were shot on the orders of the British when the truth was discovered (S. Gershel'man, *Nravstvennyi element pod Sevastopolem* (St Petersburg, 1897), p. 86).

attack Sevastopol from the north, so they now committed themselves to attack the city from the southern side, where their ships could use the harbours of Balaklava (for the British) and Kamiesh (for the French) to support their armies. The change of plan was a fatal error of judgement – and not just because the city's defences were in fact stronger on the southern side. Moving south of Sevastopol made it harder for the allied armies to block the Russian supply route from the mainland, which had been a crucial element of the strategic plan. If the city had been taken quickly, this would not have been a major problem; but once the allied commanders had ruled out a *coup de main*, they fell into the trap of conventional military thinking about how to besiege a town, ideas going back to the seventeenth century that involved the slow and methodical process of digging trenches towards the town's defences so that it could be bombarded by artillery before an assault by troops. The French favoured the idea of a longer siege, and they brought the British round to their traditional way of thinking. It seemed less risky than a quick storming. Burgoyne, the chief engineer, who had been in favour of a quick attack, changed his mind on the absurd grounds that it would cost 500 lives to seize Sevastopol in a lightning strike, losses that were 'utterly unjustifiable' in his opinion, even though the allies had already suffered 3,600 casualties at the Alma (and were to lose tens of thousands in the siege).[36]

On 23 September the march south recommenced. For two days the allied troops proceeded across the fertile valley of the Kacha and Belbek rivers, helping themselves to the grapes, peaches, pears and soft fruits ripening in the deserted farms. Exhausted and battle-weary, many soldiers collapsed from dehydration, and all along the way the columns had to stop to bury victims of the cholera. Then the armies began their flanking march around Sevastopol, winding their way through the thick oak forests of the Inkerman Heights until they reached the clearing at Mackenzie's Farm, named after an eighteenth-century Scottish settler. At this point the advance party of British cavalry crossed paths with Menshikov's rearguard troops heading north-east towards Bakhchiserai. Captain Louis Nolan of the 15th King's Hussars, who was in the vanguard with Lord Raglan's staff, felt this was an opportunity for the cavalry to deal a heavy blow to the Russians. Since the landing in the Crimea, Nolan had become increasingly frustrated with the failure of the British commanders to unleash the cavalry – first at the Bulganak and then at the Alma – against the Russian forces in retreat. So when an attack on the Russian tail- and rearguard by the Hussars was halted by Lord Lucan, Nolan was beside himself with rage. In his campaign journal, he described looking down from the Mackenzie Heights as the Russians got away:

> The guns which had escaped were tearing along the road below with some of the few carriages of the convoy which had managed to escape. Disbanded infantry were running down the sides of the steep descent without arms, without helmets, whilst a few shots from our guns hastened them along towards a Russian Army formed in dense columns below. Two regiments of our cavalry moved along the road down the valley for some distance picking up carts and horses of which we captured 22 in all, amongst them General Gorchakov's travelling carriage with two fine black horses.[37]

The allied columns became increasingly stretched out, as the exhausted stragglers fell behind or lost their way in the dense forests. Discipline broke down and many of the troops, like the Cossacks before them, began to pillage from abandoned farms and estates in the vicinity of Sevastopol. The Bibikovs' palace was vandalized and looted by French troops, who helped themselves to the champagne and burgundy from their extensive cellars and went on a rampage, throwing furniture out of the windows, smashing windows and defecating on the floors. Marshal Saint-Arnaud, who was on the scene, did nothing to prevent the pillaging, which he saw as a reward for his exhausted troops. He even accepted a small pedestal table as a gift from his troops, which he had sent to his wife in Constantinople. Some of the Zouaves (who had a tradition of theatricals) got dressed up in women's clothes from the Princess's boudoir and put on a pantomime. Others found a grand piano and began playing waltzes for the troops to dance. The owners of the palace had left it only a few hours before the arrival of the French troops, as one of their officers recalled:

> I went into a small boudoir. . . . Fresh cut flowers were still in vases on

the mantelpiece; on a round table there were some copies of [the French magazine] *Illustration*, a writing box, some pens and paper, and an uncompleted letter. The letter was written by a young girl to her fiancé who had fought at the Alma; she spoke to him of victory, success, with that confidence that was in every heart, especially in the hearts of young girls. Cruel reality had stopped all that – letters, illusions, hopes.[38]

As the allied armies marched south towards Sevastopol, panic spread among the Russian population of the Crimea. News of the defeat at the Alma was a devastating blow to morale, puncturing the myth of Russia's military invincibility, especially against the French, dating back to 1812. In Simferopol, the administrative capital of the Crimea, there was so much panic that Vladimir Pestel', its governor-general, ordered the evacuation of the town. The Russians packed their belongings onto carts and rode out of the town towards Perekop, hoping to reach the Russian mainland before it was cut off by the allied troops. Declaring himself to be ill, Pestel' was the first to leave. Since the panic started he had not appeared in public or taken any measures to prevent disorder. He had even failed to stop the Tatars of the town shipping military supplies from Russian stores to the allies. Accompanied by his gendarmes and a long retinue of officials, Pestel' rode out of the town through a large crowd of Tatars jeering and shouting at his carriage: 'See how the giaour*runs! Our deliverers are at hand!'[39]

Since the arrival of the allied armies, the Tatar population of the Crimea had grown in confidence. Before the landings, the Tatars had been careful to declare their allegiance to the Tsar. From the start of the fighting on the Danubian front, the Russian authorities in the Crimea had placed the Tatars under increased surveillance, and Cossacks had policed the countryside with ferocious vigilance. But once the allies had landed in the Crimea, the Tatars rallied to their side – in particular the younger Tatar men, who were less cowed by years of Russian rule. They saw the invasion as a liberation, and recognized the Turks as soldiers of their caliph, to whom they prayed in their mosques. Thousands of Tatars left their villages and came to Evpatoria to greet the allied armies and declare their allegiance to the new

* A pejorative Turkish term for a Balkan Christian.

'Turkish government' which they believed had been established there. The invading armies had quickly replaced the Russian governor of Evpatoria with Topal Umer Pasha, a Tatar merchant from the town. They had also brought with them Mussad Giray, a descendant of the ancient ruling dynasty of the Crimean khanate, who called on the Tatars of the Crimea to support the invasion.*

Thinking they would be rewarded, the Tatars brought in cattle, horses and carts to put at the disposal of the allied troops. Some worked as spies or scouts for the allies. Others joined the Tatar bands that rode around the countryside threatening the Russian landowners with the burning of their houses and sometimes even death if they did not give up all their livestock, food and horses to them for the 'Turkish government'. Armed with sabres, the Tatar rebels wore their sheepskin hats inside out to symbolize the overthrow of Russian power in the Crimea. 'The entire Christian population of the peninsula lives in fear of the Tatar bands,' reported Innokenty, the Orthodox Archbishop of the Kherson-Tauride diocese. One Russian landowner, who was robbed on his estate, thought the horsemen had been stirred up by their mullahs to wreak revenge against the Christians in the belief that Muslim rule would now return. It was certainly the case that in some areas the rebels carried out atrocities against not just Russians but Armenians and Greeks, destroying churches and even killing priests. The Russian authorities played on these religious fears to rally support behind the Tsar's armies. Touring the Crimea during September, Innokenty declared the invasion a 'religious war' and said that Russia had a 'great and holy calling to protect the Orthodox faith against the Muslim yoke'.[40]

On 26 September the allied armies reached the village of Kadikoi, from which they could see the southern coast. That same day, Saint-

---

* After the Russian annexation of the Crimea, the Giray clan had fled to the Ottoman Empire. In the early nineteenth century the Girays had served as administrators for the Ottomans in the Balkans and had entered into military service. The Ottoman Empire had various military units made up of Crimean émigrés. They had fought against the Russians in 1828–9, and were part of the Turkish forces on the Danubian front in 1853–4. Mussad Giray was stationed in Varna. It was there that he persuaded the allied commanders to take him with them to the Crimea to rally Tatar support for their invasion. On 20 September the allies sent Mussad Giray back to the Balkans, praising him for his efforts and considering that his job was done. After the Crimean War, the French awarded him with a Légion d'honneur medal.

Arnaud surrendered to his illness and gave up his command to Canrobert. A steamer took the marshal off to Constantinople but he died of a heart attack on the way, so the same boat took his body back to France. It also brought the false news that the siege of Sevastopol had begun, prompting Cowley, the British ambassador in Paris, to inform London that the allied armies 'would probably be in possession of the place' in a few days.[41]

In fact, the allies were still three weeks away from the beginning of the siege. With the chill of the Russian winter already in the air, they were slowly setting up their camp on the plateau overlooking Sevastopol from the southern side. For a few days, both the armies were supplied through Balaklava, a narrow inlet hardly noticeable from the sea except for the ruins of the ancient Genoese fort on the cliff top.* But it very soon became apparent that the harbour was too small for all the sailing ships to enter it. So the French moved their base to Kamiesh Bay, which was in fact superior to Balaklava as a supply base, since it was much bigger and closer to the French camp at Khersonesos – the place where the Grand Prince Vladimir had converted Kievan Rus' to Christianity.

On 1 October Captain Herbé walked onto the heights with a small group of French officers to take a closer look at Sevastopol, just 2 kilometres away. With their field glasses, they could 'see enough of this famous town to satisfy their curiosity', as Herbé wrote to his parents the next day:

> Down below one could make out the fortification works on which a large quantity of men appeared to be labouring with their picks and spades; you could even make out a few women in amongst the groups of labourers. In the port, I could perfectly distinguish, with the aid of my long-viewer, some men-of-war, of a sombre appearance, with white sails on their sides, black gangways, and guns sticking out from the embrasures. If it should please the Russians to mount all these guns on their fortifications, we can expect a jolly symphony![42]

---

*Balaklava (originally Bella Clava: 'beautiful port') was named by the Genoese, who built much of the port and saw it thrive until their expulsion by the Turks in the fifteenth century. Plundered by the Turks, the town remained a virtual ruin until the nineteenth century, although there was a monastery in the hills above the town and some Greek soldiers stationed there, who were expelled by the allies.

8

Sevastopol in the Autumn

If Herbé could have visited Sevastopol, as Tolstoy was to do in November 1854, he would have found the town in a state of high alert and feverish activity. In the sweeping opening passage of his *Sevastopol Sketches* Tolstoy takes us there in the early morning, when the city was bursting into life:

On the North Side, daytime activity is gradually supplanting the tranquillity of night: here, with a clatter of muskets, a detachment of sentries is passing by on its way to relieve the guard; here a private, having clambered from his dugout and washed his bronzed face in icy water, is turning towards the reddening east, rapidly crossing himself and saying his prayers; here a tall, heavy *madzhara* drawn by camels is creaking its way towards the cemetery, where the bloody corpses with which it is piled almost to the brim will be buried. As you approach the quay you are struck by the distinctive smells of coal, beef, manure and damp; thousands of oddly assorted articles – firewood, sides of meat, gabions, sacks of flour, iron bars and the like – lie piled up near the quayside; soldiers of various regiments, some with kitbags and muskets, others without, are milling around here, smoking, shouting abuse at one another or dragging heavy loads on to the ship that is lying at anchor, smoke coming from its funnel, by the landing stage; civilian skiffs, filled with a most various assortment of people – soldiers, sailors, merchants, women – are constantly mooring and casting off along the waterfront. . . .

The quayside contains a noisy jostle of soldiers in grey, sailors in black, and women in all sorts of colours. Peasant women are selling rolls, Russian muzhiks with samovars are shouting, 'Hot

sbitén',* and right here, lying about on the very first steps of the landing, are rusty cannonballs, shells, grapeshot, and cast-iron cannon of
various calibres. A little further off there is a large, open area strewn
with enormous squared beams, gun carriages and the forms of sleeping
soldiers; there are horses, waggons, green field guns with ammunition
boxes, infantry muskets stacked in criss-cross piles; a constant movement persists of soldiers, sailors, officers, merchants, women and
children; carts laden with hay, sacks or barrels come and go; and here
and there a Cossack or an officer is passing by on horseback, or a general in his droshky. To the right the street is blocked by a barricade, the
embrasures of which are mounted with a small cannon; beside them
sits a sailor, puffing at his pipe. To the left is a handsome building with
Roman numerals carved on its pediment, beneath which soldiers are
standing with bloodstained stretchers – everywhere you perceive the
unpleasant signs of a military encampment.[1]

Sevastopol was a military town. Its entire population of 40,000
people was connected in some way to the life of the naval base,
whose garrison numbered about 18,000 men, and from that unity
Sevastopol gained its military strength. There were sailors who had
lived there with their families since Sevastopol's foundation in the
1780s. Socially the city had a singularity: frock coats were rarely to be
seen among the naval uniforms on its central boulevards. There were
no great museums, galleries, concert halls or intellectual treasures in
Sevastopol. The imposing neoclassical buildings of the city centre
were all military in character: the admiralty, the naval school, the
arsenal, the garrisons, the ship-repair workshops, the army stores
and warehouses, the military hospital, and the officers' library, one of
the richest in Europe. Even the Assembly of Nobles (the 'handsome
building with Roman numerals') turned into a hospital during the
siege.

The town was divided into two distinct parts, a North and a South
side, separated from each other by the sea harbour, and the only direct
means of communication between the two was by boat. The North
Side of the town was a world apart from the elegant neoclassical
façades around the military harbour on the southern side. It had few

* A hot drink made with honey and spices.

built-up streets, and fishermen and sailors lived there in a semi-rural style, growing vegetables and keeping livestock in the gardens of their dachas. On the South Side there was another, less obvious, distinction between the administrative centre on the western side of the military harbour and the naval dockyards on the eastern side, where the sailors lived in garrisons or with their families in small wooden houses no more than a few yards from the defensive works. Women hung their washing on lines thrown between their houses and the fortress walls and bastions.[2]

Like Tolstoy, visitors to Sevastopol were always struck by the 'strange intermingling of camp and town life, of handsome town and dirty bivouac'. Evgeny Ershov, a young artillery officer who arrived in Sevastopol that autumn, was impressed by the way the people of the city went about their ordinary everyday business amid all the chaos of the siege. 'It was strange', he wrote, 'to see how people carried on with their normal lives – a young woman quietly out walking with her pram, traders buying and selling, children running round and playing in the streets, while all around them was a battlefield and they might be killed at any time.'[3]

People lived as if there was no tomorrow in the weeks prior to the invasion. There was non-stop revelry, heavy drinking and gambling, while the city's many prostitutes worked overtime. The allied landings had a sobering effect, but confidence ran high among the junior officers, who all assumed that the Russian army would defeat the British and the French. They drank toasts to the memory of 1812. 'The mood among us was one of high excitement,' recalled Mikhail Botanov, a young sea cadet, 'and we were not frightened of the enemy. The only one among us who did not share our confidence was the commander of a steamship who, unlike us, had often been abroad and liked to say the proverb, "In anger is not strength." Events were to show that he was longer-sighted and better informed about the true state of affairs than we were.'[4]

The defeat of the Russian forces at the Alma created panic among the civilian population of Sevastopol. People were expecting the allies to invade from the north at any time; they were confused when they saw their fleets on the southern side, supposing wrongly that they had been surrounded. 'I don't know anyone who at that moment did not say a prayer,' recalled one inhabitant. 'We all thought the enemy about to break through.' Captain Nikolai Lipkin, a battery commander in the Fourth Bastion, wrote to his brother in St Petersburg at the end of September:

> Many inhabitants have already left, but we, the servicemen, are staying here to teach a lesson to our uninvited guests. For three days in a row (24, 25 and 26 September) there were religious processions through the town and all the batteries. It was humbling to see how our fighters, standing by their bivouacs, bowed before the cross and the icons carried by our women-folk. . . . The churches have been emptied of their treasures; I say it was not needed, but people do not listen to me now, they are all afraid. Any moment now we are expecting a general attack, both by land and sea. So, my brother, that's how things are here, and what will happen next only the Lord knows.

Despite Lipkin's confidence, the Russian commanders were seriously considering abandoning Sevastopol after the battle at the Alma. There were then eight steamers on the northern side waiting for the order to evacuate the troops and ten warships on the southern side to cover their escape. Many of the city's residents made their own getaway as the enemy approached, though their path was blocked by Russian troops. Water supplies in the city were running dangerously low, the fountains having stopped and the whole population being dependent on the wells, which were always short of water at this time of year. Told by deserters that the city was supplied by water springs and pipes that ran down a ravine from the heights where they were camped, the British and the French had cut off this supply, leaving Sevastopol with just the aqueduct that supplied the naval dockyard.[5]

As the allies set up camp and prepared their bombardment of the town, the Russians worked around the clock to strengthen its defences on the southern side. With Menshikov nowhere to be seen, the main responsibility for the defence of Sevastopol passed into the hands of three commanders: Admiral Kornilov, chief of staff of the Black Sea Fleet; Totleben, the engineer; and Nakhimov, the hero of Sinope and commander of the port, who was popular among the sailors and seen as 'one of them'. All three men were military professionals of a new type that contrasted strongly with the courtier Menshikov. Their energy was remarkable. Kornilov was everywhere, inspiring the people by his daily presence in every sector of the defensive works, and promising rewards to everyone, if they could only keep the town. Tolstoy, who was to join Lipkin as a battery commander in the Fourth Bastion, wrote a letter to his brother the day after he arrived in which he described Kornilov on his rounds. Instead of hailing the men with the customary greeting, 'Health to you!', the admiral called to them, 'If you must die, lads, will you die?' 'And', Tolstoy wrote, 'the men shouted "We will die, Your Excellency, Hurrah!" And they do not say if for effect, for in every face I saw not jesting but earnestness.'[6]

Kornilov himself was far from certain that the city could be saved. On 27 September he wrote to his wife:

> We have only 5,000 reserves and 10,000 sailors, armed with various weaponry, even pikes. Not much of a garrison to defend a fortress whose defences are stretched over many miles and broken up so much that there is no direct communication between them; but what will be, will be. We have resolved to make a stand. It will be a miracle if we hold out; and if not ...

His uncertainty was increased when the sailors discovered a large supply of vodka on the wharf and went on a drunken rampage for three days. It was left to Kornilov to destroy the supplies of liquor and sober up his sailors for battle.[7]

The defensive preparations were frenzied and improvised. When the work began, it was discovered that there were no shovels in Sevastopol, so men were sent to procure as many as they could from Odessa. Three weeks later, they returned with 400 spades. Meanwhile, the people of the city worked in the main with wooden shovels they had made from torn-up planks of wood. The whole population of Sevastopol – sailors, soldiers, prisoners of war, working men and women (including prostitutes) – was involved in digging trenches, carting earth to the defences, building walls and barricades, and constructing batteries with earth, fascines and gabions,* while teams of sailors hauled up the heavy guns they had taken from their ships. Every means of carrying the earth was commandeered, and when there were

---

* Defensive tall wicker baskets filled with earth.

no baskets, bags or buckets, the diggers carried it in their folded clothes. The expectation of an imminent attack added greater urgency to their work. Inspecting these defences a year later, the allies were amazed by the skill and ingenuity of the Russians.[8]

Informed of these heroic efforts by the people of Sevastopol, the Tsar wrote to General Gorchakov at the end of September, reminding him of the 'special Russian spirit' that had saved the country from Napoleon, and urging him to summon it again against the British and the French. 'We shall pray to God, that you may call on them to save Sevastopol, the fleet and the Russian land. *Do not bow to anyone*,' he underlined in his own hand. '*Show the world that we are the same Russians who stood firm in 1812*.' The Tsar also wrote to Menshikov, at that time near the River Belbek, north-east of Sevastopol, with a message for the people of the town:

> Tell our young sailors that all my hopes are invested in them. Tell them not to bow to anyone, to put their faith in God's mercy, to remember that we are Russians, that we are defending our homeland and our faith, and to submit humbly to the will of God. May God preserve you! My prayers are all for you and for our holy cause.[9]

Meanwhile, the allies embarked on their lengthy preparations for the siege. Raglan had wanted an immediate assault. He had seen the weakness of the Russian defences, and was encouraged by the forthright and masterful Sir George Cathcart, in command of the 4th Division, whose troops had taken up positions on a hill from which he could see the whole town. It was from there that he wrote to Raglan:

> If you and Sir John Burgoyne would pay me a visit you can see everything in the way of defences, which is not much. They are working at two or three redoubts, but the place is only enclosed by a thing like a loose park wall not in good repair. I am sure I could walk into it with scarcely the loss of a man at night or an hour before day-break if all the rest of the force was up between the sea and the hill I am upon. We would leave our packs and run into it even in open day only risking a few shots whilst we passed the redoubts.

Burgoyne, formerly an advocate of a quick assault, now disagreed. Concerned with loss of lives, the army's chief engineer insisted on the need to subdue the enemy's fire with siege guns before an assault by troops was launched. The French agreed with him. So the allies settled down to the slow process of landing siege artillery and hauling it up to the heights. There were endless problems with the British guns, many of which had to be dismantled before they could be unloaded from the ships. 'The placing of our heavy ship guns in position has been most tedious,' Captain William Cameron of the Grenadier Guards wrote to his father.

> The ship guns have to be taken all to pieces, as the carriages, having only small rollers, as wheels, cannot be moved along by themselves, whereas the regular siege guns can be wheeled into their places as they stand. We have just completed a battery of five 68lb guns of 95 cwt each – all ships guns, which will tell more than any battery ever heard of at a siege before. The ground is dreadfully rocky, so that a great part of the earth for the parapet has to be carried.[10]

It was eighteen days before the guns were finally in place, days that gave the Russians crucial time to prepare their defences.

While the British were hauling up their guns, the French took the lead in digging trenches, moving slowly forward in a zigzag formation towards the defences of Sevastopol, as the Russians fired at them with artillery. The opening of the first trench was the most dangerous because there was little protection from the Russian guns. Armed with shovels and pickaxes, the first shift of 800 men crept forward under cover of the night, using rocks for shelter, until they reached a point within a kilometre of Sevastopol's Flagstaff Bastion, and on lines marked out by their commanders began digging themselves into the ground, piling up the soil in gabions in front of them to protect themselves from the Russians. On that night, 9/10 October, the sky was clear and the moon was out, but a north-west wind took the sound of digging away from the town, and by dawn, when the sleepy Russians at last discovered them, the French had dug a protected trench 1,000 metres long. Under heavy bombardment, 3,000 French soldiers went on with the works, digging new entrenchments every night and repairing trenches damaged by the Russians the next day, while shells and mortar whistled past their heads. By 16 October the first five French batteries had been built with sacks of earth and wood for palisades, fortified breastworks and parapets, and more than fifty guns (cannon, mortars and howitzers) mounted on raised platforms on the ground.[11]

Following the French, the British dug entrenchments and sited their first batteries on Green Hill (the Left Attack) and Vorontsov Hill (the Right Attack), the two positions separated by a deep ravine. Shifts of 500 men on each attack worked day and night while more than twice that number guarded them from the Russians, who launched sorties at night. 'I am off duty this morning at 4 am after 24 hours in the trenches,' Captain Radcliffe of the 20th Regiment wrote to his family.

> When we got under the breastwork that had been thrown up in the night we were pretty well under cover, but were obliged to lie down all the time for this of course was the target for the enemy's artillery day and night and the trench was only half made. However a few men were placed on the look out, their heads a few inches above the work, to give notice when they fired, by watching the smoke from the guns by day and the flash by night and calling out 'Shot' – when all in the trenches lie down and get under cover of the breastwork till it has passed, and then resume their work. By attending to this we only lost one man during the day; he was killed by a round shot.[12]

On 16 October it was finally decided to begin the bombardment of Sevastopol the following morning, even though the British works were not quite completed. There was a mood of optimistic expectation in the allied camp. 'All artillery officers – French, English and naval – say [that] after a fire of 48 hours, little will be seen of Sevastopol but a heap of ruins,' wrote Henry Clifford, a staff officer in the Light Division, to his family. According to Evelyn Wood, a midshipman who had watched the battle of the Alma from the topmast of his ship before being transferred to the land attack with the Naval Brigade,

> On 16 October the betting in our camp was long odds that the fortress would fall in a few hours. Some of the older and more prudent officers estimated that the Russians might hold out for 48 hours, but this was the extreme opinion. A soldier offered me a watch, Paris made, which

he had taken off a Russian officer killed at the Alma, for which he asked 20 s[hillings]. My messmates would not allow me to buy it, saying that gold watches would be cheaper in 48 hours.[13]

At dawn on 17 October, as soon as the fog had cleared, the Russians saw that the embrasures of the enemy batteries had been opened. Without waiting for the enemy guns to open fire, the Russians began shelling them along the line, and soon afterwards the allied counter-bombardment began with 72 British and 53 French guns. Within a few minutes the gun battle was at its height. The booming of the guns, the roaring and the whistling of the shot, and the deafening explosions of the shell drowned out the calls of the bugles and the drums. Sevastopol was completely lost in a thick black pall of smoke, which hung over the whole darkened battlefield, making it impossible for the allied gunners to hit their target with any military precision. 'We could only sit and guess and hope we were doing well,' wrote Calthorpe, who watched the bombardment with Raglan from the Quarries on Vorontsov Hill.[14]

For thousands of civilians sheltering in the bombed-out ruins of their homes in Sevastopol, these were the most terrifying moments of their lives. 'I never saw or heard of anything like it before,' wrote one resident. 'For twelve hours the wild howling of the bombs was unbroken, it was impossible to distinguish between them, and the ground shook beneath our feet. . . . A thick smoke filled the sky and blotted out the sun; it became as dark as night; even the rooms were filled with smoke.'[15]

As soon as the bombardment had begun, Kornilov had set off with his flag-lieutenant, Prince V. I. Bariatinsky, to make a tour of the defences. They went first to the Fourth Bastion, the most dangerous place in Sevastopol, which was being shelled by both the British and the French. 'Inside the No. 4 Bastion,' recalled Bariatinsky, 'the scene was frightful and the destruction enormous, whole gun teams having been struck down by shellfire; the wounded and dead were being removed by stretcher-bearers, but they were still lying round in heaps.' Kornilov went to every gun, encouraging the crews, and then moved on to the Fifth Bastion, under no less pressure from the enemy's artillery, where he met Nakhimov, dressed as he always was in a frock coat with epaulettes. Nakhimov had been wounded in the face, though he did not seem to notice it, Bariatinsky thought, as blood ran down his neck, staining the white ribbon of his St George Cross, as he talked with Kornilov. While they were conversing there, Bariatinsky recognized an officer approaching, though 'he had no eyes or face, for his features had completely disappeared underneath a mass of bloody flesh', the remains of a sailor who had been blown up, which the officer proceeded to wipe from his face, while he asked Bariatinsky for a cigarette. Ignoring the advice of his staff, who said it was too dangerous to go on, Kornilov continued his tour at the Third Bastion, the Redan, which was then being pounded by the heavy British guns with a deadly concentration of power. When Kornilov arrived, the bastion was under the command of Captain Popandul, but he was soon killed, as were the five other commanders who succeeded him that day. Kornilov passed through the trench system, within close range of the British guns, crossed the ravine, and climbed up to the Malakhov Bastion, where he talked to the wounded troops. He was just starting down the hill to complete his tour in the Ushakov Ravine when he was hit by a shell that blew away the lower part of his body. Taken to the military hospital, he died shortly afterwards.[16]

Towards midday the allied fleet joined in the bombardment, directing their heavy guns towards Sevastopol from an arc around the entrance to the sea harbour some 800 to 1,500 metres from the coast (the blockade of the harbour by the sunken Russian ships stopped them getting any closer to their target). For six hours the city was shelled by an allied broadside of 1,240 guns; its coastal batteries had just 150 guns. 'The sight was one of the most awful in the way of guns,' Henry James, a merchant seamen, wrote in his diary after watching the bombardment from further out to sea. 'Several of the liners kept up a heavy cannonade and it could be compared to the rolling of a huge drum ... We could see showers of shot striking the water at the foot of the forts and flying up in heaps at the walls.' The firing of the fleets created so much smoke that the Russian gunners could not even see the ships. Some of the gunners lost their nerve, but others showed extraordinary bravery, firing at the gun flashes of the invisible ships while shells crashed around their heads. One artillery officer on the Tenth Bastion, the main focus of the French attack, recalled seeing men who had been rewarded for their courage in previous engagements running off in panic when the firing began. 'I was caught myself between two feelings,' he recalled. 'One half of me wanted to run home to save my family, but my sense of duty told me I should stay. My feelings as a man got the better of the soldier within me and I ran away to find my family.'[17]

In fact, for all their guns, the French and British ships received better than they gave. The wooden sailing vessels of the allied fleet were unable to get close enough to the stone forts of the coastal bastions to cause them much damage (the blockade had done its job in this respect) but they could be set alight by the Russian guns, which were not so numerous but (because they were based on the land) much more accurate than the allies' long-range cannonade. After firing an estimated 50,000 rounds to little real effect on the coastal batteries, the allied fleet weighed anchor and sailed away to count its losses: five ships badly damaged, thirty sailors killed and more than 500 men wounded. Without steam-powered iron ships, the allied fleet was destined to play only a subsidiary role to the army during the siege of Sevastopol.

The first day's outcome on the land was not much more encouraging for the allies. The French made little headway against Mount Rodolph before one of their main magazines was blown up and they ceased fire, and while the British caused considerable damage to the Third Bastion, accounting for most of the 1,100 Russian casualties, they had lacked the heavy mortars to make their superior firepower count. Their much-vaunted new weapon, the 68-pounder Lancaster gun, was unreliable firing shells and was ineffective at long range against Russian earthworks, which absorbed the light projectiles. 'I fear the Lancaster is a failure,' reported Captain Lushington to General Airey the next day. 'Our guns do not go far enough out and we injure our own embrasures more than the enemy. . . . I have impressed on all the officers the necessity of slow and steady firing . . . but the distances are too great . . . and we might as well fire into a pudding as at these earthworks.'[18]

The failure of the first day's bombardment was a rude awakening for the allies. 'The town appears built of incombustible materials,' wrote Fanny Duberly, who had come to the Crimea as a war tourist with her husband, Henry Duberly, paymaster of the 8th Hussars. 'Although it was twice slightly on fire yesterday, the flames were almost immediately extinguished.'[19]

On the Russian side, the first day had destroyed the mystique of the allied armies established by their victory at the Alma. Suddenly, the enemy was no longer seen as invincible, and from that the Russians gained new hope and self-confidence. 'We all thought it was impossible for our batteries to save us,' a resident of Sevastopol wrote in a letter the next day. 'So imagine our surprise when today we found all our batteries intact, and all the guns in place! ... God has blessed Russia, and rewarded us for the insults we have suffered to our faith!'[20]

*

Having survived the first day's bombardment, the Russians now resolved to break the siege by attacking Balaklava and cutting off the British from their main base of supplies. After Alma, Menshikov had set out towards Bakhchiserai. Now, with the change in strategy, he amassed his troops in the Chernaia valley on Sevastopol's eastern side, where they were joined by the first reinforcements to arrive from the Danubian front, the 12th Infantry Division under the command of Lieutenant General Pavel Liprandi. On the evening of 24 October, a field army of 60,000 troops, 34 squadrons of cavalry and 78 artillery pieces camped around the village of Chorgun on Fediukhin Heights for an attack on the British defences of Balaklava the following morning.

The objective was well chosen. As the British were themselves aware, they were seriously overstretched and there was not much to protect their supply base from a swift attack by a large force of men. The British had constructed a total of six small redoubts along part of the Causeway Heights – the ridge-line of the Vorontsov Road separating the northern half of the Balaklava valley between the Fediukhin Heights and the road from the southern half between the road and the port itself – and placed in each of the four completed redoubts a Turkish guard (consisting mainly of raw recruits) with two or three 12-pounder guns of position. Behind the redoubts, in the southern half of the valley, the British had positioned the 93rd Highland

Infantry Brigade, under the command of Sir Colin Campbell, to whom the defence of the port was entrusted, while encamped on their flank was the cavalry division of Lord Lucan, and on the heights above the gorge descending to the port 1,000 Royal Marines with some field artillery. In the event of an attack by the Russians, Campbell could also rely on the support of the British infantry as well as two divisions of French troops under General Bosquet encamped on the heights above Sevastopol, but until they arrived the defence of Balaklava would depend on 5,000 troops.[21]

At daybreak on 25 October the Russians commenced their attack. Establishing a field battery close to the village of Kamara, they began a heavy bombardment of the No. 1 Redoubt on Canrobert's Hill (named by the British in honour of the French commander). During the night Raglan had been warned of the imminent attack by a deserter from the Russian camp, but, having sent 1,000 men to Balaklava in response to a false alarm only three days previously, he decided not to act (yet another blunder to put against his name), though he did reach the Sapoune Heights in time to get a grandstand view of the fighting in the valley below him after messages were sent to his headquarters at the start of the attack.

For more than an hour, the 500 Turkish troops defending the No. 1 Redoubt put up a stubborn resistance, as they had done against the Russians at Silistria, losing more than one-third of their men. But then 1,200 Russian troops stormed the redoubt at the point of the bayonet, forcing the exhausted defenders to abandon it to them, along with three of the seven British cannon which had been lent to the Turks. 'To our disgust,' recalled Calthorpe, who was watching from the Sapoune Heights with Raglan's staff, 'we saw a little stream of men issue from the rear of the redoubt and run down the hill-side towards our lines.' Seeing their countrymen in full retreat, the Turkish garrisons in the neighbouring three redoubts (2, 3 and 4) followed their example and withdrew towards the port, many of them carrying their blankets, pots and pans and crying 'Ship! Ship!' as they passed the British lines. Calthorpe watched as 1,000 Turkish troops streamed down the hill pursued by large parties of Cossacks. 'The yells of these wild horsemen could be heard from where we were as they galloped after these unhappy Muslims, numbers of whom were killed by their lances.'

As they ran through the settlement of Kadikoi, the Turkish soldiers were jeered at by a group of British army wives, including one, a massive washerwoman with brawny arms and 'hands as hard as horn', who seized hold of a Turk and gave him a good kicking for trampling on the washing she had laid out in the sun to dry. When she realized that the Turks had deserted her own husband's regiment, the 93rd, she scolded them: 'Ye cowardly misbelievers, to leave the brave Christian Highlanders to fecht when ye ran awa!' The Turks tried to placate her, and some called her 'Kokana',* prompting her to become even more enraged. 'Kokana, indeed! I'll Kokana ye!' she cried, and, brandishing a stick, chased them down the hill. Tired and downcast, the Turkish soldiers continued their retreat, until they reached the ravine leading to the port. Throwing their belongings on the ground, they lay down beside them to get some rest. Some spread out their prayer mats on the ground and said a prayer towards Mecca.[22]

The British accused the Turkish troops of cowardice, but this was unfair. According to John Blunt, Lord Lucan's Turkish interpreter, most of the troops were Tunisians without proper training or experience of war. They had only just arrived in the Crimea and were in a famished state: none of them had received any rations they could eat as Muslims since they had left Varna several days before and on their arrival they had disgraced themselves by attacking civilians. Blunt rode after the retreating troops and relayed to an officer Lucan's command for them to regroup behind the 93rd, but he was accosted by the soldiers 'who appeared parched with thirst and exhausted'. They asked him why no British troops had come to their support, complained that they had been left in the redoubts for several days without food or water, and declared that the ammunition they were supplied with did not fit the guns in the redoubts. One of the soldiers, his head in a bandage and smoking a long pipe, said to Blunt in Turkish: 'What can we do sir? It is God's will.'[23]

The Russian infantry took redoubts 1, 2, 3 and 4 on the Causeway Heights, abandoning the fourth after they had destroyed the gun

---

* A Turkish term for a woman who is dressed improperly. In the Ottoman period it was used to describe non-Muslim women and had sexual connotations, implying that the woman ran a brothel or was herself a prostitute.

carriages. The Russian cavalry, under General Ryzhov, moved up behind them along the North Valley and turned to attack the 93rd, the only infantry force that now prevented them from breaking through to Balaklava, since the British cavalry had been withdrawn to await the arrival of the infantry from the plateau above Sevastopol. Descending from the Causeway Heights, four squadrons of Ryzhov's cavalry, some 400 men, charged towards the Highlanders.* Watching the scene from a vineyard near the camp of the Light Brigade, Fanny Duberly was horrified. Shots 'began to fly' and 'Presently came the Russian cavalry charging over the hill-side and across the valley, right against the little line of Highlanders. Ah, what a moment! Charging and surging onward, what could that little wall of men do against such numbers and such speed? There they stood.' Forming his men into a line just two deep instead of the usual square employed by infantry against the cavalry, Campbell placed his trust in the deadly rifle power of the Minié whose effects he had seen at the Alma. As the cavalry approached, he rode along the line, calling on his men to stand firm and 'die there', according to Lieutenant Colonel Sterling of the 93rd, who thought 'he looked as if he meant it'. To Russell of *The Times*, watching from the heights, they looked like 'a thin red streak tipped with a line of steel' (later and forever misquoted as a 'thin red line'). The appearance of a steady line of redcoats caused the Russian cavalry to hesitate, and, as they did so, at a range of about 1,000 metres, Campbell gave the order for the first volley. When the smoke had cleared, Sergeant Munro of the 93rd 'saw that the cavalry were still advancing straight for the line. A second volley rang forth, and then we observed that there was a little confusion in the enemy's ranks and that they were swerving to our right.' A third volley at much closer range caught the Russians in the flank, causing them to bend sharply to their left and ride back to their own army.[24]

---

* It is something of a mystery as to why the Russians, faced by such a tiny defence force, did not make a quicker and more powerful attack against Balaklava. Various Russian commanders later claimed that they lacked sufficient troops to capture Balaklava, that the operation had been a reconnaissance, or that it was an attempt to divert the allied forces from Sevastopol rather than capture the port. But these were excuses for their failure, which perhaps could be explained by their lack of confidence against the allied armies on an open battlefield after the defeat of the Russian forces at the Alma.

Ryzhov's first four squadrons had been repulsed but the main body of the Russian cavalry, 2,000 hussars flanked by Cossack outriders, now descended from the Causeway Heights for a second charge against the Highlanders. This time the infantry was rescued just in time by the intervention of the British cavalry, eight squadrons of the Heavy Brigade, some 700 men, who had been ordered to return to the South Valley to support the 93rd by Raglan, who from his position on the Sapoune Heights had seen the danger the Highlanders were in. Riding slowly up the hill towards the enemy, the Heavy moved across their column, dressed their lines and then, from 100 metres, charged right into them, slashing wildly at them with their swords. The advance riders of the British cavalry, the Scots Greys and Inniskillings (6th Dragoons), were completely enveloped by the Russians, who had briefly halted to extend their flanks just before the charge, but the red jackets of the 4th and 5th Dragoons soon piled in to the mêlée, cutting at the Russian flanks and rear. The opposing horsemen were so tightly packed together that there was no room for swordsmanship, they could barely raise their swords or swing their sabres, and all they could do was hit or cut at anything within their reach, as if they were in a brawl. Sergeant Major Henry Franks of the 5th Dragoons saw Private Harry Herbert attacked by three Cossacks at the same time.

> He disabled one of them by a terrible cut across the back of the neck, and the second one scampered off. Herbert made a point at the third man's breast, but his sword blade broke off about three inches from the hilt . . . He threw the heavy sword hilt at the Russian, which hit him in the face, and the Cossack dropped to the ground; he was not dead, but it spoiled his visage.

Major William Forrest of the 4th Dragoons recalled his frenzied fight with a

> hussar who cut at my head, but the brass pot stood well, and my head is only slightly bruised. I cut again at him, but do not believe that I hurt him more than he hurt me. I received a blow on the shoulder at the same time, which was given by some other man, but the edge must have been very badly delivered for it has only cut my coat and slightly bruised my shoulder.

There were surprisingly few casualties, no more than a dozen killed on either side, and 300 or so wounded, mostly on the Russian side, though the combat lasted less than ten minutes. The Russians' heavy great-coats and thick shakos protected them from most sabre cuts, while their own swords were just as ineffective against the longer reach of the British cavalrymen, who sat on taller and heavier mounts.[25]

In this sort of fighting one side must eventually give way. It was the Russians who lost their nerve first. Shaken by the fighting, the hussars turned away and galloped back to the North Valley pursued by the British cavalry, until they withdrew under fire from the Russian batteries on the Causeway and Fediukhin Heights.

While the Russian cavalry withdrew, the British infantry descended from the heights of Sevastopol and marched across the South Valley to support the 93rd. The 1st Division arrived first, followed by the 4th, and then French reinforcements too – the 1st Division and two squadrons of Chasseurs d'Afrique. With the arrival of the allied infantry, it was not likely that the Russian cavalry would attack again. Balaklava had been saved.

As the Russians cut their losses and moved back to their base, Raglan and his staff on the Sapoune Heights noticed them removing the British guns from the redoubts. The Duke of Wellington had never lost a gun, or so it was believed by the keepers of his cult in the British military establishment. The prospect of these guns being paraded as trophies in Sevastopol was unbearable for Raglan, who at once sent an order to Lord Lucan, the commander of the Cavalry Division, to recover the Causeway Heights, assuring him of the support of the infantry that had just arrived. Lucan could not see the infantry, and could not believe that he was meant to act alone, with just the cavalry, against infantry and artillery, so for three-quarters of an hour he did nothing, while Raglan on the hill became more alarmed about the fate of the captured British guns. Eventually he dictated a second order to Lucan: 'Lord Raglan wishes the cavalry to advance rapidly to the front – follow the enemy and try to prevent the enemy carrying away the guns. Troop Horse Artillery may accompany. French cavalry is on your left. Immediate.'

The order was not just unclear, it was absurd, and Lucan was completely at a loss as to what to make of it. From where he was standing, at the western end of the Causeway Heights, he could see, to his right, the British guns in the redoubts captured by the Russians from the Turks; to his left, at the end of the North Valley, where he knew the bulk of the Russian forces were located, he could see a second set of guns; and further to the left, on the lower slopes of the Fediukhin Heights, he could see that the Russians also had a battery of artillery. If Raglan's order had been clearer and specified that it was the British guns on the Causeway Heights that Lucan was to take, the Charge of the Light Brigade would have ended very differently, but as it was, the order left unclear which guns the cavalry was to recover.

The only man who could tell him what it meant was the aide-de-camp who delivered it, Captain Nolan of the King's Hussars. Like many cavalrymen in the Light Brigade, Nolan had become increasingly frustrated by Lucan's failure to employ the cavalry in the sort of bold attack for which it had earned its reputation as the greatest in the world. At the Bulganak and the Alma, the cavalry had been stopped from pursuing the Russians in retreat; on the Mackenzie Heights, during the march to Balaklava, Lucan had prevented an attack on the Russian army marching east across their path; and only that morning, when the Heavy Brigade was outnumbered by the Russian cavalry, only a few minutes' ride away, Lord Cardigan, the Light Brigade's commander, declined to use them for a swift assault upon the routed enemy. The Light Brigade were made to watch while their comrades fought with the same Cossacks who had jeered at them at the Bulganak for refusing to fight. One of their officers had several times demanded of Lord Cardigan to send in the brigade, and, when Cardigan refused, slapped his saluting sword against his leg in a show of disrespect. There were signs of disobedience. Private John Doyle of the 8th King's Royal Irish Hussars recalled:

> The Light Brigade were not well pleased when they saw the Heavy Brigade and were not let go to their assistance. They stood up in their stirrups, and shouted 'Why are we kept here?' and at the same moment broke up and dashed back through our lines, for the purpose of following the Russian retreat, but they had got too far for us to overtake them.[26]

So when Lucan asked Nolan what Raglan's order meant, there was a threat of insubordination in the air. In the account he later gave in a letter to Raglan, Lucan asked the aide-de-camp where he should attack, and Nolan had replied 'in a most disrespectful but significant manner', pointing to the further end of the valley, '"There, my lord, is your enemy; there are your guns."' According to Lucan, Nolan had not pointed to the British guns on the Causeway Heights, but towards the battery of twelve Russian cannon and the main force of the Cossack cavalry at the far end of the North Valley, on either side of which, on the Causeway and Fediukhin Heights, the Russians had more cannon as well as riflemen. Lucan took the order to Cardigan, who pointed out the lunacy of charging down a valley against artillery and musket fire on three sides, but Lucan insisted that the order be obeyed. Cardigan and Lucan (who were brothers-in law) detested each other. This is usually the explanation given by historians as to why they failed to consult and find a way to circumvent the order they believed they had been given by Raglan (it would not be the first time that Raglan's orders had been disobeyed). But there is also evidence that Lucan was afraid to disobey an order that was in fact welcomed by the men of the Light Brigade, eager for action against the Russian cavalry and in danger of losing discipline if they were prevented from attacking them. Lucan himself later wrote to Raglan that he had obeyed the order because not to do so would have 'exposed me and the cavalry to aspersions against which we might have difficulty in defending ourselves' – by which he surely meant aspersions from his men and the rest of the army.[27]

The 661 men of the Light Brigade advanced at a walk down the gently sloping North Valley, the 13th Light Dragoons and 17th Lancers in the first line, led by Cardigan, the 11th Hussars immediately behind, followed by the 8th Hussars together with the 4th (Queen's Own) Regiment of Light Dragoons. It was 2,000 metres to the enemy's position at the end of the valley, and at regulation speeds it would take the Light Brigade about seven minutes to cover the distance – artillery and musket fire to the right of them, to the left of them and in front of them, along the way. As the first line broke into a trot, Nolan, who was riding with the 17th Lancers, galloped forward, waving his sword and, according to most versions, shouting to the men to hurry them along, although it has also been suggested that he realized the mistake and was attempting to redirect the Light Brigade towards the Causeway Heights and perhaps beyond to the South Valley, where they would be safe from the Russian guns. Either way, the first shell fired by the Russians exploded over Nolan and killed him. Whether it was Nolan's example, their own eagerness, or because they wanted to get through the flanking fire as fast as possible, remains unclear, but the two regiments at the head of the charge broke into a gallop long before they were ordered to. 'Come on,' shouted one man from the 13th Light Dragoons, 'don't let those bastards [the 17th Lancers] get ahead of us.'[28]

As they galloped through the crossfire from the hills, cannonballs tearing the earth up and musket fire raining in like hail, men were shot and horses fell. 'The reports from the guns and the bursting of shells were deafening,' recalled Sergeant Bond of the 11th Hussars.

> The smoke too was almost blinding. Horses and men were falling in every direction, and the horses that were not hurt were so upset that we could not keep them in a straight line for a time. A man named Allread who was riding on my left fell from his horse like a stone. I looked back and saw the poor fellow lying on his back, his right temple being cut away and his brain partly on the ground.

Trooper Wightman of the 17th Lancers saw his sergeant hit: 'He had his head clean carried off by a round shot, yet for about thirty yards further the headless body kept in the saddle, the lance at the charge, firmly gripped under the right arm.' So many men and horses from the first line were shot down that the second line, 100 metres behind, had to swerve and slow down to avoid the wounded bodies on the ground and the bewildered, frightened horses that galloped without riders in every direction.[29]

Within a few minutes, those that remained of the first line were in among the Russian gunners at the end of the valley. Cardigan, whose horse flinched from the guns' last salvo at close range, was said to be the first man through. 'The flame, the smoke, the roar were in our faces,' recalled Corporal Thomas Morley of the 17th Lancers, who compared it to 'riding into the mouth of a volcano'. Cutting down the gunners with their swords, the Light Brigade charged on with their sabres drawn to attack the Cossacks, who were ordered forward by Ryzhov to protect the guns, which some of the attackers were attempting to wheel away. Without time to form themselves before they were attacked, the Cossacks were 'thrown into a panic by the disciplined order of the mass of cavalry bearing down on them', recalled a Russian officer. They turned sharply to escape and, seeing that their way was blocked by the hussar regiments, began to fire their muskets point-blank at their own comrades, who fell back in panic, turned and charged into the other regiments behind. The whole of the Russian cavalry began a stampede towards Chorgun, some dragging the mounted guns behind them, while the advance riders of the Light Brigade, outnumbered five to one, pursued them all the way to the Chernaia river.

The panic flight of the Russian cavalry was watched from the heights above the river by Stepan Kozhukov, a junior artillery officer, who described the cavalry amassing in the area around the bridge, where the Ukrainsky Regiment and Kozhukov's battery on the hill had been ordered to block off their retreat:

> Here they were stampeding and all the time the confusion was getting worse. In a small space at the entrance of the Chorgun Ravine, where the dressing station was, were four hussar and Cossack regiments all crammed together, and inside this mass, in isolated spots, one could make out the red tunics of the English, probably no less surprised than ourselves how unexpectedly this had happened.... The enemy soon came to the conclusion that they had nothing to fear from the panic-stricken hussars and Cossacks and, tired of slashing, decided to return the way they had come through another cannonade of artillery and rifle fire. It is difficult, if not impossible, to do justice to the feat of these mad cavalry. Having lost at least a quarter of their number during the attack, and being apparently impervious to new dangers and losses, they quickly re-formed their squadrons to return over the same ground littered with their dead and dying. With desperate courage these valiant lunatics set off again, and not one of the living, even the wounded, surrendered. It took a long time for the hussars and Cossacks to collect themselves. They were convinced that the entire enemy cavalry were pursing them, and angrily did not want to believe that they had been crushed by a relatively insignificant handful of daredevils.

The Cossacks were the first to come to their senses, but they would not return to the battlefield. Instead they 'set themselves to new tasks in hand – taking prisoners, killing the wounded as they lay on the ground, and rounding up the English horses to offer them for sale'.[30]

As the Light Brigade rode back through the corridor of fire in the North Valley, Liprandi ordered the Polish Lancers on the Causeway Heights to cut off their retreat. But the Lancers had little stomach for a fight with the courageous Light Brigade, which they had just seen charge through the Russian guns and disperse the Cossacks in a panic flight, and the few attacks they made were against small groups of wounded men. Larger groups they left alone. When the retreating column of the 8th Hussars and 4th Regiment of Light Dragoons neared the Lancers, recalled Lord George Paget, the commander of the Light Dragoons, who had rallied them together before the retreat, 'down [the Lancers] came upon us at a sort of trot'.

> Then the Lancers stopped ('halted' is hardly the word) and evinced that same air of bewilderment (I know of no other word) that I had twice before remarked on this day. A few of the men on the right flank of their leading squadrons ... came into momentary collision with the right flank of our fellows, but beyond this they did nothing, and actually allowed us to shuffle, to edge away, by them, at a distance of hardly a horse's length. Well, we got by them without, I believe, the loss of a single man. How, I know not! It is a mystery to me! Had that force been composed of English *ladies*, I don't think one of us could have escaped.[31]

In fact, the English ladies were on the Sapoune Heights with all the other spectators who watched the remnants of the Light Brigade stagger back in ones and twos, many of them wounded, from the charge. Among them was Fanny Duberly, who not only watched the scene in horror but later on that afternoon rode out with her husband to get a closer look at the carnage on the battlefield:

> Past the scene of the morning we rode slowly; round us were dead and dying horses, numberless; and near me lay a Russian soldier, very still, upon his face. In a vineyard a little to my right a Turkish soldier was also stretched out dead. The horses, mostly dead, were all unsaddled,

and the attitudes of some betokened extreme pain. . . . And then the
wounded soldiers crawling to the hills![32]

Of the 661 men who set off on the charge, 113 were killed, 134
wounded, and 45 were taken prisoner; 362 horses were lost or killed.
The casualties were not much higher than those suffered on the Russian side (180 killed and wounded – nearly all of them in the first two
defensive lines) and far lower than the numbers reported in the British
press. *The Times* reported that 800 cavalry had been engaged of
whom only 200 had returned; the *Illustrated London News* that only
163 had returned safely from the charge. From such reports the story
quickly spread of a tragic 'blunder' redeemed by heroic sacrifice – the
myth set in stone by Alfred Tennyson's famous poem 'The Charge of
the Light Brigade', published only two months after the event.

> 'Forward, the Light Brigade!'
> Was there a man dismay'd?
> Not tho' the soldiers knew
>   Someone had blundered:
> Their's not to make reply,
> Their's not to reason why,
> Their's but to do and die:
> Into the valley of Death
>   Rode the Six Hundred.

But contrary to the myth of a 'glorious disaster', the charge was in
some ways a success, despite the heavy casualties. The objective of a
cavalry charge was to scatter the enemy's lines and frighten him off
the battlefield, and in this respect, as the Russians acknowledged, the
Light Brigade had achieved its aim. The real blunder of the British at
Balaklava was not so much the Charge of the Light Brigade as their
failure to pursue the Russian cavalry once the Heavy Brigade had
routed them and the Light Brigade had got them on the run and then
finish off the rest of Liprandi's army.[33]

The British blamed the Turks for their defeat at Balaklava, accusing
them of cowardice for abandoning the redoubts. They also later
claimed that they had looted property, not only from the British cavalry, but also from nearby settlements, where they were said to have

'committed some cold-blooded cruelties upon the unfortunate villa-gers around Balaklava, cutting the throats of the men and stripping their cabins of everything'. Lucan's Turkish interpreter, John Blunt, thought the accusations were unfair and that if any looting did take place, it was by the 'nondescript crowds of camp followers who prowled about . . . the battlefield'. The Turks were treated appallingly for the rest of the campaign. They were routinely beaten, cursed, spat upon and jeered at by the British troops, who sometimes even used them 'to carry them with their bundles on their backs across the pools and quagmires on the Balaklava road', according to Blunt. Seen by the British as little more than slaves, the Turkish troops were used for digging trenches or transporting heavy loads between Balaklava and the Sevastopol heights. Because their religion forbade them from eat-ing most of the available British army rations, they never received enough food; in desperation some of them began to steal, for which they were flogged by their British masters well beyond the maximum of forty-five lashes allowed for the Queen's own troops. Of the 4,000 Turkish soldiers who fought at Balaklava on 25 October, half would die from malnutrition by the end of 1854, and many of the rest would become too weak for active service. Yet the Turks behaved with dig-nity, and Blunt, for one, was 'much struck by the forbearing manner in which they endured their bad treatment and long suffering'. Rustem Pasha, the Egyptian officer in charge of the Turkish troops at Balaklava, urged them to be 'patient and resigned, and not to forget that the Eng-lish troops were the guests of their Sultan and were fighting in defence of the integrity of the Ottoman Empire'.[34]

The Russians celebrated Balaklava as a victory. The capture of the redoubts on the Causeway Heights was certainly a tactical success. The next day in Sevastopol it was marked by an Orthodox service as the British guns were paraded through the town. The Russians now had a commanding position from which to attack the British supply lines between Balaklava and the Sevastopol heights; the British were confined to their inner defence line on the hills around Kadikoi. Russian soldiers paraded through Sevastopol with trophies from the battlefield – British overcoats, swords, tunics, shakos, boots and cav-alry horses. The morale of the Sevastopol garrison was immediately lifted by the victory. For the first time since the defeat at the Alma, the

Russians sensed they were a match for the allied armies on the open battlefield.

The Tsar learned about the claimed victory in his palace at Gatchina on 31 October, when the morning courier arrived from Sevastopol. Anna Tiutcheva, who was with the Empress in the Arsenal Halls listening to a Beethoven recital, wrote in her diary later on that day:

> The news has lifted all our spirits. The Tsar, coming to the Empress to tell her the news, was so overcome with emotion that, in front of all of us, he threw himself onto his knees before the sacred icons and burst into tears. The Empress and her daughter Maria Nikolaevna, thinking that the frightful disturbance of the Tsar signified the fall of Sevastopol, also went down on their knees, but he calmed them, told them all the joyous news, and at once ordered a service of thanksgiving prayers, at which the whole court attended.[35]

*

Encouraged by their success at Balaklava, the next day the Russians launched an attack on the right flank of the British army on Cossack Mountain, a V-shaped ridge of undulating uplands, 2.5 kilometres in length, running north to south between the eastern sector of Sevastopol and the Chernaia estuary, known to the British as Mount Inkerman. On 26 October, 5,000 Russian troops under Colonel Fedorov marched east out of Sevastopol, turned right to climb Cossack Mountain, and descended on the unsuspecting soldiers of de Lacy Evans's 2nd Division, encamped at the southern end of the high plateau, at a place called Home Ridge, where the heights sloped steeply down onto the Balaklava plain. Evans had only 2,600 troops at his disposal, the rest of his division being elsewhere on trench duty, but the outlying pickets at Shell Hill held off the Russians with their Minié rifles, while Evans brought up more artillery, installing eighteen guns in positions out of sight. Drawing the enemy onto their artillery, the British dispersed them with a devastating fire that left several hundred Russians dead and wounded on the scrubland before Home Ridge.[36]

More were taken prisoner, many of them giving themselves up or deserting to the British side. They brought dreadful tales of the conditions in Sevastopol, where there was a shortage of water and the hospitals were overrun with victims of the bombing as well as cholera. A German officer who was serving with the Russians told the British 'that they were obliged to come out of Sevastopol on account of the disgraceful smell that was in the town, and his opinion was that the town would soon fall into the hands of the British as the killed and wounded was laying in the streets'. According to Godfrey Mosley, paymaster of the 20th Regiment,

> The army that came out of Sevastopol to attack the other day . . . were all drunk. The hospitals smelt so bad with them that you could not remain more than a minute in the place and we were told by an officer who they took prisoner that they had been giving them wine till they had got them to the proper pitch and asked who would go out and drive the English Dogs into the sea, instead of which we drove them back into the town with the loss of about 700 in a very short time. The same officer told us that we might have got into the town when we first came here easily, but now we should have some difficulty.[37]

In truth, the attack by the Russians was really a reconnaissance in force for a major new assault against the British forces on the heights of Inkerman. The initiative for the assault came from the Tsar, who had learned of Napoleon's intention to send more troops to the Crimea and believed that Menshikov should use his numerical superiority to break the siege as soon as possible, before the French reinforcements arrived, or at least to impose a delay on the allies until winter came to the rescue of the Russians ('I have two generals who will not fail me: Generals January and February,' Nicholas said, adopting the old cliché of 1812). By 4 November the Russians had been reinforced by the arrival of two infantry divisions of the 4th Corps from Bessarabia, the 10th Division under Lieutenant General Soimonov and the 11th under Lieutenant General Pavlov, bringing the total force at Menshikov's disposal to 107,000 men, not including the sailors. At first Menshikov had been opposed to the idea of a new offensive (he was still inclined to abandon Sevastopol to the enemy), but the Tsar was adamant and even sent his sons, the Grand Dukes Mikhail and Nikolai, to encourage the troops and to enforce his will. Under pressure, Menshikov agreed to attack, believing that the British were a less formidable opponent than the French. If the Russians could establish themselves with artillery batteries on Mount Inkerman, the allied siege lines on the right would find themselves under fire from behind, and, unless they recaptured the heights, the allies would be forced to abandon the siege.[38]

For all the Russians' losses, their sortie of 26 October had revealed the weakness of the British defences on Mount Inkerman. Raglan had been warned on a number of occasions by de Lacy Evans and Burgoyne that these crucial heights were vulnerable and needed to be occupied in strength and fortified; Bosquet, the commander of an infantry division on the Sapoune Heights to the south of Inkerman, had been adding his own warnings in almost daily letters to the British commander; while Canrobert had even offered immediate help. But Raglan had done nothing to strengthen the defences, even after the sortie by the Russians, when the French commander was amazed to learn that 'so important and so exposed a position' had been left 'totally unprotected by fortifications'.[39]

It was not just negligence that lay behind Raglan's failure but a calculated risk: the British were too few in number to protect all their positions, they were seriously overstretched, and would have been incapable of repulsing a general attack if one had been launched at several points along their line. By the first week of November, the British infantry were exhausted. They had scarcely had a rest since their landing in the Crimea, as Private Henry Smith recalled in a letter to his parents in February 1855:

> After the battle of the Alma and the march to Balaklava, we were immediately put to work, starting from 24 September during which time we never got more than 4 hours sleep out of 24, and very often did not get as much time even as to make a tin of coffee, before we were sent on some other duty, till the siege opened on 14 October, and although shell and shot fell like hail, as from the dreadful fatigue we had to undergo, we were so regardless as to lie down and sleep even at the mouth of the cannon ... We were often being 24 hours in the trenches, and I believe there was not an hour's drying in the 24, so that when we came to camp we were wet to the skin and all over mud even to the shoulders, and in

this very state we had to march to Inkerman battle without as much as a bit of bread or a sip of water to satisfy a craving hunger and thirst.[40]

Menshikov's plan was a more ambitious version of the sortie on 26 October ('Little Inkerman' as that dress rehearsal later became known). On the afternoon of 4 November, only a few hours after the arrival of the 4th Corps from Bessarabia, he ordered the offensive to begin at six o'clock the next morning. Soimonov was to lead a force of 19,000 men and 38 guns along the same route taken on 26 October. Capturing Shell Hill, they were to be joined there by Pavlov's force (16,000 men and 96 guns), which was to cross the Chernaia river and ascend the heights from the Inkerman Bridge. Under General Dannenberg, who was to take over the command at this point, the combined force was to drive the British off Mount Inkerman, while Liprandi's army distracted Bosquet's corps on the Sapoune Heights.

The plan called for a high degree of coordination between the attacking units, which was too much to expect from any army in an age before the radio, let alone from the Russians, who lacked detailed maps.* It also called for a change of commander in the middle of the battle – a recipe for disaster, especially since Dannenberg, a veteran of the Napoleonic Wars, had a record of defeat and indecisiveness that was hardly likely to inspire men. But the biggest flaw of all was the whole idea that a force of 35,000 men and 134 guns could even be deployed on the narrow ridge that was Shell Hill, a rocky piece of scrubland barely 300 metres wide. Realizing its impracticality, Dannenberg began to change the battle plan at the last minute. Late at night on 4 November he ordered Soimonov's men not to climb Mount Inkerman from the northern side, as had been planned, but to march east as far as the Inkerman Bridge to cover Pavlov's crossing of the river. From the bridge, the attacking forces were to climb the heights in three different directions and round on the British from the flanks. The sudden change was confusing; but even more confusion was to

---

* Soimonov relied on a naval map, without any markings on the land. A member of his staff showed him the way by drawing on the map with his finger (A. Andriianov, *Inkermanskii boi i oborona Sevastopolia (nabroski uchastnika)* (St Petersburg, 1903), p. 15).

come. At three o'clock in the morning, Soimonov's column was moving east from Sevastopol towards Mount Inkerman when he received another message from Dannenberg, ordering him to march in the opposite direction and attack from the west. Thinking that another change of plan would endanger the whole operation, Soimonov ignored the order, but instead of meeting Pavlov at the bridge, he now went back to his own preferred plan of attacking from the north. The three commanders thus went into the battle of Inkerman with entirely different plans.[41]

By five o'clock in the morning, Soimonov's advance guard had climbed the heights in silence from the northern side with 22 field guns. There had been heavy rain for the past three days, the steep slopes were slippery with mud; men and horses struggled with the heavy guns. The rain had stopped that night and there was now a heavy fog that shrouded their ascent from the enemy outposts. 'The fog covered us,' recalled Captain Andrianov. 'We could see no further than a few feet ahead of us. The dampness chilled our bones.'[42]

The dense fog was to play a crucial role in the fighting that lay ahead. Soldiers could not see their senior commanders, whose orders became virtually irrelevant. They relied instead on their own company officers, and when these disappeared they had to take the lead themselves, fighting on their own or alongside those comrades they could see through the fog, in a largely improvised fashion. This was to be a 'soldiers' battle' – the ultimate test of a modern army. Everything depended on the cohesion of the small unit, and every man became his own general.

In the opening hours, the fog played into the hands of the Russians. It covered their approach and brought them to within close range of the British positions, eliminating the disadvantage of their muskets and artillery against the longer range of the Minié rifles. The British pickets on Shell Hill were unaware of the Russians approaching: they had taken shelter from the bad weather by moving to the bottom of the hill, from which they could see nothing. The warning sounds of an army on the march that had been heard earlier in the night failed to trigger the appropriate alarms. Private Bloomfield was on picket duty on Mount Inkerman that night, and could hear the sounds of Sevastopol stirring for something (the bells of the churches had been ringing intermittently throughout the night) but he could not see a thing. 'There was a great fog, so much that we could not see a man 10 yards away from us, and nearly all the night there was a drizzly rain,' Bloomfield recalled. 'All went well until about midnight, when some of our sentries reported wheels and noise like the unloading of shot and shell, but the Field officer on duty took no further notice of it. All the night from about 9 o'clock in the evening the bells were ringing, and the bands were playing and a great noise was all over the town.'

Before they knew it, the pickets at Shell Hill were overrun by Soimonov's skirmishers, and then fast upon them, emerging from the fog, were the advance columns of his infantry, 6,000 men from the Kolyvansky, Ekaterinburg and Tomsky regiments. The Russians established their guns on Shell Hill and began to push the British back. 'When we retired the Russians came on with the most fiendish yells you can imagine,' recalled Captain Hugh Rowlands, in charge of the picket, who withdrew his men to the next high ground and ordered them to open fire, only to discover that their rifles would not work because their charges had been soaked by rain.[43]

The sound of firing at last sounded the alarm in the camp of the 2nd Division, where soldiers rushed about in their underwear, getting dressed and folding up their tents before grabbing their rifles and falling into line. 'There was a good deal of hurry and confusion,' recalled George Carmichael of the Derbyshire Regiment. 'A number of loose baggage animals frightened by the firing came galloping through the camp, and the men who had been away on different duties came running in to join the ranks.'[44]

The command was taken up by General Pennefather, second-in-command to de Lacy Evans, who had earlier been injured falling from his horse but was present in an advisory capacity. Pennefather chose a different tactic to the one employed by Evans on 26 October. Instead of falling back to draw the enemy onto the guns behind Home Ridge, he continued feeding the picket line with riflemen to keep the Russians as far back as possible, until reinforcements could arrive. Pennefather did not know that the division was outnumbered by the Russians by more than six to one, but his tactic rested on the hope that the thick fog would conceal his lack of numbers from the enemy.

Pennefather's men bravely held off the Russians. Fighting forward in small groups, separated from each other by fog and smoke, they were too far ahead to be seen by Pennefather, let alone controlled by him, or to be supported with any precision by the two field batteries at Home Ridge, which fired blindly in the vague direction of the enemy. Sheltering with his regiment behind the British guns, Carmichael watched the gunners do their best to keep up with the vastly superior firepower of the Russian batteries:

> They fired, I should imagine, at the flash of the enemy's guns on Shell Hill, and drew a heavy fire on themselves in return. Some [of the gunners] fell, and we also suffered, although we had been ordered to lie down to obtain what shelter we could from the ridge. One round shot, I remember, tore into my company, completely severing the left arm and both legs off a man in the front rank, and killed his rear rank man without any perceptible wound. Other casualties were also occurring in other companies. . . . The guns . . . were firing as fast as they could load, and each successive discharge and recoil brought them closer to our line . . . We assisted the gunners to run the guns into their first position, and some men also aided in carrying ammunition.[45]

The main thing at this stage was to keep the noise of the barrage up to make the Russians think that the British had more guns than they actually had, pass the ammunition and wait for reinforcements to arrive.

If Soimonov had known the weakness of the British defences, he would have ordered Home Ridge to be stormed, but he could see nothing in the fog, and the heavy firing of the enemy, whose Minié rifles were deadly accurate at the short range from which the British fired, persuaded him to wait for Pavlov's men to join him on Shell Hill before launching an assault. Within minutes Soimonov himself was killed by a British rifleman. The command was taken up by Colonel Pristovoitov, who was shot a few minutes later; and then by Colonel Uvazhnov-Aleksandrov, who was also killed. After that, it was not clear who would take up the command, nobody was keen to step up to the mark, and Captain Andrianov was sent off on his horse to consult with various generals on the matter, which wasted valuable time.[46]

Meanwhile, at 5 a.m., Pavlov's men had arrived at the Inkerman Bridge, only to discover that the naval detachment had not prepared it for their crossing, as they had been ordered to by Dannenberg. They had to wait until seven o'clock before the bridge was ready and they could cross the Chernaia. From there, they fanned out and climbed the heights in three different directions: the Okhotsky, Yakutsky and Selenginsky regiments and most of the artillery branching to the right to reach the top by the Sapper Road and join Soimonov's men, the Borodinsky ascending by the centre route along the Volovia Ravine, while the Tarutinsky Regiment climbed the steep and rocky slopes of the Quarry Ravine towards the Sandbag Battery under cover of Soimonov's guns.[47]

There were fierce gun battles across the heights – small groups of fighters dashing everywhere, using the thick bushes to conceal themselves and fire at each other like skirmishers – but the most intense was on the British right flank around the Sandbag Battery. Twenty minutes after they had crossed the bridge, the advance battalions of the Tarutinsky Regiment overpowered the small picket in the battery, but then came under a series of attacks from a combined British force of 700 men under the command of Brigadier Adams. In frenzied hand-to-hand fighting, the Sandbag Battery changed sides several times. By eight o'clock Adams's men were outnumbered by the Russians ten to one, but because of the narrow ridge on which the fighting for the battery took place, the Russians could not make their numbers tell in one assault. Once the British had regained the battery, the Russians came at them again in a series of attacks. Private Edward Hyde was in the battery with Adams's men:

> The Russian infantry got right up to it, and clambered up the front and sides of it, and we had a hard job to keep them out. Directly we saw their heads above the parapet, or looking into the embrasures, we fired at them or bayoneted them as fast as we could. They came on like ants; no sooner was one knocked backwards than another clambered over the dead bodies to take his place, all of them yelling and shouting. We in the battery were not quiet, you may be sure, and what with the cheering and shouting, the thud of blows, the clash of bayonets and swords, the ping of the bullets, the whistling of the shells, the foggy atmosphere, and the smell of powder and blood, the scene inside the battery where we were was beyond the power of man to imagine or describe.[48]

Eventually, the Russians could no longer be held back – they swarmed into the battery – and Adams and his men were forced to retreat towards Home Ridge. But reinforcements soon arrived, the Duke of Cambridge with the Grenadiers, and a new assault was launched against the Russians grouped around the Sandbag Battery, which by this stage had assumed a symbolic status far beyond its military significance to either side. The Grenadiers charged the Russians with their bayonets, Cambridge shouting at his men to keep to the high ground and not become dispersed by following the Russians down the hill, but few men could hear the Duke or see him in the fog. Among the Grenadiers was George Higginson, who witnessed the charge 'down the rugged slope, full upon the advancing host'.

> The exultant cheer ... confirmed my dread that our gallant fellows would soon get out of hand; and in fact, except for one short period during the long day when we contrived to make some kind of regular formation, the contest was maintained by groups under company officers, who were unable, owing to the mist and smoke of musketry fire, to preserve any definite touch.

The fighting became increasingly frenzied and chaotic, as one side charged the other down the hill, only to be counter-attacked by another group of men from further up the hill. The soldiers on both sides lost all discipline and became disordered mobs, uncontrolled by any officers and driven on by rage and fear (reinforced by the fact that they could not see each other in the fog). They charged and counter-charged, yelling and screaming, firing their guns, slashing out in all directions with their swords, and when they had no ammunition left they began throwing rocks at one another, striking out with their rifle butts, even kicking and biting.[49]

In this sort of fighting the cohesion of the small combat unit was decisive. Everything came down to whether groups of men and their line commanders could keep their discipline and unity – whether they could organize themselves and stick together through the fight without losing nerve or running away out of fear. The soldiers of the Tarutinsky Regiment failed this crucial test.

Chodasiewicz was one of the company officers in the 4th Battalion of the Tarutinsky Regiment. Their task was to take the eastern side of

Mount Inkerman, providing cover for Pavlov's other troops to bring up gabions and fascines for a trench work against the British positions. The unit lost its way in the thick fog, veered towards the left, and became mixed with disgruntled soldiers from the Ekaterinburg Regiment, among Soimonov's troops already on the heights, who led them back down into the Quarry. By this stage, Chodasiewicz had lost control of his men, who were totally dispersed among the Ekaterinburg Regiment. Undirected by the officers, some of the Tarutinsky men began to climb the hill again. Ahead of them they could make out some of their comrades 'standing before a small battery shouting "Hurrah!" and waving their caps for us to come on', recalled Chodasiewicz; 'the buglers continually played the advance, and several of my men broke from the ranks at a run!' At the Sandbag Battery, Chodasiewicz found his men in total disorder. Various regiments were all mixed up so that their command structures entirely broke down. He ordered his men to charge with bayonets, and they overran the British in the battery, but then they failed to push them down the hill, remaining instead inside the battery, where 'they forgot their duty and wandered about in search of booty', recalled another officer, who thought 'all this occurred because of a lack of officers and leadership'.

With all the fog and mixing-up of men, there were many instances of friendly fire on the Russian side. Soimonov's troops, in particular the Ekaterinburg Regiment, began firing at the men inside the Sandbag Battery, some thinking they were firing on the enemy, others on the orders of an officer who feared the insubordination of his men and tried to discipline them by having others shoot at them. 'The chaos was something extraordinary,' recalled Chodasiewicz: 'some of the men were grumbling at the Ekaterinburg Regiment, others were shouting for artillery to come up, the buglers constantly played the signal to advance, and drummers beat to the attack, but nobody thought of moving; there they stood like a flock of sheep.' A bugle call to manoeuvre left caused a sudden panic among the Tarutinsky men, who thought that they could hear the distant noise of the French drums. 'There were shouts on all sides of "Where is the reserve?",' recalled an officer. Fearing they had no support, the troops began to stampede down the hill. According to Chodasiewicz, 'Officers shouted to the men to halt, but to no avail, for none of them thought of stopping, but each followed the direction prompted by his fancy or his fears.' No officer, however senior, was able to reverse the panic retreat of the men, who ran down to the bottom of the Quarry Ravine and crowded around the Sevastopol aqueduct, which alone stopped their flight. When Lieutenant General Kiriakov, the commander of the 17th Infantry Division who had gone absent at the Alma, appeared at the aqueduct and rode among the men on his white charger, slashing at them with his whip and shouting at them to climb back up the hill, the soldiers paid him little attention, and then shouted back at him, 'Go up there yourself!' Chodasiewicz was ordered to collect his company, but he had only 45 men left out of a company of 120.[50]

The Tarutinsky men had not been wrong when they thought they could hear the sound of the French drums. Raglan had sent an urgent call for help to Bosquet on the Sapoune Heights at 7 a.m., after he had arrived to inspect the battle at Home Ridge (he had also sent an order for two heavy 18-pounder cannon to be brought up from the siege batteries to counter the Russian cannonade but the order had gone astray). Bosquet's men had already sensed that the British were in danger when they heard the early firing. The Zouaves had even heard the Russians on the march the night before – their African experience having taught them how to listen to the ground – and they were ready for the order to attack before it came. Nothing suited their type of fighting better than the foggy conditions and bushy scrubland of the hills: they were used to mountain warfare from Algeria and were at their best when fighting in small groups and ambushing the enemy. The Zouaves and Chasseurs were eager to advance, but Bosquet held them back, fearful of Liprandi's army, 22,000 soldiers and 88 field guns in the South Valley under the command of Gorchakov, which had begun a distant cannonade against the Sapoune Heights. 'Forward! Let's march! It's time to finish them!' the Zouaves cried impatiently when Bosquet appeared among their ranks. They were angry when the general walked before them. 'A revolt was imminent,' recalled Louis Noir, who was in the first column of Zouaves.

> The deep respect and true affection which we felt for Bosquet were tested to the limit by the impetuosity of the old Algerian bands. Suddenly

Bosquet turned and drew his sword, placed himself at the head of his Zouaves, his Turks and Chasseurs, undefeated troops he had known for years, and pointing his sword towards the 20,000 Russian troops amassed on the redoubts of the opposing heights, shouted in a thunderous voice: 'En avant! A la baïonnette!'[51]

In fact, the size of Liprandi's army was not as large as Bosquet had feared, since Gorchakov had foolishly decided to position half of them behind the Chernaia river in reserve, and had dispersed the rest between the lower slopes of the Sapoune Heights and the Sandbag Battery. But the Zouaves did not know this; they could not see their enemy in the thick fog, and attacked with fearsome energy to overcome what they believed to be their disadvantage in numbers. Charging forward in small groups, and using the brushwood for cover while they fired at the Russian columns, their tactic was to scare the Russians off by any means they could. They yelled and screamed and fired in the air as they ran forward. Their bugles sounded and their drummers beat as loud as they could. Jean Cler, a colonel of the 2nd Zouave Regiment, even told his men as they prepared to go into the battle: 'Spread out your pants as wide as they will go, and make as big a show of yourselves as you can.'[52]

The Russians were overwhelmed by the attacking force of the Zouaves, whose Minié rifles took out hundreds of men within the first few seconds of their charge. Racing up the hill-bend round Home Ridge, the Zouaves drove the Russians from the Sandbag Battery and chased them down to the bottom of St Clement's Ravine. Their momentum took them around the curving spur into Quarry Ravine, already heaving with the soldiers of the Tarutinsky Regiment, who began to panic in the crush and fired back at the new arrivals, killing mainly their own men, before the Zouaves backed out of the crossfire and climbed towards Home Ridge.

There they found the British in desperate battle with the forces on the right wing of Pavlov's pincer movement: the Okhotsky, Yakutsky and Selenginsky regiments, who had joined the remnants of Soimonov's troops and, under the command of Dannenberg, began to attack the Sandbag Battery again. The fighting was brutal, wave after wave of Russians charged with their bayonets only to be shot down by the British or tussle with them 'hand-to-hand, foot to foot, muzzle to muzzle, butt-end to butt-end', recalled Captain Wilson of the Coldstream Guards.[53] The Guards were vastly outnumbered by the Russians, and in urgent need of reinforcements when they were at last joined by six companies of Cathcart's 4th Division under the command of General Torrens. The new men were spoiling for a fight (they had missed out on the action at Balaklava and the Alma) and, ordered to attack the Russians on the ridge by the Sandbag Battery, they charged down the valley after them, losing all discipline and coming under heavy close-range fire by the Yakutsky and Selenginsky regiments from the heights above. Among those killed in the hail of bullets was Cathcart, the spot where he was buried becoming known as 'Cathcart's Hill'.

By this stage Cambridge and the Guards were down to their last 100 men in the Sandbag Battery. There were 2,000 Russians against them. They had no ammunition left. The Duke proposed to make a stand for the Sandbag Battery – an idiotic sacrifice for this relatively minor landmark on the battlefield – but his staff officers dissuaded him: it would be disastrous for the Queen's cousin and the colours of her Guards to be brought before the Tsar. Among those officers was Higginson, who led the retreat to Home Ridge. 'Clustered round the Colours,' he recalled,

> the men passed slowly backwards, keeping their front full towards the enemy, their bayonets ready at the 'charge'. As a comrade fell, wounded or dead, his fellow took his place, and maintained the compactness of the gradually diminishing group, that held on with unflinching stubbornness in protecting the flags. . . . Happily the ground on our right was so precipitous as to deter the enemy from attempting to outflank us on that side. As from time to time some Russians soldiers, more adventurous than their fellows, sprang forwards towards our compact group, two or three of our Grenadiers would dash out with the bayonet and compel steady retreat. Nevertheless our position was critical.

It was at this moment that Bosquet's men appeared on the ridge. Never had the sight of Frenchmen been so welcome to the English. The Guards cheered them as they arrived and cried, 'Vivent les Français!' and the French replied, 'Vivent les Anglais!'[54]

Stunned by the arrival of the French, the Russians withdrew to Shell Hill and attempted to consolidate. But the morale of their troops had dropped, they did not fancy their chances against the British and the French, and many of them now began to run away, using the cover of the fog to escape the attentions of their officers. For a while Dannenberg believed that he could win with his artillery: he had nearly a hundred guns, including 12-pound field guns and howitzers, more than the British at Home Ridge. But at half past nine the two heavy 18-pounders ordered up by Raglan finally arrived and opened fire on Shell Hill, their monstrous charges blasting through the Russian batteries, and forcing their artillery to withdraw from the field. The Russians were not finished. They had 6,000 men still to be used on the heights, and twice that number in reserve on the other side of the river. Some of them continued to attack, but their advancing columns were ripped apart by the heavy British guns.

Finally, Dannenberg decided to call off the action and retreat. He had to overcome the angry protests of Menshikov and the Grand Dukes, who had watched the slaughter from a safe position 500 metres behind Shell Hill and called on Dannenberg to reverse the withdrawal. Dannenberg told Menshikov, 'Highness, to stop the troops here would be to let them be destroyed to the last man. If your Highness thinks otherwise, have the goodness to give the orders yourself, and take the command from me.' The exchange was the beginning of a long and bitter argument between the two men, who could not stand each other, as each man tried to blame the other for the defeat at Inkerman – a battle where the Russians had vastly outnumbered the enemy. Menshikov blamed Dannenberg, and Dannenberg blamed Soimonov, who was dead, and everybody blamed the ordinary soldiers for their indiscipline and cowardice. But ultimately the disorder came from the absence of command, and there the blame must rest with Menshikov, the commander-in-chief, who lost his nerve completely and took no part in the action. The Grand Duke Nikolai, who saw through Menshikov, wrote to his older brother Alexander, soon to become Tsar:

We [the two Grand Dukes] had been waiting for Prince Menshikov near the Inkerman Bridge but he did not come out of his house until 6.30 a.m. when our troops had already taken the first position. We stayed with the prince all the time on the right flank, and not once did any of the generals send him a report on the course of the battle. . . . The men were disordered because they were badly directed. . . . The disorder originated from Menshikov. Staggering though it is to relate, Menshikov had no headquarters at all, just three people who work at those duties in such a fashion that, if you want to know something, you are at a loss to know whom to ask.[55]

Ordered to withdraw, the Russians fled in panic from the battle-field, their officers powerless to stop the human avalanche, while the British and French artillery fired at their backs. 'They were petrified,' recalled a French officer; 'it was no longer a battle but a massacre.' The Russians were mowed down in their hundreds, others trampled under-foot, as they ran down the hill towards the bridge and struggled to cross it, or swam across the river to the other side.[56]

Some of the French chased after them, and a dozen men or so from the Lourmel Brigade even entered Sevastopol. They were carried away by the chase and unaware that they were on their own, the rest of the French having turned back long before. The streets of Sevastopol were virtually empty, for the whole population was on the battlefield or standing guard at the bastions. The Frenchmen walked around the town, looting houses, and made their way down to the quay, where their sudden appearance caused civilians to flee in panic, thinking that the enemy had broken through. The French soldiers were equally afraid. Hoping to escape by sea, they rowed off in the first boat they could find, but just as they were rounding Fort Alexander into the open sea, their boat was sunk by a direct hit from the Quarantine Bat-tery. The story of the Lourmel soldiers became an inspiration to the French army during the long siege, giving rise to the belief that Sevas-topol could be taken with a single bold attack. Many thought their story showed that the allied armies could and should have used the moment when the Russians were in flight from the heights of Inker-man to pursue them and march into the town as those audacious men had done.[57]

The Russians lost about 12,000 men on the battlefield of Inker-man. The British listed 2,610 casualties, the French 1,726. It was an appalling number killed in just four hours of fighting – a rate of loss almost on a par with the battle of the Somme. The dead and wounded were piled on top of each others bits of bodies, torn apart by shells, lying everywhere. The war correspondent Nicholas Woods observed:

> Some had their heads taken off at the neck, as if with an axe; others their legs gone from the hips; others their arms, and others again who were hit in the chest or stomach, were literally as smashed as if they had been crushed in a machine. Across the path, side by side, lay five [Russian] Guardsmen,* who were all killed by one round shot as they advanced to charge the enemy. They lay on their faces in the same attitude, with their muskets tightly grasped in both hands, and all had the same grim, painful frown on their faces.

Louis Noir thought the Russian dead, who were mostly killed by bayonets, had a 'look of furious hatred' captured at the moment of their death. Jean Cler also walked among the wounded and the dead.

> Some were dying, but for the most part they were dead, lying pell-mell, upon one another. There were arms upraised above the mass of yellow flesh, as if begging for pity. The dead who were lying on their back had generally thrust out their hands, either as if to ward off the danger, or to beg for mercy. All of them had medals, or little copper cases, containing images of the saints, on chains around their necks.

Underneath the dead there were men alive, wounded and then buried under bodies struck down later on. 'Sometimes, from the bottom of a heap,' wrote André Damas, a French army chaplain, 'one could hear men breathing still; but they lacked the strength to lift the weight of flesh and bones that pressed them down; if their faint moans were heard, long hours passed before they could be cleared.'[58]

Major-General Codrington of the Light Division was horrified by the scavengers who robbed the dead. 'The most disgusting thing to feel is that the horrid plunderers, the prowlers of a battle-field, have been there, pockets turned inside out, things cut to look for money, everything valuable systematically searched for – officers particularly stripped for their better clothes, with just something thrown over them,' he wrote on 9 November.[59]

* Woods was mistaken: the Russian Guards were nowhere near the Crimea.

It took the allies several days to bury all their dead and evacuate the wounded to field hospitals. The Russians took much longer. Menshikov had refused the allied offer of a truce to clear the battlefield for fear that his troops would become demoralized and might even mutiny at the sight of so many dead and wounded on their side compared to the losses of the enemy. So the Russian dead and wounded lay there for several days and even weeks. Cler found four Russian wounded men alive at the bottom of the Quarry Ravine twelve days after the battle.

> The poor fellows were lying under a projecting rock; and, when asked on what they had contrived to subsist all this time, they replied by pointing, first, to Heaven, which had sent them water and inspired them with courage, and then to some fragments of mouldy, black bread, which they had found in the pouches of the numerous dead, who lay around them.

Some of the dead were not found until three months later. They were at the bottom of Spring Ravine, where they were frozen stiff, looking much like 'dried-up mummies', according to Cler. The Frenchman was struck by the contrast he had noted between the Russian dead at the Alma, who had 'an appearance of health – their clothing, underclothing, and shoes were clean and in good condition', and the dead at Inkerman, who 'wore a look of suffering and fatigue'.[60]

As at the Alma, there were claims that the Russians had engaged in atrocities against the British and the French. It was said that they had robbed and killed the wounded on the ground,* sometimes even mutilating their bodies. British and French soldiers put these actions down to the 'savagery' of the Russian troops, who they said had been well primed with vodka. 'They give no quarter,' wrote Hugh Drummond of the Scots Guards to his father on 8 November, 'and this should be represented, as it is a scandal to the world that Russia, professing to be a civilized power, should disgrace herself by such acts of barbarity.' Describing the 'dastardly conduct' of the Russian troops in his anonymous memoir, another British soldier wrote:

---

* A reasonable mistake to make amid the heavy fog and brushwood on the heights, where non-wounded soldiers lay down on the ground to ambush the enemy.

Aided by night, they emerge from the fog unexpectedly, like demons . . .
Panting with murderous intent (for fair fighting is not their aim), blessed
by inhuman Priests, promised plunder to any amount, excited by ardent
liquids, encouraged by two of their Grand Dukes . . . drunk, maddened,
every evil passion aroused, they rush wildly upon our soldiers. At Inkerman we saw the Russian soldiery bayoneting, beating out the brains,
jumping like fiends upon the lacerated bodies of the wounded Allies,
wherever they could find them. The atrocities committed by the Russians have covered their nation with infamy and made them an example
of horror and detestation to the whole world.[61]

But in fact these actions had more to do with a sense of religious outrage. When Raglan and Canrobert wrote to Menshikov on
7 November to protest against the atrocities, the Russian commander-
in-chief replied that the killings had been caused by the destruction of
the Church of St Vladimir at Khersonesos – the church built to conse-
crate the spot where the Grand Prince Vladimir had been baptized,
converting Kievan Rus' to Christianity – which had been pillaged and
then used by the French troops as part of their siege works. The 'deep
religious feeling of our troops' had been wounded by the desecration
of St Vladimir, argued Menshikov in a letter approved by the Tsar,
adding for good measure that the Russians had themselves been 'victims' of a series of 'bloody retributions' by the English troops on the
battlefield of Inkerman. Some of these facts were admitted by César
de Bazancourt, the official French historian of the expedition to the
Crimea, in his account of 1856:

> Close upon the sea-shore, amid the irregular ground upon which stand
> the remnants of the Genoese Fort, and which descends towards the
> Quarantine Bay, rose the small chapel of St Vladimir. Some scattered
> soldiers, more bold than the others, would often creep through the
> undulations of the ground towards the Quarantine establishments
> which had been abandoned by the Russians, and carry off thence any-
> thing serviceable to them – either to shelter themselves or to feed the
> fires in front of their tents; fire-wood beginning to be scarce. To these
> soldiers, already culpable, succeeded those marauders who, in every
> army, will prowl about in contempt of all laws and all discipline, in
> search of pillage. They contrived to get beyond the line of outposts, and

penetrated during the night into the small chapel placed under the guardianship of the protecting Saint of Russia.

But if the Russians had been driven to atrocities by deep religious feelings, it was certainly the case that they had been encouraged by their priests. The night before the battle, at services in churches in Sevastopol, the Russian troops were told that the British and the French were fighting for the Devil, and priests had called on them to kill them without mercy to avenge the destruction of St Vladimir.[62]

*

Inkerman was a pyrrhic victory for the British and the French. They had managed to resist the largest Russian effort yet to dislodge them from the heights around Sevastopol. But the casualties were very high, at a level that the public would find hard to tolerate, especially after they learned about the poor treatment of the dying and the wounded by the medical services. Serious questions would be asked about the wisdom of the whole campaign when the news reached home. With such heavy losses, it was no longer feasible for the allied armies to mount a fresh assault against Sevastopol's defences until fresh troops arrived.

At a joint planning conference at Raglan's headquarters on 7 November, the French took over from the British on Mount Inkerman, a tacit recognition that they had become the senior partner in the military alliance, leaving the British, now down to just 16,000 effectives, to occupy no more than a quarter of the trenches around Sevastopol. At the same meeting, Canrobert insisted on shelving any plans for an assault against Sevastopol until the following spring, when the allies would have enough reinforcements to overcome the Russian defences, which had not only withstood the first allied bombardment but had been greatly strengthened since. The French commander argued that the Russians had brought in a large number of fresh troops, increasing their numbers in Sevastopol to 100,000 men (in fact, they had barely half that number after Inkerman). He feared that they would be able to go on reinforcing their defences 'as long as the attitude of Austria with respect to the Eastern Question

allows Russia to send any number of troops she pleases from Bessarabia and Southern Russia to the Crimea'. Until the French and British
had a military alliance with the Austrians and had brought in 'very
numerous reinforcements' to the Crimea, there was no point losing
more lives in the siege. Raglan and his staff agreed with Canrobert.
The question now was how to make provision for the allied troops
to spend the winter on the heights above Sevastopol, for all they had
brought with them were lightweight tents suitable only for summer
campaigning. Canrobert believed, and the British shared his view, that
'by means of a simple stone substructure under tents, the troops might
pass the winter here'. Rose agreed. 'The climate is healthy,' he explained
to Clarendon, 'and with the exception of cold northerly winds, the
cold in winter is not vigorous.'[63]

The prospect of spending the winter in Russia filled many with a
sense of dark foreboding: they thought about Napoleon in 1812. De
Lacy Evans urged Raglan to abandon the siege of Sevastopol and
evacuate the British troops. The Duke of Cambridge proposed withdrawing the troops to Balaklava, where they could be more easily
supplied and sheltered from the cold than on the heights above Sevastopol. Raglan rejected their proposals, and resolved to keep the army
on the heights throughout the winter months, a criminal decision
prompting the resignation of Evans and Cambridge, who returned to
England, sick and disillusioned, before winter came. Their departure
began a steady homeward trail of British officers. In the two months
after Inkerman, 225 of the 1,540 officers in the Crimea departed for
warmer climes; only 60 of them would return.[64]

Among the rank and file, the realization that there would be no
quick victory was even more demoralizing. 'Why did we not make a
bold attack after being flushed with victory at Alma?' asked Lieutenant Colonel Mundy of the 33rd Regiment of Foot. He summed up the
general mood in a letter to his mother on 7 November:

> If the Russians are as strong as they say, we must quit the siege, for it is
> generally understood that even with our present strength we can do no
> good with Sevastopol. The fleet is useless and the work now so harrass-
> ing that when the cold weather comes on hundreds must fall victims to

overexertion and sickness. Sometimes not one night rest do the men get in six and oftentimes are 24 hours on. It must be remembered that they have no clothing except a thin blanket, and the cold and damp are very severe at night, and the constant state of anxiety we are always in, for fear of an attack being made on our trenches, batteries or redoubts quite puts a stop to calm wholesome sleep.

Rates of desertion from the allied trenches increased sharply as the winter cold arrived in the weeks after Inkerman, with hundreds of British and French soldiers giving themselves up to the Russian side.[65]

For the Russians, the defeat at Inkerman was a devastating blow. Menshikov became convinced that the fall of Sevastopol was unavoidable. In a letter to the Minister of War, Prince Dolgorukov, on 9 November, he recommended its abandonment so that Russian forces could be concentrated on the defence of the rest of the Crimea. The Tsar was enraged by such defeatism from his commander-in-chief. 'For what was the heroism of our troops, and such heavy losses, if we accept defeat?' he wrote to Menshikov on 13 November. 'Surely our enemies have also suffered heavily? I cannot agree with your opinion. Do not submit, I say, and do not enourage others to do so. . . . We have God on our side.' Despite such words of defiance, the Tsar was thrown into a deep depression by the news of Inkerman, and his despondent mood was clear for all at court to see. In the past Nicholas had tried to hide his feelings from his courtiers, but after Inkerman there was no more concealing it. 'The palace at Gatchina is gloomy and silent,' Tiutcheva noted in her diary: 'everywhere there is depression, people hardly daring to speak to each other. The sight of the sovereign is enough to break one's heart. Recently he has become more and more morose; his face is careworn and his look is lifeless.' Shocked by the defeat, Nicholas lost faith in the commanders who had led him to believe that the war in the Crimea could be won. He began to regret his decision to go to war against the Western powers in the first place, and turned for comfort to those advisers, such as Paskevich, who had always been against the war.[66]

'It was a treacherous, revolting business,' Tolstoy wrote of the defeat in his diary on 14 November.

The 10th and 11th divisions attacked the enemy's left flank ... The enemy put forward 6,000 riflemen – only 6,000 against 30,000 – and we retreated, having lost about 6,000 brave men.* And we had to retreat, because half our troops had no artillery owing to the roads being impassable, and – God knows why – there were no rifle battalions. Terrible slaughter! It will weigh heavy on the souls of many people! Lord, forgive them. The news of this action has produced a sensation. I've seen old men who wept aloud and young men who swore to kill Dannenberg. Great is the moral strength of the Russian people. Many political truths will emerge and evolve in the present difficult days for Russia. The feeling of ardent patriotism that has arisen and issued forth from Russia's misfortunes will long leave its traces on her. These people who are now sacrificing [so much] will be citizens of Russia and we will not forget their sacrifice. They will take part in public affairs with dignity and pride, and the enthusiasm aroused in them by the war will stamp on them for ever the quality of self-sacrifice and nobility.[67]

Since the retreat of the Russian army from Silistria, Tolstoy had led a comfortable existence in Kishinev, where Gorchakov had set up his headquarters, but he soon grew bored of attending balls and playing cards, at which he lost heavily, and dreamed of seeing action once again. 'Now that I have every comfort, good accommodation, a piano, good food, regular occupations and a fine circle of friends, I have begun to yearn for camp life again and envy the men out there,' Tolstoy wrote to his aunt Toinette on 29 October.[68]

Inspired by the wish to do something for his fellow-men, Tolstoy and a group of fellow-officers thought of setting up a periodical. The 'Military Gazette', as they called their journal, was intended to educate the soldiers, bolster their morale, and reveal their patriotism and humanity to the rest of Russian society. 'This venture of mine pleases me very much,' Tolstoy wrote to his brother Sergei. 'The journal will publish descriptions of battles – not such dull and untruthful ones as in other journals – deeds of bravery, biographies and obituaries of worthy people, especially the little known; war stories, soldiers' songs,

---

* Tolstoy is citing the official figures passed for publication by the military censors. The true Russian losses were double that amount.

popular articles about the skills of the engineers, etc.' To finance the 'Gazette', which was to be cheap enough for the troops themselves to buy, Tolstoy diverted money from the sale of the family house at Yasnaya Polyana, which he had been forced to sell that autumn to cover his losses at cards. Tolstoy wrote some of his first stories for the periodical: 'How Russian Soldiers Die' and 'Uncle Zhdanov and the Horseman Chernov', in the second of which he exposed the brutality of an army officer beating a soldier, not for something that he has done wrong, but 'because he was a soldier and soldiers must be beaten'. Realizing that this would not pass the censor, Tolstoy omitted these two stories before submitting the idea for the periodical to Gorchakov, who sent it on to the War Ministry, but even so publication was rejected by the Tsar, who did not want an unofficial soldiers' paper to challenge *Russian Invalid*, the government's own army newspaper.[69]

The defeat of Inkerman made up Tolstoy's mind to go to the Crimea. One of his closest comrades, Komstadius, with whom he had been planning to edit the 'Gazette', was killed at Inkerman. 'More than anything, it was his death that drove me to ask for a transfer to Sevastopol,' he wrote in his diary on 14 November. 'He made me feel somehow ashamed.' Tolstoy later explained to his brother that his request had been 'mostly out of patriotism – a sentiment which, I confess, is gaining an increasingly strong hold on me'.[70] But perhaps just as important to his decision to go to the Crimea was his sense of destiny as a writer. Tolstoy wanted to see and write about the war: to reveal to the public the whole truth – both the patriotic sacrifice of the ordinary people and the failures of the military leadership – and thereby start the process of political and social reform to which he believed the war must lead.

Tolstoy arrived in Sevastopol on 19 November, almost three weeks after setting out from Kishinev. Promoted to the rank of second lieutenant, he was attached to the 3rd Light Battery of the 14th Artillery Brigade and, to his annoyance, was quartered in the town itself, a long way from the city's defences. Tolstoy stayed only nine days in Sevastopol that autumn, but he saw enough to inspire much of the patriotic pride and hope in the common Russian people that filled the pages of 'Sevastopol in December', the first of his *Sevastopol Sketches*, which was to make his literary name. 'The spirit of the army is beyond all description,' he wrote to Sergei on 20 November:

A wounded soldier, almost dying, told me how they took the 24th French battery, but weren't reinforced. He was sobbing. A company of marines almost mutinied because they were to be relieved from a battery where they'd withstood bombardment for 30 days. Soldiers extract the fuses from bombs. Women carry water to the bastions and read prayers under fire. In one brigade [at Inkerman], there were 160 wounded men who wouldn't leave the front. It's a wonderful time! But now ... we've quietened down – it's beautiful in Sevastopol now. The enemy hardly fires at all and everyone is convinced that he won't take the town, and it really is impossible. There are three assumptions: either he's going to launch an assault, or he's diverting our attention with false earthworks in order to disguise his retreat, or he's fortifying his position for the winter. The first is least likely and the second most likely. I haven't managed to be in action even once, but I thank God that I've seen these people and am living at this glorious time. The bombardment [of the 17th October] will remain as the most brilliant and glorious feat not only in Russian history but in the history of the world.[71]

9

Generals January and February

Winter came in the second week of November. For three days and
nights the freezing wind and rain swept across the heights above Sevastopol, blowing down the tents of the British and French troops, who
huddled in the mud, soaked and shivering, with nothing but their
blankets and coats to cover them. And then, in the early hours of
14 November, the shores of the Crimea were hit by a hurricane. Tents
went flying like sheets of paper in the wind; boxes, barrels, trunks and
wagons were thrown headlong; tent-poles, blankets, hats and coats,
chairs and tables whirled around; frightened horses broke loose from
their pickets and stampeded through the camps; trees were uprooted;
windows smashed; and soldiers rushed around in all directions, chasing after their effects and clothes, or desperately looking for any sort
of shelter in roofless barns and stables, behind the redoubts or in holes
in the ground. 'The scene was most ridiculous, the tents being all
down and discovering everyone, some in bed, some like myself in . . .
shirts . . . all being soaked through and bellowing loudly for their
servants,' Charles Cocks of the Coldstream Guards wrote to his
brother on 17 November. 'The wind was most awful and we could
only keep our tents from going to Sevastopol by lying like spread
eagles on top of them.'[1]

All morning the storm raged, and then at two o'clock the wind died
down, allowing the men to come out from their hiding places and
retrieve their scattered possessions: soaked and dirty clothes and blankets, bits of broken furniture, pots and pans and other debris from the
muddy ground. Towards evening the temperature dropped, and the
rain changed to a heavy snow. The men tried to pitch their tents again,
their fingers numb with the freezing cold, or spent the night in barns

and sheds, huddled altogether against the walls in a hopeless search for warmth.

The devastation on the heights was nothing compared to that down in the harbour and on the open sea. Fanny Duberly, on board the *Star of the South*, looked out at a harbour seething with foam, the ships swinging terribly. 'The spray, dashing over the cliffs many hundred feet, fell like heavy rain into the harbour. Ships were crushing and crowding together, all adrift, all breaking and grinding each other to pieces.' Among those ships was the *Retribution*, on which the Duke of Cambridge was recuperating from the battle of Inkerman, which had terrified him. 'It was a fearful gale,' he wrote to Raglan the next day, 'and we had a more dreadful 24 hours of it than we ever spent.'

> It carried away two anchors & our rudder; [we] had to throw over all our upper deck guns and then we had to hold on by one anchor 200 yards from the rocks which by a merciful providence held us on . . . I find myself so completely knocked up and shattered in health by this . . . that I hope you will not object to my going for a short time to Constantinople, Gibson [his doctor] being of opinion that if I were at this moment to return to Camp in this dreadful weather I should only have to take to my bed.[2]

It was worse outside the harbour, where the bulk of the supply ships were moored in case of a new attack on Balaklava by the Russians. Smashed against the rocks, more than twenty British ships were destroyed, with the loss of several hundred lives and precious winter stores. The biggest setback was the sinking of the steamship *Prince*, which went down with all but six of its 150 crew and 40,000 winter uniforms, closely followed by the destruction of the *Resolute* and its cargo of 10 million Minié rounds. At Kamiesh, the French war fleet lost the *Henri Quatre* line-of-battle ship and the steamer *Pluton*, and the merchant navy lost two ships with all their crews and supplies. Boxes of French food were washed ashore behind the Russian lines at Quarantine Bay and as far north as Evpatoria. Ivan Kondratov, an infantryman from the Kuban, wrote to his family from a bivouac on the River Belbek on 23 November:

> The storm was so strong that huge oak trees were broken. Many of the enemy's ships were sunk. Three steamers went down near Saki. Zhirov's Cossack regiment saved 50 drowning Turks from a sunken transport

ship. They think that over thirty boats were sunk on the coast of the Crimea. That is why we have been eating English corned beef and drinking rum and foreign wines.[3]

The French recovered from the storm in a few days, but the British took much longer, and many of the problems they encountered in the winter months – the shortages of food and shelter and medical supplies – were a direct outcome of the hurricane as well as the failures of the supply system. The arrival of the winter had turned the war into a test of administrative efficiency – a test barely passed by the French and miserably failed by the British.

Confident of a quick victory, the allied commanders had made no plans for the troops to spend a winter on the heights above Sevastopol. They did not fully realize how cold it would become. The British were particularly negligent. They failed to provide proper winter clothing for the troops, who were sent to the Crimea in their parade uniforms, without even greatcoats, which arrived later on, after the first cargo of winter uniforms had gone with the steamship *Prince*. The French were better prepared. They issued their troops with sheepskins and eventually with fur-lined hooded cloaks, which became known as the *criméennes*, originally worn by officers alone. They also let the soldiers wear as many layers as they preferred, without anything remotely like that peculiar British military fetish for 'gentlemanly' dress and appearance. By the depths of winter the French troops had become so motley in their uniforms that they hardly looked like a regular army any more. But they were considerably warmer than their British counterparts. 'Rest assured,' wrote Frédéric Japy of the 3rd Zouave Regiment to his anxious mother in Beaucourt:

these are my clothes beginning with my skin: a flannel vest (*gilet*), a shirt, a wool vest, a tunic, a jacket (*caban*); on my feet some boots, and when I am not on service, leather shoes and leggings – so you see I have nothing to complain about. I have two jackets, a light one issued by the Zouaves and a monumental one which I bought in Constantinople for the cold; it weighs a little less than 50 kilograms, and I sleep in it when I am on trench duty; if it gets soaked, there is no way to carry it, nor to march with it; if I can, I shall bring it back to France as a curiosity.

Louis Noir described how the Zouaves dressed to survive the cold:

> Our battalions, and notably those who came from Africa, survived the freezing temperatures admirably. We were well dressed. Usually, on top of our uniform, we wore either a large greatcoat with a hood, perhaps a *criméenne* or a sheepskin shaped as a jacket; the legs were protected by long fur-lined leggings; and every man had been issued with a warm sheepskin hat. But there was no regulation uniform; each man dressed in his own style. One man dressed like a bedouin, another like a coachman, and another like a priest; others preferred to dress in the Greek style; and some stoics added nothing to the uniform. There were all sorts of clogs and boots – leather, rubber, wooden-soled and so on. Headgear was left entirely to the imagination of every man . . .

Dressed in summer uniforms, the British envied the warm sheep-skins and *criméennes* of the French. 'They certainly are the proper clothing for out here,' George Lawson, the army surgeon, wrote in a letter to his family:

> I wish our men had something of the sort . . . Many of them are almost shoeless and shirtless, their great coats worn to a thread and torn in all directions, having had not only to live in them during the day but sleep in them by night, covered only by the wet blanket which they have just brought up with them from the trenches.[4]

The allied commanders had also given little thought to the shelter the men would need. The tents which they had brought with them were not insulated on the ground, and provided little real protection from the elements. Many were irreparably damaged by the storm – at least half those used by the regiment of Captain Tomkinson of the Light Brigade, who complained that the tents were unfit to live in: 'They let in water to such an extent that in heavy rains the ground beneath them is flooded and the men are obliged to stand up round the pole during a whole night.' Inspecting the camp at Kadikoi, Lord Lucan found a large number of tents unfit for habitation. They were 'rotten, torn and not capable of sheltering the men', who were 'nearly all frozen to death' and suffering terribly from diarrhoea.[5]

Crimean Winter, Crimean Summer by Henry Hope Crealock, a captain
in the 90th Light Infantry Regiment. The caption reads: 'The British
Soldier – how he dressed in the depths of a Crimean winter – 0 degrees
in the sun!!! The British soldier, how he dressed in the height of a
Crimean summer – 100 degress in the shade!!'

British officers were much better sheltered than their men. Most of
them employed their servants to install a wooden floor or dig and line
with stones a hole inside their tents to insulate them from the ground.
Some had them build a dugout in the ground which they walled with
stones and covered with a brushwood roof. On 22 November Captain William Radcliffe of the 20th Regiment wrote to his parents:

My Hut is progressing steadily, I hope to be 'underground' by the end
of the week. The first operation was to dig a pit, 3 feet 6 inches deep, 8
feet wide, and 13 long. An upright post is then placed in the centre of
each end, & a cross-piece put on the top of these, & secured by rope,
nails, or anything you can get; Poles or whatever Wood you can beg,
borrow, or steal, are then placed from the earth to the cross-piece, &
secured in the same way; the Gable ends are filled up with stones, mud

and earth, & this forms the roof. ... The Walls are the sides of the pit, & we make the roof a sufficient height for a man to stand up in. Now comes the covering of the Roof, this is generally made by twining brushwood between the Poles, & then throwing mud & earth over it, but I mean to improve on it, & am covering mine by degrees, with the skins of horses and bullocks (the former dying in great numbers) & so hope to make it water-proof beyond a doubt. This takes longer doing, for the hides have to be cured, 'in a way.' [Lieutenant] McNeil and I are hutting together, I have already named it 'Hide Abbey'. He is now making the fireplace, a hole cut in one side of the Wall, & the chimney made of tin pots & clay. Oh! how I am looking forward to sitting by it.

At the top end of the social scale, British officers availed themselves of privileges which, in view of the suffering of the ordinary troops, were outrageous. Lord Cardigan (who had medical problems) slept on board his private yacht, enjoyed French cuisine, and entertained a stream of visitors from Britain. Some officers were allowed to spend the winter in Constantinople or to find accommodation at their own expense in settlements. 'As far as comfort is concerned,' Lieutenant Charles Gordon (the future 'Chinese Gordon') wrote, 'I assure you my dear – I could not be more comfortable in England.' Count Vitzthum von Eckstadt, Saxon Minister to London, later recorded that 'Several English officers, who went through that rigorous winter, have since told me with a smile that they first learned of the [army's] suffering from the newspapers'.[6]

The comfortable conditions which senior British officers were allowed to enjoy contrasted starkly with the circumstances of French officers, who lived much more closely to their men. In a letter to his family on 20 November, Captain Herbé explained the consequences of the hurricane for his living conditions:

Soldiers and officers are all lodged together in a little tent; this installation, excellent in fine weather and on the march, is gravely inconvenient during prolonged rain and cold. The ground, trampled underfoot, becomes a mass of mud, which gets everywhere, forcing everyone to splash around in the trenches and the camp. Everybody is soaked through ... In these tents, the soldiers sleep together, one against the other in a group of six; each man has just one blanket, so they stretch out three beneath them on the muddy ground, and cover themselves with the other three; their knapsacks, loaded up, serving as pillows.[7]

Generally, the French were better housed. Their tents were not only more spacious but most of them were protected from the wind by wooden palisades or walls of snow erected by the men. The French constructed various types of improvised accommodation: large huts which the soldiers called 'molehills' (*taupinères*) dug out from the ground about a metre deep, the floor lined with stone, with plaited branches for the walls and roof; 'tent-shelters' (*tentes-abris*) made up from the cloth of the soldiers' knapsacks sewn together and fastened to sticks in the ground; and cone-shaped tents (*tentes-coniques*), large enough to accommodate sixteen men, made from canvas sewn together and attached to a central pole. In all these structures there were ovens for cooking and keeping the men warm. 'Our soldiers knew how to make ovens that won the admiration and the envy of our English allies,' recalled Noir.

> The body of these ovens was sometimes made of clay, and sometimes from large bomb fragments cemented in a way to form a vault. The chimneys were constructed out of metal boxes or scrap metal pieced together on top of each other. Thanks to these ovens, our troops could warm themselves when they returned from the trenches or from sentry work half frozen to death; they could dry their clothes and sleep well without being woken by the terrible night fever that tormented the poor English. Our soldiers burnt so much wood that the great forest of Inkerman entirely disappeared in a few months; not a tree, not a bush was left. Seeing our ovens, the English complained about our cutting down the trees. . . . But they themselves made no use of these resources. None of the English soldiers wanted to build ovens for themselves; they were even less inclined to cut their own firewood. They expected everything to be given to them by their administration, without which they were destitute.[8]

Noir's disdain for the English was commonplace among the French, who thought their allies lacked the ability to adapt to field conditions. 'Ah! These English, they are men of undoubted courage but they know only how to get themselves killed,' Herbé wrote to his family on 24 November.

They have had big tents since the beginning of the siege and still don't know how to put them up. They haven't even learned how to build a little ditch around the tents to stop the rain and wind from getting into them! They eat badly, although they receive twice or three times the rations of our troops and spend a lot more than we do. They have no resilience and cannot deal with misfortune or privations.

Even the English were forced to recognize that the French were better organized than themselves. 'Oh how far superior are the French to us in every way!' noted Fanny Duberly on 27 November. 'Where are our huts? Where are our stables? All lying at *Constantinople*. The French are hutting themselves in all directions while we lie in mud and horses and men alike die of an exposure which might oh so easily be prevented. It is all alike – the same utter neglect and mismanagement runs throughout.'[9]

Unlike the French, the British could not seem to work out a system for collecting firewood. They allowed the men a ration of charcoal for burning in their fires but, because of the shortage of forage for the draught animals, it proved too difficult to haul the charcoal up from Balaklava to the heights, so the soldiers went without, though officers of course could send their servants down on their own horses to collect the fuel for them. The men suffered terribly from the freezing temperatures of December and January, with thousands of reported cases of frostbite, especially among the new recruits, who were not acclimatized to the Crimean winter. Cholera and other diseases also took their toll among the weakened men. 'I found sad misery among the men; they have next to no fuel, almost all the roots even of the brushwood being exhausted,' noted Lieutenant Colonel Sterling of the Highland Brigade:

They are entitled to rations of charcoal; but they have no means of drawing it, and their numbers are so reduced [by illness] that they cannot spare men enough to bring it six or seven miles from Balaklava. The consequence is they cannot dry their stockings or shoes; they come in from the trenches with frost-bitten toes, swelled feet, chillblains, etc.; their shoes freeze, and they cannot put them on. Those who still, in spite of their misery, continue to do their duty, often go into the trenches without shoes by preference, or they cut away the heels to get them on. . . . If this goes on, the trenches must be abandoned . . . I heard of men on their knees crying with pain.[10]

A *cantinière* in Zouave regimental uniform, 1855

It was the food supply where the British really fell down compared to the French. 'It is painful for me to compare the French and English alongside of each other in this camp,' wrote General Simpson to Lord Panmure. 'The equipage of our Allies is *marvellous*. I see continual strings of well-appointed carts and wagons . . . conveying stores, provisions, etc. . . . Everything an army ought to possess is in full working order with the French – even the daily baking of their bread – all under military control and discipline.' Every French regiment had a corps of people responsible for the basic needs of the troops – food supply and preparation, the treatment of the wounded and so on. There was a baker and a team of cooks in every regiment, which also had its own *vivandières* and *cantinières*, female sutlers, dressed in a modified version of the regimental uniform, who sold respectively food and drink from their mobile field canteens. Food was prepared collectively – every regiment having its own kitchen and appointed chefs – whereas in the British camp each man received his individual ration and was left to cook it on his own. This difference helps to explain how the French were able to maintain their health surprisingly well, compared to the British, even though they received half the rations and one-third as much meat as their allies. It was only in December that the British army moved towards the French system of mass food preparation in canteens, and as soon as they did so their circumstances began to improve.[11]

'C'est la soupe qui fait le soldat,' Napoleon once said. Soup was the mainstay of the French canteen in the Crimea. Even in the depths of winter, when fresh food supplies were at their lowest, the French could rely on an almost continuous supply of dried foodstuffs: preserved vegetables, which came in small hard cakes and needed only the adding of hot water, along with fresh or conserved meat, to make a wholesome soup; wheat biscuits, which kept for months and were more nutritious than ordinary bread because they contained less water and more fat; and plentiful supplies of coffee beans, without which the French soldier could not live. 'Coffee, hot or cold, was all I drank,' recalled Charles Mismer, a young dragoon. 'Apart from its other virtues, coffee stimulates the nerves and sustains moral courage, it is the best defence against illness.' There were many days when the French troops 'lived on a kind of soup made from coffee and crushed biscuit', Mismer wrote, though normally the rations 'were composed of salted meat, lard and rice, and fresh meat from time to time, along with a supplement of wine, sugar and coffee; only bread was sometimes lacking, but instead we had biscuit, as hard as stone, which one had to crush or slice with an axe'.[12]

All these goods were readily available because the French had set up an efficient system of supply with well-organized wagon trains and paved roads between Kamiesh and the siege lines. The harbour at Kamiesh was far more suitable for landing supplies than Balaklava. Large warehouses, slaughterhouses, private shops and trading stalls soon sprang up around the broad horseshoe bay, where three hundred ships could unload their wares from around the world. There were bars and brothels, hotels and restaurants, including one where soldiers paid a fixed price for a three-day orgy of food, wine and women, all brought in from France. 'I went to Kamiesh,' Herbé wrote to his family; 'it has become a proper town.'

> You can find whatever you want here; I even saw two fashion shops selling perfumes and hats from Paris – for the *cantinières*! I have visited Balaklava – what a pitiful comparison! The shacks constructed in the little port are full of goods for sale but everything is piled up pell-mell, without any order or attraction for the buyer. I am astonished that the English chose it as their supply base in preference to Kamiesh.[13]

Balaklava was a crowded and chaotic harbour in which the off-loading of government supplies had to compete with private traders from virtually every nationality in the Black Sea area – Greeks, Turks, Jews, Crimean Tatars, Romanians, Armenians, Bulgarians, even a handful of Russians, who were allowed to remain in the town. 'If anybody should ever wish to erect a "Model Balaklava" in England,' wrote Fanny Duberly in December, 'I will tell him the ingredients necessary.'

> Take a village of ruined houses and hovels in the extremest state of all imaginable dirt; allow the rain to pour into them, until the whole place is a swamp of filth ankle-deep; catch about, on an average, 1,000 Turks with the plague, and cram them into the houses indiscriminately; kill about 100 a day, and bury them so as to be scarcely covered with earth, leaving them to rot at leisure – taking care to keep up the supply. Onto one part of the beach drive all the exhausted *bat* ponies, dying bullocks, and worn-out camels, and leave them to die of starvation. They will generally do so in about three days, when they will soon begin to rot, and smell accordingly. Collect together from the water of the harbour all the offal of the animals slaughtered for the use of the occupants of above 100 ships, to say nothing of the town – which, together with an occasional floating human body, whole or in parts, and the driftwood of the wrecks, pretty well covers the water – and stew them all up together in a narrow harbour, and you will have a tolerable imitation of the real essence of Balaklava.[14]

Balaklava was only the beginning of the British problem. Supplies could not be taken from the port until they were released by the clerks of the commissariat through a complicated system of forms and authorizations, all filled out in triplicate. Boxes of food and bales of hay would lie around for weeks and eventually rot on the quayside before they were identified and cleared for dispatch by inefficient bureaucrats.* From Balaklava to their camps on the heights above Sevastopol the British had failed to build a proper road, so every box of bullets, every blanket and biscuit, had to be carted 10 or 11 kilometres up a steep and muddy track by horse or mule. In December and January most of these supplies had to be carried up by hand, in loads of 40 pounds a time, because there was no forage for the animals, which were rapidly dying off.

It was not just a question of poor organization. The British troops were not accustomed to foraging for food or fending for themselves. Recruited mainly from the landless and the urban poor, they had none of the peasant know-how or resourcefulness of the French soldiers, who could hunt for animals, fish in the rivers and the sea, and turn almost anything into food. 'It has become the habit of the British soldier', concluded Louis Noir, 'that every meal should be served up to him, wherever he may find himself at war. With the stubbornness which is the foundation of their character, the English would prefer to die of hunger than change any of their ways.' Unable to look after themselves, the British troops depended heavily on their regimental wives to procure and cook their food and do their laundry and any number of other menial chores that the French did for themselves – a factor that accounts for the relatively large number of women in the British army compared to the French (where there were no army wives but only *cantinières*). Marianne Young of the 28th Infantry Regiment complained that the English soldier was 'half starved upon his rations, because he could not, with three stones and a tin pot, convert them into palatable food', whereas there was 'virtually nothing the French would turn their noses up at if it could be converted into food'. They caught frogs and tortoises, which 'they cooked up to their own tastes', dug up tortoise eggs, and made a delicacy out of eating rats. The surgeon George Lawson saw a soldier cutting off the legs of a frog alive and remonstrated with

---

* So incompetent was the commissariat that it took shipments of green, unroasted coffee beans, instead of tea, the usual drink of the troops in an Empire based on the tea trade. The process of roasting, grinding and preparing the coffee was too laborious for most of the British soldiers, who threw the beans away.

him for his cruelty, but the Frenchman 'quietly smiled – I suppose at my ignorance – and patting his stomach said they were for the cuisine'.[15]

Compared to the French, the British ate badly, although – to begin with – there were plentiful supplies of meat and rum. 'Dear wife,' wrote Charles Branton, a semi-literate gunner in the 12th Battalion Royal Artillery on 21 October, 'we have lost many lives through the Corora they are dying like rotten sheep but we have plenty to eat and drink. We have two Gills of rum a day plenty of salt por and a pound and a ½ of biskit and I can ashore you that if we had 4 Gills of rum it would be a godsend.' As autumn gave way to winter, the supply system struggled to keep going on the muddy track from Balaklava to the British camp, and the rations steadily declined. By mid-December there was no fruit or vegetable in any form – only sometimes lemon or lime juice, which the men added to their tea and rum to prevent scurvy – although officers with private means could purchase cheese and hams, chocolates and cigars, wines, champagnes, in fact almost anything, including hampers by Fortnum & Mason, from the shops of Balaklava and Kadikoi. Thousands of soldiers became sick and died from illnesses, including cholera, which resurfaced with a vengeance. By January the British army could muster only 11,000 able-bodied men, less than half the number it had under arms two months before. Private John Pine of the Rifle Brigade had been suffering for several weeks from scurvy, dysentery and diarrhoea when he wrote to his father on 8 January:

> We have been living on biscuit and salt rations the greater part of the time we have been in the field, now and then we get fresh beef and once or twice we have had mutton but it is wretched stuff not fit to throw to an English dog, but it is the best that is to be got out here so we must be thankful to God for that. Miriam [his sister] tells me there is a lot of German Sausages coming out for the troops. I wish they would make haste and send them for I really think I could manage a couple of pound at the present minute. ...I have been literally starved this last 5 or six weeks ...If my dear father you could manage to send me in the form of a letter a few anti-scorbutic powders I should be obliged to you for I am rather troubled with the scurvy and I will settle with you some other time please God spares me.

Pine's condition worsened and he was shipped to the military hospital at Kulali near Constantinople, where he died within a month. Such was the chaos of the administration that there was no record of his death, and it was a year before his family found out what had happened from one his comrades.[16]

It was not long before the British troops became thoroughly demoralized and began to criticize the military authorities. 'Those out here are much in hope that peace will soon be proclaimed,' Lieutenant Colonel Mundy of the 33rd Regiment wrote to his mother on 4 February. 'It is all very fine for people at home talking of martial order and the like but *everyone* of us out here has had quite enough of hardship, of seeing our men dying by thousand from sheer neglect.' Private Thomas Hagger, who arrived in late November with the reinforcements of the 23rd, wrote to his family:

> I am sorry to say that the men that was out before I came have not had so much as a clean shirt on for 2 Mounths the people at home think that the troops out hear are well provided for I am sorry to say that they are treated worse then dogs are at home I can tell the inhabitants of old England that if the solders that are out hear could but get home again they would not get them out so easy it is not the fear of fighting it is the worse treatment that we receive.

Others wrote to the newspapers to expose the army's poor treatment. Colonel George Bell of the 1st (Royal) Regiment drafted a letter to *The Times* on 28 November:

> All the elements of destruction are against us, sickness & death, & nakedness, & uncertain ration of salt meat. Not a drop of Rum for two days, the only stand by to keep the soldier on his legs at all. If this fails we are done. The Communication to Balaklava impossible, knee deep all the way for 6 miles. Wheels can't move, & the poor wretched starved baggage animals have not strength to wade through the mud without a load. Horses – cavalry, artillery, officers' chargers & Baggage Animals die by the score every night at their peg from cold & starvation. Worse than this, the men are dropping down fearfully. I saw *nine* men of 1st Batt[alion] Royal Regt lying *Dead in one Tent* to day, and 15 more dying! All cases of Cholera. . . . The poor men's backs are never dry, their one suit of rags hang in tatters about them, they go down to the Trenches at night wet to the skin, ly there in water, mud, & slush till

morning, come back with cramps to a crowded Hosp[ital] Marquee tattered by the storm, ly down in a fetid atmosphere, quite enough of itself to breed contagion, & dy there in agony. This is no romance, it is my duty as a C.O. to see & Endeavour to alleviate the sufferings & privations of my humble but gallant comrades. I can't do it, I have no power. Everything almost is wanting in this Hospital department, so badly put together from the start. No people complain so much of it as the Medical officers of Regts & many of the Staff doctors too.

At the end of his letter, which he finished the next day, Bell added a private note to the paper's editor, inviting him to publish it and ending with the words: 'I fear to state the real state of things here.' A watered-down version of the letter (dated 12 December) was published in *The Times* on the 29th, but even that, Bell later thought, had been enough to ruin his career.[17]

*

It was through a report in *The Times* that the British public first became aware of the terrible conditions suffered by the wounded and the sick. On 12 October readers were startled by the news they took in over breakfast from *The Times* correspondent in Constantinople, Thomas Chenery, 'that no sufficient medical preparations have been made for the proper care of the wounded' who had been evacuated from the Crimea to the military hospital at Scutari, 500 kilometres away. 'Not only are there not sufficient surgeons – that, it might be urged, was unavoidable – not only are there no dressers and nurses – that might be a defect of system for which no one is to blame – but what will be said when it is known that there is not even linen to make bandages for the wounded?' An angry leader in *The Times* by John Delane, the paper's editor, the next day sparked a rush of letters and donations, leading to the establishment of a *Times* Crimean Fund for the Relief of the Sick and Wounded by Sir Robert Peel, the son of the former Prime Minister. Many letters focused on the scandal that the army had no nurses in the Crimea – a shortcoming which various well-meaning women now proposed to remedy. Among them was Florence Nightingale, the unsalaried superintendent of the Hospital for Invalid Gentlewomen in Harley Street, a family friend of Sidney

Herbert, Secretary at War. She wrote to Mrs Herbert offering to recruit a team of nurses for the East on the same day as her husband wrote to Nightingale asking her to do precisely that: the letters crossed each other in the post.

The British were far behind the French in their medical arrangements for the sick and wounded. Visitors to the French military hospitals in the Crimea and Constantinople were impressed by their cleanliness and good order. There were teams of nurses, mostly nuns recruited from the Order of St Vincent de Paul, operating under instructions from the doctors. 'We found things here in far better condition than at Scutari,' wrote one English visitor of the hospital in Constantinople:

> There was more cleanliness, comfort and attention; the beds were nicer and better arranged. The ventilation was excellent, and, as far as we could see or learn, there was no want of anything. The chief custody of some of the more dangerously wounded was confided to Sisters of Charity, of which an order (St Vincent de Paul) is founded here. The courage, energy and patience of these excellent women are said to be beyond all praise. At Scutari all was dull and silent. Grim and terrible would be almost still better words. Here I saw all was life and gaiety. These were my old friends the French soldiers, playing at dominoes by their bed-sides, and twisting paper cigarettes or disputing together ... I liked also to listen to the agreeable manner in which the doctor spoke to them. 'Mon garçon' or 'mon brave' quite lit up when he came near.

Captain Herbé was evacuated to the hospital later in the year. He described its regime in a letter to his family:

> Chocolate in the morning, lunch at 10 o'clock, and dinner at 5. The doctor comes before 10 o'clock, with another round at 4. Here is this morning's lunch menu:

> *Très bon potage au tapioca*
> *Côtelette de mouton jardinière*
> *Volaille rotie*
> *Pommes de terre roties*
> *Vin de Bordeaux de bonne qualité en carafe*
> *Raisins frais et biscuits*

Seasoned by the sea wind that breezes through our large windows, this menu is, as you can imagine, very comforting, and should soon restore our health.[18]

French death rates from wounds and diseases were considerably lower than British rates during the first winter of the war (but not the second, when French losses from disease were horrendous). Apart from the cleanliness of the French hospitals, the key factor was having treatment centres near the front and medical auxiliaries in every regiment, soldiers with first-aid training (*soldats panseurs*) who could help their wounded comrades in the field. The great mistake of the British was to transport most of their sick and wounded from the Crimea to Scutari – a long and uncomfortable journey on overcrowded transport ships that seldom had more than a couple of medical officers on board. Raglan had decided on this policy on purely military grounds ('not to have the wounded in the way') and would not listen to protests that the wounded and the sick were in no state to make such a long journey and needed treatment as soon as possible. On one ship, *Arthur the Great*, 384 wounded were laid out on the decks, packed as close as possible, much as it was on the slave ships, the dead and dying lying side by side with the wounded and the sick, without bedding, pillows or blankets, water bowls or bedpans, food or medicines, except those in the ship's chest, which the captain would not allow to be used. Fearing the spread of cholera, the navy's principal agent of transports, Captain Peter Christie, ordered all the stricken men to be put on board a single ship, the *Kanga-roo*, which was able to accommodate, at best, 250 men, but by the time it was ready to sail for Scutari, perhaps 500 were packed on board. 'A frightful scene presented itself, with the dead and dying, the sick and convalescent lying all together on the deck piled higgledy-piggledy,' in the words of Henry Sylvester, a 23-year-old assistant surgeon and one of just two medical officers on the ship. The captain refused to put to sea with such an overcrowded ship, but eventually the *Kangaroo* sailed with almost 800 patients on board, though without Sylvester, who sailed for Scutari aboard the *Dunbar*. The death toll on these ships was appalling: on the *Kangaroo* and *Arthur the Great*, there were forty-five deaths on board on each ship; on the *Caduceus*, one-third of the passengers died before they reached the hospitals of Scutari.[19]

The Russians, too, understood the need to treat the wounded as soon as possible, although conditions in their hospitals were far worse than anything that Florence Nightingale would find in Scutari. Indeed, it was a Russian, Nikolai Pirogov, who pioneered the system of field surgery that other nations came to only in the First World War. Although little known outside Russia, where he is considered a national hero, Pirogov's contribution to battlefield medicine is as significant as anything achieved by Florence Nightingale during the Crimean War, if not more so.

Nikolai Pirogov

Born in Moscow in 1810, Pirogov began his medical studies at Moscow University at the age of just 14, and became a professor at the German University of Dorpat at the age of 25, before taking up the appointment of Professor of Surgery at the Academy of Military Medicine in St Petersburg. In 1847 he was with the Russian army in the Caucasus, where he pioneered the use of ether, becoming the first surgeon to employ anaesthesia in a field operation. Pirogov reported on the benefits of ether in several Russian-language publications between 1847 and 1852, though few doctors outside Russia were aware of his articles. Apart from the relief of pain and shock through anaesthesia, Pirogov emphasized that giving ether to the wounded on arrival at the hospital kept them calm and stopped them from collapsing so that the surgeon could make a better choice in selecting between those cases requiring urgent operation and those that could wait. It was this system of triage pioneered by Pirogov during the Crimean War that marked his greatest achievement.

Pirogov arrived in the Crimea in December 1854. He was outraged by the chaos and inhuman treatment of the sick and wounded. Thousands of injured soldiers had been evacuated to Perekop on open carts in freezing temperatures, many of them arriving frozen to death or with limbs so frostbitten that they had to be cut off. Others were abandoned in dirty barns or left by the roadside for lack of transport. There were chronic shortages of medical supplies, not least because of corruption. Doctors sold off medicines and gave their patients cheaper surrogates, exacting bribes for proper treatment. The hospitals struggled to cope with the enormous numbers of wounded. At the time of the allied landings, the Russians had hospital places for 2,000 soldiers in the Crimea, but after Alma they were overwhelmed by 6,000 wounded men, and twice that number after Inkerman.[20]

Conditions in the Sevastopol hospitals were truly appalling. Two weeks after the battle of the Alma, the surgeon from Chodasiewicz's regiment visited the naval hospital:

> He found the place full of wounded men who had never had their wounds dressed from the day of the Alma, except such dressings as they could make themselves by tearing up their own shirts. The moment he entered the room he was surrounded by a crowd of these miserable creatures, who had recognized him as a doctor, some of whom held out mutilated stumps of arms wrapped up in dirty rags, and crying out to him for assistance. The stench of the place was dreadful.

Most of the surgeons in these hospitals were poorly trained, more like 'village craftsmen' than doctors, in the estimation of one Russian officer. Practising a rough-and-ready surgery with dirty butcher's knives, they had little understanding of the need for hygiene or the perils of infection. Pirogov discovered amputees who had been lying in their blood for weeks.[21]

As soon as he arrived in Sevastopol, Pirogov began to impose order on the hospitals, gradually implementing his system of triage. In his memoirs he recounts how he came to it. When he took charge of the main hospital in the Assembly of Nobles, the situation was chaotic. After a heavy bombardment, the wounded were brought in without any order, those who were dying mixed with those who needed urgent treatment and those with light wounds. At first, Pirogov dealt with the most seriously wounded as they came in, telling the nurses to transport them to the operating table directly; but even as he concentrated on one case, more and more seriously wounded men would arrive; he could not keep up. Too many people were dying needlessly before they could be treated, while he was operating on those patients too seriously wounded to be saved. 'I came to see that this was senseless and decided to be more decisive and rational,' he recalled. 'Simple organization at the dressing station was far more important than medical activity in saving lives.' His solution was a simple form of triage which he first put into practice during the bombardment of Sevastopol on 20 January. Brought into the Great Hall of the Assembly, the wounded were first sorted into groups to determine the order and priority of emergency treatment. There were three main groups: the seriously wounded who needed help and could be saved were operated on in a separate room as soon as possible; the lightly wounded were given a number and told to wait in the nearby barracks until the surgeons could treat them; and those who could not be saved were taken to a resting home, where they were cared for by medical attendants, nurses and priests until they died.[22]

In his sketch 'Sevastopol in December', Tolstoy takes his readers into the Great Hall:

No sooner have you opened the door than you are assailed without warning by the sight and smell of about forty or fifty amputees and critically wounded, some of them on camp beds, but most of them lying on the floor ... Now, if you have strong nerves, go through the doorway on the left: that is the room in which wounds are bandaged and operations performed. There you will see surgeons with pale, gloomy physiognomies, their arms soaked in blood up to the elbows, deep in concentration over a bed on which a wounded man is lying under the influence of chloroform, open-eyed as in a delirium, and uttering meaningless words which are occasionally simple and affecting. The surgeons are going about the repugnant but beneficial task of amputation. You will see the sharp, curved knife enter the white, healthy body; you will see the wounded man suddenly regain consciousness with a terrible, harrowing shrieked cursing; you will see the apothecary assistant fling the severed arm into a corner; you will see another wounded man who is lying on a stretcher in the same room and watching the operation on his companion, writhing and groaning less with physical pain than with the psychological agony of apprehension; you will see fearsome sights that will shake you to the roots of your being; you will see war not as a beautiful, orderly, and gleaming formation, with music and beaten drums, streaming banners and generals on prancing horses, but war in its authentic expression – as blood, suffering and death.[23]

The use of anaesthetics enabled Pirogov and his team of surgeons to work extremely quickly, completing over a hundred amputations in a seven-hour day by operating simultaneously on three tables (critics said he ran a 'factory system'). He developed a new type of foot amputation at the ankle, leaving part of the heel bone to give added support to the leg bone, and generally, in his amputations, cut much lower than most other doctors to minimize the trauma and loss of blood, which he understood posed the greatest threat. Above all, Pirogov was aware of the dangers of infection (which he thought came from contaminated vapours) and made a point of separating post-operative patients with clean wounds from those whose wounds were discharging pus and showing signs of developing gangrene. Through all these pioneering measures, Pirogov achieved much higher rates of survival than the British or the French – up to 65 per cent for amputations of the arm. For thigh amputations, the most dangerous and common in the armies of the Crimean War, Pirogov had survival rates of around 25 per cent, whereas only one in ten survived the operation in British and French hospitals.[24]

The British were much less enthusiastic about the use of anaesthetic than the Russians or the French. Shortly before the British army left Varna for the Crimea, the principal medical officer, Dr John Hall, issued a memorandum in which he cautioned the army's surgeons 'against the use of chloroform in the severe shock of serious gunshot wounds ... for however barbarous it may appear, the smart of the knife is a powerful stimulant; and it is much better to hear a man bawl lustily than to see him sink silently into the grave'. British medical opinion was divided on the new science of anaesthesia. Some feared the use of chloroform would weaken the patient's ability to rally, and others thought it was impractical to use it in battefield surgery because of the shortage of qualified doctors to administer it. Such attitudes were closely linked to ideas about withstanding pain that were perhaps peculiar to the British sense of manliness (keeping 'a stiff upper lip'). The notion that the British soldier was immune to pain was commonplace. As one doctor wrote from the Crimea:

> The pluck of the soldier no one has yet truly described. They laugh at pain, and will scarcely submit to die. It is perfectly marvellous, this triumph of mind over body. If a limb were torn off or crushed at home, you would have them brought in fainting, and in a state of dreadful collapse. Here they come with a dangling arm or a riddled elbow, and it's 'Now doctor, be quick, if you please; I'm not done for so bad, but I can get away back and see!' And many of these brave fellows, with a lump of towel wrung out in cold water, wrapped around their stumps, crawled to the rear of the fight, and, with shells bursting round them, and balls tearing up the sods at their feet, watched the progress of the battle. I tell you, as a solemn truth, that I took off the foot of an officer, Captain —, who insisted on being helped on his horse again, and declared that he could fight, now that his 'foot was dressed.'[25]

Like the French, Pirogov attached great importance to the role of nurses in his hospitals. Nurses helped to sort the wounded and brought comfort to the men. They dispensed medicines, brought them tea or wine, wrote letters to their families, and gave spiritual support to the dying. The affection of the nurses won the hearts of many men, who often likened them to their mothers. 'It is astonishing', wrote Pirogov to his wife, 'how the presence of a woman, nicely dressed, among the helpers in a hospital alleviates the distress of the men and relieves their suffering.' Pirogov encouraged the initiatives of Russian noblewomen to recruit teams of nurses for the Crimea. The Grand Duchess Elena Pavlovna, the Tsar's German-born sister-in-law,* founded the Community of the Holy Cross shortly after news of the defeat at Inkerman. Its first group of thirty-four nurses followed Pirogov to the Crimea, arriving in Simferopol on 1 December after a long and difficult journey over a thousand kilometres of dirt roads from St Petersburg. Most of them were the daughters, wives or widows of military men, with some from families of merchants, priests and state officials of the minor nobility, though they themselves of course had no experience of the harsh conditions of a battle zone and many of them soon fell ill with typhus and the other epidemics that raged among the men. Pirogov divided the nurses into three groups: those who were to attend to the wounded and help in operations; those who dispensed medicines; and those in charge of the general housekeeping in the hospital. For Alexandra Stakhovich, who was assigned to the operating room, the first amputation was a personal trial, but she got through it, as she wrote to tell her family:

> I was at two operations by Pirogov; we amputated an arm in one, and a leg in another; and by the grace of God I did not pass out, because in the first, where we cut off his arm, I had to hold the poor man's back and then dress his wound. Of my boldness I am writing only so that you are reassured that I am not afraid of anything. If only you knew how gratifying it can be to help these suffering men – you cannot imagine how much the doctors appreciate our presence here.[26]

In the Crimea itself, women from various communities had organized themselves into teams of nurses and made their way to the dressing stations and field hospitals of the battlefields around Sevastopol. Among them was Dasha Sevastopolskaia, the girl who had cared for the wounded at the Alma, who worked with Pirogov in the

---

* Born Princess Charlotte of Württemberg, she was received into the Russian Orthodox Church and given the name Elena Pavlovna before her marriage to the Grand Duke Mikhail Pavlovich in 1824.

operating theatre at the Assembly of Nobles. Another was Elizaveta Khlopotina, the wife of a battery commander wounded in the head at the Alma, who had followed her husband into battle and worked as a nurse in the dressing station at Kacha. Pirogov was full of admiration for the courage of these women, and battled hard against the objections of the military establishment, which was opposed to a female presence among the troops, for more teams of nurses to be organized. The influence of the Grand Duchess eventually told, and the Tsar agreed to recognize the work of the Community of the Holy Cross. Much of its early medical work in the Crimea was financed by the Grand Duchess, who had purchased medical supplies, including precious quinine, through family contacts in England and stored them in the basement of her home in the Mikhailovsky Palace in St Petersburg. But once it had the blessing of the Tsar, donations poured in from the Russian aristocracy, merchants, state officials and the Church. In January two more contingents of nurses organized by the Community arrived in Sevastopol, the second of them led by Ekaterina Bakunina, the daughter of the governor of St Petersburg and a cousin of the revolutionary anarchist Mikhail Bakunin (at that time imprisoned in the Peter and Paul Fortress in the Russian capital). Like many of the Russian upper class, she had spent her childhood summers in the Crimea, and was horrified by the invasion of her favourite holiday resort. 'I could not imagine that this beautiful little corner of our great empire could be turned into a brutal theatre of war.'[27]

Florence Nightingale had a similar administrative drive to the Grand Duchess. Born into a family of successful industrialists in Derbyshire, she was better educated than most of the men in the British government, among whom her family had a number of connections, though because of her sex she was forced to limit her activities to the field of philanthropy. Inspired by her Christian faith, she entered nursing at the age of 25, much against the will of her family, working first as a social reformer among the poor and then in a Lutheran religious community at Kaiserswerth-am-Rhein near Düsseldorf in Germany, where she observed Pastor Theodor Fliedner and his deaconesses care for the sick. Graduating from Kaiserswerth in 1851, Nightingale brought back its principles of nursing to the hospital in Harley Street, where she took over as superintendent in August 1853. It was these principles – basic cleanliness and good housekeeping on the wards – that Nightingale would take to the Crimea. There was nothing new in her ideas. The British medical officers in the Crimea were well aware of the benefits of hygiene and good order in the hospital. Their main problem in turning these commonsense ideals into active policies was a lack of manpower and resources – a problem Nightingale would only partly overcome.

In his capacity of Secretary at War, Herbert appointed Nightingale as superintendent of the Female Nursing Establishment of the English General Hospitals in Turkey, though not in the Crimea, where she had no authority until the spring of 1856, when the war was almost at an end. Nightingale's position was precarious: officially she was subordinated to the military hierarchy, but Herbert gave her instructions to report to him on the failures of the Army Medical Department, and her whole career would depend on fighting tooth and nail against its bureaucracy, which was basically opposed to female nurses at or near the front. Nightingale was domineering by nature but she needed to assume a dictatorial control over her nurses if she was to implement her organizational changes and gain the respect of the military establishment. There was no recognized body of professional nurses from which she could draw her team in Turkey, so with the help of Mrs Herbert she had to establish one herself. Her selection criteria were ruthlessly functional: she favoured younger women from the lower classes, who she thought would buckle down to the hard work and conditions that lay ahead; and she took a group of nuns with experience of nursing to supervise their work, regarding them as a practical concession to the Irish Catholics who made up one-third of the army's rank and file; but she rejected hundreds of applications from well-meaning middle-class women, whose sensitivities she feared would make them 'less manageable'.

Nightingale and her team of thirty-eight nurses arrived in Scutari on 4 November 1854, just in time for the mass transport of the wounded from the battle of Balaklava. The French had already taken over the best buildings for their hospitals, and those left for the British were badly overcrowded and in a dreadful state. The wounded and the dying were lying all together with the sick and the diseased on beds and mattresses crammed together on the filthy floor. With so many men suffering from diarrhoea, the only toilet facilities were large wooden tubs standing in the wards and corridors. There was almost no water, the old pipes having broken down, and the heating system did not work. Within days of Nightingale's arrival, the situation became much worse, as hundreds more wounded men from the battle of Inkerman flooded the hospital. The condition of these men was 'truly deplorable', as Walter Bellew, an assistant surgeon at the Hyder Pasha Hospital near Scutari, noted in his diary: 'Many were landed dead, several died on the way to the hospitals, and the rest were all in a most pitiable condition; their clothes were begrimed with filth and alvine evacuations [from the abdomen], their hands and faces blackened with gunpowder & mud &c and their bodies literally alive with vermin.' The men were dying at a rate of fifty to sixty every day: as soon as one man breathed his last he was sewn into his blanket and buried in a mass grave by the hospital while another patient took his bed. The nurses worked around the clock to feed and wash the men, give them medicines, and bring them comfort as they died. Many of the nurses were unable to cope with the strain and began drinking heavily, some of them complaining about the bossy manner of Miss Nightingale and about their menial work. They were sent home by Nightingale.[28]

By the end of December Nightingale had a second team of nurses at her disposal, and control of the *Times* Crimean Fund, enabling her to purchase stores and medicines for all the British hospitals in Scutari. She was able to act on her own initiative, without obstruction from the military authorities, who relied on her financial and administrative power to rescue them from the medical disaster they were in. Nightingale was an able administrator. Although her impact has been overestimated (and the contribution of the British medical officers, dressers and dispensers almost totally ignored) by those who later made her cult, there is no doubt that she got things moving in the main hospital at Scutari. She reorganized the kitchens, purchased new boilers, hired Turkish laundresses and supervised their work, oversaw the cleaning of the wards, and after working twenty hours every day, would make her nightly rounds, bringing words of Christian comfort to the men, for which she became known as the Lady with the Lamp. Yet despite all her efforts, the death rate continued to escalate alarmingly. In the month of January, 10 per cent of the entire British army in the East died from disease. In February, the death rate of patients at Scutari was 52 per cent, having risen from 8 per cent when Nightingale arrived in November. In all, that winter, in the four months following the hurricane, 4,000 soldiers died in the hospitals of Scutari, the vast majority of them unwounded. The British public was appalled by the loss of life. The readers of *The Times* demanded explanations, and in early March a government-appointed sanitary commission arrived in Scutari to investigate. It found that the main Barrack Hospital was built on top of a cesspool, that the sewers were leaking, with sewage spilling into the drinking water. Nightingale was unaware of the danger, for she believed that infection came from contaminated vapours, but the sanitation in the hospital was clearly inadequate. The soldiers in her care would have had a better chance of survival in any Turkish village than in her hospitals in Scutari.

*

In Britain, France and Russia, the public followed these developments with increasing interest and concern. Through daily reports in the newspapers, photographs and drawings in periodicals, people had immediate access to the latest news about the war, and a clearer grasp of its realities, than during any previous conflict. Their reactions to the news became a major factor in the calculations of the military authorities, which were exposed to a degree of public criticism never seen before during wartime. This was the first war in history in which public opinion played so crucial a role.

Britain led the way in terms of its appetite for news. Reports of the suffering of the troops and the plight of the wounded and the sick had created a state of national anxiety about the situation of the allied armies camped above Sevastopol. The severe frost in Britain that winter served only to intensify these feelings of concern for the men out in Russia. There was a huge response to the *Times* Crimean Fund, as well as to the Royal Patriotic Fund for the relief of the soldiers' wives and families, with people from all walks of life donating money, sending food parcels, and knitting warm clothing (including the 'Balaklava Helmets' that were invented at this time). The Queen herself informed the Duke of Cambridge that 'the whole female part' of Windsor Castle, including herself, was 'busily knitting for the army'.[29]

More than any other country on the Continent, Britain enjoyed a free press, and that freedom now showed its face. The abolition of the newspaper stamp duty in 1855 enabled the growth of a cheaper press, afforded even by the working man. As well as many letters from officers and soldiers, the Crimean War saw the emergence of a new breed of 'war correspondent', who brought the events of the battlefield to the breakfast tables of the middle class. During previous wars, newspapers had relied on amateur 'agents' – usually diplomats or approved officers in the armed forces – to send in reports (a tradition that lasted until the end of the nineteenth century when a young Winston Churchill reported on the Sudan as a serving army officer). These reports were normally drawn from military communiqués, and they were subject to the censorship of the authorities; it was rare for an agent to include a first-hand account of events he had himself witnessed. Things began to change in the 1840s and early 1850s, as newspapers started to employ foreign correspondents in important areas, such as Thomas Chenery, the *Times* correspondent in Constantinople since March 1854, who broke the news of the appalling conditions in the hospitals of Scutari.[30]

The advent of steamships and the telegraph enabled newspapers to send their own reporters into a war zone and print their stories within days. News travelled faster during the Crimean War as telegraphs were built in stages to link the battle zone with the European capitals. At the start of the campaign in the Crimea the fastest news could get to London in five days: two by steamship from Balaklava to Varna, and three by horseback to Bucharest, the nearest link by telegraph. By the winter of 1854, with the French construction of a telegraph to Varna, news could be communicated in two days; and by the end of April 1855, when the British laid an underwater cable between Balaklava and Varna, it could get to London in a few hours.*

* The telegraphs were meant for military use; journalists were not allowed to clog them up with long reports, so there was a time lag between the headline story in a newspaper, which arrived by cable, and the full report, which came later by steamship. There were often false reports because of this – the most famous in *The Times*, on 2 October 1854, which announced the fall of Sevastopol on the basis of telegraph communications of the victory at the Alma and Russell's first dispatch from the Crimea, covering the landing of the allied troops. It was not until 10 October that Russell's full report on the Alma got to London, by which time the true situation had been clarified by further telegraphs.

It was not just the speed of news that was important but the frank and detailed nature of the press reports that the public could read in the papers every day. Free from censorship, the Crimean correspondents wrote at length for a readership whose hunger for news about the war fuelled a boom in newspapers and periodicals. Through their vivid descriptions of the fighting, of the terrible conditions and suffering of the men, they brought the war into every home and allowed the public to be actively involved in the debate about how it should be fought. Never had so many readers written to *The Times* and other newspapers as they did in the Crimean War – nearly all of them with observations and opinions about how to improve the campaign.* Never had so many of the British middle classes been so politically mobilized. Even remote country areas were suddenly exposed to world events. In his winning memoirs, the poet Edmund Gosse recalls the impact of the war on his family, reclusive members of a small Christian sect in the Devon countryside: 'The declaration of war with Russia brought the first breath of outside life into our Calvinist cloister. My parents took in a daily newspaper, which they had never done before, and events in picturesque places, which my Father and I looked out on the map, were eagerly discussed.'[31]

The public appetite for vivid descriptions of the Crimean campaign was insatiable. War tourists like Fanny Duberly had a ready readership for their eyewitness narratives. But the greatest interest was reserved for visual images. Lithographs were quick and cheap enough to reproduce in periodicals like the *Illustrated London News*, which enjoyed a huge boom in its weekly sales during the Crimean War. Photographs aroused the interest of the public more than anything – they seemed to give a 'realistic' image of the war – and there was a substantial market for the photographic albums of James Robertson and Roger Fenton, who both made their names in the Crimea. Photography was just entering the scene – the British public had been wowed by its presentation at the Great Exhibition of 1851 – and this was the first war to be photographed and 'seen' by the public at the time of its

---

* The vicar Joseph Blakesley, who styled himself 'A Hertfordshire Incumbent', wrote so many lengthy letters to *The Times*, offering his learning on anything associated with the war, from the climate in the Crimea to the character of Russia, that he earned a reputation as a popular historian and was later even appointed to the Regius Professorship of History at Cambridge University, despite his lack of academic credentials.

Valley of the Shadow of Death (1855)

fighting. There had been daguerreotypes of the Mexican-American War of 1846–8 and calotypes of the Burmese War of 1852–3, but these were primitive and hazy images compared to the photographs of the Crimean War, which appeared so 'accurate' and 'immediate', a 'direct window onto the realities of war', as one newspaper remarked at the time. In fact they were far from that. The limitations of the wet-plate process (which required the glass plate to be exposed for up to twenty seconds) made it virtually impossible to photograph move-ment (though techniques improved to make this possible by the time of the American Civil War in the early 1860s). Most of Robertson's and Fenton's photographs are posed portraits and landscapes, images derived from genres of painting appealing to the tastes and sensibilities of their middle-class market. Although both men had seen a lot of death, neither showed it in their photographs – though Fenton referred to it symbolically in his most famous picture, *Valley of the Shadow of Death*, a desolate landscape strewn with cannonballs (which he clustered to-gether to intensify the image) – because their pictures needed to be

Men of the 68th Regiment in Winter Dress (1855)

reconciled with Victorian society's prevailing notions of it as a just and righteous war. The sanitized depiction of war in Robertson's work had more to do with commercial pressures than with any censorship, but in the case of Fenton, a royal photographer who was sent to the Crimea partly to counteract the negative depiction of the campaign in *The Times* and other newspapers, there was certainly an element of propaganda. To reassure the public that the British soldiers were warmly dressed, for example, Fenton took a portrait of some soldiers dressed in good boots and heavy sheepskin coats recently dispatched by the government. But Fenton did not arrive in the Crimea until March 1855, and that portrait was not taken until mid-April, by which time many lives had been lost to the freezing temperatures and the need for such warm clothing had long passed. With April temperatures of 26 degrees, Fenton's soldiers must have been sweltering in the heat.[32]

If Fenton's camera lied, the same could not be said of William Russell's reports in *The Times*, which did more than anything to inform the

British public of the true conditions of the war. Russell was the most important and widely read reporter from the Crimea. Born in 1820 into an Anglo-Irish family near Dublin, Russell began working for *The Times* in 1841, during the general election in Ireland. He had covered only one small border war between Prussian and Danish troops in 1850, when he was sent by John Delane, the paper's editor, with the Guards Brigade to Malta in February 1854. Delane promised the army's commander-in-chief that Russell would return before Easter, but the journalist spent the next two years with the British army, reporting on an almost daily basis on the latest news from the Crimea, and exposing many of the failures of the military authorities. Russell's Anglo-Irish background gave his writing a critical detachment from the English military establishment, whose incompetence he never hesitated to condemn. His sympathies were clearly with the ordinary troops, some one-third of them Irish, with whom he had a relaxed manner that encouraged them to talk. Henry Clifford described him as

> a vulgar low Irishman, an Apostate Catholic ... but he has the gift of the gab and uses his pen as well as his tongue, sings a good song, drinks anyone's brandy and water, and smokes as many cigars as foolish young officers will let him, and he is looked upon by most in Camp as a 'Jolly Good Fellow.' He is just the sort of chap to get information, particularly out of youngsters.[33]

The military establishment despised Russell. Raglan advised his officers not to speak to the reporter, claiming that he was a danger to security. He was particularly angered by the publication of letters in *The Times* by officers and soldiers highlighting the deplorable conditions of the troops. It was rumoured that the press was paying for such letters, some of which had not been meant for publication but had been passed on to the newspapers by relatives. The military authorities, who put more store on loyalty and obedience than on the welfare of the troops, were outraged by letter-writers who had broken ranks. 'Officers write more absurd and rascally letters than ever or else *The Times* concocts them for them, anyhow it is very bad and unsoldier-like of them,' fumed Major Kingscote of the Scots Guards and headquarters staff. 'I still maintain that the soldier is very cheerful and they always seem in good spirit. The officers I do not see much, but I observe one thing, and that is that the more aristocratic blood there is in the veins the less they grumble, in spite of the assertions of *The Times.*'

Raglan went on the attack. On 13 November he wrote to the Duke of Newcastle, Secretary of State for War, claiming that *The Times* had published information that could be useful to the enemy. There were certainly reports that the Russians had received a morale boost from Russell's articles about supply shortages and the poor condition of the troops (the Tsar himself had read them in St Petersburg). In response to Raglan's letter, the Deputy Judge Advocate William Romaine issued a warning to British reporters in the Crimea, while Newcastle wrote to their newspaper editors. But Delane resisted these attempts to curb the freedom of the press. Believing Raglan to be incompetent, he saw it as a matter of national interest to expose the poor administration of the army, and would not listen to the arguments about national security. On 23 December an editorial in *The Times* accused the high command of incompetence, official lethargy and, perhaps most damaging of all in a conflict that was fast becoming embroiled in a broader political struggle between the professional ideal of meritocracy and the old world of aristocratic privilege, obvious nepotism in the appointment of Raglan's personal staff (no less than five of his ADCs were his nephews).

Raglan's patience at last broke, and on 4 January he wrote again to Newcastle, effectively accusing Russell of treason:

> I pass over the fault the writer finds with every thing and every body, however calculated his strictures may be to excite discontent and encourage indiscipline, but I ask you to consider whether the paid agent of the Emperor of Russia could better serve his Master than does the correspondent of the paper that has the largest circulation in Europe ... I am very doubtful, now that Communications are so rapid, whether a British Army can long be maintained in the presence of a powerful Enemy, that Enemy having at his command thro' the English press, and from London to his Head Quarters by telegraph, every detail that can be required of the numbers, condition, and equipment of his opponent's force.[34]

Newcastle was not impressed. By this time, he was already feeling the political pressure created by the *Times* campaign. The scandal surrounding the condition of the army was threatening the government. Adding his own voice to the mounting criticisms of the military administration, Newcastle urged Raglan to dimiss generals Airey and Estcourt, the Quartermaster and Adjutant Generals of the army respectively, hoping this would satisfy the public demand for heads to roll. Raglan would not give them up – he did not seem to think that anybody in the high command was to blame for the army's difficulties – though he happily accepted the recall of Lord Lucan, whom he blamed (most unjustly) for the sacrifice of the Light Brigade.

By the time Lucan received his recall on 12 February, the power of the press and public criticism had brought down the government. On 29 January two-thirds of the House of Commons had voted for a motion by the Radical MP John Roebuck calling for the appointment of a select committee to investigate the condition of the army and the conduct of the government departments responsible for it – in effect, a vote of no-confidence in the government's leadership of the war campaign. Roebuck had not wanted to bring down the government – his main aim had been to make a stand for parliamentary accountability – but the pressures working on the government were no longer contained inside Parliament: they were coming from the public and the press. The next day Aberdeen resigned, and a week later, on 6 February, the Queen called on Palmerston, her least favourite politician, now aged 70, to form his first government. Palmerston was the popular choice of the patriotic middle classes – through his cultivation of the press he had captured the imagination of the British public with his aggressive foreign policy which they had come to see as the embodiment of their own national character and popular ideals – and they now looked to him to save the war campaign from the incompetent generals.

'At the stage of civilization in which we are,' the French Emperor announced in 1855, 'the success of armies, however brilliant they may be, is only transitory. In reality it is public opinion that wins the last victory.' Louis-Napoleon was well aware of the power of the press and public opinion – his rise to power had relied on them – and for that reason the French press was censored and controlled by his government during the Crimean War. Editorials were usually 'paid for' by supporters of the government and politically were often to the right of the viewpoint held by most readers of the newspaper. Napoleon saw the war as a way of winning popular support for his regime, and he pursued it with one eye on the public reaction. He instructed Canrobert (renowned for his indecision) not to order an assault 'unless perfectly certain of the result being in our favour, but also not to attempt it if the sacrifice of life should be great'.[35]

Sensitive to public criticism, Napoleon ordered his police to collect information on what people were saying about the war. Informers listened to private conversations, priests' sermons and speeches by orators, and what they heard was recorded in reports by local procurators and prefects. According to these reports, the French had never been in favour of the war, and, with the army's failure to achieve an early victory, they were becoming increasingly impatient and critical about its continuation. Much of their frustration was focused on the leadership of Canrobert and the 'cowardice' of Prince Napoleon, who had left the Crimea after Inkerman and returned to France in January, where (courting opposition views against the war) he then made well known his view that Sevastopol was 'impregnable' and that the siege should be raised. By this time, the prefects were reporting on the possibility of war-weariness becoming opposition to the government. Henri Loizillon, an engineer in the French trenches before Sevastopol, heard the soldiers talking of a revolution being planned, with strikes and demonstrations against the mobilization of further troops in France. 'The most alarming rumours circulate,' he wrote to his family. 'All the talk is of revolution: Paris, Lyon, all the major cities will be in a state of siege; in Marseille the people will rise up against the embarkation of the troops; everybody wants peace, and it seems they are ready to pay almost any price for it.' In Paris an impatient Emperor of the French was justly terrified of revolutionary violence – it was only six and a half years since crowds had taken to the barricades to bring down the July Monarchy – and made detailed plans to deal with any more disturbances in the capital. Buildings were constructed in the centre of Paris 'with the view of being capable of holding a number of troops in case of any rising', he informed Queen Victoria, and macadam was 'laid down in almost all the streets to prevent the populace from taking up the paving stones as hitherto, "pour en faire des barricades"'. To stop public criticism of the war he concluded that the

time had come to take a firmer control of the high command and go
to the Crimea himself to accelerate the capture of Sevastopol and
restore glory to the name of Napoleon.[36]

In Russia there was very little public information about the war.
There was only one Russian newspaper, the *Odessa Bulletin* (*Odesskii
Vestnik*), for the whole Black Sea area, but it did not have a correspondent in the Crimea, and it published only the most basic news
about the war, usually two or three weeks late. Strict censorship
limited what could be printed in the press. Reports of the battle on the
Alma, for example, appeared in the *Odessa Bulletin* only on 12 October, a full twenty-two days after the event, when the defeat was
described as a 'tactical withdrawal under threat from much larger
numbers of the enemy on both flanks and from the sea'. When this
laconic and mendacious bulletin failed to satisfy the reading public,
which had heard rumours of the fall of Sevastopol and the destruction
of the Black Sea Fleet, the newspaper printed a more detailed report
on 8 November, forty-nine days after the battle, in which it admitted
a defeat but failed to mention the panic flight of the Russian troops or
the superiority of the enemy's riflemen whose firepower had overwhelmed the outdated muskets of the Tsar's infantry. The public
simply could not be told that the Russian army had been poorly led
or that it was technically behind the armies of Europe.[37]

Without official information they could trust, the educated public
listened to rumours. An Englishwoman living in St Petersburg noted
some 'ridiculous ideas' about the war among the upper classes, who
were 'kept entirely in the dark by all the government accounts'. It was
rumoured, for example, that Britain was attempting to raise Poland
against Russia, that India was about to fall to the Russians, and that
the Americans would come to Russia's aid in the Crimea. Many were
convinced that a military treaty had been signed with the United
States.* 'They appeared to regard the President of the United States

---

* There was some basis to the rumours about America. US public opinion was generally pro-Russian during the Crimean War. The Northern abolitionists were sympathetic
towards the Western powers but the slave-owning South was firmly on the side of
Russia, a serf economy. There was a general sympathy for the Russians as an underdog
fighting against England, the old imperial enemy, as well as a fear that if Britain won
the war against Russia it would be more inclined to meddle once again in the affairs

with as much respect as a sailor does his sheet-anchor in a storm,' wrote the anonymous Englishwoman. Americans in Russia were fêted and showered with honours, 'and seemed rather pleased than otherwise', she added.

> It is odd that citizens of a republican nation such as that of the States should have so great a reverence for titles, orders, stars, and the like trumpery . . . The very day I left [St Petersburg], one of the attachés of their embassy showed my friends, with the greatest exultation, the Easter eggs with which the Princess so-and-so, the Countess such-an-one, and several officials of high rank about the court, had presented him: he also exhibited the portraits of the whole of the Imperial family, which he intended to hang up, he said, as household treasures, when he returned to New York.

The police struggled to contain the spread of rumours, although their informers were said to be everywhere. The Englishwoman told of two women summoned to the offices of Count Orlov, the head of the Third Section, the secret police, after they had been heard in a coffee shop voicing doubts about what was printed in the Russian press about the war. 'I was informed that they received a severe reprimand, and were *ordered to believe* all that was written under the government sanction.'[38]

The war generated varied responses throughout Russian society.

---

of the United States. Relations between the USA and Britain had been troubled during recent years because of concerns in London about America's territorial claims over Canada and its plans to invade Cuba (Clarendon had told the British cabinet that if Cuba was invaded Britain would be forced to declare war against America). Isolated in Europe, the Russians developed relations with the USA during the Crimean War. They were brought together by their common enemy – the English – although there were lingering suspicions on the Russian side of the republican Americans and, on the American side, about the despotic tsarist monarchy. Commercial contracts were signed between the Russians and Americans. A US military delegation (including George B. McClellan, the future commander of the Northern army in the early stages of the Civil War) went to Russia to advise the army. American citizens sent arms and munitions to Russia (the arms manufacturer Samuel Colt even offering to send pistols and rifles). American volunteers went to the Crimea to fight or serve as engineers on the Russian side. Forty US doctors were attached to the medical department of the Russian army. It was at this time that the USA first proposed the purchase of Russian-America, as Alaska was known, a sale that went ahead in 1867.

The invasion of the Crimea caused outrage in educated circles, which rallied round the patriotic memory of 1812. Ironically, however, most of the public anger seemed to be focused on the English rather than the French, who, as a result of the Russian victory against Napoleon, were treated 'as a people too insignificant and helpless to merit any other sentiment but that of the most profound pity and compassion', according to our unknown Englishwoman in St Petersburg. Anglophobia had a long tradition in Russia. 'Perfidious Albion' was blamed for everything in some circles of high society. 'To hear them talk one would imagine that all the evils existing in the world are to be ascribed to British influence,' the Englishwoman wrote. In the salons of St Petersburg it was a commonplace that England had been the aggressor responsible for the war, and that English money was at the root of the trouble. Some said the English had made war to gain possession of the Russian gold mines in Siberia; others that they wanted to expand their empire to the Caucasus and the Crimea. They all saw Palmerston as the prime mover of British policy and as the author of their misfortunes. Over much of the European continent, Palmerston was hated as a symbol of the bullying and dishonest British, who preached free trade and liberty as a means of advancing their own economic and imperial interests in the world. But the Russians had a special reason to despise the statesman who had spearheaded Europe's anti-Russian policy. According to the Englishwoman in St Petersburg, the names of Palmerston and Napier, the admiral in charge of the campaign in the Baltic, 'inspired the lower classes with so great a terror' that women would frighten their children off to bed by saying 'that the English Admiral was coming!'

> And among the common men, after exhausting all the opprobious terms they could think of (and the Russian language is singularly rich in that respect), one would turn to the other and say, 'You are an English dog!' Then followed a few more civilities, which they would finish by calling each other, 'Palmerston!', without having the remotest idea of what the word meant; but at the very climax of hatred and revenge, they would bawl out 'Napier!', as if he were fifty times worse than Satan himself.

A poem widely circulated among Russian officers caught the patriotic mood:

> And so in bellicose ardour
> Commander Palmerston
> Defeats Russia on the map
> With his index finger.
> Roused by his valour,
> The Frenchman, too, following fast behind,
> Brandishes his uncle's sword
> And cries: *allons courage!*[39]

The pan-Slavs and Slavophiles were the most enthusiastic supporters of the war. They had hailed the Russian invasion of the Balkans as the start of a religious war for the liberation of the Slavs, and were disappointed when the Tsar had ordered the retreat from the Danube, many of them urging him to go to war against the whole of Europe on his own. Pogodin, the editor of the Moscow journal *Moskvitianin*, became even more extreme in his pan-Slav views as a result of the retreat, calling on the Tsar to throw all caution to the wind and launch a revolutionary war against the Austrians as well as the Ottomans for the liberation of the Slavs. The allied invasion of Russia turned their calls for a European war into a reality, and their bellicose ideas were carried on a wave of patriotic sentiment that swept through society. Pogodin received the blessing of the Tsar, which gave him access to the court and the chance to write to him with opinions on foreign policy. How much influence Pogodin had on Nicholas remains unclear, but his presence at the court gave a green light to the aristocracy to subscribe openly to his ideas. According to the Englishwoman in St Petersburg: 'How much soever the Tsar might have sought to disguise his intentions concerning Turkey and Constantinople, his nobles did not attempt to do so, and that even two years ago, long ere this war was certain. "*Quant à Constantinople, nous l'aurons, soyez tranquille*,"* said a nobleman one evening.'[40]

Among the more liberal and pro-Western circles of society, however, there was less support for the war, and those with access to the

---

* 'As for Constantinople, we will have it, rest assured.'

foreign press were likely to be critical of it. Many did not see the need for Russia to become involved in the Eastern Question, let alone to become entangled in a potentially disastrous war against the Western powers. 'All sorts of dirty tricks are performed in the name of Holy Rus',' wrote Prince Viazemsky, a veteran of the war against the French in 1812, a critic and a poet of liberal persuasions, who served for twenty years in the Ministry of Finance before becoming chief of censorship in 1856. 'How will it all end? In my modest view ... we have no chance of victory. The English allied to the French will always be stronger than us.' According to the reports of the Third Section in 1854, many people in the educated classes were basically hostile to the war and wanted the government to continue with negotiations to avoid it.[41]

The opinion of the lower classes is harder to discern. Merchants were afraid of losing trade and tended to be hostile to the war. In St Petersburg, the unnamed Englishwoman noted, 'not only every street but every house gave some intimation of the struggle in which they are engaged; trade was almost at a standstill; scarcely any of the shops had customers in them; everybody seemed to be economizing their money lest poverty should come'. The serf peasants suffered most, losing young and able-bodied men from their family farms to the military drafts and at the same time shouldering most of the increased burden of taxation that resulted from the war. The peasant population declined dramatically – in some areas by as much as 6 per cent – during the Crimean War. There were crop failures, partly because of bad weather but also due to shortages of labour and draught animals that had been conscripted by the army, and around 300 serf uprisings or serious disturbances with physical attacks on landowners and the burning of their property. Among the upper classes, there was a fear of revolution, wrote the Englishwoman: 'It was the opinion of many when I left St Petersburg that the 80,000 soldiers (as the Russian said) who were bivouacked in the streets and billeted on the houses were a great deal more for the purpose of ensuring peace within the barriers of the town than for that of repelling a foreign invader.'[42]

Yet there were peasants who viewed the war as an opportunity. During the spring of 1854 a rumour spread through the countryside that freedom had been promised to any peasant serf who volunteered for the army or navy. The rumour had its roots in the decision of the government to create a fleet of galleys in the Baltic by recruiting peasant volunteers: they would be released by their landowners for the period of service provided they agreed to return to their estates afterwards. The result was a massive rush of peasants to the northern ports. Police blocked the roads, and thousands of peasants were locked up in jails, until they could be marched home in chained convoys. Once these rumours of emancipation spread, subsequent troop levies were interpreted in the same way. Priests, peasant scribes and agitators helped to spread the wrong idea. In Riazan', for example, a deacon told the serfs that if they joined the army they would be given eight silver roubles every month and that after three years of military service they and their families would be liberated from serfdom.

Everywhere the story was the same. The peasants were convinced that the Tsar Batiushka had issued a decree promising them freedom if they volunteered, and, when told that this was not true, they assumed the decree had been hidden or replaced by his evil officials. It is hard to tell how far their belief was innocent, and how far deliberate, an expression of their hopes for liberation from serfdom. In many places the rumours were confused with older peasant notions of a 'Golden Manifesto' in which the Tsar would liberate the peasants and give them all the land. One group of peasants, for example, turned up at a recuiting station, having heard that the Tsar was sitting in a 'golden chamber' on top of a mountain in the Crimea: 'he gives freedom to all who come to him, but those who do not come or are too late will remain serfs to their masters as before.' In other areas the rumours were replaced by stories that the English and the French would liberate the serfs who volunteered to join them in the Crimea, stories which began a flight of peasants to the south. In the peasant mind the south was linked to the idea of land and liberty: since medieval times it was to the steppelands of the south that the serfs had run away from their masters. The traditions of the free Cossacks remained strong among the peasantry of the southern provinces, where the volunteer movement assumed an almost revolutionary character. Bands of peasants marched to the local garrisons, demanding to be enlisted in the army and refusing to work any longer for their landowners. Armed with pikes, knives and clubs, the peasants clashed with soldiers and police.[43]

*

With no shortage of volunteers, and all the resources of their empire to draw from, the Russians had an ideal opportunity in these winter months to attack and destroy the weakened allied armies on the frozen heights above Sevastopol. But there was no initiative. The Russian high command had lost authority and self-confidence since the defeat at Inkerman. Without faith in his commanders, the Tsar had become increasingly gloomy and despondent, believing that the war could not be won and perhaps regretting that he had caused it in the first place. Courtiers described him as a broken man, physically ill, exhausted and depressed, who had aged ten years since the beginning of the war.

Perhaps the Tsar was still counting on his trusted 'Generals January and February' to defeat the British and the French. As long as they were losing men from cold, disease and hunger on the open heights, he was happy for his commanders to limit their attacks to small nightly sorties against the allies' forward positions. These sorties caused little damage but added to their exhaustion. 'Our Tsar won't let them eat or sleep,' wrote a Cossack to his family from Sevastopol on 12 January. 'It's only a shame they don't all die so we don't have to fight them.'[44]

The Russians had supply problems that prevented them developing a more ambitious strategy. With the allied fleets in control of the sea, the Russians had to bring in all their supplies by horse or oxen-driven peasant carts on snow-bound and muddy roads from south Russia. There were no railways. By the time of the hurricane, the whole of the Crimea was suffering from shortages of hay; the draft animals began to die at an alarming rate. Pirogov saw 'the swollen bodies of dead oxen at every step along the road' from Perekop to Sevastopol in the first week of December. By January the Russian army in the Crimea had just 2,000 carts to bring in supplies, one-third the number it had deployed at the start of November. In Sevastopol, rations were drastically reduced. The only meat available was rotten salted beef from the dead oxen. Transferred to Esky-Ord near Simferopol in December, Tolstoy found the soldiers there had no winter coats but plentiful supplies of vodka which they had been given to keep warm. In Sevastopol, the defenders of the bastions were just as cold and hungry as the British and the French in the trenches. Every day through these winter months at least a dozen Russians ran away.[45]

But the main reason why the Tsar would not commit to a major new offensive in the Crimea was his growing fear of an Austrian invasion of Russia. The cautious Paskevich, the only one of his senior commanders in whom he really trusted after Inkerman, had long been warning of the Austrian threat to Russian Poland, which he thought was far more serious than the danger to the Crimea. In a letter to the Tsar on 20 December, Paskevich persuaded him to keep a large corps of infantry in the Dubno, Kamenets and Galicia border regions in case of an attack by the Austrians rather than send them to the Crimea. The Austrian threat had been underlined two weeks before, when the Austrians had entered a military alliance with France and Britain promising to defend the Danubian principalities against the Russians in exchange for the allies' pledge to defend them against the Russians and guarantee their possessions in Italy for the duration of the war. In reality, the Austrians were far more concerned to use their new alliance to force the Western powers to negotiate a peace with the Russians under their own influence at Vienna than they were to go to war against Russia. But the Tsar still felt the betrayal of the Austrians, who had mobilized their troops to force the Russians out of the Danubian principalities only the previous summer, and he was afraid of them. Between 7 January and 12 February the Tsar wrote long notes in his own hand in which he planned the measures he would take if Russia faced a war against the Austrians, the Prussians and the other German states. In each memorandum he became more convinced that such a war was imminent. It was perhaps a symptom of the growing desperation that took hold of the Tsar in his final days. He was haunted by the possibility that the whole Russian Empire would collapse – that all the territorial gains of his ancestors would be lost in this foolish 'holy war' – with Britain and the Swedes attacking Russia through the Baltic, Austria and Prussia attacking through Poland and the Ukraine, and the Western powers attacking in the

16. View of the Malakhov from the Mamelon, summer 1855.

17. Interior of the Malakhov after its capture, September 1855.

18. *Sevastopol, September 1855*, by Léon-Eugène Méhédin.

19. View of Sevastopol from the Malakhov, September 1855.

20. Sevastopol from the Redan, September 1855. Note the pontoon
bridge across the sea harbour.

21 and 22. The
Guards Memorial.
Above: view of
Waterloo Place
towards the Duke of
York Column, 1885.
Below: the three
guardsmen and the
figure of Honour
with statues of
Florence Nightingale
and Sidney Herbert,
1940s.

23. *Queen Victoria's First Visit to Her Wounded Soldiers* (1856)
by Jerry Barrett.

24. *Calling the Roll after an Engagement* (1874)
by Elizabeth Thompson, Lady Butler.

25. *Three Crimean Invalids* (1855) by Joseph Cundall and Robert Howlett. The three men, who were visited by Queen Victoria at Chatham Hospital on 28 November 1855, are (*left to right*) William Young, 23rd Regiment, wounded at the Redan on 18 June 1855; Corporal Henry Burland of the 34th, both legs lost to frostbite; and John Connery of the 49th, his left leg lost to frostbite in the trenches.

26. Company Sergent Christy (*right*) and Sergeant McGifford, Royal Artillery, 1856. Photographed at Queen Victoria's request by Howlett. According to the *London Illustrated News*, 'The pictures, which they have converted into banners, were taken by these worthies from one of the churches of Sebastopol, where they decorated the wall. One picture is of St Michael, the other of St George and the Dragon. They are painted in a thoroughly Byzantine style, and in parts are illuminated with gold.'

27. The Alma Bridge, Paris, during the flood of 1910.

28. Alexandre Chauvelot's Malakoff Tower, built in 1856.

29. Fragment of the panorama *The Defence of Sevastopol* (1905). Viewers stand in the centre of events, as if on the top of the Malakhov Bastion. The painting merges into the foreground modelwork so that a real sense of perspective is created.

30. The Last Survivor of the Russians who fought at Balaklava, Moscow, 1903.

Black Sea and the Caucasus. Realizing that it was impossible to defend all sectors simultaneously, he agonized over where to place his defences, and concluded that in the last resort it would be better to lose the Ukraine to the Austrians than to weaken the defences of the centre and 'the heart of Russia'.[46]

At last, in early February, fearing that the Western powers were about to land a new invasion force to cut off the Crimea from the Russian mainland at Perekop, the Tsar ordered an offensive to recapture their likely landing base at the port of Evpatoria, which was then held by a Turkish force of around 20,000 troops under the command of Omer Pasha, supported by the guns of part of the allied fleets. The port's defensive works, which included 34 pieces of heavy artillery, were formidable, so much so that Lieutenant General Baron Wrangel, the commander of the Russian cavalry in the Evpatoria area, thought that its capture was impossible, and would not take responsibility for an offensive. But Nicholas insisted that the attack should go ahead, giving the command to Wrangel's deputy, Lieutenant General Khrulev, an artilleryman who was once described by Gorchakov as having 'not much in the head, but very brave and active, who will do exactly what you tell him'. Asked by Menshikov whether it was possible to capture Evpatoria, Khrulev was confident of success. His force of 19,000 men (with 24 squadrons of cavalry and 108 guns) set off at daylight on 17 February, by which time the Tsar was having second thoughts about the wisdom of the expedition, thinking that it might be better to let the allies land their troops and attack them on their flank as they moved to Perekop. But it was too late to stop Khrulev. The offensive lasted three hours. The Russian troops were easily repulsed, with the loss of 1,500 men, and retreated across the open country towards Simferopol. Without shelter, many of them died from exhaustion and the cold, their frozen bodies abandoned on the steppe.

By the time the news of the defeat reached the Tsar in St Petersburg on 24 February, he was already gravely ill. The Tsar had come down with influenza on 8 February, but he continued with the daily tasks of government. On the 16th, feeling slightly better and ignoring the advice of his doctors, he went out without a winter coat in a frost of 23 degrees below zero to review the troops in St Petersburg. The next day he went out again. From that evening his health began to deteriorate terminally.

He caught pneumonia. Doctors could hear liquid in his lungs, a sign that finally persuaded his personal physician, Dr Mandt, that there was no hope of a recovery. Badly shaken by the defeat at Evpatoria, on the advice of Mandt, Nicholas handed over government to his son, the Tsarevich Alexander. He asked his son to dismiss Khrulev and replace Menshikov (who was then sick himself) with Gorchakov as the commander-in-chief. But everybody knew that Nicholas had himself to blame for having ordered the attack, and he was filled with shame. According to Mandt, who was with him when he died, the Tsar's 'spiritual suffering broke him more than his physical illness', and news of the reverses at Evpatoria 'struck the final blow' to his already failing health.[47]

Nicholas died on 2 March. The public had known nothing of the Tsar's illness (he had forbidden any bulletins on his health to be published) and the announcement of his sudden death immediately gave rise to rumours that he had committed suicide. It was said that the Tsar had been distraught about Evpatoria and had asked Mandt to give him poison. A crowd assembled outside the Winter Palace, where the black flag was raised, and angry voices called for the death of the doctor with the German name. Fearing for his life, Mandt was whisked away in a carriage from the palace, and left Russia shortly afterwards.[48]

Various other rumours began to circulate: that Mandt had killed the Tsar (a version advanced by certain figures at the court to counteract the idea that Nicholas had killed himself); that Mandt was rewarded for his loyalty with a portrait of the Tsar in a diamond-studded frame; and that a doctor by the name of Gruber had been imprisoned in the Peter and Paul Fortress for showing too much interest in the Tsar's death. Rumours of the Tsar's suicide were readily believed by those who were opposed to his authoritarian rule: that he should have taken his own life seemed to them a tacit recognition of his sins. The rumours were given credence by distinguished scholars in the final decades before 1917, including Nikolai Shil'der, the author of a four-volume biography of Nicholas, whose father, Karl Shil'der, had been at his court; and they were widely cited by historians in the Soviet period. They are still believed by some historians today.[49]

In her intimate diary of life at court, Anna Tiutcheva presents enough details of the Tsar's final hours to rule out the serious possibility of suicide. But she also makes it clear that Nicholas was broken morally, that he was so filled with remorse for his mistakes, for the disastrous war that he had brought to Russia through his impulsive foreign policies, that he welcomed death. Perhaps he thought that he no longer had God on his side. Before he died, the Tsar called his son to him and asked him to tell the army and in particular the defenders of Sevastopol that 'I have always tried to do my best for them, and, where I failed, it was not for lack of good will, but from lack of knowledge and intelligence. I ask them to forgive me.'[50]

Dressed in military uniform, Nicholas was buried in the cathedral of the Peter and Paul Fortress, the burial place of all Russia's rulers since Peter the Great. Just before the lid of his coffin was closed, the Empress laid upon the heart of Nicholas a silver cross with a depiction of the Church of St Sophia in Constantinople, 'so that in Heaven he would not forget to pray for his brothers in the East'.[51]

10

Cannon Fodder

News of the Tsar's death arrived in Paris and London later on 2 March. Queen Victoria was among the first to hear. She reflected on his death in her journal:

> Poor Emperor, *he* has alas! the blood of many thousands on his conscience, but he was once a great man, and he had his great qualities, as well as good ones. What he did was from a mistaken, obstinate notion of what was right and of what he thought he had a *right* to do and to have. 11 years ago, he was here – all kindness, and certainly wonderfully fascinating and handsome. For some years afterwards, he was full of feelings of friendship for us! What the consequences of his death may be, no one can pretend to foresee.[1]

The Tsar's death was immediately announced in theatres, meeting places and other public spaces throughout the land. In Nottingham, the announcement came when the curtain fell on the first act of Donizetti's opera *Lucia di Lammermoor*. The audience cheered, the orchestra played the national anthem, and people poured into the streets to celebrate. Everyone assumed that the war was won, because Nicholas had brought about the war through his aggressive policies and, now that he was gone, Russia would at last come to its senses and sue for an early peace. *The Times* declared the death of Nicholas an act of divine intervention, God's punishment of the man responsible for the outbreak of the war, and looked forward to a rapid victory for the allies. Shares rose steeply on the Paris Bourse and the London Stock Exchange.

The news took longer to reach the allied forces in the Crimea, and it came by unexpected means. On the evening of 4 March, several days before the announcement of the Tsar's death arrived by telegram, a French trooper found a note attached to a stone that had been thrown from the Russian trenches outside the walls of Sevastopol. Written in French, the note claimed to represent the view of many Russian officers:

> The tyrant of the Russians is dead. Peace will soon be concluded, and we will have no more cause to fight the French, whom we esteem; if Sevastopol falls, it will be the despot who desired it.
>
> A true Russian,
who loves his country, but hates ambitious autocrats.[2]

Alexander II

However much such Russians may have wanted peace, the new Tsar Alexander II was not about to give up on his father's policies. He was 36 when he ascended to the throne, had been the heir apparent for thirty years, and remained firmly in the shadow of his father in the first year of his rule. He was more liberally inclined than Nicholas, having been exposed to the influence of the liberal poet Vasily Zhukovsky, his tutor at the court, and having travelled widely in Europe; to the disappointment of his father, he took no interest in military affairs, but he was a Russian nationalist with pronounced sympathies for the pan-Slav cause. On taking over from his father, Alexander quickly ruled out any talk of peace that he deemed humiliating for Russia (the only peace acceptable to the British) and pledged to go on fighting for his country's 'sacred cause' and 'glory in the world'. Through Nesselrode, however, he also made it clear that he was amenable to negotiations for a settlement in accordance with 'the integrity and honour of Russia'. Alexander was aware of the growing opposition to the war in France. The main aim of this initiative was to draw the French away from British influence by offering them the prospect of an early end to the hostilities. 'Between France and Russia the war is without hatred,' wrote Nesselrode to his son-in-law, Baron von Seebach, the Saxon Minister in Paris, who read his letter to Napoleon: 'Peace will be made when the Emperor Napoleon wants it.'[3]

Yet throughout these early months of 1855, Napoleon was under growing pressure from his British allies to commit to a more ambitious war against Russia. Palmerston, the new Prime Minister, had long been pushing for this – not just to destroy the naval base at Sevastopol but to roll back Russian power in the Black Sea region and the Caucasus, Poland, Finland and the Baltic by drawing in new allies and supporting liberation movements against tsarist rule. This assault on the Russian Empire went well beyond the Four Points agreed by the British and the French with the Austrians as the basis of the allied war plans against Russia in 1854 – plans that were carefully circumscribed by the coalition government of Aberdeen. Where Aberdeen had wanted a limited campaign to force the Russians to negotiate on these Four Points, Palmerston was determined to develop the campaign in the Crimea into a wide-ranging war against Russia in Europe and the Near East.

Almost a year earlier, in March 1854, Palmerston had outlined his 'beau ideal of the result of the war' in a letter to the British cabinet:

> Aaland (islands in the Baltic) and Finland restored to Sweden. Some of the German provinces of Russia on the Baltic ceded to Prussia. A substantive kingdom of Poland re-established as a barrier between Germany and Russia ... The Crimea, Circassia and Georgia wrested from Russia, the Crimea and Georgia given to Turkey, and Circassia either independent or given to the Sultan as Suzerain. Such results, it is true, could be accomplished only by a combination of Sweden, Prussia and Austria, with England, France and Turkey, and such results presuppose great defeats of Russia. But such results are not impossible, and should not be wholly discarded from our thoughts.

At that time Palmerston's ambitious plans had been received with a good deal of scepticism in the British cabinet (as mentioned earlier, Aberdeen had objected that they would involve the Continent in a new 'Thirty Years War'). But, now that Palmerston was the Prime Minister, Russia had been weakened and the hardships of the winter were coming to an end, the prospect of a larger war did not seem impossible at all.[4]

Behind the scenes of the British government there were powerful supporters of a broader European war against Russia. Sir Harry Verney, for example, the Liberal MP for Buckingham,* published a pamphlet, *Our Quarrel with Russia*, which circulated widely among diplomats and military leaders in the spring of 1855. It was sent by Stratford Canning, who was clearly sympathetic to its ideas, to Palmerston and Clarendon as well as to Sir William Codrington, the commander of the Light Division who was shortly to become the commander-in-chief of the eastern army, in whose papers it can still be found. Verney argued that Britain should work harder to involve the Germans in a war against Russia. Germany had a lot to fear from Russian aggression, Berlin being only a few days' march from the borders of the Tsar's empire; it was mainly Protestant, so had much in common with Britain; and strategically it was the ideal base for a war

---

* In 1857 he married Parthenope Nightingale, the elder sister of Florence Nightingale, and remained close to Florence all his life.

to liberate the Christian West from the 'barbaric' menace of Russia. In terms familiar to the standard discourse of European Russophobia, Verney argued that the Russians should be driven 'eastwards beyond the Dnieper to the Asiatic steppe'.

> Russia is a country which makes no advances in any intellectual or industrial pursuits, and wholly omits to render her influence beneficial to the world. The government from the highest to the lowest is thoroughly corrupt. It lives on the intrigues of agents and on the reports of highly paid spies at home and abroad. It advances into countries more civilized and better governed than its own, and strives to reduce them to its own level of debasement. It opposes the circulation of the Bible and the work of the missionary. . . . The Greeks in Turkey have so little maintained the Christian character that they have done more to injure Christianity than ever the Turks have been able to effect; they are the allies throughout the Turkish empire on whose aid the Russians rely in furnishing them with intelligence and carrying out their designs. Russia seeks to obtain excellence only in the arts of war – for that there is no sum she will not pay.
>
> Our contest with her involves the question, whether the world shall make progress, according to the highest interpretation of that word, in civilisation, with all its most precious accompaniments. On its issue depend religious, civil, social and commercial liberty; the empire of equal laws; order consistent with freedom; the circulation of the Word of God; and the promulgation of principles founded on the Scripture.[5]

Napoleon was generally sympathetic to Palmerston's idea of using the war to redraw the map of Europe. But he was less interested in the anti-Russian campaign in the Caucasus, which mainly served British interests. Moreover, his fear of domestic opposition, which had risen to alarming levels after the army's failure to achieve an early victory, made him wary of committing France to a long and open-ended war. Napoleon was torn. On a practical level, his instinct was to concentrate on the Crimea, to capture Sevastopol as a symbol of the satisfaction of French 'honour' and 'prestige' which he needed to strengthen his regime, and then bring the war to a quick and 'glorious' end. But the vision of a European war of liberation on the model of the great Napoleon was never far away from the Emperor's thoughts. He flirted with the idea that the French might rediscover their enthusiasm for the war if it offered them that old revolutionary dream of a Europe reconstructed out of democratic nation states.

Napoleon wanted to return the Crimea to the Ottoman Empire. He was a strong supporter of Italian independence, believing that the war was an opportunity to impose this on the Austrians by giving them control of the Danubian principalities as compensation for the loss of Lombardy and Venetia. But above all he sympathized with the Polish cause, the most pressing foreign issue in French politics. He thought the Austrians and Prussians might agree to the restoration of an independent Poland as a buffer state between themselves and Russia, whose expansionism had been demonstrated by the war, and he tried to persuade Palmerston that the re-creation of a Polish kingdom should be made a condition of any peace negotiations. But the British were afraid that the restoration of Poland would give new life to the Holy Alliance and even spark revolutionary wars in Italy and Germany; if that happened, Europe might become entangled in a new round of Napoleonic Wars.

All these factors contributed to the failure of the Vienna Conference, the diplomatic peace initiative sponsored by the Austrians, in the first months of 1855. Austria had joined the military alliance with the Western powers the previous December, but not in order to encourage a prolonged war against Russia which would only damage its own economy and unsettle its Slav minorities. Rather, the Austrians hoped to use their new alliance to pressure the British and the French to negotiate a peace with the Russians under their own patronage at Vienna.

January was a good moment to return to diplomacy. The military stalemate and hardships of the winter had increased public pressure on the Western governments to find a conclusion to the war. The French, in particular, were happy to explore the diplomatic possibilities. Senior ministers such as Drouyn and Thouvenal had begun to doubt that a military victory could be achieved. They feared that the longer the fighting continued – and the French were doing most of it – the more the public would react against a war which they already felt was being fought for mainly British interests. Such considerations helped to bring Napoleon round to the idea of a peace initiative – he hoped it might promote his ideals in Poland and Italy – even though he remained an ally of Palmerston, who did not believe in or desire peace. In the early weeks of 1855, however, when Palmerston was obliged to display a degree of moderation to form a cabinet with the peace-loving Peelites, even he was under pressure to consider (or give the appearance of considering) the Austrian initiatives.

On 7 January, Prince Alexander Gorchakov, the Tsar's ambassador in Vienna,* announced Russia's acceptance of the Four Points, including the controversial third point ending Russian domination of the Black Sea. In the last weeks of his life Nicholas was eager to get peace talks under way. With the entry of Austria into a military alliance with the Western powers, he had been haunted by the prospect of a general European war against Russia, and was prepared to look for an 'honourable' exit from the conflict in the Crimea. The British were mistrustful of the Russians' intentions. On 9 January Queen Victoria informed Clarendon, the Foreign Minister, that in her view Russia's acceptance of the Four Points was no more than a 'diplomatic manoeuvre' designed to stop the allies from capturing the Crimea. The Queen believed that the military campaign should not stop, that Sevastopol should be captured to ensure Russia's acceptance of the Four Points. Palmerston agreed. He had no intention of allowing any peace initiative to hold back the military blows he planned to strike against the Russians in the spring campaigning season.[6]

The French ministers were more inclined to take the Russian offer at its face value and explore the possibilities of a negotiated settlement. Their willingness to do so was greatly strengthened during February, when Napoleon announced his firm intention – against the many warnings of his ministers and allies, who feared for his life – to go to the Crimea and take personal charge of the military operations there. Palmerston agreed with Clarendon that every effort must be made to stop the Emperor's 'insane' idea, even if it meant beginning peace negotiations in Vienna. For the sake of the alliance, and to give his government the appearance of being serious about peace talks following the resignation of three senior Peelites (Gladstone, Graham

---

* Not to be confused with Mikhail Gorchakov, his commander-in-chief.

and Herbert) who had doubted his sincerity after just a fortnight in office, Palmerston named Lord John Russell as Britain's representative at the Vienna Conference.*

The appointment of Russell, a long-time member of the war party, seemed at first to be a way for Palmerston to kill off the peace talks. But Russell soon became converted to the Austrian initiative and even came to question the principles and motives of British policy in the Eastern Question and the Crimean War. In a brilliant memorandum which he wrote in March, Russell listed various ways for Britain to protect the Ottoman Empire against Russian aggression – by empowering the Sultan to summon the allied fleets into the Black Sea, for example, or by fortifying and garrisoning the Bosporus against surprise attacks – without a war whose main aim, he concluded, was to bring the Russians to their knees. Russell was also very critical of Britain's doctrinaire approach to the liberal reform of Muslim–Christian relations in the Ottoman Empire – its tendency to impose a single reformed system based on British administrative principles rather than to work in a more conservative and pragmatic way with existing local institutions, religious networks and social practices to promote improvements on the ground. Such thinking was very Austrian and set alarm bells ringing in Whitehall. Palmerston was suddenly confronted with the prospect of being forced to sign up to a peace he did not want, under pressure from the French and from the growing number of supporters of the Austrian initiative, including Prince Albert. The Prince Consort had by early May come round to the view that a diplomatic alliance of the four great powers plus Germany was a better guarantee of security for Turkey and Europe than the continuation of the war against Russia.

The longer the Vienna talks continued, the more determined Palmerston became to break them up and resume the fighting on a larger

---

* Herbert's resignation from the cabinet (as Secretary to the Colonies) came after weeks of harsh and xenophobic criticism in the British press, which had focused on his family connections to Russia. It was said, for example, in the *Belfast News-Letter* (29 Dec. 1854) that his mother Lady Herbert was the sister of a prince with a 'splendid palace in Odessa' that had been deliberately spared by the British during the bombardment of that town (in fact Vorontsov's palace had been badly damaged during the bombardment of Odessa). In the *Exeter Flying Post* (31 Jan. 1855), Herbert was accused of attempting to 'obstruct the way [of the government] and favour the designs of the Czar'.

scale. But the ultimate decision over war or peace rested with the vacillating Emperor of the French. In the end, it came down to whether he would listen to the counsel of Drouyn, his Foreign Minister, who recommended a peace plan based on the Austrian proposals to limit Russian naval power in the Black Sea, or whether he would listen to Lord Cowley, the British ambassador, who tried to convince him that any such proposal was no substitute for the destruction of the Russian fleet and that it would be a national humiliation to sign any peace before that goal had been achieved. The crucial meeting took place in Paris on 4 May, when Marshal Vaillant, the Minister of War, joined with Cowley in emphasizing the disgrace of accepting peace without a military victory and the dangerous impact that such a peace might have on the army and the political stability of the Second Empire. The peace plans were rejected, and Drouyn soon resigned, as Napoleon grudgingly committed to the British alliance and the idea of an enlarged war against Russia.[7]

There was no shortage of new allies for such a war. On 26 January a military convention had been signed by France and Britain with the Kingdom of Piedmont-Sardinia, the one Italian state that had broken free of Austrian political control, by which 15,000 troops under the command of the Italian General Alfonso La Marmora were sent to join the British in the Crimea, where they arrived on 8 May. For Camillo Cavour, the Piedmontese Prime Minister, the sending of this expeditionary force was an opportunity to forge an alliance with the Western powers so as to promote the cause of Italian unification under Piedmont's leadership. Cavour supported the idea of a general war against Russia and the Holy Alliance to redraw the map of Europe on liberal national lines. The commitment of Italian troops was a risky strategy, though, without any formal promises of help from the British or the French, who could not afford to alienate the Austrians (on 22 December the French had even signed a secret treaty with the Austrians agreeing to maintain the status quo in Italy as long as they were allies in the war against Russia). But the Piedmontese would have no real leverage on the international scene until they proved their usefulness to the Western powers, and, since it seemed unlikely that the Austrians would join the war as combatants, this was a chance for the Piedmontese to prove that they were more valuable than the

Austrians. Certainly, the allied commanders thought that the Sardinians were 'smart fine-looking fellows' and first-rate troops. One French general, who watched them disembark at Balaklava, thought they all seemed 'well looked after and turned out, organized and disciplined, and all fresh in their new and shiny dark blue uniforms'.[8] They behaved well and bravely in the Crimea.

The Poles too supported the idea of a general European war against Russia. With the encouragement of Adam Czartoryski and the Hôtel Lambert group, the French and British sponsored the creation of a Polish legion under the command of Zamoyski. Made up of 1,500 Polish exiles, prisoners of war and deserters from the tsarist army, the legion was equipped by the Western powers but disguised with the name of the 'Sultan's Cossacks' to fight against the Russians in the Crimea and the Caucasus.* According to a Russian officer, who had been imprisoned by the allies at Kinburn, most of the 500 Poles who had been recruited by the allies from his prison had been given money to join the Polish Legion, and those who had refused had been beaten.[9] The legion did not come into active operation until the autumn of 1855, but the project had been endlessly discussed from the spring. It became entangled in the thorny issue of whether the Western powers would recognize the legion as a national force, which would therefore mean giving their support to the Polish cause as an objective of the war, an issue that was never really explored or clarified.

Eager to enlist more troops for a larger war against Russia, Palmerston called for the recruitment of mercenaries from around the world. He talked of raising 40,000 troops. 'Let us get as many Germans and Swiss as we can,' he declared in the spring; 'let us get men from Halifax, let us enlist Italians, and let us increase our bounty without raising the standard. The thing must be done. We must have troops.' Without a system of conscription to build up trained reserves, the British army was historically dependent on foreign mercenaries,

---

* There were many Poles who ran away from the Russian army and joined the Sultan's forces, some of them quite senior officers who adopted Turkish names, partly to disguise themselves from the Russians: Iskander Bey (later Iskander Pasha), Sadyk Pasha (Micha Czaykowski) and 'Hidaiot' (Hedayat) with Omer Pasha's army in the Danube area; Colonel Kuczynski, chief of staff of the Egyptian army at Evpatoria; and Major Kleczynski and Major Jerzmanowski of the Turkish army in the Crimea.

but the heavy losses of the winter months made it more than usually reliant on the enlistment of a foreign legion. British troops were out-numbered by the French by at least two to one, which meant the French had the upper hand in deciding allied aims and strategy. During December a Foreign Enlistment Bill was rushed through Parliament. There was considerable public opposition, mainly based on mistrust of the foreigner, which forced the Bill to be amended so that no more than 10,000 troops were to be recruited from abroad. The largest group of mercenaries came from Germany, some 9,300 men, mostly artisans and agricultural labourers, about half of whom had military training or experience, followed by the Swiss, who numbered about 3,000 men. They arrived in Britain in April, each man receiving a bounty of £10. Trained at Aldershot, a combined force of 7,000 Swiss and German soldiers was sent off to Scutari in November 1855. As it turned out, they were too late to join the fighting in the Crimea.[10]

*

The question facing the British and the French was not just how to enlist new allies and recruits for a broader war against Russia, but where to focus that attack. By the spring of 1855 Russia's forces had become extremely thinly spread and there were many weak points in the empire's defences, so it made good sense to broaden the campaign with new assaults in these places. The only problem was deciding where. Of the 1.2 million Russian soldiers in the field, 260,000 were guarding the Baltic coast, 293,000 were in Poland and western Ukraine, 121,000 were in Bessarabia and along the Black Sea coast, while 183,000 were stationed in the Caucasus.[11]

So stretched were the Russians' defences, and so frightened were they that the allies would break through, that plans were made for a partisan war on the lines of 1812. A secret memorandum ('On National Resistance in the Event of the Enemy's Invasion of Russia') was drawn up by General Gorchakov in February. Gorchakov was worried by the build-up of the allied European armies for a new offensive in the spring, and feared that Russia would not have enough forces to defend all its borders against them. Like Paskevich and Tsar Nicholas, he was most afraid of an Austrian invasion through Poland and Ukraine, where the largest Russian forces were deployed, because of the ethnic and religious composition of these borderlands: if the Austrians broke through, they were likely to be joined, not only by the Poles, but by the Catholic Ruthenians in Volhynia and Podolia. Gorchakov proposed that Russia's line of partisan defence should be drawn up on religious lines in areas behind these borderlands, in Kiev and Kherson provinces, where the population was Orthodox and might be persuaded by their priests to join partisan brigades. Under the command of the Southern Army, the brigades would destroy bridges, crops and cattle, following the scorched-earth policies of 1812, and then take to the forests, from which they would ambush the invading troops. Approved by Alexander, Gorchakov's proposals were put into operation during March. Priests were sent to the Ukraine. Armed with copies of a manifesto written by the Tsar on his deathbed, they called on the Orthodox peasants to wage a 'holy war' against the invaders. This initiative was not a success. Bands of peasants did appear in the Kiev area, some of them with as many as 700 men, but most were under the impression that they would be fighting for their liberation from serfdom, not against a foreign enemy. They marched with their pitchforks and hunting guns against the local manors, where they had to be dispersed by soldiers from the garrisons.[12]

Meanwhile the allies discussed where to direct new offensives in the spring. Many British leaders pinned their hopes on a campaign in the Caucasus, where the Muslim rebel tribes under the command of the Imam Shamil had already linked up with the Turkish army to attack the Russians in Georgia and Circassia. In July 1854, Shamil had launched a large-scale assault on the Russian positions in Georgia. With 15,000 cavalry and troops, he had advanced to within 60 kilometres of Tbilisi, at that time defended by only 2,000 Russian troops. But the Turks had failed to move their forces up from Kars to join in his attack on the tsarist military headquarters, so he had retreated into Daghestan. Some of Shamil's forces under the command of his son Gazi Muhammed attacked the summer house of the Georgian Prince Chavchavadze in Tsinandali, taking off as prisoners the Prince's wife and her sister (granddaughters of the last Georgian king) with their children and their French governess. Shamil had hoped to exchange them for his son Jemaleddin, a prisoner in St Petersburg, but news of their capture caused an international sensation, and French and British representatives demanded their unconditional release. But by the time their letters reached Shamil, in March 1855, the Imam had in fact successfully exchanged the women and their children for Jemaleddin and 40,000 silver roubles from the Russian court.[13]

The British had been running guns and ammunition to the rebel Muslim tribes since 1853, but so far they had been reluctant to commit wholeheartedly to Shamil's army or indeed to the Turks in the Caucasus, both of whom they looked on with colonial contempt. The capture of the princesses did not win Shamil any friends in London. But in the spring of 1855, prompted by the hunt for new ways to bring Russia to its knees, the British and the French began to explore the possibility of developing relations with the Caucasian tribes. In April the British government sent a special agent, John Longworth, its former consul in Monastir and a close associate of David Urquhart, the Turcophile supporter of the Circassians, on a secret mission to make contact with Shamil and encourage him to unite the Muslim tribes in a 'holy war' against Russia by promising British military support. The French government sent its own agent, Charles Champoiseau, its vice-consul in Redutkale, on a separate mission to the Circassian tribes around Sukhumi in Georgia.[14]

The British pledged to arm Shamil's army and expel the Russians from Circassia. On 11 June Stratford Canning reported to the Foreign Office that he had got the Porte 'to issue a firman on Circassian independence in the event of the expulsion of Russia from their country' (a dubious concept in this complex tribal area). By this time Longworth himself had arrived in Circassia, and had reported that the mountain tribes were well armed with Minié rifles and hunting guns. The British agent thought the Turks could lead the Circassian tribes on the Kuban plain in a war against Russia. Mustafa Pasha, the commander-in-chief of the Turkish forces in Batumi, had met with the Circassian tribal leaders and had 'virtually become the governor-general of Circassia', Longworth reported. There were rumours of Mustafa raising a large Circassian army, up to 60,000 strong, to raid southern Russia from the Caucasus. But Longworth was afraid that the Ottomans were using the situation to reassert their power in the Caucasus, and he warned the British to oppose them. The local pashas were taking advantage of their renewed links with the Porte to rule despotically, and this had alienated many tribes from the British and the French as the allies of the Turks. Longworth also rejected the idea of supporting Shamil's movement on the grounds that it had been infiltrated by Islamic fundamentalists, most notably by Shamil's emissary (Naib) in Circassia, Muhammed Emin, who had pledged to expel all the Christians from the Caucasus and had forbidden Shamil's followers from having any contact with the non-Muslims. According to Longworth, the Naib planned to build 'a feudal empire based upon the principles of Islamic fanaticism'. Longworth's reservations about supporting Shamil were shared by many Eastern experts at the Foreign Office in London. They warned against the use of Muslim forces (especially the Turks) against the Russians in Georgia and Armenia on the grounds that only a European army could have any real authority among the Christian population there.[15]

Unwilling to send in their own forces to the Caucasus, and frightened of depending upon Muslim troops, the British and the French delayed making a decision on what sort of policy they should develop in this crucial area. With an effective force in the Caucasus, the allies might have dealt a much swifter and more devastating blow to Russia than they achieved by laying siege to Sevastopol for eleven months. But they were too wary to exploit this potential.

The allies also had high hopes for the naval campaign in the Baltic, which was renewed in the spring. With a new fleet of steamships and floating batteries, and a new commander, Rear Admiral Sir Richard Dundas, in place of Napier, who had been widely blamed for the perceived failure of the campaign in 1854, there was optimistic talk of taking Kronstadt and Sveaborg, the Russian fortresses that Napier had failed to attack, and then of threatening St Petersburg itself. The naval surveyor and hydrographer who was placed in charge of planning the campaign was Captain Bartholomew Sulivan, who had accompanied Charles Darwin on the *Beagle* expedition. From his preliminary researches, Sulivan concluded that the fortresses could be captured by ships alone, without the need of land troops. When Clarendon went to Paris at the beginning of March to try to dissuade Napoleon from carrying out his threat to go to the Crimea, he took Sulivan's report with him. It was warmly received by the Emperor, who thought that the decision not to attack Kronstadt in 1854 had been a disgrace. Like the British, Napoleon believed that Kronstadt's capture would encourage Sweden to join the alliance against Russia.

The first British warships left Spithead on 20 March, with more following a fortnight later; the French fleet under Admiral Pénaud arrived in the Baltic on 1 June. In a vain attempt to reinforce the allied blockade of Russian trade – a blockade that was circumvented by trade through Germany – the British fleet attacked and destroyed various Russian coastal stations. But their main targets remained Kronstadt and Sveaborg. From his ship, 8 kilometres from Kronstadt, Prince Ernest of Leiningen wrote to his cousin Queen Victoria on 3 June:

> There is the town before us with its numerous churches and spires and its endless batteries all showing their teeth ready to bite us if we give them a chance. The entrance of the harbour is guarded by two huge forts, Alexander and Menshikov, and to arrive at these ships must first pass the three tiers (78 guns) of Fort Risbank ... From our masthead we can distinctly see the gilt cupolas and towers of St Petersburgh and right opposite the fleet is the magnificent palace of Oranienbaum, built of some white stone that looks very much like marble ... It is still cold up here, but the weather is clear and we hardly have any night at all, only about two hours darkness from eleven to one.[16]

While they waited for the French to arrive, Sulivan carried out a careful reconnaissance of the Baltic's shallow waters, including the coastline of Estonia, where he was invited to a surreal dinner by an Anglophile noble family at their country house. 'It really all seemed like a dream,' he wrote:

> three miles inland in an enemy's country, and going over all this quite English-like scenery with a nice young lady speaking as good English as I did, except with a slightly foreign accent ... We had a splendid dinner, but more plain meats, game etc. than I expected. Coffee and tea were carried out under a tree, and we left about ten, just at dusk, the baron driving me at a rattling pace in a light phaeton with English horses and a thoroughly English-dressed groom, leather belts, boots and all.

In early June Sulivan submitted his report. He was now pessimistic about the possibility of overcoming the powerful defences at Kronstadt, as Napier had been in 1854. During the past year the Russians had reinforced their fleet (Sulivan counted thirty-four gunboats) and strengthened the seaward defences with electrical and chemical underwater mines (described as 'infernal machines') and a barrier made up of timber frames secured to the seabed and filled with rocks. It would be difficult to remove it without suffering severe losses from the heavy guns of the fortress. The planned attack on Kronstadt was abandoned – and with it went the hopes of a decisive allied breakthrough in the Baltic.[17]

Meanwhile the allies also thought of ways to broaden their campaign in the Crimea. The military stalemate of the winter months led many to conclude that continuing to bombard Sevastopol from the south would not produce results, as long as the Russians were able to bring in supplies and reinforcements from the mainland via Perekop and the Sea of Azov. For the siege to work, Sevastopol had to be encircled on its northern side. That had been the rationale of the original allied plan in the summer of 1854 – a plan which had been overturned by Raglan, who feared that his men would suffer in the heat if they occupied the Crimean plain to cut the Russians off from Perekop. By the end of the year the foolishness of Raglan's strategy had become clear for all to see, and military leaders were calling for a broader strategy. In a memorandum of December, for example, Sir John Burgoyne, Raglan's chief engineer, urged the creation of an allied force of 30,000 men on the River Belbek, 'with a view to further operations against Bakhchiserai and Simferopol' which would cut off Sevastopol from one of its two main routes of supply (the other being via Kerch in the eastern Crimea).[18]

The Russian attack on Evpatoria in February prompted more plans for a stronger allied presence to interrupt the Russian supply lines from Perekop. Allied troops were sent to Evpatoria to reinforce the Turkish force during March. They found an appalling situation there – a real humanitarian crisis – with up to 40,000 Tatar peasants living in the streets, without food or shelter, having fled their villages out of fear of the Russians. The crisis encouraged the allied commanders to think about committing further troops to the north-west Crimean plain, if only to protect and mobilize the Tatar population against the Russians.[19]

But it was in April that the allies really got down to the serious business of rethinking their military strategy in the Crimea. On 18 April, Palmerston, Napoleon, Prince Albert, Clarendon, Lord Panmure (the new Secretary of State for War), Vaillant, Burgoyne and Count Walewski (Drouyn's successor at the Ministry of Foreign Affairs in Paris) met in a council of war at Windsor Castle. Palmerston and Napoleon were decidedly in favour of a change in strategy, running down the bombardment of Sevastopol in order to concentrate on the conquest of the Crimea as a whole, which both men saw as the beginning of a larger war against Russia. The new plan would have the advantage of involving the Crimean Tatars on the allied side. Above all, it would represent a return to the sort of fighting in the open field in which the allied armies had proved themselves technically superior to the Russians at Alma and Inkerman. It was in the skill and rifle power of their infantry that the allies had their greatest superiority over the Russians – advantages that counted for very little in the siege warfare of Sevastopol. In engineering and artillery, the Russians were at least the equal of the British and the French.

Napoleon was the most enthusiastic about a change of strategy. Though the occupation of Sevastopol was central to his aims, he was convinced that the town would not fall until it was fully encircled, but, when it was, it would fall without a fight. He proposed that instead of bombarding the city from the south, the allies should land an army at Alushta, 70 kilometres to the east, and march from there towards Simferopol, through which most of the Russian army's supplies were transported. The British agreed with the broad outlines of Napoleon's strategy, although as part of the bargain they managed to dissuade him from his daring idea of going to the Crimea to take command of the military operations himself. The 'Emperor's plan' (as the Alushta expedition became known in French circles) was included as one of three options for a diversionary attack on the Crimean interior, the others being an offensive by allied troops based at Sevastopol against Bakhchiserai, and the landing of a force at Evpatoria which would march across the plain to Simferopol. The two war ministers signed a memorandum of the agreed plan, which Panmure sent to Raglan on the authority of the British cabinet. Panmure's instructions left it up to Raglan to choose between the three alternatives, but made it clear that he was being ordered to embark on one of them. The trenches at Sevastopol were to be left in the hands of 60,000 men (30,000 Turks and 30,000 French), whose new task would be to maintain a barrage to prevent the Russians from breaking out of the city rather than continue with any intention of taking the offensive.

Raglan was sceptical of the new plan. He wanted to continue with the bombardment, which he was convinced was on the point of a breakthrough, and believed that a field offensive would not leave enough troops to defend the allied positions before Sevastopol. In an act of open defiance, if not mutiny, against his political superiors, Raglan convened a council of war in the Crimea at which he told his allied commanders, Canrobert and Omer Pasha, that Panmure's memorandum was only a 'suggestion' and that he (Raglan) could proceed with it or not as he thought fit. Raglan dragged his heels over the new plan, coming up with various excuses not to take men away from the siege, until Canrobert, who was in favour of the field campaign and had several times offered to place his troops under Raglan's command if only he would start it, exploded in frustration. 'The field plan worked out by Your Majesty', Canrobert informed Napoleon, 'has been rendered practically impossible by the non-cooperation of the Commander in Chief of the English Army.'[20]

For many years the French would blame the British for the failure of the plan to march on Simferopol and conquer the rest of the Crimea. They had good reason to be enraged by Raglan, who could have been removed by Palmerston for insubordination, if not incompetence, after his refusal to implement the order for an attack on the Crimean interior. With their superior rifle power, and the support of the Tatar population on the plain, there was good reason to suppose that a field campaign would have captured Simferopol and cut off the Russians' main route of supply through the peninsula. This was exactly the scenario the Russians had feared most, which was why the Tsar had ordered the attack on Evpatoria in February. The Russians knew how vulnerable they were to an attack on their supply lines, and had always seen the route from Evpatoria as the most likely one for an allied offensive towards Simferopol or Perekop. As they later admitted, they were amazed that the British and the French had never tried to launch such an attack.[21]

The one serious effort the allies made to cut off Sevastopol from its bases of supply was their raid on the port of Kerch, which controlled the supply lines across the Sea of Azov, although it took two attempts to accomplish it. Plans for an attack had been advanced at the start of the campaign, but the first order for the action was not made until 26 March, when Panmure wrote to Raglan instructing him to organize a 'combined operation by sea and land' to 'reduce the defences of Kerch'. It was an attractive proposal, not least because it would involve the Royal Navy, which had hardly been used so far, at a time when the British contribution to the allied effort was being seriously questioned by the French. Canrobert was initially doubtful about the operation, but on 29 April he gave his agreement for a squadron of French warships under the command of Admiral Bruat and 8,500 soldiers to join the expedition, which would be led by Lieutenant General Brown, the veteran commander of the Light Division. The allied fleet set off on 3 May, sailing north-west towards Odessa to disguise its intentions from the Russians before doubling back towards Kerch. But just before it reached its destination, a fast boat caught up with the fleet and delivered an order from Canrobert for the French ships to return. Shortly after the fleet had left, the new telegram line to Paris had brought an order from Napoleon for Canrobert, instructing him to bring up the reserves from Constantinople: since Bruat's ships would be required, Canrobert reluctantly decided to withdraw from the Kerch attack. The Royal Navy was forced to turn back, and Canrobert was disgraced in British (and many French) eyes.[22]

The recall of the expedition antagonized the already worsening relations between the British and the French. It played a major part in Canrobert's decision to resign his command on 16 May. He felt that his position had been undermined, that he had let the British down, and hence had no authority to compel Raglan to carry out the plans for a field campaign. The new French commander-in-chief, General Pélissier, a short, stocky man with a rough-and-ready manner, was far more decisive, more a man of action, than Canrobert, who had long been nicknamed 'Robert Can't' by the British. Pélissier's appointment was greeted with enthusiasm in the British camp. Colonel Rose, the British commissioner at the headquarters of the French army, who had been close to Canrobert, wrote to Clarendon that the time had come for a more 'can-do' approach to the war and that Pélissier was the man to deliver it:

> General Pélissier will never allow a half and half execution of his orders; if it can be done, it must be done. He is of a violent temper and rough manner, but I believe him to be just and sincere; and I think that in all important matters these two qualities will triumph over his ebulliations of temper. He has a quick conception, plenty of common sense, and a resolute mind, which thinks of overcoming, not yielding to difficulties.[23]

Eager to repair relations with the British, Pélissier agreed to revive the operation against Kerch, although he concurred with Raglan that the main target of the allied operations should remain the Sevastopol

General Pélissier

defences. On 24 May sixty ships of the allied fleet set off with a combined force of 7,000 French, 5,000 Turks and 3,000 British troops under Brown's command. Seeing the approach of the armada, most of the Russian inhabitants of Kerch fled to the countryside. After a brief bombardment, the allied troops were able to come ashore without opposition. Brown was met by a deputation of the Russian civilians who were left. They told him they were frightened of attacks by the local Tatar population and begged him to protect them. Brown ignored their pleas. Ordering the destruction of the arsenal in Kerch, Brown left a small force of mainly French and Turkish toops in the town and marched with the remainder of his troops to the important fort at Yenikale, further along the coast, where the looting of Russian property continued under Brown's supervision. Meanwhile, the allied warships entered the Sea of Azov, sailed towards the Russian coastline, destroyed Russian shipping, and laid waste to the ports of Mariupol and Taganrog.*

The attacks on Russian property in Kerch and Yenikale soon descended into a drunken rampage, and some terrible atrocities by the allied troops. The worst took place in Kerch, where the local Tatar population took advantage of the allied occupation to carry out a violent revenge against the Russians of the town. Aided by the Turkish troops, the Tatars looted shops and houses, raped Russian women, and killed and mutilated hundreds of Russians, including even children and babies. Among the excesses was the destruction of the town's

---

* Taganrog had insufficient military forces to defend itself, just one battalion of infantry and a Cossack regiment, along with a unit of 200 armed civilians, in all some 2,000 troops, but no artillery. In a desperate effort to save the town from bombardment, the governor sent a delegation to meet the commanders of the allied fleet with an offer to decide the fate of Taganrog by combat in the field. He even offered to make the sides unequal to reflect the allied advantage at sea. It was an extraordinary act of chivalry that could have come directly from the pages of medieval history. The allied commanders were unimpressed, and returned to their ships to begin the bombardment of Taganrog. The entire port, the dome of the cathedral and many other buildings were destroyed. Among the many inhabitants who fled the besieged city was Evgenia Chekhova, the mother of the future playwright Anton Chekhov, who was born in Taganrog five years afterwards (L. Guerrin, *Histoire de la dernière guerre de Russie (1853–1856)*, 2 vols. (Paris, 1858), vol. 2, pp. 239 –40; N. Dubrovin, *Istoriia krymskoi voiny i oborony Sevastopolia*, 3 vols. (St Petersburg, 1900), vol. 3, p. 191).

museum, with its rich and magnificent collection of Hellenic art, an outrage reported by Russell in *The Times* on 28 May:

> The floor of the museum is covered in depth with the debris of broken glass, of vases, urns, statuary, the precious dust of their contents, and charred bits of wood and bone, mingled with the fresh splinters of the shelves, desks, and cases in which they had been preserved. Not a single bit of anything that could be broken or burnt any smaller had been exempt from reduction by hammer or fire.

For several days Brown did nothing to stop the atrocities, even though he had received reports that a contingent of French and British troops had taken part in the looting. Brown saw the Tatars as allies, taking the view that they were engaged in a 'legitimate rebellion' against Russian rule. Eventually, having been informed of the worst atrocities, Brown dispatched a tiny force (just twenty British cavalrymen) to restore order. They were far too few in number to have any real effect, though they did shoot some British troops whom they had caught committing rape.[24]

According to Russian witnesses, it was not just the allied soldiers who had taken part in the looting, the violence and rape; it was also officers. 'I saw several English officers carrying to their ship furniture and sculptures, and all sorts of other items they had plundered from our homes,' recalled one resident of Kerch. Several women claimed they had been raped by British officers.[25]

*

The development of all these broader plans was held back because, with the coming of the spring, the British and French troops got bogged down once again in the siege of Sevastopol, which still held first place in the allied strategy. Despite the recognition that a change of plan was needed for the siege to work, the allies remained wedded to the idea that one last surge would bring the walls of Sevastopol tumbling down and force Russia to accept a humiliating peace.

In terms of actual fighting, the siege had gone through a quiet period in the winter months, as both sides concentrated on the strengthening of their defensive works. The French did most of the trench digging on the allied side, mainly because the British-held ground was very rocky. According to Herbé, they dug 66 kilometres of trenches, and the British just 15, during the eleven months of the siege. It was slow, exhausting, dangerous work, cutting into the hard ground in freezing temperatures, dynamiting the rock that lay underneath, under constant fire from the enemy. 'Every metre of our trenches was literally at the cost of one man's life and often two,' recalled Noir.[26]

The Russians were particularly active in their defensive works. Under the direction of their engineering genius Totleben, they developed their earthworks and trenches on a more sophisticated level than ever before seen in the history of siege warfare. In the early stages of the siege the Russian fortifications were little more than hastily improvised earthworks reinforced with wickerwork, fascines and gabions; but new and more formidable defences were added in the winter months. The bastions were reinforced by the addition of casemates – fortified gun emplacements dug several metres underground and covered with thick ship-timbers and earthworks that made them proof to the heaviest bombardment. Inside the most heavily fortified bastions, the Malakhov and the Redan (the Third), there was a maze of bunkers and apartments, including one, in the Redan, with a billiard table and ottomans, and in each there was a small chapel and a hospital.[27]

To protect these crucial bastions the Russians built new works outside the city walls: the Mamelon (the Kamchatka Lunette) to defend the Malakhov, and the Quarry Pits in front of the Redan. The Mamelon was constructed by the soldiers of the Kamchatka Regiment (from which it derived its Russian name) under almost constant fire from the French during most of February and early March. So many men were killed in building it that not all of them could be evacuated, even under cover of the night, and many dead were left in the earthworks. The Mamelon was itself a complex fortress system protected by the twin redoubts of the White Works on its left flank (so named because of the white clay soil exposed by the excavation of the defences). Henri Loizillon, a French engineer, described the surprise of his fellow-soldiers at what else they found inside the Mamelon when they captured it in early June:

Everywhere there were shelters in the ground covered up with heavy timbers where the men had taken cover from the bombs. In addition, we discovered an enormous underground capable of holding several hundred men, so the losses which they suffered were much less than we supposed. These shelters were all the more curious for the surprising comfort we found there: there were beds with eiderdowns, porcelains, complete tea services, etc., so the soldiers had not been badly served. There was also a chapel whose only remarkable object was a rather beautiful gilded wooden sculpture of Christ.[28]

Amid all this frenzied building there was little major fighting. But the Russians launched sporadic raids at night against the trenches of the British and the French. Some of the most daring were led by a seaman called Pyotr Koshka, whose exploits were so famous that he became a national hero in Russia. It was not entirely clear to the allied troops what the purpose of these sorties was. They seldom caused any lasting damage to their defensive works, and the losses they inflicted on the men were trifling, usually less than the Russians lost themselves. Herbé thought their aim was to add to the allies' fatigue because the constant threat of an attack at night made it impossible for them to sleep in the trenches (that was in fact the Russians' intention). According to Major Whitworth Porter of the Royal Engineers, the first intimation of an imminent attack would be 'the discovery of several dusky forms creeping over the parapet'.

The alarm is instantly given, and in another moment they are upon us. Our men, scattered as they are, are taken by surprise, give way step by step before the advancing foe, until at length they make a stand. And now a hand-to-hand struggle ensues. The cheers, the shouts, and the hallos of our men; the yells of the Russians raging like so many maniacs from the effects of the vile spirit with which they have been maddened before making the onslaught; the sharp cracks of the rifles, resounding momentarily on all sides; the hastily shouted words of command; the blast of the Russian bugle, ringing out clear in the midst of all of the din, sounding their advance – all conspire to render it a scene of confusion, enough to bewilder the steadiest nerves. When to this is added the probability that the scene of the struggle may be in a battery, where the numerous traverses, guns and other obstacles cumber up the space, and render it difficult for either party to act, some idea may be formed of this extraordinary spectacle. Sooner or later – generally in the course of a very few minutes – our men, having gathered together in sufficient numbers, make a bold dash forward, and drive the enemy headlong over the parapet. One smart volley is rattled after them to increase the speed of their flight, and the loud, ringing British cheer . . .[29]

The allies also launched surprise attacks against the Russian out-works – their aim being not to capture these positions but to weaken the morale of the Russian troops. The Zouaves were the ideal soldiers to carry out these raids: in hand-to-hand fighting they were the most effective in the world. On the night of 23/4 February, their celebrated 2nd Regiment stormed and briefly occupied the newly constructed White Works, just to show the Russians that they could capture them at will, before retreating with 203 wounded men, and 62 officers and soldiers dead, whom they carried back, under heavy fire, rather than abandon them to the Russians.[30]

In contrast to the sorties of the allies, some of the attacks by the Russians were large enough to suggest that their intention was to drive the allies from their positions, though in reality they were never powerful enough for that. On the night of 22/3 March, the Russians launched a sortie of some 5,000 men against the French positions opposite the Mamelon. It was their largest sortie yet. The brunt of the assault was taken by the 3rd Zouaves, who held off their attackers in fierce hand-to-hand fighting in the dark, illuminated only by the flashes of the rifles and muskets. The Russians spread out in a flanking movement and quickly captured the weakly defended British trenches on their right, from which they aimed their fire into the French side, but the Zouaves continued to hold firm, until at last British reinforcements arrived, enabling the Zouaves to push the Russians back towards the Mamelon. The sortie cost the Russians a great deal: 1,100 men were wounded, and more than 500 killed, nearly all of them in or near the trenches of the Zouaves. After the fighting was over, the two sides agreed to a six-hour armistice to collect the dead and wounded who were clogging up the battlefield. Men who had been at war only a few moments previously began to fraternize, speaking to each other with hand signals and the odd word in each other's language, though nearly all the Russian officers could speak French well, the adopted language of the Russian aristocracy. Captain

Nathaniel Steevens of the 88th Regiment of Foot witnessed the scene:

> Here we saw a crowd of English officers & Men mingled with some Russian Officers & escort, who had brought out the Flag of Truce; this was the most curious sight of all; the Officers chatted together as freely and gaily as if the warmest friends, and as for the Soldiers, those who 5 minutes before had been firing away at each other, might now be seen smoking together, sharing tobacco and drinking Rum, exchanging the usual compliments of 'bono Ingles' &c; the Russian Officers were very gentlemanly looking men, spoke French and one English; at length on reference to watches it was found 'time was nearly up' so both Parties gradually receded from each others' sight to their respective works, not however without our men shaking hands with the Russian soldiers & some one calling out, 'Au revoir.'[31]

Apart from these sorties, the troops stayed on their respective sides in the early months of 1855. 'The siege is now only nominal,' Henry Clifford wrote to his family on 31 March. 'We fire a few shots during the day, but all seems at a standstill.' It was a strange situation, since there was plenty of artillery sitting idle, implying almost a loss of belief in the siege. In these months there was far more digging than shooting to be done – a fact that did not please many of the troops. According to Whitworth Porter of the Royal Engineers, the British soldier did not like 'spade-work', thinking it not soldier-like. He quotes an Irishman in the infantry:

> 'Shure, now, I didn't 'list for this here kind o' work. When I tuk the shillen, it was to be a sodger, and take me senthry go, right and proper, and use me bayonet when I was tould to; but I never dhreamt o' nothen o' this kind. Shure, one o' the very raisins why I listed was because I hated spade-work; and the Sargent as tuk me swore by St. Pathrick that I should niver see a spade agin; and yet, no sooner does I come out here, than I gits a pick and shovel put in me hand, just as bad as iver it was in Ould Ireland.' And then he would go on with his work, grumbling all the time, and uttering fierce denunciations against the Russians, who he vowed he would make pay for all this, if ever he got inside that blessed town.[32]

As the siege settled into a monotonous routine of exchanging fire with the enemy, the soldiers in the trenches became accustomed to living under constant bombardment. To an outsider, they seemed almost nonchalant about the dangers that surrounded them. On his first visit to the trenches, Charles Mismer, a 22-year-old dragoon in the French cavalry, was amazed to see the soldiers playing cards or sleeping in the trenches while bombs and shells fell around them. The troops came to recognize the various bombs and shells from their different sounds, which told them what evasive action they should take: the round shot, 'rushing through the air with a sharp, shrill shriek, very startling to the nerves of the young soldier', as Porter recalled it; the volley of grape, 'buzzing along with a sound not unlike that of a covey of birds very strong on the wing'; the 'bouquet', a shower of small shells enclosed in a bomb, 'each one leaving a long curved trail of light in its track and, as they reach their destination, lighting up the atmosphere with short, fitful flashes, as they burst in succession'; and the larger mortar shell, 'rising proudly and grandly in the air, easily to be discerned in the night by the fiery train of its burning fuse, tracing a majestic curve high in mid-air, until, having attained its extreme altitude, it commences to descend, falling faster and faster, till down it swoops ... making a sound in its passage through the air like the chirping of a pee-wit'. It was impossible to tell where the mortar shell would land, or where its splinters would explode, so 'all one could do when one heard the birdlike noise was to lie face down against the earth and hope'.[33]

Gradually, as the siege dragged on without any gains by either side, the exchange of fire assumed a symbolic character. In quiet periods, when the men grew bored, they turned it into sport. François Luguez, a captain in the Zouaves, recalled how his men would play shooting games with the Russians: one side would raise on the end of their bayonet a piece of cloth for the other side to shoot – each shot being greeted with a cheer and laughter if it hit, and jeering if it missed.[34]

With less and less to fear, the sentries in the picquets began to venture into no man's land to entertain themselves or warm themselves at night. From time to time there was some fraternization with the Russians, whose own outposts were no further than a football-pitch length away. Calthorpe recorded one such incident, when a group of unarmed Russian soldiers approached the British picquets:

> They made signs that they wanted a light for their pipes, which one of our men gave them, and then they stayed a few minutes talking to our sentries, or rather trying to do so, the conversation being something after this wise:
>
> 1st Russian soldier – 'Englise bono!'
>
> 1st English soldier – 'Russkie bono!'
>
> 2nd Russian soldier – 'Francis bono!'
>
> 2nd English soldier – 'Bono!'
>
> 3rd Russian soldier – 'Oslem no bono!'
>
> 3rd English soldier – 'Ah, ah! Turk no bono!'
>
> 1st Russian soldier – 'Oslem!' making a face, and spitting on the ground to show his contempt.
>
> 1st English soldier – 'Turk!' pretending to run away, as if frightened, upon which all the party go into roars of laughter, and then after shaking hands, they return to their respective beats.[35]

To while away the time the soldiers developed a wide variety of pursuits and games. In the bastions of Sevastopol, noted Ershov, 'card games of all sorts were played around the clock'. Officers played chess and read voraciously. In the casemate of the Sixth Bastion there was even a grand piano, and concerts were arranged with musicians from the other bastions. 'To begin with,' writes Ershov, 'the concerts were dignified and ceremonious with proper attention to the rules of listening to classical music, but gradually, as our mood changed, there was a corresponding tendency towards national melodies or folk songs and dances. Once a masked ball was arranged, and one cadet appeared in a woman's dress to sing folk songs.'[36]

Theatrical amusements were very popular in the French camp, where the Zouaves had their own theatre troupe, a transvestite vaudeville, that entertained huge crowds of noisy soldiers in a wooden shed. 'Imagine a Zouave dressed up as a shepherdess and flirting with the men (*faisant la coquette*)!' recalled André Damas, a chaplain in the French army. 'And then another Zouave dressed up as a young lady of society, and playing hard to get (*jouant la précieuse*)! I have never seen anything as funny or as talented as these gentlemen. They were hilarious.'[37]

Horse racing was also popular, especially among the British, whose cavalry was almost totally unoccupied. But it was not only the cavalry horses that took part in these races. Whitworth Porter attended a meeting organized by the 3rd Division on the downs. 'The Day was bitterly cold,' he noted in his diary on 18 March,

> a keen west wind cutting into one's very bones: still the course was crowded with stragglers from all parts of the army; every one who could contrive to raise a pony for the occasion had done so, and queer-looking they most of them were. I saw one huge specimen of a British officer, who could not have measured less than six foot three in his stockings, bestriding the smallest, skinniest, shaggiest pony I have ever seen.[38]

There was a lot of drinking in these relatively idle months. In all the armies it resulted in a growing general problem of indiscipline, swearing, insolence, drunken brawls and violence, as well as acts of insubordination by the men, all of which suggested that morale among the troops was becoming dangerously low. In the British army (and there is no reason to suppose that it was worse affected than the Russian or the French) a staggering 5,546 men (roughly one in eight of the entire army in the field) behaved so badly that they were court-martialled for various acts of drunkenness during the Crimean War. Most soldiers drank a good-sized tumbler of alcohol with their breakfast – vodka for the Russians, rum for the British and wine for the French – and another with dinner. Many also drank during the day – and some were never sober throughout the entire siege. Drinking was the primary recreation of soldiers in all the armies, including the Turks, who liked the sweet Crimean wine. Henry Clifford recalled the drinking culture in the allied camps:

> Almost every regiment has a canteen, and at the door of each of these stood, no they did not stand, for very few could, but lay and rolled about, groups of French and English soldiers, in every state of intoxication. Merry, laughing, crying, dancing, fighting, sentimental, affectionate, singing, talking, quarrelsome, stupid, beastly, brutal, and dead-drunk.

French just as bad as English, and English just as bad as French ... What a mistake to over-pay a soldier! Give him one farthing more than he really wants, and he gives way to his brutal propensities and immediately gets *drunk*. ... Let him be English, French, Turk, Sardinian, give him enough money and he will get drunk.[39]

The sudden arrival of warm spring weather raised the morale of the allied troops. 'Today it is spring,' Herbé wrote on 6 April; 'the sun has not left us for three weeks, and eveything has changed in appearance.' The French soldiers planted gardens near their tents. Many, like Herbé, shaved their winter beards, washed their linen, and generally spruced up their appearance, so that 'if the ladies of Sevastopol should give a ball and invite the French officers, our uniforms would still shine brightly among their elegant costumes'. After such a cruel winter, when all was hidden under mud and snow, the Crimea appeared to be suddenly transformed into a place of great beauty, with a profusion of colourful spring flowers on the heathlands, fields of rye grass a metre or so high, and birdsong everywhere. 'We have had a few warm days only,' wrote Russell of *The Times* on 17 March,

and yet the soil, wherever a flower has a chance of springing up, pours forth multitudes of snowdrops, crocuses, and hyacinths ... The finches and larks here have a Valentine's-day of their own, and still congregate in flocks. Very brilliant goldfinches, large buntings, golden-crested wrens, larks, linnets, titlarks, and three sorts of tomtits, the hedge sparrow, and a pretty species of wagtail, are very common all over the Chersonese; and it is strange to hear them piping and twittering about the bushes in the intervals of the booming of the cannon, just as it is to see the young spring flowers forcing their way through the crevices of piles of shot and peering out from under shells and heavy ordnance.[40]

In the British camp, the spirit of the troops was lifted by improvements in the supply of foodstuffs and other basic goods, mainly as a result of the private enterprise that took advantage of the opportunities offered by the failure of the government to provide for the troops in the Crimea. By the spring of 1855 a vast array of private traders and sutlers had set up stalls and shops in Kadikoi. Although prices were extortionate, anything could be purchased there, from potted meats and pickles, bottled beer and Greek raki to roasted coffee, tins of Albert biscuits, chocolate, cigars, toiletries, paper, pens and ink, and the best champage from Oppenheim's or Fortnum & Mason, which both had outlets in the main bazaar. There were saddlers, cobblers, tailors, bakers and hoteliers, including the famous Mary Seacole, a Jamaican woman who provided hearty meals and hospitality, herbal remedies and medicines at the 'British Hotel' she set up at a place she named Spring Hill near Kadikoi.

Born in Kingston in 1805 to a Scottish father and Creole mother, this extraordinary woman had worked as a nurse in the British military stations in Jamaica and had married an Englishman called Seacole, who died within a year. She had later run a hotel and general store with her brother in Panama, where she had coped with outbreaks of disease. At the start of the Crimean War she travelled to England and attempted to get herself recruited as a nurse with Florence Nightingale, but she was rejected several times, no doubt partly because of the colour of her skin. Determined to make money and to help the war effort as a sutler and hotelier, she teamed up with Thomas Day, one of her husband's distant relatives, to set up a company, 'Seacole and Day'. Setting sail from Gravesend on 15 February, they collected stores in Constantinople, where they also recruited a young Greek Jew (whom she would call 'Jew Johnny'). Although rather grandly named, the 'British Hotel' was really just a restaurant and general store in what Russell described as 'an iron storehouse with wooden sheds', but it was much loved by British officers, its main clientele, for whom it was a sort of club, where they could indulge themselves and enjoy comfort food that reminded them of home.[41]

For the ordinary troops, Mary Seacole and the private stores of Kadikoi had less significance in improving food provisioning than the celebrated chef Alexis Soyer, who also arrived in the Crimea during the spring. Born in France in 1810, Soyer was the head chef at the Reform Club in London, where he came to the attention of the leaders of the Whig and Liberal governments. He was well known for his *Shilling Cookery Book* (1854), found in every home of the self-improving middle class. In February 1855 he wrote a letter to *The Times* in response to an article about the poor condition of the hospital kitchens in Scutari. Volunteering to advise the army on cooking, Soyer travelled to Scutari, but soon left with Nightingale for the Crimea, where she visited the hospitals at Balaklava and fell dangerously ill herself, forcing her to return to Scutari. Soyer took over the running of the kitchens at the Balaklava Hospital, cooking daily for more than a thousand men with his team of French and Italian chefs. Soyer's main significance was his introduction of collective food provisioning to the British army through mobile field canteens – a system practised in the French army since the Napoleonic Wars. He designed his own field stove, the Soyer Stove, which remained in British military service until the second half of the twentieth century, and he had 400 stoves shipped in from Britain, enough to feed the whole army in the Crimea. He set up army bakeries and developed a type of flat bread that could keep for months. He trained in every regiment a soldier-cook, who would follow his simple but nutritious recipes. Soyer's genius was his ability to convert army rations into palatable food. He specialized in soups, like this one for fifty men:

1. Put in the boiler 30 quarts, 7½ gallons, or 5½ camp-kettles of water
2. Add to it 50 lbs of meat, either beef or mutton
3. The rations of preserved or fresh vegetables
4. Ten small tablespoonfuls of salt
5. Simmer for three hours, and serve.[42]

The construction of a railway from Balaklava to the British camp above Sevastopol was the key to the improvement of supply. The idea for the Crimean railway – the first in the history of warfare – went back to the previous November, when news of the terrible conditions of the British army first broke in *The Times*, and it became apparent that one of the main problems was the need to transport all supplies along the muddy track from Balaklava to the heights. These reports were read by Samuel Peto, a railwayman who had made his mark as a successful London building contractor* before moving into railways in the 1840s. With a grant of £100,000 from the Aberdeen government, Peto assembled the materials for the railway and recruited

---

* Peto & Grissell, the company he ran with his cousin Thomas Grissell, built many well-known London buildings, including the Reform Club, the Oxford & Cambridge Club, the Lyceum and Nelson's Column.

a huge team of mainly Irish and very unruly navvies. They started to arrive in the Crimea at the end of January. The navvies worked at a furious pace, laying up to as much as half a kilometre of track a day, and by the end of March the entire railway line of 10 kilometres connecting Balaklava with the loading bays near the British camp had been completed. It was just in time to help with the transport of the newly arrived heavy guns and mortar shells that Raglan had instructed to be taken up from Balaklava to the heights in preparation for a second bombardment of Sevastopol which the allies had agreed to begin on Easter Monday, 9 April.[43]

*

The plan was to overwhelm Sevastopol with ten days of continual bombardment, followed by an assault on the town. With five hundred French and British guns firing round the clock, almost twice as many as in the first bombardment of October, this now became not only the heaviest bombardment of the siege, but the heaviest in history until that time. Among the allied troops, desperate for an ending of the war, there were high expectations for the attack, making them impatient for it to begin. 'The works are continuing, as always, and we are hardly advancing!' Herbé wrote to his family on 6 April. 'The impatience of the officers and soldiers has created a certain discontent, everybody blames each other for the mistakes of the past, and one senses that an energetic breakthrough is now needed to reimpose order . . . Things cannot go on like this much longer.'[44]

The Russians knew about the preparations for a bombardment. Deserters from the allied camp had warned them about it, and they could see with their own eyes the intense activity in the enemy's redoubts, where new guns appeared every day.[45] On the night of Easter Sunday, a few hours before the shelling was due to begin, prayers had been held in churches throughout the town. There were also prayers in all the bastions. Priests processed along the Russian defences with icons, including the holy icon of St Sergius which had been sent by the Troitsky Monastery in Sergiev Posad on the orders of the Tsar. It had accompanied the early Romanovs on their campaigns and had been with the Moscow militia in 1812. Everybody felt the immense significance of these holy rituals. There was a general sense that the city's destiny was about to be decided by divine providence, a feeling reinforced by the fact that both sides were celebrating Easter, which that year fell on the same day in the Orthodox and Latin calendars. 'We prayed with fervency,' wrote a Russian nurse. 'We prayed with all our might for the city and ourselves.'

At the midnight Mass at the main church, so brightly lit with candles that it could be seen from the enemy's trenches, a vast crowd spilled onto the streets and stood in silent prayer. Every person held a candle, bowing periodically to cross themselves, many people kneeling on the ground, while priests processed with icons and the choir sang. In the middle of the night there was a violent storm and the rain came pouring down. But no one moved: they thought the storm was an act of God. The worshippers remained out in the rain until first light, when the bombardment started and they dispersed, still dressed in their finest Easter clothes, to help in the defence of the bastions.[46]

A storm picked up that morning, so intense that the booms of the first guns were 'almost overpowered by the howling of the wind, and the dull monotonous plashing of the rain, which continued to descend with unabated violence', according to Whitworth Porter, who watched the bombardment from the heights. Sevastopol was completely shrouded in black gunsmoke and the morning fog. Inside the town, people could not tell where the bombs and shells were coming from. 'We knew that there was an enormous allied fleet at the harbour entrance just in front of us but we could not see it through the smoke and fog, the driving wind and pouring rain,' recalled Ershov. Confused and frightened crowds of screaming people ran about the streets in search of cover, many of them heading towards Fort Nicholas, the one remaining place of relative safety, which now began to function like a sort of bustling ghetto within Sevastopol. In the centre of the town, there were bombed-out houses everywhere. The streets were filled with building debris, broken glass and cannonballs, which 'rolled around like rubber balls'. Ershov noticed little human dramas everywhere:

A sick old man was being carried through the streets in the arms of his son and daughter while cannonballs and shells exploded around them –

an old woman following behind. . . . Some young women, dressed up prettily, leaning up against railings of the gallery, exchanged looks with a group of hussars from the garrison. Beside them, three Russian merchants in conversation – crossing themselves every time a bomb exploded. 'Lord! Lord! This is worse than Hell!' I heard them say.

In the Assembly of Nobles, the main hospital, nurses struggled to cope with the wounded, who arrived by the thousand. In the operating room, Pirogov and his fellow-surgeons went on amputating limbs while a wall collapsed from a direct hit. There was no attempt by the allies to avoid the bombing of the city's hospitals. Their firing was indiscriminate, and among the wounded there were many women and children.[47]

Inside the Fourth Bastion, the most dangerous place throughout the siege, the soldiers 'hardly ever slept', according to Captain Lipkin, one of the battery commanders in the bastion, who wrote to his brother on 21 April. 'The most we could allow ourselves was a few minutes' sleep dressed in our full uniforms and boots.' The bombardment from the allied guns, only a couple of hundred metres away, was incessant and deafening. The bombs and shells came in so quickly that the defenders had no sense of their danger until they landed. One wrong move could get them killed. Living under constant fire bred a new mentality. Ershov, who visited the bastion during the bombardment, felt 'like an inexperienced tourist entering a different world', although he himself was a seasoned artilleryman. 'Everybody rushed about, there seemed to be confusion everywhere; I could not understand or make out anything.'[48]

Tolstoy returned to Sevastopol in the middle of the bombardment. He had heard the bombs from the River Belbek, 12 kilometres away, where he had spent the winter in the Russian camp attached to the 11th Artillery Brigade. Having decided that he could best serve the army with his pen, and wanting time to write, he had applied to join the staff of General Gorchakov as an aide-de-camp. But instead, much to his annoyance, he had been transferred with his battery to the Fourth Bastion, right in the thick of the battle. 'I'm irritated,' he wrote in his diary, 'especially now when I am ill [he had caught a cold], by the fact that it doesn't occur to anybody that I'm good for anything except *chair à canon* [cannon fodder], and the most useless kind at that.'

In fact, once he had got over his cold, Tolstoy's spirits rose, and he started to enjoy himself. He was on quartermaster duty at the bastion four days out of eight. Off duty, he stayed in Sevastopol in a modest but clean dwelling on the boulevard, where he could hear the military band playing. But when he was on duty he slept in the casemate in a small cell furnished with a campbed, a table littered with papers, the manuscript of his memoir *Youth*, a clock and an icon with its vigil light. A fir post held up the ceiling, from which was suspended a tarpaulin sheet to catch falling rubble. Throughout his stay in Sevastopol, Tolstoy was accompanied by a serf called Alexei, who had been with him since he had gone to university (he figures in more than one of Tolstoy's works as 'Alyosha'). When Tolstoy was on duty at the bastion, his rations from the city were carried out to him by Alexei, a duty involving considerable danger.[49]

The cannonade was incessant. Every day, 2,000 shells landed on the bastion. Tolstoy was afraid, but he quickly got the better of his fear, and discovered a new courage in himself. Two days after grumbling at being treated as cannon fodder, he confided to his diary: 'The constant charm of danger and my observations of the soldiers I'm living with, the sailors and the very methods of war are so pleasant that I don't want to leave here.' He began to feel a close attachment to his fellow-soldiers in the bastion, one of whom would later remember him as a 'fine comrade' whose stories 'had captured the spirit of us all in the heat of the battle'. As Tolstoy wrote to his brother, expressing an idea that would lie at the heart of *War and Peace*, he 'liked the experience of living under fire' with these 'simple and kind men, whose goodness is apparent during a real war'.[50]

For ten days the bombing never stopped. At the end of the bombardment the Russians counted 160,000 shells and mortars that hit Sevastopol, destroying hundreds of buildings, and wounding or killing 4,712 soldiers and civilians. The allies did not have it all their own way. The Russians counter-attacked with 409 guns and 57 mortars, firing 88,751 cannonballs and shells during the ten days. But it soon became apparent that the Russians lacked the ammunition to maintain their resistance. Orders had been given to the battery commanders to fire once for every two shots fired by the enemy. Captain Edward Gage of the Royal Artillery wrote home on the evening of 13 April:

> The Defence, as regards long Balls, is as obstinate as the impetuosity of the attack, and every thing that genius & bravery can accomplish is conspicuous in the Russians. However, it cannot but be perceived that their fire is comparatively weak tho' the effects is very distressing to our Gunners. We have had more casualties than during the last siege, but we have had more men & Batteries engaged. . . . I do not suppose the fire will last much more than a day longer, for the men are completely beat, having been in the trenches every 12 hours since the fire opened and human flesh & blood cannot stand this much longer.[51]

The reduction of the Russian fire handed the initiative to the allies, whose barrage steadily increased. The Mamelon and the Fifth Bastion were almost entirely destroyed. Expecting an assault, the Russians frantically reinforced their garrisons, and put most of their defenders into the bunkers underground, ready to ambush the storming parties. But the assault never came. Perhaps the allied commanders were put off by the stubborn and courageous resistance of the Russians, who rebuilt their battered bastions under heavy bombardment. But the allies were also divided among themselves. It was during this period that Canrobert began openly to express his frustrations. He supported the new allied strategy, which entailed running down the bombardment of Sevastopol to concentrate on the conquest of the Crimea as a whole, and was reluctant to commit his troops to an assault which he understood would cost a lot of lives when they might be better used for this new plan. He was further discouraged from an attack by his chief engineer, General Adolphe Niel, who had received secret instructions from Paris to delay a move against Sevastopol until the Emperor Napoleon – then still considering a journey to the Crimea – arrived to take command of the assault himself.

Unwilling to act alone, the British confined themselves to a sortie on the night of 19 April against the Russians' rifle pits on the eastern edge of the Vorontsov Ravine which prevented them from developing their works towards the Redan. The pits were captured by the 77th Regiment after heavy fighting with the Russians, but the victory came at a price, in the loss of its commander, Colonel Thomas Egerton, a giant of a man at over 2 metres, and his second-in-command, the 23-year-old Captain Audley Lemprière, who stood less than 1.5 metres tall, as Nathaniel Steevens, a witness to the fighting, described in a letter to his family on 23 April:

> Our loss was *severe*, 60 men killed & wounded, and *seven Officers*, of whom Col. Egerton (a tall powerful man) & Capt. Lemprière of the 77th were *killed*; the latter was very young, had just got his company and was about the *smallest* officer in the Army, a great pet of the Colonel's and called by him his *child*; he was killed, poor fellow at the first attack in the rifle pit; the Colonel, tho' wounded, snatched him up in his arms & carried him off declaring 'they shall never take my child'; the Colonel then returned and in the second attack was killed.[52]

For the moment, without the French, this was as much as the British could achieve. On 24 April Raglan wrote to Lord Panmure: 'We must prevail upon Gen. Canrobert to take the Mamelon, otherwise we cannot move forward with any prospect of success or safety.' It was vital for the French to clear the Russians out of the Mamelon before they could mount an assault on the Malakhov, just as it was crucial for the British to occupy the Quarry Pits before they could attack the Redan. Under Canrobert the action was delayed. But once he handed over his command to Pélissier on 16 May, who was as determined as Raglan to take Sevastopol by an assault, the French committed to a combined attack on the Mamelon and the Quarries.

The operation began on 6 June with a bombardment of the outworks which lasted until six o'clock the following evening, when the allied assault was scheduled to begin. The signal for the start of the attack was to be given by Raglan and Pélissier, who were to meet on the field of action. But at the agreed hour the French commander was fast asleep, having thought to take a nap before the beginning of the fighting, and no one dared to wake the fiery general. Pélissier arrived an hour late for his rendezvous with Raglan, by which time the battle had begun – the French troops rushing forward first, followed by the British, who had heard their cheers.* The order for attack had been given by General Bosquet, in whose entourage was Fanny Duberly:

---

* This incident is the origin of the famous phrase, originally coined by Totleben: 'The French army is an army of lions led by donkeys.' The phrase was later used to describe the British army in the First World War.

General Bosquet addressed them in companies; and as he finished each speech, he was responded to by cheers, shouts, and bursts of song. The men had more the air and animation of a party invited to a marriage than a party going to fight for life or death. To me how sad a sight it seemed! The divisions begin to move and to file down the ravine, past the French battery, opposite the Mamelon. General Bosquet turns to me, his eyes full of tears – my own I cannot restrain, as he says, '*Madame, à Paris, on a toujours l'Exposition, les bals, les fêtes; et – dans une heure et demie la moitié de ces braves seront morts!*'[53]

Led by the Zouaves, the French rushed forward, without any order, towards the Mamelon, from which a tremendous volley of artillery fire forced them back. Many of the troops began to scatter in panic and had to be regrouped by their officers before they were ready to attack again. This time the attackers, running through a storm of musket fire, reached the ditch at the bottom of the Mamelon's defensive walls, which they climbed, while the Russians fired down on them or (without time to reload their muskets) threw down the stones of the parapet. 'The wall was four metres high,' recalled Octave Cullet, who was in the first line of attack; 'it was difficult to climb, and we had no ladders, but our spirit was irrepressible':

Hoisting one another up, we scaled the walls, and overcoming the resistance of the enemy on the parapet, launched a furious avalanche of fire into the crowd defending the redoubt. . . . What happened next I cannot describe. It was a scene of carnage. Fighting like madmen, our soldiers spiked their guns, and the few Russians who were brave enough to fight us were all slaughtered.[54]

The Zouaves did not stop in the Mamelon but continued to rush on towards the Malakhov – a spontaneous action by soldiers caught up in the fury of the fight – only to be mowed down in their hundreds by the Russian guns. Lieutenant Colonel St George of the Royal Artillery, who watched the dreadful scene, described it in a letter on 9 June:

Then such a fire opened from the Malakhov tower as never was seen before I am sure: sheets of flame, with their explosion, followed each other in the rapidest succession. The Russians worked the guns wonderfully well (and it is my trade, I am a judge) and fired like fiends upon the multitudes of poor little Zouaves, whose pluck had carried them to the edge of a ditch they had no means of crossing, & who stood in hesitation till they were knocked over. It was too much for them, and they wavered and retreated into the Mamelon; and even this became too hot for them, and they had to retire into their trenches again. Reinforcements came in strength. Again they dashed into the Mamelon, whose guns they had already spiked, and killed its defenders, and again, foolishly I think, went through to try the Malakhov. They failed a second time and had to retire, but this time no farther than the Mamelon, which they are holding still, having won it with admirable courage, and left between 2 and 3 thousand killed and wounded on the field.[55]

Meanwhile the British attacked the Quarries. The Russians had left only a small force in the Quarry Pits, relying on their ability to retake them with reinforcements from the Redan should they be stormed. The British took the Quarries easily but soon found that they had not enough men to hold them, as wave after wave of Russians attacked them from the Redan. For several hours, the two sides were engaged in fierce hand-to-hand fighting, as one side expelled the other from the rifle pits, only to be forced back yet again by reinforcements from the other side. By five o'clock in the morning, when the last Russian attack was finally repulsed, there were heaps of dead and wounded on the ground.

At midday on 9 June a white flag was raised from the Malakhov, and another appeared on the Mamelon, now in the hands of the French, signalling a truce to collect the bodies from the battlefield. The French had made enormous sacrifices to capture the crucial Mamelon and White Works, losing almost 7,500 dead and wounded men. Herbé went out into no man's land with General Failly to agree the arrangements with the Russian General Polussky. After the exchange of a few formalities, 'the conversation took a friendly turn – Paris, St Petersburg, the hardships of the previous winter', Herbé noted in a letter to his family that evening, and while the dead were cleared away, 'cigars were exchanged' between the officers. 'One might have thought we were friends meeting for a smoke in the middle of a hunt,' Herbé wrote. After a while some officers appeared with a magnum of champagne, and General Failly, who had ordered them to fetch it, proposed a 'toast to peace' that was heartily accepted by the Russian officers. Six hours later, when several thousand bodies had been cleared away, it was time to end the truce. After each side had been given time to check that none of their own men had been left in no man's land, the white flags were taken down and, as Polussky had suggested, a blank shot was fired from the Malakhov to signal the resumption of hostilities.[56]

With the capture of the Mamelon and the Quarry Pits, everything was ready for an assault on the Malakhov and the Redan. The date set for the attack was 18 June – the 40th anniversary of the battle of Waterloo. It was hoped that an allied victory would heal the old divisions between the British and the French and give them something new to celebrate together on that day.

Victory was bound to cost a lot of lives. To storm the Russian forts, the attackers would have to carry ladders and run uphill across several hundred metres of open ground, traversing ditches and abbatis* under heavy fire from the Russian guns on the Malakhov and the Redan, as well as flanking fire from the Flagstaff Bastion. When they reached the forts, they would have to use their ladders to get into the ditch and climb the walls, under point-blank fire from the enemy above, before overcoming the defenders on the parapets and fighting off the Russians, amassed behind more barricades inside the forts, until reinforcements could arrive.

It was agreed by the allies that the French would attack the Malakhov first, and then, as soon as they had silenced the Russian guns, the British infantry would begin their storming of the Redan. On Pélissier's insistence, the assault would be limited to the Malakhov and the Redan rather than a broad attack against the town. The assault on the Redan was probably superfluous because the Russians were almost certain to abandon it once the French were able to bring their artillery to bear against it from the Malakhov. But Raglan thought that it was essential for the British to storm *something*, even at the cost of unnecessary losses, if this battle was to achieve its symbolic aim as a joint operation on the anniversary of Waterloo. The French had been consistently critical of Britain's failure to match their own troop commitments in the Crimea.

---

* A barrier about 2 metres high and a metre or so wide, made up of felled trees, timber and brushwood.

Heavy casualties were expected. The French were told that half the stormers would be killed before even reaching the Malakhov. Those in the first line of attack had to be offered money or promotion before they could be persuaded to take part. In the British camp, the stormers were known as the Forlorn Hope, derived from the Dutch, *Verloren hoop*, which actually meant 'lost troops', but the English mistranslation was appropriate.[57]

The night before the assault on the Malakhov, the French soldiers settled down in their bivouacs, each man trying to prepare himself for the events of the next day. Some tried to get some sleep, others cleaned their guns, or talked among themselves, and still others found a quiet place to say a prayer. There was a general sense of foreboding. Many soldiers wrote their name and home address on a ticket which they hung around their neck so that anyone who found them if they died would be able to inform their family. Others wrote a farewell letter to their loved ones, giving it to the army chaplain to send off in case they died. André Damas had a large postbag. The chaplain was impressed by the calmness of the men in these final moments before battle. Few, it seemed to him, were animated by a hatred of the enemy or by the desire for revenge stirred up by the rivalry between nations. One soldier wrote:

> I am calm and confident – I am surprised at myself. In face of such a danger, it is only you, my brother, I dare tell this. It would be arrogant to confess it to anybody else. I have eaten to gain strength. I have drunk only water. I do not like the over-excitements of alcohol in battle: they do no good.

Another wrote:

> As I write these lines to you, the call to battle can be heard. The great day has arrived. In two hours we begin our assault. I am wearing with devotion the medal of the Blessed Virgin and the scapular I was given by the nuns. I feel calm, and tell myself that God shall protect me.

A captain wrote:

> I shake you by the hand, my brother, and want you to know that I love you. Now, my God, have pity on me. I commend myself to you with

sincerity – let Your will be done! Long Live France! Today our eagle must soar above Sevastopol![58]

Not all the allied preparations went to plan. During the evening there were desertions from the French and British camps – not only by soldiers but by officers who had no stomach for the imminent assault and crossed over to the enemy. The Russians were warned of the assault by a French corporal who had deserted from the General Staff and carried to the Russians a detailed plan of the French attack. 'The Russians knew, in precise detail, the position and strength of all our battalions,' wrote Herbé, who was later told this by a senior Russian officer. They had also received warnings from British desert- ers, including one from the 28th (North Gloucestershire) Regiment. But even without these warnings, the Russians were alerted by the noisy preparations of the British on the evening of the 17th. Lieuten- ant Colonel James Alexander of the 14th Regiment recalled that 'the men, being excited, did not go to sleep but remained up till we were directed to fall in at midnight. Our camp looked like a fair, lighted up, with a buzz of voices everywhere. The Russians must have remarked on this.'[59]

They certainly did. Prokofii Podpalov, an orderly to General Golev in the Redan, recalled noticing the steady build-up of activity in the Quarries in the evening – the 'sound of voices, of footsteps in the trenches, and the rumbling of the wheels of the gun carriages being moved towards us', which 'made it obvious that the allies were pre- paring to give the signal for an assault'. At that moment the Russians had been withdrawing their forces from the Redan. Men were going back into town for the night. But noticing these signs of an imminent attack, Golev ordered all his troops to return to the Redan, where they mounted the cannon and took up their positions on the para- pets. Podpalov recalled the 'extraordinary silence' of the men as they waited for the assault to begin. 'That grave-like silence contained within it something sinister: everybody felt that something terrible was approaching, something powerful and threatening, with which we would fight for life and death.'[60]

The French attack had been scheduled to begin well before first light, at three o'clock, with three hours of bombardment, followed by the storming of the Malakhov at 6 a.m., an hour after sunrise. During the evening of the 17th, however, Pélissier made a sudden change of plan. He had decided that in those first minutes of daylight the Russians could not fail to see the French preparing to attack, and they would bring up infantry reserves to defend the Malakhov. Late that evening he issued a new order for the stormers to attack the Malakhov directly at 3 a.m., when the rocket signal to begin would be fired from the Victoria Redoubt, behind the French lines near the Mamelon. This was not the only sudden change that evening. In a fit of temper, and seeking to claim the expected success, Pélissier also removed General Bosquet, who had questioned his decision to begin the assault without a bombardment. Bosquet had a detailed knowledge of the Russian positions, and he had the confidence of the soldiers; he was replaced by a general who had neither. The French troops were unsettled by the sudden changes – none more so than General Mayran, the man chosen to lead the assault with the 97th Regiment, who was personally insulted by the fiery Pélissier in another argument, prompting Mayran to storm off to his post saying, 'Il n'y a plus qu'à se faire tuer' ('There's nothing left to do but get killed').[61]

It was Mayran, in his eagerness, who made a fatal blunder, when he mistook a shell trailing light from its fuse as the rocket signal to attack, and ordered the 97th to begin the assault fifteen minutes too early, when the rest of the French troops were not ready. According to Herbé, who was with the 95th Regiment in the second column just behind Mayran, the general had been provoked by an incident shortly after two o'clock in the morning, when two Russian officers had crept up to the French trenches and called out in the dark,

'Allons, Messieurs les Français, quand il vous plaira, nous vous atten-dons' ['Come on, gentlemen of France, when you are ready, we shall be waiting']. We were stupefied. It was obvious that the enemy knew all our plans, and that we would find a well-prepared defence. General Mayran was inflamed by this audacious provocation, and formed his men in columns, ready to attack the Malakhov as soon as the signal was given . . . All eyes were fixed on the Victoria Redoubt. Suddenly, at about a quarter to three, a trailing light followed by a streak of smoke was seen to cross the sky. 'It's the signal,' cried several officers who were grouped around Mayran. A second trail of light appeared soon afterwards. 'There is no doubt,' the general said, 'it is the signal: besides, it is better to be too early than too late: Forward the 97th!'

The 97th rushed forward – only to be met by a deadly barrage of artillery and musket fire by the Russians, who were well armed and ready on every parapet. 'Suddenly the enemy was coming towards us in a huge wave,' recalled Podpalov, who watched the scene from the Redan.

> Soon, in the dim light, we could just make out that the enemy was carrying ladders, ropes, spades, boards, etc. – it looked like an army of ants on the move. They came closer and closer. Suddenly, right across the line, our bugles sounded, followed by the booming of our cannon and the firing of our guns; the earth shook, there was a thunderous echo, and it was so dark from the gunsmoke that nothing could be seen. When it cleared, we could see that the ground in front of us was covered with the bodies of the fallen French.

Mayran was among those who were hit in the first wave. Helped to his feet by Herbé, he was badly wounded in the arm, but refused to retreat. 'Forward the 95th!' he called back to the second line. The reinforcements moved forward, but they too were shot down in huge numbers by the Russians guns. This was not a battle but a massacre. Following their instincts, the attackers lay down on the ground, ignoring Mayran's orders to advance, and engaged the Russians in a gun battle. After twenty minutes, by which time the battlefield was littered with their dead, the French troops saw a rocket in the sky: it was the real signal to attack.[62]

Pélissier had ordered the rocket to be fired in a desperate attempt to coordinate the French assault. But if Mayran had advanced too early, his other generals were not ready: expecting a later start, they had not managed to prepare in time. The troops from the reserve lines were rushed forward to join in the attack, but the sudden order to advance unsettled them, and many of the men 'refused to leave the trenches, even when their officers threatened them with the harshest punishments', according to Lieutenant Colonel Dessaint, the head of the army's political department, who concluded that the soldiers 'had an intuition of the disaster that awaited them'.[63]

Watching from the Vorontsov Ridge, Raglan could see that the disjointed French assault was a bloody fiasco. One French column, to the left of the Malakhov, had broken through, but its supports were being devastated by the Russian guns on the Malakhov and the Redan. Raglan might have helped the French by bombarding the Redan, as agreed in the original allied plan, before launching an assault; but he felt bound by a sense of duty and honour to support the French by storming the Redan immediately, without a preliminary bombardment, even though he must have known, if only from the events of the previous hour, that such a policy was bound to end in disaster and the needless sacrifice of many men. 'I always guarded myself from being tied down to attack at the same moment as the French, and I felt that I ought to have some hope of their success before I committed our troops,' Raglan wrote to Panmure on 19 June, 'but when I saw how stoutly they were opposed, I considered it was my duty to assist them by attacking myself ... Of this I am quite certain, that, if the troops had remained in our trenches, the French would have attributed their non-success to our refusal to participate in the operation.'[64]

The British assault began at 5.30 a.m. The attacking troops ran forward from the Quarries and the trenches on either side, followed by the supporting parties carrying ladders to scale the walls of the Redan. It soon became apparent that it was a hopeless task. 'The troops no sooner began to show themselves beyond the parapet of the trenches, than they were assailed by the most murderous fire of grape that ever was witnessed,' reported Sir George Brown, who had been given the command of the assault. The first Russian volley took out one-third of the attackers. From the trenches on the left, Codrington observed the devastating effect of the barrage on the troops attempting to run across 200 metres of open ground towards the Redan:

> The moment they showed themselves, fire of grape was opened upon
> them – it ploughed the ground – it knocked over many, the dust blinded
> them, and I saw many swerve away to the trenches on their left. The

officers told me afterwards they were blinded by the dust thrown up by the grape; and one told me he was quite blown – out of breath – before he got halfway.[65]

Overwhelmed by the torrent of grape-shot, the troops began to waver; some lost their nerve and ran away, despite the efforts of their officers to regroup the men by shouting threats. Eventually, the first line of attackers and the leading ladder-men reached the abbatis, about 30 metres from the ditch of the Redan. While they struggled to squeeze through the gaps of the abbatis, the Russians 'mounted the parapets of the Redan and delivered volley after volley into us', recalled Timothy Gowing:

> They hoisted a large black flag and defied us to come on. The cry of 'Murder' could be heard on that field, for the cowardly enemy fired for hours upon our countrymen as they lay writhing in agony and blood. As some of our officers said, 'This will never do – we'll pay them for this yet!' We would have forgiven them all had they not shot down poor, defenceless, wounded men.

The storming party dwindled to the last hundred men, who started to retreat, in defiance of their officers, whose threats to shoot them were ignored. According to one officer, who had urged a group of men to continue the attack, 'they became impressed with the conviction that another step forward and they would be blown into the air; they would fight any number of men, they said, but they would not step forward to be blown up'.[66] It had been widely rumoured that the Redan was mined.

Meanwhile, 2,000 men from the 3rd Division under the command of Major-General Eyre on the left flank broke through into the suburbs of Sevastopol itself. They had been instructed to occupy some Russian rifle pits and, if the attack on the Redan allowed it, to advance further down the Picquet House Ravine. But Eyre had exceeded his orders and had pushed on his brigade, defeating the Russians in the Cemetery, before coming under heavy fire in Sevastopol's streets. They found themselves in a 'cul-de-sac', recalled Captain Scott of the 9th Regiment: 'we could neither advance nor retire, and had to hold our ground from 4 a.m. to 9 p.m., 17 hours under a tremendous fire of shot, shell, grape, canister, and hundreds of their sharpshooters, our only cover being the houses which crumbled about us at every discharge.' According to Lieutenant Colonel Alexander of the 14th Regiment, the storming of the city became something of an escapade, as some of the Irish soldiers 'rushed on into part of Sevastopol, got among houses with women in them, pictures, mahogany, furniture and pianos; they got also among strong wine ... Some of the Irish boys dressed themselves up as women and so fought; some of them brought back looking glasses, tables and a gooseberry bush with the berries on it!' But for the rest of the troops, sheltering in bombed-out and crumbling buildings from the enemy's fire, the day passed with no such amusements. It was only under cover of darkness that they were able to retreat, carrying hundreds of wounded men with them.[67]

The next morning a truce was called to clear the killed and wounded from the battlefield. The casualties were enormous. The British lost about 1,000 men, killed and wounded; the French perhaps six times that number, though the precise figure was suppressed. A Zouave captain who was part of the team sent out into no man's land to collect the dead described what he saw in a letter home on 25 June:

> I will not tell you all the horrible sensations I experienced on arriving on that ground, strewn with bodies rotting in the heat, among which I recognized some of my comrades. There were 150 Zouaves with me, carrying stretchers and flasks with wine. The doctor with us told us to care first for the wounded who could still be saved. We found a lot of these unfortunates – they all asked to drink and my Zouaves poured them wine ... There was an intolerable smell of corruption everywhere; the Zouaves had to cover their noses with a handkerchief while carrying away the dead bodies, whose heads and feet were left dangling.[68]

Among the dead was General Mayran, who was blamed for the defeat in Pélissier's account to Napoleon, although, if truth be told, Pélissier himself was at least as responsible for his last-minute changes to the plan. Raglan certainly believed that Pélissier was principally at fault, not just for the changes of plan but for his decision to limit the attack to the Malakhov and the Redan rather than commit to a broader assault on the town which might have had the effect of scattering the Russian defenders – a decision he believed Pélissier had made from worries that the French troops might 'run riot' in the town, as he explained in his letter to Panmure.

But Raglan's criticisms were no doubt coloured by his own sense of guilt for the needless sacrifice of so many British troops. According to one of his physicians, Raglan fell into a deep depression following the failure of the assault, and when he was on his deathbed, on 26 June, it was not from cholera that he was suffering, as had been rumoured, but 'a case of acute mental anguish, producing first great depression, and subsequently complete exhaustion of the heart's action'.[69] He died on 28 June.

11

The Fall of Sevastopol

'My dear father,' Pierre de Castellane, an aide-de-camp to General Bosquet, wrote on 14 July. 'All my letters should begin, I think, with the same words, "nothing new", which is to say: we dig, we organize our batteries, and every night we sit and drink around the campfire; every day two companies of men are taken off to hospital.'[1]

With the failure of the assaults on the Malakhov and the Redan, the siege returned to the monotonous routine of trench-digging and artillery fire, without any signs of a breakthrough. After nine months of this trench warfare, there was a general sense of exhaustion on both sides, a demoralizing sense that the stalemate might continue indefinitely. Such was the desire for the war to end that all sorts of suggestions were made to break the deadlock. Prince Urusov, a first-rate chess player and a friend of Tolstoy, attempted to persuade Count Osten-Sacken, commander of the Sevastopol garrison, that a challenge should be sent to the allies to play a game of chess for the foremost trench, which had changed hands many times, at the cost of several hundred lives. Tolstoy suggested that the war should be decided by a duel.[2] Although this was the first modern war, a dress rehearsal for the trench fighting of the First World War, it was fought in an age when some ideas of chivalry were still alive.

Demoralization soon set in among the allied troops. No one thought a renewed attack had much prospect of success – the Russians were building even stronger defences – and everybody feared they would have to spend a second winter on the heights above Sevastopol. All the soldiers now began to write of wanting to go home. 'I have fully made up my mind to come home somehow,' Lieutenant Colonel Mundy wrote to his mother on 9 July. 'I cannot and will not stand another winter. I know if I did, I should be a useless decrepit old man in a year and I would rather be a live jackass than a dead lion.' Soldiers envied wounded comrades who were taken home. According to one British officer, 'many a man would gladly lose an arm to get off these heights and leave this siege'.[3]

Despair that the war would never end led many troops to question why they were fighting. The longer the slaughter continued, the more they came to see the enemy as suffering soldiers like themselves, and the more senseless it all seemed. The French army chaplain André Damas cited the case of a Zouave who came to him with religious doubts about the war. The Zouave had been told (as all the soldiers were) that they were waging war against 'barbarians'. But during the ceasefire to collect the dead and wounded following the fighting on 18 June he had helped a badly injured Russian officer, who as a mark of gratitude had taken from his neck and given him a leather pendant embossed with the image of the Madonna and Child. 'This war has to stop,' the Zouave told Damas; 'it is cowardly. We are all Christians; we all believe in God and religion, and without that we would not be so brave.'[4]

Trench fatigue was the big enemy of the summer months. By the tenth month of the siege soldiers had become such nervous wrecks from living under constant bombardment, so exhausted from the lack of sleep, that many of them could no longer cope. In their memoirs, many soldiers wrote of 'trench madness' – a mixed bag of mental illnesses, as far as one can tell, from claustrophobia to what later would be known as 'shell shock' or 'combat stress'. Louis Noir, for instance, recalled many cases when 'entire companies' of battle-hardened Zouaves would 'suddenly get up in the middle of the night, seize their guns, and call to others hysterically for help to fight imaginary enemies. These incidents of nervous over-excitation became a contagion affecting many men; remarkably, it affected first of all those who were the strongest physically and morally.' Jean Cler, a colonel in the Zouaves, also recalled seasoned fighters who 'suddenly went mad' and ran away to the Russians, or who were unable to bear it any more and shot themselves. Suicides were noted by many memoirists. One wrote of a Zouave, 'a veteran of our African wars', who appeared all right until, one day, sitting by his tent and drinking coffee with his comrades, he said that he had had enough; taking up his gun, he walked away and put a bullet through his head.[5]

The loss of comrades was a major strain on soldiers' nerves. It was not the sort of thing that men would often write about, even in the British army where there was no real censorship of their letters home; stoical acceptance of death in battle was expected of the soldier, and perhaps was needed to survive. Yet in the frequent outpouring of sorrow at the loss of friends we may perhaps catch a glimpse of deeper and more troubling emotions than such letter-writers felt able to express. Commenting on the published correspondence of his fellow-officer, Henri Loizillon, for example, Michel Gilbert was struck by the anguish and remorse in a letter to his family on 19 June. The letter contained a long list of names, a 'funereal accounting' of the soldiers who had fallen in the previous day's assault on the Malakhov, and yet, Gilbert thought, one could feel from it 'how much his soul was haunted by the breath of death (*souffle de la mort*). The list of names goes on and on, endlessly despairing, friends who disappeared, the names of officers who have been killed.' Loizillon appeared lost in grief and guilt – guilt because he had survived – and it was only with the final humorous lines of his letter, in which he described the unsuccessful prayers of a fellow-soldier, that his 'vigorous spirit of self-preservation reappeared':

> My poor friend Conegliano [Loizillon wrote], at the moment when we were leaving for the attack, told me (he is very religious): 'I have brought my rosary, which the Pope blessed, and I have said a dozen prayers for the general [Mayran], a dozen for my brother, and for you as well.' Poor boy! Of the three, it was only me his prayers helped to save.[6]

Apart from the effect of witnessing so many deaths, the soldiers in the trenches must have been worn down by the horrendous scale and nature of the injuries endured by all the armies in the siege. Not until the First World War would the human body suffer so much damage as it did in the fighting at Sevastopol. Technical improvements to artillery and rifle fire made for much more serious wounds than those inflicted on the soldiers of the Napoleonic or Algerian wars. The modern elongated conical rifle shot was more powerful than the old round shot, and heavier as well, so it went straight through the body, breaking any bones along its way, whereas the lighter round shot tended to deflect on its passage through the body, usually without breaking bones. At the beginning of the siege the Russians used a conical bullet weighing 50 grams, but from the spring of 1855 they began to use a larger and heavier rifle bullet, 5 centimetres long and weighing twice as much as the British and French bullets. When these new bullets struck the soft part of the human body, they left a bigger hole, which could heal, but when they hit the bone, they would break it more extensively, and if an arm or leg was fractured, it would almost certainly require amputation. The Russian practice of holding their fire until the final moment, and then shooting at the enemy from point-blank range, guaranteed that their rifle power caused the maximum damage.[7]

In the allied hospitals there were soldiers with some gruesome wounds, but there were just as many in the Russian hospitals, victims of the even more advanced artillery and rifle fire of the British and the French. Khristian Giubbenet, a professor of surgery who worked in the military hospital in Sevastopol, wrote in 1870:

> I do not think that I ever saw such awful injuries as I was forced to deal with during the final period of the siege. The worst without a doubt were the frequently occurring stomach wounds, when the bloody guts of men would be hanging out. When such unfortunates were brought to the dressing stations, they could still speak, were still conscious, and went on living for a few hours. In other cases the guts and the pelvis were ripped out at the back: the men could not move their lower bodies but they retained their consciousness until they died in a few hours' time. Without a doubt, the most terrible impression was created by those whose faces had been blown up by a shell, denying them the image of a human being. Imagine a creature whose face and head have been replaced by a bloody mass of tangled flesh and bone – there are no eyes, nose, mouth, cheeks, tongue, chin or ears to be seen, and yet this creature continues to stand up on its own feet, and moves and waves its arms about, forcing one to assume that it still has a consciousness. In other cases in the place where we would see a face, all that remained were some bloody bits of dangling skin.[8]

The Russians had far heavier casualties than the allies. By the end of July 65,000 Russian soldiers had been killed or wounded in

Sevastopol – more than twice the number lost by the allies – not including losses from illness or disease. The bombardment of the town in June had added several thousand wounded, not just soldiers but civilians, to the already overcrowded hospitals (4,000 casualties were added on 17 and 18 June alone). In the Assembly of Nobles 'the wounded were laid out on the parquet floor not only side by side but on top of each other', recalled Dr Giubbenet. 'The moans and screams of a thousand dying men filled the gloomy hall, which was only dimly lit by the candles of the orderlies.' At the Pavlovsk Battery another 5,000 wounded Russian soldiers were just as tightly packed on the bare floors of wharves and stores. To relieve the overcrowding, the Russians built a large field hospital towards the River Belbek, 6 kilometres from Sevastopol, in July, where the less seriously wounded were evacuated, as dictated by Pirogov's system of triage. There were other reserve hospitals at Inkerman, on the Mackenzie Heights and in the former khan's palace in Bakhchiserai. Some of the wounded were taken as far as Simferopol, and even to Kharkov, 650 kilometres away, by horse and cart on country roads, where all the hospitals were filled to overflowing with casualties of the siege. But this was still not enough to cope with the ever-growing number of sick and wounded men. In June and July at least 250 Russians were added to the list of casualties every day. During the last weeks of the siege, the number rose to as many as 800 casualties a day, twice the losses officially reported by Gorchakov, according to Russian prisoners later captured by the allies.[9]

The Russians were coming under growing strain. With the allied occupation of Kerch and the blockade of their supply lines through the Sea of Azov from the start of June, they began to suffer from serious shortages of ammunition and artillery. Small mortar shells were the main problem. Battery commanders were ordered to limit their fire to one shot for every four received from the enemy. Meanwhile, the allies were now reaching levels of concentrated fire never before seen in a siege war – their industries and transport systems enabling their artillery to fire up to 75,000 rounds per day.[10] This was a new type of industrial warfare and Russia, with its backward serf economy, could not compete.

Morale was running dangerously low. In June the Russians lost their two inspirational leaders in Sevastopol: Totleben was seriously wounded during the bombardment of 22 June and was forced to retire; and six days later Nakhimov was hit by a bullet in the face while he was inspecting the batteries at the Redan. Taken to his quarters, he lay unconscious for two days before dying on 30 June. His funeral was a solemn ceremony attended by the entire population of the town, and watched by the allied troops, who ceased their bombardment to watch the funeral cortège pass below them by the city walls. 'I cannot find words to describe to you the profound sadness of the funeral,' wrote a Sevastopol nursing sister to her family.

> The sea with the great fleet of our enemies, the hills with our bastions where Nakhimov spent his days and nights – these said more than words can express. From the hills where their batteries threaten Sevastopol, the enemy could see and fire directly on the procession; but even their guns were respectfully silent and not one round was fired during the service. Imagine the scene – and above it all the dark storm clouds, reflecting the mournful music, the sad tolling of the bells, and the doleful funeral chants. This was how the sailors buried their hero of Sinope, how Sevastopol laid to rest its own fearless and heroic defender.[11]

By the end of June the situation in Sevastopol had become so desperate, with not just ammunition but supplies of food and water running dangerously low, that Gorchakov began preparing to evacuate the town. Much of the population had already left, fearing they would starve to death, or fall victim to the cholera or typhus that spread as epidemics in the summer months. A special committee to fight the epidemics in Sevastopol reported thirty deaths a day from cholera alone in June. Most of those who stayed had long been forced to abandon their bombed-out homes and take refuge in Fort Nicholas, at the far end of the town by the entrance to the sea harbour, where the main barracks, offices and shops were all enclosed within its walls. Others found a safer home on the North Side. 'Sevastopol began to resemble a graveyard,' recalled Ershov, the artillery officer.

> With every passing day even its central avenues became more empty and gloomy – it looked like a town that had been destroyed by an earthquake. Ekaterinskaia Street, which in May had still been a lively

and handsome thoroughfare, was now, in July, deserted and destroyed. Neither on it nor on the boulevard would one see a female face, nor any person walking freely any more; only solemn groups of troops. . . . On every face there was the same sad expression of tiredness and foreboding. There was no point going into town: nowhere did one hear the sound of joy, nowhere did one find any amusement.

In Tolstoy's 'Sevastopol in August', a story based on true events and characters, a soldier at the River Belbek asks another who has just arrived from the besieged town whether his room there is still in one piece. 'My dear fellow,' the other one replies, 'the building was shelled to kingdom come ages ago. You won't recognize Sevastopol now; there's not a single woman left in the place, no taverns, no brass bands; the last pub closed down yesterday. It's about as cheerful as a morgue.'[12]

It was not only civilians who were abandoning Sevastopol. Soldiers were deserting in growing numbers during the summer months. Those who ran away to the allies claimed that desertion was a mass phenomenon, and this is supported by the fragmentary figures and communications of the Russian military authorities. There was a report in August, for example, that the number of desertions had 'dramatically increased' since June, especially among those reserve troops who were called up to the Crimea: a hundred men had run away from the 15th Reserve Infantry Division, as had three out of every four reinforcements sent from the Warsaw Military District. From Sevastopol itself, around twenty soldiers went missing every day, mostly during sorties or bombardments, when they were not so closely watched by their commanding officers. According to the French, who received a steady flow of deserters in the summer months, the main reason the men gave for their desertion was that they had been given virtually no food, or only rotten meat, to eat. There were various rumours of a mutiny by some of the reservists in the Sevastopol garrison during the first week of August, though the uprising was brutally put down and all evidence of it suppressed by the Russians. 'There has been a report that one hundred Russian soldiers have been shot by a sentence of Court Martial in the Town for Mutiny,' Henry Clifford wrote to his father shortly afterwards. Several regiments were broken up and put in the reserve because they had become unreliable.[13]

*

Realizing that Sevastopol could not withstand the siege for much longer, the Tsar ordered Gorchakov to launch one last attempt to break the ring of allied troops. Gorchakov was doubtful that it could be done. An offensive 'against an enemy superior in numbers and entrenched in such solid positions would be folly', the commander-in-chief reasoned. But the Tsar insisted that *something* should be done: he was looking for a way to end the war on terms acceptable to Russia's national honour and integrity, and needed a military success to begin peace talks with the British and the French from a stronger position. Sending three of his reserve divisions to the Crimea, Alexander bombarded Gorchakov with instructions to attack (though not suggesting where) before the allies sent more troops, as he believed they were about to do. 'I am convinced that we must go on the offensive,' he wrote to Gorchakov on 30 July; 'otherwise all the reinforcements I have sent to you, as has happened in the past, will be sucked into Sevastopol, that bottomless pit.'[14]

The only line of action that Gorchakov believed had any chance of success was an attack on the French and Sardinian positions on the Chernaia river. By 'capturing the enemy's watering places, it might be possible to threaten his flank and limit his attacks on Sevastopol, maybe opening the way for further advantageous operations', he wrote to the Tsar. 'But we should not deceive ourselves, for there is little hope of success in such an initiative.' Alexander would not listen to Gorchakov's reservations. On 3 August he wrote to him again: 'Your daily losses in Sevastopol underline what I have told you many times before in my letters – *the necessity to do something decisive to end this frightful massacre* [the Tsar's italics].' Alexander knew that Gorchakov was essentially a courtier, an acolyte of the cautious Paskevich, and suspected that he was reluctant to take the responsibility for an offensive. He concluded his letter with the words: 'I want a battle, but if you as commander-in-chief fear the liability, then convene a military council to take it for you.'[15]

A council of war met on 9 August to discuss a possible attack. Many of the senior commanders were against an offensive. Osten-Sacken, who had been much affected by the death of Nakhimov and was now convinced that the loss of Sevastopol was unavoidable, argued that enough men had been sacrificed and that it was time to evacuate the naval base. Most of the other generals shared Osten-Sacken's pessimistic view but no one else was brave enough to speak out in such terms. Instead they went along with the idea of an offensive to please the Tsar, though few had any confidence in any detailed plan. The most audacious proposal came from the gung-ho General Khrulev, who had led the failed attack on Evpatoria. Khrulev now favoured the complete destruction of Sevastopol (even bettering the example of Moscow 1812) followed by a mass assault on the enemy's positions by every man available. When Osten-Sacken objected that the suicidal plan would end in tens of thousands of needless deaths, Khrulev answered: 'Well, so what? Let everybody die! We will leave our mark upon the map!' Cooler heads prevailed, and the meeting ended with a vote in favour of Gorchakov's idea of an attack on the French and Sardinian positions on the Chernaia, though Gorchakov himself remained extremely doubtful that it could succeed. 'I am marching on the enemy because if I don't, Sevastopol will soon be lost,' he wrote on the eve of the offensive to Prince Dolgoruky, the Minister of War. But if the attack did not succeed, 'it would not be [his] fault', and he would 'try to evacuate Sevastopol with as little loss as possible'.[16]

The attack was scheduled for the early morning of 16 August. The evening before, the French troops had been celebrating the *fête de l'empereur* – also (not coincidentally) the Feast of the Assumption, a major holiday for the Italians, who, like the French, had been drinking late into the night. They had only just gone off to bed, when, at 4 a.m., they were woken by the sound of Russian cannon.

Using the cover of an early morning fog, the Russians advanced towards the Traktir Bridge with a combined force of 47,000 infantry, 10,000 cavalry and 270 field guns under the command of General Liprandi on the left (opposite the Sardinians) and General Read, the son of a Scottish engineer who had emigrated to Russia, on the Russian right (opposite the French). The two generals were under orders not to cross the river before receiving orders from Gorchakov, the commander-in-chief, who was not sure whether to deploy his reserve divisions against the French on the Fediukhin Heights or the Sardinians on Gasfort Hill. He was relying on the opening artillery bombardment to expose the enemy's positions and help him make up his mind.

The Russians' opening cannon shots failed to reach their targets, however. They merely served to raise the alarm for the 18,000 French troops and 9,000 Sardinians to prepare themselves for battle and for those in the forward position to move up to the Traktir Bridge. Frustrated with the lack of progress, Gorchakov sent his aide-de-camp, a Lieutenant Krasovsky, to hurry out to Read and Liprandi and tell them it was 'time to start'. By the time the message got to Read, its meaning was far from clear. 'Time to start what?' Read asked Krasovsky, who did not know. Read decided that the message could not mean to begin the artillery fire, which had started already, but the start of an infantry attack. He ordered his men to cross the river and storm the Fediukhin Heights – even though the cavalry and infantry reserves that were supposed to support an attack had not arrived. Gorchakov, meanwhile, had decided to concentrate his reserve forces on the left, having been encouraged by the ease with which Liprandi's skirmishers had driven off the Sardinian outposts from Telegraph Hill (known by the Italians as the *Roccia dei Piemontesi*). Hearing the sound of muskets firing from Read's men in front of the Fediukhin, Gorchakov redirected some of his reserves to support them, but, as he acknowledged afterwards, he knew already that the battle had been lost: his troops were divided and attacking on two fronts when the whole point of the offensive had been to deal a single mighty blow.[17]

Read's men crossed the river near the Traktir Bridge. Without cavalry or artillery support, they marched towards their almost certain destruction by the French artillery and riflemen firing down on them from the slopes of the Fediukhin Heights. Within twenty minutes 2,000 Russian infantry had been gunned down. Reserves arrived, in the form of the 5th Infantry Division. Its commander suggested that the whole division should be committed to the attack. Perhaps by weight of numbers, they might have broken through. But Read chose instead to commit them piecemeal to the battle, regiment by regiment, and each one, in turn, was shot down by the French, who by this time were entirely confident of their ability to defeat the Russian columns and held off their fire until they were at close hand. 'Our artillery played havoc with the Russians,' recalled Octave Cullet, a French infantry captain who was on the Fediukhin.

> Our soldiers, confident and strong, fired at them from two lines with a calm and deadly volley that can only be achieved by battle-hardened troops. Each man that morning had been given eighty cartridges but few had been shot; no one paid attention to the firing from our flanks but concentrated only on the approaching Russian troops.... Only when they were right onto us and threatening to envelop us, did we start our firing – not one shot was lost on this vast semicircle of attackers. Our men displayed admirable composure (*sang-froid*) and no one thought of retreating.[18]

At last, Gorchakov put an end to Read's bungling and ordered the entire division to join in the attack. For a while, they pushed the French back up the hill, but the deadly salvoes of the enemy's rifles eventually forced them to retreat and cross over to the other side of the river. Read was killed by a shell splinter during the retreat, and Gorchakov took over his command, ordering eight battalions from Liprandi's forces on the left to support him at the eastern end of the Fediukhin Heights. But these troops came under heavy rifle fire from the Sardinians, who had moved across from Gasfort Hill to protect the open flank, and were forced back towards Telegraph Hill. The situation was hopeless. Shortly after 10 a.m. Gorchakov ordered a general withdrawal, and with one last round from all their cannon, as if to sound a note of defiance in defeat, the Russians retreated to lick their wounds.[19]

The allies lost 1,800 casualties on the Chernaia river. The Russians counted 2,273 dead, almost 4,000 men wounded and 1,742 missing, most of them deserters who had used the morning mist and confusion of the battle to run away.* It was several days before the dead and

---

* In an attempt to stop them from deserting, the Russian officers had told their men that if they gave themselves up to the enemy their ears would be cut off and given to the Turks (whose military custom was to cut off ears to receive a reward); but even this had not prevented Russian troops from running off in large numbers.

wounded were cleared away (the Russians did not even come to collect theirs) and in that time there were many visitors who saw the frightful scene, not just nurses who came to help the wounded, but war tourists, who took trophies from the bodies of the dead. At least two British army chaplains took part in the plundering for souvenirs. Mary Seacole describes the ground 'thickly numbered with the wounded, some of them calm and resigned, others impatient and restless, a few filling the air with their cries of pain – all wanting water, and all grateful to those who administered it'. Thomas Buzzard, a British doctor with the Turkish army, was struck by how most of the dead 'lay on their faces, literally, to use the Homeric phrase, "biting the dust"', in contrast to the way they were usually depicted on their backs in classical paintings of battles (most of the Russians had been shot from the front while advancing up the hill and so had fallen forwards naturally).[20]

Somehow the Russians had contrived to lose against an enemy less than half their size. In his explanation to the Tsar, Gorchakov put the entire blame on the unfortunate General Read, arguing that he had failed to understand his order when he moved his men against the French on the Fediukhin Heights. 'It is grievous to think that if Read had carried out my orders to the letter, we might have ended with something like success and that at least a third of those brave troops who have been killed might have been alive today,' he wrote to the Tsar on 17 August. Alexander was not impressed by Gorchakov's attempt to shift the blame onto the dead general. He had wanted a success to approach the allies with proposals for a peace on favourable terms, and this setback had ruined all his plans. 'Our brave troops', he replied to Gorchakov, 'have suffered enormous losses *without any gain* [the Tsar's italics].' The truth was that both men were to blame for the needless slaughter: Alexander for insisting on an offensive when none was really possible; and Gorchakov for failing to withstand his pressure for attack.[21]

The defeat on the Chernaia was a catastrophe for the Russians. It was now only a question of time before Sevastopol would fall to the allies. 'I am sure that this is the second-to-last bloody act of our operations in the Crimea,' wrote Herbé to his parents on 25 August, after being wounded on the Chernaia; 'the last will be the capture of Sevastopol.' According to Nikolai Miloshevich, one of the defenders of the naval base, after the defeat 'the Russian troops lost all their trust in their officers and generals'. Another soldier wrote: 'The morning of 16 August was our last hope. By the evening it had disappeared. We began to say farewell to Sevastopol.'[22]

Realizing that the situation was hopeless, the Russians now prepared to evacuate Sevastopol, as Gorchakov had warned they would have to do if they were defeated on the Chernaia in his letter to the Minister of War on the eve of the battle. The evacuation plan centred on the building of a floating bridge across the sea harbour to the North Side, where the Russians would have a commanding position against the allied forces if they occupied the town on the southern side. The idea of a bridge was first advanced by General Bukhmeier, a brilliant engineer, in the first week of July. It was rejected by scores of engineers on the grounds that it would be impossible to build, especially where Bukhmeier had suggested, between Fort Nicholas and the Mikhailov Battery, where the sea harbour was 960 metres wide (which would make it one of the longest pontoon bridges ever built) and strong winds often made the water very rough. But the urgency of the situation persuaded Gorchakov to give his backing to the dangerous plan, and with several hundred soldiers to cart the timbers from as far as Kherson, 300 kilometres away, and vast teams of sailors to link them to the pontoons, Bukhmeier organized the building of the bridge, which was finally completed on 27 August.[23]

*

Meanwhile the allies were preparing for another assault on the Malakhov and the Redan. By the end of August they had come to realize that the Russians could not hold out much longer. The flow of deserters from Sevastopol had become a flood after the defeat on the Chernaia – and they all told the same stories of the terrible conditions in the town. Once the allied commanders recognized that a new assault would probably succeed, they were all the more determined to launch it as soon as possible. September was approaching, the weather would soon turn, and there was nothing they feared more than a second winter in the Crimea.

Pélissier took the lead. His position had been greatly strengthened by the routing of the Russians on the Chernaia. Napoleon had had his doubts about Pélissier's policy of persisting with the siege – he had been in favour of a field campaign – but with this new victory he set aside these reservations and gave his full support to his commander to push ahead for the victory he craved.

Where the French commander led, the British were obliged to follow: they lacked the troops or record of success to impose their military policies. After the catastrophe of 18 June, Panmure was determined to prevent a repeat of the unsuccessful British attack against the Redan, and for a while it seemed a new assault involving the British had been ruled out. But, with the victory at the Chernaia, things looked very different, and from the momentum of events a new logic developed that drew the British into a new assault.

By this time the French had sapped up to the abbatis of the Malakhov, only 20 metres from the fortress ditch, and were taking heavy casualties from the Russian guns. They had dug so close to the Malakhov that when they talked they could be clearly heard by the Russians. The British too had dug as far as they were able in the rocky ground towards the Redan – they were 200 metres from the fort – and were also losing many men. From the top of the naval library, the Russians could make out the facial features of the British soldiers in the exposed trenches. Their sharpshooters in the Redan could take them out without any difficulty as soon as they raised their heads. Every day, the allied armies were losing between 250 and 300 men. The situation was untenable. There was no point delaying an assault: if it could not succeed now, it would probably never do so, in which case the whole idea of continuing the siege should be abandoned before the onset of winter. That was the logic by which the British government now permitted Raglan's replacement, General James Simpson, to join Pélissier in planning a last attempt to take Sevastopol by an infantry assault.[24]

The date for the operation was set for 8 September. This time, in contrast to the botched attempt of 18 June, the assault was preceded by a massive bombardment of the Russian defences, beginning on 5 September, though even before that, from the last days of August, the intensity of the allies' artillery fire had been steadily growing. Firing

50,000 shells a day, and from a much closer range than ever before, the French and British guns caused immense damage. Hardly a building was left standing in the centre of the town, which looked as if it had been hit by an earthquake. The casualties were horrendous – something like a thousand Russians were killed or wounded every day from the last week of August and nearly 8,000 in the three days of the bombardment – but the last brave defenders of Sevastopol dared not think of abandoning the town. 'On the contrary,' recalled Ershov,

> even though we were defending a half-destroyed Sevastopol, essentially a phantom of a town, without any more significance except for its name, we prepared ourselves to fight for it to the last man in the streets: we moved our stores to the North Side, put up barricades and got ready to transform every ruined building into an armed citadel.[25]

The Russians were expecting an assault – the bombardment left no room for doubt about the allies' intentions – but they thought that it would come on 7 September, the anniversary of the battle of Borodino, their famous victory against the French in 1812 when one-third of Napoleon's army had been destroyed. When the attack did not come, the Russian defenders let down their guard. They were even more confused on the morning of the 8th, when the bombardment started up again with a furious intensity at 5 a.m. – the French and British guns firing more than 400 shells a minute – until suddenly at ten o'clock it stopped. Again the assault did not come. The Russians had anticipated that the allies would attack either at dawn or at dusk, as they had always done before. So they interpreted this new bombardment as an indication of a possible assault that evening. That idea was reinforced at 11 a.m. when the Russian lookouts on the Inkerman Heights reported what they believed to be a preparatory build-up of allied ships. The lookouts were not mistaken: the allied plan had called for the navy to join the assault by attacking the coastal defences of the city, but that morning the fine hot weather broke and a strong north-west wind and a heavy sea forced this part of the operation to be cancelled at the last moment; so the ships that had gathered at the mouth of the sea harbour did not look as if they could be ready for an imminent attack. And yet that is precisely what the allies had in store. On Bosquet's wise insistence, the assault had been set to start at noon – just when the Russians would be changing the guard and would expect it least.[26]

The allied plan was simple: to repeat the actions they had tried to carry out on 18 June but with a larger force and without the mistakes. This time, instead of the three divisions they had used on 18 June, the French would employ ten and a half divisions (five and a half against the Malakhov and five against the other bastions on the Town Front), a massive assault force of 35,000 men, supported by 2,000 brave Sardinians. The French commanders, who would give the signal for the assault to begin, had watches that were synchronized so as to avoid a repetition of the confusion caused by General Mayran's mistaking of the rocket signal to attack. At midday they gave the order to begin. The drummers beat their drums, the bugles sounded, the band played the *Marseillaise*, and with a resounding cheer of '*Vive l'Empereur!*', General MacMahon's Division, some 9,000 men in all, surged out of the French trenches, followed by the rest of the French infantry. Led by the courageous Zouaves, they ran towards the Malakhov, and, using planks and ladders to cross the ditch, climbed the walls of the fortress. The Russians were caught by surprise. At the time of the attack the garrison was being changed and many of the soldiers had retired for their lunch, thinking that the halt in the bombardment meant that all was safe. 'The French were in the Malakhov before our boys had a chance to grab their guns,' recalled Prokofii Podpalov, who watched in horror from the Redan. 'In a few seconds they had filled the fort with hundreds of their men, and hardly a shot was fired from our side. A few minutes later, the French flag was raised on the turret.'[27]

The Russians were overwhelmed by the sheer force of the French attack. They turned their backs and fled in panic from the Malakhov. Most of the soldiers in the bastion were teenagers from the 15th Reserve Infantry Division who had no experience of combat. They were no match for the Zouaves.

Once they had overrun the Malakhov, MacMahon's men swarmed across the Russian defences, joining the Zouaves in fearsome hand-to-hand fighting against the Russians on the Zherve (Gervais) Battery, on the left flank of the Malakhov, while other units launched attacks against the other bastions along the line. The Zouaves captured the Zherve Battery but on the right they were unable to dislodge the Kazan Regiment, who bravely stood their ground until reinforcements were brought up from Sevastopol, enabling the Russians to launch a counter-attack. There followed some of the fiercest fighting of the war. 'Time after time we charged them with our bayonets,' recalled one of the Russian soldiers, Anatoly Viazmitinov. 'We had no idea what our objective was, and never asked ourselves if it could succeed. We simply hurled ourselves forward, totally intoxicated by the excitement of the fight.' Within minutes the ground between the Zherve Battery and the Malakhov was covered with the dead, the Russians and the French all entangled; and with each successive charge another layer of dead was added to the heap, on which the two sides went on fighting, treading on the wounded and the dead, until the battlefield became a 'mound of bodies', as Viazmitinov later wrote, 'and the air was filled with a thick red dust from the bloody ground, making it impossible for us to see the enemy. All we could do was fire through the dust in their direction, making sure to keep our muskets parallel to the ground in front of us.' Eventually, with more troops arriving all the time, MacMahon's infantry overwhelmed the Russians with their superior rifle power and forced them to retreat. Then they consolidated their control of the Malakhov by building makeshift barricades – using the dead and even wounded Russians as human sandbags along with reclaimed gabions, fascines and embrasures from the half-destroyed defences – behind which they turned their heavy guns towards Sevastopol.[28]

Meanwhile, the British launched their own assault on the Redan. In some ways the Redan was much harder to capture than the Malakhov. The British could not dig their trenches in the rocky ground in front of it and would therefore have to run across this open space and then clamber over the abbatis under close-range fire from the enemy. The broad V-shape of the Redan also meant that the storming parties would be exposed to flanking fire as they crossed the ditch and climbed the parapet. It was also rumoured that the Redan had been mined by the Russians. But once the French had occupied the Malakhov, the Redan was more vulnerable to attack.

As in June, the British waited for the French to take the lead, but as soon as they saw the tricolour on the Malakhov they raced forward towards the Redan. Running through a storm of roundshot, grape and musketry, a good number of the storming party of a thousand men managed to cross the abbatis and climb down into the ditch, although at least half the ladders had been dropped along the way. There was chaos in the ditch as the stormers came under point-blank fire from the Russian gunners on the parapets above their heads. Some began to waver, unsure how to climb the parapet; others tried to find some shelter at the bottom of the ditch. But in the end a group of men succeeded in scrambling up the wall and climbing into the fortress. Most were killed, but they had set an example, and others followed them. Among them was Lieutenant Griffith of the 23rd (Royal Welch) Fusiliers:

> We rushed madly along the trenches, grapeshot flying about our ears. Several officers we met coming back wounded said they had been in the Redan and that the supports were only wanted to complete the victory. On we rushed impeded more and more by the wounded officers and men carried back from the front. . . . 'On the 23rd! This way!' cried the staff officers. We scrambled out of the trench into open ground. That was a fearful moment. I rushed across the space about 200 yards, I think, grapeshot striking the ground all the way and men falling down on all sides. When I got to the edge of the ditch of the Redan I found our men all mixed up in confusion but keeping up a steady fire on the enemy . . . [In the ditch] there were lots of men of different regiments all huddled together – scaling ladders placed against the parapet crowded with our fellows. Radcliffe and I got hold of the ladder and went up it to the top of the parapet where we were stopped by the press – wounded and dead men kept tumbling down on us – it was indeed an exciting and fearful scene.[29]

The ditch and the slopes leading up to the parapet quickly filled with new arrivals, like Griffith, who could not climb the parapet because of the 'press' created by the fighting above them. The interior of the Redan was strongly defended with a series of traverses manned by the Russians feeding in their supports from behind; the few stormers who managed to fight their way into the fortress were hemmed in by them, vastly outnumbered and subjected to a devastating crossfire from both flanks at the northern end of the V-shape. The morale of the soldiers crowded in the ditch began to fall apart. Ignoring the commands of their officers to climb the parapet, 'the men clung to the outside of the salient angle in hundreds', recalled Lieutenant Colin Campbell, watching from the trenches, 'although they were swept down by the flanking fire in scores'. Many lost their nerve entirely and ran back to the trenches, which themselves were full of men waiting for the order to attack. Discipline broke down. There was a general stampede to the rear. Griffith joined the panic flight:

> Feeling disgraced, tho' I had done my best, unwillingly I turned to follow the men. I saw our trench at some distance but I never expected to reach it. The fire was fearful and I kept tumbling over the dead and wounded men who literally covered the ground. At last to my great joy I gained our Parallels and tumbled somehow into the trench . . . I should have said that on the way a bullet hit my water-bottle, which was slung at my side, spilt all the water and glanced off. A stone thrown up by a grapeshot hit me in the leg but didn't hurt me much. Soon after we found . . . a few men and by degrees mustered most of the unhurt. It was very melancholy we found so many missing.

Henry Clifford was among the officers who tried in vain to restore discipline: 'When the men ran in from the parapet of the Redan. . . . we drew our swords and beat the men and implored them to stand and not run, that all would be lost; but many fled. The trench where they ran in was so crowded that it was impossible to move without walking over the wounded who lay under our feet.'[30]

It was hopeless to attempt to renew the attack with these panic-stricken troops, most of whom were young reservists. General Codrington, the commander of the Light Division in charge of the assault, suspended further action for the day – a day when the British had counted 2,610 fallen men, 550 of them dead. Codrington intended to renew the attack with the battle-hardened troops of the Highland Brigade the next day. But it never came to that. Later that evening the Russians decided that they could not defend the Redan against the French guns installed in the Malakhov, and evacuated the fortress. As one Russian general explained in perhaps the earliest account of these events, the Malakhov was 'only one fortress, but it was the key to Sevastopol, from which the French would be able to bombard the town at will, killing thousands of our soldiers and civilians, and probably destroying the pontoon bridge to cut off our escape to the North Side'.[31]

Gorchakov ordered the evacuation of the entire South Side of Sevastopol. Military installations were blown up, stores were set alight, and crowds of soldiers and civilians prepared themselves to cross the floating bridge to the North Side. A good number of the Russian soldiers believed the decision to evacuate the city was a betrayal. They had seen the previous day's fighting as a partial victory, in so far as they had beaten off the enemy's attacks on all the bastions except the Malakhov, and they did not understand, or refused to acknowledge, that what they had just lost was indispensable to the continued defence of the town. Many of the sailors did not want to leave Sevastopol, where they had spent their lives, and some even protested. 'We cannot leave, there is no authority to order us,' proclaimed one group of sailors, referring to the absence of a naval chief following the death of Nakhimov.

> The soldiers can leave but we have our naval commanders, and we have not been told by them to go. How could we leave Sevastopol? Surely, everywhere the assault has been repulsed, only the Malakhov has been taken by the French, but tomorrow we can take it back, and we will remain at our posts! ... We must die here, we cannot leave, what would Russia say of us?[32]

The evacuation began at seven o'clock in the evening and went on all night. On the sea harbour quayside at Fort Nicholas a huge crowd of soldiers and civilians assembled to cross the floating bridge. The wounded and the sick, women with young children, the elderly with walking sticks, were all mixed up with soldiers, sailors, horses and artillery on carriages. The evening sky was illuminated by the flames of burning buildings, and the sound of the guns on the distant bastions was confused with explosions in Sevastopol, forts and ships, as the Russians blew up anything of use to the enemy that could not be removed. Expecting the British and the French to appear at any moment, people in the crowd began to panic, to push and shove each other to get closer to the bridge. 'You could smell the fear,' recalls Tatyana Tolycheva, who was waiting at the bridge with her husband and her son. 'There was a terrific racket – people screaming, weeping, wailing, the wounded groaning, and shells flying in the sky.' Bombs were dropping on the harbour all the time: one killed eight allied prisoners of war with a direct hit on the crowded quayside. The soldiers, horses and artillery were the first to cross, followed by the ox-drawn carts laden down with cannonballs, stacks of hay and wounded men. There was silence as they crossed the bridge – nobody was sure if they would make it to the other side. The sea was rough, the north-west wind still blowing strong, and the rain was coming down into their faces as they made their way across the sea harbour. The civilians formed a line to cross the bridge. They could take only what they carried in their arms. Among them was Tolycheva:

> On the bridge there was a crush – nothing but confusion, panic, fear! The bridge almost gave way from the weight of all of us, and the water came up to our knees. Suddenly someone became scared and began to shout, 'We're drowning!' People turned around and tried to make it back onto the shore. There was a struggle, with people stepping over each other. The horses became scared and began to rear. . . . I thought we were going to die and said a prayer.

By eight o'clock the next morning the crossing was complete. A signal was given to the last defenders to leave the bastions and set fire to the town. With the sole remaining pieces of artillery they sank the last ships of the Russian Black Sea Fleet in the sea harbour before crossing to the North Side.[33]

From the Star Fort, Tolstoy watched the downfall of Sevastopol. During the storming he had been placed in charge of a five-gun battery and had been one of the town's last defenders to cross the pontoon bridge. It was his birthday, he was 27, but the sight before him now was enough to break his heart. 'I wept when I saw the town in flames and the French flags on our bastions,' he wrote to his aunt, 'and generally, in many respects, it was a very sad day.'[34]

Looking back on the burning city that morning was Alexandra Stakhova, a nurse engaged in the removal of the wounded from Sevastopol. She described the scene in a letter to her family the following day:

> The whole city was engulfed in flames – from everywhere the sound of explosions. It was a scene of terror and chaos! . . . Sevastopol was covered in black smoke, our own troops were setting fire to the town.

The sight brought tears to my eyes (I seldom cry) and that eased the burden on my heart, for which I thank God ... How hard it has been to experience and see all this, it would have been easier to die.[35]

The Great Fire of Sevastopol – a repeat of Moscow 1812 – continued for several days. Parts of the city were still burning when the allied armies entered it on 12 September. There they found some dreadful scenes. Not all the wounded had been taken from Sevastopol – there were too many of them to transport – and about 3,000 were abandoned without food or water in the town. Dr Giubbenet, who had been responsible for the evacuation of the hospitals, had left the wounded there on the assumption that they would soon be found by the allies. He had no idea it would be four days before the allies occupied the town. He was later mortified to read the Western press reports, like this one by Russell of *The Times*:

> Of all the pictures of the horrors of war which have ever been presented to the world, the hospital of Sevastopol offered the most heartrending and revolting. Entering one of these doors, I beheld such a sight as few men, thank God, have ever witnessed: ... the rotten and festering corpses of the soldiers, who were left to die in their extreme agony, untended, uncared for, packed as close as they could be stowed ... saturated with blood which oozed and trickled through upon the floor, mingling with the droppings of corruption. Many lay, yet alive, with maggots crawling about in their wounds. Many, nearly mad by the scene around them, or seeking escape from it in their extremest agony, had rolled away under the beds and glared out on the heart stricken spectators. Many, with legs and arms broken and twisted, the jagged splinters sticking through the raw flesh, implored aid, water, food, or pity, or, deprived of speech by the approach of death or by dreadful injuries in the head or trunk, pointed to the lethal spot. Many seemed bent alone on making their peace with Heaven. The attitudes of some were so hideously fantastic as to root one to the ground by a sort of dreadful fascination. The bodies of numbers of men were swollen and bloated to an incredible degree; and the features, distended to a gigantic size, with eyes protruding from the sockets and the blackened tongue lolling out of the mouth, compressed tightly by the teeth which had set upon it in the death-rattle, made one shudder and reel round.[36]

The sight of the devastated city inspired awe in all who entered it. 'Sevastopol presents the most curious spectacle that one can imagine,' wrote Baron Bondurand, the French military intendant, to Marshal de Castellane on 21 September.

> We ourselves had no idea of the effects of our artillery. The town is literally crushed to bits. There is not a single house that our projectiles missed. There are no roofs left at all, and almost all the walls have been destroyed. The garrison must have taken huge casualties in this siege where all our blows counted. It is a testimony to the indisputable spirit and endurance of the Russians, who held on for so long and only surrendered when their position became untenable with our capture of the Malakhov.

There were signs of destruction everywhere. Thomas Buzzard was startled by the beauty of the ruined town:

> In one of the handsomest streets there was a fine classical building, said to be a church, built of stone, much in the style of the Parthenon of Athens. Some of its huge columns had been almost knocked to pieces. On entering we found that a shell had come through the roof and exploded on the floor, shattering it to pieces. It was strange to turn from this and look into a green and peaceful garden close to it with the trees in full leaf.[37]

For the troops, the occupation of Sevastopol was an opportunity for pillage. The French were organized in their looting and it was endorsed by their officers, who joined in plundering Russian property and sending home their stolen trophies, as if this were a completely normal part of war. In a letter to his family on 16 October, Lieutenant Vanson made a long list of the souvenirs he was sending them, including a silver and gold medallion, a porcelain service, and a sabre taken from a Russian officer. A few weeks later he wrote again: 'We are continuing to pillage Sevastopol. There are no real curiosities remaining to be found, but there was one thing I really wanted, a nice chair, and I am pleased to inform you that I found one yesterday. It is missing a foot and the upholstered seat, but the back is beautifully carved.' Compared to the French, the British troops were slightly more restrained. On 22 September Thomas Golaphy wrote to his family on the back of a Russian document. He talked of the soldiers

> taking everything we could lay hands upon and selling it to anyone who would like to buy it and there was some splendid articles sold very cheap but there was no one here but the Greeks to buy it, we was not allowed to plunder the town the same as the French, they could go into all parts of it but there was only one part that was facing our works that we was allowed to enter.[38]

If the British trailed the French in pillaging, they far outstripped them in their binge drinking. The occupying troops found a huge supply of alcohol in Sevastopol, and the British, in particular, set about the task of drinking it with the licence they assumed they had been given by their officers for their hard-earned victory. Drunken fights, insubordination and indiscipline became a major problem in the British camp. Alarmed by reports of 'mass drunkenness' among the troops, Panmure wrote to Codrington, warning him of 'the extreme hazard to your army physically which must exist if this evil be not speedily arrested, as well as the disgrace which is daily accumulating on our national character'. He called for the soldiers' field allowance to be cut, and for the full force of martial law to be applied. From October to the following March, 4,000 British troops were court-martialled for drunkenness; most of them were given fifty lashes for their misbehaviour, and many also lost up to a month's pay, but the drunkenness continued until the stocks of alcohol ran out, and the troops left the Crimea.[39]

*

The downfall of Sevastopol was cheered by crowds in London and Paris. There was dancing and drinking and much singing of patriotic anthems in the streets. Many people thought that this meant the end of the war. The capture of the naval base and the destruction of the Tsar's Black Sea Fleet had been the focus of the allied war plans, at least in so far as these were communicated to the general public, and these had now been achieved. But in fact, in military terms, the loss of Sevastopol was a long way from the defeat of Russia: a large-scale land invasion to capture Moscow or a victory in the Baltic against St Petersburg would be needed to accomplish that.

If some Western leaders hoped that the capture of Sevastopol would force the Tsar to sue for peace, they were quickly disappointed. The Imperial Manifesto announcing the loss to the Russian people struck a note of defiance. On 13 September Alexander moved to Moscow, entering it in a staged re-enactment of Alexander I's dramatic appearance in the 'national' capital after the invasion by Napoleon in July 1812, when cheering crowds had greeted him on his way to the Kremlin. 'Remember 1812,' the Tsar wrote to Gorchakov, his commander-in-chief, on 14 September. 'Sevastopol is not Moscow. The Crimea is not Russia. Two years after the burning of Moscow, our victorious troops were in Paris. We are still the same Russians and God is with us.'[40]

Alexander thought of ways to carry on the war. In late September he wrote a detailed plan for a new Balkan offensive in 1856: it would take the war to Russia's enemies on European soil by instigating partisan and nationalist revolts among the Slavs and Orthodox. According to Tiutcheva, Alexander 'reprimanded anyone who talked of making peace'. Nesselrode was certainly in favour of peace negotiations, and told the Austrians that he would welcome proposals from the allies if they were 'compatible with our honour'. But for the moment all the talk in St Petersburg and Moscow was about continuing the war, even if that talk was largely bluff to pressure the allies into offering better peace terms to Russia. The Tsar knew that the French were tired of the war, and that Napoleon would favour peace, once he had achieved the 'glorious victory' that the fall of Sevastopol symbolized. It was the British who would be less inclined to end the war, Alexander realized. For Palmerston, the campaign in the Crimea had always been the start of a broader war to reduce the power of the Russian Empire in the world, and the British public, as far as one can tell, were generally in favour of continuing. Even Queen Victoria could not endure the idea that the British army's 'failure on the Redan should be', as she put it, 'our last *fait d'armes*'.[41]

After neglecting the fronts in Asia Minor and the Caucasus for so long, the main concern for Britain was the Russian siege of Kars. Alexander stepped up pressure on the Turkish fortress town to strengthen his negotiating position in peace talks with the British following the downfall of Sevastopol. The capture of Kars would open the way for the Tsar's troops to advance towards Erzurum and Anatolia, threatening British interests on the land route to India. Alexander had ordered the attack against Kars in June in the hope of diverting allied troops from Sevastopol. A Russian force of 21,000 infantry, 6,000 Cossacks and 88 guns led by General Muraviev advanced from the Russian–Turkish border to Kars, 70 kilometres away, where a Turkish force of 18,000 troops under the command of the British General William Williams, knowing they would be defeated in an open battlefield, had spent all their energies on the fortification of the town. Among the many foreign officers in the Turkish force at Kars – a legion of Polish, Italian and Hungarian refugees from the failed rebellions of 1848–9 – there were many skilful engineers. The Russians launched their first attack on 16 June, but when this was vigorously repulsed they laid siege to the city, intending to starve the city's defenders into surrendering. The Russians saw the siege of Kars as their answer to the allied siege of Sevastopol.

The Turks favoured sending an expeditionary force to relieve Kars. Omer Pasha pleaded with the British and the French to let him redeploy his Turkish forces in Kerch and Evpatoria (some 25,000 infantry and 3,000 cavalry) and 'throw myself upon some point of the coast of Circassia, and by menacing from thence the communication of the Russians, oblige them to abandon the siege of Kars'. The allied commanders were reluctant to make a decision and passed the matter on to the politicians in London and Paris, who were at first unwilling to move the Turkish contingent from the Crimea, and then approved the plan in general terms but argued over the best way to get to Kars. It was only on 6 September that Omer Pasha left the Crimea for Sukhumi, on the Georgian coast, from where it would take his army of 40,000 men several weeks to cross the southern Caucasus.

Meanwhile Muraviev was getting restless before Kars. The siege had taken a terrible toll on the town's defenders, who suffered from shortages of food and from cholera; but Sevastopol had fallen, the Tsar needed Kars quickly, and with Omer Pasha's army on its way, he could not wait for the blockade to break the morale of the Turks. On 29 September the Russians launched a full-scale assault on the bastions of Kars. Despite their weakened state, the Turkish forces fought extremely well, deploying their artillery to great effect, and the Russians suffered heavy casualties, about 2,500 dead and twice that number wounded, compared to about 1,000 Turkish casualties. Muraviev returned to his siege tactics. By mid-October, when Omer Pasha, after several delays, was only just beginning his long march south from Sukhumi, the defenders of Kars were starving; the hospital was packed with victims of scurvy. Women were bringing their children to the house of General Williams and leaving them there for him to feed. The horses of the town had all been slaughtered for their meat. People were reduced to eating grass and roots.

On 22 October word arrived that Selim Pasha, Omer Pasha's son, had landed an army of 20,000 men on the north coast of Turkey and was marching towards Erzurum. But by the time he reached the town, only a few days' march away, the situation in Kars had become even worse: a hundred people were dying every day, and soldiers were deserting all the time. Among those who were fit to struggle on, morale sank to an all-time low. Heavy snowfalls at the end of October made it practically impossible for the Turkish relief forces to reach Kars. Omer Pasha's army was held up by Russian forces in Mingrelia, and then showed no sign of hurrying towards Kars, resting for five days in Zugdedi, the capital of Mingrelia, where the troops became distracted by pillaging and kidnapping children to sell as slaves. From there, they failed to make much headway in very heavy rain through the deeply forested and marshy territory. Selim Pasha's forces were even slower to advance from Erzurum. It turned out that he did not have 20,000 men, but less than half that number, far too few to defeat Muraviev's forces on their own, so Selim Pasha decided not to try. On 22 November a note was handed by a British diplomat to General Williams, informing him that Selim Pasha's army would not come to Kars. With all hope gone, Williams surrendered the garrison to Muraviev, who, to his credit, ensured that the 4,000 sick and wounded Turkish soldiers were well cared for, and distributed food to the 30,000 soldiers and civilians he had starved into submission.[42]

Having taken Kars, the Russians controlled more enemy territory than the allied powers. Alexander saw his victory at Kars as a counterbalance to the loss of Sevastopol, and now thought the time was right to put out peace feelers to the Austrians and the French. Direct contact was established between Paris and St Petersburg at the end of November, when Baron von Seebach, Nesselrode's son-in-law, who looked after Russia's interests in the French capital, was approached by Count Walewski, Napoleon's cousin and Foreign Minister. Walewski was 'personally well-inclined' towards peace talks with Russia, Seebach reported back to Nesselrode, but had warned that Napoleon was 'dominated by his fear of England' and determined to maintain his alliance with that country. If Russia wanted peace, it would have to make proposals – starting with the limitation of Russia's naval power in the Black Sea – that enabled France to overcome the reluctance of the British to start talks.[43]

That was not going to be easy. With the fall of Kars, the British government was even more determined to go on with the war and take it into new theatres. In December the cabinet discussed sending half the force in the Crimea to Trebizond to cut off a potential Russian advance from Kars towards Erzurum and Anatolia. Plans for the operation were prepared for consideration by the allied war council in January. There was also talk of a major new campaign in the Baltic, where the destruction of the naval base at Sveaborg on 9 August had shown the allied leaders what could be achieved with steam-powered armoured ships and long-range guns. Beyond Westminster, there was an almost unanimous consensus that the fall of Sevastopol should be only the start of a broader war against Russia. Even Gladstone, a firm advocate of peace, was obliged to ackowledge that the British public did not want the war to end. The Russophobic press called on Palmerston to launch a spring campaign in the Baltic. It called for the destruction of Kronstadt, the blockade of St Petersburg, and the expulsion of the Russians from Finland: Russia was to be destroyed as a threat to European liberty and to British interests in the Near East.[44]

Palmerston and his 'war party' had their own agenda for a broad crusade against Russia. It went well beyond the original objective of the war – the defence of Turkey – in its plans for the permanent containment and weakening of Russia as an imperial rival to Britain. 'The main and real object of the war is to curb the aggressive ambition of Russia,' Palmerston had written to Clarendon on 25 September. 'We went to war not so much to keep the Sultan and his Musselmen in Turkey, as to keep the Russians out of Turkey; but we have an equally strong interest in keeping the Russians out of Norway and Sweden.' Palmerston proposed continuing the war on a pan-European scale as well as in Asia 'to contain the power of Russia'. As he saw it, the Baltic states, like Turkey, if they joined this enlarged war, would be established as '*part of a long line of circumvallation* to confine the future extension of Russia'. Palmerston insisted that Russia had 'not yet been beaten half enough' and demanded that the war go on for at least another year – until the Crimea and the Caucasus had been detached from Russia and Polish independence had been won.[45]

It was not just a question of surrounding Russia with Western-aligned states, but of a broader 'war of nationalities' to break up the Russian Empire from within. The idea was first advanced by Palmerston in his memorandum to the cabinet in March 1854. Then he had proposed to return the Crimea and the Caucasus to the Ottoman Empire; to give Finland to Sweden, the Baltic provinces to Prussia, and Bessarabia to Austria; and to restore Poland as a kingdom independent from Russia. Such ideas had been discussed and tacitly acknowledged as the unofficial war aims of the British cabinet by various figures in the Westminster establishment during the Crimean War. The basic premise, as explained by the Duke of Argyll in a letter to Clarendon in October 1854, was that while the Four Points were 'good and sufficient' as war aims in so far as they allowed 'for any amount of change or extension', the dismemberment of Russia would become desirable and possible 'if and when a successful war can place it within our reach'. With the fall of Sevastopol, these ideas were advanced once again within the inner circles of Palmerston's war cabinet. 'I suspect Palmerston would wish the war to glide imperceptibly into a war of nationalities, as it is called, but would not like to profess it openly now,' the political diarist Charles Greville wrote on 6 December.[46]

Throughout the autumn of 1855 Palmerston supported the idea of preparing for a continuation of the war the following spring, if only as a means of keeping up the pressure on the Russians to accept the punitive peace terms he had in mind. He was furious with the French and the Austrians for opening direct talks with the Russians, and for considering relatively moderate terms based on the Four Points. He was convinced, as he wrote to Clarendon on 9 October, that 'Nessel-rode and his spies' were 'working on the French in Paris and Brussels', and that, 'with the Austrians and Prussians cooperating in Nessel-rode's endeavours', it would require 'all our steadiness and skill to avoid being drawn into a peace which would disappoint the first expectations of the country and leave unaccomplished the real objects of the war'. In the same note Palmerston outlined what he saw as the minimum conditions of a settlement: Russia was to end its interference in the Danubian principalities, where the Sultan was to 'give the princes a good constitution to be previously agreed to by England and France'; the Danube delta was to be given up by Russia to Turkey; and the Russians were to lose all their naval bases in the Black Sea, along with any 'portions of territory which are in their hands rallying places for attacks upon her neighbours', territories among which he included the Crimea and the Caucasus. As for Poland, Palmerston was no longer sure whether Britain could support a war of independence, but he thought the French should run with the idea, which had been advanced by Walewski, to put further pressure on the Russians to accept a diminution of their power in the world.[47]

But the French were less enthusiastic. Having done most of the fighting, their views carried at least as much weight as Palmerston's. Without the support of France, Britain could not think of continuing the war, let alone involving new allies from among the European powers, who mostly preferred French to British leadership.

France had suffered more than Britain from the war. Apart from its losses on the battlefield, the French army was very badly hit by various diseases, mainly scurvy and typhus but also cholera, during the autumn and winter of 1855. The problems were similar to those of the British the previous winter: the situation of the two armies had been reversed. Where the British had drastically improved their sanitation and medical provision during the past year, the French had let their standards drop as more troops had arrived in the Crimea and they lacked the resources to cope with the increased demand.

In these circumstances it was impracticable for Napoleon to think of fighting on. He could suspend operations until the following spring, by which time his army might have recovered. But the soldiers were becoming dangerously demoralized, as their letters home made clear, and they would not stand for another winter in the Crimea. Writing on 13 October, Captain Charles Thoumas, for example, thought there was a danger of a revolt by the army if it was not brought back to France soon. Frédéric Japy, a lieutenant in the Zouaves, also thought the soldiers would rise up against their officers; they were not prepared to go on with a war which they now felt had been for mainly British interests. Henri Loizillon was afraid a new campaign would draw the French into an endless war against a country that was too big to defeat – a lesson he believed they should have learned from 1812.[48]

Public opinion in France would not support the military campaign for much longer. The French economy had been badly affected by the war: trade was down; agriculture suffered labour shortages as a result of military conscriptions that had already taken 310,000 Frenchmen to the Crimea; and in the cities there were shortages of food which began to be widely felt in November 1855. According to the reports of the local prefects and procurators, there was a real danger of civil unrest if the war went on through the winter. Even the provincial press, which had led the calls for war in 1854, were now urging an end to it.[49]

Always sensitive to public pressure, Napoleon spent the autumn looking for a way to end the war without alienating the British. He was keen to make the most politically of the 'glorious victory' that the fall of Sevastopol symbolized, but did not want to endanger his alliance with Britain, which was the cornerstone of his foreign policy. Napoleon was not opposed in principle to the idea of a broader war. He was sympathetic to Palmerston's vision of using the war against Russia to redraw the map of Europe, fostering national revolutions to break down the 1815 system and leave France in a dominant position on the Continent at the expense of Russia and the Holy Alliance. But he would not get involved in a campaign against Russia in the Caucasus and Asia Minor, where he felt that British interests were mainly served. As Napoleon saw it, the only way he could justify the continuation of a large-scale war against Russia would be if it achieved his grand dreams for the European continent. On 22 November Napoleon wrote to Queen Victoria suggesting three alternatives: a limited defensive war of attrition; peace negotiations on the basis of the Four

Points; or an 'appeal to all the nationalities, the re-establishment of Poland, the independence of Finland and of Hungary'. As Napoleon explained, he personally favoured peace, but offered to discuss this grand proposal for a broader European war, if Britain felt that peace was not acceptable on the Four Points. 'I could comprehend a policy', he wrote to Victoria, 'which would have a certain grandeur and would put the results aimed at on a level with the sacrifices to be made.'

Napoleon's proposal was almost certainly disingenuous, a clever ploy to force the British to join peace talks. He knew that the British were not prepared for a Napoleonic war of national liberation on the Continent. Yet there are hints that he might have been prepared to launch this broader war if Palmerston had called his bluff. In 1858 Napoleon would tell Cowley that France had wanted peace and that was why he had been forced to end the war; but equally, if he had been forced into a renewal of the war by Palmerston, he would have been determined 'not to make peace until a better equilibrium [had been] secured for Europe'.[50]

Whatever the Emperor's intentions, Walewski, his Foreign Minister, who strongly favoured an immediate peace, was evidently using the threat of Napoleon supporting a revolutionary war to bring Britain, Austria and Russia to peace negotiations on the basis of the Four Points. Napoleon took part in this game of threats. He wrote to Walewski for the attention of Clarendon:

> I want peace. If Russia agrees to the neutralization of the Black Sea, I will make peace with them whatever the objections of England. But if, in the spring, it has come to nothing, I will appeal to the nationalities, above all to the nation of the Poles. The war will have as its principle, not the rights of Europe, but the interests of individual states.

If Napoleon's threat of a revolutionary war was almost certainly empty, his threat of a separate peace with Russia certainly was not. Behind the establishment of direct contact with St Petersburg was the influential party led by the Emperor's half-brother, the Duc de Morny, a railway speculator who saw in Russia 'a mine to be exploited by France'. In October Morny had established contact with Prince Gorchakov, the Russian ambassador in Vienna and shortly to become the Foreign Minister, with the offer of a Franco-Russian deal.[51]

Alarmed by these French initiatives, the Austrians intervened. Count Buol, their Foreign Minister, approached Bourqueney, the French ambassador in Vienna, and together with Morny, who ascertained from Gorchakov what terms the Russians were likely to accept, they worked out a set of peace proposals to be imposed on Russia as an Austrian ultimatum with French and British support 'for the integrity of the Ottoman Empire'. The Franco-Austrian terms were essentially a rewording of the Four Points, though Russia was now to surrender part of Bessarabia so as to be separated altogether from the Danube, and the neutralization of the Black Sea was to be achieved through a Russo-Turkish convention rather than a general peace treaty. Although the Russians had already accepted the Four Points as a basis of negotiations, a fifth was now added reserving the right of the victorious powers to include further undefined conditions at the peace conference 'in the interest of Europe'.[52]

The French and Austrian peace proposals arrived in London on 18 November. The British government, which had merely been informed of the progress of the Austro-French negotiation, was offended at the manner in which the agreement had been reached by the two Catholic powers, Palmerston suspecting that Russian influence had played a part in softening the proposed terms, which he was determined to reject. There was no mention of the Baltic, and no guarantee against Russian aggression in the Black Sea. 'We stick to the great Principles of Settlement which are required for the future security of Europe,' he wrote to Clarendon on 1 December. 'If the French government change their opinion, responsibility will rest with them, and the People of the two countries will be told of it.' Clarendon was more cautious, as ever. He feared that France might make a separate peace, and that, if it did so, Britain would be unable to fight alone. The Foreign Minister won some minor amendments to the terms – the neutralization of the Black Sea was to be agreed by a general treaty and the fifth point was to contain 'particular conditions' – but otherwise he favoured acceptance of the French and Austrians terms. With the help of the Queen, he persuaded Palmerston to go along with the plan, at least for the time being, to prevent a separate Franco-Russian peace, arguing that the Tsar was likely to reject the proposals in any case, allowing Britain to resume hostilities and press for harsher terms.[53]

Clarendon was almost right. The Tsar was in a warlike mood throughout that autumn. According to a senior Russian diplomat, he 'was little disposed to make terms with our adversaries' at a moment when they were about to experience the difficulties of a second winter in the Crimea. Napoleon's desire for peace suggested to the Tsar that Russia might still have a chance to secure a better ending to the war, if it kept fighting long enough to bring the internal problems of France to a head. In a revealing letter to his commander-in-chief, Gorchakov, Alexander declared that he saw no hope of an early termination of hostilities. Russia would continue with the war until France was forced to sign a peace by the outbreak of disorders, caused by the bad harvest and the growing discontent of the lower classes:

> Former revolutions always began in this manner and it may well be that a general revolution is not far away. This I regard as the most probable conclusion to the present war; neither from Napoleon nor from England do I expect a sincere desire for peace on terms compatible with our views and, as long as I live, I will accept no others.[54]

Nobody was able to persuade the Tsar to back down from his belligerent stance. Seebach came with a personal message from Napoleon urging him to accept the proposals, or run the risk of losing half his empire, if hostilities against Russia were resumed. News arrived that Sweden had finally agreed a military treaty with the Western powers on 21 November – an ominous development for Russia if the allies were to launch a new campaign in the Baltic. Even Frederick William IV, the Prussian king, declared that he might be forced to join the Western powers against Russia, if Alexander continued with a war that 'threatened the stability of all legitimate government' on the Continent. 'I beg you, my dear nephew,' he wrote to Alexander, 'go as far as you can in your concessions, weighing carefully the consequences for the true interests of Russia, for Prussia and the whole of Europe, if this atrocious war is continued. Subversive passions, once unchained, could have revolutionary effects that nobody could calculate.' Yet, in the face of all these warnings, Alexander remained adamant. 'We have reached the utmost limit of what is possible and compatible with Russia's honour,' he wrote to Gorchakov on 23 December. 'I will never accept humiliating conditions and am convinced that every true

Russian feels as I do. It only remains for us – crossing ourselves – to march straight ahead and by our united efforts to defend our native land and our national honour.'[55]

Two days later Alexander finally received the Austrian ultimatum with the allied terms. The Tsar called a council of his father's most trusted advisers to consider the Russian reply. Older and calmer heads than the Tsar's prevailed at this meeting in the Winter Palace in St Petersburg. The key speech was made by Kiselev, the reformist Minister of State Domains, who had charge of the 20 million peasants owned by the state. He clearly spoke for the other councillors. Russia lacked the means to continue with the war, Kiselev argued. The neutral powers were moving to the side of the Western alliance, and it would be imprudent to run the risk of fighting against the whole of Europe. Even a resumption of hostilities against the Western powers was unwise: Russia could not win, and it would result in even harsher peace terms from the enemy. While the mass of the Russian people shared the Tsar's patriotic feelings, Kiselev believed, there were elements that might begin to waver if the war became prolonged – there was the possibility of revolutionary disturbances. There were already signs of serious unrest among the peasantry, who were carrying the main burden of the war. They should not reject the Austrian proposals, argued Kiselev, but they might propose amendments to uphold Russia's territorial integrity. The council agreed with Kiselev's views. A reply was sent to the Austrians accepting their peace terms, but rejecting the cession of Bessarabia and the addition of the fifth point.

The Russian counter-proposals divided the allies. The Austrians, who had an interest in Bessarabia, immediately threatened to break off relations with Russia; but the French were not prepared to jeopardize the peace negotiations 'for a few scraps of land in Bessarabia!' as Napoleon explained to Queen Victoria in a letter on 14 January. The Queen was of the opinion that they should postpone negotiations to exploit divisions between Russia and the Austrians. It was sound advice. Like his father, Alexander feared the prospect of a war with Austria more than anything, and perhaps only this would bring him round to accept their proposals. On 12 January Buol informed the Russians that Austria would break off relations six days later if they failed to accept the peace terms. Frederick William expressed his support for the Austrian proposals in a telegraph to St Petersburg. The Tsar was now on his own.

On 15 January Alexander called another meeting of his council in the Winter Palace. This time Nesselrode made the key speech. He warned the Tsar that in the coming year the allies had decided to concentrate their forces on the Danube and Bessarabia, close to the Austrian border. Austria was likely to be drawn into the hostilities against Russia, and its decision would affect the remaining neutral powers, Sweden and Prussia, most decisively. If Russia refused to make peace now, it was in danger of finding itself in a war against the whole of Europe. The old Prince Vorontsov, formerly the viceroy of the Caucasus, supported Nesselrode. Speaking in a voice charged with emotion, he urged the Tsar to accept the Austrian terms, however painful they might be. Nothing more could be achieved through a continuation of the struggle, and resistance might lead to an even more humiliating peace, perhaps the loss of the Crimea, the Caucasus, even Finland and Poland. Kiselev agreed, adding that the people of Volhynia and Podolia in the Ukraine were just as likely as the Finns and Poles to rise up against Russian rule, if the war went on and Austrian troops approached those Western borderlands. Compared to these dangers, the sacrifices demanded by the ultimatum were insignificant. One by one, the Tsar's officials urged him to accept the terms for peace. Only Alexander's younger brother, the Grand Duke Constantine, advocated fighting on, but he had no office in the government, and however patriotic his appeal to the spirit of resistance of 1812 may have sounded to their Russian hearts, it lacked the reasoning to change their minds. The Tsar had decided. The next day the Austrians received a note from Nesselrode announcing his acceptance of their peace terms.[56]

*

In Sevastopol, the troops had been preparing to spend a second winter in the Crimea. No one really knew if they would have to fight again, but there were all sorts of rumours about being sent to the Danube or the Caucasus or some other quarter of the Russian Empire for a spring campaign. 'What will become of us?' wrote the battalion commander Joseph Fervel to Marshal de Castellane on 15 December. 'Where will we find ourselves next year? That is the question everybody asks but no one can answer.'[57]

Meanwhile, the troops occupied themselves with the daily business of survival on the heights above Sevastopol. Supplies improved and the soldiers were provided with better tents and wooden huts. The bars and shops at Kamiesh and Kadikoi were always full, and Mary Seacole's hotel did a roaring trade. There were various amusements to keep the soldiers occupied – theatre, gambling, billiards, hunting and horse racing on the plain while the weather allowed it. Boatloads of tourists arrived from Britain to see the famous battle sites and collect souvenirs – a Russian gun or sword, or a bit of uniform plundered from the bodies of the Russian dead that remained in the trenches for weeks and even months following the capture of Sevastopol. 'Only the English could have such ideas,' noted a French officer, who was amazed by the morbid fascinations of these war tourists.[58]

Towards the end of January, as news of the impending peace arrived, the allied soldiers began to fraternize increasingly with the Russians. Prokofii Podpalov, the young soldier who had taken part in the defence of the Redan, was among the Russians encamped by the Chernaia river, the site of the bloody battle in August. 'Every day we became more friendly with the French soldiers on the other side of the river,' he recalled. 'We were told by our officers to be polite to them. Usually, we would go up to the river and throw across (the river wasn't wide) some things for them: crosses, coins and so on; and the French would throw us cigarettes, leather purses, knives, money. This is how we talked: the French would say "Russkii camarade!" and the Russians: "Franchy brothers!"' Eventually, the French ventured over the river and visited the Russians in their camp. They drank and ate together, sang their songs for each other, and conversed in sign language. The visits became regular. One day, on leaving the Russian camp, the French soldiers handed out some cards on which they had written their names and regiments, and invited the Russians to visit them in their camp. They did not return for a few days, so Podpalov and some of his comrades decided to visit the French camp. They were amazed by what they saw. 'It was clean and tidy everywhere, there were even flowers growing by the tents of the officers,' Podpalov recalled. The Russians found their friends, and they were invited to their tents, where they drank rum with them. The French soldiers walked them back to the river, embraced them many times, and invited them to come again. A week later Podpalov returned to the French camp on his own, but he could not find his friends. They had left for Paris, he was told.[59]

12

Paris and the New Order

The Peace Congress was scheduled to begin at the French Foreign Ministry on the Quai d'Orsay in the afternoon of 25 February. By midday a large and excited crowd of spectators had gathered along the Quai d'Orsay to watch the arrival of the delegates. Stretching from the Pont de la Concorde to the rue d'Iéna, the onlookers had to be kept back by infantrymen and the gendarmerie to allow the carriages of the foreign dignitaries to pass by and pull up outside the newly completed buildings of the Foreign Ministry. The delegates arrived from one o'clock, each one cheered with cries of *'Vive la paix!'* and *'Vive l'Empereur!'* as they stepped out and entered into the building. Dressed in morning coats, the delegates assembled in the magnificent Hall of Ambassadors, where a large round table covered with green velvet and twelve armchairs around it had been laid out for the conference. The hall was a showcase for the decorative arts of the Second Empire. Satin crimson drapes hung from the walls. The only pictures were life-size portraits of Napoleon III and the Empress Eugénie, whose dominating gaze was a constant reminder to the delegates of France's new position as the arbiter of international affairs. On a console by the fireplace was a marble bust of Napoleon I – *persona non grata* in diplomatic circles for more than forty years. The Paris congress marked what Napoleon III wanted to believe was the return of Napoleonic France to the Concert of Europe.[1]

The choice of Paris as the venue for the congress was a sign of France's new position as the pre-eminent power on the Continent. The only other city where it might have taken place was Vienna, where the 1815 treaty had been signed, but the idea was rejected by the British, who had been suspicious of the diplomatic efforts of the Austrians since the beginning of the war. With diplomatic power shifting briefly to Paris, Vienna now appeared a city of the past. 'Who could deny that France comes out of all of this enlarged,' wrote Count Walewski to Napoleon, after learning that he would become the host of the congress. 'France alone will have profited in this struggle. Today she holds first place in Europe.'

The congress came only three months after the ending of the *Exposition Universelle*, a glittering international event rivalling London's Great Exhibition of 1851. Five million visitors had made their way through the exhibition halls on the Champs-Elysées. The two events placed Paris at the centre of Europe. This was a major victory for Napoleon III, whose decision to enter the war had always been influenced by his need for prestige at home and abroad. From the start of the peace talks the previous autumn, he had emerged as the key player, on whom all the other powers depended for the satisfaction of their interests. 'I am struck by the general deference to the Emperor Napoleon,' wrote Princess Lieven to Baroness Meyendorff on 9 November. 'The war has carried him pretty high, him and France: it has not enhanced England.'[2]

Peace talks had been going on throughout the winter, and by the time the delegates arrived in Paris, most of the controversial issues had already been resolved. The main sticking point was the tough stance of the British, who were in no hurry to end a war in which they had not had a major victory to satisfy their honour and justify their losses of the previous eighteen months. The capture of Sevastopol had, after all, been a French success. Urged on by a belligerent press and public, Palmerston reiterated the minimum conditions he had set out on 9 October, and threatened to keep on with the war, starting with a spring campaign in the Baltic, if the Russians failed to come to peace on British terms. He pressed Clarendon, his Foreign Secretary, to accept nothing less than complete Russian submission to his conditions at the Paris congress.

Despite his assertions, Palmerston's demands were in a state of flux. By November he had given up on the idea of securing independence for Circassia: no representative from that confused territory could be found to sign a treaty on its behalf. Yet he continued to insist that Russia should be deprived of the Caucasus and Central Asia, and was adamant that British firmness could obtain this. Russia was negotiating from a weak position, he wrote to Clarendon on 25 February, and was showing 'impudence' by arguing against the latest version of the British terms: the complete removal of Russian ships and arsenals from the Black Sea and the evacuation 'of every part of Turkish territory [including Kars] now occupied by Russian troops'. These conditions, Palmerston maintained, were 'not dishonourable to Russia . . . but only calculated to be manifest and patent pledges of the sincerity of her disclaimer of aggressive intentions'. Warning Clarendon about Count Orlov, the leader of the Russian delegation to Paris, he revealed his Russophobic attitudes:

> As to Orloff, I know him well – he is civil and courteous externally, but his inward mind is deeply impregnated with Russian insolence, arrogance and pride. He will do his best to bully without appearing to do so. He will stand out for every point which he thinks he has a chance of carrying, and he has all the cunning of a half civilized savage.[3]

The French and the Italians were disgusted by Palmerston's behaviour (Victor Emmanuel, the Piedmontese king, described him as a 'rabid animal'). Eager for peace, the French did not share the British inclination to punish Russia. They needed a rapprochement with the Russians to realize Napoleon's plans in Italy. Sympathetic to the cause of Italian unification, the French Emperor calculated that he could regain Savoy and Nice – captured by the French in 1792 but returned to Piedmont by the Congress of Vienna in 1815 – by helping the Piedmontese to conquer Lombardy-Venetia from the Austrians and expel the Habsburgs from the rest of Italy. Requiring the support or armed neutrality of the Russians to defeat the Austrians, the French were unwilling to go along with Palmerston's punitive initiatives against Russia. Their main point of difference with the British concerned the boundary of Bessarabia, a territory to be given back by Russia to Ottoman Moldavia. Palmerston, supported by Austria, took a tough line, arguing that Russia must not have any means of access to the Danube, the key Austrian anxiety. The Russians wanted to use Kars as a counterweight to Bessarabia, and the French supported them. But, under pressure from the British and the Austrians, Napoleon persuaded Orlov to accept a compromise at Paris. Overall, the Russians lost about a third of the Bessarabian land they had taken from the Turks in 1812, including the Danube delta, but they retained the Bulgarian communities of Bessarabia and the strategically important mountain ridge running south-east from Chotin. The British claimed a victory; Austria celebrated the liberation of the Danube; and the Russians felt the loss of (southern) Bessarabia as a national humiliation. It was the first territory the Russians had ceded to the Turks since the seventeenth century.[4]

On the other major issues the powers largely came to terms before the Paris congress met, guided by the Four Points agreed by the allies in 1854. The British had attempted to add a fifth point that would take away from Russia all its lands in the southern Caucasus (Circassia, Georgia, Erivan and Nakhichevan) but the Russians insisted that they held these territories by the Treaty of Adrianople and the Turks backed up their claims. However, the Russians were forced to surrender Kars. They also lost out in their efforts to avoid the full effect of the Third Point – the demilitarization of the Black Sea – by negotiating an exclusion for Nikolaev (20 kilometres inland from the coastline on the Bug river) and for the Sea of Azov.

On the question of the two Danubian principalities (the main subject of the First Point), there was a lively exchange of ideas. The British were broadly in favour of restoring Ottoman control. The French gave their backing to the Romanian liberals and nationalists who wanted to unite the principalities as an independent state. The Austrians were flatly opposed to the establishment of a nation state on their south-eastern border, as they had significant Slav minorities with national aspirations of their own. The Austrians rightly suspected that the French were backing the Romanians as a way of putting pressure on the Austrians to give up their interests in northern Italy. The three powers all agreed to end the Russian protectorate over the Danubian principalities and to guarantee the free commercial navigation of the Danube (the Second Point). But they could not agree on what to replace it with – other than the collective guarantee of the great powers under the nominal sovereignty of the Ottoman Empire with vague plans for elections at some point in the future to determine the views of the population in Moldavia and Wallachia.

As for the question of protecting the Christian subjects of the

Ottoman Empire (the Fourth Point), representatives of the allied powers met with the Grand Vizier Ali Pasha and the Tanzimat reformer Fuad Pasha (the Sultan's delegates to the Paris congress) in Constantinople in early January to impress on them the need for the Porte to show that it was serious about granting full religious and civil equality to the Empire's non-Muslims (including Jews). Reporting on the conference to Clarendon on 9 January, Stratford Canning was sceptical about the Turkish ministers' expressions of commitment to reform. He thought they were resentful of the foreign imposition of reform, that they saw it as undermining Ottoman sovereignty, and concluded that it would be difficult to get any protection for the Christians implemented properly. The Turks had always lived in the belief that the Christians were inferior, and no law passed by the Sultan could overcome that prejudice in the short period of time expected by the West. 'We may expect procrastination on the ground of respect of religious antipathies, popular prejudices, and unassociating habits,' wrote the veteran diplomat, who further warned that forcing through reforms might lead to a revolt by the Muslims against the Sultan's Westernizing policies. In response to a 21-point draft programme presented by the allies' representatives, the Sultan issued the Hatt-i Hümayun on 18 February. The decree promised to his non-Muslim subjects full religious and legal equality, rights of property, and open entry on merit to the Ottoman military and civil service. The Turks hoped that the reform would prevent any further European intervention into Ottoman affairs. They wanted the Hatt-i Hümayun excluded from the Paris talks, on the grounds of Turkish sovereignty. But the Russians – who had been named in the Fourth Point as one of the five great powers that would guarantee the security of the Sultan's Christian subjects – insisted that the issue was brought up. They were satisfied with the compromise solution – an international declaration joined by the Porte on the importance of Christian rights in the Ottoman Empire – and in their domestic propaganda the Russians even used it as a symbol of their 'moral victory' in the Crimean War. In one sense they were right, in so far as the Paris congress restored the status quo in the Church of the Nativity in Bethlehem and the Holy Sepulchre in Jerusalem, as Russia had demanded on behalf of the Greeks against the Latin claims, a point made by the Tsar many times. In a manifesto published on the day the peace was signed, Alexander invoked Providence for bringing to pass 'the original and principal aim of the war ... Russians! Your efforts and sacrifices have not been in vain!'[5]

Finally, there was the unspoken question of Poland. The idea of restoring Polish independence from Russia had first been advanced among the wartime allied diplomats by Walewski, the son of Napoleon I by the Polish Countess Marie Walewska. After the capture of Sevastopol, the French Emperor wanted to do something for Poland: an independent Polish kingdom fitted the Napoleonic ideal of a new Europe based on nation states to overthrow the 1815 settlement. At first Napoleon III supported Czartoryski's programme for the restoration of Congress Poland, the autonomous kingdom established by the Vienna treaty, whose freedoms had been undermined by the Russians. Later on, as the pre-congress talks got under way and it became apparent that none of the other powers would come out in favour of the Poles, Napoleon gave his backing to Czartoryski's pared-down list of conditions for Polish language rights and the defence of Poland against Russification. But Orlov would have none of this, insisting that Russia's rights in Poland were based, not on the 1815 treaty, but on the Russian conquest of Poland during the suppression of the Polish insurrection of 1830–31. In the interests of improving his relations with Russia, whose support would be needed against the Austrians in Italy, Napoleon decided to give up on the Poles. Nothing more was said about the Polish question at the Paris congress. Even Palmerston, who rarely missed a chance to confront Russia, advised Clarendon not to make an issue of the Poles. 'It would not be expedient,' he explained, 'to require Russia to restore the Kingdom of Poland.'

> The advantage to the Poles would be very doubtful; if they could be made independent of Russia, that indeed would be a great advantage both for the Poles and for Europe, but the difference either for the Poles or for Europe between the present condition of the Kingdom of Poland and that which was established by the Treaty of Vienna would be hardly worth all the difficulties which we should have to encounter in endeavouring to carry such a change into effect. The Russian Govt would say as it said in former years that Poland had rebelled and was conquered,

and that consequently it is held now by right of conquest and not by the Treaty of Vienna, and that therefore Russia is freed from the obligation of that Treaty. The Russians would moreover say that to make such a demand is to interfere in the internal affairs of Russia.

'Poor Poland!' remarked Stratford Canning to Lord Harrowby, one of Czartoryski's supporters. 'Her revival is a regular flying Dutchman. Never is – always to be.'[6]

With all the major issues resolved beforehand, the Paris congress proceeded smoothly without any major arguments. Just three sessions were required to draft the settlement. There was plenty of spare time for a full range of social engagements – banquets, dinners, concerts, balls and receptions, and a special celebration to mark the birth of the Prince Imperial, Louis-Napoleon, the only child of Napeolon III and the Empress Eugénie – before the diplomats finally assembled for the formal signing of the peace treaty at one o'clock on Sunday, 30 March.

Announcements of the peace were made throughout Paris. Telegraphs worked overtime to spread the news across the world. At two o'clock, the ending of the war was signalled by a thunderous cannonade fired by the guns at Les Invalides. Cheering crowds assembled in the streets, restaurants and cafés did a roaring trade, and in the evening the Paris sky was lit by fireworks. The next day, there was a parade on the Champ de Mars. French troops passed by the Emperor and Prince Napoleon, senior French commanders and foreign dignitaries, watched by tens of thousands of Parisians. 'There was an electrical tremor of excitement in the crowd,' claimed the official history of the congress, published the next year, 'and from the people there was a deafening cheer of national pride and enthusiasm that filled the Champ de Mars better than a thousand cannon could.'[7] Here was the glory and popular acclaim Napoleon had wanted when he went to war.

*

News of the peace arrived in the Crimea the next day – as long as it took for the telegram to be relayed from Paris to Varna and communicated by the underwater cable to Balaklava. On 2 April the allied guns in the Crimea were fired for the final time – in salute to mark the end of the war.

Six months were given to the allies to evacuate their armed forces. The British used the port of Sevastopol, where they oversaw the destruction of the magnificent docks by a series of explosions, while the French destroyed Fort Nicholas. There were enormous quantities of war *matériel* to be counted, loaded onto ships and taken home: captured guns and cannon, munitions, scrap metal and food supplies, including vast amounts of booty from the Russians. It was a complicated logistical operation to allocate it all to the various departments of the ministries of war, and many things were left behind, sold off to the Russians, or, like the English wooden huts and barracks, donated to them on condition that they were used 'for the inhabitants of the Crimea who had been made homeless by the war' (the Russians accepted the English offer but kept the huts and barracks for the army). 'It is an enormous endeavour to carry off, in just a few months, everything that was brought here over a period of two years,' wrote Captain Herbé to his family on 28 April. 'A large number of the horses and mules will have to be abandoned or sold off cheaply to the population of the Crimea, and I don't count on ever seeing mine again.' The animals were not the only means of transport to be sold off privately. The Balaklava railway was purchased by a company established by Sir Culling Eardly and Moses Montefiore, who wanted to use the equipment to build a new railroad between Jaffa and Jerusalem, a communication that would 'civilize and develop the resources of a district now wild and disorderly', according to Palmerston, who authorized the sale. It would serve the growing traffic of religious pilgrims to the Holy Lands. The Jaffa railway was never built and in the end the Balaklava line was sold to the Turks as scrap.[8]

Considering how long it took to ship all these supplies to the Crimea, the evacuation was completed speedily. By 12 July Codrington was ready to hand over possession of Balaklava to the Russians before departing with the final British troops on HMS *Algiers*. A stickler for military etiquette, the commander-in-chief was offended by the low rank and appearance of the Russian delegation sent to meet him and receive control of Balaklava:

There were about 30 Cossacks of the Don mounted and about 50 infantry. But such a lot! I could not have conceived the Russians would have sent such a dirty specimen of their troops. Never were [there] such figures in grey coats – so badly armed too – disreputable looking – we were all surprised and amused. I hope they intended to insult us by such specimens: if so, it must have rather turned the tables if they heard the remarks. The Guard marched on board – the Russians posted their sentries – and the evacuation was completed.[9]

Left behind in the Crimea were the remains of many thousands of soldiers. During the last weeks before their departure, the allied troops laboured hard to build graveyards and erect memorials to those comrades they would leave behind. In one of his last reports from the Crimea, William Russell described the military cemeteries:

The Chersonese is covered with isolated graves, with longer burial grounds, and detached cemeteries from Balaklava to the verge of the roadstead of Sevastopol. Ravine and plain – hill and hollow – the roadside and secluded valley – for miles around, from the sea to the Chernaia, present those stark-white stones, singly or in groups, stuck upright in the arid soil, or just peering over the rank vegetation which springs from beneath them. The French have taken but little pains with their graves. One large cemetery has been formed with great care and good taste near the old Inkerman camp, but in general our allies have not enclosed their burial places. ... The burial ground of the non-commissioned officers and men of the Brigade of Guards is enclosed by a substantial wall. It is entered by a handsome double gate, ingeniously constructed of wood, and iron hoops hammered out straight, and painted, which is hinged on two massive pillars of cut stone, with ornamental capitals, each surmounted by a cannon ball. There are six rows of graves, each row containing thirty or more bodies. Over each of these is either a tomb-stone or a mound, fenced in by rows of white stones, with the initials or sometimes the name of him who lies below, marked on the mound by means of pebbles. Facing the gate, and close to it stands a large stone cross. ... There are but few monumental stones in this cemetery; one is a stone cross, with the inscription, 'Sacred to the memory of Lieutenant A. Hill, 22nd Regiment, who died June 22, 1855. This stone was erected by his friends in the Crimea.' Another is 'In memory of Sergeant-Major Rennie, 93rd Highlanders. Erected by a friend.' . . . [Another] is to 'Quarter-master J. McDonald, 72nd Regiment, who died, on the 16th of September, from a wound received in the trenches before Sevastopol on the 8th of December, aged thirty-five years.'[10]

The British cemetery at Cathcart's Hill, 1855

After the allied armies left, the Russians, who had withdrawn towards Perekop during their evacuation, moved back to the southern towns and plains of the Crimea. The battlefields of the Crimean War returned to farms and grazing lands. Cattle roamed across the grave-yards of the allied troops. Gradually, the Crimea recovered from the economic damage of the war. Sevastopol was rebuilt. Roads and bridges were repaired. But in other ways the peninsula was permanently changed.

Most dramatically, the Tatar population had largely disappeared. Small groups had begun to leave their farms at the start of the conflict, but their numbers grew towards the end of the war, in line with their fear of reprisals by the Russians after the departure of the allied troops. There had already been reprisals for the atrocities at Kerch, with mass arrests, confiscations of property, and summary executions of 'suspicious' Tatars by the Russian military. The inhabitants of the Baidar valley petitioned Codrington to help them leave the Crimea, fearing what would happen to them if their villages should fall into the hands of the Russians, 'as our past experience of them gives us little ground to hope for good treatment'. Written and translated into English by a local Tatar scribe, their supplication continued:

> In return for the kindness shown us by the English we should as soon cease to remember God as to forget Her Majesty Queen Victoria and General Codrington, for whom we will pray the five times a day that the Mahometan religion enjoins us to say our prayers, and our prayers to preserve them and the whole English nation shall be handed down to our children's children.

> Signed in the names of the priests, nobles and inhabitants of the following twelve villages: Baidar, Sagtik, Kalendi, Skelia, Savatka, Baga, Urkusta, Uzunyu, Buyuk Luskomiya, Kiatu, Kutchuk Luskomiga, Varnutka.[11]

Codrington did nothing to help the Tatars, even though they had provided the allies with foodstuffs, spies and transport services throughout the Crimean War. The idea of protecting the Tatars against Russian reprisals never crossed the minds of the allied diplomats, who might have included a stronger clause about their treatment in the peace treaty. Article V of the Paris Treaty obliged all warring nations to 'give full pardon to those of their subjects who appeared guilty of actively participating in the military affairs of the enemy' – a clause that appeared to protect not only the Crimean Tatars but the Bulgarians and Greeks of the Ottoman Empire, who had sided with the Russians during the Danubian campaigns. But Count Stroganov, the governor-general of New Russia, found a way around this clause by claiming that the Tatars had lost their treaty rights, if they had broken Russian law by departing from their place of residence without prior approval from the military authorities – as tens of thousands of them had been forced to do during the Crimean War. In other words, any Tatar who had left his home without a stamp in his passport was deemed to be a traitor by the Russian government, and was subject to penal exile in Siberia.[12]

As the allied armies began their evacuation of the Crimea, the first large groups of Tatars also left. On 22 April, 4,500 Tatars set sail from Balaklava for Constantinople in the belief that the Turkish government had invited them to relocate in the Ottoman Empire. Alarmed by the mass exodus, which was a threat to the Crimean agricultural economy, Russian local officials looked for guidance from St Petersburg as to whether they should stop the departure of the Tatars. Having been informed that the Tatars had collaborated en masse with the enemy, the Tsar responded that nothing should be done to prevent their exodus, adding that in fact it 'would be advantageous to rid the peninsula of this harmful population' (a concept re-enacted by Stalin during the Second World War). Communicating Alexander's statement to his officials, Stroganov interpreted it as a direct order for the expulsion of the Muslim population from the Crimea by claiming that the Tsar had said that it was 'necessary' (and not just 'advantageous') to make the Tatars leave. Various pressures were applied to encourage their departure: there were rumours of a planned mass deportation to the north, of Cossack raids on Tatar villages, of campaigns to force the Tatars to learn Russian in Crimean schools, or to convert to Christianity. Taxes were increased on Tatar farms, and Tatar villages were deprived of access to water, forcing them to sell their land to Russian landowners.

Between 1856 and 1863 about 150,000 Crimean Tatars and perhaps 50,000 Nogai Tatars (roughly two-thirds of the combined Tatar population of the Crimea and southern Russia) emigrated to the Ottoman Empire. Precise figures are hard to calculate, and some historians have put the figures much higher. Concerned about growing labour shortages in the region, in 1867 the Russian authorities tried to work out from police statistics how many Tatars had left the peninsula since the ending of the war. It was reported that 104,211 men and 88,149 women had left the Crimea. There were 784 deserted villages, and 457 abandoned mosques.[13]

Along with the removal of the Tatar population, the Russian authorities pursued a policy of Christianizing the Crimea after 1856. More than ever, as a direct consequence of the Crimean War, they saw the peninsula as a religious borderland between Russia and the Muslim world over which they needed to consolidate their hold. Before the war, the relatively liberal governor-general, Prince Vorontsov, had opposed the spread of Christian institutions to the Crimea, on the grounds that it would 'germinate among the [Tatar] natives unfounded dangerous thoughts about intentions of deflecting them from Islam and converting them to Orthodoxy'. But Vorontsov retired from his post in 1855, to be replaced by the aggressively Russian nationalist Stroganov, who actively supported the Christianizing goals of Innokenty, the Archbishop of the Kherson-Tauride diocese, within which the Crimea fell. Towards the end of the Crimean War, Innokenty's sermons had been widely circlated to the Russian troops in the form of pamphlets and illustrated prints (*lubki*). Innokenty portrayed the conflict as a 'holy war' for the Crimea, the centre of the nation's Orthodox identity, where Christianity had arrived in Russia. Highlighting the ancient heritage of the Greek Church in the peninsula, he depicted the Crimea as a 'Russian Athos', a sacred place in the 'Holy Russian Empire' connected by religion to the monastic centre of Orthodoxy on the peninsula of Mount Athos in north-eastern Greece. With Stroganov's support, Innokenty oversaw the creation of a separate bishopric for the Crimea as well as the establishment of several new monasteries in the peninsula after the Crimean War.[14]

To encourage the Christian settlement of the Crimea, the tsarist government introduced a law in 1862 granting special rights and subsidies to colonists from Russia and abroad. Land abandoned by the Tatars was set aside for sale to foreigners. The influx of new Christian populations during the 1860s and 1870s transformed the ethnic profile of the Crimea. What had once been Tatar settlements were now populated by Russians, Greeks, Armenians, Bulgarians, even Germans and Estonians – all of them attracted by promises of cheap and fertile land or by special rights of entry into urban guilds and corporations not ordinarily available to newcomers. Armenians and Greeks turned Sevastopol and Evpatoria into major trading centres, while older Tatar towns like Kefe (Theodosia), Gözleve and Bakhchiserai fell into decline. Many of the rural immigrants were Bulgarian or other Christian refugees from Bessarabia, territory ceded by the Russians to the Turks after the Crimean War. They were settled by the government in 330 villages once occupied by the Tatars, and were helped financially to transform mosques into churches. Meanwhile, many of the Tatars who had fled from the Crimea were resettled on the lands abandoned by the Christians in Bessarabia.[15]

All around the Black Sea rim, the Crimean War resulted in the uprooting and transmigration of ethnic and religious groups. They crossed in both directions over the religious line separating Russia from the Muslim world. Greeks emigrated in their tens of thousands from Moldavia and Bessarabia to southern Russia after the Crimean War. Moving in the opposite direction, from Russia into Turkey, were tens of thousands of Polish refugees and soldiers who had fought in the Polish Legion (the so-called 'Ottoman Cossacks') against Russia in the Crimea and the Caucasus. They were settled by the Porte on Turkish lands in the Dobrudja region of the Danube delta, in Anatolia and other areas, while others ended up in Adampol (Polonezkoi), the Polish settlement established by Adam Czartoryski, the leader of the Polish emigration, on the outskirts of Constantinople in 1842.

On the other side of the Black Sea, tens of thousands of Christian Armenians left their homes in Anatolia and emigrated to Russian-controlled Transcaucasia in the wake of the Crimean War. They were fearful that the Turks would see them as allies of the Russians and carry out reprisals against them. The European commission appointed by the Paris Treaty to fix the Russian–Ottoman border found Armenian villages 'half inhabited' and churches in a state of 'advanced decay'.[16]

Meanwhile, even larger numbers of Circassians, Abkhazians and other Muslim tribes were forced out of their homelands by the Russians, who after the Crimean War stepped up their military campaign against Shamil, engaging in a concerted policy of what today would be defined as 'ethnic cleansing' to Christianize the Caucasus. The campaign was largely driven by the strategic demands created by the Paris settlement in the Black Sea, where the Royal Navy could freely operate and the Russians had no means of self-defence in their vulnerable coastal areas where the Muslim population was hostile to Russia. The Russians focused first on the fertile lands of Circassia in the western Caucasus – territories close to the Black Sea coast. Muslim villages were attacked by Russian troops, men and women massacred, farms and homes destroyed to force the villagers to leave or starve. The Circassians were presented with the choice of moving north to the Kuban plains – far enough away from the coastal areas for them not to be a threat in case of an invasion – or emigrating to the Ottoman Empire. Tens of thousands resettled in the north but equally large numbers of Circassians were herded by the Russians to the Black Sea ports, where, sometimes after weeks of waiting by the docks in terrible conditions, they were loaded onto Turkish boats and taken off to Trebizond, Samsun and Sinope in Anatolia. The Ottoman authorities were unprepared for the mass influx of refugees and several thousands of them died from disease within months of their arrival in Turkey. By 1864 the Muslim population of Circassia had been entirely cleared. The British consul C. H. Dickson claimed that one could walk a whole day in formerly Circassian territories and not meet a living soul.[17]

After the Circassians, it was the turn of the Abkhazian Muslims, at that time settled in the Sukhumi–Kale region, where the Russian campaign to clear them off their lands began in 1866. The tactics were essentially the same as those employed against the Circassians, except this time the Russians had a policy of keeping back the able-bodied male workers out of fear for the economy, and forcing out their women, children and the elderly. The British consul and Arabic scholar William Gifford Palgrave, who made a tour of Abkhazia to collect information on the ethnic cleansing, estimated that three-quarters of the Muslim population had been forced to emigrate. Overall, counting both Circassians and Abkhazians, around 1.2 million Muslims were expelled from the Caucasus in the decade following the Crimean War, most of them resettling in the Ottoman Empire, and by the end of the nineteenth century the Muslims of these two regions were outnumbered by new Christian settlers by more than ten to one.[18]

*

As a signal of his intention to grant religious toleration, the Sultan agreed to attend two foreign balls in the Turkish capital, one at the British embassy, the other at the French, in February 1856. It was the first time in the history of the Ottoman Empire that a sultan had accepted invitations to a Christian entertainment in the house of a foreign ambassador.

Abdülmecid arrived at the British embassy wearing the Order of the Garter presented to him a few weeks before to mark the allied victory. Stratford Canning, the ambassador, met the Sultan at the carriage door. As the Sultan alighted, a signal was transmitted by electric wire to the British fleet, anchored in the Bosporus, which saluted then with prolonged salvoes of cannon. It was a costume ball and princes, pirates, musketeers, fake Circassians and shepherdesses were in attendance. Lady Hornby wrote down her impressions the next day.

> It would take me a day to enumerate half the costumes. But everyone who had been to the Queen's *bals costumés* agreed that they did not approach this one in magnificence; for besides the gathering of French, Sardinian and English officers, the people of the country appeared in their own superb and varied costumes; and the groups were beyond all description beautiful. The Greek Patriarch, the Armenian Archbishop, the Jewish High Priest were there in their robes of state. Real Persians, Albanians, Kurds, Servians, Armenians, Greeks, Turks, Austrians, Sardinians, Italians and Spaniards were there in their different dresses, and many wore their jewelled arms. Abdülmecid quietly walked up the ballroom with Lord and Lady Stratford, their daughters, and a gorgeous array of Pashas in the rear. He paused with evident delight and pleasure at the really beautiful scene before him, bowing on both sides, and smiling as he went ... Pashas drink vast quantities of champagne, of which they pretend not to know the exact genus, and slyly call it '*eau gazeuse*'.

At the ball at the French embassy the Sultan appeared wearing the medal of the Légion d'honneur that had been presented to him by Thouvenel, the French ambassador. Welcomed by a military salute, he talked to foreign dignitaries and moved among the dancers, who improvised to the Turkish marches performed by the army band.[19]

One of the things that pleased the Sultan most at these events was the appearance of the European women, whose dress he claimed greatly to prefer to that of Muslim women. 'If socializing with these ladies is like their outer appearance,' he told his Austrian physician, 'then I certainly envy you Europeans.' Encouraged by the Sultan, palace women and high officials' wives began to adopt more elements of Western dress – corsets, silk capes and transparent veils. They appeared more often in society and socialized more frequently with men.

Domestic culture was also Westernized, with the appearance of European table manners, cutlery and crockery, furniture and decorative styles in the homes of the Ottoman élites in Constantinople.[20]

In almost every sphere of life, the Crimean War marked a watershed in the opening up and Westernization of Turkish society. The mass influx of refugees from the Russian Empire was only one of many ways in which the Ottoman Empire became more exposed to external influence. The Crimean War brought new ideas and technologies into the Ottoman world, accelerated Turkey's integration into the global economy, and greatly increased contacts between Turks and foreigners. More Europeans came to Constantinople during and immediately after the Crimean War than at any other time in its previous history; the many diplomats, financiers, military advisers and soldiers, engineers, tourists, merchants, missionaries and priests left a deep impression on Turkish society.

The war also led to a vast expansion of foreign capital investment in the Ottoman Empire, and with it an increase in Turkey's financial dependence on Western banks and governments (foreign loans to finance the war and Tanzimat reforms spiralled from about £5 million in 1855 to a staggering £200 million by 1877). It stimulated the development of telegraphs and railways, and accelerated the emergence of what might be called Turkish public opinion through newspapers and a new type of journalistic writing that came about directly as a result of the huge demand for information during the Crimean War. With the New Ottomans (*Yeni Osmanlilar*), a loose group of journalists and would-be reformers who briefly came together in something like a political party during the 1860s, the war also triggered a reaction against some of these changes and fostered the emergence of the first Ottoman (Turkish) nationalist movement. The New Ottomans' belief in adopting Western institutions within a framework of Muslim tradition made them in many ways the 'spiritual fathers' of the Young Turks, the creators of the modern Turkish state.[21]

The New Ottomans were opposed to the growing intervention of the European powers in the Ottoman Empire. They were against reforms which they believed had been imposed on Turkey by Western governments to promote the special interests of Christians. In particular, they disapproved of the Hatt-i Hümayun decree of 1856, which had indeed been imposed by the European powers. The decree was written by Stratford Canning along with Thouvenel and then presented to the Porte as a condition of the continuation of foreign loans. It reiterated the principles of religious toleration articulated in the Hatt-i Sharif of 1839 but defined them more clearly in Western legal terms, without reference to the Koran. In addition to promising toleration and civil rights for non-Muslims, it introduced some new political principles to Ottoman governance stipulated by the British: strict annual budgets by the government; the establishment of banks; the codification of criminal and civil law; the reform of Turkish prisons; and mixed courts to oversee a majority of cases involving Muslims and non-Muslims. It was a thoroughgoing programme of Westernization for the Ottoman Empire. The New Ottomans had supported the principles contained in the Hatt-i Sharif of 1839 as a necessary element of the Tanzimat reforms; unlike the decree of 1856, it had some domestic origins and had not threatened the privileged position of Islam in the Ottoman Empire. But they saw the Hatt-i Hümayun as a special dispensation for the non-Muslims conceded under pressure by the great powers, and they feared that it would compromise the interests of Islam and Turkish sovereignty.

The foreign origins and terminology of the Hatt-i Hümayun stirred even greater resentment among Muslim clerics and conservatives. Even the old Tanzimat reformer Mustafa Reshid – who returned for a brief spell as Grand Vizier after Stratford had insisted on his reappointment in November 1856 – thought it went too far in its concessions to the Christians. Angered by the Hatt-i Hümayun, a group of Muslim theologians and students plotted a conspiracy against the Sultan and his ministers, but they were arrested in 1859. Under interrogation their leaders claimed that the Hatt-i Hümayun was a contravention of shariah law because it had granted Christians equal rights to Muslims. Sheikh Ahmet, one of the main conspirators, claimed that the Christians had obtained these rights only through the help of foreign powers, and that the concessions would mean the end of the privileged position of Islam in the Ottoman Empire.[22]

Their views were shared by many power-holders and beneficiaries of the old Muslim hierarchy – local pashas, governors, landowners and notables, clerics and officials, tax-farmers and moneylenders – who were all afraid that the better-educated and more active Christian minorities would soon come to dominate the political and social order, if they were granted civil and religious equality. For centuries the Muslims of the empire had been told that the Christians were inferior. Faced with the loss of their privileged position, the Muslims became increasingly rebellious. There were riots and attacks by Muslims against Christians in Bessarabia, in Nablus and in Gaza in 1856, in Jaffa during 1857, in the Hijaz during 1858, and in Lebanon and Syria, where 20,000 Maronite Christians were massacred by Druzes and Muslims during 1860. In each case religious and economic divisions reinforced each other: the livelihood of Muslims engaged in agriculture and small trades was directly threatened by the import of European goods by Christian middlemen. Rioters attacked Christian shops and houses, foreign churches and missionary schools, even embassies, after they had been stirred up by Muslim clerics opposed to the Hatt-i Hümayun.

In Nablus, to take just one example, the troubles began on 4 April, shortly after Muslim leaders had denounced the Hatt-i Hümayun at Friday prayers. There were 5,000 Christians in Nablus, a town of 10,000 people, and before the Crimean War they had lived peacefully with the Muslims. But the war had increased tensions between them. The defeat of Russia was seen as a 'Muslim victory' by the local Palestinians, whose religious pride was offended by the new laws of religious toleration in the Hatt-i Hümayun. Christians, for their part, saw it as an allied triumph. They raised French and British flags on their houses in Nablus and placed a new bell over the Protestant mission school. These were provocations to Islamic sentiment. At Friday prayers, the ulemas condemned these signs of Western domination, arguing that Muslims would soon be called to prayer by the English bell, unless they rose up to destroy the Christian churches, which, they said, would be 'a proper form of prayer to God'. Calling for jihad, crowds spilled out onto the streets of Nablus, many of them gathering by the Protestant mission, where they tore down the British flag.

Amid these heightened tensions, violence was sparked by a bizarre incident involving the Reverend Mr Lyde, a Protestant missionary and Fellow of Jesus College, Cambridge, who had accidentally shot a beggar attempting to steal his coat. 'The cup of fanaticism was full, and one drop more caused it to run over,' wrote James Finn, the British consul in Jerusalem, who reported on the incident. Lyde had taken refuge from the mob in the house of the town governor, Mahmud Bek, who pacified the family of the dead man and proposed to bury him. But the ulemas were not satisfied with this. After a religious council, they forbade the burial and suspended public prayers in all the mosques 'until the price of the blood of Islam should be paid'. Calling for 'Vengeance on the Christians!' a large crowd assembled outside the governor's house and demanded to be given Lyde, who offered to sacrifice himself, but Mahmud Bek refused, whereupon the the mob began to rampage through the town, pillaging and destroying any property on which they could lay their hands. Christian houses, schools and churches were ransacked and burned. Several Prussian consular officials were murdered, along with a dozen Greeks, according to Finn, who also reported that 'eleven women are known to have given premature birth to infants from the effect of fright'. Order was eventually restored by the intervention of the Sultan's troops, and on 21 April Lyde was put on trial in a Turkish court in Jerusalem, where a mixed Muslim and Christian jury acquitted him of murder but ordered him to pay a large sum in compensation to the beggar's family.* Lyde returned to England in a deranged mental state: he had delusions of himself as Christ. The ringleaders of the Muslim riots were never brought to trial, and attacks on Christians in the area continued for many months. In August 1856 the violence spread from Nablus to Gaza. In February 1857 Finn reported that 300 Christians were 'still living in a state of terror in Gaza', for 'no one could control the Muslim fanatics', and the Christians would not testify for fear of reprisals.[23]

Faced with the prospect of this sort of violence almost anywhere, the Ottoman authorities dragged their heels over implementing the new laws of religious toleration in the Hatt-i Hümayun. Stratford Canning was increasingly frustrated with the Porte. 'Turkish ministers are very little disposed to meet the demands of Her Majesty's Government on the subject of religious persecution,' he wrote to

---

* Lyde's accusers claimed that he had fired wilfully at the beggar but the only witnesses of the shooting were three women. The testimony of women was inadmissible in a Turkish court.

Clarendon. 'They pretend to entertain apprehensions of popular discontent among the Mussulmans, if they were to give way.' Turkish participation in the Crimean War had led to a resurgence of 'Muslim triumphalism', Stratford reported. As a result of the war, the Turks had become more protective of their sovereignty, and more resentful of Western intervention into their affairs. There was a new generation of Tanzimat reformers at the head of the Turkish government who were more secure in their personal position and less dependent on the patronage of foreign powers and ambassadors than Reshid's generation of reformers had been before the Crimean War; they could afford to be more cautious and more practical in their implementation of reforms, carrying out the economic and political requirements of the Western powers but not hurrying to fulfil the religious promises contained in the Hatt-i Hümayun. Throughout his last year as ambassador, Stratford urged the Turkish leaders to be more serious about the protection of the Christians in the Ottoman Empire: it was the price, he told them, that Turkey had to pay for British and French help in the Crimean War. He was particularly exercised by the continued execution of Muslims for converting to Christianity, despite the Sultan's promises to secure the Christians from religious persecution and abolish the 'barbarous practice of putting seceders to death'. Citing numerous cases of Christian converts being driven from their homes and killed, Stratford wrote to the Porte on 23 December 1856:

> The great European powers can never consent to perpetuate by the triumphs of their fleets and armies the enforcement in Turkey of a law [apostasy], which is not only a standing insult to them, but a source of cruel persecution to their fellow Christians. They are entitled to demand, the British Government distinctly demands, that the Mohamedean who turns Christian shall be as free from every kind of punishment on that account as the Christian who embraces the Mohamodean faith.[24]

Yet by the time of his return to London the next year, very little had been done by the Porte to satisfy the demands of the European governments. 'Among the Christians,' Finn reported in July 1857, 'a strong feeling of discontent is on the increase because of the slowness of the Turkish government to implement religious toleration.'

The Christians complain that they are insulted in the streets, that they are not placed in equal rank at public courts with Muslim fellow subjects, that they are ousted from almost every office of government employment, and that they are not allowed the honour of military service but instead of it have the old military tax doubled upon them.

In the rural areas of Palestine, according to Finn, the Hatt-i Hümayun remained unobserved for many years. Local governors were corrupt, ill-disciplined and closely linked to the Muslim notables, clerics and officials, who kept the Christians in their place, while the Porte was too remote and weak to curb their excesses, let alone to force them to uphold the new laws of equality.[25]

But it was in the Balkans that the failure of the Porte to carry out reforms would have the most lasting consequences for the Ottoman Empire. Throughout the Balkan region, Christian peasants would rise up against their Muslim landlords and officials, beginning in Bosnia in 1858. The continuation of the *millet* system would give rise to nationalist movements that would involve the Ottomans and the European powers in a long series of Balkan wars, culminating in the conflicts that would bring about the First World War.

*

The Paris Treaty did not make any major territorial changes to the map of Europe. To many at the time, the outcome did not appear worthy of a war in which so many people died. Russia ceded southern Bessarabia to Moldavia. But otherwise the treaty's articles were statements of principle: the independence and integrity of the Ottoman Empire were confirmed and guaranteed by the great powers (the first time a Muslim state was recognized by international law, the Congress of Vienna having specifically excluded Turkey from the European powers regulated by its international laws); the protection of the non-Muslim subjects of the Sultan was guaranteed by the signatory powers, thereby annulling Russia's claims to protect the Christians of the Ottoman Empire; Russia's protectorate over the Danubian principalities was negated by an article confirming the autonomy of these two states under Ottoman sovereignty; and, most humiliating of all for the

Russians, Article XI declared the Black Sea to be a neutral zone, open to commercial shipping but closed to all warships in peacetime, thus depriving Russia of its naval ports and arsenals on this crucial southern coastal frontier.[26]

But if the Paris Treaty made few immediate changes to the European map, it marked a crucial watershed for international relations and politics, effectively ending the old balance of power, in which Austria and Russia had controlled the Continent between themselves, and forging new alignments that would pave the way for the emergence of nation states in Italy, Romania and Germany.

Although it was Russia that was punished by the Paris Treaty, in the longer term it was Austria that would lose the most from the Crimean War, despite having barely taken part in it. Without its conservative alliance with Russia, which never quite forgave it for its armed neutrality in favour of the allies in 1854, and equally mistrusted by the liberal Western powers for its reactionary politics and 'soft-on-Russia' peace initiatives during the war, Austria found itself increasingly isolated on the Continent after 1856. Consequently it would lose out in Italy (in the war against the French and Piedmontese in 1859), in Germany (in the war against the Prussians in 1866) and in the Balkans (where it steadily retreated from the 1870s until 1914).

None of that was yet apparent in April 1856, when Austria joined France and Britain in a Triple Alliance to defend the Paris settlement. The three powers signed an agreement that any breach of the Paris Treaty would become a cause of war. Palmerston saw it as a 'good additional Security and Bond of Union' against Russia, which he fully expected to re-emerge in due course as a major threat to the Continent. He wanted to expand the *entente* into an anti-Russian league of European states.[27] Napoleon was not so sure. Since the fall of Sevastopol, there had been a growing rapprochement between the French and the Russians. Napoleon needed Russia for his plans against the Austrians in Italy. Meanwhile, for the Russians, and in particular for their new Foreign Minister, Alexander Gorchakov, who replaced Nesselrode in 1856, France represented the most likely power to support their efforts to remove the humiliating Black Sea clauses of the Paris Treaty. Both France and Russia were revisionist powers: where Russia wanted revisions to the treaty of 1856, France wanted to remove the remnants of the 1815 settlement. A deal between them could be made.

Unlike Nesselrode, a firm supporter of the Holy Alliance and its legitimist principles, Gorchakov took a pragmatic view of Russia's role on the Continent. In his opinion, Russia should not form alliances that committed it to general principles, such as the defence of legitimate monarchies, as it had done before the Crimean War. The war had shown that Russia could not rely in any way on the solidarity of legitimate European monarchies. Nesselrode's policy had made Russia vulnerable to the failings of other governments, Austria in particular, a power Gorchakov despised from his time as ambassador in Vienna. Instead, Gorchakov believed Russia should focus its diplomacy on its own national interests, and ally with other powers regardless of their ideology to further those interests. Here was a new type of diplomacy, the realpolitik later practised by Bismarck.

The Russians tested the Paris Treaty from the start, focusing on minor issues which they could exploit to open up divisions in the Crimean alliance. In May 1856 they claimed ownership of a lighthouse on tiny Serpent Island, in Turkish waters near the mouth of the Danube delta, and landed seven men with an officer to take up residence in the lighthouse. Walewski was inclined to let the Russians have the insignificant island, but Palmerston was adamant that they had to be ejected, on the grounds that they were infringing Turkish sovereignty. When the captain of a British ship made contact with the Turks on Serpent Island, he was told that they did not mind the Russians being there: they saw them as guests and were happy to sell them their supplies. Palmerston put his foot down. 'We must avoid the fatal mistake made by Aberdeen in permitting the early movements and indications of Russian aggression to go on unnoticed and unrepressed,' he wrote to Clarendon on 7 August. Orders were prepared to send the gunboats in to remove the Russians physically, but John Wodehouse, the British envoy in St Petersburg, was doubtful whether Britain had the right to do this, and the Queen shared these doubts, so Palmerston backed down and diplomatic pressure was used instead. Gorchakov insisted that the island had been owned by the Russians since 1833, and appealed to the French, who were thus manoeuvred into a position of international mediation between Britain and Russia.[28]

Meanwhile, the Russians launched a second challenge to the Paris Treaty in connection with the border between Russian Bessarabia and Turkish-controlled Moldavia. By an accident of mapping and confusion over names, the allies had drawn the border running to the south of an old village called Bolgrad, 3 kilometres to the north of New Bolgrad, a market town situated on the shores of Lake Yalpuk, which runs into the Danube. The Russians made use of the lack of clarity, claiming that they should be given both Bolgrads, and thus joint ownership of Lake Yalpuk. Palmerston insisted that the border should remain at the old village – the intention of the treaty having been to deprive the Russians of access to the Danube. He urged the French to remain firm and show a united front against the Russians, who would otherwise exploit their differences. But the French were happy to concede the Russian claim as a matter of good faith, though they then proposed that the boundary should run along a narrow strip of land between the market town and Lake Yalpuk, thereby granting more territory to the Russians but depriving them of access to the lake. Once again, the French acted as intermediaries between Russia and Britain.

By mid-November the Duc de Morny had persuaded Gorchakov to give up Russia's claim to Serpent Island, provided Russia was given New Bolgrad, without access to the lake, and territorial compensation for their loss in a form decided by the French Emperor. The deal was linked to a proposal by the Tsar and Gorchakov (drawn up with the help of Morny in St Petersburg) for a Franco-Russian convention for the protection of the neutrality of the Black Sea and the Danubian principalities, as set out in the Paris Treaty, but now necessitated, it was claimed by the Russians, 'by the fact that the treaty has been violated by England and Austria', who had 'tried to cheat' the Russians of legitimate possessions in the Danube area. Morny recommended the Russian proposal to Napoleon and passed on to the French Emperor a promise made to him by Gorchakov: Russia would support French acquisitions on the European continent if France signed the convention. 'Mark well,' Morny wrote, 'Russia is the only power that will ratify the territorial gains of France. I have already been assured of that. Try and get the same from the English! And who knows, with our demanding and capricious people, one day we might have to come to Russia for their satisfaction.' Details of the Russian attitude to French territorial acquisitions had been outlined in a secret instruction to Count Kiselev, the former governor of the Danubian principalities who became ambassador to France after the Crimean War: protocol required that a senior statesman represent the Tsar's new policy of friendship towards France. Should Napoleon direct his attention to the Italian peninsula, Kiselev was told, Russia 'would consent in advance to the reunion of Nice and Savoy with France, as well as to the union of Lombardy with Sardinia'. If his ambitions were directed to the Rhine, Russia would 'use its good offices' to help the French, while continuing to honour its commitments to Prussia.[29]

A conference of the powers' representatives in Paris brought about a speedy resolution of the two disputes in January 1857: Turkish ownership of Serpent Island was confirmed with an international commission to control the lighthouse; and New Bolgrad was given to Moldavia, with Russia compensated by a boundary change elsewhere in Bessarabia. On the face of it, the Russians had been forced to back down on both issues, but they had scored a political victory by weakening the bonds of the Crimean alliance. The French had made it clear that the integrity of the Ottoman Empire was of secondary significance to them, and they were ready to enter into a deal with the Russians to redraw the European map.

Over the next eighteen months a number of high-level Russian visitors appeared in France. In 1857, the Grand Duke Constantine, the Tsar's younger brother and the admiral in charge of the much-needed reform of the Russian navy after the Crimean War, made a trip to Paris, having decided that a partnership with France was the best way to get the technical assistance Russia needed to modernize its backward fleet (he gave to French firms all the orders that could not be fulfilled by Russian shipbuilders). On his way, he stopped at the Bay of Villafranca, near Nice, where he negotiated an agreement with Cavour for the Odessa Shipping Company to rent a coaling station from the Turin government, thereby providing Russia with a foothold in the Mediterranean.* Napoleon gave a splendid reception to the

---

* It was from this time that Nice became a favourite resort of the Russian aristocracy, a 'Russian Brighton', according to the British press, which was alarmed by the appearance of Russian merchant ships in the Mediterranean, a sea dominated by the Royal Navy.

Grand Duke in Paris, and drew him into private conversations about the future of Europe. The French Emperor knew that the Grand Duke was trying to assert himself as a force in Russian foreign policy, and that he had pan-Slav views at odds with those of Gorchakov, so he played to his political ambitions. Napoleon referred specifically to the possibility of an Italian uprising against the Austrians and the eventual unification of Italy under Piedmont's leadership, and talked about the likelihood of Christian uprisings in the Ottoman Empire, a subject of great interest to Constantine, suggesting that in both cases it would suit their interests to encourage the formation of smaller nation states.[30]

Encouraged by the Grand Duke, Napoleon entered into direct contact with the Tsar with the aim of securing his support for a French-Piedmontese war against the Austrians in Italy. Having met the Tsar at Stuttgart in September 1857, Napoleon became so confident of his support that when he met Cavour the following July at Plombières to draw up war plans he assured the Piedmontese Prime Minister that he had Alexander's solemn promise to back their plans in Italy: after the defeat of the Austrians in Lombardy-Venetia, an enlarged Piedmont would form a Kingdom of Northern Italy (as had emerged briefly in 1848–9) and become united with Tuscany, a reduced Papal State and the Kingdom of the Two Sicilies in an Italian Confederation; and for his efforts on behalf of the Italian cause, Napoleon would be rewarded with the return of Nice and Savoy to France. Cavour had pinned his hopes for Italy on the Franco-British alliance. That was why he had committed his Sardinian troops to the Crimean War. At the Paris congress he had won the sympathies of the British and the French through his influence behind the scenes, and although he had gained nothing tangible, no firm promise of support for the idea of Italy, he continued to believe that the Western powers were his only hope. Hardly believing that a Russian tsar would give his

_____

There were dire warnings of an intrigue between Russia and the Catholic powers. When rumours later circulated that the Russians were intending to set up coaling stations in other parts of the Mediterranean, in 1858, Palmerston (by this stage out of office) called for a show of naval strength against the Sardinians. But the Conservative government of Lord Derby was less concerned, seeing Russia's deal with the Sardinians as no more than a commercial agreement. The Villafranca contract lasted until 1917.

blessing to a national revolution, Cavour rushed to the nearby spa resort of Baden-Baden, where the 'run-down kings and princes' of Europe congregated, to consult with the Grand Duchess Elena Pavlovna (Alexander's influential liberal aunt), who confirmed that Russia could be counted on. 'The Grand Duchess told me', Cavour wrote to General Marmora, 'that if France were to unite with us, public opinion would force the Russian government to participate.'[31]

But in truth, the Tsar was not keen to get involved in any war. In return for French commitments to cancel their support for the Black Sea clauses of the Paris Treaty, Alexander promised only armed neutrality, mobilizing a large Russian force on the border with Galicia to prevent the Austrians from sending troops to Italy. The Austrians had used armed neutrality in favour of the allies during the Crimean War, and Alexander's decision to follow the same tactic let him take revenge on Austria for its betrayal. Napoleon, for his part, was unwilling to give a firm pledge on the Black Sea clauses, fearing it would damage his relations with Britain, so no formal treaty with the Russians could be reached. But there was a gentlemen's agreement between the emperors, signed in March 1859, by which the Russians would adopt a stance of 'benevolent neutrality' in the event of a Franco-Austrian war in exchange for French 'good offices' at a 'future date'.[32]

It was on this basis that the French and Piedmontese began their war against Austria in April 1859, in the knowledge that the Russians would advance 300,000 troops towards the Austrian frontier while they attacked in Italy. Only a few years before, Russia would have given military support to Austria against any French attempts to revise the Vienna treaty. The Crimean War had changed everything.

Under the command of Napoleon III and Victor Emmanuel, the Franco-Piedmontese army won a series of rapid victories, destroying the Austrian forces under the command of Emperor Franz Joseph at the battle of Solferino on 24 June, the last major battle in history in which all the armies were under the personal command of their monarchs. By this time, Napoleon was afraid that the German states might take up arms in support of Austria; therefore, without telling the Piedmontese, he signed an armistice with the Austrians at Villafranca, by which most of Lombardy, including its capital, Milan, was transferred to the French, who immediately gave it to Piedmont, as agreed by

Napoleon and Cavour at Plombières. The Villafranca deal restored the monarchs of the central Italian states (Parma, Modena and Tuscany) who had been unseated by the popular revolts that broke out at the beginning of the war – a deal that enraged the Piedmontese, though it pleased the Russians, who had deep concerns about the way the Italian movement was taking a revolutionary turn. The Piedmontese army proceeded to annex the central states. Savoy and Nice were transferred to France, its agreed reward for helping the Italian cause. Their cession was opposed by the revolutionary general Giuseppe Garibaldi, a hero of the war against the Austrians, who had been born in Nice. In the spring of 1860, he led his thousand Redshirts on an expedition to conquer Sicily and Naples and unite them with the rest of Italy under Piedmont's leadership.

The revolutionary turn taken by the Garibaldians placed a severe strain on the Tsar's relations with Napoleon. It brought home to him that giving his support to the French Emperor's policies could have dangerous consequences. There was nothing to prevent the tide of nationalism spreading into Habsburg lands and from there into Poland and other Russian territories. In October 1860 Russia broke off relations with Piedmont as a protest against its annexation of Naples. Gorchakov condemned Piedmont for promoting revolution, pledged to oppose the territorial changes taking place in Italy unless they were approved by a new international congress, and gave his cautious backing to the Austrians in Italy (there was no chance of the Russians actually fighting to keep the Habsburgs in Venetia, the only part of the peninsula, along with the papal city of Rome, that had not yet been unified under the control of the first Italian parliament, which met at Turin in 1861). When Victor Emmanuel took the title of King of Italy, in March 1861, the Russians and the Austrians agreed together to refuse him recognition, despite pressure from the British and French. When the British asked Gorchakov to use his influence on the Prussians to recognize the King, the Russian Foreign Minister refused. The Holy Alliance was not quite dead, it seemed. Justifying his refusal to cooperate with Britain's plans for Italy, Gorchakov maintained that Austria and Turkey might be undermined by revolutionary movements if the powers left unchecked the nationalist uprisings started by the Piedmontese. With tongue in cheek, perhaps,

François Rochebrune

given how the British had justified their actions in the Crimean War, Gorchakov informed Lord Napier, the British ambassador in St Petersburg: 'We have two cardinal objects: the preservation of Turkey and the preservation of Austria.'[33]

The Polish uprising of 1863 was the final breaking point for Russia's policy of friendship towards France. Inspired by Garibaldi, Polish students began demonstrations in 1861, prompting General Lambert, the Tsar's viceroy, to impose martial law. The Polish leaders gathered secretly, some supporting the idea of a popular democratic revolution uniting peasants and workers, others, led by Czartoryski, more conservative, seeking to establish a national movement led by nobles and intellectuals. The uprising began as a spontaneous protest against conscription into the Russian army. Small groups of insurgents fought the mighty Russian army from guerrilla strongholds mainly in the forests of Lithuania, Poland, Belarus and western (Catholic) Ukraine. Some of them had fought against the Russians during the Crimean

War, including many of the 'Zouaves of Death', organized by François Rochebrune, who had served as an officer with the French Zouaves in the Crimea and had taken part in the Anglo-French expedition to China in the Second Opium War of 1857 before settling in Cracow in Austrian Poland, where he set up a fencing school. Dressed in a black uniform with a white cross and a red fez, and many of them armed with Minié rifles from the Crimean War, the Polish Zouaves swore to die rather than surrender to the Russians.

A clandestine revolutionary government was established in Warsaw. It declared 'all sons of Poland free and equal citizens', gave the peasants ownership of land, and appealed for help to the nations of Europe. Pope Pius IX ordered special prayers for the victory of Catholic Poland against Orthodox Russia, and was active in arousing sympathy for the Polish rebels in Italy and France. Napoleon wanted to land troops in the Baltic to support the Poles, but was held back by the British, who feared a renewal of the Crimean War. In the end, the competing French invasion of Mexico prevented troops from being sent. The diplomatic intervention of the Western powers on behalf of Poland angered the Russians, who felt betrayed by the French, in particular. It made the Russians even more determined to crush the Polish insurrectionaries. The Russian army burned whole towns and villages. Tens of thousands of Polish men and women were exiled to Siberia, and hundreds of insurgents were publicly hanged.

Alarmed by the consequences of their pro-French policies, the Russians moved away from France in the wake of the Polish uprising and returned to their old alliance with Prussia, another ruler of annexed Polish territory and the only power that had supported them against the Poles (a military convention had allowed the Russians to transport troops on Prussian trains). To Alexander, who had always had his doubts about the liberal French, Prussia seemed a more reliably conservative ally, and a counterbalance to the growing influence and power of the French on the Continent. The Russians gave considerable backing to Otto von Bismarck, the Prussian Prime Minister, whose conservatism had been noted by the Tsar during his period as ambassador in St Petersburg between 1859 and 1862. Bismarck himself placed a high priority on his good relations with Russia, which consistently supported Prussia in its wars against Denmark (in 1864),

Austria (in 1866) and France (in 1870). With the defeat of France and the support of a grateful Germany, united by Bismarck, in 1871 Russia finally succeeded in getting the removal of Article XI of the Paris Treaty, allowing it to recommission its Black Sea Fleet. Events moved so rapidly in the fifteen years since the treaty that the international landscape was almost unrecognizable: with Napoleon III in exile in England following his removal by the forces of the Third Republic, Austria and France reduced in power and prestige, and the establishment of Germany and Italy as new states, the issues and passions of the Crimean War rapidly receded into the distance.

*

Russia did not lose a lot in terms of territory but it was humbled by the Paris Treaty. Apart from the loss of its Black Sea Fleet and Bessarabia, it lost prestige in the Balkans and forfeited the gains that it had made in the Eastern Question since the eighteenth century. Russia did not recover the dominant position it had held in Europe until after 1945.

The demilitarization of the Black Sea was a major strategic blow to Russia, which was no longer able to protect its vulnerable southern coastal frontier against the British or any other fleet, should the Sultan call on them in the event of war. The destruction of the Russian Black Sea Fleet, Sevastopol and other naval docks was a humiliation. No compulsory disarmament had ever been imposed on a great power previously. Not even France had been disarmed after the Napoleonic Wars. The way Russia had been treated was unprecedented for the Concert of Europe, which was supposed to honour the principle that no great power should be humbled by others. But the allies did not really think that they were dealing with a European power in Russia. They regarded Russia as a semi-Asiatic state. During the negotiations at the Paris congress, Walewski had asked the British delegates whether it would not be too humiliating for the Russians if the Western powers installed consuls in their Black Sea ports to police the demobilization. Cowley insisted that it would not, pointing out that a similar condition had been imposed on China by the Treaty of Nanking after the First Opium War.[34]

In Russia itself, the Crimean defeat discredited the armed services and highlighted the need to modernize the country's defences, not just in the strictly military sense, but also through the building of railways, industrialization, sound finances and so on. The Ministry of War lost the favoured position it had held in the government system of Nicholas I and became overshadowed by the ministries of Finance and the Interior, although unavoidably it continued to receive the lion's share of state expenditure.

The image many Russians had built up of their country – the biggest, richest and most powerful in the world – had suddenly been shattered. Russia's backwardness had been exposed. Calls for reform were heard from every quarter of society. Everything was open to question. The Crimean disaster had exposed the shortcomings of every institution in Russia – not just the corruption and incompetence of the military command, the technological backwardness of the army and the navy, or the inadequate roads and lack of railways that accounted for the chronic problems of supply, but the poor condition and illiteracy of the serfs who had made up the armed forces, the inability of the serf economy to sustain a state at war against the industrial powers, and the failures of autocracy itself. Critics focused on Nicholas I, whose arrogant and wilful policies had led the country to ruin and sacrificed so many lives. 'Public opinion is now very scornful of the memory of Nicholas,' Tiutcheva noted in her diary.

> With every new setback there are bitter reproaches against his name. They accuse him of pursuing a purely personal policy, which for the sake of his own pride and glory renounced the historical traditions of Russia, failed our brothers, the Orthodox Slavs, and turned the Tsar into the Gendarme of Europe when he could and should have brought new life to the East and the Church.

Even in the governing élite the bankruptcy of the Nicholaevan system was recognized. 'My God, so many victims,' wrote the tsarist censor Alexander Nikitenko in his diary. 'All at the behest of a mad will, drunk with absolute power and arrogance. . . . We have been waging war not for two years, but for thirty, maintaining an army of a million men and constantly threatening Europe. What was the point of it all? What profit, what glory has Russia reaped from this?' A few years earlier, Nikitenko reflected, the pan-Slav nationalists in Moscow had been preaching that the West was in decline, that a new Slavic civilization under Russian leadership would take its place. 'And now Europe has proved to us in our ignorance and apathy, our arrogant contempt for her civilization, just how decayed Russia really is! Oh what wretches we are!'[35]

One of the voices calling for reform belonged to Tolstoy, whose *Sevastopol Sketches* had catapulted him to literary fame. Tolstoy's experience of the Crimean War shaped his ideas on life and literature. He had witnessed at first hand the incompetence and corruption of many officers, and their often brutal treatment of the ordinary soldiers and sailors, whose courage and resilience had inspired him. It was in his diary of the campaign that he first developed his ideas for radical reform and vowed to fight injustice with his pen. On his way from Odessa to Sevastopol in November 1854, he was told by the pilot of his boat about the transport of the soldiers: 'how a soldier lay down in the pouring rain on the wet bottom of the boat and fell asleep; how an officer beat a soldier for scratching himself; and how a soldier shot himself during the crossing for fear of having overstayed his leave by two days and how he was thrown overboard without burial.' The contrast with the way he thought the ordinary soldier was treated in the Western armies brought home the need for change. 'I spent a couple of hours chatting with French and English wounded,' Tolstoy noted in his diary at Eski-Orda near Simferopol the same month.

> Every soldier is proud of his position and respects himself, for he feels himself to be an effective spring in the army machine. Good weapons and the skill to use them, youth, and general ideas about politics and the arts give them an awareness of their own worth. With us, stupid foot and arms drills, useless weapons, oppression, age, lack of education, and bad food and keep destroy the men's last spark of pride, and even give them too high an opinion of the enemy.[36]

It is doubtful whether many private soldiers in the French or British army had strong ideas about the arts. As with so much Russian admiration of 'the West', there was a good deal of naivety in Tolstoy's assessment, but such ideals gave energy to his reformist zeal.

On the death of Nicholas I, Tolstoy drafted 'A Plan for the Reform of the Army' and presented it to Count Osten-Sacken, the commander of the Sevastopol garrison, in the hope that he would forward it to the new Tsar Alexander, who was said to favour more humane policies.

On the strength of this rumour, Tolstoy opened his proposal with a bold declaration of principle that was true in part yet hardly a fair comment on the brave defenders of Sevastopol:

> My conscience and sense of justice forbid me to keep silent in the face of the evil being openly perpetrated before me, causing the deaths of millions and sapping our strength and undermining our country's honour. . . . We have no army, we have a horde of slaves cowed by discipline, ordered about by thieves and slave traders. This horde is not an army because it possesses neither any real loyalty to faith, tsar and fatherland – words that have been so much misused! – nor valour, nor military dignity. All it possesses are, on the one hand, passive patience and repressed discontent, and on the other, cruelty, servitude and corruption.

Tolstoy strongly condemned the harsh treatment of the serf soldiers. In an early version of his proposals he even went so far as to maintain that in 'every beaten soldier' there was a buried 'feeling of revenge' that was 'too suppressed to appear yet as a real force' but was waiting to erupt ('and Oh Lord what horrors lie in wait for our society if that should occur'). He later cut this inflammatory sentence, on the calculation that it would scotch his reform ideas in government circles. Tolstoy called for an end to corporal punishment in the army, blaming Russia's poor performance in the Crimean War on the brutalization of the troops. He advanced plans for the reform of the artillery, which had been shown to be so ineffective against the Minié rifles. Putting forward his ideas about how to improve the command, he delivered a devastating critique of the officers in the Crimea, denouncing them as cruel and corrupt, concerned mainly with the minutiae of the soldiers' uniforms and drill, and serving in the army only because they were unfit for anything else. But once again he cut out a fiery passage – in which he had claimed that the senior commanders were courtiers, selected because the Tsar liked them and not for their competence – on the grounds that it would lessen his chances of getting a hearing for his plans. It was already being rumoured that he was the anonymous author of a satirical army song in which the defeats in the Crimea were blamed on the incompetence of the officers with the biggest epaulettes. The ballad circulated widely in the army and society, earning Tolstoy, as its suspected author, a reprimand from the Grand

Duke Mikhail Nikolaevich, the Tsar's brother, who accused the verses of destroying the morale of the soldiers.* Though Tolstoy's authorship was never established, he was denied promotion beyond second lieutenant, a rank he had obtained before his arrival in Sevastopol.[37]

Tolstoy's experience in the Crimean War had led him to question more than just the military system. The poet Afanasy Fet, who first met Tolstoy in Turgenev's St Petersburg apartment in the winter of 1855, was struck by the young man's 'automatic opposition to all generally accepted opinions'. Living side by side with the ordinary soldiers in the Crimea had opened Tolstoy's eyes to the simple virtues of the peasantry; it had set him on a restless search for a new truth, for a way to live morally as a Russian nobleman and landowner, given the injustices of serfdom. He had touched on these matters before. In *A Landowner's Morning* (1852), he wrote about a landowner (for which read: Tolstoy) who seeks a life of happiness and justice in the country and learns that it can only be found in constant labour for the good of others less happy than himself. At around the same time, he had proposed to reduce the dues of the serfs on his estate at Yasnaya Polyana, but the serfs were suspicious of his intentions (they were not accustomed to such benevolence) and had turned his offer down. But it was only in the Crimea that Tolstoy began to feel a close attachment to the serfs in uniform – those 'simple and kind men, whose goodness is apparent during a real war'. He was disgusted with his former life – the gambling, the whoring, the excessive feasting and drinking, the embarrassment of riches, and the lack of any real work or purpose in his life. And after the war, he threw himself into the task of living with the peasants in 'a life of truth' with new determination.[38]

By the time of Tolstoy's return, there was a new reformist spirit in the air. Among the more liberal and enlightened noblemen it was generally accepted that the time had come to liberate their serfs. In

---

* In 1857 the army song was published by the socialist exile Alexander Herzen in his periodical the *Polar Star*. The ballad was well known in the student revolutionary circles of the 1860s and was later even cited by Lenin. In fact, Tolstoy was not wholly responsible for the song, which expressed a discontent that was widely felt in the army. It originated with a group of artillery officers, including Tolstoy, who gathered round the piano in the rooms of their commander on an almost daily basis to drink and sing and make up songs. As he was already known for his writing, Tolstoy, who no doubt played a leading role in the composition of the verses, took most of the blame for them.

the words of Sergei Volkonsky, the famous Decembrist and one of Tolstoy's distant relatives, who was released from his Siberian exile in 1856, the abolition of serfdom was 'the least the state could do to recognize the sacrifice the peasantry has made in the last two wars: it is time to recognize that the Russian peasant is a citizen as well'. The peasant soldiers who had fought in the Crimea had been led to expect their freedom. In the spring of 1854 thousands of peasants had turned up at the recruiting stations after hearing rumours that freedom had been promised by the Tsar to any serf who volunteered for the army or navy, and there had been clashes with the soldiers and police when they were turned away. Expectations of emancipation mounted after the Crimean War. In the first six years of Alexander's reign there were 500 peasant uprisings and strikes against the gentry on the land.[39]

The new Tsar believed that the liberation of the serfs was a necessary measure to prevent a revolution. 'It is better to abolish serfdom from above than to wait for the time when it begins to abolish itself from below,' he told a group of Moscow noblemen in 1856. The defeat in the Crimean War had persuaded Alexander that Russia could not compete with the Western powers until it swept aside its old serf economy and modernized itself. The gentry had very little idea how to make a profit from their estates. Most of them knew next to nothing about agriculture or accounting. Yet they went on spending in the same old lavish way as they had always done, mounting up enormous debts. By 1859 one-third of the estates and two-thirds of the serfs owned by the landed nobles had been mortgaged to the state and noble banks. The economic argument for emancipation was becoming irrefutable, and many landowners were shifting willy-nilly to the free labour system by contracting other people's serfs. Since the peasantry's redemption payments would cancel out the gentry's debts, the economic rationale was becoming irresistible.*

---

* Under the terms of the emancipation, the peasants were obliged to pay redemption dues on the land transferred to them. These repayments, calculated by the gentry's own land commissions, were to be repaid over a forty-nine-year period to the state, which recompensed the gentry in 1861. Thus, in effect, the serfs bought their freedom by paying off their masters' debts. The redemption payments became increasingly difficult to collect, not least because the peasantry regarded them as unjust from the start. They were finally cancelled in 1905.

In 1858 the Tsar appointed a special commission to formulate proposals for the emancipation in consultation with provincial gentry committees. Under pressure from diehard squires to limit the reform or to fix the rules for the land transfers in their favour, the commission became bogged down in political wrangling for the best part of two years. In the end, the reactionary gentry were defeated and the moderate reformists got their way, thanks in no small measure to the personal intervention of the Tsar. The Edict of Emancipation was signed by Alexander on 19 February 1861 and read to the peasants by their parish priests. It was not as far-reaching as the peasantry had expected. The Edict allowed the landowners considerable leeway in choosing the bits of land for transfer to the peasantry, and in setting the redemption dues the peasant communes would have to pay for them, whereas the peasants had expected to be given all the land without payment.* There were rebellions in many areas, sometimes after rumours circulated that the published law was not the one the Tsar had meant to sign but a forgery by nobles and officials who wanted to prevent the real emancipation, the long-awaited 'Golden Manifesto' in which the Tsar would liberate the peasants and give them all the land.

Despite the disappointment of the peasantry, the emancipation was a crucial watershed. Freedom of a sort, however limited it may have been in practice, had at last been granted to the mass of the people, and there were grounds to hope for a national rebirth. Writers compared the Edict to the conversion of Russia to Christianity in the tenth century. They spoke about the need for Young Russia to liberate itself from the sins of its past, whose riches had been purchased by the people's sweat and blood, about the need for the landlord and the peasant to overcome their old divisions and become reconciled by nationality. For, as Fedor Dostoevsky wrote in 1861, 'every Russian is a Russian first of all'.[40]

Along with the emancipation of the serfs, the defeat in the Crimean War accelerated the Tsar's plans for a reform of the army. Tolstoy was not the only officer to advance proposals for reform during the Crimean War. In the summer of 1855, Count Fedor Ridiger, commander of the

---

* Overall, perhaps half the farming land in European Russia was transferred from the gentry's ownership to the communal tenure of the peasantry, although the precise proportion depended largely on the landowner's will.

Guards and Grenadiers, endorsed many of Tolstoy's criticisms of the officers corps in a memorandum to the Tsar. Blaming Russia's imminent defeat on the gross incompetence of the senior command and the army's administration, Ridiger advised that officers should be trained in military science rather than in parades and reviews, and that those with talent should be given wider scope to take responsibility on the battlefield. Shortly afterwards, similar ideas were put forward by another high-ranking member of the military establishment, Adjutant General V. A. Glinka, who also criticized the army's system of supply. Proposals were advanced for the building of railways, the lack of which, it was agreed by everyone, had been a major reason for the supply problems of the military during the Crimean War.[41]

The Tsar set up a 'Commission for the Improvement of the Military Sphere' under General Ridiger, but then began to waver over implementing its proposed reforms, with which he clearly sympathized, although plans for a network of railways to link Moscow and St Petersburg with the major centres of agriculture and the border areas were approved by the Tsar as early as January 1857. Alexander was afraid of a possible reaction by the aristocracy at a time when he needed its support for the emancipation of the serfs. He put in charge of the War Ministry a man well known for his loyalty and military incompetence, General Nikolai Sukhozanet, who oversaw a period of tinkering reforms, mostly minor statutes altering the appearance of the Guards' uniforms, but including two initiatives that were to have more significance: a revision of the Military Criminal Statute to reduce the maximum number of lashes permissible as corporal punishment from 6,000 to 1,500 (a figure still quite adequate to kill any soldier); and measures to improve the education and military training of the peasant soldiers, who were nearly all illiterate and unfit for modern war, as the Crimean War had clearly shown.

One of the results of these attempts to improve the army's education was the creation of a new journal, *Voennyi sbornik* (Military Miscellany). Its aim was to appeal to officers and soldiers by presenting them with lively articles about military science and affairs, stories, poems and articles about society written in a liberal spirit of reform. Exempted from military censorship, it was similar in conception to the 'Military Gazette' which Tolstoy had proposed in 1854. Its literary section was edited by Nikolai Chernyshevsky, editor of the hugely influential democratic journal the *Contemporary*, in which Tolstoy's own works had appeared. Chernyshevsky was himself the author of the novel *What Is to Be Done?* (1862) which would inspire several generations of revolutionaries, including Lenin. By the 1860s, *Voennyi sbornik* was rivalling the sales of the *Contemporary*, with more than 5,000 subscribers, demonstrating that ideas of reform had a receptive audience in the Russian army after the Crimean War.

The idea of setting up *Voennyi sbornik* had come from Dmitry Miliutin, the main driving force behind the military reforms after the Crimean War. A professor at the Military Academy, where he had taught since being gravely wounded in the campaign against Shamil in the Caucasus in 1838, Miliutin was a brilliant military analyst who quickly took on board the lessons of the defeat in the Crimea: the need to reform and modernize the military on the model of the Western forces that had so roundly beaten Russia's backward serf army. He soon had a chance to apply these lessons to the Tsar's ongoing struggles in the Caucasus.

In 1856 the Tsar had appointed his long-time confidant Prince A. I. Bariatinsky as viceroy of the Caucasus, with extraordinary powers to finish off the war against Shamil. Bariatinsky was an advocate of expanding Russia's influence in the Caucasus and Central Asia as an antidote to the curtailment of her influence in Europe after the Crimean War. Alexander was persuaded by his arguments. Even before the Paris Treaty was announced, the Tsar announced his intention to step up the campaign against the Muslim rebels in the Caucasus. He exempted units in the Caucasus from the general military demobilization, mobilized new regiments, and ordered a consignment of 10,000 Minié rifles purchased from abroad to be sent to Bariatinsky, who by the end of 1857 had overall control of more than one-sixth of the military budget and 300,000 men. Bariatinsky brought in Miliutin as his chief of staff to introduce the military reforms which he saw were needed in the Caucasus: if they were successful there, they would reinforce the arguments for the reform of the Russian army as a whole. Drawing on Western military thinking as well as the proposals of General Ridiger, Miliutin proposed to rationalize the chain of command, giving more initiative and control of resources to local commanders to exercise their judgement in response to local conditions, an idea predicated on a general improvement in the training of officers.[42]

The end of the Crimean War had left Shamil's movement completely demoralized. Without the intervention of the Western powers and little real assistance from the Ottomans, the guerrilla movement of the Muslim tribes came to the end of its ability to continue fighting the Russians. The Chechens were exhausted by the war, which had lasted forty years, and delegations from all over Chechnya were appealing to Shamil to make peace with the Russians. Shamil wanted to fight on. But against the massive surge of military forces deployed by Bariatinsky he was unable to hold out for long and he finally surrendered to the Russians on 25 August 1859.*

On the basis of the army's triumph in the Caucasus, in November 1861 Miliutin was appointed Minister of War on Bariatinsky's recommendation to the Tsar. Once the Edict of Emancipation had been passed, Alexander felt the time had at last come to push through the military reforms. The legislative package presented by Miliutin to the Tsar built upon his earlier plans. The most important piece of legislation (passed only in 1874) was the introduction of universal conscription, with military service declared compulsory for all males at the age of 20. Organized through a territorial system of military districts for the maintenance of a peacetime standing army, the new Russian system was similar to the modern conscript armies of other European states, although in tsarist Russia, where government finances were inadequate and class, religious and ethnic hierarchies continued to be felt in the application of every policy, the universal principle was never fully realized. The main emphasis of Miliutin's legislation was on military efficiency but humanitarian concerns were never far behind in his reform. His fundamental mission was to reshape the

---

* Shamil was sent to St Petersburg for a meeting with the Tsar. There he was treated as a celebrity by the Russian public, which for years had lived on tales of his courage and daring. Exiled to Kaluga, Shamil suffered from the cold. In 1868 he was moved to the warmer climate of Kiev, where he was given a mansion and a pension, and placed under only loose surveillance by the authorities. In 1869 he was allowed to leave for a pilgrimage to Mecca on condition that he left his oldest sons in Russia as hostages. After completing his pilgrimage to Mecca, he died in Medina in 1871. Two of his sons became officers in the Russian army, but two others fought for the Turks against the Russians in 1877–8.

army's culture so that it related to the peasant soldier as a citizen and no longer as a serf. The army schools were modernized, with greater emphasis on the teaching of military science and technology. Elementary schooling was made compulsory for all recruits, so that the army became an important means of education for the peasantry. The military justice system was reformed and corporal punishment was abolished, in theory at least, for in practice the Russian soldier continued to be punished physically and sometimes even flogged for relatively minor infringements of discipline. The army's culture of serfdom continued to be felt by the common soldier until 1917.

*

The Crimean War reinforced in Russia a long-felt sense of resentment against Europe. There was a feeling of betrayal that the West had sided with the Turks against Russia. It was the first time in history that a European alliance had fought on the side of a Muslim power against another Christian state in a major war.

No one resented Europe more than Dostoevsky. At the time of the Crimean War, he was serving as a soldier in the fortress of Semipalatinsk in Central Asia following his release from a Siberian prison camp, to which he had been exiled for his involvement in the left-wing Petrashevsky circle in 1849. In the only published verse he ever wrote (and the poetic qualities of 'On the European Events of 1854' are such that one can see why this was so), Dostoevsky portrayed the Crimean War as the 'crucifixion of the Russian Christ'. But, as he warned the Western readers of his poem, Russia would arise and, when she did so, she would turn towards the East in her providential mission to Christianize the world.

> Unclear to you is her predestination!
> The East – is hers! To her a million generations
> Untiringly stretch out their hands. . . .
> And the resurrection of the ancient East
> By Russia (so God has commanded) is drawing near.[43]

Having been defeated by the West, Russia turned towards Asia in its imperial plans. For Bariatinsky and the War Ministry, the defeat of

Shamil in the Caucasus was to serve as a springboard for the Russian conquest of the independent khanates of Central Asia. Gorchakov and the Foreign Ministry were not so sure, fearing that an expansionist policy would set back their attempts to mend relations with the British and the French. Caught at first between these opposing policies, in 1856–7 the Tsar moved towards the view that Russia's destiny lay in Asia and that only Britain stood in the way of its fulfilment. Deeply influenced by the climate of mutual suspicion between Russia and Britain after the Crimean War, it was a viewpoint that would define Russia's policies in the Great Game, its imperial rivalry with Britain for supremacy in Central Asia.

The Tsar was concerned by the growing presence of the British in Persia following their victory in the Anglo-Persian War of 1856–7. By the Paris Treaty of March 1857, the Persians withdrew from Herat, the north-western Afghan city they had occupied with Russian backing in 1852 and 1856. From his correspondence with Bariatinsky, it is clear that Alexander was afraid that the British would use their influence in Tehran to install themselves on the southern shores of the Caspian. He shared Bariatinsky's gloomy prediction that 'the appearance of the British flag on the Caspian would be a fatal blow not only to our influence in the East, not only to our foreign trade, but also to the political independence of the [Russian] Empire'.

Alexander commissioned a report from Sukhozanet, 'On the Possibility of an Armed Clash between Russia and England in Central Asia'. Although the report rejected the idea of a British military threat, the Tsar persisted in his fear that the British might deploy their Indian army to conquer Central Asia and expel the Russians from the Caucasus. In the spring of 1857 the British steamer *Kangaroo* and several smaller vessels carrying military supplies for Shamil's forces had been caught on the Circassian coast. Russia no longer had a Black Sea Fleet to block such acts of intervention into its affairs by the British. Alexander demanded 'categorical explanations' from the British government, but received none. The 'unmentionable infamy', as he called the *Kangaroo* affair, reinforced the Tsar's belief that Russia would not be secure against the British threat as long as the Caucasus remained unconquered and the Central Asian steppe beyond her political control.

Throughout the Crimean War the Russians had considered various ideas for an attack through Central Asia towards Kandahar and India, mainly as a means of diverting British troops from the Crimea. Although these plans were all rejected as impracticable, rumours of a Russian invasion were widely circulated and believed in India, where inflammatory pamphlets called on Muslims and Hindus to take advantage of the exhaustion of the British in the Crimea to rise up against their rule. The outbreak of the Indian Mutiny in the early summer of 1857 encouraged the Tsar to reconsider his Central Asia plans. The Royal Navy could threaten Russia's coastline in the Baltic, in the Pacific Ocean and in the Black Sea, which was now defenceless as a result of the demilitarization imposed on the Russians by the Paris Treaty. The only place where the Russians could even pretend to mount a counter-threat was in India. The British were extremely sensitive to any threat against their Indian empire, mainly because of their fragile tax-base there, which they dared not increase for political reasons. Few Russians strategists believed in the reality of a campaign against India, but exploiting British nervousness was good tactics.

In the autumn of 1857 the Tsar commissioned a strategic memorandum on Central Asia by a brilliant young military attaché, Nikolai Ignat'ev, who had been brought to his attention after he had represented Russia on the question of its disputed border with Moldavia at the Paris congress. Considering the possibility of a renewed war against Britain, Ignat'ev argued that the only place where Russia stood a chance of victory was in Asia. Russia's strength in Central Asia was the 'best guarantee of peace', so Russia should exploit the Indian crisis to strengthen its position at the expense of Britain in 'the countries which separate Russia from the British possessions'. Ignat'ev proposed sending expeditions to explore and map the 'undiscovered' steppe of Central Asia for the benefit of Russian trade and military intelligence. By developing commercial and diplomatic ties with the khanates of Kokand, Bukhara and Khiva, Russia could turn them into buffer states against British expansion. Giving his approval to the plan, the Tsar sent an exploratory party to Khiva and Bukhara under the leadership of Ignat'ev which concluded economic treaties with the two khanates in the summer of 1858. Officially, the mission had been sent by the Foreign Ministry, but unofficially it was also working for the War Ministry, collecting topographical, statistical and 'general military information' on various routes into Central Asia. From the start of the Russian initiative there was a more forward policy, favoured by the followers of Bariatinsky in the War Ministry, to set up protectorates and military bases in the khanates for the conquest of Turkestan and the Central Asian steppe right up to the borders of Afghanistan.[44]

The Russian advance into Central Asia was led by two veterans of the Crimean War. One was Mikhail Cherniaev, who had fought against the Turks on the Danube in 1853 and had distinguished himself for his bravery at Inkerman and Sevastopol, before being transferred to defend Russian colonists against the raids of the Central Asian tribes on the steppes of southern Orenburg. From 1858 Cherniaev began launching his own raids deep into the territory of Turkestan, destroying Kirghiz and other hostile tribal settlements and supporting rebellions against the khanates of Khiva and Kokand by other Central Asian tribes who were willing to declare their allegiance to Russia. Cherniaev's military initiatives, quietly supported but not endorsed officially by the War Ministry, led by stealth to the Russian annexation of Turkestan. In 1864, Cherniaev led a force of a thousand men across the steppes of Turkestan to occupy the fortress of Chimkent. Joined by a second Russian column from Semipalatinsk, they then seized Tashkent, 130 kilometres to the south, effectively imposing Russian rule on this vital power-base of the Central Asian cotton trade. Cherniaev was awarded the St George Cross and appointed military governor of Turkestan in 1865. After angry diplomatic protests by the British, who were afraid that the Russian troops might continue their advance from Tashkent to India, the Russian government disowned responsibility for the invasion carried out by Cherniaev. The general was forced into retirement in 1866. But unofficially he was received as a hero in Russia. The nationalist press proclaimed him the 'Ermak of the nineteenth century'.*

Meanwhile, the conquest of the Central Asian steppe was carried on by General Kaufman, a second veteran of the Crimean War, who

---

* Ermak Timofeevich, the sixteenth-century Cossack leader and folk hero who began the exploration and military conquest of Siberia.

had led the sappers at the siege of Kars before becoming Miliutin's chief of engineers at the War Ministry. Kaufman replaced Cherniaev as the military governor of Turkestan. In 1868 he completed the conquest of Samarkand and Bukhara. Five years later Khiva also fell to the Russians, followed by Kokand in 1876. Left in the hands of their respective khans as far as their internal government was concerned, but subject to the control of the Russians in their foreign relations, Bukhara and Khiva became essentially protectorates along the lines of the Princely States of British India.

Cherniaev and Ignat'ev became leading figures in the pan-Slav movement of the 1860s and 1870s. Along with Russia's turn towards the East, pan-Slavism was the other main reaction by the Russians to their defeat in the Crimean War, as their feelings of resentment against Europe led to an explosion of nationalist sentiment. With censorship relaxed by the liberal reforms of the new Tsar, a new slew of pan-Slav journals forcefully criticized Russia's foreign policy before the Crimean War. In particular, they attacked the legitimist policies of Nicholas I for having sacrificed the Balkan Christians to Muslim rule in the interests of the Concert of Europe. 'For the sake of the balance of Europe,' Pogodin wrote in the first number of the pan-Slav journal *Parus* in January 1859, 'ten million Slavs are forced to groan, suffer, and agonize under the yoke of the most savage despotism, the most unbridled fanaticism, and the most desperate ignorance.'[45] With Gorchakov's abandonment of these legitimist principles, the pan-Slavs renewed their calls on the government to support the liberation of the Balkan Slavs from Turkish rule. Some went so far as to claim that Russia should protect itself against a hostile West by uniting all the Slavs of Europe under Russian leadership – an idea first put forward by Pogodin during the Crimean War and repeated with even more insistence in his writings afterwards.

As pan-Slav ideas gained influence in Russian intellectual and government circles, there was a proliferation of philanthropic organizations to promote the pan-Slav cause by sending money to the Balkan Slavs for schools and churches, or by bringing students to Russia. The Moscow Slavic Benevolent Committee was established in 1858, with separate branches opening in St Petersburg and Kiev in the 1860s. Funded by private benefactors and the Ministry of Education, it brought together officials and miltary men (many of them veterans of the Crimean War who had fought in the Balkans) with academics and writers (including Dostoevsky and Tiutchev, who both belonged to the St Petersburg Committee).

During the first post-war years the pan-Slavs were cautious not to discuss openly their more radical ideas of Slavic political unification, nor to criticize too severely the foreign policy of the government (the views expressed by Pogodin led to *Parus* being banned). But by the early 1860s, when Ignat'ev emerged as a pan-Slav supporter and became a leading figure in the government, they became more vocal in their views. Ignat'ev's growing influence in foreign affairs was based largely on his highly successful negotiation of the Sino-Russian Treaty of Beijing, in November 1860, which gave Russia possession of the Amur and Ussuri regions as well as Vladivostok in the Far East. In 1861 Ignat'ev became Director of the Asiatic Department of the Foreign Ministry, the office responsible for Russia's policy in the Balkans. Three years later he was appointed as the Tsar's envoy to Constantinople – a post he held until the Russo-Turkish war of 1877–8. Throughout these years Ignat'ev pushed for a military solution to the Eastern Question in the Balkans: Russian-sponsored Slav uprisings against Turkish rule and the intervention of the tsarist army, leading to the liberation of the Slavs and the creation of a Slavic Union under Russian leadership.

Pan-Slav ambitions for the Balkans focused first on Serbia, where the restoration of the Europeanized but autocratic Prince Mihailo to the throne in 1860 was seen as a victory for Russian influence and yet another defeat for the Austrians. Gorchakov supported the Serb movement for liberation from the Turks, fearing otherwise that, if they gained independence on their own, the Serbs would fall under Austrian or Western influence. Writing to the Russian consul in Bucharest, the Foreign Minister underlined that 'our policy in the East is directed mainly toward strengthening Serbia materially and morally and giving her the opportunity to stand at the head of the movement in the Balkans'. Ignat'ev went further, advocating an immediate solution to the Eastern Question by military means. Taking up a proposal by Mihailo, he urged the Russian government to support the Serbs in a war against the Turks and help them form a confederation with the Bulgarians, to which Bosnia, Herzegovina and Montenegro could be joined.

Under pan-Slav pressure, the Russian Foreign Ministry increased its support for the Serb movement. After a Turkish bombardment of Belgrade in 1862, the Russians called a special conference of the signatories of the Paris Treaty at Kanlidze near Constantinople and eventually succeeded in getting the removal of the final Turkish garrisons from Serbia in 1867. It was their first major diplomatic victory since the end of the Crimean War. Encouraged by their success, the Russians gave their backing to the Serbian attempt to create a Balkan League. Serbia formed a military alliance with Montenegro and Greece and a pact of friendship with the Romanian leadership, and established closer ties with Croatian and Bulgarian nationalists. The Russians subsidized the Serb army, though a mission sent by Miliutin to inspect it found it in a chronic state. Then in the autumn of 1867 Prince Mihailo backed away from war against the Turks, prompting Russia to suspend its war credits. The assassination of Mihailo the following June confirmed the end of Russian–Serb cooperation and the collapse of the Balkan League.[46]

The next seven years were a period of relative calm in the Balkans. The imperial monarchies of Russia, Austria-Hungary and Germany (the Three Emperors' League of 1873) guaranteed the preservation of the status quo in the Balkans. Official Russian policy in these years was based on a firm commitment to the European balance of power, and on that basis Gorchakov secured a major diplomatic victory with the annulment of the Paris Treaty's Black Sea clauses at a conference of the European powers in London in 1871. But unofficially the policy of Russia remained the encouragement of the pan-Slav movement in the Balkans – a policy coordinated by Ignat'ev from the Russian embassy in Constantinople through its consulates in the Balkan capitals. In his memoirs, written at the end of his long life in the 1900s, Ignat'ev explained that his aim in the Balkans in the 1860s and 1870s had been to destroy the Treaty of Paris, to recover southern Bessarabia, and to control the Turkish Straits, either directly through military conquest or indirectly through a treaty with a dependent Turkey, of the kind Russia had enjoyed before the Crimean War. 'All my activities in Turkey and among the Slavs', he wrote, 'were inspired by ... the view that Russia alone could rule in the Balkan peninsula and Black Sea ... Austria-Hungary's expansion would be halted and the Balkan peoples, especially the Slavs, would direct their gaze exclusively to Russia and make their future dependent on her.'[47]

In the summer of 1875 revolts by Christians against Turkish rule in Herzegovina spread north into Bosnia, and then into Montenegro and Bulgaria. The revolts had been sparked by a sharp increase in taxes levied by the Turkish government on the Christian peasants after harvest failures had left the Porte in a financial crisis. But they soon took on the character of a religious war. The leaders of the uprisings looked to Serbia and Russia for support. Encouraged by Ignat'ev, Serbian nationalists in Belgrade called on their government to send in troops to defend the Slavs against the Turks and unite them in a Greater Serbia.

In Bulgaria, the rebels were badly armed and organized, but their hatred of the Turks was intense. In the spring of 1876 the revolt spilled over into massacres against the Muslim population, which had increased massively since the Crimean War as a result of the immigration of about half a million Crimean Tatars and Circassians fleeing from the Russians to Bulgaria. Tensions with the Christians were intensified when the newcomers reverted to a semi-nomadic way of life, launching raids on the Christian settlements and stealing livestock in a way not experienced before by the peasants in the area. Lacking enough regular troops to quell the Bulgarians, the Ottoman authorities used the Bashi Bazouks, irregulars mostly drawn from the local Muslim population, who brutally suppressed their Christian neighbours, massacring around 12,000 people in the process. In the mountain village of Batak, where a thousand Christians had taken refuge in a church, the Bashi Bazouks set fire to the building, burning to death all but one old woman, who survived to tell the tale.[48]

News of the Bulgarian atrocities spread throughout the world. The British press claimed that 'tens of thousands' of defenceless Christian villagers had been slaughtered by 'fanatical Muslims'. British attitudes to Turkey changed dramatically. The old policy of promoting the Tanzimat reforms in the belief that the Turks were willing pupils of English liberal governance was seriously questioned, and for many Christians completely undermined, by the Bulgarian massacres. Gladstone, the leader of the Liberal opposition whose views on foreign policy were closely linked to his High Church Anglican moral principles, took the lead in a popular campaign for British intervention to protect the Balkan Christians against Turkish violence. Gladstone had only cautiously supported the Crimean War. He was hostile to the presence of the Turks in Europe on religious grounds, and had long wanted to use British influence to secure more autonomy for the Christians in the Ottoman Empire. In 1856 he had even advanced the idea of a new Greek empire in the Balkans to protect the Christians, not just against the Muslims of Turkey, but against the Russians and the Pope.[49]

The strongest reaction to the Bulgarian atrocities was in Russia. Sympathy for the Bulgarians engulfed the whole of educated society in a surge of patriotic feeling, intensified by a national desire for revenge against the Turks after the Crimean War. Calls for intervention to protect the Bulgarians were heard from all quarters: from Slavophiles, such as Dostoevsky, who saw in a war for the liberation of the Balkan Slavs the fulfilment of Russia's historical destiny to unite the Orthodox; and from Westernizers, such as Turgenev, who thought it was the duty of the liberal world to liberate enslaved Bulgaria. Here was a golden opportunity for the pan-Slavs to realize their dreams.

Officially, the Russian government denounced the Christian revolts in the Balkans. It was on the defensive, having been accused by Western governments of instigating the revolts. But pan-Slav opinion, and in particular the journal *Russkii mir* (Russian World), owned and edited by Cherniaev, the former military governor of Turkestan, came out in support of the Balkan Christian cause and called on the government to support it. 'Speak but one word, Russia,' *Russkii mir* predicted, 'and not only the entire Balkans ... but all the Slav peoples ... will rise in arms against their oppressors. In alliance with her 25 million fellow Orthodox, Russia will strike fear into all of Western Europe.' Everything depended on the actions of Serbia, the 'Piedmont of the Balkans', in the phrase of Cherniaev. The Tsar and Gorchakov warned the Serbian leaders not to intervene in the uprisings, though privately they sympathized with the pan-Slavs ('Do anything you like provided we do not know anything about it officially,' Baron Jomini, the acting head of the Russian Foreign Ministry, told a member of the St Petersburg Committee). Encouraged by Ignat'ev and the Russian consul in Belgrade, as well as by the arrival of Cherniaev as a volunteer for the Slav cause in April, the Serb leaders declared war on Turkey in June 1876.[50]

The Serbs were counting on the armed intervention of Russia. Cherniaev was in charge of their main army. Along with his presence, Ignat'ev's promises had led them to believe that this would be a repetition of the Balkan war of 1853–4, when Nicholas I had sent his army into the Danubian principalities in the expectation – ultimately disappointed – that it would encourage a war of liberation by the Slavs. Public opinion in Russia was increasingly belligerent. The nationalist press called on the army to defend the Christians against the Turks. Pan-Slav groups sent volunteers to fight on their behalf – and about five thousand made their way to Serbia.* Subscriptions were organized to send money to the Slavs. Pro-Slav feeling swept across society. People talked about the war as a crusade – a repeat of the war against the Turks in 1854.

By the autumn of 1876 war fever had spread to the Russian court and government circles. Cherniaev's army faced defeat. Responding to his desperate pleas for help, the Tsar sent an ultimatum to the Porte and mobilized his troops. This was enough to force the Turks to end hostilities against the Serbs, who duly made their peace with them. Abandoning the Serbs, the Russians shifted their support to the Bulgarians and demanded autonomy for them, which the Turks would not accept. With Austria's neutrality assured through promises of gains in Bosnia and Herzegovina, in April 1877 Russia declared war on Turkey once again.

From the start, the Russian offensive in the Balkans assumed the character of a religious war. It was overwhelmingly redolent of the opening Russo-Turkish phase of the Crimean War. As the Russians crossed the Danube under the command of the Grand Duke Nikolai, they were joined by Slav irregulars, Bulgarians and Serbs, some of them demanding money to fight, but most fighting for their national cause against the Turks. This was the sort of Christian war that Nicholas had wanted when his troops had crossed the Danube in 1853–4. Encouraged by the rising of the Slavs, Alexander considered pushing on to seize Constantinople and impose a Russian settlement on the

---

* Including the character of Vronsky at the end of Tolstoy's novel *Anna Karenina*.

Balkans. He was urged to do so not only by the pan-Slav press but by his own brother, the Grand Duke Nikolai, who wrote to him after his armies had captured Adrianople, a short march from Constantinople, in January 1878: 'We must go to the centre, to Tsargrad, and there finish the holy cause you have assumed.' Pan-Slav hopes were at their height. 'Constantinople must be ours,' wrote Dostoevsky, who saw its conquest by the Russian armies as nothing less than God's own resolution of the Eastern Question and as the fulfilment of Russia's destiny to liberate Orthodox Christianity.

> It is not only the magnificent port, not only the access to the seas and oceans, that binds Russia so closely to the resolution . . . of this fateful question, nor is it even the unification and regeneration of the Slavs. Our goal is more profound, immeasurably more profound. We, Russia, are truly essential and unavoidable both for the whole of Eastern Christendom and for the whole fate of future Orthodoxy on the earth, for its unity. This is what our people and their rulers have always understood. In short, this terrible Eastern Question is virtually our entire fate for years to come. It contains, as it were, all our goals and, mainly, our only way to move out into the fullness of history.[51]

Alarmed by the advance of the Russian troops to Adrianople, the British ordered their Mediterranean fleet to enter the Dardanelles and agreed in Parliament to raise £6 million for military purposes. It was a repeat of the movements that had led to the Crimean War. Under pressure from the British, the Russians agreed to an armistice with the Ottomans but continued advancing towards Constantinople, halting only under threat from the Royal Navy at San Stefano, a village just outside the Turkish capital, where on 3 March they signed a treaty with the Turks. By the Treaty of San Stefano, the Porte agreed to recognize the full independence of Romania, Serbia and Montenegro, as well as the autonomy of a large Bulgarian state (to include Macedonia and part of Thrace). In exchange for a narrow strip of land to the south of the Danube, Romania ceded back to Russia southern Bessarabia, the territory taken from the Russians by the Treaty of Paris. With the restoration of her Black Sea status completed seven years before, Russia had succeeded in reversing all the losses she had suffered after the Crimean War.

The Treaty of San Stefano was mainly Ignat'ev's doing. It was the realization of most of his pan-Slav dreams. But it was totally unacceptable to the Western powers, which had not gone to war to stop the Russians bullying the Turks in 1854 only to allow them to do so again twenty-four years afterwards. In Britain, the old warlike feelings against Russia were expressed in 'jingoism', a new aggressive mood of can-do foreign policy summed up by the current hit song of pubs and music halls:

> We don't want to fight but by Jingo if we do
> We've got the ships, we've got the men, we've got the money too
> We've fought the Bear before, and while we're Britons true
> The Russians shall not have Constantinople.

Afraid of British intervention and a possible repeat of the Crimean War, the Tsar ordered the Grand Duke to withdraw his troops to the Danube. As they did so they took part in revenge attacks against the Muslims of Bulgaria which were joined and sometimes instigated by Christian volunteers: several hundred thousand Muslims fled Bulgaria for the Ottoman Empire at the end of the Russo-Turkish war.

Determined to halt the extension of Russian power into the Balkans, the great powers met at the Congress of Berlin to revise the Treaty of San Stefano. The main objection of the British and the French was the establishment of a greater Bulgaria, which they viewed as a Russian Trojan horse threatening the Ottoman Empire in Europe. With direct access to the Aegean Sea in Macedonia, this enlarged Bulgarian state could easily be used by the Russians to attack the Turkish Straits. The British forced the Russians to agree to the division of Bulgaria, returning Macedonia and Thrace to direct Ottoman control. A week before the Berlin congress, Benjamin Disraeli, the British Prime Minister, had concluded a secret alliance with the Ottomans against Russia, whereby Britain was allowed to occupy the strategic island of Cyprus and bring in troops from India. The revelation of this alliance, along with Disraeli's threats of war, forced the Russians to concede to his demands.

The Congress of Berlin ended Russia's pan-Slav hopes. Ignat'ev was dismissed as the Tsar's envoy to Constantinople and went into retirement. Arriving back in London to a hero's welcome, Disraeli claimed that he had brought back 'Peace with honour' from Berlin. He told the House of Commons that the Treaty of Berlin and the Cyprus Convention would protect Britain and its route to India against Russian aggression for years to come. But tensions in the Balkans would remain. In many ways the congress sowed the seeds of the future Balkan wars and the First World War by leaving so many border disputes unresolved. Above all, the fundamental problem of the Eastern Question, the 'sick man of Europe', Turkey, remained without a cure. As the British Foreign Secretary, the Marquess of Salisbury, acknowledged on his return from Berlin, 'We shall set up a rickety sort of Turkish rule south of the Balkans once again. But it is a mere respite. There is no vitality left in it.'[52]

*

In Jerusalem, where all these international conflicts had begun, the end of the Crimean War was proclaimed on 14 April 1856. A salute from the Castle guns announced that the Pasha had been informed of the peace, and his troops assembled on the public square outside the Jaffa Gate for thanksgiving prayers led by the imam. It was to the same square that they had been summoned in September 1853 to go and fight for their Sultan against Russia.[53] History had come full circle in Jerusalem.

Twelve days later, on 26 April, the old religious rivalries began once again. Fights broke out between the Greeks and the Armenians during the ceremony of the Holy Fire in the Church of the Holy Sepulchre. For several days before the sacred ceremony, rival groups of pilgrims had smuggled various weapons into the church and concealed them there. Others were supplied with knives and iron spikes thrown from a window near the roof of the St Nicholas Convent. It was not clear how the fighting started, the British consul Finn, who witnessed it, reported three days afterwards, but 'during the conflict the missiles were also flung upwards to the galleries, demolishing rows of lamps and tearing church pictures representing the most sacred subjects of faith – glass and oil pouring down upon their heads – and silver lamps on silver chains were beaten down and the materials have since vanished'. The Pasha left his place in the gallery and ordered up his guard to separate the fighters. But he was badly hurt by a blow to his head and had to be carried away on his men's shoulders – the crowd in the church being too thick to allow a passage otherwise – while his secretary was also beaten up. Eventually, a squadron of the Pasha's soldiers rounded up the rioters, the church attendants cleared up all the mess, and the ceremony of the Holy Fire proceeded as usual, the monks standing guard before the tomb of Christ, the congregation chanting 'Lord have mercy', until the patriarch emerged bearing lighted candles, and, as the church bells rang, the pilgrims pressed towards him to light their torches from the miraculous flames.[54]

Epilogue: The Crimean War in Myth and Memory

The end of the Crimean War was marked by modest festivities in Britain. There was general disappointment that peace had come before the troops had scored a major victory to equal that of the French at Sevastopol and that they had failed to carry out a broader war against Russia. Mixed with this sense of failure was a feeling of outrage and national shame at the blunders of the government and military authorities. 'I own that peace rather sticks in my throat,' Queen Victoria noted in her journal on 11 March, 'and so it does in that of the *whole* Nation.' There was no great victory parade in London, no official ceremony to welcome home the troops, who arrived at Woolwich looking 'very sunburnt', according to the Queen. Watching several boatloads of soldiers disembark on 13 March, she thought they were 'the picture of *real* fighting men, such fine tall strong men, some strikingly handsome – all with such proud, noble, soldier-like bearing. . . . They all had long beards, and were heavily laden with large knapsacks, their cloaks and blankets on the top, canteens and full haversacks, and carrying their muskets.'[1]

But if there were no joyous celebrations, there were memorials – literally hundreds of commemorative plaques and monuments, paid for in the main by groups of private individuals and erected in memory of lost and fallen soldiers in church graveyards, regimental barracks, hospitals and schools, city halls and museums, on town squares and village greens across the land. Of the 98,000 British soldiers and sailors sent to the Crimea, more than one in five did not return: 20,813 men died in the campaign, 80 per cent of them from sickness or disease.[2]

Reflecting this public sense of loss and admiration for the suffering troops, the government commissioned a Guards Memorial to commemorate the heroes of the Crimean War. John Bell's massive ensemble – three bronze Guardsmen (Coldstream, Fusilier and Grenadier) cast from captured Russian cannon and standing guard beneath the classical figure of Honour – was unveiled on Waterloo Place at the intersection of Lower Regent Street and Pall Mall in London in 1861. Opinion was divided on the monument's artistic qualities. Londoners referred to the figure of Honour as the 'quoits player' because the oak-leaf coronels in her outstretched arms resembled the rings used in that game. Many thought the monument lacked the grace and beauty needed for a site of such significance (Count Gleichen later said that it looked best in the fog). But its symbolic impact was unprecedented. It was the first war memorial in Britain to raise to hero-status the ordinary troops.[3]

The Crimean War brought about a sea change in Britain's attitudes towards its fighting men. It laid the basis of the modern national myth built on the idea of the soldier defending the nation's honour, right and liberty. Before the war the idea of military honour was defined by aristocracy. Gallantry and valour were attained by high-born martial leaders like the Duke of York, the son of George III and commander of the British army against Napoleon, whose column was erected in 1833, five years after the Duke's death, from the funds raised by deducting one day's pay from every soldier in the army. Military paintings featured the heroic exploits of dashing noble officers. But the common soldier was ignored. Placing the Guards Memorial opposite the Duke of York's column was symbolic of a fundamental shift in Victorian values. It represented a challenge to the leadership of the aristocracy, which had been so discredited by the military blunders in the Crimea. If the British military hero had previously been a gentleman all 'plumed and laced', now he was a trooper, the 'Private Smith' or 'Tommy' ('Tommy Atkins') of folklore, who fought courageously and won Britain's wars in spite of the blunders of his generals. Here was a narrative that ran through British history from the Crimean to the First and Second World Wars (and beyond, to the wars of recent times). As Private Smith of the Black Watch wrote in 1899, after a defeat for the British army in the Boer War,

> Such was the day for our regiment,
> Dread the revenge we will take.

> Dearly we paid for the blunder
> A drawing-room General's mistake.
> Why weren't we told of the trenches?
> Why weren't we told of the wire?
> Why were we marched up in column,
> May Tommy Atkins enquire . . .[4]

As the American writer Nathaniel Hawthorne wrote in his *English Notebooks*, the year of 1854 had 'done the work of fifty ordinary ones' in undermining aristocracy.[5]

The war's mismanagement also triggered a new assertiveness in the middle classes, which rallied round the principles of professional competence, industry, meritocracy and self-reliance in opposition to the privilege of birth. The Crimean War had furnished them with plenty of examples of professional initiatives having come to the rescue of the badly managed military campaign – the nursing work of Florence Nightingale, the culinary expertise of Alexis Soyer, Samuel Peto's Balaklava railway, or Joseph Paxton's navvies, who were sent to build the wooden huts that sheltered British soldiers from a second winter on the Sevastopol Heights. Thanks to the press, to which they wrote with their practical advice and opinions, the middle classes became actively involved in the daily running of the war. Politically, they were the real victors, since by its end the war was being run on professional principles. It was a sign of their triumph that in the decades afterwards, Whig, Conservative and Liberal governments alike all passed reforms promoting middle-class ideals: the extension of the franchise to the professional and artisan classes, freedom of the press, greater openness and accountability in government, meritocracy, religious toleration, public education, and a more caring attitude towards the labouring classes and 'deserving poor' which had its origin in, among other things, a concern for the suffering of the soldiers during the Crimean War. (That concern was the impetus for a series of army reforms brought in by Lord Cardwell, Gladstone's War Minister, between 1868 and 1871. The purchase of commissions was replaced by a merit-based system of promotions; the period of enlistment for privates was drastically reduced; pay and conditions were improved; and flogging was abolished in peacetime.)

The new-found confidence of the British middle classes was epitomized by Florence Nightingale. She returned from the Crimea as a national heroine, and her image was sold widely on commemorative postcards, figurines and medallions to the public. *Punch* depicted her as Britannia carrying a lamp rather than a shield, a lancet rather than a lance, and in verse suggested that she was more worthy of the public's adoration than any dashing noble officer:

> The floating froth of public praise
> blown lightly by each random gust,
> Settles on trophies, bright for days, to
> lapse in centuries of rust.
>
> The public heart, that will be fed, but has
> no art its food to choose,
> Grasps what comes readiest, stones for
> bread, rather than fast, will not refuse.
>
> Hence hero-worship's hungry haste takes
> meanest idols, tawdriest shrines,
> Where CARDIGAN struts, plumed and laced,
> or HUDSON in brass lacquer shines.
>
> Yet when on top of common breaths a
> truly glorious name is flung,
> Scorn not because so many wreaths
> before unworthiest shrines are hung.
>
> The people, howe'er wild or weak, have
> noble instincts still to guide:
> Oft find false gods, when true they seek;
> but true, once found, have ne'er denied.
>
> And now, for all that's ill-bestowed or
> rash in popular applause,
> Deep and true England's heart has
> glow'd in this great woman's holy cause.[6]

In popular plays and drawing-room ballads, Nightingale's patriotic dedication and professionalism served to compensate for the damage done to national pride by the recognition that stupidity and misman-agement had caused greater suffering to the soldiers than anything inflicted by the enemy. In one play, *The War in Turkey*, produced in the Britannia Saloon in London, for example, there was a series of comic scenes ridiculing the incompetence of the British authorities, followed by a scene in which 'Miss Bird' (Nightingale) appears and sorts out all the problems left behind. The scene ends with a moral lesson: 'In that young lady we behold true heroism – the heart that beats in her bosom is capable of any heroic deed.'[7]

The legend of the Lady with the Lamp became part of Britain's national myth, retold in countless histories, schoolbooks and biog-raphies of Florence Nightingale. It contained the basic elements of the middle-class Victorian ideal: a Christian narrative about womanly care, good works and self-sacrifice; a moral one of self-improvement and the salvation of the deserving poor; a domestic tale of cleanliness, good housekeeping and the improvement of the home; a story about individual determination and the assertion of the will that appealed to professional aspirations; and a public narrative of sanitary and hospital reform, to which Nightingale would dedicate herself for the rest of her long life after her return from the Crimea.

In 1915, when Britain was at war again, this time with Russia on its side, a statue of the Lady with the Lamp was added to the Crimean War Memorial, which was moved back towards Regent Street to accommo-date the new figure. The statue of Nightingale was joined by one brought in from the War Office of a thoughtful Sidney Herbert, the Secretary at War who had sent her to the Crimea.[8] It was belated public recognition for a man who had been hounded out of office during the Crimea War partly on account of his family connections to Russia.

*

On a sunny Friday morning, 26 June 1857, the Queen and Prince Albert attended a parade of Crimean veterans in Hyde Park. By a royal warrant the previous January, the Queen had instituted a new medal, the Victoria Cross, to reward bravery by servicemen regardless of their class or rank. Other European countries had long had such awards – the French, the Légion d'honneur, since 1802; the Dutch, the Military Order of William, and even the Russians had a merit medal before 1812. In Britain, however, there was no system of military honours to recognize the bravery of the troops on the basis of merit, only one to reward officers. The war reports by Russell of *The Times* and other journalists had brought to the attention of the British public many acts of bravery by ordinary troops; they had portrayed the suffering of the soldiers in heroic terms, giving rise to a widespread feeling that a new award was needed to recognize their deeds. Sixty-two Crimean veterans were chosen to receive the first Victoria Crosses – a small bronze medal supposed to be cast from the captured Russian cannon of Sevastopol.* At the ceremony in Hyde Park, each one took his turn to bow before the Queen as Lord Panmure, Secretary of State for War, read out his name and gave the citation for gallantry. Among these first recipients of Britain's highest military honour were sixteen privates from the army, four gunners and one sapper, two seamen and three boatswains.[9]

The institution of the Victoria Cross not only confirmed the change in the idea of heroism; it also marked a new reverence for war and warriors. The troops who had received the Victoria Cross found their deeds commemorated in a multitude of post-war books that exalted the bravery of men at arms. The most popular, *Our Soldiers and the Victoria Cross*, was brought out by Samuel Beeton, best known as the publisher of his wife's book, *Mrs Beeton's Book of Household Management*, in 1861. Written to inspire and teach boys, the preface of *Our Soldiers* claimed:

> Boys – worthy to be called boys – are naturally brave. What visions are those which rise up before the young – what brave words to speak, what brave actions to do – how bravely – if need be – to suffer! . . . This is the leading thought in this book about Soldiers – it is meant to keep alive the bravery of youth in the experience of manhood.[10]

This didactic cult of manliness animated the two major British novels set against the background of the Crimean War: Charles Kingsley's *Two Years Ago* (1857) and Henry Kingsley's *Ravenshoe* (1861). It was also the pervading theme of Charles Kingsley's *Westward Ho!* (1855), a New World adventure story set at the time of the Spanish Armada,

---

* It has since been shown that the metal in fact came from antique Chinese guns (J. Glanfield, *Bravest of the Brave: The Story of the Victoria Cross* (London, 2005)).

which was inspired by the militarism and xenophobia of Britain during the Crimean War. Its author himself described it in 1854 as 'a most ruthless and bloodthirsty book (just what the times want, I think)'.[11]

The argument for war was also at the heart of Thomas Hughes's hugely influential novel *Tom Brown's Schooldays* (1857), whose most famous scene, the fight between Tom and the bully Slogger Williams, was clearly meant to be read by the public as a moral lesson on the recent war against Russia:

> From the cradle to the grave, fighting, rightly understood, is the business, the real highest, honestest business of every son of man. Every one who is worth his salt has his enemies, who must be beaten, be they evil thoughts and habits in himself, or spiritual wickednesses in high places, or Russians, or Border-ruffians, or Bill, Tom, or Harry, who will not let him live his life in quiet till he has thrashed them. It is no good for Quakers, or any other body of men, to uplift their voices against fighting. Human nature is too strong for them, and they don't follow their own precepts. Every soul of them is doing his own piece of fighting, somehow and somewhere. The world might be a better world without fighting, for anything I know, but it wouldn't be our world; and therefore I am dead against crying peace when there is no peace, and isn't meant to be. . . . [Saying 'no' to a challenge to fight is] a proof of the highest courage, if done from true Christian motives. It's quite right and justifiable, if done from a simple aversion to physical pain and danger. But don't say 'No' because you fear a licking, and say or think it's because you fear God, for that's neither Christian nor honest.[12]

Here was the origin of the cult of 'muscular Christianity' – the notion of 'Christian soldiers' fighting righteous wars that came to define the Victorian imperial mission. This was a time when Britons began to sing in church:

> Onward, Christian soldiers, marching as to war,
> With the cross of Jesus going on before.
> Christ, the royal Master, leads against the foe;
> Forward into battle see His banners go!   (1864)

The argument for 'muscular Christianity' was first made in a review of Kingsley's novel *Two Years Ago* in 1857, a year when the idea of the 'Christian soldier' was reinforced by the actions of the British troops in putting down the Indian Mutiny. But the idea of training boys to fight for Christian causes was also prominent in Hughes's sequel to *Tom Brown's Schooldays*, *Tom Brown at Oxford* (1861), where athletic sport is extolled as a builder of manly character, teamwork, chivalry and moral fortitude – qualities that had made Britons good at war. 'The least of the muscular Christians has hold of the old chivalrous and Christian belief that a man's body is given him to be trained and brought into subjection, and then used for the protection of the weak, the advancement of all righteous causes, and the subduing of the earth which God has given to the children of men.'[13] At the heart of this ideal was a new concentration on physical training and the mastery of the body as a form of moral strengthening for the purposes of holy war. It was a quality associated with the hardiness of the suffering soldiers in the Crimea.

But that suffering, too, played a role in transforming the public image of the British troops. Before the war the respectable middle and upper classes had viewed the rank and file of the British army as little more than a dissolute rabble – heavy-drinking and ill-disciplined, brutal and profane – drawn from the poorest sections of society. But the agonies of the soldiers in the Crimea had revealed their Christian souls and turned them into objects of 'good works' and Evangelical devotion. Religious ministering to the rank and file dramatically increased during the war. The army doubled its number of chaplains and every man was given a Bible free of charge, courtesy of middle-class donations to the Society for Promoting Christian Knowledge and the Naval and Military Bible Society.[14]

The soldiers were recast as saintly figures, martyrs of a holy cause, in the eyes of many Evangelicals. Among them was Catherine Marsh, whose lively and sentimental hagiography, *Memorials of Captain Hedley Vicars, Ninety-Seventh Regiment* (1856), sold more than 100,000 copies in its first few years of publication and reappeared in numerous abridged and juvenile editions up until the First World War. Compiled from Vicars's diary and his letters to his mother from the Crimea, *Memorials* was dedicated to the 'noble ideal of the Christian soldier' and offered to the public as a 'fresh and ample refutation to those who, in the face of examples to the contrary, still maintain that entire devotion of the heart to God must withdraw a man from many of the active duties of life and ... that in making a good Christian you may spoil a good soldier'. Vicars is portrayed as a soldier-saint, a selfless hero who bears the burdens of his fellow-men on the Sevastopol heights by sharing his food and tent, caring for them and reading them the Bible when they are sick. Vicars leads his men to 'Holy War' against the Russians, who are described as 'heathens', 'infidels' and 'savages'. He is mortally wounded during the sortie of 22–3 March 1855, and his death is compared to the martyrdom of Christ in Marsh's final chapter ('Victory'), which is prefaced by Longfellow's verse (a translation from the Spanish poet Jorge Manrique):

> His soul to Him who gave it rose,
> God led it to its long repose,
> Its glorious rest!
> And though the warrior's sun has set,
> Its light shall longer round us yet,
> Bright, radiant, blest.

Vicars was buried in Sevastopol but in St George's Church on Bromley Road in Beckenham, Kent, there is a white marble tablet carved in the shape of a scroll with a sheathed sword behind on which these words are inscribed:

TO THE GLORY OF GOD AND TO THE BELOVED MEMORY OF HEDLEY VICARS CAPTAIN 97TH REGIMENT WHO THROUGH FAITH IN THE WORD OF GOD THAT 'THE BLOOD OF JESUS CHRIST HIS SON CLEANSETH US ALL IN SIN' PASSED FROM THE DEATH OF SIN TO THE LIFE OF RIGHTEOUSNESS. HE FELL IN BATTLE, AND SLEPT IN JESUS, ON THE NIGHT OF 22ND OF MARCH, 1855. AND WAS BURIED BEFORE SEBASTOPOL AGED 28 YEARS.[15]

Beyond the sanctification of soldiers and the new manly ideal, the common effort of the war seemed to offer the possibility of national unity and reconciliation needed to end the class divisions and industrial strife of the 1830s and 1840s. In Dickens's *Household Words*, alongside the serialization of Elizabeth Gaskell's *North and South* (1855), a novel on the theme of ending the class conflict, there appeared a series of poems by Adelaide Anne Procter, Queen Victoria's favourite poet, including 'The Lesson of the War'.

> The rulers of the nation,
>   The poor ones at their gate,
> With the same eager wonder
>   The same great news await!
> The poor man's stay and comfort,
>   The rich man's joy and pride,
> Upon the bleak Crimean shore
>   Are fighting side by side.[16]

A similar idea can be found in Tennyson's poetic monodrama *Maud* (1855), where a state of 'civil war' created by the 'lust of gain' at home gives way to an ending in which the narrator looks to war abroad as a higher and more godly cause:

> Let it go or stay, so I wake to the higher aims
> Of a land that has lost for a little her lust of gold,
> And love of a peace that was full of wrongs and shames,
> Horrible, hateful, monstrous, not to be told;
> And hail once more to the banner of battle unroll'd!
> Tho' many a light shall darken, and many shall weep
> For those that are crush'd in the clash of jarring claims,
> Yet God's just wrath shall be wreak'd on a giant liar;
> And many a darkness into the light shall leap,
> And shine in the sudden making of splendid names,
> And noble thought be freer under the sun,
> And the heart of a people beat with one desire;
> For the peace, that I deem'd no peace, is over and done,
> And now by the side of the Black and the Baltic deep,
> And deathful-grinning mouths of the fortress, flames
> The blood-red blossom of war with a heart of fire.
>
> Let it flame or fade, and the war roll down like a wind,
> We have proved we have hearts in a cause, we are noble still,
> And myself have awaked, as it seems, to the better mind;

476

It is better to fight for the good, than to rail at the ill;

I have felt with my native land, I am one with my kind,

I embrace the purpose of God, and the doom assign'd.

Painters picked up the same theme. In John Gilbert's *Her Majesty the Queen Inspecting the Wounded Coldstream Guards in the Hall of Buckingham Palace* (1856), a painting (sadly lost) that was popular enough to be reproduced as a coloured lithograph as late as 1903, there is a touching poignancy in the meeting between the Queen and the wounded heroes of the Crimea which suggests the prospect of post-war unity between the highest and the lowest of the land. Jerry Barrett's large painting *Queen Victoria's First Visit to Her Wounded Soldiers* (1856) played on this emotion too. This sentimental picture of the royal family visiting Crimean invalids at the Chatham army hospital was such a success when it was first shown at Thomas Agnew's gallery in Piccadilly that several thousand prints were subsequently sold to the public in various editions costing between three and ten guineas.[17]

The Queen herself was a collector of photographic souvenirs of Crimean veterans. She commissioned commercial photographers like Joseph Cundall and Robert Howlett to make a series of commemorative portraits of maimed and wounded soldiers in various military hospitals, including Chatham, for the royal collection at Windsor. Cundall and Howlett's striking photographs reached beyond their patroness's hands. Through photographic exhibitions and their reproduction in the illustrated press, they brought home to the public in explicit terms the suffering of the soldiers and the human costs of war. These pioneering photographs were very different from Fenton's genteel images. In Cundall and Howlett's *Three Crimean Invalids* (1855), for example, the wounded infantrymen are seated on a hospital bed displaying their loss of limbs. There is no emotion in their expressions, no romanticism or sentimentality in their representation, only the documentary evidence in black and white of the impact made by iron shot and frostbite on the body. In their notes in the royal archives, Cundall and Howlett identified the men as William Young of the 23rd Regiment, wounded at the Redan on 18 June 1855; Henry Burland of the 34th, both legs lost to frostbite in the trenches before Sevastopol; and John Connery of the 49th, his left leg lost to frostbite in the trenches.[18]

Memories of the Crimean War continued to provide a winning subject for British artists well into the 1870s. The best known of these Crimean pictures was *Calling the Roll after an Engagement, Crimea* (1874) by Elizabeth Thompson (Lady Butler), which caused a sensation when it was exhibited at the Royal Academy. So great were the crowds that came to see it that a policeman was put on guard to provide protection. Already known for her earlier paintings on military themes, Thompson had conceived *The Roll Call* (as it became popularly known) in the immediate aftermath of the Cardwell reforms, when army matters were prominent in public life. From detailed sketches of Crimean veterans, she created a striking composition, in which the remnants of the Grenadiers, wounded, cold and utterly exhausted, assemble after a battle to be counted by their mounted officer. The painting was completely different from conventional depictions of war that focused on the glorious deeds of gallant officers: apart from the mounted officer, the 2-metre-high canvas was entirely dominated by the suffering of the rank and file. It stripped away the heroics and let the viewer look into the face of war. After its showing at the Royal Academy *The Roll Call* went on national tour, drawing immense crowds. In Newcastle, it was advertised by men with sandwich boards which simply read '*The Roll Call* is Coming!' In Liverpool, 20,000 people saw the picture in three weeks – a huge number for the time. People came away profoundly moved by the painting, which had clearly touched the nation's heart. The Queen purchased *The Roll Call* from its original buyer, a Manchester industrialist, but a printing company retained the right to reproduce it in a popular edition of engravings. Thompson herself became a national heroine overnight. A quarter of a million cartes-de-visite photographs of the artist were sold to the public, who put her on a par with Florence Nightingale.[19]

*

What will they say in England
When the story there is told
Of deeds of might, on Alma's height,
Done by the brave and bold?
Of Russia, proud at noontide,

Humbled ere set of sun?
They'll say "Twas like Old England!'
They'll say "Twas noble done!'

What will they say in England
When, hushed in awe and dread,
Fond hearts, through all our happy homes
Think of the mighty dead,
And muse, in speechless anguish,
On father – brother – son?
They'll say in dear Old England
'God's holy will be done.'

What will they say in England?
Our names, both night and day
Are in their hearts and on their lips,
When they laugh, or weep, or pray.
They watch on earth, they plead with heaven,
Then, forward to the fight!
Who droops or fears, while England cheers,
And God defends the right?

Reverend J. S. B. Monsell in
The Girls' Reading Book (1875)[20]

The Crimean War left a deep impression on the English national identity. To schoolchildren, it was an example of England standing up against the Russian Bear to defend liberty – a simple fight between Right and Might, as *Punch* portrayed it at the time. The idea of John Bull coming to the aid of the weak against tyrants and bullies became part of Britain's essential narrative. Many of the same emotive forces that took Britain to the Crimean War were again at work when Britain went to war against the Germans in defence of 'little Belgium' in 1914 and Poland in 1939.

Today, the names of Alma, Balaklava, Inkerman, Sebastopol, Cardigan and Raglan continue to inhabit the collective memory – mainly through the signs of streets and pubs. For decades after the Crimean War there was a fashion for naming girls Florence, Alma, Balaklava, and boys Inkerman. Veterans of the war took these names to every

"RIGHT AGAINST WRONG."

APRIL 8, 1854.]   [PUNCH, No. 665.

'Right Against Wrong' (*Punch*, 8 April 1854)

corner of the world: there is a town called Balaklava in South Australia and another in Queensland; there are Inkermans in West
Virginia, South and West Australia, Queensland, Victoria and New
South Wales in Australia, as well as Gloucester County, Canada; there
are Sebastopols in California, Ontario, New South Wales and Victoria, and a Mount Sebastopol in New Zealand; there are four towns
called Alma in Wisconsin, one in Colorado, two in Arkansas, and ten
others in the United States; four Almas and a lake with the same name
name in Canada; two towns called Alma in Australia, and a river by
that name in New Zealand.

   In France, too, the names of the Crimea are found everywhere,
reminders of a war in which 310,000 Frenchmen were involved. One
in three did not return home. Paris has an Alma Bridge, built in 1856
and rebuilt in the 1970s, which is now mainly famous for the scene of

Princess Diana's fatal car crash in 1997. Until then it was better known for its Zouave statue (the only one of four to be kept from the old bridge) by which water levels are still measured by Parisians (the river is declared unnavigable when the water passes the Zouave's knees). Paris has a place de l'Alma, and a boulevard de Sébastopol, both with metro stations by those names. There is a whole suburb in the south of Paris, originally built as a separate town, with the name of Malakoff (Malakhov). Initially called 'New California', Malakoff was developed in the decade after the Crimean War on cheap quarry land in the Vanves valley by Alexandre Chauvelot, the most successful of the property developers in nineteenth-century France. Chauvelot cashed in on the brief French craze for commemorating the Crimean victory by building pleasure-gardens in the new suburb to increase its appeal to artisans and workers from the overcrowded centre of Paris. The main attraction of the gardens was the Malakoff Tower, a castle built in the image of the Russian bastion, set in a theme-park of ditches, hills, redoubts and grottoes, along with a bandstand and an outside theatre, where huge crowds gathered to watch the re-enactments of Crimean battles or take in other entertainments in the summer months. It was with the imprimatur of Napoleon that New California was renamed Malakoff, in honour of his regime's first great military victory, in 1858. Developed as private building plots, the suburb grew rapidly during the 1860s. But after the defeat of France by Prussia in 1870, the Malakoff Tower was destroyed on the orders of the Mayor of Vanves, who thought it was a cruel reminder of a more glorious past.

Malakoff towers were built in towns and villages throughout provincial France. Many of them survive to this day. There are Malakoff towers in Sivry-Courtry (Seine-et-Marne), Toury-Lurcy (Nièvre), Sermizelles (Yonne), Nantes and Saint-Arnaud-Montrond (Cher), as well as in Belgium (at Dison and Hasard-Cheratte near Liège), Luxembourg and Germany (Cologne, Bochum and Hanover), Algeria (Oran and Algiers) and Recife in Brazil, a city colonized by the French after the Crimean War. In France itself, nearly every town has its rue Malakoff. The French have given the name of Malakoff to public squares and parks, hotels, restaurants, cheeses, champagnes, roses and *chansons*.

481

But despite these allusions, the war left much less of a trace on the French national consciousness than it did on the British. The memory of the Crimean War in France was soon overshadowed by the war in Italy against the Austrians (1859), the French expedition to Mexico (1862–6) and, above all, the defeat in the Franco-Prussian War. Today the Crimean War is little known in France. It is a 'forgotten war'.

In Italy and Turkey, as in France, the Crimean War was eclipsed by later wars and quickly dropped out of the nationalist myths and narratives that came to dominate the way these countries reconstructed their nineteenth-century history.

In Italy, there are very few landmarks to remind Italians of their country's part in the Crimean War. Even in Piedmont, where one might expect to see the war remembered, there is very little to commemorate the 2,166 soldiers who were killed in the fighting or died from disease, according to official statistics, though the actual number was almost certainly higher. In Turin, there is a Corso Sebastopoli and a Via Cernaia, in memory of the only major battle in which the Italians took part. The nationalist painter Gerolamo Induno, who went with the Sardinian troops to the Crimea and made many sketches of the fighting there, painted several battle scenes on his return in 1855, including *The Battle of the Chernaia*, commissioned by Victor Emmanuel II, and *The Capture of the Malakoff Tower*, both of which excited patriotic sentiment for a few years in northern Italy. But the war of 1859 and everything that happened afterwards – the Garibaldi expedition to the south, the conquest of Naples, the annexation of Venetia from the Austrians during the war of 1866 and the final unification of Italy with the capture of Rome in 1870 – soon overshadowed the Crimean War. These were the defining events of the Risorgimento, the popular 'resurrection' of the nation, by which Italians would come to see the making of modern Italy. As a foreign war led by Piedmont and Cavour, a problematic figure for the populist interpretation of the Risorgimento, the campaign in the Crimea had no great claim for commemoration by Italian nationalists. There were no public demonstrations for the war, no volunteer movements, no great victories or glorious defeats in the Crimea.

In Turkey the Crimean War has been not so much forgotten as

obliterated from the nation's historical memory, even though it was there that the war began and Turkish casualties were as many as 120,000 soldiers, almost half the troops involved, according to official statistics. In Istanbul, there are monuments to the allied soldiers who fought in the war, but none to the Turks. Until very recently the war was almost totally ignored by Turkish historiography. It did not fit the nationalist version of Turkish history, and fell between the earlier 'golden age' of the Ottoman Empire and the later history of Atatürk and the birth of the modern Turkish state. Indeed, if anything, despite its victorious conclusion for the Turks, the war has come to be seen as a shameful period in Ottoman history, a turning point in the decline of the empire, when the state fell into massive debt and became dependent on the Western powers, who turned out to be false friends. History textbooks in most Turkish schools charge the decline of Islamic traditions to the growing intervention of the West in Turkey as a result of the Crimean War.[21] So do the official Turkish military histories, like this one, published by the General Staff in 1981, which contains this characteristic conclusion, reflecting many aspects of the deep resentments nationalists and Muslims in Turkey feel towards the West:

> During the Crimean War Turkey had almost no real friends in the outside world. Those who appeared to be our friends were not real friends ... In this war Turkey lost its treasury. For the first time it became indebted to Europe. Even worse, by participating in this war with Western allies, thousands of foreign soldiers and civilians were able to see closely the most secret places and shortcomings of Turkey ... Another negative effect of the war was that some semi-intellectual circles of Turkish society came to admire Western fashions and values, losing their identity. The city of Istanbul, with its hospitals, schools and military buildings, was put at the disposal of the allied commanders, but the Western armies allowed historic buildings to catch fire through their carelessness ... The Turkish people showed their traditional hospitality and opened their seaside villas to the allied commanders, but the Western soldiers did not show the same respect to the Turkish people or to Turkish graves. The allies prevented Turkish troops from landing on the shores of the Caucasus [to support Shamil's war against the

Russians] because this was against their national interests. In sum, Turkish soldiers showed every sign of selflessness and shed their blood on all the fronts of the Crimean War, but our Western allies took all the glory for themselves.[22]

*

The effect of the war in Britain was matched only by its impact in Russia, where the events played a significant role in shaping the national identity. But that role was contradictory. The war was of course experienced as a terrible humiliation, inflaming profound feelings of resentment against the West for siding with the Turks. But it also fuelled a sense of national pride in the defenders of Sevastopol, a feeling that the sacrifices they made and the Christian motives for which they had fought had turned their defeat into a moral victory. The idea was articulated by the Tsar in his Manifesto to the Russians on learning of the fall of Sevastopol:

> The defence of Sevastopol is unprecedented in the annals of military history, and it has won the admiration not just of Russia but of all Europe. The defenders are worthy of their place among those heroes who have brought glory to our Fatherland. For eleven months the Sevastopol garrison withstood the attacks of a stronger enemy against our native land, and in every act it distinguished itself through its extraordinary bravery ... Its courageous deeds will always be an inspiration to our troops, who share its belief in Providence and in the holiness of Russia's cause. The name of Sevastopol, which has given so much blood, will be eternal, and the memory of its defenders will remain always in our hearts together with the memory of those Russian heroes who fought on the battlefields of Poltava and Borodino.[23]

The heroic status of Sevastopol owed much to the influence of Tolstoy's *Sevastopol Sketches*, which were read by almost the entire Russian literate public in 1855–6. *Sevastopol Sketches* fixed in the national imagination the idea of the city as a microcosm of that special 'Russian' spirit of resilience and courage which had always saved the country when it was invaded by a foreign enemy. As Tolstoy wrote in the closing passage of 'Sevastopol in December', composed in April 1855, at the height of the siege:

So now you have seen the defenders of Sevastopol on the lines of defence themselves, and you retrace your steps, for some reason paying no attention now to the cannonballs and bullets that continue to whistle across your route all the way back to the demolished theatre [i.e. the city of Sevastopol], and you walk in a state of calm exaltation. The one central, reassuring conviction you have come away with is that it is quite impossible for Sevastopol ever to be taken by the enemy. Not only that: you are convinced that the strength of the Russian people cannot possibly ever falter, no matter in what part of the world it may be put to the test. This impossibility you have observed, not in that proliferation of traverses, parapets, ingeniously interwoven trenches, mines and artillery pieces of which you have understood nothing, but in the eyes, words and behaviour – that which is called the spirit – of the defenders of Sevastopol. What they do, they do so straightforwardly, with so little strain or effort, that you are convinced they must be capable of a hundred times as much . . . they could do anything. You realize now that the feeling which drives them has nothing in common with the vain, petty and mindless emotions you yourself have experienced, but is of an altogether different and more powerful nature; it has turned them into men capable of living with as much calm beneath a hail of cannonballs, faced with a hundred chances of death, as people who, like most of us, are faced with only one such chance, and of living in those conditions while putting up with sleeplessness, dirt and ceaseless hard labour. Men will not put up with terrible conditions like these for the sake of a cross or an honour, or because they have been threatened: there must be another, higher motivation. This motivation is a feeling that surfaces only rarely in the Russian, but lies deeply embedded in his soul – a love of his native land. Only now do the stories of the early days of the siege of Sevastopol, when there were no fortifications, no troops, when there was no physical possibility of holding the town and there was nevertheless not the slightest doubt that it would be kept from the enemy – of the days when Kornilov, that hero worthy of ancient Greece, would say as he inspected his troops: 'We will die, men, rather than surrender Sevastopol,' and when our Russian soldiers, unversed in phrase-mongering, would answer: 'We will die! Hurrah!' – only now do the stories of those days cease to be a beautiful historic legend and become a reality, a fact. You will suddenly have a clear and vivid awareness that those men you have just seen are the very same heroes who in those difficult days did not allow their spirits to sink but rather felt them rise as they joyfully prepared to die, not for the town but for their native land. Long will Russia bear the imposing traces of this epic of Sevastopol, the hero of which was the Russian people.[24]

The 'epic of Sevastopol' turned defeat into a national triumph for Russia. 'Sevastopol fell, but it did so with such glory that Russians should take pride in such a fall, which is worth a brilliant victory,' wrote a former Decembrist.[25] Upon this grand defeat, the Russians built a patriotic myth, a national narrative of the people's selfless heroism, resilience and sacrifice. Poets likened it to the patriotic spirit of 1812 – as did Aleksei Apukhtin in his well-known ballad 'A Soldier's Song about Sevastopol' (1869), which came to be learned by many Russian schoolboys in the final decades of the nineteenth century:

> The song I'll sing to you, lads, isn't a jolly one;
> It's not a mighty song of victory
> Like the one our fathers sang at Borodino,
> Or our grandfathers sang at Ochakov.
>
> I'll sing to you of how a cloud of dust
> Swirled up from the southern fields,
> Of how countless enemies disembarked
> And how they came and defeated us.
>
> But such was our defeat that since then
> They haven't come back looking for trouble,
> Such was our defeat that they sailed away
> With sour faces and bashed noses.
>
> I'll sing of how leaving hearth and home behind
> The rich landowner joined the militia,
> Of how the peasant, bidding his wife farewell,
> Came out of his hut to serve as a volunteer.
>
> I'll sing of how the mighty army grew
> As warriors came, strong as iron and steel,
> Who knew they were heading for death,
> And how piously did they die!

Of how our fair women went as nurses
To share their cheerless lot,
And how for every inch of our Russian land
Our foes paid us with their blood;

Of how through smoke and fire, grenades
Thundering, and heavy groans all round,
Redoubts emerged one after another,
Like a grim spectre the bastions grew –

And eleven months lasted the carnage,
And during all these eleven months
The miraculous fortress, shielding Russia,
Buried her courageous sons . . .

Let the song I sing to you not be joyful:
It's no less glorious than the song of victory
Our fathers sang at Borodino
Or our grandfathers at Ochakov.[26]

This was the context in which Tolstoy wrote his own 'national epic', *War and Peace*. Tolstoy's conception of the war against Napoleon as Russia's national awakening – the rediscovery of 'Russian principles' by the Europeanized nobility and the recognition of the patriotic spirit of the serf soldiers as the basis of a democratic nationhood – was a reflection of his reaction to the heroic deeds of the Russian people during the Crimean War. Written between 1862 and 1865, in the years immediately after the emancipation of the serfs, when Russian liberal society was inspired by ideals of national reform and reconciliation between the landed classes and the peasantry, *War and Peace* was originally conceived as a Decembrist novel set in the aftermath of the Crimean War. In the novel's early form ('The Decembrist'), the hero returns after thirty years of exile in Siberia to the intellectual ferment of the late 1850s. A second Alexandrine reign has just begun, with the accession of Alexander II to the throne, and once again, as in 1825, high hopes for reform are in the air. But the more Tolstoy researched the Decembrists, the more he realized that their intellectual roots lay in the war of 1812, and so set his novel then.

The memory of 1812 was bitterly contested after the Crimean War, which had opened up a new perspective on the national character. Democrats like Tolstoy, inspired by the recent sacrifices of the Russian peasant soldiers, saw 1812 as a people's war, a victory attained by the patriotic spirit of the whole nation. To conservatives, on the other hand, 1812 represented the holy triumph of the Russian autocratic principle, which alone saved Europe from Napoleon.

The commemoration of the Crimean War was entangled in a similar ideological conflict. Conservatives and Church leaders portrayed it as a holy war, the fulfilment of Russia's divine mission to defend Orthodoxy in the broader world. They claimed that this had been achieved with the international declaration to protect the Christians of the Ottoman Empire and the Paris Treaty's preservation of the status quo, as the Russians had demanded, in the Holy Places of Jerusalem and Bethlehem. In their writings and sermons on the war, they described the defenders of the Crimea as selfless and courageous Christian soldiers who had sacrificed their lives as martyrs for the 'Russian holy land'. They re-emphasized the sanctity of the Crimea as the place where Christianity had first appeared in Russia. From the moment the war had ended, the monarchy sought to connect its commemoration to the memory of 1812. The Tsar's visit to Moscow following the surrender of Sevastopol was staged as a re-enactment of Alexander I's dramatic appearance in the former Russian capital in 1812, when he had been greeted by vast crowds of Muscovites. In 1856 the Tsar delayed his coronation until the anniversary of the battle of Borodino, Russia's victory against Napoleon in September 1812. It was a symbolic move to compensate for the painful loss of the Crimean War and reunite the people with the monarchy on the basis of a more glorious memory.[27]

For the democratic intellectual circles in which Tolstoy moved, however, the thread connecting the Crimean War to 1812 was not the holy mission of the Tsar but the patriotic sacrifice of the Russian people, who laid down their lives in the defence of their native land. That sacrifice, however, was hard to quantify. No one knew how many soldiers died. Precise figures for Russian casualties were never collected, and any information about heavy losses was distorted or concealed by the tsarist military authorities, but estimates of the Russians killed during the Crimean War vary between 400,000 and

600,000 men for all theatres of the war. The Medical Department of the Ministry of War later published a figure of 450,015 deaths in the army for the four years between 1853 and 1856. This is probably the most accurate estimate.[28] Without precise figures, the people's sacrifice grew to assume a mythic status in the democratic imagination.

Sevastopol itself was elevated to a quasi-sacred site in the collective memory. The veneration of the fallen heroes of the siege began as soon as the war ended, not on the initiative of the government and official circles, but through popular efforts, by families and groups of veterans erecting monuments or founding churches, cemeteries and benevolent funds with money raised from public donations. The focal point of this democratic cult was the commemoration of admirals Nakhimov, Kornilov and Istomin, the popular heroes of Sevastopol. They were idolized as 'men of the people', devoted to the welfare of their troops, who had all died as martyrs in the defence of the town. In 1856 a

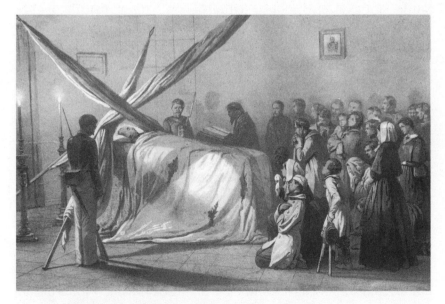

The Death of Admiral Nakhimov by Vasily Timm (1856)

national fund was organized to pay for the erection of a monument to the admirals in Sevastopol, and there were similar initiatives in many other towns. Kornilov was the central figure of numerous histories of the war. Nakhimov, the hero of Sinope and virtually a saint in the folklore of the siege, appeared in tales and prints as a brave and selfless soldier, a martyr of the people's holy cause, who was ready for his death when he was struck down while inspecting the Fourth Bastion. It was entirely through private funding that the Museum of the Black Sea Fleet was established in Sevastopol in 1869. On display to the crowds who came on the opening day were various weapons, artefacts and personal items, manuscripts and maps, drawings and engravings collected from veterans. It was the first historical museum of this public nature in Russia.*

The Russian state became involved in the commemoration of Sevastopol only in the later 1870s, around the time of the Russo-Turkish war, mainly as a result of the growing influence of the pan-Slavs in government circles, but government initiatives focused on court favourites, such as General Gorchakov, and virtually neglected the people's hero Nakhimov. By this time the admiral had become an icon of a popular nationalist movement that the regime attempted to subordinate to its own Official Nationality by building monuments to the Crimean War. In 1905, a year of revolution and war against Japan, a splendid panorama of *The Defence of Sevastopol* was opened to commemorate the fiftieth anniversary of the siege, in a purpose-built museum on a site where the Fourth Bastion had once stood. Government officials insisted on replacing the portrait of Nakhimov with one of Gorchakov in Franz Roubaud's life-size painting-model re-creating the events of 18 June, when the defenders of Sevastopol had repelled the assault by the British and the French.[29] Nakhimov did not appear in the museum, which was built upon the very ground where he had been mortally wounded.

The Soviet commemoration of the war returned the emphasis to the popular heroes. Nakhimov came to stand for the patriotic sacrifice and heroism of the Russian people in the defence of their motherland – a propaganda message that took on a new force during the war of 1941–5. From 1944, Soviet naval officers and sailors were decorated with the Nakhimov Medal, and trained in special cadet schools established in his name. In books and films he became a

* The Rumiantsev Library and Museum, opened in Moscow in 1862, was not a public collection in this sense. It was donated to the public by a single nobleman.

symbol of the Great Leader rallying the people against an aggressive foreign foe.

Production of Vsevolod Pudovkin's patriotic film *Admiral Nakhimov* (1947) began in 1943, when Britain was an ally of the Soviet Union. Planned as a Soviet counterpart to Alexander Korda's wartime epic about Lord Nelson, *Lady Hamilton* (1941), its first cut made light of Britain's role as an enemy of Russia during the Crimean War, focusing instead on Nakhimov's private life and on his relations with the population of Sevastopol. But as it went through editing, the film got caught up in the opening skirmishes of the Cold War – a conflict that arose in the Turkish Straits and the Caucasus, the starting points of the Crimean War. From the autumn of 1945, the Soviets pushed for a revision of the 1936 Montreux Convention on the neutrality of the Straits. Stalin demanded joint Soviet–Turkish control of the Dardanelles and the cession to the Soviet Union of Kars and Ardahan, territories conquered by tsarist Russia but ceded to the Turks in 1922. Mindful of the build-up of Soviet troops in the Caucasus, the United States sent warships to the eastern Mediterranean in August 1946. It was precisely at this moment that Stalin demanded changes to Pudovkin's film: the focus shifted from Nakhimov as a man to Nakhimov as a military leader against the foreign foe; and Britain was depicted as the enemy of Russia who had used the Turks to pursue its aggressive imperialist aims in the Black Sea, just as Stalin claimed the Americans were doing in the early stages of the Cold War.[30]

A similar patriotic line was taken by the great historian of the Stalin era, Evgeny Tarle, in his two-volume history of *The Crimean War* (1941–3), his biography *Nakhimov* (1948), and in his later book, *The City of Russian Glory: Sevastopol in 1854–55* (1955), published to commemorate the centenary. Tarle was very critical of the tsarist leadership, but he glorified the patriotic courage and resilience of the Russian people, led and inspired by the example of such heroic leaders as Nakhimov and Kornilov, who laid down their lives for the defence of Russia against the 'imperialist aggression' of the Western powers. The fact that Russia's enemies in the Crimean War – Britain, France and Turkey – were now all NATO members and adversaries of the newly founded Warsaw Pact in 1955 added greater tension to the Soviet celebration of the war's centenary.

Pride in the heroes of Sevastopol, the 'city of Russian glory', remains an important source of national identity, although today it is situated in a foreign land – a result of the transfer of the Crimea to Ukraine by Nikita Khrushchev in 1954 and the declaration of Ukrainian independence on the dissolution of the Soviet Union in 1991. In the words of one Russian nationalist poet:

> On the ruins of our superpower
> There is a major paradox of history:
> Sevastopol – the city of Russian glory –
> Is . . . outside Russian territory.[31]

The loss of the Crimea has been a severe blow to the Russians, already suffering a loss of national pride after the collapse of the Soviet empire. Nationalists have actively campaigned for the Crimea to return to Russia, not least nationalists in Sevastopol itself, which remains an ethnic Russian town.

Memories of the Crimean War continue to stir profound feelings of Russian pride and resentment of the West. In 2006 a conference on the Crimean War was organized by the Centre of National Glory of Russia with the support of Vladimir Putin's Presidential Administration and the ministries of Education and Defence. The conclusion of the conference, issued by its organizers in a press release, was that the war should be seen not as a defeat for Russia, but as a moral and religious victory, a national act of sacrifice in a just war; Russians should honour the authoritarian example of Nicholas I, a tsar unfairly derided by the liberal intelligentsia, for standing up against the West in the defence of his country's interests.[32] The reputation of Nicholas I, the man who led the Russians into the Crimean War against the world, has been restored in Putin's Russia. Today, on Putin's orders, Nicholas's portrait hangs in the antechamber of the presidential office in the Kremlin.

At the end of the Crimean War a quarter of a million Russians had been buried in mass graves in various locations around Sevastopol. All around the battle sites of Inkerman and Alma, the Chernaia valley, Balaklava and Sevastopol there are unknown soldiers buried underground. In August 2006 the remains of fourteen Russian infantrymen from the Vladimir and Kazan regiments were discovered not far from the spot where they were killed during the battle at the Alma. Alongside their skeletons were their knapsacks, water-bottles, crucifixes and grenades. The bones were reburied with military honours in a ceremony attended by Ukrainian and Russian officials at the Museum of the Alma near Bakhchiserai, and there are plans in Russia to build a chapel on the site.

Notes

INTRODUCTION

1. L. Liashuk, *Ofitsery chernomorskogo flota pogubshie pri zashchite Sevastopolia v 1854–1855 gg.* (Simferopol, 2005); G. Arnold, *Historical Dictionary of the Crimean War* (London, 2002), pp. 38–9.

2. *Losses of Life in Modern Wars: Austria-Hungary; France* (Oxford, 1916), p. 142; *Histoire militaire de la France*, 4 vols. (Paris, 1992), vol. 2, p. 514; D. Murphy, *Ireland and the Crimean War* (Dublin, 2002), p. 104. The best recent survey of allied effectives and casualties is T. Margrave, 'Numbers & Losses in the Crimea: An Introduction', *War Correspondent*, 21/1 (2003), pp. 30–32; 21/2 (2003), pp. 32–6; 21/3 (2003), pp. 18–22.

3. J. Herbé, *Français et russes en Crimée: Lettres d'un officier français à sa famille pendant la campagne d'Orient* (Paris, 1892), p. 337; A. Khrushchev, *Istoriia oborony Sevastopolia* (St Petersburg, 1889), pp. 157–8.

CHAPTER I. RELIGIOUS WARS

1. FO 78/446, Finn to Aberdeen, 27 May 1846; 78/705 Finn to Palmerston, 5 Apr. 1847; H. Martineau, *Eastern Life: Present and Past*, 3 vols. (London, 1848), vol. 3, pp. 162–5.

2. Ibid., pp. 120–21.

3. FO 78/368, Young to Palmerston, 14 Mar. 1839.

4. Quoted in D. Hopwood, *The Russian Presence in Palestine and Syria, 1843–1914: Church and Politics in the Near East* (Oxford, 1969), p. 9.

5. A. Kinglake, *The Invasion of the Crimea: Its Origin and an Account of Its Progress down to the Death of Lord Raglan*, 8 vols. (London, 1863), vol. 1, pp. 42–3; N. Shepherd, *The Zealous Intruders: The Western Rediscovery of Palestine* (London, 1987), p. 23; Martineau, *Eastern Life*, vol. 3, p. 124; R. Curzon, *Visits to Monasteries in the Levant* (London, 1849), p. 209.

6. FO 78/413, Young to Palmerston, 29 Jan. and 28 Apr. 1840; 78/368, Young to Palmerston, 14 Mar. and 21 Oct. 1839.

7. R. Marlin, *L'Opinion franc-comtoise devant la guerre de Crimée*, Annales Littéraires de l'Université de Besançon, vol. 17 (Paris, 1957), p. 23.

8. E. Finn (ed.), *Stirring Times, or, Records from Jerusalem Consular Chronicles of 1853 to 1856*, 2 vols. (London, 1878), vol. 1, pp. 57–8, 76.

9. FO 78/705, Finn to Palmerston, 2 Dec. 1847.

10. On the various interpretations of the treaty, see R. H. Davison, *Essays in Ottoman and Turkish History, 1774–1923: The Impact of the West* (Austin, Tex., 1990), pp. 29–37.

11. *Mémoires du duc De Persigny* (Paris, 1896), p. 225; L. Thouvenal, *Nicolas Ier et Napoléon III: Les préliminaires de la guerre de Crimée 1852–1854* (Paris, 1891), pp. 7–8, 14–16, 59.

12. A. Gouttman, *La Guerre de Crimée 1853–1856* (Paris, 1995), p. 69; D. Goldfrank, *The Origins of the Crimean War* (London, 1995), pp. 76, 82–3;

Correspondence Respecting the Rights and Privileges of the Latin and Greek Churches in Turkey, 2 vols. (London, 1854–6), vol. 1, pp. 17–18.

13. A. Ubicini, *Letters on Turkey*, trans. Lady Easthope, 2 vols. (London, 1856), vol. 1, pp. 18–22.

14. S. Montefiore, *Prince of Princes: The Life of Potemkin* (London, 2000), pp. 244–5.

15. W. Reddaway, *Documents of Catherine the Great* (Cambridge, 1931), p. 147; *Correspondence artistique de Grimm avec Cathérine II*, Archives de l'art français, nouvelle période, 17 (Paris, 1932), pp. 61–2; *The Life of Catherine II, Empress of Russia*, 3 vols. (London, 1798), vol. 3, p. 211; *The Memoirs of Catherine the Great* (New York, 1955), p. 378.

16. Davison, *Essays in Ottoman and Turkish History*, p. 37; H. Ragsdale, 'Russian Projects of Conquest in the Eighteenth Century', in id. (ed.), *Imperial Russian Foreign Policy* (Cambridge, 1993), pp. 83–5; V. Aksan, *Ottoman Wars 1700–1870: An Empire Besieged* (London, 2007), pp. 160–61.

17. Montefiore, *Prince of Princes*, pp. 274–5.

18. Ibid., pp. 246–8.

19. G. Jewsbury, *The Russian Annexation of Bessarabia: 1774–1828. A Study of Imperial Expansion* (New York, 1976), pp. 66–72, 88.

20. M. Gammer, *Muslim Resistance to the Tsar: Shamil and the Conquest of Chechnya and Dagestan* (London, 1994), p. 44; J. McCarthy, *Death and Exile: The Ethnic Cleansing of Ottoman Muslims 1821–1922* (Princeton, 1995), pp. 30–32.

21. M. Kozelsky, 'Introduction', unpublished MS.

22. K. O'Neill, 'Between Subversion and Submission: The Integration of the Crimean Khanate into the Russian Empire, 1783–1853', Ph.D. diss., Harvard, 2006, pp. 39, 52–60, 181; A. Fisher, *The Russian Annexation of the Crimea, 1772–1783* (Cambridge, 1970), pp. 144–6; M. Kozelsky, 'Forced Migration or Voluntary Exodus? Evolution of State Policy toward Crimean Tatars during the Crimean War', unpublished paper; B. Williams, 'Hijra and Forced Migration from Nineteenth-Century Russia to the Ottoman Empire', *Cahiers du monde russe*, 41/1 (2000), pp. 79–108; M. Pinson, 'Russian Policy and the Emigration of the Crimean Tatars to the Ottoman Empire, 1854–1862', *Güney-Dogu Avrupa Arastirmalari Dergisi*, 1 (1972), pp. 38–41.

23. A. Schönle, 'Garden of the Empire: Catherine's Appropriation of the Crimea', *Slavic Review*, 60/1 (Spring 2001), pp. 1–23; K. O'Neill, 'Constructing Russian Identity in the Imperial Borderland: Architecture, Islam, and the Transformation of the Crimean Landscape', *Ab Imperio*, 2 (2006), pp. 163–91.

24. M. Kozelsky, *Christianizing Crimea: Shaping Sacred Space in the Russian Empire and Beyond* (De Kalb, Ill., 2010), chap. 3; id., 'Ruins into Relics: The

Monument to Saint Vladimir on the Excavations of Chersonesos, 1827-57', *Russian Review*, 63/4 (Oct. 2004), pp. 655-72.

CHAPTER 2. EASTERN QUESTIONS

1. R. Nelson, *Hagia Sophia, 1850–1950: Holy Wisdom Modern Monument* (Chicago, 2004), pp. 29-30.

2. Ibid., p. 30.

3. N. Teriatnikov, *Mosaics of Hagia Sophia, Istanbul: The Fossati Restoration and the Work of the Byzantine Institute* (Washington, 1998), p. 3; *The Russian Primary Chronicle: Laurentian Text*, trans. S. Cross and O. Sherbowitz-Wetzor (Cambridge, Mass., 1953), p. 111.

4. T. Stavrou, 'Russian Policy in Constantinople and Mount Athos in the Nineteenth Century', in L. Clucas (ed.), *The Byzantine Legacy in Eastern Europe* (New York, 1988), p. 225.

5. Nelson, *Hagia Sophia*, p. 33.

6. A. Ubicini, *Letters on Turkey*, trans. Lady Easthope, 2 vols. (London, 1856), vol. 1, pp. 18-22.

7. D. Hopwood, *The Russian Presence in Palestine and Syria, 1843-1914: Church and Politics in the Near East* (Oxford, 1969), p. 29.

8. S. Pavlowitch, *Anglo-Russian Rivalry in Serbia, 1837-39* (Paris, 1961), p. 72; B. Lewis, *The Emergence of Modern Turkey* (Oxford, 2002), p. 31.

9. F. Bailey, *British Policy and the Turkish Reform Movement, 1826-1853* (London, 1942), pp. 19-22; D. Ralston, *Importing the European Army: The Introduction of European Military Techniques and Institutions into the Extra-European World, 1600-1914* (Chicago, 1990), pp. 62-3.

10. W. Miller, *The Ottoman Empire, 1801-1913* (Cambridge, 1913), p. 18.

11. V. Aksan, *Ottoman Wars 1700-1870: An Empire Besieged* (London, 2007), p. 49.

12. D. Goldfrank, *The Origins of the Crimean War* (London, 1995), pp. 41-2.

13. A. Bitis, *Russia and the Eastern Question: Army, Government and Society, 1815-1833* (Oxford, 2006), pp. 33-4, 101-4; Aksan, *Ottoman Wars*, pp. 290-96; T. Prousis, *Russian Society and the Greek Revolution* (De Kalb, Ill., 1994), pp. 31, 50-51.

14. A. Zaionchkovskii, *Vostochnaia voina 1853-1856*, 3 vols. (St Petersburg, 2002), vol. 1, pp. 8, 19; L. Vyskochkov, *Imperator Nikolai I: Chelovek i gosudar'* (St Petersburg, 2001), p. 141; M. Gershenzon, *Epokha Nikolaia I* (Moscow, 1911), pp. 21-2.

15. A. Tiutcheva, *Pri dvore dvukh imperatov: Vospominaniia, dnevnik, 1853-1882* (Moscow, 1928-9), pp. 96-7.

16. R. Wortman, *Scenarios of Power: Myth and Ceremony in Russian Monarchy*, vol. 1: *From Peter the Great to the Death of Nicholas I* (Princeton, 1995), p. 382; D. Goldfrank, 'The Holy Sepulcher and the Origin of the Crimean War', in E. Lohr and M. Poe (eds.), *The Military and Society in Russia: 1450–1917* (Leiden, 2002), pp. 502–3.

17. Bitis, *Russia and the Eastern Question*, pp. 167–76.

18. Ibid., p. 187.

19. Aksan, *Ottoman Wars*, pp. 346–52.

20. P. Schroeder, *The Transformation of European Politics, 1763–1848* (Oxford, 1994), pp. 658–60.

21. A. Seaton, *The Crimean War: A Russian Chronicle* (London, 1977), p. 36.

22. Bitis, *Russia and the Eastern Question*, pp. 361–2, 366.

23. FO 97/404, Ponsonby to Palmerston, 7 July 1834; R. Florescu, *The Struggle against Russia in the Romanian Principalities 1821–1854* (Monachii, 1962), pp. 135–60.

24. F. Lawson, *The Social Origins of the Egyptian Expansionism during the Muhammad Ali Period* (New York, 1992), chap. 5; Aksan, *Ottoman Wars*, pp. 363–7; A. Marmont, *The Present State of the Turkish Empire*, trans. F. Smith (London, 1839), p. 289.

25. Bitis, *Russia and the Eastern Question*, pp. 468–9.

26. Zaionchkovskii, *Vostochnaia voina*, vol. 1, p. 235.

27. FO 181/114, Palmerston to Ponsonby, 6 Dec. 1833; P. Mosely, *Russian Diplomacy and the Opening of the Eastern Question in 1838 and 1839* (Cambridge, Mass., 1934), p. 12; Bailey, *British Policy*, p. 53.

28. L. Levi, *History of British Commerce, 1763–1870* (London, 1870), p. 562; Bailey, *British Policy*, p. 74; J. Gallagher and R. Robinson, 'The Imperialism of Free Trade', *Economic History Review*, 2nd ser., 6/1 (1953); FO 78/240, Ponsonby to Palmerston, 25 Nov. 1834; D. Urquhart, *England and Russia* (London, 1835), p. 110.

29. B. Kingsley Martin, *The Triumph of Lord Palmerston: A Study of Public Opinion in England before the Crimean War* (London, 1963), p. 85.

30. J. Gleason, *The Genesis of Russophobia in Great Britain* (Cambridge, Mass., 1950), p. 103.

31. Ibid., pp. 211–12, 220.

32. *India, Great Britain, and Russia* (London, 1838), pp. 1–2.

33. R. Shukla, *Britain, India and the Turkish Empire, 1853–1882* (New Delhi, 1973), p. 27.

34. M. Gammer, *Muslim Resistance to the Tsar: Shamil and the Conquest of Chechnya and Dagestan* (London, 1994), p. 121.

35. J. Pardoe, *The City of the Sultan; and Domestic Manners of the Turks in 1836*, 2 vols. (London, 1854), vol. 1, p. 32.

36. C. White, *Three Years in Constantinople; or, Domestic Manners of the Turks in 1844*, 3 vols. (London, 1846), p. 363. See also E. Spencer, *Travels in Circassia, Krim-Tartary, &c., including a Steam Voyage down the Danube from Vienna to Constantinople, and round the Black Sea in 1836*, 2 vols. (London, 1837).

37. Urquhart, *England and Russia*, p. 86.

38. S. Lane-Poole, *The Life of the Right Honourable Stratford Canning*, 2 vols. (London, 1888), vol. 2, p. 17.

39. Ibid., p. 104. On Freemasonry in nineteenth-century Turkey, see the many works of Paul Dumont, including 'La Turquie dans les archives du Grand Orient de France: Les loges maçonniques d'obédience française à Istanbul du milieu du XIXe siècle à la veille de la Première Guerre Mondiale', in J.-L. Bacqué-Grammont and P. Dumont (eds.), *Économie et société dans l'empire ottoman (fin du XVIIIe siècle–début du XXe siècle)* (Paris, 1983), pp. 171–202.

40. A. Cunningham, *Eastern Questions in the Nineteenth Century: Collected Essays*, 2 vols. (London, 1993), vol. 2, pp. 118–19.

41. B. Abu Manneh, 'The Islamic Roots of the Gülhane Rescript', in id., *Studies on Islam and the Ottoman Empire in the Nineteenth Century* (Istanbul, 2001), pp. 83–4, 89.

42. FO 97/413, Stratford to Palmerston, 7 Feb. 1850; Lane-Poole, *The Life of the Right Honourable Stratford Canning*, vol. 2, p. 215.

CHAPTER 3. THE RUSSIAN MENACE

1. S. Tatishchev, 'Imperator Nikolai I v Londone v 1844 godu', *Istoricheskii vestnik*, 23/3 (Feb. 1886), pp. 602–4.

2. E. Stockmar, *Denkwürdigkeiten aus den Papieren des Freiherrn Christian Friedrich V. Stockmar* (Brunswick, 1872), p. 98; T. Martin, *The Life of His Royal Highness the Prince Consort*, 5 vols. (London, 1877), vol. 1, p. 215.

3. G. Bolsover, 'Nicholas I and the Partition of Turkey', *Slavonic Review*, 27 (1948), p. 135.

4. Tatishchev, 'Imperator Nikolai', pp. 355–8.

5. Martin, *The Life of His Royal Highness*, vol. 1, p. 224.

6. Tatishchev, 'Imperator Nikolai', p. 604; Stockmar, *Denkwürdigkeiten*, p. 98.

7. Tatishchev, 'Imperator Nikolai', p. 604.

8. *The Letters of Queen Victoria: A Selection from Her Majesty's Correspondence between the Years 1837 and 1861*, 3 vols. (London, 1907–8), vol. 2, pp. 16–17; Martin, *The Life of His Royal Highness*, vol. 1, p. 219; Tatishchev, 'Imperator Nikolai', p. 609.

9. Martin, *The Life of His Royal Highness*, vol. 1, p. 223; Stockmar, *Denkwürdigkeiten*, pp. 397, 400.

10. Tatishchev, 'Imperator Nikolai', p. 615; Stockmar, *Denkwürdigkeiten*, p. 399.

11. Ibid., pp. 396–9.

12. H. Ragsdale, 'Russian Projects of Conquest in the Eighteenth Century', in id. (ed.), *Imperial Russian Foreign Policy* (Cambridge, 1993), pp. 75–7; O. Subtelnyi, 'Peter I's Testament: A Reassessment', *Slavic Review*, 33 (1974), pp. 663–78.

13. Ragsdale, 'Russian Projects', pp. 79–80.

14. Ibid., p. 81.

15. J. Gleason, *The Genesis of Russophobia in Great Britain* (Cambridge, Mass., 1950), pp. 39, 43.

16. R. Wilson, *A Sketch of the Military and Political Power of Russia in the Year 1817* (London, 1817); Gleason, *Genesis of Russophobia*, p. 56.

17. [Lieut. Col.] Sir George de Lacy Evans, *On the Designs of Russia* (London, 1828), pp. 191, 199–219.

18. *The Portfolio; or a Collection of State Papers, etc. etc., Illustrative of the History of Our Times*, 1 (1836), p. 103.

19. Ibid., pp. 187–95. See further, M. Kukiel, *Czartoryski and European Unity 1770–1861* (Princeton, 1955), p. 236.

20. Hansard, HC Deb. 23 Feb. 1848, vol. 96, pp. 1132–1242; HC Deb. 1 Mar. 1848, vol. 47, pp. 66–123 (Palmerston quotation at p. 122).

21. *The Times*, 20 July 1831; *Northern Liberator*, 3 Oct. 1840.

22. Gleason, *Genesis of Russophobia*, p. 126.

23. Kukiel, *Czartoryski*, p. 205.

24. R. McNally, 'The Origins of Russophobia in France: 1812–1830', *American Slavic and East European Review*, 17/2 (Apr. 1958), pp. 179–83.

25. A. Mickiewicz, *Livre des pèlerins polonais, traduit du polonais d'A. M. par le Comte C. de Montalembert; suivi d'un hymne à la Pologne par F. de La Menais* (Paris, 1833).

26. *Cinq millions de Polonais forcés par la czarine Catherine, les czars Paul, Alexandre et récemment Nicolas d'abjurer leur foi religieuse. Eclaircissements sur la question des Grecs-Unis sous le rapport statistique, historique et religieux* (Paris and Strasburg, 1845); *Journal des débats*, 23 Oct. 1842.

27. *The Nuns of Minsk: Narrative of Makrena Mieczysławska, Abbess of the Basilian Convent of Minsk; The History of a Seven Years' Persecution Suffered for the Faith, by Her and Her Nuns* (London, 1846), pp. 1–16; Hansard, HL Deb. 9 Mar. 1846, vol. 84, p. 768; M. Cadot, *La Russie dans la vie intellectuelle française, 1839–1856* (Paris, 1967), p. 464.

28. [Count] V. Krasinski, *Is the Power of Russia to be Reduced or Increased by the Present War? The Polish Question and Panslavism* (London, 1855), p. 4.

29. Marquis de Custine, *Russia*, 3 vols. (London, 1844), vol. 3, pp. 21, 353; G. Kennan, *The Marquis de Custine and His Russia in 1839* (London, 1971).

30. Cadot, *La Russie dans la vie intellectuelle française*, p. 471.

31. S. Pavlowitch, *Anglo-Russian Rivalry in Serbia, 1837–39* (Paris, 1961).

32. N. Tsimbaev, *Slavianofil'stvo: Iz istorii russkoi obshchestvenno-politicheskoi mysli XIX veka* (Moscow, 1986), p. 36.

33. A. Bitis, *Russia and the Eastern Question: Army, Government and Society, 1815–1833* (Oxford, 2006), pp. 93–7.

34. N. Riasanovsky, *Nicholas I and Official Nationality in Russia 1825–1855* (Berkeley, 1959), p. 152.

35. Ibid., p. 166.

36. P. Mérimée, *Correspondence générale*, 18 vols. (Paris, 1941–65), vol. 5, p. 420; Cadot, *La Russie dans la vie intellectuelle française*, p. 516; L. Namier, *1848: The Revolution of the Intellectuals* (Oxford, 1946), pp. 40–42.

37. Cadot, *La Russie dans la vie intellectuelle française*, p. 468.

38. R. Florescu, *The Struggle against Russia in the Romanian Principalities 1821–1854* (Monachii, 1962), chaps. 7 and 8.

39. FO 195/321, Colquhoun to Palmerston, 16 Aug. 1848.

40. FO 195/332, Colquhoun to Stratford Canning, 2 July 1849.

41. Florescu, *Struggle against Russia*, pp. 217–18.

42. D. Goldfrank, *The Origins of the Crimean War* (London, 1995), pp. 68–71.

CHAPTER 4. THE END OF PEACE IN EUROPE

1. On British naval defence against France, see A. Lambert, *The Crimean War: British Grand Strategy, 1853–56* (Manchester, 1990), pp. 25–7.

2. RA VIC/MAIN/QVJ/1855, 16 Apr.

3. *Mémoires du duc De Persigny* (Paris, 1896), p. 212.

4. A. J. P. Taylor, *The Struggle for Mastery in Europe 1848–1918* (Oxford, 1955), p. 49.

5. *Mémoires du duc De Persigny*, p. 225; E. Bapst, *Les Origines de la Guerre en Crimée: La France et la Russie de 1848 à 1851* (Paris, 1912), pp. 325–7.

6. FO 78/895, Rose to Malmesbury, 28 Dec. 1852.

7. K. Vitzthum von Eckstadt, *St Petersburg and London in the Years 1852–64*, 2 vols. (London, 1887), vol. 1, p. 38; D. Goldfrank, *The Origins of the Crimean War* (London, 1995), pp. 109–10.

8. FO 65/424, Seymour to Russell, 11 and 22 Jan., 22 Feb. 1853.

9. FO 65/424, Seymour to Russell, 11 Jan., 21 Feb. 1853; A. Cunningham,

Eastern Questions in the Nineteenth Century: Collected Essays, 2 vols. (London, 1993), vol. 2, p. 136.

10. FO 65/424, Seymour to Russell, 22 Feb. 1853; FO 65/425, Seymour to Clarendon, 29 Mar. 1853.

11. Cunningham, *Eastern Questions*, vol. 2, pp. 139–40.

12. FO 65/424, Seymour to Russell, 10 Feb. 1853.

13. RGAVMF, f. 19, op. 7, d. 135, l. 37; FO 65/424, Seymour to Russell, 7 Jan. 1853; *Correspondence Respecting the Rights and Privileges of the Latin and Greek Churches in Turkey*, 2 vols. (London, 1854–6), vol. 1, pp. 121–4.

14. RGAVMF, f. 19, op. 7, d. 135, l. 43; J. Curtiss, *Russia's Crimean War* (Durham, NC, 1979), p. 94.

15. FO 65/420, Clarendon to Seymour, 23 Mar., 5 Apr. 1853; Goldfrank, *Origins of the Crimean War*, pp. 136–8.

16. *Mémoires du duc De Persigny*, pp. 226–31; Bapst, *Origines de la Guerre en Crimée*, p. 354.

17. *Mémoires du comte Horace de Viel-Castel sur le règne de Napoléon III, 1851–1864*, 2 vols. (Paris, 1979), vol. 1, p. 180; J. Ridley, *Napoleon III and Eugenie* (London, 1979), p. 365; S. Lane-Poole, *The Life of the Right Honourable Stratford Canning*, 2 vols. (London, 1888), vol. 2, p. 237.

18. *Correspondence Respecting the Rights and Privileges of the Latin and Greek Churches*, vol. 1, pp. 256–8; Cunningham, *Eastern Questions*, pp. 159–62; Goldfrank, *Origins of the Crimean War*, pp. 147–8, 156–7; A. Saab, *The Origins of the Crimean Alliance* (Charlottesville, Va., 1977), pp. 135–7; Lane-Poole, *The Life of the Right Honourable Stratford Canning*, vol. 2, p. 248.

19. BOA, AMD, 44/81, Musurus to Reshid Pasha, 13 May 1853; RGAVMF, f. 19, op. 7, d. 135, l. 52; C. Badem, 'The Ottomans and the Crimean War (1853–1856)', Ph.D. diss. (Sabanci University, 2007), pp. 74–6.

20. A. Zaionchkovskii, *Vostochnaia voina 1853–1856*, 3 vols. (St Petersburg, 2002), vol. 1, pp. 739–40.

21. *Russkii arkhiv*, 1891, no. 8, p. 169; 'Voina s Turtsiei 1828–1829 i 1853–1854', *Russkaia starina*, 16 (1876), pp. 681–7; P. Schroeder, *Austria, Great Britain and the Crimean War: The Destruction of the European Concert* (Ithaca, NY, 1972), p. 76.

22. RGVIA, f. 846, op. 16, d. 5407, ll. 7–11; d. 5451, ll. 13–14; Zaionchkovskii, *Vostochnaia voina*, vol. 1, p. 74.

23. *Za mnogo let: Zapiski (vospominaniia) neizvestnogo 1844–1874 gg.* (St Petersburg, 1897), p. 74; RGB OR, f. 743, T. Klemm, 'Vospominaniia starogo-soldata, rasskazannye synu, kadetu VII klacca Pskovskogo kadetskogo korpusa', l. 6.

24. F. Kagan, *The Military Reforms of Nicholas I: The Origins of the Modern*

Russian Army (London, 1999), p. 221; E. Brooks, 'Reform in the Russian Army, 1856–1861', *Slavic Review*, 43/1 (Spring 1984), p. 64; E. Wirtschafter, *From Serf to Russian Soldier* (Princeton, 1990), p. 24.

25. Brooks, 'Reform', pp. 70–71; K. Marx, *The Eastern Question: A Reprint of Letters Written 1853–1856 Dealing with the Events of the Crimean War* (London, 1969), pp. 397–8; J. Curtiss, *The Russian Army under Nicholas I, 1825–1855* (Durham, NC, 1965), p. 115; P. Alabin, *Chetyre voiny: Pokhod-nye zapiski v voinu 1853, 1854, 1855 i 1856 godov*, 2 vols. (Viatka, 1861), vol. 1, p. 43.

26. Curtiss, *Russian Army*, pp. 248–9.

27. *Za mnogo let*, pp. 34–5, 45–7; RGB OR, f. 743, T. Klemm, 'Vospominaniia starogo-soldata', ll. 4, 7–8; Wirtschafter, *From Serf to Russian Soldier*, p. 87.

28. BOA, I, HR, 328/21222; S. Kiziltoprak, 'Egyptian Troops in the Crimean War (1853–1856)', in *Vostochnaya (Krymskaya) Voina 1853–1856 godov: Novye materialy i novoe osmyslenie*, 2 vols. (Simferopol, 2005), vol. 1, p. 49; Lane-Poole, *The Life of the Right Honourable Stratford Canning*, vol. 2, p. 296.

29. A. Slade, *Turkey and the Crimean War: A Narrative of Historical Events* (London, 1867), p. 186; E. Perret, *Les Français en Orient: Récits de Crimée 1854–1856* (Paris, 1889), pp. 86–7.

30. T. Buzzard, *With the Turkish Army in the Crimea and Asia Minor* (London, 1915), p. 121; J. Reid, *Crisis of the Ottoman Empire: Prelude to Collapse 1839–1878* (Stuttgart, 2000), p. 257.

31. RGVIA, f. 450, op. 1, d. 33, ll. 4–12; *A Visit to Sebastopol a Week after Its Fall: By an Officer of the Anglo-Turkish Contingent* (London, 1856), p. 53; *Vospominaniia ofitsera o voennyh deistviyah na Dunae v 1853–54 gg.: Iz dnevnika P.B.* (St Petersburg, 1887), p. 566.

32. M. Chamberlain, *Lord Aberdeen: A Political Biography* (London, 1983), p. 476; FO 65/421, Palmerston to Seymour, 16 July 1853; *Correspondence Respecting the Rights and Privileges of the Latin and Greek Churches*, vol. 1, p. 400.

33. R. Florescu, *The Struggle against Russia in the Romanian Principalities 1821–1854* (Monachii, 1962), pp. 241–6.

34. FO 65/422, Palmerston to Seymour, 2 Aug. 1853.

35. *Correspondence Respecting the Rights and Privileges of the Latin and Greek Churches*, vol. 1, pp. 400–404.

36. Goldfrank, *Origins of the Crimean War*, pp. 190–213.

37. *The Greville Memoirs 1814–1860*, ed. L. Strachey and R. Fulford, 8 vols. (London, 1938), vol. 1, p. 85.

38. H. Maxwell, *The Life and Letters of George William Frederick, Fourth Earl of Clarendon*, 2 vols. (London, 1913), vol. 2, p. 25.

39. Slade, *Turkey and the Crimean War*, pp. 101–2, 107; Saab, *Origins of the Crimean Alliance*, p. 64; Cunningham, *Eastern Questions*, pp. 198–9.

40. Saab, *Origins of the Crimean Alliance*, p. 81; Badem, 'The Ottomans and the Crimean War', pp. 80, 90.

41. *The Times*, 27 Sept. 1853; *Correspondence Respecting the Rights and Privileges of the Latin and Greek Churches*, vol. 1, pp. 562–3.

42. A. Türkgeldi, *Mesâil-i Mühimme-i Siyâsiyye*, 3 vols. (Ankara, 1957–60), vol. 1, pp. 319–21; Badem, 'The Ottomans and the Crimean War', p. 93.

CHAPTER 5. PHONEY WAR

1. BOA, HR, SYS, 907/5.

2. BOA, HR, SYS, 903/2–26.

3. RGVIA, f. 846, op. 16, d. 5429, ll. 11–17; 'Vospominaniia A. A. Genritsi', *Russkaia starina*, 20 (1877), p. 313.

4. 'Vostochnaia voina: Pis'ma kn. I. F. Paskevicha k kn. M. D. Gorchakovu', *Russkaia starina*, 15 (1876), pp. 163–91, 659–74 (quotation, p. 182); E. Tarle, *Krymskaia voina*, 2 vols. (Moscow, 1944), vol. 1, pp. 216–18.

5. 'Voina s Turtsiei 1828–1829 i 1853–1854', *Russkaia starina*, 16 (1876), pp. 700–701; S. Nikitin, 'Russkaia politika na Balkanakh i nachalo vostochnoi voiny', *Voprosy istorii*, 4 (1946), pp. 3–29.

6. A. Zaionchkovskii, *Vostochnaia voina 1853–1856*, 3 vols. (St Petersburg, 2002), vol. 2, pp. 523–4; 'Voina s Turtsiei 1828–1829 i 1853–1854', p. 708.

7. Zaionchkovskii, *Vostochnaia voina*, vol. 1, pp. 321–2, 564.

8. 'Voina s Turtsiei 1854 g.', *Russkaia starina*, 18 (1877), p. 141; *Correspondence Respecting the Rights and Privileges of the Latin and Greek Churches in Turkey*, 2 vols. (London, 1854–6), vol. 1, pp. 415–18; RGVIA, f. 846, op. 16, d. 5417, l. 7.

9. RGIA, f. 711, op. 1, d. 35, ll. 1–3; A. Tiutcheva, *Pri dvore dvukh imperatov: Vospominaniia, dnevnik, 1853–1882* (Moscow, 1928–9), pp. 129–30, 146–8, 162–3.

10. Zaionchkovskii, *Vostochnaia voina*, vol. 1, pp. 702–8.

11. Ibid., pp. 559–61.

12. L. Vyskochkov, *Imperator Nikolai I: chelovek i gosudar'* (St Petersburg, 2001), pp. 296–7.

13. Zaionchkovskii, *Vostochnaia voina*, vol. 1, p. 535.

14. 'Vostochnaia voina: Pis'ma kn. I. F. Paskevicha k kn. M. D. Gorchakovu', p. 190.

15. M. Pinson, 'Ottoman Bulgaria in the First Tanzimat Period – the Revolts in Nish (1841) and Vidin (1850)', *Middle Eastern Studies*, 11/2 (May 1975),

pp. 103–46; H. Inalcik, *Tanzimat ve Bulgar Meselesi* (Ankara, 1943), pp. 69–71; 'Vospominaniia o voine na Dunae v 1853 i 1854 gg.', *Voennyi sbornik*, 14/8 (1880), p. 420; *Rossiia i Balkany: Iz istorii obshchestvenno-politicheskikh i kul'turnykh sviazei (xviii veka–1878 g.)* (Moscow, 1995), pp. 180–82.

16. FO 195/439, Grant to Clarendon, 11 Jan. 1854; FO 78/1014, Grant to Clarendon, 9 Jan. 1854; *Vospominaniia ofitsera o voennyh deistviyah na Dunae v 1853–54 gg.: Iz dnevnika P.B.* (St Petersburg, 1887), pp. 531, 535, 543; 'Vospominaniia A. A. Genritsi', p. 313; A. Ulupian, 'Russkaia period-icheskaia pechat' vremen krymskoi voiny 1853–56 gg. o Bolgarii i bolgarakh', in *Rossiia i Balkany*, pp. 182–3; A. Rachinskii, *Pokhodnye pis'ma opolchentsa iz iuzhnoi Bessarabii 1855–1856* (Moscow, 1858), pp. 8–11.

17. *Vospominaniia ofitsera o voennyh deistviyah na Dunae*, pp. 585–9; A. Baumgarten, *Dnevniki 1849, 1853, 1854 i 1855* (n.p., 1911), pp. 82–7.

18. FO 78/1008, Fonblanque (consul in Belgrade) to Stratford Canning, 31 Dec. 1853, 11, 17, 24 and 26 Jan. 1854.

19. L. Guerrin, *Histoire de la dernière guerre de Russie (1853–1856)*, 2 vols. (Paris, 1858), vol. 1, p. 63; J. Koliopoulos, 'Brigandage and Insurgency in the Greek Domains of the Ottoman Empire, 1853–1908', in D. Gondicas and C. Issawi (eds.), *Ottoman Greeks in the Age of Nationalism: Politics, Economy, and Society in the Nineteenth Century* (Princeton, 1999), pp. 147–8.

20. *Shamil' – stavlennik sultanskoi Turtsii i angliiskikh kolonizatorov: Sbornik dokumental'nykh materialov* (Tbilisi, 1953), p. 367; 'Voina s Turtsiei 1828–1829 i 1853–1854', p. 696.

21. E. Adamov and L. Kutakov, 'Iz istorii proiskov inostrannoy agentury vo vremya Kavkazskikh voyn', *Voprosy istorii*, 11 (Nov. 1950), pp. 101–25.

22. M. Gammer, 'Shamil and the Ottomans: A Preliminary Overview', in *V. Milletlerarasi Türkiye Sosyal ve Iktisat Tarihi Kongresi: Tebligler. Istanbul 21–25 Agustos 1989* (Ankara, 1990), pp. 387–94; M. Budak, '1853–1856 Kırım Harbi Baslarinda Dogu Anadolu-Kafkas Cephesi ve Seyh Samil', *Kafkas Arastirmalari*, 1 (1988), pp. 132–3; Tarle, *Krymskaia voina*, vol. 1, p. 294.

23. B. Lewis, 'Slade on the Turkish Navy', *Journal of Turkish Studies/Türklük Bilgisi Araştırmaları*, 11 (1987), pp. 6–7; C. Badem, 'The Ottomans and the Crimean War (1853–1856)', Ph.D. diss. (Sabanci University, 2007), pp. 107–9.

24. FO 195/309, Slade to Stratford Canning, 7 Dec. 1853.

25. A. Slade, *Turkey and the Crimean War: A Narrative of Historical Events* (London, 1867), p. 152.

26. BOA, HR, SYS, 1346/38; S. Lane-Poole, *The Life of the Right Honourable Stratford Canning*, 2 vols. (London, 1888), vol. 2, pp. 333–5; *Correspondence Respecting the Rights and Privileges of the Latin and Greek Churches*, vol. 1, p. 814.

27. *Morning Post*, 16 Dec. 1853; *The Times*, 13 and 18 Dec. 1853; *Sheffield and Rotherham Independent*, 17 Dec. 1853; *Chronicle*, 23 Dec. 1853.

28. *The Letters of Queen Victoria: A Selection from Her Majesty's Correspondence between the Years 1837 and 1861*, 3 vols. (London, 1907–8), vol. 2, p. 126.

29. RA VIC/MAIN/QVJ/1853, 13 Nov. and 15 Dec.

30. FO 65/423, Palmerston to Seymour, 27 Dec. 1853; RA VIC/MAIN/QVJ/1853, 15 Dec.; P. Schroeder, *Austria, Great Britain and the Crimean War: The Destruction of the European Concert* (Ithaca, NY, 1972), p. 122.

31. Ibid., pp. 123–6.

32. A. Saab, *The Origins of the Crimean Alliance* (Charlottesville, Va., 1977), pp. 126–7; A. Lambert, *The Crimean War: British Grand Strategy, 1853–56* (Manchester, 1990), p. 64.

33. Quoted in S. Brady, *Masculinity and Male Homosexuality in Britain, 1861–1913* (London, 2005), p. 81; G. Henderson, *Crimean War Diplomacy and Other Historical Essays* (Glasgow, 1947), p. 136.

34. M. Taylor, *The Decline of British Radicalism, 1847–1860* (Oxford, 1995), pp. 230–31; R. Seton Watson, *Britain in Europe 1789–1914: A Survey of Foreign Policy* (Cambridge, 1937), pp. 321–2; RA VIC/MAIN/QVJ/1853, various entries, Nov. and Dec.

35. RA VIC/MAIN/QVJ/1853, 8 Dec.; RA VIC/MAIN/QVJ/1854, 15 Feb.

36. Saab, *Origins of the Crimean Alliance*, p. 148; id., *Reluctant Icon: Gladstone, Bulgaria, and the Working Classes, 1856–1878* (Cambridge, Mass., 1991), p. 31.

37. O. Anderson, 'The Reactions of Church and Dissent towards the Crimean War', *Journal of Ecclesiastical History*, 16 (1965), pp. 211–12; B. Kingsley Martin, *The Triumph of Lord Palmerston: A Study of Public Opinion in England before the Crimean War* (London, 1963), pp. 114–15, 164.

38. R. Marlin, *L'Opinion franc-comtoise devant la guerre de Crimée*, Annales Littéraires de l'Université de Besançon, vol. 17 (Paris, 1957), pp. 19–20; Taylor, *Decline of British Radicalism*, p. 226.

39. Marlin, *L'Opinion franc-comtoise*, pp. 22–3.

40. L. Case, *French Opinion on War and Diplomacy during the Second Empire* (Philadelphia, 1954), pp. 16–24.

41. Tarle, *Krymskaia voina*, vol. 1, pp. 405–28.

42. See e.g. V. Vinogradov, 'The Personal Responsibility of Emperor Nicholas I for the Coming of the Crimean War: An Episode in the Diplomatic Struggle in the Eastern Question', in H. Ragsdale (ed.), *Imperial Russian Foreign Policy* (Cambridge, 1993), pp. 159–70.

43. GARF, f. 678, op. 1, d. 451, l. 306.

44. T. Schiemann, *Geschichte Russlands unter Kaiser Nikolaus I*, 4 vols. (Berlin, 1904–19), vol. 4, p. 430.

45. E. Boniface, Count de Castellane, *Campagnes de Crimée, d'Italie, d'Afrique, de Chine et de Syrie, 1849–1862* (Paris, 1898), pp. 75–6; J. Ridley, *Napoleon III and Eugenie* (London 1979), p. 365.

46. Lambert, *The Crimean War*, pp. 64 ff.

47. Schroeder, *Austria, Great Britain and the Crimean War*, p. 150; Lady F. Balfour, *The Life of George, Fourth Earl of Aberdeen*, 2 vols. (London, 1922), vol. 2, p. 206.

48. RA VIC/MAIN/QVJ/1854, 6 Mar.; W. Baumgart, *The Peace of Paris 1856: Studies in War, Diplomacy and Peacemaking* (Oxford, 1981), p. 13; Henderson, *Crimean War Diplomacy*, p. 72; BLO Clarendon Papers, Stratford Canning to Clarendon, 7 Apr. 1854, c. 22; Lane-Poole, *The Life of the Right Honourable Stratford Canning*, vol. 2, pp. 354–8; PRO 30/22/11, Russell to Clarendon, 26 Mar. 1854.

49. RA VIC/MAIN/QVJ/1854, 26 Mar.

50. K. Vitzthum von Eckstadt, *St Petersburg and London in the Years 1852–64*, 2 vols. (London, 1887), vol. 1, pp. 83–4; A. Kinglake, *The Invasion of the Crimea: Its Origin and an Account of Its Progress down to the Death of Lord Raglan*, 8 vols. (London, 1863), vol. 1, pp. 476–7.

51. See R. Ellison, *The Victorian Pulpit: Spoken and Written Sermons in Nineteenth-Century Britain* (Cranbury, NJ, 1998), pp. 43–9.

52. H. Beamish, *War with Russia: God the Arbiter of Battle. A Sermon Preached on Sunday April 2, 1854* (London, 1854), p. 6; T. Harford Battersby, *Two First-Day Sermons Preached in the Church of St John, Keswick* (London, 1855), p. 5; J. James, *The War with Russia Imperative and Righteous: A Sermon Preached in Brunswick Chapel, Leeds, on the Day of National Humiliation* (London, 1854), pp. 14–15.

53. G. Croly, *England, Turkey, and Russia: A Sermon Preached on the Embarkation of the Guards for the East in the Church of St Stephen, Walbrook, February 26, 1854* (London, 1854), pp. 8, 12–13, 26–7, 30–31. For similar sermons, see H. Bunsen, *'The War is a Righteous War': A Sermon Preached in Lilleshall Church on the Day of Humiliation and Prayer* (London, 1854); R. Burton, *The War of God's Sending: A Sermon Preached in Willesden Church on the Occasion of the Fast, April 26, 1854* (London, 1854); R. Cadlish, *The Sword of the Lord: A Sermon Preached in the Free St George's Church, Edinburgh on Wednesday, April 26, 1854* (London, 1854); H. Howarth, *Will God Be for Us? A Sermon Preached in the Parish Church of St George's, Hanover Square, on Wednesday, April 26, 1854* (London, 1854); *A Sermon Preached by the Rev. H. W. Kemp, Incumbent of St John's Church,*

Hull, on Wednesday, April 26th: Being the Day Appointed by Her Gracious Majesty the Queen for the Humiliation of the Nation on the Commencement of the War with Russia (London, 1854); J. Cumming, *The War and Its Issues: Two Sermons* (London, 1854); J. Hall, *War with Russia Both Just and Expedient: A Discourse Delivered in Union Chapel, Brixton Hill, April 26, 1854* (London, 1854); John, Bishop of Lincoln, *War: Its Evils and Duties: A Sermon Preached in the Cathedral Church of Lincoln on April 26th, 1854* (London, 1854).

54. FO 195/445, Finn to Clarendon, 28 Apr. 1854; E. Finn (ed.), *Stirring Times, or, Records from Jerusalem Consular Chronicles of 1853 to 1856*, 2 vols. (London, 1878), vol. 2, pp. 130–31.

CHAPTER 6. FIRST BLOOD TO THE TURKS

1. *Tolstoy's Letters*, ed. and trans. R. F. Christian, 2 vols. (London, 1978), vol. 1, p. 38.
2. A. Maude, *The Life of Tolstoy: First Fifty Years* (London, 1908), pp. 96–7.
3. 'Voina s Turtsiei 1854 g.', *Russkaia starina*, 18 (1877), p. 327.
4. RGADA, f. 1292, op. 1, d. 6, l. 68; E. Tarle, *Krymskaia voina*, 2 vols. (Moscow, 1944), vol. 1, p. 273; 'Vospominaniia kniazia Emiliia Vitgenshteina', *Russkaia starina*, 104 (1900), p. 190.
5. A. Khomiakov, *Polnoe sobranie sochinenii*, 8 vols. (Moscow, 1900), vol. 8, p. 350.
6. FO 78/1014, Cunningham to Stratford Canning, 4, 20, 23 and 30 Mar. 1854.
7. E. Jouve, *Guerre d'Orient: Voyage à la suite des armées alliées en Turquie, en Valachie et en Crimée* (Paris, 1855), p. 115; FO 78/1008, Fonblanque to Stratford Canning, 27 Mar. 1854; FO 78/1014, Cunningham to Stratford Canning, 23 Mar. 1854.
8. RGVIA, f. 9198, op. 6/264, cb. 6, d. 14, ll. 101, 104, 106.
9. FO 78/1009, Fonblanque to Palmerston, 27 May 1854; Palmerston to Fonblanque, 10 July 1854.
10. RGVIA, f. 846, op. 16, d. 5417, ll. 41–4; E. Kovalevskii, *Voina s Turtsiei i razryv s zapadnymi derzhavami v 1853–1854* (St Petersburg, 1871), pp. 203–15; S. Plaksin, *Shchegolovskii al'bom: Sbornik istoricheskikh faktov, vospominanii, zapisok, illiustratsii i.t.d. za vremia bombardirovki Odessy v 1854* (Odessa, 1905), pp. 43–7.
11. RGVIA, f. 481, op. 1, d. 89, ll. 1–5; M. Bogdanovich, *Vostochnaia voina 1853–1856*, 4 vols. (St Petersburg, 1876), vol. 2, pp. 89–93; L. Guerrin, *Histoire de la dernière guerre de Russie (1853–1856)*, 2 vols. (Paris, 1858), vol. 1, pp. 111–15; J. Reid, *Crisis of the Ottoman Empire: Prelude to Collapse*

1839–1878 (Stuttgart, 2000), pp. 255–7; NAM 1968–03–45 ('Journal of Captain J. A. Butler at the Siege of Silistria').

12. NAM 1968–03–45 ('Journal of Captain J. A. Butler at the Siege of Silistria'); RGVIA, f. 846, op. 16, d. 5520, ch. 2, l. 62.

13. *Tolstoy's Letters*, vol. 1, pp. 39–40.

14. Tarle, *Krymskaia voina*, vol. 1, pp. 445–7.

15. B. Gooch, *The New Bonapartist Generals in the Crimean War* (The Hague, 1959), pp. 82, 109; NAM 1973–11–170 (Kingscote letter, 15 May, p. 2).

16. J. Herbé, *Français et russes en Crimée: Lettres d'un officier français à sa famille pendant la campagne d'Orient* (Paris, 1892), p. 30.

17. L. Noir, *Souvenirs d'un simple zouave: Campagnes de Crimée et d'Italie* (Paris, 1869), p. 222.

18. P. de Molènes, *Les Commentaires d'un soldat* (Paris, 1860), pp. 58–9.

19. *The Times*, 26 Apr. 1854.

20. C. Bayley, *Mercenaries for the Crimean: The German, Swiss, and Italian Legions in British Service 1854–6* (Montreal, 1977), p. 20. On the Irish in the British army, see D. Murphy, *Ireland and the Crimean War* (Dublin, 2002), pp. 17–25.

21. NAM 1968–07–289 (Raglan to Herbert, 15 May 1854).

22. NAM 1994–01–215 (Bell letter, June 1854).

23. A. Slade, *Turkey and the Crimean War: A Narrative of Historical Events* (London, 1867), p. 355.

24. NAM 1973–11–170 (Kingscote letter, 29 Apr. 1854, p. 3); Noir, *Souvenirs d'un simple zouave*, p. 212.

25. J. Howard Harris, Earl of Malmesbury, *Memoirs of an Ex-Minister*, 2 vols. (London, 1884), vol. 1, p. 412; *The Diary and Correspondence of Henry Wellesley, First Lord Cowley, 1790–1846* (London, 1930), p. 54.

26. *Tolstoy's Letters*, vol. 1, pp. 40–41.

27. A. Tiutcheva, *Pri dvore dvukh imperatov: Vospominaniia, dnevnik, 1853–1882* (Moscow, 1928–9), p. 195; *Akten zur Geschichte des Krimkriegs: Österreichische Akten zur Geschichte des Krimkriegs*, ser. 1, vol. 2 (Munich, 1980), p. 248.

28. Bogdanovich, *Vostochnaia voina*, vol. 2, pp. 107–8.

29. Jouve, *Guerre d'Orient*, p. 121; A. Kinglake, *The Invasion of the Crimea: Its Origin and an Account of Its Progress down to the Death of Lord Raglan*, 8 vols. (London, 1863), vol. 2, p. 56; Guerrin, *Histoire de la dernière guerre*, vol. 1, pp. 123–5.

30. Jouve, *Guerre d'Orient*, pp. 108, 116.

31. *Tolstoy's Letters*, vol. 1, p. 41.

32. Jouve, *Guerre d'Orient*, p. 123; Guerrin, *Histoire de la dernière guerre*, vol. 1, p. 127; FO 195/439, Colquhoun to Clarendon, 13 Aug. 1854.

33. Tarle, *Krymskaia voina*, vol. 1, pp. 454–5; M. Levin, 'Krymskaia voina i russkoe obshchestvo', in id., *Ocherki po istorii russkoi obshchestvennoi mysli, vtoraia polovina XIX veka* (Leningrad, 1974), pp. 293–304.

34. P. Schroeder, *Austria, Great Britain and the Crimean War: The Destruction of the European Concert* (Ithaca, NY, 1972), pp. 207–9; R. Florescu, *The Struggle against Russia in the Romanian Principalities 1821–1854* (Monachii, 1962), pp. 284–6.

35. La Vicomte de Noë, *Les Bachi-Bazouks et les Chasseurs d'Afrique* (Paris, 1861), pp. 9–11; Noir, *Souvenirs d'un simple zouave*, p. 215.

36. Noë, *Les Bachi-Bazouks*, pp. 34, 38–42, 56–68; J. Reid, 'Social and Psychological Factors in the Collapse of the Ottoman Empire, 1780–1918', *Journal of Modern Hellenism*, 10 (1993), pp. 143–52.

37. C. Mismer, *Souvenirs d'un dragon de l'armée de Crimée* (Paris, 1887), p. 34; Molènes, *Les Commentaires d'un soldat*, p. 30; FO 78/1009, Fonblanque to Palmerston, 10 June 1854; C. Hibbert, *The Destruction of Lord Raglan: A Tragedy of the Crimean War, 1854–1855* (London, 1961), p. 164; J. Spilsbury, *The Thin Red Line: An Eyewitness History of the Crimean War* (London, 2005), p. 26; H. Rappaport, *No Place for Ladies: The Untold Story of Women in the Crimean War* (London, 2007), pp. 61–2.

38. M. Thoumas, *Mes souvenirs de Crimée 1854–1856* (Paris, 1892), pp. 107–9; Herbé, *Français et russes en Crimée*, p. 55.

39. K. Marx, *The Eastern Question: A Reprint of Letters Written 1853–1856 Dealing with the Events of the Crimean War* (London, 1969), p. 451.

40. A. Lambert, *The Crimean War: British Grand Strategy, 1853–56* (Manchester, 1990), p. 106.

41. L. Noir, *Souvenirs d'un simple zouave*, pp. 218–19.

42. Lambert, *The Crimean War*, p. 84.

43. WO 28/199, Newcastle to Raglan, 29 June 1854.

44. W. Mosse, *The Rise and Fall of the Crimean System, 1855–1871: The Story of the Peace Settlement* (London, 1963), p. 1; W. Baumgart, *The Peace of Paris 1856: Studies in War, Diplomacy and Peacemaking* (Oxford, 1981), p. 13.

45. Schroeder, *Austria, Great Britain and the Crimean War*, pp. 193–4.

46. Ibid., p. 204; Lambert, *The Crimean War*, pp. 86–7.

47. S. Harris, *British Military Intelligence in the Crimean War* (London, 2001), p. 37; H. Small, *The Crimean War: Queen Victoria's War with the Russian Tsars* (Stroud, 2007), pp. 36–7; V. Rakov, *Moi vospominaniia o Evpatorii v epohu krymskoi voiny 1853–1856 gg.* (Evpatoriia, 1904), p. 10; FO 881/550, Raglan to Newcastle, 19 July 1854.

48. E. Boniface, Count de Castellane, *Campagnes de Crimée, d'Italie, d'Afrique, de Chine et de Syrie, 1849–1862* (Paris, 1898), pp. 90–91; L. de Saint-Arnaud, *Lettres du Maréchal Saint-Arnaud*, 2 vols. (Paris, 1858), vol. 2, p. 462.

49. Herbé, *Français et russes en Crimée,* p. 59; R. Portal, *Letters from the Crimea, 1854–55* (Winchester, 1900), pp. 17, 25; FO 78/1040, Rose to Clarendon, 6 Sept. 1854.

50. Kinglake, *Invasion of the Crimea,* vol. 2, pp. 148–9.

CHAPTER 7. ALMA

1. J. Cabrol, *Le Maréchal de Saint-Arnaud en Crimée* (Paris, 1895), p. 312; L. Noir, *Souvenirs d'un simple zouave: Campagnes de Crimée et d'Italie* (Paris, 1869), p. 219; M. O. Cullet, *Un régiment de ligne pendant la guerre d'orient: Notes et souvenirs d'un officier d'infanterie 1854–1855–1856* (Lyon, 1894), p. 68; NAM 2000–02–94 (Rose letter, 28 Aug. 1854).

2. P. de Molènes, *Les Commentaires d'un soldat* (Paris, 1860), p. 5; E. Vanson, *Crimée, Italie, Mexique: Lettres de campagnes 1854–1867* (Paris, 1905), p. 23; NAM 1978–04–39–2 (Hull letter, 12 July 1854); NAM 2000–02–94 (Rose letter, 28 Aug. 1854).

3. A. de Damas, *Souvenirs religieux et militaires de la Crimée* (Paris, 1857), pp. 147–8.

4. RGVIA, f. 846, op. 16, d. 5492, ll. 50–51; V. Rakov, *Moi vospominaniia o Evpatorii v epohu krymskoi voiny 1853–1856 gg.* (Evpatoriia, 1904), pp. 13–14, 21–2; A. Markevich, *Tavricheskaia guberniia vo vremia krymskoi voiny: Po arkhivnym materialam* (Simferopol, 1905), pp. 18–23; A. Kinglake, *The Invasion of the Crimea: Its Origin and an Account of Its Progress down to the Death of Lord Raglan,* 8 vols. (London, 1863), vol. 2, p. 166.

5. RGVIA, f. 846, op. 16, d. 5450, ll. 29–32; N. Mikhno, 'Iz zapisok chinovnika o krymskoi voine', in N. Dubrovin (ed.), *Materialy dlia istorii krymskoi voiny i oborony sevastopolia; Sbornik izdavaemyi komitetom po ustroistvu sevastopol'skogo muzeia,* vyp. 3 (St Petersburg, 1872), p. 7.

6. W. Baumgart, *The Crimean War, 1853–1856* (Oxford, 1999), p. 116.

7. R. Hodasevich, *A Voice from within the Walls of Sebastopol: A Narrative of the Campaign in the Crimea and the Events of the Siege* (London, 1856), p. 35.

8. Cullet, *Un régiment,* p. 68; Molènes, *Les Commentaires d'un soldat,* p. 45.

9. L. de Saint-Arnaud, *Lettres du Maréchal Saint-Arnaud,* 2 vols. (Paris, 1858), vol. 2, p. 490.

10. V. Bonham-Carter (ed.), *Surgeon in the Crimea: The Experiences of George Lawson Recorded in Letters to His Family* (London, 1968), p. 70.

11. NAM 2003–03–634 ('The Diary of Bandmaster Oliver', 15, 16, 17 Sept. 1854); J. Hume, *Reminiscences of the Crimean Campaign with the 55th Regiment* (London, 1894), p. 47.

12. H. Small, *The Crimean War: Queen Victoria's War with the Russian Tsars* (Stroud, 2007), p. 44.

13. N. Dubrovin, *Istoriia krymskoi voiny i oborony Sevastopolia*, 3 vols. (St Petersburg, 1900), vol. 1, pp. 215-17; Hodasevich, *A Voice*, pp. 47, 68; Damas, *Souvenirs*, p. 11; M. Bot'anov, *Vospominaniia sevastopoltsa i kavkatsa, 45 let spustia* (Vitebsk, 1899), p. 6; Noir, *Souvenirs d'un simple zouave*, p. 235.

14. E. Perret, *Les Français en Orient: Récits de Crimée 1854-1856* (Paris, 1889), p. 103.

15. Dubrovin, *Istoriia krymskoi voiny*, vol. 1, p. 222; id., *349-dnevnaia zashchita Sevastopolia* (St Petersburg, 2005), p. 52; A. Seaton, *The Crimean War: A Russian Chronicle* (London, 1977), pp. 75-6.

16. Hodasevich, *A Voice*, pp. 55-6.

17. Perret, *Les Français en Orient*, p. 106; Hodasevich, *A Voice*, p. 32; M. Vrochenskii, *Sevastopol'skii razgrom: Vospominaniia uchastnika slavnoi oborony Sevastopolia* (Kiev, 1893), p. 21.

18. R. Egerton, *Death or Glory: The Legacy of the Crimean War* (London, 2000), p. 82.

19. Small, *The Crimean War*, p. 47; N. Dixon, *On the Psychology of Military Incompetence* (London, 1994), p. 39.

20. M. Masquelez, *Journal d'un officier de zouaves* (Paris, 1858), pp. 107-8; Noir, *Souvenirs d'un simple zouave*, pp. 226-8; Molènes, *Les Commentaires d'un soldat*, pp. 232-3; A. Gouttman, *La Guerre de Crimée 1853-1856* (Paris, 1995), pp. 294-8; RGVIA, f. 846, op. 16, d. 5575, l. 4.

21. Small, *The Crimean War*, p. 50; Noir, *Souvenirs d'un simple zouave*, pp. 230-31; E. Tarle, *Krymskaia voina*, 2 vols. (Moscow, 1944), vol. 2, p. 20; Hodasevich, *A Voice*, pp. 69-70.

22. Ibid., p. 70; J. Spilsbury, *The Thin Red Line: An Eyewitness History of the Crimean War* (London, 2005), p. 61; A. Massie, *The National Army Museum Book of the Crimean War: The Untold Stories* (London, 2004), p. 36.

23. Spilsbury, *Thin Red Line*, pp. 64-5; Kinglake, *Invasion of the Crimea*, vol. 2, pp. 332 ff.; NAM 1976-06-10 ('Crimean Journal, 1854', pp. 54-5).

24. Small, *The Crimean War*, pp. 51-4; Spilsbury, *Thin Red Line*, pp. 65-9; E. Totleben, *Opisanie oborony g. Sevastopolia*, 3 vols. (St Petersburg, 1863-78), vol. 1, p. 194.

25. A. Khrushchev, *Istoriia oborony Sevastopolia* (St Petersburg, 1889), p. 13; Hodasevich, *A Voice*, pp. 73-6; Tarle, *Krymskaia voina*, vol. 2, p. 20.

26. A. du Picq, *Battle Studies* (Charleston, SC, 2006), pp. 112, 223.

27. Dubrovin, *Istoriia krymskoi voiny*, vol. 1, pp. 267-8; Baron de Bazancourt, *The Crimean Expedition, to the Capture of Sebastopol*, 2 vols. (London, 1856), vol. 1, pp. 260-62.

28. NAM 1974–02–22–86–4 (21 Sept. 1872); Bonham-Carter, *Surgeon in the Crimea*, p. 73.

29. S. Calthorpe, *Letters from Headquarters; or the Realities of the War in the Crimea by an Officer of the Staff* (London, 1858), pp. 76–7.

30. Seaton, *The Crimean* War, pp. 96–7; Kh. Giubbenet, *Slovo ob uchastii narodov v popechenii o ranenyh voinakh i neskol'ko vospominanii iz krymskoi kampanii* (Kiev, 1868), p. 15.

31. *The Times*, 1 Dec. 1854.

32. Noir, *Souvenirs d'un simple zouave*, p. 234; Egerton, *Death or Glory*, pp. 219–20; H. Drummond, *Letters from the Crimea* (London, 1855), pp. 49–50.

33. RGVIA, f. 846, op. 16, d. 5450, ll. 41–2; H. Elphinstone, *Journal of the Operations Conducted by the Corps of Royal Engineers* (London, 1859), pp. 21–2; J. Curtiss, *Russia's Crimean War* (Durham, NC, 1979), pp. 302–5; Totleben, *Opisanie*, vol. 1, pp. 66 ff.

34. Dubrovin, *Istoriia krymskoi voiny*, vol. 1, pp. 268–9.

35. *Den' i noch' v Sevastopole: Stseny iz boevoi zhizni (iz zapisok artillerista)* (St Petersburg, 1903), pp. 4–5; Gouttman, *La Guerre de Crimée*, p. 305.

36. Egerton, *Death or Glory*, p. 92.

37. NAM 1989–06–41 (Nolan diary, p. 35).

38. Noir, *Souvenirs d'un simple zouave*, p. 239; Perret, *Les Français en Orient*, pp. 119–20.

39. RGVIA, f. 846, op. 16, d. 5492, ll. 62–3; Dubrovin, *Istoriia krymskoi voiny*, vol. 1, pp. 293–302; Tarle, *krymskaia voina*, vol. 2, p. 23; Hodasevich, *A Voice*, pp. 119–21.

40. RGVIA, f. 846, op. 16, d. 5492, ll. 57–8; Markevich, *Tavricheskaia guberniia*, pp. 9–10; '1854 g.', *Russkaia starina*, 19 (1877), p. 338; Rakov, *Moi vospominaniia*, pp. 16–39; Molènes, *Les Commentaires d'un soldat*, pp. 46, 71–2.

41. T. Royle, *Crimea: The Great Crimean War 1854–1856* (London, 1999), p. 244.

42. J. Herbé, *Français et russes en Crimée: Lettres d'un officier français à sa famille pendant la campagne d'Orient* (Paris, 1892), p. 104.

CHAPTER 8. SEVASTOPOL IN THE AUTUMN

1. L. Tolstoy, *The Sebastopol Sketches*, trans. D. McDuff (London, 1986), pp. 39, 42–3. Reproduced by permission.

2. M. Vrochenskii, *Sevastopol'skii razgrom: Vospominaniia uchastnika slavnoi oborony Sevastopolia* (Kiev, 1893), p. 9; N. Berg, *Desiat' dnei v Sevastopole* (Moscow, 1855), p. 15.

3. Tolstoy, *Sebastopol Sketches*, p. 43; E. Ershov, *Sevastopol'skie vospominaniia artilleriiskogo ofitsera v semi tetradakh* (St Petersburg, 1858), p. 29.

4. M. Bot'anov, *Vospominaniia sevastopoltsa i kavkatsa 45 let spustia* (Vitebsk, 1899), p. 6.

5. E. Totleben, *Opisanie oborony g. Sevastopolia*, 3 vols. (St Petersburg, 1863–78), vol. 1, p. 218; *Vospominaniia ob odnom iz doblestnykh zashchitnikov Sevastopolia* (St Petersburg, 1857), p. 7; *Sevastopol' v nyneshnem sostoianii: Pis'ma iz kryma i Sevastopolia* (Moscow, 1855), p. 19; WO 28/188, Burgoyne to Airey, 4 Oct. 1854; FO 78/1040, Rose to Clarendon, 8 Oct. 1854.

6. *Tolstoy's Letters*, ed. and trans. R. F. Christian, 2 vols. (London, 1978), vol. 1, p. 44. The scene was reproduced in *Sebastopol Sketches* (p. 57).

7. S. Gershel'man, *Nravstvennyi element pod Sevastopolem* (St Petersburg, 1897), p. 84; R. Egerton, *Death or Glory: The Legacy of the Crimean War* (London, 2000), p. 91.

8. E. Tarle, *Krymskaia voina*, 2 vols. (Moscow, 1944), vol. 2, p. 38; Gershel'man, *Nravstvennyi element*, pp. 70–71; Totleben, *Opisanie*, vol. 1, pp. 198 ff.; J. Herbé, *Français et russes en Crimée: Lettres d'un officier français à sa famille pendant la campagne d'Orient* (Paris, 1892), p. 133.

9. RGVIA, f. 846, op. 16, d. 5613, l. 12; N. Dubrovin, *Istoriia krymskoi voiny i oborony Sevastopolia*, 3 vols. (St Petersburg, 1900), vol. 2, p. 31.

10. NAM 1968–07–292 (Cathcart to Raglan, 27 Sept. 1854); NAM 1983–11–13–310 (12 Oct. 1854).

11. E. Perret, *Les Français en Orient: Récits de Crimée 1854–1856* (Paris, 1889), pp. 142–4; Baron de Bazancourt, *The Crimean Expedition, to the Capture of Sebastopol*, 2 vols. (London, 1856), vol. 1, pp. 343–8.

12. NAM 1982–12–29–13 (Letter, 12 Oct. 1854).

13. H. Clifford, *Letters and Sketches from the Crimea* (London, 1956), p. 69; E. Wood, *The Crimea in 1854 and 1894* (London, 1895), pp. 88–9.

14. S. Calthorpe, *Letters from Headquarters; or the Realities of the War in the Crimea by an Officer of the Staff* (London, 1858), p. 111.

15. *Sevastopol' v nyneshnem sostoianii*, p. 16.

16. V. Bariatinskii, *Vospominaniia 1852–55 gg.* (Moscow, 1904), pp. 39–42; A. Seaton, *The Crimean War: A Russian Chronicle* (London, 1977), pp. 126–9.

17. NAM 1969–01–46 (Private journal, 17 Oct. 1854); *Den' i noch' v Sevastopole: Stseny iz boevoi zhizni (iz zapisok artillerista)* (St Petersburg, 1903), pp. 7, 11.

18. A. Khrushchev, *Istoriia oborony Sevastopolia* (St Petersburg, 1889), p. 30; WO 28/188, Lushington to Airey, 18 Oct. 1854.

19. *Mrs Duberly's War: Journal and Letters from the Crimea*, ed. C. Kelly (Oxford, 2007), p. 87.

20. *Sevastopol' v nyneshnem sostoianii*, p. 16.

21. WO 28/188, Burgoyne to Raglan, 6 Oct. 1854; J. Spilsbury, *The Thin Red Line: An Eyewitness History of the Crimean War* (London, 2005), p. 138.

22. Calthorpe, *Letters*, p. 125; NAM 1968-07-270 ('Letters from the Crimea Written during the Years 1854, 55 and 56 by a Staff Officer Who Was There'), p. 125; H. Rappaport, *No Place for Ladies: The Untold Story of Women in the Crimean War* (London, 2007), pp. 82-3.

23. D. Austin, 'Blunt Speaking: The Crimean War Reminiscences of John Elijah Blunt, Civilian Interpreter', *Crimean War Research Society: Special Publication*, 33 (n.d.), pp. 24, 32, 55.

24. *Mrs Duberly's War*, p. 93; NAM 1968-07-270 ('Letters from the Crimea Written during the Years 1854, 55 and 56 by a Staff Officer Who Was There'), pp. 119-20; W. Munro, *Records of Service and Campaigning in Many Lands*, 2 vols. (London, 1887), vol. 2, p. 88.

25. H. Franks, *Leaves from a Soldier's Notebook* (London, 1904), p. 80; NAM 1958-04-32 (Forrest letter, 27 Oct. 1854).

26. Spilsbury, *Thin Red Line*, pp. 155-6; H. Small, *The Crimean War: Queen Victoria's War with the Russian Tsars* (Stroud, 2007), pp. 71-2.

27. Small, *The Crimean War*, pp. 73-82.

28. R. Portal, *Letters from the Crimea, 1854-55* (Winchester, 1900), p. 112. For a version of events that has Nolan trying to redirect the charge, see D. Austin, 'Nolan Did Try to Redirect the Light Brigade', *War Correspondent*, 23/4 (2006), pp. 20-21.

29. Spilsbury, *Thin Red Line*, pp. 161-2.

30. S. Kozhukov, 'Iz krymskikh vospominanii o poslednei voine', *Russkii arkhiv*, 2 (1869), pp. 023-025.

31. G. Paget, *The Light Cavalry Brigade in the Crimea* (London, 1881), p. 73.

32. *Mrs Duberly's War*, p. 95.

33. Small, *The Crimean War*, pp. 64, 86-8; RGVIA, f. 846, op. 16, d. 5585, l. 31; Dubrovin, *Istoriia krymskoi voiny*, vol. 2, pp. 144-7.

34. N. Woods, *The Past Campaign: A Sketch of the War in the East*, 2 vols. (London, 1855), vol. 2, pp. 12-14; Austin, 'Blunt Speaking', pp. 54-6.

35. N. Dubrovin, *349-dnevnaia zashchita Sevastopolia* (St Petersburg, 2005), p. 91; A. Tiutcheva, *Pri dvore dvukh imperatov: Vospominaniia, dnevnik, 1853-1882* (Moscow, 1928-9), p. 161.

36. A. Kinglake, *The Invasion of the Crimea: Its Origin and an Account of Its Progress down to the Death of Lord Raglan*, 8 vols. (London, 1863), vol. 5, pp. 1-24.

37. NAM 1963-11-151 (Letter, 27 Oct. 1854); NAM 1986-03-103 (Letter, 31 Oct. 1854).

38. Tarle, *Krymskaia voina*, vol. 2, p. 140.

39. B. Gooch, *The New Bonapartist Generals in the Crimean War* (The Hague, 1959), p. 145.

40. NAM 1994–02–172 (Letter, 22 Feb. 1855).

41. Khrushchev, *Istoriia oborony Sevastopolia*, pp. 38–42; Seaton, *The Crimean War*, pp. 161–4.

42. A. Andriianov, *Inkermanskii boi i oborona Sevastopolia (nabroski uchastnika)* (St Petersburg, 1903), p. 16.

43. Dubrovin, *Istoriia krymskoi voiny*, vol. 2, pp. 194–5; Spilsbury, *Thin Red Line*, pp. 196–8.

44. NAM 1968–07–264–1 ('The 95th Regiment at Inkerman').

45. Ibid.

46. Andriianov, *Inkermanskii boi*, p. 20.

47. P. Alabin, *Chetyre voiny: Pokhodnye zapiski v voinu 1853, 1854, 1855 i 1856 godov*, 2 vols. (Viatka, 1861), vol. 2, pp. 74–5; Dubrovin, *Istoriia krymskoi voiny*, vol. 2, pp. 203–5.

48. Spilsbury, *Thin Red Line*, pp. 211–12.

49. G. Higginson, *Seventy-One Years of a Guardsman's Life* (London, 1916), pp. 197–8; Kinglake, *Invasion of the Crimea*, vol. 5, pp. 221–57.

50. R. Hodasevich, *A Voice from within the Walls of Sebastopol: A Narrative of the Campaign in the Crimea and the Events of the Siege* (London, 1856), pp. 190–8; Seaton, *The Crimean War*, p. 169.

51. L. Noir, *Souvenirs d'un simple zouave: Campagnes de Crimée et d'Italie* (Paris, 1869), p. 278.

52. J. Cler, *Reminiscences of an Officer of Zouaves* (New York, 1860), p. 211; *Historique de 2e Régiment de Zouaves 1830–1887* (Oran, 1887), pp. 66–7.

53. Spilsbury, *Thin Red Line*, p. 214.

54. Higginson, *Seventy-One Years*, p. 200; Spilsbury, *Thin Red Line*, p. 232.

55. Seaton, *The Crimean War*, pp. 175–6.

56. M. O. Cullet, *Un régiment de ligne pendant la guerre d'orient: Notes et souvenirs d'un officier d'infanterie 1854–1855–1856* (Lyon, 1894), p. 112.

57. Noir, *Souvenirs d'un simple zouave*, pp. 281–3.

58. Woods, *The Past Campaign*, vol. 2, pp. 143–4; Noir, *Souvenirs d'un simple zouave*, p. 278; Cler, *Reminiscences*, p. 216; A. de Damas, *Souvenirs religieux et militaires de la Crimée* (Paris, 1857), p. 70.

59. RA VIC/MAIN/F/1/38.

60. Cler, *Reminiscences*, pp. 219–20.

61. RA VIC/MAIN/F/1/36 (Colonel E. Birch Reynardson to Colonel Phipps, Sebastopol, 7 Nov.); H. Drummond, *Letters from the Crimea* (London, 1855), p. 75; *A Knouting for the Czar! Being Some Words on the Battles of Inkerman, Balaklava and Alma by a Soldier* (London, 1855), pp. 5–9.

62. RGVIA, f. 846, op. 16, d. 5634, ll. 1–18; Bazancourt, *The Crimean Expedition*, pp. 116–17; Noir, *Souvenirs d'un simple zouave*, pp. 278–9; Kinglake, *Invasion of the Crimea*, vol. 5, pp. 324, 460–63.

63. FO 78/1040, Rose to Clarendon, 7 Nov. 1854.

64. Small, *The Crimean War*, p. 209.

65. NAM 1984–09–31–63 (Letter, 7 Nov. 1854); *Vospominaniia ob odnom iz doblestnykh zashchitnikov Sevastopolia*, pp. 11, 15; RGVIA, f. 846, op. 16, d. 5629, l. 7; d. 5687, l. 1; Dubrovin, *Istoriia krymskoi voiny*, vol. 2, p. 384.

66. RGVIA, f. 846, op. 16, d. 5450, ll. 34–42; d. 5452, ch. 2, ll. 16–18; Dubrovin, *Istoriia krymskoi voiny*, vol. 2, pp. 272–3; Tiutcheva, *Pri dvore dvukh imperatov*, p. 165.

67. *Tolstoy's Diaries*, vol. 1: *1847–1894*, ed. and trans. R. F. Christian (London, 1985), p. 95.

68. H. Troyat, *Tolstoy* (London, 1970), pp. 161–2.

69. *Tolstoy's Letters*, vol. 1, p. 45; A. Opul'skii, *L. N. Tolstoi v krymu: Literaturno-kraevedcheskii ocherk* (Simferopol, 1960), pp. 27–30.

70. Troyat, *Tolstoy*, p. 162.

71. *Tolstoy's Letters*, vol. 1, pp. 44–5.

CHAPTER 9. GENERALS JANUARY AND FEBRUARY

1. NAM 1988–06–29–1 (Letter, 17 Nov. 1854).

2. *Mrs Duberly's War: Journal and Letters from the Crimea*, ed. C. Kelly (Oxford, 2007), pp. 102–3; NAM 1968–07–288 (Cambridge to Raglan, 15 Nov. 1854).

3. Ia. Rebrov, *Pis'ma sevastopol'tsa* (Novocherkassk, 1876), p. 26.

4. *Lettres d'un soldat à sa mère de 1849 à 1870: Afrique, Crimée, Italie, Mexique* (Montbéliard, 1910), p. 66; L. Noir, *Souvenirs d'un simple zouave: Campagnes de Crimée et d'Italie* (Paris, 1869), p. 288; V. Bonham-Carter (ed.), *Surgeon in the Crimea: The Experiences of George Lawson Recorded in Letters to His Family* (London, 1968), p. 104.

5. WO 28/162, 'Letters and Papers Relating to the Administration of the Cavalry Division'.

6. NAM 1982–12–29–23 (Letter, 22 Nov. 1854); D. Boulger (ed.), *General Gordon's Letters from the Crimea, the Danube and Armenia* (London, 1884), p. 14; K. Vitzthum von Eckstadt, *St Petersburg and London in the Years 1852–64*, 2 vols. (London, 1887), vol. 1, p. 143.

7. J. Herbé, *Français et russes en Crimée: Lettres d'un officier français à sa famille pendant la campagne d'Orient* (Paris, 1892), p. 144.

8. J. Baudens, *La Guerre de Crimée: Les campements, les abris, les ambulances, les hôpitaux, etc.* (Paris, 1858), pp. 63–6; Noir, *Souvenirs d'un simple zouave*, p. 248.

9. Herbé, *Français et russes en Crimée*, p. 151; *Mrs Duberly's War*, pp. 110–11.

10. NAM 1968–07–270 ('Letters from the Crimea Written during the Years 1854, 55 and 56 by a Staff Officer Who Was There'), pp. 188–9.

11. I. G. Douglas and G. Ramsay (eds.), *The Panmure Papers, Being a Selection from the Correspondence of Fox Maule, 2nd Baron Panmure, afterwards 11th Earl of Dalhousie*, 2 vols. (London, 1908), vol. 1, pp. 151–2; B. Gooch, *The New Bonapartist Generals in the Crimean War* (The Hague, 1959), pp. 159–60.

12. C. Mismer, *Souvenirs d'un dragon de l'armée de Crimée* (Paris, 1887), pp. 59–60, 96–7.

13. Noir, *Souvenirs d'un simple zouave*, p. 291; Herbé, *Français et russes en Crimée*, pp. 225–6.

14. *Mrs Duberly's War*, p. 118.

15. Noir, *Souvenirs d'un simple zouave*, p. 288; H. Rappaport, *No Place for Ladies: The Untold Story of Women in the Crimean War* (London, 2007), p. 38; Bonham-Carter, *Surgeon in the Crimea*, p. 65.

16. NAM 1996–05–4–19 (Pine letter, 8 Jan. 1855); Mismer, *Souvenirs d'un dragon*, pp. 124–5; NAM 1996–05–4 (Letter, 8 Jan. 1855).

17. NAM 1984–09–31–79 (4 Feb. 1855); NAM 1976–08–32 (Hagger letter, 1 Dec. 1854); G. Bell, *Rough Notes by an Old Soldier: During Fifty Years' Service, from Ensign G.B. to Major-General, C.B.*, 2 vols. (London, 1867), vol. 2, pp. 232–3.

18. K. Chesney, *Crimean War Reader* (London, 1960), p. 154; Herbé, *Français et russes en Crimée*, p. 343.

19. Baudens, *La Guerre de Crimée*, pp. 101–3; J. Shepherd, *The Crimean Doctors: A History of the British Medical Services in the Crimean War*, 2 vols. (Liverpool, 1991), vol. 1, pp. 135–6, 237; *Health of the Army in Turkey and Crimea: Paper, being a medical and surgical history of the British army which served in Turkey and the Crimea during the Russian war*, Parliamentary Papers 1857–8, vol. 38, part 2, p. 465.

20. N. Pirogov, *Sevastopol'skie pis'ma i vospominaniia* (Moscow, 1950), pp. 28–37, 66, 147–8, 220–23; *Za mnogo let: Zapiski (vospominaniia) neizvestnogo 1844–1874 gg.* (St Petersburg, 1897), pp. 82–3; Kh. Giubbenet, *Ocherk meditsinskoi i gospital'noi chasti russkih voisk v Krymu v 1854–1856 gg.* (St Petersburg, 1870), p. 2.

21. N. Berg, *Desiat' dnei v Sevastopole* (Moscow, 1855), pp. 17–19; R. Hodasevich, *A Voice from within the Walls of Sebastopol: A Narrative of the Campaign in the Crimea and the Events of the Siege* (London, 1856), p. 129;

E. Kovalevskii, *Voina s Turtsiei i razryv s zapadnymi derzhavami v 1853–1854* (St Petersburg, 1871), p. 82; Pirogov, *Sevastopol'skie pis'ma*, pp. 151–2.

22. Ibid., pp. 155–6, 185.

23. L. Tolstoy, *The Sebastopol Sketches*, trans. D. McDuff (London, 1986), pp. 44, 47–8.

24. Giubbenet, *Ocherk*, pp. 5, 7.

25. H. Connor, 'Use of Chloroform by British Army Surgeons during the Crimean War', *Medical History*, 42/2 (1998), pp. 163, 184–8; Shepherd, *The Crimean Doctors*, vol. 1, pp. 132–3.

26. Pirogov, *Sevastopol'skie pis'ma*, p. 27; *Istoricheskii obzor deistvii krestovozdvizhenskoi obshchiny sester' popecheniia o ranenykh i vol'nykh k voennykh gospitaliakh v Krymu i v Khersonskoi gubernii c 1 dek. 1854 po 1 dek. 1855* (St Petersburg, 1856), pp. 2–4; *Sobranie pisem sester Krestovozd-vizhenskoi obshchiny popecheniia o ranenykh* (St Petersburg, 1855), p. 22.

27. *Gosudarstvennoe podvizhnoie opolchenie Vladimirskoi gubernii 1855–56: Po materialam i lichnym vospominaniiam* (Vladimir, 1900), p. 82; Rappaport, *No Place for Ladies*, pp. 115–17.

28. NAM 1951–12–21 (Bellew journal, 23 Jan. 1855); Rappaport, *No Place for Ladies*, pp. 101, 125.

29. G. St Aubyn, *Queen Victoria: A Portrait* (London, 1991), p. 295.

30. A. Lambert and S. Badsey (eds.), *The War Correspondents: The Crimean War* (Strand, 1994), p. 13; S. Markovits, *The Crimean War in the British Imagination* (Cambridge, 2009), p. 16.

31. E. Gosse, *Father and Son* (Oxford, 2004), p. 20.

32. M. Lalumia, *Realism and Politics in Victorian Art of the Crimean War* (Epping, 1984), p. 120.

33. H. Clifford, *Letters and Sketches from the Crimea* (London, 1956), p. 146.

34. NAM 1968–07–284 (Raglan to Newcastle, 4 Jan. 1855).

35. Gooch, *The New Bonapartist Generals*, p. 192.

36. L. Case, *French Opinion on War and Diplomacy during the Second Empire* (Philadelphia, 1954), pp. 2–6, 32; H. Loizillon, *La Campagne de Crimée: Lettres écrites de Crimée par le capitaine d'état-major Henri Loizillon à sa famille* (Paris, 1895), p. 82; RA VIC/MAIN/QVJ/1856, 19 Apr.

37. *Za mnogo let*, pp. 75–8.

38. *The Englishwoman in Russia: Impressions of the Society and Manners of the Russians at Home* (London, 1855), pp. 292–3, 296–8.

39. Ibid., pp. 294–5; *Za mnogo let*, p. 73.

40. E. Tarle, *Krymskaia voina*, 2 vols. (Moscow, 1944), vol. 1, pp. 454–9; *The Englishwoman in Russia*, p. 305.

41. A. Zaionchkovskii, *Vostochnaia voina 1853–1856*, 3 vols. (St Petersburg, 2002), vol. 2, p. 76; GARF, f. 109, op. 1, d. 353 (*chast'* 2), l. 7.

42. I. Ignatovich, *Pomeshchichie krest'iane nakanune osvobozhdeniia* (Leningrad, 1925), pp. 331–7; *The Englishwoman in Russia*, pp. 302–3, 313.

43. J. Curtiss, *Russia's Crimean War* (Durham, NC, 1979), pp. 532–46; D. Moon, 'Russian Peasant Volunteers at the Beginning of the Crimean War', *Slavic Review*, 51/4 (Winter 1992), pp. 691–704. On a similar phenomenon in the Kiev, Podol'e and Volhynia regions in the early months of 1855, see RGVIA, f. 846, op. 16, d. 5496, ll. 18–52.

44. RGVIA, f. 846, op. 16, d. 5452, ch. 2, l. 166; Rebrov, *Pis'ma sevastopol'tsa*, p. 3.

45. Pirogov, *Sevastopol'skie pis'ma*, p. 148; A. Markevich, *Tavricheskaia guberniia vo vremia krymskoi voiny: Po arkhivnym materialam* (Simferopol, 1905), pp. 107–51; A Opul'skii, *L. N. Tolstoi v krymu: Literaturno-kraevedcheskii ocherk* (Simferopol, 1960), p. 12; Hodasevich, *A Voice*, pp. 24–5; RGVIA, f. 9198, op. 6/264, sv. 15, d. 2.

46. 'Vostochnaia voina: Pis'ma kn. I. F. Paskevicha k kn. M. D. Gorchakovu', *Russkaia starina*, 15 (1876), pp. 668–70; Tarle, *Krymskaia voina*, vol. 2, pp. 224–8.

47. RGVIA, f. 846, op. 16, d. 5450, ll. 50–54; RGVIA, f. 846, op. 16, d. 5452, ch. 2, ll. 166, 199–201; 'Doktor Mandt o poslednikh nedeliiakh imperatora Nikolaia Pavlovicha (iz neizdannykh zapisok odnogo priblizhennogo k imperatoru litsa)', *Russkii arkhiv*, 2 (1905), p. 480.

48. *Poslednie minuty i konchina v bozhe pochivshego imperatora, nezabvennogo i vechnoi slavy dostoinogo Nikolaia I* (Moscow, 1855), pp. 5–6; 'Noch' c 17-go na 18 fevralia 1855 goda: Rasskaz doktora Mandta', *Russkii arkhiv*, 1 (1884), p. 194; 'Nekotorye podrobnosti o konchine imperatora Nikolaia Pavlovicha', *Russkii arkhiv*, 3/9 (1906), pp. 143–5; Tarle, *Krymskaia voina*, vol. 2, p. 233.

49. See e.g. V. Vinogradov, 'The Personal Responsibility of Emperor Nicholas I for the Coming of the Crimean War: An Episode in the Diplomatic Struggle in the Eastern Question', in H. Ragsdale (ed.), *Imperial Russian Foreign Policy* (Cambridge, 1993), p. 170.

50. A. Tiutcheva, *Pri dvore dvukh imperatov: Vospominaniia, dnevnik, 1853–1882* (Moscow, 1928–9), p. 178.

51. Ibid., pp. 20–21.

CHAPTER 10. CANNON FODDER

1. RA VIC/MAIN/QVJ/1856, 2 Mar.

2. L. Noir, *Souvenirs d'un simple zouave: Campagnes de Crimée et d'Italie* (Paris, 1869), p. 312.

3. F. Charles-Roux, *Alexandre II, Gortchakoff et Napoléon III* (Paris, 1913), p. 14.

4. *The Later Correspondence of Lord John Russell, 1840–1878*, ed. G. Gooch, 2 vols. (London, 1925), vol. 2, pp. 160–61; Lady F. Balfour, *The Life of George, Fourth Earl of Aberdeen*, 2 vols. (London, 1922), vol. 2, p. 206.

5. H. Verney, *Our Quarrel with Russia* (London, 1855), pp. 22–4.

6. G. B. Henderson, 'The Two Interpretations of the Four Points, December 1854', in id., *Crimean War Diplomacy and Other Historical Essays* (Glasgow, 1947), pp. 119–22; *The Letters of Queen Victoria: A Selection from Her Majesty's Correspondence between the Years 1837 and 1861*, 3 vols. (London, 1907–8), vol. 3, pp. 65–6.

7. P. Schroeder, *Austria, Great Britain and the Crimean War: The Destruction of the European Concert* (Ithaca, NY, 1972), pp. 256–77.

8. P. Jaeger, *Le mura di Sebastopoli: Gli italiani in Crimea 1855–56* (Milan, 1991), p. 245; C. Thoumas, *Mes souvenirs de Crimée 1854–1856* (Paris, 1892), p. 191.

9. RGVIA, f. 846, op. 16, d. 5855, ll. 36–7.

10. H. Bell, *Lord Palmerston*, 2 vols. (London, 1936), vol. 2, p. 125; Hansard, HC Deb. 21 May 1912, vol. 38, p. 1734; C. Bayley, *Mercenaries for the Crimean: The German, Swiss, and Italian Legions in British Service 1854–6* (Montreal, 1977).

11. F. Kagan, *The Military Reforms of Nicholas I: The Origins of the Modern Russian Army* (London, 1999), p. 243.

12. RGVIA, f. 846, op. 16, d. 5496, ll. 1–4, 14, 18–19, 22–8.

13. C. Badem, 'The Ottomans and the Crimean War (1853–1856)', Ph.D. diss. (Sabanci University, 2007), pp. 182–4.

14. FO 881/1443, Clarendon to Cowley, 9 Apr. 1855.

15. FO 881/1443, Clarendon to Cowley, 13 Apr. 1855; Stratford to Clarendon, 11 June 1855; Longworth to Clarendon, 10 June, 2 and 26 July 1855; FO 881/547, Brant memo on Georgia, 1 Feb. 1855; L. Oliphant, *The Transcaucasian Provinces the Proper Field of Operation for a Christian Army* (London, 1855).

16. RA VIC/MAIN/F/2/96.

17. T. Royle, *Crimea: The Great Crimean War 1854–1856* (London, 1999), pp. 377–8; B. Greenhill and A. Giffard, *The British Assault on Finland* (London, 1988), p. 321.

18. WO 28/188, Burgoyne to Raglan, Dec. 1854.

19. A. de Damas, *Souvenirs religieux et militaires de la Crimée* (Paris, 1857), pp. 149–50; NAM 6807–295–1 (Sir Edward Lyons to Codrington, March 1855).

20. H. Small, *The Crimean War: Queen Victoria's War with the Russian Tsars* (Stroud, 2007), pp. 125–33.

21. V. Rakov, *Moi vospominaniia o Evpatorii v epohu krymskoi voiny 1853–1856 gg.* (Evpatoriia, 1904), pp. 52–6; E. Tarle, *Krymskaia voina*, 2 vols. (Moscow, 1944), vol. 2, p. 217; *The Times*, 14 June 1856, p. 5.

22. WO 6/74, Panmure to Raglan, 26 Mar. 1855; Royle, *Crimea*, p. 370.

23. FO 78/1129/62, Rose to Clarendon, 2 June 1855.

24. A. Kinglake, *The Invasion of the Crimea: Its Origin and an Account of Its Progress down to the Death of Lord Raglan*, 8 vols. (London, 1863), vol. 8, pp. 48–55; E. Perret, *Les Français en Orient: Récits de Crimée 1854–1856* (Paris, 1889), pp. 287–9; *The Times*, 28 May 1855.

25. RGVIA, f. 846, op. 16, d. 5563, l. 322; N. Dubrovin, *Istoriia krymskoi voiny i oborony Sevastopolia*, 3 vols. (St Petersburg, 1900), vol. 3, p. 179.

26. J. Herbé, *Français et russes en Crimée: Lettres d'un officier français à sa famille pendant la campagne d'Orient* (Paris, 1892), p. 337; Noir, *Souvenirs d'un simple zouave*, p. 314.

27. *A Visit to Sebastopol a Week after Its Fall: By an Officer of the Anglo-Turkish Contingent* (London, 1856), p. 34.

28. M. Vrochenskii, *Sevastopol'skii razgrom: Vospominaniia uchastnika slavnoi oborony Sevastopolia* (Kiev, 1893), pp. 77–84; H. Loizillon, *La Campagne de Crimée: Lettres écrites de Crimée par le capitaine d'état-major Henri Loizillon à sa famille* (Paris, 1895), pp. 106–7.

29. Herbé, *Français et russes en Crimée*, p. 199; RGVIA, f. 846, op. 16, d. 5452, ch. 2, l. 166; W. Porter, *Life in the Trenches before Sevastopol* (London, 1856), p. 111.

30. E. Boniface, Count de Castellane, *Campagnes de Crimée, d'Italie, d'Afrique, de Chine et de Syrie, 1849–1862* (Paris, 1898), pp. 168–73.

31. Noir, *Souvenirs d'un simple zouave*, p. 313; E. Ershov, *Sevastopol'skie vospominaniia artilleriiskogo ofitsera v semi tetradakh* (St Petersburg, 1858), pp. 167–73; NAM 1965–01–183–10 (Steevens letter, 26 Mar. 1855).

32. H. Clifford, *Letters and Sketches from the Crimea* (London, 1956), p. 194; Porter, *Life in the Trenches*, pp. 64–5.

33. C. Mismer, *Souvenirs d'un dragon de l'armée de Crimée* (Paris, 1887), p. 140; Porter, *Life in the Trenches*, pp. 68–9.

34. F. Luguez, *Crimée-Italie 1854–1859: Extraits de la correspondence d'un officier avec sa famille* (Nancy, 1895), pp. 61–2.

35. J. Cler, *Reminiscences of an Officer of Zouaves* (New York, 1860), pp. 233–4; S. Calthorpe, *Letters from Headquarters; or the Realities of the War in the Crimea by an Officer of the Staff* (London, 1858), pp. 215–16.

36. Ershov, *Sevastopol'skie vospominaniia*, pp. 224–30.

37. Damas, *Souvenirs*, p. 265.

38. Porter, *Life in the Trenches*, p. 127.

39. WO 28/126, Register of Courts Martial; Clifford, *Letters and Sketches*, p. 269. For some of the many voluminous reports on drunkenness in the Russian army, see RGVIA, f. 484, op. 1, dd. 398–403.

40. Herbé, *Français et russes en Crimée*, p. 225; *The Times*, 17 Mar. 1855.

41. M. Seacole, *Wonderful Adventures of Mrs Seacole in Many Lands* (London, 2005), p. 117.

42. A. Soyer, *Soyer's Culinary Campaign* (London, 1857), p. 405.

43. B. Cooke, *The Grand Crimean Central Railway* (Knutsford, 1990).

44. Herbé, *Français et russes en Crimée*, p. 223.

45. RGVIA, f. 481, op. 1, d. 18, ll. 1–8.

46. V. Kolchak, *Voina i plen 1853–1855 gg.: Iz vospominanii o davno perezhitom* (St Petersburg, 1904), pp. 41–2; Vrochenskii, *Sevastopol'skii razgrom*, p. 113; *Sobranie pisem sester Krestovozdvizhenskoi obshchiny popecheniia o ranenykh* (St Petersburg, 1855), pp. 37–40; Ershov, *Sevastopol'skie vospominaniia*, p. 91.

47. Porter, *Life in the Trenches*, p. 144; Ershov, *Sevastopol'skie vospominaniia*, pp. 97–107; *Sobranie pisem sester Krestovozdvizhenskoi obshchiny*, pp. 49–55; N. Pirogov, *Sevastopol'skie pis'ma i vospominaniia* (Moscow, 1950), p. 62.

48. *Vospominaniia ob odnom iz doblestnykh zashchitnikov Sevastopolia* (St Petersburg, 1857), pp. 14–18; Ershov, *Sevastopol'skie vospominaniia*, p. 34.

49. H. Troyat, *Tolstoy* (London, 1970), pp. 170–71; *Tolstoy's Diaries*, vol. 1: *1847–1894*, ed. and trans. R. F. Christian (London, 1985), p. 103; A. Maude, *The Life of Tolstoy: First Fifty Years* (London, 1908), pp. 111–12.

50. *Tolstoy's Diaries*, vol. 1, p. 104; V. Nazar'ev, 'Zhizn' i liudi bylogo vremeni', *Istoricheskii vestnik*, 11 (1890), p. 443; M. Vygon, *Krymskie stranitsy zhizni i tvorchestva L. N. Tolstogo* (Simferopol, 1978), p. 37.

51. Vrochenskii, *Sevastopol'skii razgrom*, p. 117; N. Dubrovin, *349-dnevnaia zashchita Sevastopolia* (St Petersburg, 2005), pp. 161–7; NAM 1968–07–484 (Gage letter, 13 Apr. 1855).

52. J. Jocelyn, *The History of the Royal Artillery (Crimean Period)* (London, 1911), p. 359; NAM 1965–01–183–10 (Letter, 23 Apr. 1855).

53. Mismer, *Souvenirs d'un dragon*, pp. 179–80; *Mrs Duberly's War: Journal and Letters from the Crimea*, ed. C. Kelly (Oxford, 2007), pp. 186–7.

54. M. O. Cullet, *Un régiment de ligne pendant la guerre d'orient: Notes et souvenirs d'un officier d'infanterie 1854–1855–1856* (Lyon, 1894), pp. 165–6; Herbé, *Français et russes en Crimée*, pp. 260–65.

55. NAM 1974–05–16 (St George letter, 9 June 1855).

56. A. du Casse, *Précis historique des opérations militaires en orient de mars 1854 à septembre 1855* (Paris, 1856), p. 290; Herbé, *Français et russes en Crimée*, pp. 267–72.

57. Cullet, *Un régiment*, p. 182; J. Spilsbury, *The Thin Red Line: An Eyewitness History of the Crimean War* (London, 2005), pp. 278–9.

58. Cullet, *Un régiment*, pp. 278, 296–9.

59. Herbé, *Français et russes en Crimée*, p. 285; NAM 1962–10–94–2 (Alexander letter, 22 June 1855).

60. V. Liaskoronskii, *Vospominaniia Prokofiia Antonovicha Podpalova* (Kiev, 1904), p. 17.

61. Small, *The Crimean War*, p. 159.

62. Herbé, *Français et russes en Crimée*, pp. 280–81; Liaskoronskii, *Vospominaniia*, p. 17.

63. Boniface, *Campagnes de Crimée*, p. 235.

64. Kinglake, *Invasion of the Crimea*, vol. 8, pp. 161–2.

65. A. Massie, *The National Army Museum Book of the Crimean War: The Untold Stories* (London, 2004), pp. 199–200.

66. T. Gowing, *A Soldier's Experience: A Voice from the Ranks* (London, 1885), p. 115; Spilsbury, *Thin Red Line*, pp. 282–6; *A Visit to Sebastopol*, pp. 31–2.

67. NAM 1966–01–2 (Scott letter, 22 June 1855); NAM 1962–10–94–2 (Alexander letter, 24 June 1855).

68. Luguez, *Crimée-Italie*, pp. 47–9.

69. NAM 1968–07–287–2 (Raglan to Panmure, 19 June 1855); NAM 1963–05–162 (Dr Smith to Kinglake, 2 July 1877).

CHAPTER 11. THE FALL OF SEVASTOPOL

1. E. Boniface, Count de Castellane, *Campagnes de Crimée, d'Italie, d'Afrique, de Chine et de Syrie, 1849–1862* (Paris, 1898), p. 247.

2. A. Maude, *The Life of Tolstoy: First Fifty Years* (London, 1908), p. 119.

3. NAM 1984–09–31–129 (Letter, 9 July 1855); NAM 1989–03–47–6 (Ridley letter, 11 Aug. 1855).

4. A. de Damas, *Souvenirs religieux et militaires de la Crimée* (Paris, 1857), pp. 84–6.

5. L. Noir, *Souvenirs d'un simple zouave: Campagnes de Crimée et d'Italie* (Paris, 1869), p. 282; J. Cler, *Reminiscences of an Officer of Zouaves* (New York, 1860), pp. 231–2; C. Mismer, *Souvenirs d'un dragon de l'armée de Crimée* (Paris, 1887), p. 117.

6. H. Loizillon, *La Campagne de Crimée: Lettres écrites de Crimée par le capitaine d'état-major Henri Loizillon à sa famille* (Paris, 1895), pp. x–xi, 116–17.

7. J. Baudens, *La Guerre de Crimée: Les campements, les abris, les ambu-*

lances, les hôpitaux, etc. (Paris, 1858), pp. 113–15; G. Guthrie, *Commentaries on the Surgery of the War in Portugal ... with Additions Relating to Those in the Crimea* (Philadelphia, 1862), p. 646.

8. Kh. Giubbenet, *Ocherk meditsinskoi i gospital'noi chasti russkih voisk v Krymu v 1854–1856 gg.* (St Petersburg, 1870), pp. 143–4.

9. Ibid., pp. 10, 13, 88–90; RA VIC/MAIN/QVJ/1856, 12 Mar.

10. M. Vrochenskii, *Sevastopol'skii razgrom: Vospominaniia uchastnika slavnoi oborony Sevastopolia* (Kiev, 1893), pp. 164–9; W. Baumgart, *The Crimean War, 1853–1856* (London, 1999), p. 159.

11. E. Tarle, *Krymskaia voina*, 2 vols. (Moscow, 1944), vol. 2, p. 328.

12. RGVIA, f. 846, op. 16, d. 5732, l. 28; E. Ershov, *Sevastopol'skie vospominaniia artilleriiskogo ofitsera v semi tetradakh* (St Petersburg, 1858), pp. 244–5; L. Tolstoy, *The Sebastopol Sketches*, trans. D. McDuff (London, 1986), p. 139.

13. RGVIA, f. 9196, op. 4, sv. 2, d. 1, ch. 2, ll. 1–124; f. 9198, op. 6/264, sv. 15, d. 2/2, ll. 104, 112; f. 484, op. 1, d. 264, ll. 1–14; d. 291, ll. 1–10; Boniface, *Campagnes de Crimée*, p. 267; Loizillon, *La Campagne de Crimée*, pp. 105, 139; H. Clifford, *Letters and Sketches from the Crimea* (London, 1956), p. 249.

14. A. Seaton, *The Crimean War: A Russian Chronicle* (London, 1977), p. 195.

15. Ibid., p. 196.

16. A. Khrushchev, *Istoriia oborony Sevastopolia* (St Petersburg, 1889), pp. 120–22; Tarle, *Krymskaia voina*, vol. 2, pp. 344–7; Seaton, *The Crimean War*, p. 197.

17. M. O. Cullet, *Un régiment de ligne pendant la guerre d'orient: Notes et souvenirs d'un officier d'infanterie 1854–1855–1856* (Lyon, 1894), pp. 199–203; Seaton, *The Crimean War*, p. 202; D. Stolypin, *Iz lichnyh vospominanii o krymskoi voine i o zemledel'cheskih poryadkakh* (Moscow, 1874), pp. 12–16; I. Krasovskii, *Iz vospominanii o voine 1853–56* (Moscow, 1874); P. Jaeger, *Le mura di Sebastopoli: Gli italiani in Crimea 1855–56* (Milan, 1991), pp. 306–9.

18. Cullet, *Un régiment*, pp. 207–8.

19. Seaton, *The Crimean War*, p. 205; J. Herbé, *Français et russes en Crimée: Lettres d'un officier français à sa famille pendant la campagne d'Orient* (Paris, 1892), p. 318.

20. Jaeger, *Le mura di Sebastopoli*, p. 315; Loizillon, *La Campagne de Crimée*, pp. 168–70; M. Seacole, *Wonderful Adventures of Mrs Seacole in Many Lands* (London, 2005), p. 142; T. Buzzard, *With the Turkish Army in the Crimea and Asia Minor* (London, 1915), p. 145.

21. Seaton, *The Crimean War*, pp. 206–7.

22. Herbé, *Français et russes en Crimée*, p. 321; N. Berg, *Zapiski ob osade Sevastopolia*, 2 vols. (Moscow, 1858), vol. 2, p. 1.

23. Vrochenskii, *Sevastopol'skii razgrom*, p. 201.

24. H. Small, *The Crimean War: Queen Victoria's War with the Russian Tsars* (Stroud, 2007), pp. 169–70; Ershov, *Sevastopol'skie vospominaniia*, pp. 157, 242–3; Cullet, *Un régiment*, p. 220.

25. *Za mnogo let: Zapiski (vospominaniia) neizvestnogo 1844–1874 gg.* (St Petersburg, 1897), pp. 90–91; Giubbenet, *Ocherk*, p. 148.

26. RGVIA, f. 846, op. 16, d. 5758, l. 57; Vrochenskii, *Sevastopol'skii razgrom*, pp. 213–20; Tarle, *Krymskaia voina*, vol. 2, pp. 360–61. On Russian intelligence from allied prisoners, see RGVIA, f. 846, op. 16, d. 5687, l. 7.

27. A. Niel, *Siège de Sébastopol: Journal des opérations du génie* (Paris, 1858), pp. 492–502; E. Perret, *Les Français en orient: Récits de Crimée 1854–1856* (Paris, 1889), pp. 377–9; Herbé, *Français et russes en Crimée*, pp. 328–9; V. Liaskoronskii, *Vospominaniia Prokofiia Antonovicha Podpalova* (Kiev, 1904), pp. 19–20; *Tolstoy's Letters*, ed. and trans. by R. F. Christian, 2 vols. (London, 1978), vol. 1, p. 52.

28. RGVIA, f. 846, op. 16, d. 5758, ll. 58–60; A. Viazmitinov, 'Sevastopol' ot 21 marta po 28 avgusta 1855 goda', *Russkaia starina*, 34 (1882), pp. 55–6; Ershov, *Sevastopol'skie vospominaniia*, pp. 277–9.

29. J. Spilsbury, *The Thin Red Line: An Eyewitness History of the Crimean War* (London, 2005), p. 303.

30. Spilsbury, *Thin Red Line*, p. 304; C. Campbell, *Letters from Camp to His Relatives during the Siege of Sebastopol* (London, 1894), pp. 316–17; Clifford, *Letters and Sketches*, pp. 257–8.

31. RGVIA, f. 846, op. 16, d. 5758, l. 65.

32. M. Bogdanovich, *Vostochnaia voina 1853–1856*, 4 vols. (St Petersburg, 1876), vol. 4, p. 127.

33. RGVIA, f. 846, op. 16, d. 5758, l. 68; T. Tolycheva, *Rasskazy starushki ob osade Sevastopolia* (Moscow, 1881), pp. 87–90.

34. *Tolstoy's Letters*, vol. 1, p. 52.

35. *Sobranie pisem sester Krestovozdvizhenskoi obshchiny popecheniia o ranenykh* (St Petersburg, 1855), pp. 74, 81–2.

36. Giubbenet, *Ocherk*, pp. 19, 152–3; *The Times*, 27 Sept. 1855.

37. Boniface, *Campagnes de Crimée*, pp. 295–6; Buzzard, *With the Turkish Army*, p. 193.

38. E. Vanson, *Crimée, Italie, Mexique: Lettres de campagnes 1854–1867* (Paris, 1905), pp. 154, 161; NAM 2005–07–719 (Golaphy letter, 22 Sept. 1855).

39. WO 28/126; NAM 6807–379/4 (Panmure to Codrington, 9 Nov. 1855).

40. S. Tatishchev, *Imperator Aleksandr II: Ego zhizn' i tsarstvovanie*, 2 vols. (St Petersburg, 1903), vol. 1, pp. 161–3.

41. RGVIA, f. 481, op. 1, d. 36, ll. 1–27; A. Tiutcheva, *Pri dvore dvukh imperatov: Vospominaniia, dnevnik, 1853–1882* (Moscow, 1928–9), p. 65; W. Mosse, 'How Russia Made Peace September 1855 to April 1856', *Cambridge Historical Journal*, 11/3 (1955), p. 301; W. Baumgart, *The Peace of Paris 1856: Studies in War, Diplomacy and Peacemaking* (Oxford, 1981), p. 7.

42. Tarle, *Krymskaia voina*, vol. 2, pp. 520–24; H. Sandwith, *A Narrative of the Siege of Kars* (London, 1856), pp. 104 ff.; *Papers Relative to Military Affairs in Asiatic Turkey and the Defence and Capitulation of Kars: Presented to Both Houses of Parliament by Command of Her Majesty* (London, 1856), p. 251; C. Badem, 'The Ottomans and the Crimean War (1853–1856)', Ph.D. diss. (Sabanci University, 2007), pp. 197–223.

43. Mosse, 'How Russia Made Peace', pp. 302–3.

44. Baumgart, *The Peace of Paris 1856*, pp. 5–7.

45. BLMD, Add. MS 48579, Palmerston to Clarendon, 25 Sept. 1855.

46. Argyll, Duke of, *Autobiography and Memoirs*, 2 vols. (London, 1906), vol. 1, p. 492; *The Greville Memoirs 1814–1860*, ed. L. Strachey and R. Fulford, 8 vols. (London, 1938), vol. 7, p. 173.

47. BLMD, Add. MS 48579, Palmerston to Clarendon, 9 Oct. 1855.

48. C. Thoumas, *Mes souvenirs de Crimée 1854–1856* (Paris, 1892), pp. 256–60; *Lettres d'un soldat à sa mère de 1849 à 1870: Afrique, Crimée, Italie, Mexique* (Montbéliard, 1910), pp. 106–8; Loizillon, *La Campagne de Crimée*, pp. xvii–xviii.

49. A. Gouttman, *La Guerre de Crimée 1853–1856* (Paris, 1995), p. 460; L. Case, *French Opinion on War and Diplomacy during the Second Empire* (Philadelphia, 1954), pp. 39–40; R. Marlin, *L'Opinion franc-comtoise devant la guerre de Crimée*, Annales Littéraires de l'Université de Besançon, vol. 17 (Paris, 1957), p. 48.

50. W. Echard, *Napoleon III and the Concert of Europe* (Baton Range, La., 1983), pp. 50–51.

51. Gouttman, *La Guerre de Crimée*, p. 451; A. J. P. Taylor, *The Struggle for Mastery in Europe 1848–1918* (Oxford, 1955), p. 78.

52. Mosse, 'How Russia Made Peace', p. 303.

53. BLMD, Add. MS 48579, Palmerston to Clarendon, 1 Dec. 1855; Baumgart, *The Peace of Paris*, p. 33.

54. Mosse, 'How Russia Made Peace', p. 304.

55. Ibid., pp. 305–6.

56. Ibid., pp. 306–13.

57. Boniface, *Campagnes de Crimée*, p. 336.

58. D. Noël, *La Vie de bivouac: Lettres intimes* (Paris, 1860), p. 254.

59. Liaskoronskii, *Vospominaniia*, pp. 23–4.

CHAPTER 12. PARIS AND THE NEW ORDER

1. E. Gourdon, *Histoire du Congrès de Paris* (Paris, 1857), pp. 479–82.

2. W. Baumgart, *The Peace of Paris 1856: Studies in War, Diplomacy and Peacemaking* (Oxford, 1981), p. 104.

3. P. Schroeder, *Austria, Great Britain and the Crimean War: The Destruction of the European Concert* (Ithaca, NY, 1972), p. 347; BLMD, Add. MS 48579, Palmerston to Clarendon, 25 Feb. 1856.

4. Schroeder, *Austria, Great Britain and the Crimean War*, p. 348; W. Echard, *Napoleon III and the Concert of Europe* (Baton Rouge, La., 1983), p. 59.

5. FO 78/1170, Stratford Canning to Clarendon, 9 Jan. 1856; Baumgart, *The Peace of Paris 1856*, pp. 128–30.

6. Ibid., pp. 140–41; BLMD, Add. MS 48579, Palmerston to Clarendon, 4 Mar. 1856; M. Kukiel, *Czartoryski and European Unity 1770–1861* (Princeton, 1955), p. 302.

7. Gourdon, *Histoire*, pp. 523–5.

8. RGVIA, f. 846, op. 16, d. 5917, ll. 1–2; J. Herbé, *Français et russes en Crimée: Lettres d'un officier français à sa famille pendant la campagne d'Orient* (Paris, 1892), p. 402; BLMD, Add. MS 48580, Palmerston to Clarendon, 24 Mar. 1856.

9. NAM 1968–07–380–65 (Codrington letter, 15 July 1856).

10. *The Times*, 26 July 1856.

11. RGVIA, f. 846, op. 16, d. 5838, ll. 10–12; NAM 6807–375–16 (Vote of thanks to Codrington, undated).

12. M. Kozelsky, 'Casualties of Conflict: Crimean Tatars during the Crimean War', *Slavic Review*, 67/4 (2008), pp. 866–91.

13. M. Kozelsky, *Christianizing Crimea: Shaping Sacred Space in the Russian Empire and Beyond* (De Kalb, Ill., 2010), p. 153. For more on the statistics of the emigration, see A. Fisher, 'Emigration of Muslims from the Russian Empire in the Years after the Crimean War', *Jahrbücher für Geschichte Osteuropas*, 35/3 (1987), pp. 356–71. The highest recent estimate is 'at least 300,000', in J. McCarthy, *Death and Exile: The Ethnic Cleansing of Ottoman Muslims 1821–1922* (Princeton, 1995), p. 17.

14. Kozelsky, *Christianizing Crimea*, p. 151.

15. Ibid., p. 155; A. Fisher, *Between Russians, Ottomans and Turks: Crimea and Crimean Tatars* (Istanbul, 1998), p. 127.

16. BLMD, Add. MS 48580, Palmerston to Clarendon, 24 Mar. 1856.

17. FO 195/562, 'Report on the Political and Military State of the Turkish Frontier in Asia', 16 Nov. 1857; FO 97/424, Dickson to Russell, 17 Mar. 1864; *Papers Respecting Settlement of Circassian Emigrants in Turkey, 1863-64* (London, 1864).

18. McCarthy, *Death and Exile*, pp. 35-6.

19. FO 78/1172, Stratford to Clarendon, 31 Jan. 1856; *Journal de Constantinople*, 4 Feb. 1856; Lady E. Hornby, *Constantinople during the Crimean War* (London, 1863), pp. 205-8; C. Badem, 'The Ottomans and the Crimean War (1853-1856)', Ph.D. diss. (Sabanci University, 2007), p. 290; D. Blaisdell, *European Financial Control in the Ottoman Empire* (New York, 1929), p. 74.

20. Badem, 'The Ottomans', pp. 291-2.

21. Ibid., pp. 281-3; R. Davison, 'Turkish Attitudes Concerning Christian-Muslim Equality in the 19th Century', *American Historical Review*, 59 (1953-4), pp. 862-3.

22. Ibid., p. 861.

23. FO 195/524, Finn to Clarendon, 10, 11, 14 and 29 Apr., 2 May, 6 June 1856; 13 Feb. 1857; E. Finn (ed.), *Stirring Times, or, Records from Jerusalem Consular Chronicles of 1853 to 1856*, 2 vols. (London 1878), vol. 2, pp. 424-40.

24. *Correspondence Respecting the Rights and Privileges of the Latin and Greek Churches in Turkey*, 2 vols. (London, 1854-6), vol. 2, p. 119; FO 78/1171, Stratford to Porte, 23 Dec. 1856.

25. FO 195/524, Finn to Stratford, 22 July 1857; Finn, *Stirring Times*, vol. 2, pp. 448-9.

26. See H. Wood, 'The Treaty of Paris and Turkey's Status in International Law', *American Journal of International Law*, 37/2 (Apr. 1943), pp. 262-74.

27. W. Mosse, *The Rise and Fall of the Crimean System, 1855-1871: The Story of the Peace Settlement* (London, 1963), p. 40.

28. BLMD, Add. MS 48580, Palmerston to Clarendon, 7 Aug. 1856; Mosse, *The Rise and Fall*, pp. 55 ff.

29. Ibid., p. 93.

30. G. Thurston, 'The Italian War of 1859 and the Reorientation of Russian Foreign Policy', *Historical Journal*, 20/1 (Mar. 1977), pp. 125-6.

31. C. Cavour, *Il carteggio Cavour-Nigra dal 1858 al 1861: A cura della R. Commissione Editrice*, 4 vols. (Bologna, 1926), vol. 1, p. 116.

32. Mosse, *The Rise and Fall*, p. 121.

33. K. Cook, 'Russia, Austria and the Question of Italy, 1859-1862', *International History Review*, 2/4 (Oct. 1980), pp. 542-65; FO 65/574, Napier to Russell, 13 Mar. 1861.

34. A. J. P. Taylor, *The Struggle for Mastery in Europe 1848-1918* (Oxford, 1955), p. 85.

35. A. Tiutcheva, *Pri dvore dvukh imperatov: Vospominaniia, dnevnik, 1853–1882* (Moscow, 1928–9), p. 67; A. Kelly, *Toward Another Shore: Russian Thinkers between Necessity and Chance* (New Haven, 1998), p. 41.

36. *Tolstoy's Diaries*, vol. 1: *1847–1894*, ed. and trans. R. F. Christian (London, 1985), pp. 96–7.

37. M. Vygon, *Krymskie stranitsy zhizni i tvorchestva L. N. Tolstogo* (Simferopol, 1978), pp. 29–30, 45–6; H. Troyat, *Tolstoy* (London, 1970), p. 168.

38. Kelly, *Toward Another Shore*, p. 41; Vygon, *Krymskie stranitsy*, p. 37.

39. IRL, f. 57, op. 1, n. 7, l. 16; RGIA, f. 914, op. 1, d. 68, ll. 1–2.

40. F. Dostoevskii, *Polnoe sobranie sochinenii*, 30 vols. (Leningrad, 1972–88), vol. 18, p. 57.

41. N. Danilov, *Istoricheskii ocherk razvitiia voennogo upravleniia v Rossii* (St Petersburg, 1902), *prilozhenie 5; Za mnogo let: Zapiski (vospominaniia) neizvestnogo 1844–1874 gg.* (St Petersburg, 1897), pp. 136–7.

42. E. Brooks, 'Reform in the Russian Army, 1856–1861', *Slavic Review*, 43/1 (Spring 1984), pp. 66–78.

43. Quoted in J. Frank, *Dostoevsky: The Years of Ordeal, 1850–1859* (London, 1983), p. 182.

44. E. Steinberg, 'Angliiskaia versiia o "russkoi ugroze" v XIX–XX vv', in *Problemy metodologii i istochnikovedeniia istorii vneshnei politiki Rossii, sbornik statei* (Moscow, 1986), pp. 67–9; R. Shukla, *Britain, India and the Turkish Empire, 1853–1882* (New Delhi, 1973), pp. 19–20; *The Politics of Autocracy: Letters of Alexander II to Prince A. I. Bariatinskii*, ed. A. Rieber (The Hague, 1966), pp. 74–81.

45. M. Petrovich, *The Emergence of Russian Panslavism, 1856–1870* (New York, 1956), pp. 117–18.

46. D. MacKenzie, 'Russia's Balkan Policies under Alexander II, 1855–1881', in H. Ragsdale (ed.), *Imperial Russian Foreign Policy* (Cambridge, 1993), pp. 223–6.

47. Ibid., pp. 227–8.

48. Lord P. Kinross, *Ottoman Centuries: The Rise and Fall of the Turkish Empire* (London, 1977), p. 509.

49. A. Saab, *Reluctant Icon: Gladstone, Bulgaria, and the Working Classes, 1856–1878* (Cambridge, Mass., 1991), pp. 65–7.

50. Ibid., p. 231.

51. F. Dostoevsky, *A Writer's Diary*, trans. K. Lantz, 2 vols. (London, 1995), vol. 2, pp. 899–900.

52. Taylor, *The Struggle for Mastery in Europe*, p. 253; *The Times*, 17 July 1878.

53. Finn, *Stirring Times*, vol. 2, p. 452.

54. FO 195/524, Finn to Canning, 29 Apr. 1856.

EPILOGUE

1. RA VIC/MAIN/QVJ/1856, 11 and 13 Mar.

2. T. Margrave, 'Numbers & Losses in the Crimea: An Introduction. Part Three: Other Nations', *War Correspondent*, 21/3 (2003), pp. 18–22.

3. R. Burns, *John Bell: The Sculptor's Life and Works* (Kirstead, 1999), pp. 54–5.

4. T. Pakenham, *The Boer War* (London, 1979), p. 201.

5. N. Hawthorne, *The English Notebooks, 1853–1856* (Columbus, Oh., 1997), p. 149.

6. 'Florence Nightingale', *Punch*, 29 (1855), p. 225.

7. S. Markovits, *The Crimean War in the British Imagination* (Cambridge, 2009), p. 68; J. Bratton, 'Theatre of War: The Crimea on the London Stage 1854–55', in D. Brady, L. James and B. Sharatt (eds.), *Performance and Politics in Popular Drama: Aspects of Popular Entertainment in Theatre, Film and Television 1800–1976* (Cambridge, 1980), p. 134.

8. M. Bostridge, *Florence Nightingale: The Woman and Her Legend* (London, 2008), pp. 523–4, 528; M. Poovey, 'A Housewifely Woman: The Social Construction of Florence Nightingale', in id., *Uneven Developments: The Ideological Work of Gender in Victorian Fiction* (London, 1989), pp. 164–98.

9. W. Knollys, *The Victoria Cross in the Crimea* (London, 1877), p. 3.

10. S. Beeton, *Our Soldiers and the Victoria Cross: A General Account of the Regiments and Men of the British Army: And Stories of the Brave Deeds which Won the Prize 'For Valour'* (London, n.d.), p. vi.

11. Markovits, *The Crimean War*, p. 70.

12. T. Hughes, *Tom Brown's Schooldays* (London, n.d.), pp. 278–80.

13. T. Hughes, *Tom Brown at Oxford* (London, 1868), p. 169.

14. O. Anderson, 'The Growth of Christian Militarism in Mid-Victorian Britain', *English Historical Review*, 86/338 (1971), pp. 46–72; K. Hendrickson, *Making Saints: Religion and the Public Image of the British Army, 1809–1885* (Cranbury, NJ, 1998), pp. 9–15; M. Snape, *The Redcoat and Religion: The Forgotten History of the British Soldier from the Age of Marlborough to the Eve of the First World War* (London, 2005), pp. 90–91, 98.

15. *Memorials of Captain Hedley Vicars, Ninety-Seventh Regiment* (London, 1856), pp. x, 216–17.

16. Quoted in Markovits, *The Crimean War*, p. 92.

17. M. Lalumia, *Realism and Politics in Victorian Art of the Crimean War* (Epping, 1984), pp. 80–86.

18. Ibid., pp. 125–6.

19. Ibid., pp. 136–44; P. Usherwood and J. Spencer-Smith, *Lady Butler, Battle Artist, 1846–1933* (London, 1987), pp. 29–31.

20. Mrs H. Sandford, *The Girls' Reading Book* (London, 1875), p. 183.

21. See e.g. R. Basturk, *Bilim ve Ahlak* (Istanbul, 2009).

22. Genelkurmay Askeri Tarih ve Stratejik Etüt Başkanlığı, *Selçuklular Döneminde Anadoluya Yapılan Akınlar – 1799–1802 Osmanlı-Fransız Harbinde Akka Kalesi Savunması – 1853–1856 Osmanlı-Rus Kırım Harbi Kafkas Cephesi* (Ankara, 1981), quoted in C. Badem, 'The Ottomans and the Crimean War (1853–1856)', Ph.D. diss. (Sabanci University, 2007), pp. 20–21 (translation altered for clarity).

23. A. Khrushchev, *Istoriia oborony Sevastopolia* (St Petersburg, 1889), pp. 159–6.

24. L. Tolstoy, *The Sebastopol Sketches*, trans. D. McDuff (London, 1986), pp. 56–7.

25. N. Dubrovin, *349-dnevnaia zashchita Sevastopolia* (St Petersburg, 2005), p. 15.

26. A. Apukhtin, *Sochineniia*, 2 vols. (St Petersburg, 1895), vol. 2, p. iv. Translation by Luis Sundkvist and the author.

27. M. Kozelsky, *Christianizing Crimea: Shaping Sacred Space in the Russian Empire and Beyond* (De Kalb, Ill., 2010), pp. 130–39; R. Wortman, *Scenarios of Power: Myth and Ceremony in Russian Monarchy*, vol. 2: *From Alexander II to the Abdication of Nicholas II* (Princeton, 2000), p. 25; O. Maiorova, 'Searching for a New Language of Self: The Symbolism of Russian National Belonging during and after the Crimean War', *Ab Imperio*, 4 (2006), p. 199.

28. RGVIA, f. 481, op. 1, d. 27, l. 116; M. Bogdanovich (ed.), *Istoricheskii ocherk deiatel'nosti voennago upravlennia v Rossii v pervoe dvatsatipiatiletie blagopoluchnago tsarstvoivaniia Gosudaria Imperatora Aleksandra Nikolaevicha (1855–1880 gg.)*, 6 vols. (St Petersburg, 1879–81), vol. 1, p. 172.

29. S. Plokhy, 'The City of Glory: Sevastopol in Russian Historical Mythology', *Journal of Contemporary History*, 35/3 (July 2000), p. 377.

30. S. Davies, 'Soviet Cinema and the Early Cold War: Pudovkin's *Admiral Nakhimov* in Context', *Cold War History*, 4/1 (Oct. 2003), pp. 49–70.

31. Quoted in Plokhy, 'The City of Glory', p. 382.

32. The conference papers are online: http://www.cnsr.ru/projects.php?id=10.

Select Bibliography

Aksan, V., *Ottoman Wars 1700–1870: An Empire Besieged* (London, 2007).

Akten zur Geschichte des Krimkriegs: Französische Akten zur Geschichte des Krimkriegs, 3 vols. (Munich, 1999–2003).

Akten zur Geschichte des Krimkriegs: Österreichische Akten zur Geschichte des Krimkriegs, 3 vols. (Munich, 1979–80).

Akten zur Geschichte des Krimkriegs: Preussische Akten zur Geschichte des Krimkriegs, 2 vols. (Munich, 1990–91).

Alabin, P., *Chetyre voiny: Pokhodnye zapiski v voinu 1853, 1854, 1855 i 1856 godov*, 2 vols. (Viatka, 1861).

Alberti, M., *Per la storia dell'alleanza e della campagna di Crimea, 1853–1856: Lettere e documenti* (Turin, 1910).

Anderson, M., *The Eastern Question* (London, 1966).

Anderson, O., *A Liberal State at War: English Politics and Economics during the Crimean War* (London, 1967).

——'The Growth of Christian Militarism in Mid-Victorian Britain', *English Historical Review*, 86/338 (1971), pp. 46–72.

Andriianov, A., *Inkermanskii boi i oborona Sevastopolia (nabroski uchastnika)* (St Petersburg, 1903).

[Anon.] *The Englishwoman in Russia: Impressions of the Society and Manners of the Russians at Home* (London, 1855).

Ascherson, N., *Black Sea* (London, 1995).

Baddeley, J., *The Russian Conquest of the Caucasus* (London, 1908).

Badem, C., 'The Ottomans and the Crimean War (1853–1856)', Ph.D. diss. (Sabanci University, 2007).

Bailey, F., *British Policy and the Turkish Reform Movement, 1826–1853* (London, 1942).

Bapst, E., *Les Origines de la Guerre en Crimée: La France et la Russie de 1848 à 1851* (Paris, 1912).

Baudens, J., *La Guerre de Crimée: Les campements, les abris, les ambulances, les hôpitaux, etc.* (Paris, 1858).

Baumgart, W., *The Peace of Paris 1856: Studies in War, Diplomacy and Peace-making* (Oxford, 1981).

Bayley, C., *Mercenaries for the Crimean: The German, Swiss, and Italian Legions in British Service 1854–6* (Montreal, 1977).

Bazancourt, Baron de, *The Crimean Expedition, to the Capture of Sebastopol*, 2 vols. (London, 1856).

Berg, M., *Desiat' dnei v Sevastopole* (Moscow, 1855).

Bestuzhev, I., *Krymskaia voina 1853–1856* (Moscow, 1956).

Bitis, A., *Russia and the Eastern Question: Army, Government and Society, 1815–1833* (Oxford, 2006).

Bogdanovich, M., *Vostochnaia voina 1853–1856*, 4 vols. (St Petersburg, 1876).

Bolsover, G., 'Nicholas I and the Partition of Turkey', *Slavonic Review*, 27 (1948), pp. 115–45.

Bonham-Carter, V. (ed.), *Surgeon in the Crimea: The Experiences of George Lawson Recorded in Letters to His Family* (London, 1968).

Boniface, E., Count de Castellane, *Campagnes de Crimée, d'Italie, d'Afrique, de Chine et de Syrie, 1849–1862* (Paris, 1898).

Bostridge, M., *Florence Nightingale: The Woman and Her Legend* (London, 2008).

Bresler, F., *Napoleon III: A Life* (London, 1999).

Brown, D., *Palmerston and the Politics of Foreign Policy, 1846–55* (Manchester 2002).

Buzzard, T., *With the Turkish Army in the Crimea and Asia Minor* (London, 1915).

Cadot, M., *La Russie dans la vie intellectuelle française, 1839–1856* (Paris, 1967).

Calthorpe, S., *Letters from Headquarters; or the Realities of the War in the Crimea by an Officer of the Staff* (London, 1858).

Case, L., *French Opinion on War and Diplomacy during the Second Empire* (Philadelphia, 1954).

Cavour, C., *Il carteggio Cavour-Nigra dal 1858 al 1861: A cura della R. Commissione Editrice*, 4 vols. (Bologna, 1926).

Charles-Roux, F., *Alexandre II, Gortchakoff et Napoléon III* (Paris, 1913).

Cler, J., *Reminiscences of an Officer of Zouaves* (New York, 1860).

Clifford, H., *Letters and Sketches from the Crimea* (London, 1956).

Cooke, B., *The Grand Crimean Central Railway* (Knutsford, 1990).

Correspondence Respecting the Rights and Privileges of the Latin and Greek Churches in Turkey, 2 vols. (London, 1854–6).

Crimée 1854–6, Exhibition catalogue, Musée de l'Armée (Paris, 1994).

Cullet, M. O., *Un régiment de ligne pendant la guerre d'orient: Notes et souvenirs d'un officier d'infanterie 1854–1855–1856* (Lyon, 1894).

Cunningham, A., *Eastern Questions in the Nineteenth Century: Collected Essays*, 2 vols. (London, 1993).

Curtiss, J., *The Russian Army under Nicholas I, 1825–1855* (Durham, NC, 1965).

—— *Russia's Crimean War* (Durham, NC, 1979).

Damas, A. de, *Souvenirs religieux et militaires de la Crimée* (Paris, 1857).

Dante, F., *I cattolici e la guerra di Crimea* (Rome, 2005).

David, S., *The Homicidal Earl: The Life of Lord Cardigan* (London, 1997).

—— *The Indian Mutiny* (London, 2002).

Davison, R. H., 'Turkish Attitudes Concerning Christian–Muslim Equality in the 19th Century', *American Historical Review*, 59 (1953–4), pp. 844–64.

—— *Reform in the Ottoman Empire, 1856–1876* (Princeton, 1963).

—— *Essays in Ottoman and Turkish History, 1774–1923: The Impact of the West* (Austin, Tex., 1990).

Doré, G., *Histoire pittoresque, dramatique et caricaturale de la Sainte Russie* (Paris, 1854).

Dubrovin, N., *Istoriia krymskoi voiny i oborony Sevastopolia*, 3 vols. (St Petersburg, 1900).

Egerton, R., *Death or Glory: The Legacy of the Crimean War* (London, 2000).

Ershov, E., *Sevastopol'skie vospominaniia artilleriiskogo ofitsera v semi tetradakh* (St Petersburg, 1858).

Fisher, A., *The Russian Annexation of the Crimea, 1772–1783* (Cambridge, 1970).

—— *The Crimean Tatars* (Stanford, Calif., 1978).

—— 'Emigration of Muslims from the Russian Empire in the Years after the Crimean War', *Jahrbücher für Geschichte Osteuropas*, 35/3 (1987), pp. 356–71.

Florescu, R., *The Struggle against Russia in the Romanian Principalities 1821–1854* (Monachii, 1962).

Gammer, M., *Muslim Resistance to the Tsar: Shamil and the Conquest of Chechnya and Dagestan* (London, 1994).

Gershel'man, S., *Nravstvennyi element pod Sevastopolem* (St Petersburg, 1897).

Giubbenet, Kh., *Ocherk meditsinskoi i gospital'noi chasti russkih voisk v Krymu v 1854–1856 gg.* (St Petersburg, 1870).

Gleason, J., *The Genesis of Russophobia in Great Britain* (Cambridge, Mass., 1950).

Goldfrank, D., *The Origins of the Crimean War* (London, 1995).

—— 'The Holy Sepulcher and the Origin of the Crimean War', in E. Lohr and M. Poe (eds.), *The Military and Society in Russia: 1450–1917* (Leiden, 2002), pp. 491–506.

Gondicas, D., and Issawi, C. (eds.), *Ottoman Greeks in the Age of Nationalism: Politics, Economy, and Society in the Nineteenth Century* (Princeton, 1999).

Gooch, B., *The New Bonapartist Generals in the Crimean War* (The Hague, 1959).

Gouttman, A., *La Guerre de Crimée 1853–1856* (Paris, 1995).

Guerrin, L., *Histoire de la dernière guerre de Russie (1853–1856)*, 2 vols. (Paris, 1858).

Harris, S., *British Military Intelligence in the Crimean War* (London, 2001).

Henderson, G., *Crimean War Diplomacy and Other Historical Essays* (Glasgow, 1947).

Herbé, J., *Français et russes en Crimée: Lettres d'un officier français à sa famille pendant la campagne d'Orient* (Paris, 1892).

Hibbert, C., *The Destruction of Lord Raglan: A Tragedy of the Crimean War, 1854–1855* (London, 1961).

Hodasevich, R., *A Voice from within the Walls of Sebastopol: A Narrative of the Campaign in the Crimea and the Events of the Siege* (London, 1856).

Hopwood, D., *The Russian Presence in Palestine and Syria, 1843–1914: Church and Politics in the Near East* (Oxford, 1969).

Ingle, H., *Nesselrode and the Russian Rapprochement with Britain, 1836–1844* (Berkeley, 1976).

Jaeger, P., *Le mura di Sebastopoli: Gli italiani in Crimea 1855–56* (Milan, 1991).

Jewsbury, G., *The Russian Annexation of Bessarabia: 1774–1828. A Study of Imperial Expansion* (New York, 1976).

Jouve, E., *Guerre d'Orient: Voyage à la suite des armées alliées en Turquie, en Valachie et en Crimée* (Paris, 1855).

Kagan, F., *The Military Reforms of Nicholas I: The Origins of the Modern Russian Army* (London, 1999).

Keller, U., *The Ultimate Spectacle: A Visual History of the Crimean War* (London, 2001).

Khrushchev, A., *Istoriia oborony Sevastopolia* (St Petersburg, 1889).

King, C., *The Black Sea: A History* (Oxford, 2004).

——*The Ghost of Freedom: A History of the Caucasus* (Oxford, 2008).

Kinglake, A., *The Invasion of the Crimea: Its Origin and an Account of Its Progress down to the Death of Lord Raglan*, 8 vols. (London, 1863).

Kovalevskii, E., *Voina s Turtsiei i razryv s zapadnymi derzhavami v 1853–1854* (St Petersburg, 1871).

Kozelsky, M., *Christianizing Crimea: Shaping Sacred Space in the Russian Empire and Beyond* (De Kalb, Ill., 2010).

Krupskaia, A., *Vospominaniia krymskoi voiny sestry krestovozdvizhenskoi obshchiny* (St Petersburg, 1861).

Kukiel, M., *Czartoryski and European Unity 1770–1861* (Princeton, 1955).

Lalumia, M., *Realism and Politics in Victorian Art of the Crimean War* (Epping, 1984).

Lambert, A., *Battleships in Transition: The Creation of the Steam Battlefleet, 1815–1860* (Annapolis, Md., 1984).

—— *The Crimean War: British Grand Strategy, 1853–56* (Manchester, 1990).

——and Badsey, S. (eds.), *The War Correspondents: The Crimean War* (Stroud, 1994).

Lane-Poole, S., *The Life of the Right Honourable Stratford Canning*, 2 vols. (London, 1888).

The Letters of Queen Victoria: A Selection from Her Majesty's Correspondence between the Years 1837 and 1861, 3 vols. (London, 1907–8).

Lettres du maréchal Bosquet à sa mère 1829–58, 4 vols. (Pau, 1877–9).

Lettres du maréchal Bosquet à ses amis, 1837–1860, 2 vols. (Pau, 1879).

Lettres d'un soldat à sa mère de 1849 à 1870: Afrique, Crimée, Italie, Mexique (Montbéliard, 1910).

Levin, M., 'Krymskaia voina i russkoe obshchestvo', in id., *Ocherki po istorii russkoi obshchestvennoi mysli, vtoraia polovina XIX veka* (Leningrad, 1974), pp. 293–304.

Loizillon, H., *La Campagne de Crimée: Lettres écrites de Crimée par le capitaine d'état-major Henri Loizillon à sa famille* (Paris, 1895).

Luguez, F., *Crimée-Italie 1854–1859: Extraits de la correspondence d'un officier avec sa famille* (Nancy, 1895).

McCarthy, J., *Death and Exile: The Ethnic Cleansing of Ottoman Muslims 1821–1922* (Princeton, 1995).

MacKenzie, D., 'Russia's Balkan Policies under Alexander II, 1855–1881', in H. Ragsdale (ed.), *Imperial Russian Foreign Policy* (Cambridge, 1993), pp. 219–46.

McNally, R., 'The Origins of Russophobia in France: 1812–1830', *American Slavic and East European Review*, 17/2 (Apr. 1958), pp. 179–83.

Markevich, A., *Tavricheskaia guberniia vo vremia krymskoi voiny: Po arkhivnym materialam* (Simferopol, 1905).

Markovits, S., *The Crimean War in the British Imagination* (Cambridge, 2009).

Marlin, R., *L'Opinion franc-comtoise devant la guerre de Crimée*, Annales Littéraires de l'Université de Besançon, vol. 17 (Paris, 1957).

Martin, K., *The Triumph of Lord Palmerston: A Study of Public Opinion in England before the Crimean War* (London, 1963).

Marx, K., *The Eastern Question: A Reprint of Letters Written 1853–1856 Dealing with the Events of the Crimean War* (London, 1969).

Masquelez, M., *Journal d'un officier de zouaves* (Paris, 1858).

Massie, A., *A Most Desperate Undertaking: The British Army in the Crimea, 1854–56* (London, 2003).

—— *The National Army Museum Book of the Crimean War: The Untold Stories* (London, 2004).

Mémoires du comte Horace de Viel-Castel sur le règne de Napoléon III, 1851–1864, 2 vols. (Paris, 1979).

Mémoires du duc De Persigny (Paris, 1896).

Mismer, C., *Souvenirs d'un dragon de l'armée de Crimée* (Paris, 1887).

Molènes, P. de, *Les Commentaires d'un soldat* (Paris, 1860).

Moon, D., 'Russian Peasant Volunteers at the Beginning of the Crimean War', *Slavic Review*, 51/4 (Winter 1992), pp. 691–704.

Mosse, W., *The Rise and Fall of the Crimean System, 1855–1871: The Story of the Peace Settlement* (London, 1963).

Mrs Duberly's War: Journal and Letters from the Crimea, ed. C. Kelly (Oxford, 2007).

Niel, A., *Siège de Sébastopol: Journal des opérations du génie* (Paris, 1858).

Nilojkovic-Djuric, J., *Panslavism and National Identity in Russia and in the Balkans, 1830–1880* (Boulder, Colo., 1994).

Noël, D., *La Vie de bivouac: Lettres intimes* (Paris, 1860).

Noir, L., *Souvenirs d'un simple zouave: Campagnes de Crimée et d'Italie* (Paris, 1869).

Osmanli Belgelerinde Kirim Savasi (1853–1856) (Ankara, 2006).

Pavlowitch, S., *Anglo-Russian Rivalry in Serbia, 1837–39* (Paris, 1961).

Perret, E., *Les Français en orient: Récits de Crimée 1854–1856* (Paris, 1889).

Petrovich, M., *The Emergence of Russian Panslavism, 1856–1870* (New York, 1956).

Picq, A. du, *Battle Studies* (Charleston, SC, 2006).

Pirogov, N., *Sevastopol'skie pis'ma i vospominaniia* (Moscow, 1950).

Plokhy, S., 'The City of Glory: Sevastopol in Russian Historical Mythology', *Journal of Contemporary History*, 35/3 (July 2000), pp. 369–83.

Ponting, C., *The Crimean War: The Truth behind the Myth* (London, 2004).

Prousis, T., *Russian Society and the Greek Revolution* (De Kalb, Ill., 1994).

Rachinskii, A., *Pokhodnye pis'ma opolchentsa iz iuzhnoi Bessarabii 1855–1856* (Moscow, 1858).

Ragsdale, H. (ed.), *Imperial Russian Foreign Policy* (Cambridge, 1993).

Rakov, V., *Moi vospominaniia o Evpatorii v epohu krymskoi voiny 1853–1856 gg.* (Evpatoriia, 1904).

Rappaport, H., *No Place for Ladies: The Untold Story of Women in the Crimean War* (London, 2007).

Rebrov, Ia., *Pis'ma sevastopol'tsa* (Novocherkassk, 1876).

Reid, D., *Soldier-Surgeon: The Crimean War Letters of Dr Douglas A. Reid, 1855–1856* (Knoxville, Tenn., 1968).

Reid, J., *Crisis of the Ottoman Empire: Prelude to Collapse 1839–1878* (Stuttgart, 2000).

Riasanovsky, N., *Nicholas I and Official Nationality in Russia 1825–1855* (Berkeley, 1959).

Rich, N., *Why the Crimean War?* (New York, 1985).

Royle, T., *Crimea: The Great Crimean War 1854–1856* (London, 1999).

Russell, W., *The British Expedition to the Crimea* (London, 1858).

Saab, A., *The Origins of the Crimean Alliance* (Charlottesville, Va., 1977).

——*Reluctant Icon: Gladstone, Bulgaria, and the Working Classes, 1856–1878* (Cambridge, Mass., 1991).

Sandwith, H., *A Narrative of the Siege of Kars* (London, 1856).

Schiemann, T., *Geschichte Russlands unter Kaiser Nikolaus I*, 4 vols. (Berlin, 1904–19).

Schroeder, P., *Austria, Great Britain and the Crimean War: The Destruction of the European Concert* (Ithaca, NY, 1972).

Seacole, M., *Wonderful Adventures of Mrs Seacole in Many Lands* (London, 2005).

Seaton, A., *The Crimean War: A Russian Chronicle* (London, 1977).

Shepherd, J., *The Crimean Doctors: A History of the British Medical Services in the Crimean War*, 2 vols. (Liverpool, 1991).

Slade, A., *Turkey and the Crimean War: A Narrative of Historical Events* (London, 1867).

Small, H., *Florence Nightingale, Avenging Angel* (London, 1998).

—— *The Crimean War: Queen Victoria's War with the Russian Tsars* (Stroud, 2007).

Southgate, D., *The Most English Minister: The Policies and Politics of Palmerston* (New York, 1966).

Soyer, A., *Soyer's Culinary Campaign* (London, 1857).

Spilsbury, J., *The Thin Red Line: An Eyewitness History of the Crimean War* (London, 2005).

Stockmar, E., *Denkwürdigkeiten aus den Papieren des Freiherrn Christian Friedrich V. Stockmar* (Brunswick, 1872).

Stolypin, D., *Iz lichnyh vospominanii o krymskoi voine i o zemledel'cheskih poryadkakh* (Moscow, 1874).

Strachan, H., *From Waterloo to Balaclava: Tactics, Technology and the British Army* (London, 1985).

Sweetman, J., *War and Administration: The Significance of the Crimean War for the British Army* (London, 1984).

Tarle, E., *Krymskaia voina*, 2 vols. (Moscow, 1944).

Taylor, A. J. P., *The Struggle for Mastery in Europe 1848–1918* (Oxford, 1955).

Thoumas, M., *Mes souvenirs de Crimée 1854–1856* (Paris, 1892).

Thouvenal, L., *Nicolas Ier et Napoléon III: Les préliminaires de la guerre de Crimée 1852–1854* (Paris, 1891).

Thurston, G., 'The Italian War of 1859 and the Reorientation of Russian Foreign Policy', *Historical Journal*, 20/1 (Mar. 1977), pp. 121–44.

Tiutcheva, A., *Pri dvore dvukh imperatov: Vospominaniia, dnevnik, 1853–1882* (Moscow, 1928–9).

Tolstoy, L., *The Sebastopol Sketches*, trans. D. McDuff (London, 1986).

Tolstoy's Diaries, ed. and trans. R. F. Christian, 2 vols. (London, 1985).

Tolstoy's Letters, ed. and trans. R. F. Christian, 2 vols. (London, 1978).

Totleben, E., *Opisanie oborony g. Sevastopolia*, 3 vols. (St Petersburg, 1863–78).

Ubicini, A., *Letters on Turkey*, trans. Lady Easthope, 2 vols. (London, 1856).

Urquhart, D., *England and Russia* (London, 1835).

Vanson, E., *Crimée, Italie, Mexique: Lettres de campagnes 1854–1867* (Paris, 1905).

A Visit to Sebastopol a Week after Its Fall: By an Officer of the Anglo-Turkish Contingent (London, 1856).

Vrochenskii, M., *Sevastopol'skii razgrom: Vospominaniia uchastnika slavnoi oborony Sevastopolia* (Kiev, 1893).

Vyskochkov, L., *Imperator Nikolai I: Chelovek i gosudar'* (St Petersburg, 2001).

Warner, P., *The Crimean War: A Reappraisal* (Ware, 2001).

Wirtschafter, E., *From Serf to Russian Soldier* (Princeton, 1990).

Zaionchkovskii, A., *Vostochnaia voina 1853–1856*, 3 vols. (St Petersburg, 2002).

Za mnogo let: Zapiski (vospominaniia) neizvestnogo 1844–1874 gg. (St Petersburg, 1897).

Index

Pages with illustrations have italic numbers. Foot of page references have *n* following the page number.

Astrakhan (Mongol khanate) 9
atrocities: alleged after Balaklava 252–3;
alleged after Inkerman 270–71; allied
troops in Kerch 344–5; Bashi Bazouks
190, 459–60; in Bulgaria 459–60; in
Constantinople (1821) 34; Giurgevo
186; religious justification for 271–2;
Tatar bands 228, 344–5
Attwood, Thomas 82
Austria-Hungary: neutrality assured by
future territorial gains 461; Three
Emperors' League (1873) 458;
see also Austrian Empire
Austrian army, in Wallachia (1854) 189
Austrian Empire: armed neutrality in
favour of allies 184–5; benevolent
neutrality with respect to Russia 273;
demands Napoleon III's peaceful
intentions 101; demands Russian
withdrawal from principalities 170,
184–5; direct talks with Russians
401–2; fearful of Slav uprisings
184–5, 329; Four Points for Peace
with Russia (1854) 195–6, 326, 401;
Franco-Austrian peace ultimatum
405, 407–8; hopes for alliance with
Russia 13–14, 16; hoping to negotiate
a peace 329–30; Italian independence
and 132–3; military alliance with
France and Britain 320; mobilizes
troops (1853 & 1854) 124, 170, 184;
motives for invading principalities
189; negotiations with Britain and
France 158, 159, 327, 401; Paris
Peace Congress (1856) 411–12, 414,
433; peace initiative, the Vienna Note
(1853) 124–5; ready to march into
Serbia 155, 170; 1848 revolutions 92,
96–8; Russian foreign policy and 115;
Russian partition plans (1852) 104;
and Russian plans for Greece (1820s)
36; steps back from war with
Ottomans 39–40; support from
Gorchakov over revolution in Italy
439–40; threatens to join anti-Russian
alliance xx, 170; Triple Alliance
(1856) 433; and Tsar Nicholas'
Ottoman partition plans 62–3, 68–9,
106, 115; Vienna Conference (1855)

329–32; war with French and
Piedmontese (1859) 433, 437–9; war
with Prussia (1866) 433, 442; wary
of Russia in Slav lands 89, 115,
131, 155, 170, 184–5; *see also*
Austria-Hungary

Bakhchiserai 22, 222, 241, 423;
Museum of the Alma 493; reserve
hospital 377
Bakunin, Mikhail 301
Bakunina, Ekaterina (nurse) 301
Balaklava, British supply base 225,
229&n, 288
Balaklava, battle of (1854) xix, 241–54
Balaklava helmets 304
Balaklava Railway 355–6, 418, 469
Balkan League 458
Balkan War (1853–4) 461
Balkans: continuing conflict between
Christians and Muslims 59–60, 432,
459–62; Czartoryski's plan 82; hoped
for Slav/Christian uprisings 131,
167–8, 170, 437, 457, 459, 461–2;
Nationalism 29, 89–90; pan-Slavism
89–92, 115–16, 133–9, 456–62;
retreat of Austria 433; Russia and 29,
32, 89–92, 456–64; Russian partition
plans (1852) 104; seeds of future wars
464; status quo guaranteed by Three
Emperors' League (1873) 458; theatre
of war xix; *see also* European Turkey
Balta Liman, Act of (1849) 95–6
Baltic campaign (1854) xx, 14, 159,
193&n, 315–16
Baltic campaign (1855) 337
Baltic provinces, of Russia, Palmerston's
plans for 159, 327, 401
Bariatinsky, Prince Alexander I (viceroy of
the Caucasus) 450–51, 452–3; fears
British presence on the Caspian Sea 453
Bariatinsky, Prince Vladimir I (Flag Lt to
Adm Kornilov) 238–9
Barrett, Jerry, *Queen Victoria's First Visit
to Her Wounded Soldiers* 477
Bashi Bazouks 120, 141; atrocities 190,
459–60; cholera and retreat to Varna
190–91; in French service 189–91; at
Giurgevo 186

Ottoman army: make up of 120–22, 173; atrocities alleged in Kerch 344–5; drinking 352; European officers 120, 121, 172–4, 186; ill-treatment by British 253; language a major problem 120; pursuit of retreating Russians 185–7; religious nature of reprisals 186; Silistria and Danubian front 168, 170, 172–5; terror tactics 138; at Varna 182–3; at Alma 208, 209; at Balaklava 241, 242–3, 252–3; in Kars 398–9

Ottoman Empire: border line with Orthodox Russia 10–11; British commercial interests (1830s) 46–8; British foreign policy and 52–3; Congress of Berlin resolutions 463; corrupt bureaucracy 30; Crimea obliterated from national memory 482–4; Crimean War casualties 483; cultural and religious make up 27–9; customs and permissions in the Holy Land 6–7; declaration of war on Russia (1853) 128–9, 130; declares jihad after Navarino 38; effect on of Crimean War xxi–xxii; exposure to Western culture 426–7; foreign capital investment 427; France and 436; fudges issue of Holy Sepulchre roof repairs 7; Grand Council agrees to accept Vienna peace terms (1853) 143; Grand Council refuses Menshikov's demands 112–14; and Greek independence 33–6; Hatt-i Hümayun decree 415, 427–32; Holy Land religious rights and 8, 11, 12, 34, 103, 104, 107–8, 415; hostility to interference from Britain 60; lack of communications infrastructure 59; liberal political reform in 52–60; loss of the Crimea 16; military backwardness 30; Muslim institutions a brake on progress 29; organizes support in Britain (1853) 130; Orthodox subjects 9–10, 27–9, 58–60, 90; Palmerston's plans 159, 327; Paris Peace Congress (1856) 414–16, 432; parliament established (1876) 57; peace negotiations (1853) 124; plan

to meet further incursions by Russia 400; planned to be a vassal state 106; at point of collapse (1829) 39–40; political asylum offered to Hungarian Poles 97, 98; reaction to Greek uprising in Moldavia and Wallachia 33–4; resentment against Christians 427–32, 483–4; response to Tsar Alexander I's ultimatum 34–5; Romanian revolution 1848 and 94; Russia invades and takes Kars 398–9; Russian annexation of Crimea recognized (1792) 17; Russian plans to partition 62–70, 104–7; San Stefano Treaty 462–3; secular Ottomanism 57; seeks help from Britain and France against Russians 109; the 'sick man of Europe' 105; signs Act of Balta Liman (1849) 95–6; Slav subjects and Tsar Nicholas 90–91; Tanzimat reforms see Tanzimat reforms; treatment/persecution of Christians 27–8, 30, 429–31; unaffected by Sinope 143; war with Russia (1787–92; 1806–12; 1828–29) 17, 18, 19, 21, 38–40; war with Russia (1853–6) 128–9, 130, 139–42; war with Russia (1877–8) 461–2; war with Serbia (1876) 461; weakness of 29, 31, 41–3, 49; Westernizing liberal reforms 25, 31, 53–60, 426–8; see also Eastern Question; millet system; Ottoman army; Ottoman navy

Ottoman navy, at Sinope (1853) 141–3
Oudinot, General Charles Nicolas 134n

pacifists, vilified by Russophobes 149
paintings, Crimean War subjects 477–8, 482, 489, 490
Palestine, riots and attacks on Christians 429–30
Palgrave, William Gifford (British consul in Abkhazia) 425
Palmerston, Henry Temple, 3rd Viscount 3, 5, 44–5, 46, 56, 60, 67, 110&n, 148; Aberdeen's foreign policies and 146, 326, 434; aggressive campaign wanted 158–9, 193; anti-Russian

Stalin, Joseph: demands changes to
Pudovkin's film 491; demands joint
Soviet–Turkish control of
Dardanelles 491
The Standard (newspaper) 50
Stanley, Edward, Lord Stanley (14th Earl
of Derby) 78
Star Fort (Sevastopol) 222–3, 224, 393
Star of the South (ship), lodgings for
British officers and wives 279
steamships, enable fast movement of
news 305
Steevens, Capt Nathaniel (88th Foot):
ceasefire fraternization 349; death of
Col Egerton 361
Sterling, Lt-Col Anthony (93rd Highland
Bde) 244, 285
Stockmar, Christian Friedrich, Baron 67
Straits Convention (1841) *see*
Convention of London
Stroganov, Count, governor-general of
New Russia 421–2, 423
Sturdza, Alexandru 32, 34
Sturdza, Michael, Prince of Moldavia 42
Sukhozanet, Gen Nikolai 449;
reports on British threat in Central
Asia 453
Sukhumi 398
Suleiman Pasha (Ottoman commissioner
in Bucharest) 94
Sulivan, Captain Bartholomew, reports
on Baltic fortresses 337–8, 338–9
Sunni Muslims, the Caucasus 18
supply ships, destroyed by the hurricane
(1854) 279
Sveaborg (Baltic fortress) 193, 337, 400
Sweden: Baltic sea war and 193n;
military treaty with Western powers
406; Palmerston's plans and 159,
327, 401
Switzerland, source of mercenary
soldiers 334
Sylvester, Henry (Asst. Surgeon) 294
Syria, riots and attacks on Christians 429

Taganrog, destruction of part of allied
Kerch raid 344&n
Talleyrand-Périgord, Charles Maurice
de 71

Tanzimat reforms 57–60, 99, 106, 121,
150; cost of 427; Hatt-i Sharif and 428;
opposition to 59–60, 127–8; support
for questioned in Britain 459–60
Tarle, Evgeny (Stalin era historian) 491
Tashkent 455
Tatars 9, 10–11; submit to Catherine the
Great 16; in Bulgaria 459; exodus
from the Crimea 420–23, 459;
misinform allies about Sevastopol
defences 224&n; plan to involve in
open field war 340; refugees in
Evpatoria 339; reprisals by Russians
420–21; resettled in Bessarabia 424;
revenge attacks in Kerch 344–5,
421; rise up against Russians upon
arrival of allies 202, 227–8; Russian
policy towards 20–21, 421–2
Tatischev, Vasily 13
Taylor, Sir Herbert, Urquhart and 74
telegraph: speeds reception of news from
the front 305&n; underwater cable
(Balaklava to Varna) 305
Tennyson, Alfred, Lord: *Maud* 475–7;
'The Charge of the Light Brigade' 252
'Testament of Peter the Great' 70–72
Theodosia (Kefe) 22, 423
Thiers, Adolphe 83
Third Section (Russian secret police)
104; attempt to contain rumours 314;
reports on more educated classes 317
Thompson, Elizabeth *see* Butler,
Elizabeth (née Thompson)
Thoumas, Capt Charles (French army),
letters home 403
Thouvenal, Édouard-Antoine de (French
ambassador to the Porte) 103, 329,
426; Hatt-i Hümayun decree 428
Three Emperors' League (1873) 458
Thunderer (Russian steam frigate)
108, 114
Tiger, HMS, aground and captured at
Odessa 171
The Times (newspaper) 73, 76, 80;
'Anglicus' articles 77; attacked by
Raglan 310; comment on the death of
the Tsar 324; draws attention to poor
medical conditions in Crimea 292;
influence on politics 147–8, 310–11;

About the Author

ORLANDO FIGES *is the author of* The Whisperers, Natasha's Dance, *and* A People's Tragedy, *which have been translated into over twenty languages. The recipient of the Wolfson History Prize and the Los Angeles Times Book Award, among others, Figes is a professor of history at Birkbeck College, University of London.*